Beowulf & Other Stories

To whom it may concern

Beowulf & Other Stories:

A New Introduction to Old English, Old Icelandic and Anglo-Norman Literatures

Edited by Richard North and Joe Allard

PEARSON

Longman

Harlow, England • London • New York • Boston • San Francisco • Toronto
Sydney • Tokyo • Singapore • Hong Kong • Seoul • Taipei • New Delhi
Cape Town • Madrid • Mexico City • Amsterdam • Munich • Paris • Milan

PEARSON EDUCATION LIMITED

Edinburgh Gate
Harlow CM20 2JE
United Kingdom
Tel: +44 (0)1279 623623
Fax: +44 (0)1279 431059
Website: www.pearsoned.co.uk

First edition published in Great Britain in 2007

© Pearson Education Limited 2007

ISBN: 978-1-4058-3572-5

British Library Cataloguing in Publication Data
A CIP catalogue record for this book can be obtained from the British Library

Library of Congress Cataloging in Publication Data
Beowulf & other stories : a new introduction to Old English, Old Icelandic, and
  Anglo-Norman literatures / edited by Richard North and Joe Allard.
       p. cm.
    Includes bibliographical references and index.
    ISBN 978-1-4058-3572-5 (pbk.)
      1. Literature, Medieval—History and criticism. 2. English literature—Old English,
  ca. 450–1100—History and criticism. 3. Old Norse literature—History and criticism.
  4. Anglo-Norman literature—History and criticism. I. North, Richard, 1961– II. Allard,
  Joe, 1948–

PN681.B38 2007
809'02—dc22

                                                                                    2006051568

10 9 8 7 6 5 4 3 2 1
10 09 08 07

Set by 35 in 9/13.5pt Stone Serif
Printed and bound in Malaysia, (CTP-VVP)

The Publisher's policy is to use paper manufactured from sustainable forests.

Contents

List of plates and maps

(In central plate section)

Plates

Maps

Acknowledgements

This book was written in the Dark Ages of the early twenty-first century in order to illuminate the old and medieval glories of the late seventh to fourteenth. Forgive the sentimentality – we wanted to show you how good the poem *Beowulf* really is and how interesting the other stories in Old English, Old Icelandic or Anglo-Norman literatures really are. Some people of our generation never learned this, but we acknowledge them anyway for their stimulating words. One is a former restaurant critic and winner of the 2005 Bad Sex in Fiction Award, Giles Coren, who finally settled *Beowulf*'s hash in *The Times* on 17 September the same year when the film *Beowulf and Grendel* premiered in Toronto. 'A cultural artefact fit for modern consumption?', he asked. 'I'm not convinced. For *Beowulf* is by no means a work of complexity and depth.' He had read some *Beowulf* in Old English at Oxford (OE *gecoren* means 'chosen') and still had the book on his shelves. 'There is no growth in *Beowulf*', he claimed, 'No learning. No more moral or intellectual development than in a gory video game.' He summed it up by saying '*Beowulf* is rubbish, its popularity based, as the Queen Mother's was, purely on the coincidence of survival.' This was too much. Republicans also read *Beowulf*. The poem is popular because it is good.

Even more sadly, its quality escaped A.N. Wilson, author of *Betjeman* and other famous biographies. In his view, the poet of *Beowulf* never existed. 'The *Beowulf* poet was created', Wilson writes, 'by Victorian and early 20th century Eng Lit scholars' who were suffering from an inferiority complex about German literature. Long ago A.N. taught this poem in the original for seven years ('seven years, I should say, largely wasted') to students in Oxford. 'When I think I could have spent seven years', he lamented, 'teaching Goethe's *Faust* or Dante's *Inferno*, I very nearly weep at the waste.' This neurasthenia was published in *The Sunday Telegraph* on 30 January 2000. The occasion was the award of the Whitbread Prize a week earlier to Seamus Heaney for his translation of *Beowulf* (Faber), about which Mr Wilson was (and presumably still is) not very happy. That was because he had wanted *Harry Potter* to win it instead. '*Beowulf* is just a rather dull folk tale', he retorted, 'set to repetitive verse forms, about a Dark Age Desperate Dan killing fictitious monsters.' If that is what his students had learned, clearly something had to be done.

A third old Oxfordian would tell you *Beowulf* is not an English poem at all. When *The Guardian* extracted from modern poet James Fenton's *An Introduction to English Poetry* on 25 May 2002, the puff was that he 'celebrates English poetry in all its variety'. Not enough variety to include Old English poems! 'English poetry', he says, 'begins whenever we decide to say the modern English language begins, and it extends as far as we decide to say that the English language extends.' So is reading English poetry now a kind of convenience shopping? 'Some people think that English poetry begins with the Anglo-Saxons', writes Fenton. 'I don't, because I can't accept that there is any continuity between the traditions of Anglo-Saxon poetry and those established in English poetry by the time of, say, Shakespeare.' So no Old English poetry is English unless it takes us into the Renaissance! How enlightened. Looking at these and other gems from the flâneur profession, the editors decided that something had to be done.

So we started this book and got some friends to help write it. This book will be in all the good bookshops and we hope in many of the bad ones. It aims to counter prejudice and put the record straight about *Beowulf* and the other subjects above. Ours is not a gathering of separate essays or articles such as you would find in a commemorative volume. It is, so we could put it given the above mentioned video games, a collaborative venture heading in one direction, two or three drivers in the cab and a platoon of mercenaries in the back, all driving down damnation alley with the cops in hot pursuit. Our mission, could we as teachers but choose to neglect it, is to bring our subjects into the minds of the generations to come.

We had a lot of fun editing and writing this book and credit must go where it is due. We acknowledge ourselves for any and all errors in this book. Positively, we acknowledge Daisy, Chris, Pamela, Inma, Sanae and Jon, who read draft chapters and always gave us the right steer. Many thanks to them and also to Gavin, who didn't read the chapter we gave him (that was useful too). Thanks go to our anonymous first reviewers. Among other friends, colleagues and simple associates special praise must be reserved for Fu, who, in the darkest days of this project two autumns ago, kept up our spirits by cracking the *Peitsche* in her inimitable way. Clive tried out his chapter on the girls of the Queen's School, Chester, to whom we are grateful. Here and there our students in UCL and Essex also gave advice. Our thanks, of course, to all those contributing chapters to this book for their enthusiasm, erudition and sense of guilt. In the last respect, there are several contenders for the prize, but here we think it is Andy who shone in particular because he best of all knew how to submit his chapters only when they were just right. Last, but not least, we thank Philip from Pearson Education for supporting the project, getting it rolling and paying for several bibulous lunches in exchange for adding his words to the text. We think we could have had some more wine, Philip, but without your words the book might have been dry too. A big thank you, then, to Chris Allard, Peter Baker, Stewart Brookes, Jayne Carroll, Melanie Carter, Pamela Clunies-Ross, David Crystal, Patricia Gillies, Terry Gunnell, Susan Irvine, Sanae Kasahara, F.C. Koffrae, Philip Langeskov, Daisy Neijmann, Jennifer Neville, Éamonn Ó Carragáin, Andy Orchard, Steve Orchard Gavin Phipps, Inma Ridao, R.T. Rumple, Clive Tolley, Jon Wood, Bryan Weston Wyly and all the girls at the Queen's School, Chester.

Richard North and Joe Allard

Publisher's acknowledgements

We are grateful to the following for permission to reproduce copyright material:

Plate 1 courtesy of the Sheffield Galleries & Museums Trust; plate 2 courtesy of the Master and Fellows of Corpus Christi College, Cambridge; plate 3 courtesy of York Archaeological Trust; plate 4 courtesy of the British Museum; plate 5 courtesy of the Dean and Chapter of Exeter; plate 6 courtesy of the Cathedral Library, Vercelli; plate 9 courtesy of Ross Trench-Jellicoe; plate 10 courtesy of the Department of Archaeology, Durham University, photograph by T. Middlemass; plate 11 courtesy of Trinity College Library, Dublin; plate 12 courtesy of the Bodleian Library, University of Oxford; plate 12 courtesy of the Ashmolean Museum, Oxford; plates 14, 15 and 17 courtesy of the Árni Magnússon Institute, Iceland; plate 16 courtesy of the Mary Evans Picture Library; plates 19 and 21 courtesy of the British Library; plate 20 courtesy of the British Film Institute. Maps 4 and 6 courtesy of Professor Simon Keynes.

In some instances we have been unable to trace the owners of copyright material, and would appreciate any information that would enable us to do so.

CHAPTER 1

An introduction to this book

Richard North, David Crystal and Joe Allard

Not a lot of people know about Old English literature, but you can if you read this book. If you like reading literature, then these pages have got something for you. An undiscovered country like ours is more than just one more name to acquire in a list of 'been there done that'. It is really a whole landscape to explore. There is more than Old English here, too. Besides Old English literature, there is also Old Icelandic and early medieval Celtic and French. Together they could all be called the imaginative equivalent of a terrain full of forests, rivers, marshes, lakes and mountains all peopled by the strangest, most unusual beings in the sunniest but also the most changeable weather. Come and join us there for a day. The following chapters have been written to give you the road into this wild interior. Starting with Old English, we will give you answers – or leads to answers – to questions that you might have about Old English or, further afield, about Old Icelandic or Anglo-Norman literature.

Of course, the first question is what these things are. 'Old English' is English literature written in the language of its time in England from around the year 600 to 1100. 'Old Icelandic' is poems and prose works from around 850 to 1400 composed and written in Norway and Iceland. 'Anglo-Norman' covers literature in England, the Celtic lands and France in the period 1066 to about 1200 and leads into Middle English literature such as *The Canterbury Tales* of Geoffrey Chaucer. The Anglo-Saxons who spoke Old English fought, settled down and intermarried with Vikings, i.e. Danes and Norwegians who spoke 'Old Norse', a language which was written down in Iceland and is also called 'Old Icelandic'. Many of the Icelandic sagas – which are rather like historical novels – tell stories about the Vikings in England. The Normans who invaded England in 1066 were themselves of Viking origin and spoke a French which, in due course, changed the English language into its present form. They also cleared the way for new forms of literature from France such as rhyming poetry and 'romance'. Because Old English, Old Icelandic and Anglo-Norman overlap in this way we are putting them together in this book. The promiscuity of this venture is such, indeed, that we are going one step further and mixing these subjects quite deliberately up. Old English is the leading theme, which you will find dealt with in this and the following chapters until the *Anglo-Saxon Chronicle* and Viking wars in Chapter 11. The other subjects will have been brought in here or there but Chapter 11 is where we start the Icelandic theme by including a potted introduction to Old Norse. Thereafter, Chapters 12 and 13 go large on the Old Icelandic literary tradition as such, before our book turns back to Old English literature in Chapter 14, via its mature prose tradition as seen in the writers of the English Benedictine Reform. All this sets the scene for the third main theme in Chapter 15, the rich literary fusions of Anglo-Norman, Irish, Welsh, Cornish, Breton, Middle Eastern and French.

Teaching these various subjects has been both a challenge and great fun; the editors hope it will remain so. Each in our own area, we and all the contributors in this book have got years of experience of reading the literature, of researching the literature and – most importantly – of teaching the literature. These days, however, we are beginning to feel that the subjects should get a higher profile in education. The figures speak for themselves. In 99% of schools not only the world over, of course, but also in the UK where Old English came from, the coverage of Old English literature is zero. In 90% of university English departments in the whole Anglophone world it is also zero. Old Icelandic hardly gets a look in. French is mostly taken at the modern end. 'Celtic' has become a catch-all for something between the Romans and Chaucer. This state of affairs is ironic at a time and in a culture where much of the public imagination is enthralled by stories and images, whether in book or film, cartoon or computer game – which are drawn directly from Old English and Old Icelandic and from Celtic and medieval Romance. In his creation of *The Lord of the Rings*, J.R.R. Tolkien, himself a professor of Anglo-Saxon and Middle English, drew deeply from *Beowulf*, Celtic mythology and heathen Norse poetry recorded in Iceland in the twelfth and thirteenth centuries (see Chapter 2).

Just as Tolkien drew on Old English, in particular, so Peter Jackson drew on Tolkien, for a trilogy of films at the dawn of the new millennium. Jackson's three films on *The Lord of the Rings* have become a phenomenon, tapping into a remarkable seam of international interest. Tolkien's original, too, was a global phenomenon. There is a connection and it is a very human connection at that. Just as we have been entertained – enthralled, even – by Jackson's films, so our forebears, more than 1000 years ago, were enthralled by the works we will discuss in the chapters that follow. As we hope the book will make clear, we have an affiliation with these people who, though far away in time, are not so far away in spirit. We can infer from the works that remain that they, like us, could be moved by the written word; that they, like us, could be inspired by heroism; that they, like us, could laugh at themselves and those around them. It is quite an inheritance, and we well might ask where we would be without all the runes and Vikings. To put it less whimsically, where would the world of entertainment and the imagination be without them? If you want to know where it all came from, read on.

To take the leading subject here, Old English literature, we feel that the recent academic attitude that Old English no longer has the right to be considered part of the English literary canon is stupid. French, German, Italian and Spanish have no such abundance of literature in their own languages going back as far as the seventh century. And what do we do? We call it inconvenient and pretend it's not there. There are also those who are more considered in their opposition. They would say that there is a lack of continuity between Old English and that of later periods, given that literary English fell out of general use from about 1100 to 1300. That is true, while there is also the huge influx of French, Latin and Greek vocabulary in the twelfth, fourteenth and sixteenth centuries, which nowadays accounts for more than half the English word-stock. But that doesn't mean Old English is finished, or that it is not relevant to a wider understanding of our rich literary heritage. As you can find in Chapter 10, the remaining vocabulary, most of it derived from Old English and a significant amount from Old Norse, is used with far higher frequency than later additions from French, Latin and Greek, and the underlying syntax is more or less the same. Although Old English literature stopped short before its Norman–French successor, it was long ago clear, bizarrely so you might think, that the poetry of the moderns has turned back to the accentual, alliterating, compound-building verse craft of Old English poets for much of its inspiration. By this we mean poets such as Gerard Manly Hopkins, Ezra Pound, W.H. Auden, Ted Hughes, Geoffrey Hill, Tony Harrison, E.H. Prynne and Seamus Heaney. But there will be others out there, too. Some of the negative attitudes current today are the result simply of laziness. They are lazy because those who espouse them won't take the time or make the effort to learn to read the old texts in the original, or even in translation. We hope to recommend some good translations, mainly our own. But we also hope to show that the originals themselves are neither so difficult, nor quite so distant, as people have been led to believe.

We have subtitled our book a 'new' introduction because many of the recent and available introductions to the subject are far too specialised for the ordinary reader. This collection of essays should be both scholarly and accessible. It aims to give the reader a reliable panorama of the literature of the period. Let's call it 'Anglo-Saxon' for the people and history, 'Old English' for literature. Ditto 'Old Norse' for the general period (and some of the poetry) and 'Old Icelandic' for the literature.

The Anglo-Saxon period starts with an invitation from King Vortigern to the Jutes Hengest and Horsa in 449 to sort out some unruly local tribes. They came, they conquered, they remained. We read about these brothers in the work of the Venerable Bede in the early eighth century. Bede also tells us about the remarkable Cædmon, the first recorded English performance poet, divinely inspired to verse in the later seventh century. In this book we'll find out about important intellectual and literary developments in Old English in the work of Alcuin. He was a scholar at the court of King Charlemagne, whose empire was the blueprint of modern France, Germany and Italy all rolled into one. We will look at King Alfred the Great, who made much better books than he did cakes. Looming large through much of our book are the tumultuous years recorded in *The Anglo-Saxon Chronicle*. An entry for 793 tells us of the first Viking raid at Lindisfarne. This heralds a long period of horror stories of Scandinavian raids and battles and a lot of immigration, settlement and intermarriage. Indeed, for a long time large parts of the country were run by the Danes and in the early decades of the eleventh century the entire country was under Danish rule, part of a confederation of states with Denmark, Norway and parts of Sweden. How does that grab you for an early alternative to the European Union?

This Viking peril that we so vividly love to imagine finally drew to a close in the eleventh century with the triumph of William the Conqueror (aka the Bastard) of Normandy. He defeated the Anglo-Saxon King Harold Godwinson at the Battle of Hastings in 1066. Only two weeks earlier, Harold had cut down the seven-foot Norwegian, King Haraldr, 'the Harsh Ruler' at Stamford Bridge (in Yorkshire, *not* the London football ground). These events signal the start of serious Anglo-Norman influence on the literature and language and the end of Old English as a working literary tool. When English popped up again it had French words and looked different. But actually Middle English, as it is called, consisted of dialects of Old English with a new extra power.

Diversity is strength: the people in the British Isles have always been diverse and the literature of all this early period reflects that no less than English texts of the twenty-first century. Old English and the other languages and cultures were anything but pure. The Anglo-Saxons were the latest in a long line of immigrants to Britain and they knew it. They often feared they would not be the last. In Northumbria in the seventh century the Anglian royal family learned to speak Irish Gaelic and Welsh as well as Northumbrian Old English, no doubt some Pictish too. Their priests spoke Latin and when they started building monasteries they added Italian to the list and blended all these cultures together. So multiculturalism is not simply the invention of some twentieth-century sociologist; we have been there before. If you hear people question the relevance of Old English to today – or deride it for being alien or ideologically unsound – remember that 'relevance' can be the puritan's opening gambit for a monocultural takeover.

Obviously, the world around us today, in the early twenty-first century, is facing a raft of new challenges of mass migration and potential conflict. American English is absorbing Latin American Spanish and Spanish is doing the same by English, and so on. But the challenges here are actually not new at all, not by the standards of the period featured in this book. In this period there was a fluid interchange and development of a variety of languages *all the time*. And, indeed, regular changes of allegiances, boundaries and laws. You can find this fluidity almost anywhere in Britain. The town of Colchester in Essex, for example, is not only where one of the authors of this chapter is gainfully employed; it was also the original Roman capital of Britain. Queen Boudicca of the Iceni torched the place and the Romans moved the capital to London leaving an important garrison behind. Colchester became part of the Danelaw in 886 with the agreement of King Alfred and a Danish earl named Guthrum. A Saxon church in the town centre has a door scarred with what the tourist office claims are axe marks from marauding heathen Vikings in the tenth century. Just down the road is the town of Maldon, immortalised in verse (*The Battle of Maldon*) for the last stand of Byrhtnoth, the local earl, against an army of Norwegian heavies in 991. These raiders were probably led by a man who became king of Norway four years later and converted Iceland to Christianity four years after that, one Óláfr Tryggvason. We see a lot of this human dynamo in the *Sagas of Icelanders*. Back in Colchester in 1066 when the Normans arrived, they found a pretty usable Roman fortress itself built on a temple to old Emperor Claudius. They built this up into their keep, the biggest in Britain. And so, like the history of most towns in England, Colchester's is in constant flux. It's all change and none of it is unimportant.

This is why we are going to depart from the specialised convention of restricting our pursuit to *only* Anglo-Saxon history and culture or Old English literature. Chapters are included here on heathen mythology, the

Sagas of Icelanders and the poetry of early Middle English, Anglo-Norman and Provençale French. All areas are interesting in their own right, of course, but they also reflect the international comings and goings of life in northern Europe in the past. We get a sense of this as early as *Beowulf*, whose story is set in Scandinavia although it was written in Old English verse. The poet of *Beowulf* doesn't mention England because at the time of his story England does not yet exist. By the same token, in *Beowulf* we run into Frisians, Franks, Goths as well as Danes, Geats, Swedes and Norwegians. Grendel is already known as an Alien-like horror lurking here and there in the haunted monster Mere and in the great hall of Hrothgar, king of Denmark (see Chapter 3). Yet it turns out Grendel is descended from Adam and Eve, just like the Danes are, although in his case the line is of Cain rather than Abel. His mother seems to have mated with the devil. He is both us and the Other at one and the same time. The minor Old English heroic poems, such as *Widsith* and *Deor*, show a range of tribes and places that is truly astonishing (see Chapter 4). These reflect the so-called Age of Migrations, a period from the fourth to the sixth century when whole wagon convoys of refugees from different Germanic tribes could be seen making their way across what was left of the Roman Empire (see Map 1).

The Goths, for example, were so many things at different times that we doubt they would have minded being related also to high medieval church architecture, early nineteenth-century ladies' novels or twentieth-century lifestyle choice. They started in the first century BC on the tranquil isle of Gotland in the Baltic, crossed to Pomerania near Poland and curved east into Ukraine until they reached the north coast of the Black Sea, from where the Huns, coming from northern China, drove them south-westwards through what is now Romania across the Danube into Thrace in northern Greece. They are just one example, and that was just the start of their travels. They went on into Asia Minor or west across to Illyria (the former Yugoslavia), up to the north Italian plain and down to Rome where they stayed only a few days. One of them thought city buildings were like 'walled tombs', and they preferred to move around outside. By then the Roman Empire was finished. Some of them stayed behind to run Italy for the new Byzantine Empire in the east. Others pushed further west, founded one kingdom around Toulouse in southwest France and then another in Toledo in central Spain, where they remained until the Berbers and Arabs from North Africa conquered Iberia from 711 to 720. The Vandals, originally from Vendelsyssla in Sweden, followed the same path as the Goths and gave their name to Andalucía (from *Wandalusia*) in southern Spain, before crossing the straits and heading to Carthage in Tunisia, which they ruled into the

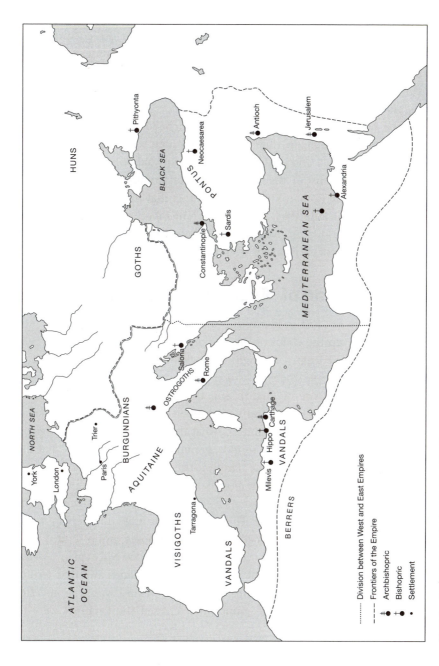

Map 1 Barbarians in the late Roman Empire

sixth century. Burgundy in central France is named after a smaller tribe which hailed from Bornholm (Old Norse *Borgundarhólmr*), another island in the Baltic. In due course all these Germanic migrants blended into the background. Spanish and Portuguese have still got a few Gothic words today. It will be clear, even from this lightning tour, that the European cultures of today are still mightily influenced by the culture of the distant past. Perhaps, you might think, this cultural inheritance is something worth clinging on to, rather than shaving off. If so, read on.

The Angles, Saxons, Jutes and others migrated westwards at about the same time, although, in their case, the journey was shorter. They sailed across the Channel and settled in Britannia, an old outpost of the Roman Empire where many of them and other non-Romans had been living as auxiliaries in the Roman army. The reality is that most of them had been migrating for so long they could barely remember where they came from and often made this up. Nonetheless, they gave us what became the Old English language. Let us take it from the ground up.

The beginning of 'England' and Old English

Languages do not just suddenly appear: they gradually evolve out of other languages. Given the chaos of the Age of Migrations, can we say anything certain about the origins of English? One thing is clear. If we look at the languages of Europe today, we can see immediately many similarities between the structure of English and the structure of such languages as German, Dutch and Danish. During the nineteenth century, the new science of comparative philology established that these and a few other languages had so much in common – in sounds, grammar, and vocabulary – that they just had to belong to the same 'family'. The philologists called the family *Germanic* and worked out that it must have been spoken by people in northern Europe about 2500 years ago. As we have seen, the Germanic people did not all stay in the same place. They migrated in huge numbers in several directions. To put it more broadly than before, some groups ended up in Scandinavia and their speech evolved into present-day Norwegian, Swedish and Danish. Other groups went towards the Netherlands and that resulted in Dutch and Frisian. The groups that stayed behind were the ancestors of modern German. And the groups that crossed the Channel were the originators of English.

Thanks to the monk from Jarrow, the Venerable Bede (*c.* 673–735), we have a rough idea about who the English groups were. In Chapter 1 of his *History of the English Church and People* (*Historia ecclesiastica gentis*

Anglorum), written *c.* 730, he paints a picture of a multiethnic and multi-lingual Britain:

> This island at present . . . contains five nations, the English, Britons, Scots, Picts, and Latins, each in its own peculiar dialect cultivating the sublime study of Divine truth. The Latin tongue is, by the study of the Scriptures, become common to all the rest.

Later chapters describe in detail how this situation had arisen. The first arrivals, Bede says, were Britons (we would now call them Celts) and they gave their name to the land. A tribe known as the Picts then arrived in the north, from Scythia via northern Ireland, where the resident Scots would not let them stay. The Scots (Latin *Scotti*, 'Irish') themselves arrived in Caledonia in northwest Britain some time later, secured their own settlements in the Pictish regions and gave their name to the country: Scotland. Then, 'in the year of Rome 798' (that is, 43 AD), Emperor Claudius sent an expedition which rapidly established a Roman presence in much of the island.

The Romans ruled in Britain until the early fifth century, when Rome was taken by the Goths, and the military garrisons at the edges of the Roman Empire had to be withdrawn to help protect the homeland. As a result, the Britons found themselves in trouble. With no Roman protection, the Picts and Scots attacked them repeatedly from the north. The Britons appealed to Rome for help, but the Romans were preoccupied with their own wars and could do nothing. The attacks continued, so the Britons made a momentous decision. Bede tells the story in Chapters 14 and 15 of his *History*:

> They consulted what was to be done, and where they should seek assistance to prevent or repel the cruel and frequent incursions of the northern nations; and they all agreed with their King Vortigern to call over to their aid, from the parts beyond the sea, the Saxon nation. [. . .] Then the nation of the Angles, or Saxons, being invited by the aforesaid king, arrived in Britain with three long ships.

Something of this story is also told in *The Anglo-Saxon Chronicle*, written in Old English from the eighth century onwards. The *Chronicle* reports the Saxon landing in Ebbsfleet – Pegwell Bay, near Ramsgate, in Kent – in 449 AD. The fifth nation, led by the brother-commanders Hengest and Horsa, had arrived.

Bede tells us that the Germanic arrivals were the ancestors of the English peoples that surrounded him in the eighth century:

> Those who came over were of the three most powerful nations of Germany – Saxons, Angles, and Jutes. From the Jutes are descended the people of Kent, and of the Isle of Wight, and those also in the province of the West-Saxons who are to this day called Jutes, seated opposite to the Isle of Wight.

From the Saxons, that is, the country which is now called Old Saxony, came the East-Saxons, the South-Saxons, and the West-Saxons.

From the Angles, that is, the country which is called Anglia [*Angulus*, modern Angeln], and which is said, from that time, to remain desert to this day, between the provinces of the Jutes and the Saxons, are descended the East-Angles, the Midland-Angles, Mercians, all the race of the Northumbrians, that is, of those nations that dwell on the north side of the river Humber, and the other nations of the English.

The account was influential. It was incorporated into *The Anglo-Saxon Chronicle* for the year 449. But we have to be very careful when we read such statements as the 'nations' were 'Saxons, Angles, and Jutes'. We dare not trust the names and the descriptions. Nowadays we are used to interpreting community names as if they reflected a social reality that is essentially coherent, territorial and culturally homogeneous: the Poles live in Poland and do things that are typically Polish, the Danes live in Denmark and do things typically Danish. Of course, we know that such characterisations hide a host of variations, not least those arising from immigration and ethnic mixing. But in the days described by Bede, the names bore an even greater unpredictability in relation to social conditions.

Some names were 'tribal', in the sense that all the members of the group would be originally related through kinship: the Angles may well have been a tribe, in this sense, though doubtless mixed with other stock. Other names reflected a much looser sense of 'tribal', being little more than a collection of bands gathered together under a leader. The *-ing* names of English towns suggest this interpretation: *Reading*, for example, was where the 'people of Rēad' ('Red') lived.

Yet another interpretation of a name is as a label for a confederation of groups who came together for defence or attack. This description seems to suit the Saxons, whose identity was based on their fighting ability with the type of short sword known as the *seax*. As long as a man carried a *seax*, he would be called Saxon, regardless of his ethnic or geographical origins. In a similar way, later, all Vikings would be called 'Danes', regardless of whether they came from Denmark or not. The names, accordingly, are not as clear-cut as they might appear. In particular, it was perfectly possible for an Angle to 'become' a Saxon by joining one of the *seax*-wielding groups. And as the Saxons moved westwards from their homeland in southwest Denmark, doubtless many Frisians, Franks and others would have been incorporated into their ranks.

We know least of all about the Jutes. The name Jutland, in northern Denmark, suggests an original homeland, but there is evidence that by the time the Jutes arrived in England they had lived elsewhere and adopted other ways. Their burial practice, for example, was inhumation – like that used by the Franks and other tribes on the middle Rhine – and not like that usual among the tribes of northwest Germany, who practised cremation. Many of the trappings found in graves in Kent, Sussex and along the Thames are similar to those discovered in Frankish and Frisian territories. All this mixing suggests that the Jutes had no clear ethnic identity when they crossed the Channel: they may have given their name to Jutland, but they left no name in Britain other than in Bede's Latin and Old English heroic poetry. In Chapter 4 of this book, we will return to the Jutes in relation to Hengest, for *Beowulf* and the *Finnsburh Fragment* have a story about him in Frisia. It can be argued that the Anglo-Saxons believed Hengest and his people were Jutes.

Tribal and national names for the English

The linguistic situation, always a reflex of social structure, must accordingly have been much messier than any simple classification could ever reflect. When the invaders arrived in England, they did not bring with them three 'pure' Germanic dialects – Anglian, Saxon and Jutish – but a wide range of spoken varieties, displaying different kinds of mutual influence. A modern analogy is hard to find, but television these days sometimes allows us to observe a battalion of British troops abroad. They are brought together by their military purpose, not by speech: when we listen to them talk, we hear all kinds of accents. Their Anglo-Saxon counterparts would have been even more varied in their speech. The age they lived in, especially earlier in the so-called Age of Migrations, allowed a free proliferation of accents and dialects in the language they spoke.

It is not possible to say how intelligible the Angles, Saxons and Jutes found one another. There was a great deal that unified them culturally, of course. They had a common oral literary heritage and a common set of religious beliefs. Probably their dialects would have been mutually comprehensible, for the most part, albeit with islands of difficulty due to distinctive local pronunciations and vocabulary. The variation may have been no more than that which differentiates, say, present-day Glasgow, Newcastle or London. The speech of these cities can be extremely difficult for outsiders to understand, when spoken rapidly and colloquially. Yet it becomes accessible when people speak slowly and regular contact with the speakers quickly increases comprehension. Doubtless such variations in style existed in early Germanic, too. But there were significant differences separating the eastern and western branches of Germanic. If a Goth from southern Europe met a northern Saxon in the fifth century, they would probably have had great difficulty understanding one another.

Not only was there a great deal of linguistic variety among the continental peoples before they crossed the Channel and the North Sea, there was substantial variation in Britain already. Bede gives the impression that there were no Germanic people in Britain before the Anglo-Saxon invasions, but we now know that Hengest and Horsa were by no means the first Germanic people to arrive in Britain from the European continent. There is archaeological evidence of a Germanic presence in the Roman towns and forts of the south and east before the end of the Roman occupation. For example, Germans in Roman military service in Gaul wore belt buckles of a distinctive type and these have been found in early fifth-century graves at locations along the River Thames. And early runic inscriptions using the Germanic 'runic alphabet' have been found. The earliest runic inscription known in England was found in a cremation cemetery at the former Roman town of Caistor-by-Norwich, in Norfolk. It is written on the anklebone of a deer, and reads *raihan*, 'roe deer'. The object was probably a plaything of some kind. What is interesting is that the shape of one of the runes, the symbol for H, has a single crossbar. This was typical of northern runic writing and suggests that the person who used this script came from Scandinavia, possibly southern Denmark. The important thing, however, is that this find can be dated to around the year 400. In other words, the writer was living in East Anglia well before the Anglo-Saxon invasions began – and he spoke some form of Germanic.

Kent must have been an especially mixed sociolinguistic region. The name long precedes the Anglo-Saxon invasions. It is Celtic in origin. Philologists have suggested that it comes from an early form *canto-*, probably meaning 'rim' or 'border': hence, 'the land on the border'. The British tribe that lived there were known as the *Cantii*. As the region on the 'rim' of England and the part closest to the European mainland, it is likely that there had long been contact with the Germanic peoples. Kent early became a trade route to and from the European mainland and, as a result, was exposed to a wide range of continental influences, especially from Frisians and Franks. During the late sixth century, in the reign of Æthelberht (who married the Christian daughter of a Frankish king), it would become a major cultural and political centre, doubtless highly cosmopolitan in outlook.

If there had long been Germanic people in Kent, then they may have been responsible for the naming of the Saxon peoples, as they heard of their arrival. Those to the south came to be called the South Saxons (Sussex) and to the west the West Saxons (Wessex), with those in between the Middle Saxons (Middlesex). Those to the north, curiously, were not called North Saxons (unfortunately, there is no Northsex), but East Saxons (Essex), which suggests that the naming took place at a time when the arrivals on the east coast had moved along the Thames until they could be seen to be 'east' of the other groups. An interesting point is that these names are the names of the people, not the place they lived in. If the names had been made after the places, they would have appeared as *Sussexland* or the like. Later it happened like that anyway, with *Englaland* ('land of the Angles').

To start with it seems the Angles established themselves in one half of the country and the Saxons in the other. So why did the name *England* derive from the former group? The historical evidence, though meagre, does not suggest that the Angles were any more numerous than the Saxons or had greater military successes. The Welsh, too, call 'English' *Saesneg*, the Scots, *Sassenach*: in both cases after *Saxon*. So why is the country called *England* and not *Saxonland*, *Saxland* or some other such form? It is a puzzle, but we can make some good guesses.

The original use of the name *Angli* (for the people) and *Anglia* (for the country) is found in Latin writers during the seventh century, but only with reference to the Angles (as opposed to the Saxons and Jutes). One king of Kent, Æthelberht, is called *rex Anglorum* – 'king of the Angles'. *Angl-* is later found in Old English as both *Angel-* and *Engl-*. In the Alfredian translation of Bede (Book IV, Chapter 26), for example, we find the phrase *on Engla lande*, translating *in regione Anglorum*, which meant 'in the country of the Angles'. Bede never used *Anglia* for the country as a whole: his name for it was *Brittania* or *Britannia* ('Britain').

There was one context, however, where the early Latin writers did give the *Angl-* element prominence. This was in the phrase *Angli Saxones*, used at least from the eighth century to mean the 'English Saxons' (of Britain) as opposed to the 'Old Saxons' (of the continent). A long time afterwards, as the historical facts began to blur in the popular mind, *Anglo-Saxons* came to be interpreted as 'Angles and Saxons', the combined Germanic people of Britain, which is how the term is used today. But in the eighth century *Angl-* did not have this sense. Rather, it was the crucial, contrastive element in the phrase – the *English* Saxons, as opposed to any other kind. Issues of identity being so important, perhaps it was this prominence that fixed *Angl-* in the intuitions of the people, as a label for the people as a whole?

Whatever the reason, we can see the name broadening its meaning in the ninth century. The Old English translation of Bede uses the term *Angelcynn* (literally, 'Angle-kin', i.e. 'race of the Angles', Bede's *gens Anglorum*) to refer to all the Germanic peoples. The adjective *English* makes its first appearance at that time, too – long pre-dating the name *England*. In a treaty made between King Alfred and the Danish invader Guthrum (*c.* 886) we see *English* opposed to *Danish* and it plainly refers to all of the non-Danish population, not just the Angles. Also, at around the same time, *English* is used for the language: the translation of Bede at one point (Book III, Chapter 19) talks about a monastery *nemned on Englisc* ('named in English') *Cneoferisburh* and Alfred quite often uses the name in this way. From there it was a natural move to call the whole country after the language, although this happened slowly. More than a century after Alfred, we find the phrase *Engla lande* referring to the whole country, by the writers of the eleventh-century *Chronicle*. There was then a long period of varied usage and we find such forms as *Engle land*, *Englene londe*, *Engle lond*, *Engelond* and *Ingland*. The spelling *England* emerged in the fourteenth century and soon after became established as the norm.

Back in 449, a cross-section of British society would show people of many different backgrounds. These people were Celts, Romano-Celts, Germanic immigrants of various origins, doubtless some Germano-Celts, for the invaders did not always bring their wives with them. They lived in tiny communities of perhaps just a few hundred people. But this is not the only dimension we have to consider, in understanding the forces that influenced the development of Old English. The diachronic dimension, the way language changes over time, must also be taken into account, for waves of immigration and invasion do not take place all at once. If Germanic people were arriving in Britain in, say, 400, their speech would be very different from those who arrived a century later, even if the two groups of people originated in exactly the same part of the continental mainland. And at least a century was involved, with Angles and Jutes coming a half-century after the Roman auxiliaries, South Saxons another half-century after Angles and Jutes, West Saxons a generation after that. These names are, in any case, terms of convenience, but a lot can happen to pronunciation in a hundred years. If you listen today to recordings made by the British or American media in the 1920s you will be struck by the very different 'far back' sound of the announcers then. How much more different would a century of pronunciation change have been, at a time when there was so little contact between people?

Once in the country, mobility did not cease. Population growth within the Anglo-Saxon groups, plus the continual pressure from new arrivals in the east, forced people to move inland. Although frequently halted through conflict with the British, the Anglo-Saxons rapidly spread throughout central, southern and north-eastern England. By 600 they had reached the area of present-day Dorset and occupied land north to the River Severn, across central England into Yorkshire and north along the coast towards the River Tyne. The paths taken by the Angles followed the major rivers. Some entered the country via the Wash, at the River Ouse, eventually moving northwest to form the kingdom of Lindsey. A major grouping moved south to form the kingdom of East Anglia.

One group that settled in an area west of modern Cambridge in the early sixth century came to be known as Middle Angles. Some entered via the River Humber, taking the Trent tributary southwards towards central England: these came to be called Mercians (a name which meant 'marchmen' or 'people on the frontier'). Some moved north from the Humber, along the Yorkshire River Ouse, forming the kingdom of Deira. Further north still, the kingdom of Bernicia, Bede's country, came to be established through a series of incursions, initially from the sea and then from the south. There was no movement at that time into Cornwall, Wales, Cumbria or southern Scotland, where the British were still dominant.

In all this, we are talking about small groups meeting small groups. No national armies existed in the sixth century or for some time after. Accordingly, it is not possible to generalise about the social consequences of the expansion. In some places, an Anglo-Saxon victory would mean the total displacement of the British. In others, the British would have stayed nearby. They often preferred to live on the higher ground, while the Anglo-Saxons preferred the lower. In other places again, cultural assimilation would have taken place. The traditional view that the Anglo-Saxons arrived and pushed all the British back into Wales and Cornwall, destroying every-thing en route, is now known to be simplistic. Although there are several reports in the *Anglo-Saxon Chronicle* of towns being sacked (such as Pevensey, in Sussex, in 491), the archaeological evidence suggests that most towns were not. And although some Britons fled to the Welsh mountains, the far north, the Cornish moors or further afield to Armorica, the great western French peninsula now known after them as 'Brittany', many stayed in sub-jection and adopted the new culture.

There would have been a great deal of mutual linguistic influence between people. Accents and dialects come closer together when communities are at peace with each other, diverge when they are at odds. Many people must have been bilingual or even trilingual. There are tantalising hints of bilingual awareness in some of the place names. The British name for *Dover*, for example, was *Dubris*, which was a plural form meaning 'waters'. When the name was adopted by the Anglo-Saxons it became *Dofras*, which was likewise a plural form. This suggests that those who named the place had some awareness of Celtic grammar. *Wendover* ('white waters' – a stream) in Berkshire and *Andover* ('ash-tree stream') in Hampshire had a similar history.

Place names provide intriguing evidence about the developing relationships between the British and the Anglo-Saxons. There are large numbers of Celtic place names in England. A small selection would include *Arden, Avon, Exe, Leeds* and *Severn,* as well as the hundreds of compound names which contain a Celtic component. Most of the forms found in these names (insofar as they can be interpreted at all) have meanings to do with features of the landscape, such as *cumb/comb* 'deep valley', *dun* 'hill fort', *lin* 'lake' and several words for 'hill' – *torr, pen, crug, bre.* The Celtic element is italicised in the following selection: *Berk*shire, *Bray, Bre*don, *Cam*bridge, *Car*lisle, *Ciren*cester, *Don*caster, *Glou*cester, Ilfra*combe,* Lan*caster,* Lei*cester,* Lin*coln,* Mal*vern,* Man*chester, Penkridge, Penrith, Pen*zance Wilt*shire, Win*chester, Wor*cester.

The Celtic names are not evenly distributed across England. If there are few such names in an area, presumably this was a location where few British people remained or where the assimilation into Anglo-Saxon society was complete. Conversely, where there are clusters of Celtic names, we must assume a culture where the British survived with their own identity for some time, coexisting with their Anglo-Saxon neighbours, who were presumably fewer in number compared with their compeers in the east. On this basis, we can see a steady increase in Celtic place names as we look from east to west across England, until we reach Wales and Cornwall, where there are hardly any Germanic names at all. Celtic names in the east are by no means entirely absent, but they do tend to be names of major centres and features, such as *Thames, London, Dover* and *Kent.* In such cases, we are probably seeing the workings of convenience: the Anglo-Saxons took over the Celtic name simply because it was widely known.

In an age of great mobility, contacts would have been very transient and of variable status. At one point, two groups might be trading partners; at another, they might be enemies. There was a continual shifting of local alliances between bands. There must have been dozens of fiefdoms throughout the period. By 700 seven 'kingdoms' had been established throughout the country: the so-called Anglo-Saxon Heptarchy of Kent, Sussex, Wessex, Essex, East Anglia, Mercia and Bernicia (Northumberland) – although it would be misleading to think of these domains as being particularly large (some were more like a modern county in size) or as having clear-cut political boundaries. The entire population of England in those days was probably less than half a million.

Neither is the balance of power between these kingdoms stable during the next 200 years. East Anglia and Kent were important areas in the seventh century, the latter especially following the arrival of St Augustine and other Roman Catholic missionaries in 597. By the end of that century Northumbria had become a major religious and cultural centre (as Bede would later demonstrate). Mercia's power grew in the eighth century, especially under King Offa (757–96). In the ninth century, political power moved south again, with Wessex dominant after a battle on the frontier near Swindon in 825. Wessex was saved from Danish conquest by King Alfred (ruled 871–99) whose descendants increased West Saxon power until their language, 'West Saxon', became the Old English literary and adminstrative standard.

Then, as now, power politics controlled language trends. Power residing in Kent meant that initially the Kentish dialect would gain prestige. Power in the north would lead to a corresponding boost for Northumbrian. And for the first time in the history of English we can see the effect of such power on language, through the medium of writing. The missionaries introduced the Roman alphabet to the country and large numbers of manuscripts, initially all in Latin, were soon being produced by monastic scribes. By the middle of the seventh century, these scribes were beginning to incorporate Old English forms into their work, devising a new alphabet in the process. It was an uncertain, experimental period, for this was the first time anyone had tried to write down what English people said, and conventions of handwriting, layout, spelling and style had to be established. The texts soon began to display distinctive features, some of which reflected the regional background of the scribe or the location where he was working. The written language immediately added a new dimension to the language, a fresh set of opportunities for expression. The writing down of Old English dialects, first Kentish, then Northumbrian, then Mercian and West Saxon, was in fact the seedbed for an Old English literature.

Looking at new languages in this book

Throughout this book all the authors pay an acute attention to the languages themselves. Reading Old English and Old Icelandic texts through translations, but usually accompanied by the originals, will help you with the art of close reading. We reckon that the reader of two texts at once, old and modern, can be stimulated by a pace slower than that to which he or she is accustomed with later works of English literature. This is undeniably an intense focus. We presume that where you, the reader, are concerned, Old English and Old Norse are new languages. The speed of all this is is slow, but the reward worth waiting for. There is a craft in Old English and other early medieval verse, in its charge and sound and accent and imagery, which no translation can deliver. In looking at the original from time to time, we hope you will engage with its arresting content. The translations plus bits of the original may help you to new perspectives on problems relating to the history of ideas. Topics such as textual authority, prose-poetic boundaries, genre, gender or even heathen substrata within Christianity, will all confront you at some stage while you read this book. In the manuscripts that preserve them, Old English poems are written virtually all in prose format and without authorial attribution, without titles, without dates of composition, with hardly any punctuation and in some cases without even the boundaries between texts being clear. Similarly, all of the many *Sagas of Icelanders* are anonymous.

If we turn to some famous Old English poems, we see first that *The Wanderer* is a challenge to read in most of these respects (see Chapter 5). There are heathen substrata in another great work, *The Dream of the Rood*, which is nonetheless renowned for a vivid use of Christian symbolism (see Chapter 6). Later Old English writers, working often in prose narratives, play with the boundaries between verse and prose in ways that are impossible to mimic now (see Chapters 9 and 11). Some Old English compounds have no equivalent in any one modern English word. And some of these conceptual challenges have re-emerged within literary theory in the modern era.

In at the deep end: how to think of translation

It's not the same if you read it in translation. True, you have an overview and a guide to the original, which, in the best cases, can almost take you there. That is what the contributors' translations are aiming to do here. Sometimes you will meet different translations in this book of the same Old English text. That's all part of the fun, a sort of challenge for you to make your own. A bad translation, a paraphrase, can be like a plot summary on the internet or one in a standard A-Level *Companion to English Literature*. It gives you the outline but leaves you cold, stripping the humanity clean off until reading the text becomes no more than a trite exercise. Avoiding paraphrase is a constant challenge for a translator. Even with the best translations, such as Heaney's *Beowulf*, you are at a remove from the original. It is the same kind of remove as when you read ancient authors such as Plato or Virgil in modern English. Old English is, in antiquity if nothing else, the classical language of English heritage, yet the relative difficulty with its language often means that after the taking or leaving of a few translations, Old English poems are sidelined in favour of later, more accessible English works.

The fact that no Old English texts seem to lead into these later English works adds further to the sense that it is remote. Reading it solely in translation may then seem rather pointless. Whereas the classics can be read in translation to gain insight into the meanings of later English works whose authors read Latin and Greek, without the same continuity with later periods it is hard to see how translations of Old English works can be regarded by anyone as equal in status to original texts from the later periods of English literature. Anyway, that's enough negativity!

The only remedy is to learn a bit of the language on which the translations are based. For one thing, learning Old English can give you a sense of the earliest history of our language that no translation can communicate. Also, the surviving corpus of Old English literature is large. We can show you that this has the merit to be studied for its own sake. Old English works have the same right to commentary and analysis as English works from the later periods. The key to good commentary is language and here Old English is no different. This ancient tongue must be learned deliberately, like any other language that is new, with the aid of guided texts for reading and grammar. But there are some advantages. Half the battle is spelling, since many words are odd-looking versions of words we have now. For instance: *enġel* ('angel', noun); *ðæt*, 'that' (pronoun); *forð*, 'forth' (i.e. 'forwards in time and space', adverb); *blīþe*, 'blithe' (i.e. 'cheerful', adjective). No doubt you notice the odd letters *æ* ('ash'), *ð* ('eth') and *þ* ('thorn'). These letters are older ways of writing the modern *a* and *th*. They are also part of the Old Norse alphabet (and still used in Iceland today). There are frequent vowel combinations (diphthongs: *eo, ea, ie*) and the letter *y* was pronounced like *u* in French *tu*. OE *ġe-* sounded like 'ye'. OE *sc-* is spelt for our *sh-*: *sċip*, 'ship', for instance; or *ġe-sċeaft* [/ye-sha:ft/], 'shaping', i.e. 'creation'. Similarly, OE *ċ-* is often spelt for our *ch-*: *ċiriċe*, 'church' [/chi:richeh/]; or *iċ* [/ich/] 'I'. Here the spelling makes Old English look decidedly alien, less familiar to us than it really is. But it is largely a matter of appearances. In these words, the letters *c* and *g* can be written dotless and vowels without length marks. They will be, with a few exceptions, in the rest of this book. You will see more on all this in Peter S. Baker's chapter on language (Chapter 10).

Translation and its discontents

So – and this is where the fun begins – there is only one way to show you what you are missing with translations even while you rely on them as guides to the original. That is to show you their perpetual shifts and instability over time. The best way to do that is to lead you through two practice commentaries on poems which will crop up later in this book, *The Wanderer* and *The Dream of the Rood*.

Ultimately *The Wanderer* (115 lines) can be read as a work of theology or philosophy. Yet its opening image, of a wandering man (a Christian hermit?, a pagan mercenary?) pulling an oar across a cold expanse of sea, is as uncanny as anything in Coleridge's *Rime of the Ancient Mariner*. On line 8 this aged figure recalls the past, then speaks to us of sorrows which, for reasons of stoicism or safety, he can reveal to no one. His king died and he has roamed the world since looking for a lord who could show him the same bond. He dreams of his lost king; then appears to hallucinate his lost kinsmen before him on the sea, confusing them with seabirds. A voice intrudes in *The Wanderer*, on line 58, to tell us of the world's transience and imminent end, of the need for resignation before this time, of the revelry of lost ages and the Creator's ability to destroy his own work. In lines 92–110 another speaker (perhaps the same man) laments the passing of joys, the coming of crazy weather before the end of the world; yet with hope of a world to come. The speech ends and the poet concludes with an affirmation to the effect that a resigned faith can lead to grace in heaven.

As a poem *The Wanderer* first presents the modern reader with an editor's conceptual problem of deciding, in the almost total absence of manuscript punctuation, at what point the poet's narrator finishes his opening speech (from *The Wanderer*, line 8). If at line 110, shortly before the poet's conclusion, then we are dealing with a persona which itself creates a sub-persona (a second speaker often known as 'the Wise Man') with a speech starting at line 92. If somewhere earlier (lines 11, 14, 16, 29, 33, 36, 44, 48 have all been suggested), then we have not one narrator, but two, in which case the speech demarcated at 92–110 belongs to the second speaker. The conceptual problem challenges every reader of this poem. Just about every translator has opted for the 'one narrator' solution. In part, this is a simplification of an American critical view from the early 1970s, one influenced by the 'stream of consciousness' of early modernism, that we can now deal with two or more 'voices' or 'planes' in this work without worrying too much about who speaks where. But mostly it is true that translators of *The Wanderer* have taken the 'one narrator' option because, if they can sell to today's novel readers the notion of a single 'character' transforming itself from despair to optimism (or deeper despair), they will do so.

R.K. Gordon (1926, rev. 1954) thus gives lines 8–110 to the Wanderer, who himself creates a 'Wise Man's' speech within his own, on lines 92–110. Similarly Crossley-Holland (1984), but more stream than consciousness in this case, blends the Wise Man's speech into the Wanderer's, which he punctuates on lines 8–110. The American Burton Raffel starts off the Wanderer's speech at line 8, ends it at line 110, but confusingly starts off the Wise Man's speech (at line 92) without finishing it. On these compromises the translators then ground interpretations. Gordon sees the Wanderer as one man reasoning until he finds hope; his translation of lines 1–2:

> Often the solitary man prays for favour, the mercy of the Lord.

Later, at 107:

> the decree of fate changes the world under the heavens.

Crossley-Holland, in the same place, modulates Gordon's hopefulness into a post-war English bleakness:

> Often the wanderer pleads for pity
> and mercy from the Lord.

Then, later:

> the world beneath the heavens is in the hands of fate.

Raffel, insofar as his interpretations bear close resemblance to *The Wanderer*, is at first religious:

> This lonely traveller longs for grace,
> For the mercy of God.

then existentialist:

> Firmly clutched by a fickle Fate.

as if his Wanderer were a fool in a godless universe.

What these three influential translators do best here is bleakness. But what if it is really quite an optimistic poem? The original lines they translate go as follows:

> Oft him anhaga   are gebideð,
> metudes miltse.

Taken more literally, this is something like 'Often the solitary man experiences grace, the mercy of the Measurer.' To compare the above translations: 'favour', 'pity' and 'grace' are all OK for *are* on line 1. Informing today's reader, however, of semantic variants is not a thing any good translator wants to do. But Gordon and Crossley-Holland go on to read *gebideð* (*bideth*, i.e. 'experiences') on line 1 for *gebiddeð* (*biddeth*, i.e. 'prays for', 'pleads for'). Raffel, with 'longs', seems to want to render both words: an ambiguous fudge. With the flat terms 'Lord' (Gordon and Crosley-Holland) and 'God' (Raffel) for *metud* in *metudes*, none of them seems interested in capturing the implications of God as the 'Measurer'. The more literal meaning of *metud* is the Deity who knows the count of days. And take line 107:

> onwendeð wyrda gesceaft   weoruld under heofonum.

More literally: 'the power that shapes events (i.e. Providence) changes the world beneath the heavens' (which is possibly a reference to a belief in the power of the planets to enact God's will by influencing human behaviour on earth). The complex phrase *wyrda gesceaft*, translated as 'the decree of fate', 'the hands of fate' and 'clutched by fickle Fate', becomes more alien to the original sense the later the translation. Only Gordon's rendering may come close. Even here, however, by removing the sense of 'shaping' in *gesceaft*, Gordon loses for you any optimistic Boethian sense of the physical connection between the Shaper of Events and us, the people whose lives He shapes. Just as little connection, you can be sure, will most translations of Old English poems give you between the poet's thoughts and your own.

The Dream of the Rood (156 lines) is thought to have been written in the early eighth century in Anglo-Saxon Northumbria. Lines from an older version survive in runes on the sides of the Ruthwell Cross from Dumfriesshire, Scotland. The complete text is found in a book, the Vercelli Book, which ended up a thousand years ago in a monastery of that name in northern Italy (see Chapter 6). In this poem we meet a man asleep at midnight who sees a vision of the Cross. The Cross tells him the story of the Crucifixion from its own unique point of view, whereupon the man promises to us his (and thus our) new resolve to lead a better life. The brilliance of the poet's image of the Cross in the opening section of his poem is overwhelming, its scale panoramic. The man giving us the frame narrative soon becomes emotionally devastated. Presently, in the words of Crossley-Holland, this narrator exclaims:

> Wondrous was the tree of victory, and I was stained
> by sin, stricken by guilt.

How close is this translation to the Old English? It is hard to know. Crossley-Holland appears to be influenced by Gordon, whose version is prose:

> Wondrous was the cross of victory, and I, stained with sins, stricken with foulness.

Raffel sets out the dreamer's words in verse:

> It was a tree of victory/
> > and splendor, and I tainted,
> Ulcered with sin.

So which of these is our closest guide to the original? It's hard to tell without looking at the original.

The original lines in this case (*The Dream of the Rood*, lines 13–14) look strange, but they go as follows:

> S̲yllic wæs se s̲igebeam,   and ic s̲ynnum f̲ah,
> forw̲undod mid w̲ommum.

A literal guide to their meaning is 'Resplendent was the victory-tree/-ray [mod. English *beam*], and I [was] stained with crimes [mod. English *sins*], wounded with defilements.' This can be stronger than what you find in the influential translations, although all translators suffer from the fact that modern English verse does not carry the same semantic charge with the same symmetry and within the same tightly compacted space.

While we are at this, the blank space on the above verse line is called a *caesura* [/sezu:ra/], a slight pause for breath. There is a caesura on every Old English verse line. A caesura divides the line's first half from its second, and sentences often start and finish at this point. Verse lines themselves, a bit like 'modern' accentual verse, are not held together by end rhyme or syllable count, but by alliteration: regularly there are four stressed syllables per line, the third one alliterating with either or both of the two before it. In this case, it is with both first and second syllables: 1. *s̲yllic*, 2. *s̲igebeam*, 3. *s̲ynnum*, and 4. *f̲ah*. As we shall see, alliteration is also of critical importance in Old Norse Eddic (anonymous balladic) and skaldic (occasional author-named) poetry (Chapters 12 and 13).

Straight off you can see that none of these translators has rendered this metrical pattern, because the modern English language will not support it. You can also see that only Raffel has attempted a caesura; wider acquaintance with his work, however, will show you that he usually leaves this out. Yet here he still leaves out the rhetorical effects of the original, which could be called *chiaroscuro* (bright–dark contrasts) and *chiasmus* (syntax rendering word types as A-B-B-A). The first effect is represented in the contrast of *syllic* ('resplendent'), with *fah* and *forwundod* ('stained', i.e. 'painted dark'; '(badly) wounded', i.e. 'dark with blood'). The second, in the pattern 'adjective – noun subject, noun subject – adjective': i.e. *syllic – sigebeam, ic – synnum fah, forwundod mid wommum* ('resplendent – victory-tree/-ray, I – stained with crimes etc.'). Crossley-Holland almost gets these effects, although he misses the mark by putting 'by sin' at the start of the next line. Gordon, whose translation he may have consulted here, dilutes these effects in prose. With 'stricken', neither's language is strong enough anyway. Crossley-Holland, in particular, muffles the power of the original with 'guilt': *wommum* is a word that more literally denotes an unhealed wound. Raffel, although he has captured some of the poet's power with the striking words 'splendor', 'tainted', 'ulcer', misses the poet's chiaroscuro and chiasmus by placing 'and splendor' not before but after the caesura and by losing the colour darkness of OE *fah* with the novelty of 'tainted'.

In fact, although Raffel uses 'cross' on his line 4, Gordon on his line 5, Crossley-Holland on his line 6, the cross in *The Dream of the Rood* is not actually called a cross (Old English *rod*) until line 44 of the poem, not until we are well within the reported direct speech of *the Cross itself* (for in this poem, the Cross speaks as a living object, in a technique known as prosopopoeia). Thus the poet's indirectness is lost, along with the full force of his doctrinal strangeness. In his book, the Cross is variously a living tree, a ray of light, a bonfire, a military standard, a gallows, a warrior (a warhorse, too, maybe), and an angel (*Dream*, 9–10):

> Beheoldon þær engel Dryhtnes ealle
> fægere þurh forðgesceaft.

More literally, 'All people and things dazzling-fair through creation beheld in that place the angel of the Lord.' (Old English *forðgesceaft* seems to mean shaping of things ('creation') forwards ('forth') through time as well as space, but no one has been able to conceptualise this word so far. Gordon's words are straightforward, as usual:

> All the Angels of God, fair by creation, looked on there.

Crossley-Holland reduces the original, then oversimplifies:

> All the angels of God,
> fair creations, guarded it.

Raffel even more so:

> Angels looked on,
> The loveliest things in creation.

All three have got their grammar wrong: *engel* on *Dream* 9 cannot be nominative plural as they have it ('angels', as subject), because this is what *englas* is later on *The Dream of the Rood*, line 106. Old English *engel* on *Dream* 9 is accusative singular ('angel', direct object of the verb *beheoldon*, 'they beheld'); the implication, worrying for some translators as it clearly is, is that the poet considered the Cross to be an angel (his view of the Crucifixion is extraordinary in more ways than this). This and other points can be argued; you will be unable to argue them, however, until you have first tried to read the poem in the original language.

Ultimately, only the translation which you make yourself can reveal effects such as those above, or allow you to feel the mind of the Anglo-Saxon author still alive, and at work, in his text after more than 1000 years. In other words, the reader's connection with the original is best made personal to the reader by the reader himself. Learning the basics of the Old English language is the best way you can begin to accomplish this. The translations available, as you have seen, differ among themselves in accuracy and in the separate literary aims and cultural distortions of their modern authors. Some translations lay off-beat trails, while all work at varying removes from the thoughts, aims and mindset of the original authors. Who can do better?, you may ask. That is true: translation is always relative, never absolute. But were you never to read more than other people's translations of Old English and Old Icelandic literature such as are represented in this book, you would remain barred from coming closer, powerless to engage with the authors, simply unable to do what you do elsewhere: read for yourself.

We hope, too, that we have not misled you about the challenges you will face: Old English and Old Icelandic *are* challenging fields. But rich rewards await those who take up the challenge. An understanding of this literature will enrich your broader understanding of literature, but, more than that, it will help you to ponder those deeper questions that lie somewhere near the heart of any humane culture: why do we write? And why, come to think of it, do we read?

The attempt to learn Old English and Old Icelandic is not a futile one. Long ago in the 890s – a period covered in this book – King Alfred became concerned about the decay of a language. Latin, in this case. A principal motive for his remarkable translation programme, which lays the basis for the development of Old English prose (see Chapter 9) was the inability of English monks and priests to read the Latin in the books housed in their monasteries. No fool, Alfred saw in the loss of a language not just the loss of a tool of communication, but the loss of a shared ritual, too. Rituals bind us together, as families, as communities and, to some degree, as nations. That the study of Old English and Old Icelandic is in decline is not in doubt. It has become marginalised by its difficulty, its otherness, but also because of laziness and the ease agenda. We believe that this decline need not become terminal and that by halting – then reversing – the decline we will bring ourselves to a closer understanding of our shared literary and social heritage, those rituals and practices that long ago helped us on a path to becoming the people we are today. And that, we think, is not a bad way to start.

Translations and texts

Crossley-Holland, Kevin, trans., *The Anglo-Saxon World: An Anthology* (Oxford, 1984).

Gordon, R.K., trans., *Anglo-Saxon Poetry* (London, 1954, repr. 1974 [first published 1926]).

Heaney, Seamus, trans., *Beowulf: A New Translation* (London, 1999).

Lapidge, Michael and John Blair, Simon Keynes and Donald Scragg, eds, *The Blackwell Encyclopaedia of Anglo-Saxon England* (Oxford, 1999).

Raffel, Burton, trans., *Poems and Prose from the Old English* (Yale, NH, 1998).

Further reading

Gneuss, Helmut, 'The Old English Language', in Godden, Malcolm, and Michael Lapidge, eds, pp. 23–54.

Godden, Malcolm and Michael Lapidge, eds, *The Cambridge Companion to Old English Literature* (Cambridge, 1991).

Mitchell, Bruce and Fred C. Robinson, *A Guide to Old English*, 6th edn (Oxford, 2000) (the 5th edn, 1992, is also OK to use).

Names to look out for

Apollonius of Tyre. Noble suitor who eventually finds the right woman. Subject of a fragmentary novel in late West Saxon.

Aragorn. Son of Arathorn, aka 'Strider'. Last in the line of Numenor and king in waiting of Gondor in *The Lord of the Rings*.

Ari inn fróði ('the learned') Þorgilsson. First Icelandic historian in the vernacular with *Íslendingabók* (*c.* 1125). The sagas regularly acknowledge his influence.

Ármóðr. Farmer in Vermaland in western Sweden. Nearly drowns in Egill's vomit one winter.

Arthur. World-famous king of the Britons. Crushes all Europe beneath him in the Insular tradition, gets crushed by Lancelot's affair with Guinevere, his queen, in the Continental.

Ásdís Stýrsdóttir. Fancied by Halli the Swedish berserk. Later married to Snorri the Goði.

Ætla. Old English name for Attila the Hun, who died of a nosebleed in 454. In the background of *Widsith* and the *Waldere* story. Known in Old Norse poetry as King Atli, second husband of Guðrún the Burgundian.

Baldr inn góði ('the good' or 'the beautiful'). Norse sacrificial lamb, son of Óðinn and Frigg. Killed accidentally on purpose by Loki who gets Hǫðr to stab him with a mistletoe spear.

Beadohild. Daughter of King Nithad and made pregnant by Weland in revenge for his captivity. Gives birth to Widia, a hero of the Goths. Old Norse version is called Bǫðvildr in *The Lay of Wayland* (*Vǫlundarkviða*).

Beowulf. Geatish prince, son of Ecgtheow. Destroys Grendel and Grendel's mother for King Hrothgar of Denmark, then dies 50 years later, as a king, in action against the Dragon that threatens his people.

Bergþóra. Njáll's wife and mother of Skarpheðinn. A powerful force at Bergþórshvol. Dies in the burning.

Bolli Bollason 'the Courteous'. Son of Guðrún by Bolli Þorleiksson. Takes revenge on Helgi, his father's killer. Later distinguishes himself as a member of the Varangian Guard in Constantinople.

Bolli Þorleiksson. Father of the above. Kjartan Óláfsson's cousin and blood brother. Marries Guðrún and kills Kjartan with 'Leg-Biter'.

Broddi Bjarnarson. Successfully saves Ale-Hood's miserable skin from outlawry by humiliating six powerful *goðar*.

Brynhildr. Warrior woman, fancies Sigurðr but finds out that he wooed her anyway in the shape of Gunnarr, now her husband. Heavy scene. To make up for this she lies to Gunnarr about Sigurðr's performance in bed.

Bǫðvarr bjarki. Great warrior with the nature of a bear. Champion of King Hrólfr of Denmark and friend of Hjalti, speaker of the surviving Norse poem *Bjarkamál*. Norse counterpart of Beowulf.

Bǫðvarr Egilsson. Drowns as a young man and is lamented by his father, along with another deceased brother, in *The Hard Loss of Sons* (*Sonatorrek*, *c.* 960).

Culhwch. Hero in the Mabinogion. Name means 'pig-run'. Needs King Arthur's help to win Olwen, a giant's daughter.

Deor. Poet of the Heodenings. Services no longer required by the king (Heoden), who caps it by giving Deor's estates to a rival, the poet Heorrenda.

Detrih. Old High German name for Theodric, the exiled Gothic king of Italy.

Eadwacer. Name given to the female speaker's possessive husband in *Wulf and Eadwacer*. Role therein unknown, but as the Old English form of Odoacer, the king who exiles Theodric from Italy, Eadwacer here may be a reference to this story.

Egill Skalla-Grímsson. The great Viking from Borg in Iceland. Rune master, warrior, poet, prolific drinker, sailor and berserk.

Eiríkr Bloodaxe. King of Norway but later reduced to ruling York. Husband of Gunnhildr. Enemy of Egill and his family.

Eiríkr the Red. Names and settles Greenland during a sentence of outlawry. Father of Leifr the Lucky.

Eormanric. Magically gifted king of the Goths and married to Ealhhid in *Widsith*. Has a 'wolvish intention' in *Deor*. Known as Jǫrmunrekkr in Old Norse, an aged despot who kills his new wife Svanhildr along with her presumed lover, his own son. Survives his mother-in-law Guðrún's attempt to kill him, albeit as a talking head.

Éomer. Prince of the Rohirrim in *The Lord of the Rings*. Name taken from *Eomer*, son of Offa of Angeln in *Beowulf*.

Éowyn. Niece of Théoden, a princess of Rohan. Name means 'horse joy'.

Fenrir. Cosmic wolf, born to swallow Óðinn whole in Ragnarǫk. As a pup, bites off the right hand of Týr as a punishment for being lied to about the strength of the chain the gods put on his paw.

Finn. Son of Folcwalda and king of the Frisians at Finnsburh. Attacks Hnæf, his brother-in-law, but is later killed himself.

Flosi Þórðarson. From Svínafell in Southeast Iceland. Kinsman to Hildigunnr the Healer, widow of Hǫskuldr Hvítanessgoði, he is the leader of the avenging burners of Bergþórshváll.

Freawaru. Daughter of Hrothgar and Wealhtheow. Betrothed to Ingeld, but Beowulf knows the marriage will not work out.

Freyja. Norse goddess of fertility, sunshine, beauty and plenty of sex. Keeps cats and lots of male friends. Lover of her brother Freyr and daughter of Njǫrðr. One of the Vanir.

Freyr. Norse god of fertility and penis enlargement. Prince of the Vanir, brother of Freyja and son of Njǫrðr. Worshipped a lot in Sweden. Sometimes called Ingvi-freyr and corresponds to the name Ingui or Ing in heathen Anglo-Saxon England.

Fricco. Apparently a Swedish name for the god Freyr as he was worshipped in Uppsala, Sweden, in the eleventh century. Stands out in more than one way.

Frigg. Norse goddess of responsible love. Unfaithful wife of Óðinn and grieving mother of Baldr. Leader of the female deities.

Gandalf. Helpful guardian wizard in *The Hobbit* and *The Lord of the Rings*. Name is taken from Gandálfr in *Vǫluspá*, a dwarf, but means 'magic demon'.

Gawain. Arthur's sister's son. Becomes the king's enforcer in the Insular tradition, although the Continental tradition doesn't really like him. Something not quite right in him, but later adopted as an English answer to Lancelot.

Geirmundr the Noisy. A Norwegian Viking brought to Iceland by Óláfr the Peacock. He marries Þuríðr Óláfsdóttir. She steals his prize sword 'Leg-Biter' from him when the marriage breaks down.

Gilli the Russian. Rich merchant in Norway and Sweden who traffics women among other commodities.

Glámr. Swedish shepherd who becomes a monstrous living dead in the North of Iceland. Re-killed by Grettir the Strong whom he curses with the fear of the dark.

Glæsir the Bull. The final incarnation of Þórólfr Lame-Foot. He kills Þóroddr Þorbrandsson.

Grendel and Grendel's mother. *Beowulf*'s single-parent family. Both descended from Cain. Grendel is a cannibal and haunts Heorot for 12 years until Beowulf kills him by ripping off his arm.

Grettir 'the Strong' Ásmundarson. The strongest man in Iceland. An outlaw for nearly 20 years. He is afraid of the dark after a curse from Glámr the ghost.

Gríma. 'Masked'. Called Wormtongue. Bad counsellor to Théoden in *The Lord of the Rings*. His real patron is Saruman, who gets it in the end.

Grímnir. 'Masked One', an itinerant wizard tortured between two fires. Óðinn in disguise, unfortunately for King Geirrǫðr, whose hall it is.

Guðrún Gjúkadóttir. Burgundian princess. Intelligent and beautiful, happily married to Sigurðr until he is killed on the orders of Brynhildr. Marries Atli and avenges her brothers on him and their children. Makes a third marriage whose sons she then loses to avengeing Svanhildr on King Jǫrmunrekkr of the Goths.

Guðrún Ósvífrsdóttir. Intelligent and beautiful. Marries Bolli Þorleiksson instead of her (we think) true love Kjartan Óláfsson. It ends in tears. One of several impressive women in *Laxdæla saga*.

Guinevere. Errant queen of King Arthur. Has a celebrated affair with Lancelot, which, in the Continental rather than Insular tradition, leads to the destruction of Camelot.

Gunnarr Gjúkason. King of the Burgundians, brother of Guðrún and Hǫgni. Kills Sigurðr, Guðrún's husband, at Brynhildr's insistence. Later goes on a one-way trip to King Atli of the Huns. Counterpart of King Guthere in *Waldere*.

Gunnarr Hámundarson. Friend of Njáll. Hallgerðr's third husband. Besieged at Hlíðarendi and killed by his enemies. Hallgerðr refuses to give him locks of her long hair to mend his bow because he had slapped her once upon a time.

Gunnarr Lambason. Þráinn's nephew. Taunts Skarpheðinn during the burning at Bergþórshváll. Loses an eye when Skarpheðinn flings one of Þráinn's teeth at him. Loses his head in more than one way on Orkney.

Gunnhildr. Queen of King Eiríkr Bloodaxe in Norway and York. Queen Mother of Haraldr Grey-Cloak. Egill's nemesis. A nymphomaniacal witch who gives Hrútr Herjólfsson an enlargement when he goes back to his fiancée.

Guthere, son of Gifica. King of the Burgundians in *Waldere*. Ambushes Waldere and his woman on their way back to Aquitaine.

Gylfi. King of Sweden in Snorri's treatise *The Beguiling of Gylfi* who tries to discover the secrets of the Æsir, the Norse gods.

Hagena. Hero in *Waldere*. Best friend of Waldere, now forced by his kinsman Guthere to ambush Waldere and his woman in the Vosges. Counterpart of Hǫgni in Old Norse and Hagen in medieval German literature.

Halldórr Snorrason. Eleventh of Snorri the Goði's 19 children. Fights alongside Haraldr Harðráði as a Varangian mercenary in Constantinople. He brings stories of these adventures to Iceland.

Hallgerðr Hǫskuldsdóttir. Half-sister of Óláfr the Peacock and aunt of Kjartan. She has beautiful long legs and hair but is mischievous, being 'extremely mixed'. Complicit in the deaths of her three husbands, most notably Gunnarr.

Halli and Leiknir. Swedish berserk brothers. Halli fancies Ásdís Stýrsdóttir. They come to a bad end through the machinations of Stýrr and Snorri the Goði.

Hallr of Síða. Convert to Christianity during Þangbrandr's mission. Chosen as Christian lawspeaker in 999. Bribes the heathen lawspeaker Þorgeirr the Goði of Ljósavatn to pronounce the law. Christianity is accepted.

Hama. Best friend of Widia. In *Beowulf*, said to steal the *Brosinga mene*, a great necklace, from King Eormanric of the Goths, but then seems to dump or donate this somewhere in exchange for the Christian faith.

Haraldr Harðráði ('hard ruler') Sigurðsson. Leader of the Varangian Guard and, later, King of Norway. A great friend of the Icelanders. A poet himself and patron of Icelandic skalds. Takes on Harold Godwinson at Stamford Bridge and loses everything.

Heimdallr. Known as 'the whitest [probably blondest] of the gods'. Gods' sentinel for the coming of Ragnarǫk. Can hear the grass grow and see infinite distance. Held by some to be identical with the Norse World Tree.

Helgi Harðbeinsson. Kills Bolli Þorleiksson in a mountain hut and is, in turn, killed by Bolli's son.

Hengest. Probably a Jute, but lieutenant of Hnæf among the Half-Danes. Takes part in the Danish vengeance for Hnæf in Finnsburh. As 'Hengistus', later invades Kent to make the first Germanic settlement of Britain.

Heorrenda. Clever poet who gets Deor's lands and position among the Heodenings. Medieval German version, Hôrant, is regarded as one of the greatest singers there ever was.

Hildebrand. Old champion in the Old High German *Hildebrandslied*. Clears the way for King Detrih's restoration in Italy by killing Hadubrand, his own son.

Hildeburh. Queen of Finn and sister of Hnæf. Pivot for all the grief going on in Finnsburh that winter and spring. Harbinger of Wealhtheow in Heorot in a similar role.

*Hildegyth. Name is reconstructed from Hiltgunt, Waldere's lover in the corresponding *Waltharius*. In *Waldere*, stands by her man in the Vosges.

Hjalti Skeggjason. The Byron of millennial Iceland. Outlawed for calling Freyja (and Óðinn) a bitch. Son-in-law of Gizurr the White, brother-in-law of Ísleifr Gizurarson, first bishop of Iceland.

Hnæf. Captain of the Half-Danes, brother of Hildeburh and through her the brother-in-law of King Finn of the Frisians. Dies at Finnsburh after the first five days.

Hondscio. Unfortunate Geat who falls asleep at his post in Heorot. Eaten by Grendel. Name means 'glove', as in Beowulf's words *glof hangode* ('the glove hung out', *Beowulf*, line 2085). 'Hung out' of Grendel's mouth?

Hrefna. Kjartan marries her on the rebound from Gúðrun. When he is killed she dies of a broken heart.

Hrethel. Old king of the Geats who brings up Beowulf and loses his favourite son Herebeald to another son Hæthcyn. Dies of grief.

Hrólfr Helgason. King of Denmark and patron of Bǫðvarr bjarki, among others. Celebrated as a wise king. Has his Custer moment in a famous last stand in Lejre. Counterpart of Hroth(w)ulf in *Beowulf*.

Hrothgar. Son of Healfdene in *Beowulf*. Aged king of the Danes, master of Heorot and victim of Grendel's depredations for 12 years. Gives Beowulf some wisdom to go home with.

Hroth(w)ulf. Son of Halga and nephew of Hrothgar. Legend has it that he takes Denmark by killing Hrethric, his cousin and Hrothgar's son. Counterpart of Hrólfr who is the patron of Bǫðvarr bjarki.

Hrútr ('ram') Herjólfsson. Hǫskuldr's half-brother. Marries Unnr Marðardóttir but it ends in divorce when Gunnhildr's ironic magic prevents him from consummating the marriage. With two later wives he has 26 children.

Hygelac. Son of Hrethel. King of the Geats and Beowulf's best friend and mother's brother. Comes to grief on a raid in Friesland.

Hǫðr. Name means 'battle'. The blind Norse god and brother of Baldr. Not the best person to be with on a quail shoot.

Hǫgni Gjúkason. Burgundian prince and counterpart of Hagena in *Waldere*. Can take open-heart surgery without anaesthetic.

Hǫskuldr Dala-Kolsson. Given Laxárdalr by Unnr the Deep-Minded. Father of Óláfr the Peacock by his Irish slave girl Melkorka.

Iðunn. Norse goddess of regeneration, keeper of the golden apples of youth. Betrayed into Þjazi's clutches, then rescued back again, by Loki.

Ingeld. Son of Froda and king of the Heathobards. Marries Freawaru but is predicted to repudiate her and assault Heorot instead. As 'Hinieldus', the subject of some songs denounced by Alcuin in a letter of 797.

Ísleifr Gizurarson. Iceland's first native-born bishop.

Jǫrmunrekkr. See *Eormanric, Guðrún Gjúkadóttir, Svanhildr*.

Kári Sǫlmundarsson. Brother-in-law of the Njálssons. Escapes the burning at Bergþórshváll and wreaks revenge on the burners.

Kjartan Óláfsson. A real dreamboat. Named for his royal Irish great-grandfather. His grandfathers are Hǫskuldr and Egill. Doesn't quite manage to marry Guðrún and it all ends in blood and tears.

Kormákr. Skaldic poet and frustrated lover.

Lancelot. Famous French gallant at Camelot. Invincible, loyal to Arthur and loving to Guinevere, all at the same time.

Leifr inn heppni ('the Lucky') Eiríksson. Erstwhile lover of Þórgunna. Said to lead expeditions to North America (*Vínland*) from Greenland.

Loki. Norse god of mischief, to put it mildly. Half-god and half-giant. Starts off a prankster and ends up looking like the Antichrist. Changes sex a few times. Biggest feat is the elimination of Baldr the Beautiful.

Melkorka. Daughter of the Irish king Mýrkjartan. Taken captive in a Viking raid at 15 and sold into slavery. Bought by Hǫskuldr in Sweden from Gilli the Russian. Mother of Óláfr the Peacock.

Merlin. Arthur's resident wizard who is also responsible for getting Arthur engendered by a man not his mother's husband.

Mordred. Arthur's nephew and also his son (by Morgan le Faye, Arthur's wicked sister). Betrays his uncle by usurping power while Arthur is on business abroad.

Nithad. King who has Weland chained and hamstrung so as to be his favourite craftsman. Old Norse version is called Níðuðr in *The Lay of Wayland* (*Vǫlundarkviða*).

Njáll Þorgeirsson. Farmer at Bergþórshvol. Wise and prescient, he is well versed in the law. Can't grow a beard. Burned at home in the end.

Njǫrðr. Norse god of the sea, fisheries and oceanic strength. Patrician deviant and father of Freyr and Freyja. Leader of the Vanir among the Æsir or main Norse gods.

Óðinn. One-eyed Norse god of poetry, magic, warfare and the dead. Patron of Egill Skalla-Grímsson and counterpart of Woden in Anglo-Saxon England. Has lots of names. See *Grímnir*.

Offa of Angeln. King of a region on the east side of the neck of the Schleswig-Holstein peninsular. Famous because he was regarded as an ancestor by King Offa of Mercia (757–96).

Óláf Pái ('the Peacock') Hǫskuldsson. Handsome bastard son of Hǫskuldr and Melkorka. Marries Þorgerðr Egilsdóttir. Builds a famous hall. Father of Kjartan and Þuríðr.

Óláfr Tryggvason. King of Norway. Probably involved in the Battle of Maldon. Forces Christianity on Iceland in 1000. Holds Kjartan hostage in Norway at just the wrong moment. His sister is the beautiful Ingibjǫrg who distracts Kjartan from Guðrún.

Ragnarǫk. End of the world, Norse style. A mixture of Armageddon, pyroclastic flow and asteroid strikes.

Roland. Charlemagne's great champion who lets himself be tricked by Ganelon, his stepfather, into taking the rearguard in a retreat up through the Pyrenees.

Saruman. 'Crafty'. The white wizard in *The Lord of the Rings* who goes bad. Patron of Wormtongue.

Scyld Scefing. Mythical founder of the Scylding dynasty in *Beowulf*. Arrives as a baby in a boat, departs as an old man likewise.

Sif. Wife of Þórr, with a son Ullr ('brilliance') by a previous marriage. Name means 'family'. Has hair made of gold. Make of that what you can.

Sigmundr. Brother of Signý, unwitting father of their son Sinfjǫtli, her designer vengeance baby. He and Sinfjǫtli are Norse versions of Sigemund and Fitela in *Beowulf*.

Signý. Sister of Sigmundr and architect of their grand vengeance against her husband Sigarr, who killed her father and 11 other brothers. Coldest woman in literature.

Sigurðr Hlǫðvisson. Earl of Orkney when Gunnarr Lambason has his head chopped off by Kári for lying about the burning of Njáll and his family. This was the Christmas before the Battle of Clontarf.

Sigurðr Sigmundarson. Brought up to kill the dragon Fáfnir for its treasure. Kills his evil mentor Reginn and takes the hoard to Gunnarr of the Burgundians. Marries Gunnarr's sister Guðrún but is killed by his brothers-in-law on the insistence of Brynhildr, Gunnarr's wife.

Skaði. Norse giantess and a goddess on skis. Hunts in the winter ranges with bow and arrow. Daughter of the giant Þjazi and divorced wife of Njǫrðr.

Skalla-Grímr Kveldúlfsson ('Baldy-Grímr son of Evening Wolf'). Settles at Borg in Iceland. Egill's demonic father.

Skarpheðinn. Njáll's eldest son. A real Viking, with crooked nose, protruding teeth and a wicked grin.

Skjǫldungar. Norse form of *Scyldingas*, Old English name for the dynasty of Danish kings in *Beowulf*.

Sleipnir. Óðinn's eight-legged stallion on which he rides to and from the world of the dead. His father is the stallion Svaðilfari. His mother is Loki (in mare's shape, of course).

Snorri the Goði ('the Broker Chieftain') Þorgrímsson. A clever man with an appetite for revenge. Lives at Helgafell. Confidant of Guðrún Ósvífrsdóttir. Conspires with Stýrr to get rid of the Swedish berserks Halli and Leiknir. Marries Ásdís Stýrsdóttir.

Starkaðr Stórvirksson. Giant-descended tall guy fighting as a mercenary in all major northern wars. Devotee also of Óðinn to whom he owes his special powers. Also a Norse version of the unnamed 'old spear-fighter' imagined by Beowulf in his prediction about the undoing of Ingeld's marriage.

Stúfr inn blindi ('the blind'). Son of Þórðr the Cat. Skaldic poet who entertains King Haraldr Harðráði in Norway.

Stýrr Þorgrímsson. Farms at Hraun. Neighbour of Snorri the Goði. Father of Ásdís.

Svanhildr Sigurðardóttir. Flaxen-haired daughter of Guðrún Gjúkadóttir. Unwisely married off to King Jǫrmunrekkr of the Goths.

Théoden. King of the Rohirrim in *The Lord of the Rings*. Name means 'king' in Old English verse.

Theodric. King of the Goths in Italy. Exiled by his enemy Odoacar (Old English Eadwacer). Known as Detrih in Old High German and Þjóðrekr or Þiðrekr in Old Norse.

Tristan. With Iseut, the Irish queen of King Mark of Cornwall, his uncle, Tristan is the first sympathetic adulterer in romance literature.

Týr. Norse god with one hand (he loses the other in a misunderstanding with Fenrir). Derived from an ancient Norse version of Jupiter or Zeus.

Ulysses. Greek lord trying to get home, otherwise known as Odysseus. Made to illustrate weakness of mind in King Alfred's version of Boethius's *On the Consolation of Philosophy* because of his whirlwind romance with Circe the witch.

Unferth. Son of Ecglaf. Hrothgar's *maitre d'* in Heorot. Has an altercation with Beowulf in which he is accused of fratricide.

Unnr in djúpúðga ('the Deep-Minded') Ketilsdóttir. Matriarchal settler of a large swath of Breiðafjǫrðr. Stands at the beginning of *Laxdœla saga*, facing Guðrún at the end.

Unnr Marðardóttir. Her divorce from Hrútr lies at the very root of the feuds that lead to the deaths of Gunnarr and Njáll.

Vafþrúðnir. Giant who contends with, and loses to, the disguised Óðinn in a lethal general knowledge quiz.

Waldere. Hero of the eponymous poem. Refugee from the court of King Ætla of the Huns, ambushed by the greedy Guthere on the way back to Aquitaine.

Wealhtheow. Hrothgar's queen. Depending on how you look at her, either wears the trousers in Heorot or is a sad victim of circumstance. Seems to turn Hrothgar off the idea of adopting Beowulf as his son.

Weland the Smith. Demon craftsman who avenges his imprisonment by killing the sons of King Nithad and raping his daughter Beadohild. Found on the Frank's Casket and known as Vǫlundr, a shaman, in Old Norse.

Widia. Gothic hero known from the poems *Deor* and *Waldere*. Gets King Theodric out of a tight spot. Best friend of Hama.

Wiglaf. Son of Weohstan. Remote kinsman of Beowulf who helps him kill the Dragon.

Wudga. See *Widia*

Þangbrandr. Son of Count Willibald of Saxony. Ferocious German born-again missionary for King Óláfr Tryggvason in Iceland.

Þjazi. Father of Skaði. Takes Iðunn to the giants' world but loses her back to Loki. Killed by the Norse gods with fire.

Þorgeirr lǫgsǫgumaðr. The 'lawspeaker' of year 1000 from Ljósavatn in the north. A heathen who makes Iceland convert to Christianity by vote of parliament.

Þorgerðr Egilsdóttir. Marries Óláfr 'the Peacock'. Agrees that Geirmundr 'the Noisy' can marry her daughter Þuríðr. Tricks Egill out of suicide after Bǫðvarr's drowning and encourages him to compose *The Hard Loss of Sons* (*Sonatorrek*).

Þorkell Eyjólfsson. Guðrún's fourth husband. Father of Gellir and great-grandfather of Ari the Learned Þorgilsson.

Þóroddr 'the Tribute Taker'. Farmer at Fróða. Rather unhappily married to Þuríðr. He drowns then returns for his funeral feast. Summonsed and banished by Þórðr 'the Cat'.

Þóroddr Þorbrandsson. Snorri the Goði's blood-brother. Burns the corpse of Þórólfr 'Lame-Foot'. Is killed by Glæsir the Bull.

Þórgunna. Imposing middle-aged Hebridean woman who moves into Fróða farm the year of the hauntings. Brings with her beautiful English linen of which Þuríðr is envious. Ex-mistress of Leifr 'the Lucky', she is buried at Skálholt.

Þórhallr. Called 'Ale-Hood'. Brews not always very drinkable ale for the Althing. Quite a miserable little man in many respects.

Þórðr Kǫttr ('the Cat'). Father of Stúfr 'the Blind'. He summons the ghosts at Fróða farm.

Þórólfr Geiríðisson. Called 'Lame-Foot'. Arnkell's father. Neighbour of Snorri the Goði. One of the nastiest and most persistent revenants in the literature. His final incarnation is as Glæsir the bull.

Þórólfr Skalla-Grímsson. Egill's handsome and capable brother. Egill doesn't like him. Mark-II version of his like-named uncle. This one is killed at the Battle of Vinheiðr or *Brunanburh*.

Þórr. Norse god of thunder, the weather, winds and sailing at sea. Packs a big iron hammer which he uses to smash the skulls of giants. Not the intellectual among Norse gods.

Þórsteinn the Red. Son of Unnr the Deep-Minded. Ruler of half of Scotland. Killed at Caithness.

Þráinn Sigfússon. Gunnarr's uncle. Killed by Skarphéðinn in spectacular fashion in a skate-by head splitting, which causes his teeth to spill famously on to the ice.

Þuríðr. Snorri Goði's half-sister. Married to Þoroddr at Fróða farm. Mother (we suspect by Bjǫrn from Breiðavík) of young Kjartan.

CHAPTER 2

Old English influence on *The Lord of the Rings*

Clive Tolley

Pearl of delight that a prince doth please
To grace in gold enclosed so clear,
I vow that from over orient seas
Never proved I any in price her peer.
So round, so radiant ranged by these,
So fine, so smooth did her sides appear
That ever in judging gems that please
Her only alone I deemed as dear.
Alas! I lost her in garden near:
Through grass to the ground from me it shot;
I pine now oppressed by love-wound drear
For that pearl, mine own, without a spot.

These lines were written by J.R.R. Tolkien (1892–1973) who also wrote *The Lord of the Rings* (1954–5). As everyone knows, the three books which make up *The Lord of the Rings* were adapted in the early years of the twenty-first century into a world-famous film trilogy by the New Zealand director Peter Jackson. Tolkien was a professor of Old and Middle English in the University of Oxford. The lines above are his translation of the opening stanza of *Pearl*, which is one of the greatest Middle English poems of Chaucer's time, the late fourteenth century. In the stanza above, the narrator of *Pearl* describes the loss of a precious pearl and his search for it. But the pearl, it emerges, is a symbol of his young daughter. Perhaps her name was Margaret, which means 'pearl'. At any rate, the exuberant poetic descriptions in *Pearl* are expressions both of the father's loss and his quest to find her, concluding with his vision of her, resplendent in paradise, but separated by the great gulf of death, no longer to please a prince of this world, but the Prince of Heaven himself.

Old English literature might be looked upon as just such a pearl. The study of Old English is the study of a past culture: death separates us from its creators. Yet the people of those days were men and women like us, with the same depths of experience and the same ability to express those depths. Some of their creations indeed emerge as pearls of great price, for those who seek to find them. The father in *Pearl* sets out from the familiar surroundings of his garden and it is only by following this route that the otherworldly splendours of paradise are finally revealed. In this chapter, I would like to come to Old English along a similar path, starting from what (probably) is the more familiar world of Tolkien's fiction or, rather, taking a further step back, from Peter Jackson's film adaptation of *The Lord of the Rings*. The film presents the viewer with a rich array of visual and emotional ravishment. And the uncut versions, drawing also from *The Silmarillion* (1977), are rich in characterisation. Striding through Middle Earth, from *The Fellowship of the Ring* through *The Twin Towers* to his crowning in *The Return of the King*, is 'Strider' Aragorn, son of Arathorn, last of the kings of Gondor. He is in some way reminiscent of Beowulf, son of Ecgtheow, monster-slayer general and the future king of Geatland. Like Beowulf, whose father Ecgtheow is at best a violent renegade passing through one kingdom after another, Aragorn is a man with a dubious family past. He is wary of his own lineage and in *The Return of the King*, just like the hero of *Beowulf*, he takes up the crown not with ambition, but with much persuasion after harbouring doubts about his own suitability for the role. Aragorn, to the extent of this likeness, was probably based on the Geatish hero of whom we shall read so much in this book and especially in the following chapter. And Rohan, the kingdom of horsemen into which Aragorn leads two of his fellowship in the second part of *The Lord of the Rings*, was based in large part on the country and great hall of Hrothgar, king of Denmark, in the first two-thirds of *Beowulf*. It is obvious, but needs restating, that the books could not have been written, the films made, without the great Old English poem named *Beowulf*.

From among the many striking scenes in Tolkien's novels and Jackson's films, I will pick one that relates to the court of Rohan and particularly to Théoden, its king. Here I have to assume you are to some extent familiar with the film, if not the novel, *The Lord of the Rings*. Let us look now at the arrival of Gandalf and his companions at the 'Golden Hall' in Edoras, court of Théoden, king of Rohan. Here we see two worlds confronting one another and finally uniting. One of these worlds is the Quest of the Ring, with Gandalf as its guide and mentor; the other is that of the proud Rohirrim, led by the decrepit Théoden, who is under the thumb of the treacherous counsellor Gríma ('Masked'), nicknamed Wormtongue. There are some splendid touches in the film. For example, the tossing of the banner of Rohan as rubbish in the wind in *The Two Towers* is not something Tolkien wrote, but surely he would have been gratified to see this symbolic representation of the inner collapse of Rohan presented in a form which works well in this visual format. The character of Wormtongue is also presented outstandingly well, even though in details it differs from what Tolkien wrote. Above all, the lady Éowyn ('Equine joy'), niece to the king, is finely presented in all her complexity, exceeding the sometimes stereotypical depiction Tolkien affords her. How subtle, for example, is the moment when she almost yields to Wormtongue, then turns on him in fury.

But – and I feel that amidst all the adulation that has surrounded the film it is owed to Tolkien to point such matters out – the exorcism of 'Théoden King', one of the most dramatic events in the 'Golden Hall' in the court of Edoras, capital of Rohan, misses Tolkien's point. In the film we are presented, essentially, with a contest of wizardry between Gandalf and his fellow wizard Saruman ('Crafty'), who, having turned to evil, has somehow possessed Théoden and who is finally exorcised from the king by Gandalf. In this show of strength Gandalf reveals that he is no longer Gandalf the Grey, but Gandalf the White, appropriating Saruman's erstwhile colour, the symbol of the purity he has now lost. The reason the scene is unfortunate – apart from its simply departing from the book – is that moral uprightness and freedom, and their opposites, are presented as imposed from outside. All that is needed to solve the problem is a powerful enough magician to impose his will on the situation. In other words, *might is right* – a principle which Tolkien explicitly says Gandalf refuses to adopt. In the book, Gandalf *persuades* the king to relinquish the counsel of Wormtongue. This isn't as visually dramatic, but it is far more adult and, what is more, it is an important part of Tolkien's message. The free peoples of Middle Earth are free not so much because of political structures, but because they choose to be so, even in the face of ill advice and pressure from outside. Freedom is defined from within, not imposed from outside. It relates to our stance on good and evil, rather than to political systems. In our own world, we see regimes around us appropriating to themselves the moral high ground and seeking to impose what they usually term 'democracy' by force, acting in much the same way as Gandalf does in Jackson's film. Tolkien has often been criticised for writing an indulgent fantasy work with no relevance to the real world. I would like to suggest, without engaging in a detailed political debate, that the point he is making here is strikingly pertinent to many of the events being perpetrated on the world stage around us.

What has this got to do with Old English?

Attitudes towards Tolkien and Old English are often the same. Both are seen as irrelevant. Prejudices like this should always be countered. Picking a scene from the film and – without being swayed by the hype – comparing it with what Tolkien actually wrote is a straightforward and graphic way of developing a vital skill: a critical approach, by means of which we may hope to uncover the meaning of the scene and the details of how this meaning is realised. This goes for whether the scene is by Tolkien or by Jackson. In the process we should be able to come to an appreciation of the true extent – even if in the end we may decide that extent is limited – to which a work such as *The Lord of the Rings* is a serious book, about serious, adult issues which will always remain current. The same approach is called for with any work of Old English literature.

Having realised that Tolkien deserves a serious critical approach, we must, of course, apply this not only to the derivative film, but also to Tolkien's own text. Doing this reveals a second reason for unease with Jackson's approach in the Golden Hall 'exorcism' scene. One of the best-known influences on Tolkien is the Old English epic – or, more correctly, extended elegiac – poem *Beowulf*. As you see, our book is named after *Beowulf* and the chapter after this one is especially focused on the poem. *Beowulf* was immensely important to Tolkien when he wrote *The Lord of the Rings*. While there are many points throughout Tolkien's work which can be traced back to the poem, the Golden Hall scene forms a sort of cluster, a concentrate. And yet in large part Jackson has chosen not to follow Tolkien here, but to go his own way in this scene. This may well be due to the general exigencies of film making rather than a specific decision, but it is nonetheless unfortunate. Before showing how Tolkien handled this scene, let us take a broader view of his influences.

The Rohirrim are a proud race of horse lords. They clearly belong to a pre-urban, and pre-urbane, society, where the code of honour is defined by truth, loyalty and courage. They are, in fact, the Anglo-Saxons, as imagined and idealised by Tolkien. Indeed, the language they speak in the book is Old English. The foundation legend of the English, as you have seen in the previous chapter, is that they came from northern Germany and Denmark in 449 at the invitation of the British king, King Vortigern of Kent, to act as mercenaries, and were given the isle of Thanet as reward. In their greed they seized Kent for themselves and, subsequently, the whole of England, driving the British out. Likewise, in the prehistory of the novels, the Rohirrim ride from the north and fight as confederates at the Battle of Celebrant and are given Rohan by the realm of Gondor. 'Gondor' is parallel to the Roman Empire, which still nominally existed when the English came to England, although it had no authority in Britain any longer. The land the Rohirrim have been given is said to be largely empty, however, and there is no tale of rebellion and seizing of more land: the Rohirrim stay loyal to Gondor. In one essential, the Rohirrim differ markedly from the English, in their mastery of horses. The Riders of Rohan have many names in *Éo-* such as Éomer and Éowyn. That is because the word *eoh* is the Old English for 'horse' (an ancient word related to (but not borrowed from) the Latin word *equus*). There are complex reasons for Tolkien's choice here, but I would like to mention just one. The first kings of the English when they settled in Kent were called Hengest and Horsa. These names mean 'stallion' and 'horse'. Yet there are no legends associating the English with horses. But inspired by the implications of the names, and enticed into recreating a lost legend, Tolkien forged a whole race of Anglo-Saxon horsemen.

Arrival at the court of Rohan

Having created a (slightly modified) race of Anglo-Saxons, Tolkien naturally crafted a scene among them where he could closely echo his favourite Old English literary work, *Beowulf*. The arrival of Gandalf, Aragorn, Gimli and Legolas at *Meduseld* ('mead hall' in Old English), the hall of King *Théoden* (Old English for 'lord'), in the settlement of *Edoras* (Old English for 'courts') in Rohan (Book III, Chapter 6) is based precisely on an extended scene in *Beowulf*. This is the arrival of the Geatish hero, Beowulf, and his men at the Danish hall of Heorot. In the poem, Beowulf, a man with the strength of 30, has come to Denmark to rid King Hrothgar, king of the Danes, of Grendel, a cannibalistic monster who has preyed on Heorot for 12 years. To see the influences from *Beowulf* to *The Lord of the Rings*, have a look at some passages set side by side in the box on page 43. Precise points of similarity in the two are linked by means of numbers.

My comparison will use a translation of *Beowulf*, although Tolkien would have had the original poem in mind. Finding the right translation is a matter of some importance, since Tolkien had an acute sensitivity to linguistic registers. Not surprisingly, given the difference in backgrounds, the scriptwriters of Jackson's film version don't have Tolkien's knowledge of the English language, or his sensitivity to its use, but thankfully a great deal of the dialogue in the films derives directly from the book. In what follows I shall use the recent translation of Seamus Heaney. It is a version with its own faults and foibles, but whose isn't?, one might well ask. And it is appropriate to render the words of the greatest poet writing in English over a millennium ago with those of one of the most respected poets of our day, one who has himself been moved by the poetic splendour of the original work.

Arrivals at Heorot and Meduseld

A *Beowulf*, lines 224–490

Beowulf and his followers disembark from their ship and are met by the Danish coastguard, who greets them in the following words:

[1] 'What kind of men are you who arrive [2] rigged out for combat in coats of mail, [3] sailing here [4] over the sea-lanes [5] in your steep-hulled boat? [6] I have been stationed

as lookout on this coast for a long time.

My job is to watch the waves for raiders, any danger to the Danish shore.

[7] Never before has a force under arms disembarked [8] so openly – not bothering to ask

if the sentries allowed them safe passage or the clan had consented. [9] Nor have I seen

a mightier man-at-arms on this earth than the one standing here: [10] unless I am mistaken,

[11] he is truly noble. This is no mere

hanger-on in a hero's armour.

So now, before you fare inland

[12] as interlopers, [13] I have to be informed

about who you are and where you hail from.

Outsiders from across the water,

I say it again: [14] the sooner you tell where you come from and why, the better.'

Beowulf replies that they have come from Hygelac of the Geats to help Hrothgar against the ravages of the monster. The coastguard replies:

[15] 'Anyone with gumption

and a sharp mind will take the measure

B *The Lord of the Rings*, Book III, Chapter 6

As the company approaches Edoras, Legolas is able to discern the scene and the details of the royal hall Meduseld: 'And it seems to my eyes that it is [18] thatched with gold. [19] The light of it shines far over the land.'

As they approach, Aragorn sings a song in the language of Rohan, 'Where now the horse and the rider?' [in the film, this song is sung by Théoden at the Battle of Helm's Deep, where, it could be argued, it acquires greater pertinence and poignancy]: this is inspired by a passage in the Old English poem *The Wanderer*, but its theme of the passing of things is common to *Beowulf*.

The company is greeted by a warden at the gates:

It is the will of Théoden King that none should enter his gates, save those who know our tongue and are our friends. None are welcome here in days of war but our own folk, and those that come from Mundburg in the land of Gondor. [1] Who are you that [3] come [8] heedless [4] over the plain thus [2] strangely clad, [5] riding horses like to our own horses? [6] Long have we kept guard here, and we have watched you from afar. [7] Never have we seen other riders so strange, [9] nor any horse more proud than is one of these that bear you. [11] He is one of the *Mearas*, [10] unless our eyes are cheated by some spell. [13] Say, are you not a wizard, some [12] spy from Saruman, or phantoms of his craft? [14] Speak now and be swift!

Aragorn and Gandalf explain they had met Éomer, but the guard replies that Wormtongue has forbidden any to see the king; Gandalf says his [26] errand is with the king and no one else, and bids the guard go and tell Théoden. The guard asks of two things: what's said and what's done. I believe what you have told me: that you are a troop

loyal to our king. So come ahead
with your arms and your gear, [16] and I will guide you.'

He promises Beowulf's ship will be [17] carefully guarded. The Geats march on, the poet commenting on the boar images on their helms, towards the hall, Heorot, adorned in gold:

They marched in step,
hurrying on till the timbered hall
rose before them, [18] radiant with gold.
Nobody on earth knew of another
building like it. Majesty lodged there,
[19] its light shone over many lands.

The guard returns to his post on the shore:

[20] 'It is time for me to go.

May the Almighty
Father keep you and in His kindness watch over your exploits. I'm away to the sea, back on alert against enemy raiders.'

The Geats make their way up the [21] stone paved street. They put their [22] weapons against the wall of the hall, and sit on a [23] bench. Wulfgar, King Hrothgar's [24] officer ['I am Hrothgar's herald and officer'], comes to question them, and comments on their [25] boldness. Beowulf declares who he is, and says he wants to report his [26] errand to Hrothgar himself. Wulfgar says he will ask, [27] 'then hurry back with whatever reply it pleases him to give'. He advises Hrothgar not to refuse the request. The king gives a speech: he knows Beowulf by name and reputation, and bids the Geats enter. [28] Wulfgar returns with the message, telling them they may go in in their helms, but [29] must leave their weapons outside. Beowulf greets Hrothgar and offers to fight without weapons against the monster Grendel. Hrothgar gladly accepts Beowulf's offer, and after telling him a little about Grendel asks him to join the feast in the hall. [30] The old king Hrothgar has Unferth below him in the hall, and his wife Wealhtheow serves.

what names he should give, and remarks that they seem [25] fell and grim beneath their tiredness; they give their names. The guard says he will go in, and tells them to [27] 'wait here a little while, and I will bring you such answer as seems good to him.' He goes in and then [28] returns, saying they may come in, but [29] must leave their weapons, which the doorwardens will [17] keep. The company goes through the gates; 'they found a broad path, [21] paved with hewn stones'. The hall and its surrounds are described; at the top of the stair were stone [23] seats. The guard, who has [16] guided them up, now says farewell: [20] 'There are the doors before you. I must return now to my duty at the gate. Farewell! And may the Lord of the Mark be gracious to you!' They ascend the stair, and are greeted by Háma [24] the doorwarden ['I am the doorward of Théoden'], who asks for their weapons. There is a heated debate over this, but the weapons are laid aside – Aragorn lays Andúril [22] against the wall – and in the end Háma allows only the staff of Gandalf to pass: [15] 'in doubt a man of worth will trust to his own wisdom. I believe you are friends and folk worthy of honour, who have no evil purpose. You may go in.'

[30] In the hall, the aged Théoden sits with Éowyn behind and Gríma at his feet.

Wormtongue and Unferth

From this point Tolkien's narrative diverges from *Beowulf*. Théoden greets Gandalf coldly, whereas Hrothgar greets Beowulf warmly. Wormtongue immediately adds to Théoden's coldness with further insult. It is on Wormtongue that the influence from *Beowulf* now focuses. Whereas the scene of arrival shows a point by point, but ultimately fairly superficial influence from *Beowulf* to *The Lord of the Rings*, with Wormtongue we encounter a more imaginative development that springs, largely, from a philological consideration. Specifically, the focus of Tolkien's inspiration lies in a name. For Wormtongue is based, in part, on *Beowulf*'s 'Unferth', a fractious Danish courtier who delivers a personal attack on Beowulf straight after the passage summarised in the box on pages 43 and 44. In Old English Unferth's name means 'strife', although it has other implications such as 'senseless'. It is typical that Tolkien should focus his interest on such a linguistically complex character as Unferth, who seems to have been specially invented by the poet of *Beowulf* to cause strife. Unferth's main role in the poem is to accuse Beowulf of not being up to the job of dealing with Grendel, on the basis of his bad performance in a swimming (or rowing) match he once had with another hero at sea. Beowulf tries to put the record straight, rounds on Unferth and defends himself by pointing out that Unferth has hardly shown himself the hero lately given that Grendel is still there. Moreover, the word is that Unferth killed his own brothers. Unferth's speech is strange being so incongruous with Hrothgar's warm welcome earlier, especially considering that Unferth is his official 'spokesman' (Old English *þyle*; compare p. 205). It is no surprise that Unferth has been the topic of a great deal of discussion by scholars of Old English literature.

Unferth shows up again later in *Beowulf* when Beowulf has the task of killing Grendel's mother in her underwater lair. She lives in the 'Mere' a few miles away from Heorot, and from there she came the night before to avenge her son whom Beowulf killed. When Beowulf is about to dive into this gloomy pool to fight Grendel's mother, Unferth lends him his sword, which is called Hrunting. Beowulf requests that if he is killed this sword should go back to its owner. The difference between this Unferth and the previous chagrin-driven criminal by that name is noted by the poet of *Beowulf*, who says he must have been drunk when he spoke before. He also points out that Unferth is too much of a coward to undertake the exploit himself.

Several times the poet mentions how the Danish court is now at peace, but will not always be so. Later the king's nephew, Hrothulf, will stage his coup, engaging in strife with, and indeed slaying, his cousins who are the sons of King Hrothgar. One scene in *Beowulf* where this contrast is pointed out goes as far as citing Unferth as the man sitting at the king's feet. Does the poet mean that Unferth was to be involved in stirring up strife between the two sides of the family, supporting the upstart Hrothulf?

Going back to *The Lord of the Rings*, we see that Wormtongue steals the king's sword and cravenly refuses to march to war against the Orcs. While he is not accused of fratricide, later on, back in the Shire, it turns out that Wormtongue has murdered Lotho. This accusation is poured on him with scorn by Saruman, his once 'white wizard' master. Not a good move for Saruman, for Wormtongue is thus egged on to murder him. Wormtongue is a traitor, a spy of Saruman in the court of Théoden, who has gained the trust of the king against his better judgement. He also sticks loyally to his master Saruman, even in beggary, up to the last moment when he murders him. In *Beowulf*, likewise, it may be supposed that Unferth serves King Hrothgar until he betrays him in Hrothulf's rebellion.

Théoden's enmity towards his nephew Éomer, and the death of his son Théodred, which Wormtongue mentions in one breath, is based on this family struggle in the Danish royal house. In *Beowulf* there is little doubt that Hrothulf is already a villainous traitor in this way. Yet in the Old Icelandic version of this story, which calls Hrothulf 'Hrólfr Pole-Ladder' (*kraki*), this man is regarded as a great hero and the epitome of kingship (see p. 27). In Tolkien's *The Lord of the Rings*, Théoden's shift from blame to praise of his nephew seems to reflect a vacillation in the author between these Old English and Old Norse traditions, which he exploits for imaginative purposes. Tolkien chooses to exonerate Éomer. In line with this, Tolkien retains the tragic death of the king's son, but divorces this from any action of Éomer's.

Unferth is an ambiguous character; Tolkien was invariably drawn to ambiguous sources when they offered the opportunity for imaginative resolution. In *The Lord of the Rings* Tolkien does indeed resolve many of the ambiguities of Unferth in Wormtongue. In contrast to the strange behaviour of Unferth as a favoured counsellor, there is no real doubt of Wormtongue's position as a disloyal coward. It is just that the old king – and he alone – has been deceived and is himself undeceived in the course of events. Hence Wormtongue's presence at court, and his attack on Gandalf, are both explained naturally. The inexplicable change of character of Unferth in generously offering Beowulf his sword is made use of by Tolkien. However, Tolkien maintains a consistency of character in Wormtongue and so turns the action in *Beowulf* on its head; far from Wormtongue offering a sword to anyone, he steals the king's. Wormtongue's unwillingness to march to war with Théoden matches Unferth's unwillingness to fight the monster in the Mere.

Tolkien has been able to rationalise Wormtongue out of the ambiguous Unferth by using the most elusive of all the latter's characteristics, his treachery. He follows a creative urge to tie up the loose ends left by the *Beowulf* poet. And he reads other things into the original scene in the hall in *Beowulf*, more than could ever be justified on a scholarly basis, yet which show his highly creative attention to the human complexity of the scene. Here I am thinking of a detail about Wormtongue vis à vis Éowyn, the king's niece. The princess Éowyn fulfils the same role in Meduseld as Wealhtheow, the queen of King Hrothgar, does in Heorot. The poet says nothing of the relationship between Wealhtheow and Unferth, but merely juxtaposes them by presenting the king and his nephew with Unferth at their feet and Wealhtheow coming to speak to the king. What is the faithless Unferth likely to be thinking of as he sits there looking up at the beautifully adorned queen as she speaks? He answers by telling us that Wormtongue had his eye on Éowyn. As noted, Peter Jackson goes one further in the film and lends Éowyn a momentary hesitation towards Wormtongue, a scene acted with fine delicacy by Miranda Otto.

The situation in Edoras is far plainer than that in Heorot and it is by imbuing the scene with strife that Tolkien makes it so. The major difference between the two arrival scenes, which we have just compared, is that the Geats are welcomed by the Danes, whereas Aragorn and friends are cold shouldered by the Rohirrim as a result, it emerges, of the machinations of Wormtongue's strife. It is clear that Tolkien paid homage to *Beowulf* with the detailed, but circumstantial, similarity of these arrival scenes. But it is also clear that this homage was less important to him than his imaginative development of Unferth, the ambiguous character whose name means 'strife'.

The importance of *Beowulf*

The detailed use Tolkien made of *Beowulf* in the depiction of the court of Rohan should now be clear. But why did he feel the ancient poem was so important that he should enter into such a dialogue with it – and indeed, on the wider scale, devote his whole life to its exposition?

As if he knew this question would come up some time, Tolkien attempts something of an answer to it in a lecture which was then published as the essay '*Beowulf*: The Monsters and the Critics'. This lecture had a profound effect within the field of Old English studies when it was delivered in 1936.

It continues to be essential reading to this day, a rare commendation for any academic work. Tolkien's achievement was to salvage *Beowulf* from the hands of critics who were blind to the factor that made the poem great. It is hard to imagine, but *Beowulf* was once studied either as Scandinavian history, a repository of artefacts for archaeologists or as an archive of Old English linguistic features and grammatical forms. In his own day Tolkien helped to rescue the poem for posterity. One method he adopts is rather extraordinary for an academic, but is actually the key to the success of his piece. He uses like to defend like, that is to say he adopts a mantle of heightened poetic, almost mantic, expression in order to defend the poetic craft of the work he is discussing. Needless to say, my words here are scarcely sufficient to explain why Tolkien's article is so striking and so I will give a few further indications.

In the first place, Tolkien stresses the obvious. One problem for critics of the poem was that, on the one hand, they felt it to be great, but, on the other hand, they were embarrassed by the subject matter, the slaying of three monsters. To use a modern, if itself soon to become dated, image, this is as if a great poet decided to make use of his PlayStation as a source of inspiration for the composition of his greatest work and yet succeeded in producing a masterpiece. Or, as Tolkien puts it, as if Milton had decided to recount the fairytale of Jack and the Beanstalk in noble verse. Tolkien stresses that this is entirely the wrong way to look at things. He points out that the universally acknowledged greatness of the poem's style would be felt merely incongruous, not dignified, if the subject the poet chose to place at the centre – the fights with the three monsters – were not well suited to the expression of greatness in the hands of a gifted artist. 'I would suggest, then', he says, 'that the monsters are not an inexplicable blunder of taste; they are essential, fundamentally allied to the underlying ideas of the poem, which give it its lofty tone and high seriousness.' As a parallel, he points out that the outline story of Shakespeare's masterpiece *King Lear* is quite as trite as that of *Beowulf*.

For Tolkien, the poet's choice of subject has resulted in a poem with greater depth and applicability than if he had chosen a 'realistic' human situation from history:

> It is just because the main foes in *Beowulf* are inhuman that the story is larger and more significant than this imaginary poem of a great king's fall. It glimpses the cosmic and moves with the thought of all men concerning the fate of human life and efforts; it stands amid but above the petty wars of princes, and surpasses the dates and limits of historical periods, however important. At the

beginning, and during its process, and most of all at the end, we look down as if from a visionary height upon the house of man in the valley of the world.

In particular, he focuses on the 'ancient theme: that man, each man and all men, and all their works shall die': 'for the universal significance which is given to the fortunes of the hero it is an enhancement and not a detraction, in fact it is necessary, that his final foe should be not some Swedish prince, or treacherous friend, but a dragon: a thing made by imagination for just such a purpose.'

Tolkien highlights some of the artistry involved in the presentation of this theme:

> It is essentially a balance, an opposition of ends and beginnings. In its simplest terms it is a contrasted description of two moments in a great life, rising and setting; an elaboration of the ancient and intensely moving contrast between youth and age, first achievement and final death. It is divided in consequence into two opposed portions, different in matter, manner, and length.

In Tolkien's view, this structure is a reflection of the very essence of Old English alliterative metre: each line of verse is composed of two balanced, but not rhythmically equal, half-lines.

Another impressive aspect of the essay is Tolkien's gift of expression, reflecting a well-read and considered understanding of his subject. He says the greatness of fine poetry cannot be communicated by analysis. Cornered, however, into trying to do just this, Tolkien responds by composing a piece of writing which is itself infused with poetic expression. He alludes to 'Jabberwocky', a poem in Lewis Carroll's *Through the Looking Glass and What Alice Found There* (1871). Who could better this metaphor for *Beowulf*'s learned but short-sighted researchers at this time?

> For it is of their nature that the jabberwocks of historical and antiquarian research burble in the tulgy wood of conjecture, flitting from one tum-tum tree to another. Noble animals, whose burbling is on occasion good to hear; but though their eyes of flame may sometimes prove searchlights, their range is short.

Even today, perhaps as a result of this passage, you find the name 'Jabberwocky' sometimes used by academics outside the field as shorthand mockery for Old English, Old Norse, anything medieval like that. But that is their loss, not yours. Tolkien, however, wishes to shift the study of Old English away from such uninspired and short-sighted 'jabberwocky'. In the same piece he went on to use an image resonant of biblical parable to express the generally deficient approach of those critics who viewed *Beowulf* as a great artefact composed out of elements from yet older tales:

> I would express the whole industry in yet another allegory. A man inherited a field in which was an accumulation of old stone, part of an older hall. Of the old stone some had already been used in building the house in which he actually lived, not far from the old house of his fathers. Of the rest he took some and built a tower. But his friends coming perceived at once (without troubling to climb the steps) that these stones had formerly belonged to a more ancient building. So they pushed the tower over, with no little labour, in order to look for hidden carvings and inscriptions, or to discover whence the man's distant forefathers had obtained their building material. Some suspecting a deposit of coal under the soil began to dig for it, and forgot even the stones. They all said: 'This tower is most interesting.' But they also said (after pushing it over): 'What a muddle it is in!' And even the man's own descendants, who might have been expected to consider what he had been about, were heard to murmur: 'He is such an odd fellow! Imagine his using these old stones just to build a nonsensical tower! Why did not he restore the old house? He had no sense of proportion.' But from the top of that tower the man had been able to look out upon the sea.

But Tolkien is at his best when he is expounding the implications of a short expression, from which the poem's overall significance may be gleaned:

> It is in *Beowulf* that a poet has devoted a whole poem to the theme [of 'this indomitability, this paradox of defeat inevitable yet unacknowledged'], and has drawn the struggle in different proportions, so that we may see man at war with the hostile world, and his inevitable overthrow in Time. The particular is on the outer edge, the essential in the centre.
>
> Of course, I do not assert that the poet, if questioned, would have replied in the Anglo-Saxon equivalents of these terms. Had the matter been so explicit to him, his poem would certainly have been the worse. None the less we may still, against his great scene, hung with tapestries woven of ancient tales of ruin, see the *hæleð* walk. When we have read his poem, as a poem, rather than as a collection of episodes, we perceive that he who wrote *hæleð under heofenum* may have meant in dictionary terms 'heroes under heaven', or 'mighty men upon earth', but he and his hearers were thinking of the *eormengrund*, the great earth, ringed with *garsecg*, the shoreless sea, beneath the sky's inaccessible roof; whereon, as in a little circle of light about their halls, men with courage as their stay went forward to that battle with the hostile world and the offspring of the dark which ends for all, even the kings and champions, in defeat. [. . .] Death comes to the feast, and they say He gibbers: He has no sense of proportion.

No one could fail to be impressed by the sustained quality of this writing. Yet more lies in these passages (and in the whole essay) than meets the eye.

Lewis Carroll, like Tolkien, was an Oxford don who spent much time in recounting fabulous adventure stories. In Carroll's case, these were centred on the little girl Alice who visits *Wonderland* (1865) and then steps *Through the Looking Glass* (1871). Tolkien, in his way, is hinting that his lecture on *Beowulf* was about more than just the Old English poem. It pointed to his own work as well, and indeed to much other literary work besides. What his essay amounts to is, at the very least, the intimation of a general approach to literature. More specifically, when we look at Carroll's third great work, his nonsense poem *The Hunting of the Snark* (1876), we find what appears to be a deep concern over the bewildering quest of life which concludes in death. In Tolkien's view of it, this is the theme at the centre of *Beowulf*, of Tolkien's own works and, indeed, of great literature in general.

In my second quotation above from 'The Monster and the Critics', we see Tolkien imagining the use of old stone to build a new tower, from which to see the sea. This is an image which celebrates the renewal of poetic life from older materials. Tolkien's target here was allegory, a textual reading of hidden or symbolic or secondary meanings, which, in his view, amounted to fragmenting the text, pulling it apart, with a resulting loss in understanding. Tolkien in fact castigates allegorical readings of his work in his introduction to *The Lord of the Rings*. The rise of Hitler in World War II? Forget it. It is as if he resented being forced in these books to hold back something powerful, something symbolic, in the chains of an allegory which he says he never intended. In Tolkien's creative writing the tower and the sea are recurrent and important themes, second, probably, only to the tree, which provided Tolkien with another image for story in his work *On Fairy Stories*. In fact, Tolkien's tower-and-sea image in 'The Monsters and the Critics' has a twofold derivation which reflects how this essay looks both outwards to the great tradition of literature of which *Beowulf* is part and inwards, to his own fictional world. Outwardly, more or less the same image was used by the great Victorian writer and poet Matthew Arnold in his critical discussion (1888) of the thirteenth-century *Mabinogion*, a collection of 11 tales in medieval Welsh. Inwardly, this image is central to Tolkien's private tales of Earendil (the wellspring, indeed, of the world of Middle Earth), which I consider later. Of course, the tower is an ancient image, one redolent of associations in literature from the most ancient up to the present. There is no doubt Tolkien meant to touch on this network of allusion as well.

In my third quotation from 'The Monsters and the Critics' above, on man's inevitable overthrow in Time, Tolkien brilliantly encapsulates the main theme of *Beowulf* by recreating for us something of the flavour of the poem itself. Tolkien focuses on a few words fraught with dim echoes of a lost mythology (*heofen, eormengrund, garsecg*). Tolkien is writing more as a poet than an academic here – but it is nonetheless scholarly writing at its best. What he writes may be applied to his own work almost as pertinently as to *Beowulf.* This indicates not merely that he has his own works in mind, but that the influence of the Old English poem, not so much in superficial plot terms, but in what it is *about*, its ethos, has been enormous. While *The Lord of the Rings* is a celebration of what Tolkien found beautiful, more deeply it is an elegy for the passing of such things.

Other sources for *The Lord of the Rings*

It would be wrong to leave you with the impression that *Beowulf*, or even Old English, are the only sources that inspired Tolkien. His writings are saturated with a familiarity and respect for the great works of classical and medieval literature. *The Lord of the Rings* can scarcely be understood without recognising the huge importance of the great Roman epic, the *Aeneid*. The fall of Gondolin, an ancient legend by the time of the hobbits but one which was formative of the world they live in, is based on the fall of Troy in the second book of the *Aeneid* (and the description of Gondolin's fall in *The Silmarillion* closely matches that in the *Aeneid*). More importantly, Frodo owes much to the depiction of the dutiful Aeneas, founder of Rome, in the Roman epic. Not all Tolkien's sources were such masterpieces, however.

If we turn back to Wormtongue, we find a quite different source, in addition to *Beowulf*. Wormtongue is more fully drawn than Unferth, and in this matter Tolkien was inspired by another fictional character, namely the old witch Gagool, spokeswoman of the king and regaler of newcomers, in Henry Rider Haggard's *King Solomon's Mines* (1885). Rider Haggard was a popular Victorian adventure story writer, who managed to compose stories of remarkable narrative force without, however, having much of a gift for putting words together in a well-crafted manner. His better-known stories are set in southern Africa, where Tolkien grew up. Tolkien was heavily influenced by Rider Haggard, at least in terms of incident and plot, although fortunately the constant and vapid philosophising in Haggard has completely washed over Tolkien. There is a journey for four companions across a waterless desert and freezing mountains also in *King Solomon's Mines*. The picture of Wormtongue as a snivelling wretch, 'a queer twisted sort of creature' as he is described, faithfully adhering to his dispossessed master when all others have abandoned him, coincides with Gagool, the withered and wicked witch in Haggard's novel, who stays loyal to the evil king Twala when all others have gone over to Ignosi, the rightful king of the Kukuanas. Gagool's end comes when she stabs one of those she has guided to the mines and she is crushed under the gate stone as she runs away. With more narrative significance in Tolkien's *The Lord of the Rings*, Wormtongue stabs Saruman, his very master, before meeting an immediate death at the hands of the hobbits.

The combination in Wormtongue of two such disparate characters, Unferth and Gagool, may be viewed as a minor stroke of genius on Tolkien's part. Viewed from a different angle, however, it could also be viewed as a lost opportunity. As we have seen, Unferth is a mystery, full of inconsistencies. There are two opposing opportunities for anyone who wishes to use him as an inspiration. One of them would be to create a complex character in which these inconsistencies are amplified and investigated. The other is to realign the elements in a new, but straightforward individual. Tolkien has chosen the latter approach. It is interesting that in fleshing out his character, he turned to a relatively modern writer whose characters were really cardboard cut-outs. This is not intended necessarily as a criticism of Tolkien, since his writings do not operate chiefly on the basis of deep characterisation, but it emphasises that his response to Old English sources represents merely one approach among many, a fact which ought to encourage others to develop their own varied responses.

Tolkien's wizard Gandalf

Another character who turns up in Rohan and is central to the whole story of the Ring is worth discussing a little. Tolkien declared in an interview for *The Diplomat*: 'To me a name comes first and the story follows.' Nowhere is this more vividly illustrated than with the wizard Gandalf, with whom we move from Old English into the closely related area of Old Norse. In *The Hobbit* (1937) and *The Lord of the Rings* (1954–5), the character of Gandalf, the Grey Wanderer, wielder of the fire of Anor (the sun), has various sources. A major one is surely the Norse god Óðinn, who is a wanderer among men and, in some way, an image of the sun (compare p. 357). The dark side of this Norse god has been hived off onto Sauron, Gandalf's evil counterpart, whose eye provides such a memorable image in Peter Jackson's three films. The possession of just one burning eye is the prime characteristic of Óðinn in all the sources we have of him. But to return to Gandalf's name. 'Gandálfr' is listed as one of the dwarfs in a verse sequence called *The Catalogue of Dwarfs* (*Dvergatal*) which is contained within an Icelandic poem called *The Seeress' Prophecy* (*Vǫluspá*). The latter poem is one of the finest and most obscure in Old Icelandic literature. It was composed, perhaps, around the year 1000. Through a seeress, or sibyl, it tells the whole history of the Norse mythological cosmos from first creation to final destruction and subsequent rebirth, but does so in a highly allusive style, using only a few select myths from which highlights are picked and juxtaposed in a non-narrative manner. There are three reasons why the name Gandálfr in particular would have attracted Tolkien's attention, besides the implication that, since we know nothing of the norse tale that must have attached to Gandálfr's name, we know nothing really about Gandalf either. The first reason is that *The Catalogue of Dwarfs* is an interpolation into *The Seeress' Prophecy*. The second is that *álfr*, the second part of the Norse Gandalf-name, means 'elf', yet the name is included among a list of dwarfs. Third, and most interestingly, is the word *gandr* which is the first element in Gandalf's name. It appears that in pre-Christian Scandinavian religion the *gandr* was a sort of spirit that helped certain special 'seers', communicators with the other world. Today's popular culture would call these people 'shamans', although real shamans belong to different types of society, mainly in Siberia. In the far north of Europe, however, when the Norwegians met their neighbours the Sami (Lapps), they used the word *gandr* to describe the helping spirit which the Sami shaman used to make his contact with the other world. I quote here an account (translated from Latin) from the twelfth-century *History of Norway* (*Historia Norwegiae*). This piece is of interest in its own right and it shows the sort of thing that lies behind Tolkien's creation:

> Moreover their intolerable paganism, and the amount of devilish superstition they practise in their magic, will seem credible to almost no one. For there are some of them who are venerated as prophets by the ignorant populace, since by means of an unclean spirit that they call a *gandr* they predict, when petitioned, many things to many people, even as these things are turning out; and they draw desirable things to themselves from far off regions in a wondrous way, and amazingly, though themselves far away, they produce hidden treasures. By some chance while some Christians were sitting at the table among the Sami for the sake of trade their hostess suddenly bowed over and died; hence the Christians mourned greatly, but were told by the Sami, who were not at all distressed, that she was not dead but stolen away by the *gandar* of rivals, and they would soon

get her back. Then a magician stretched out a cloth, under which he prepared himself for impious magic incantations, and with arms stretched up lifted a vessel like a tambourine, covered in diagrams of whales and deer with bridles and snow-shoes and even a ship with oars, vehicles which that devilish *gandr* uses to go across the depths of snow and slopes of mountains or the deep waters. He chanted a long time and jumped about with this piece of equipment, but then was laid flat on the ground, as black as an Ethiopian all over his body, and foaming from the mouth as if wearing a bit. His stomach was ripped open and with the loudest roaring ever he gave up the ghost. Then they consulted the other one who was versed in magic about what had happened to them both. He performed his job in a similar way but not with the same outcome – for the hostess rose up cured – and indicated that the deceased sorcerer had perished by the following sort of accident: his *gandr*, transformed into the shape of a water beast, had by ill-luck struck against an enemy's *gandr* changed into sharpened stakes as it was rushing across a lake, for the stakes lying set up in the depths of that same lake had pierced his stomach, as appeared on the dead magician at home.

Some of all this seeps through into Gandalf in *The Lord of the Rings*. Gandalf's contest with the Balrog, in the mines of Moria, is partly comparable to this sort of shamanistic contest, although it should be added immediately that a more significant source is medieval vision literature, such as *St Patrick's Purgatory*, where a sinner beholds in a dream the trials imposed on the sinful soul in Purgatory. To some extent Tolkien even seems to have used Dante's thirteenth-century masterpiece, *The Divine Comedy*. There is no space in this chapter to give this discussion the detail it needs. The point here is just to illustrate the breadth, and vividness, of Tolkien's sources.

Tolkien's wizard Saruman

Whereas Gandalf has a firmly Norse origin, Saruman is formed out of Old English. It is worth adding that a third important wizard in *The Lord of the Rings*, Radagast, is derived linguistically from Slavonic. Where Saruman is concerned, Tolkien appears to have created him almost out of a couple of pages of the standard Old English dictionary, *An Anglo-Saxon Dictionary*, by Joseph Bosworth in 1838, revised by T. Northcote Toller in 1898 and 1921. In this book the Old English base word *searu* has a long entry because there are many compound words in which *searu* forms the first element. The basic sense of *searu* is 'cunning' or 'treacherous', but a secondary sense of 'weapons' occurs in some cases. Bosworth's and Toller's main entry (s.v.

'searu') begins by noting that in the immediately following examples of the word, 'it is uncertain whether the word is being used with a good or a bad meaning'. Already we begin to see the origins of a clever character who is wily and given to treachery, with intentions that are uncertain and with the propensity to take up arms against those he has deceived. So it is that Saruman deceives all who trust him, Gandalf included. Further entries for *searu* add flesh to this outline. The (unrelated, but similar-sounding) verb *seárian* is glossed as meaning 'to grow sear, wither, pine away' and the examples given refer to leaves withering. The image of the aged wizard surely stems from this, in particular as he grows more wizened after being cast down by Gandalf and there may be a sideways glance at Saruman's searing or defoliation of the woods around Orthanc, his great tower. This tower itself seems to derive in part from another unconnected, but similar-sounding, entry in the dictionary. *Searoburh* was the Anglo-Saxon name for the city of Salisbury in southwest England, as it was before it was moved from its first location in Old Sarum. This old place is a striking site, now deserted, atop an ancient hill fort, surrounded by great defences and once topped by the spire of the cathedral. In fact, Sarum was a Roman and Iron Age fort far antedating the occurrence of *Searoburh* in Old English. There could be more than a passing similarity here to Saruman's dwelling in *The Lord of the Rings*, for Orthanc is said to have been an ancient construction before Saruman took it over. The word *orthanc* itself is firmly Old English, meaning 'original thought, ingenuity', with an obvious semantic connection to a *searuman*, a 'cunning man'. In fact, in Old English the word *searo-þanc* occurs, 'cunning thought', which directly links Orthanc with Saruman. *Orþanc*, however, has two other meanings: one is glossed in Latin as *machinamenta*, 'mechanical devices'; the other is 'thoughtlessness' or folly. All these meanings come together in the contrivances Saruman was engaged in at Orthanc, in the machines he installed there and in the complete folly of his exploits.

It will be noted that Tolkien uses the form *Saruman*, not *Searuman*, as we would expect from the dictionary entries. This stems from different Old English dialects. *Searuman* is a West Saxon, *Saruman* a Mercian form. Tolkien has deliberately given Saruman a Mercian name in order to connect with the position of this character within the realm of Rohan. The Rohirrim in the books call their land 'the Mark'. This is an English form of *Mercia*, a name which is really a Latinised form of Old English *merce* [/meh:rche/], 'people of the frontier'. 'Mark' means a boundary and 'March', a variant of this word, is still used of the Welsh Marches. 'Mark' also describes the region within a boundary, a borderland. So Tolkien is telling us that Rohan is specifically Mercia, the kingdom in the midlands of England which was ruled by the great King Offa from 757 to 796 (see Chapter 8, p. 233). To some extent, Tolkien is keen to redress, through his fiction, the imbalance of the fact that most of the surviving Old English documents are written in West Saxon. Tolkien felt a strong affinity to the West Midlands, within the ancient realm of Mercia, were his mother's farmily sprang from.

In some of the other examples we have seen how a story would act as an impulse to Tolkien. The case of Saruman, by way of contrast, illustrates the extent to which his inspiration could be purely linguistic in nature, or rather, how he was inspired by patterns perceived in webs of words that contained something particularly suggestive for him. Whenever we look into the particular ways this inspiration worked, we find an extraordinary depth of knowledge on Tolkien's part, to do with the sources he is using, be they literary or lexical. His fictional works operate on several levels. It is possible to enjoy the scenes in Rohan without a deep knowledge of the sources, but beneath the surface we find further dimensions of meaning penetrating to the depths. We have the history of Middle Earth itself, represented in the meanings of names such as 'Saruman' within the languages (Old English, Old Norse, Welsh, Irish and Scots Gaelic) that Tolkien knew. At the same time we encounter in Tolkien's work an engagement, often of a detailed kind, with the words and the tales of Anglo-Saxon, Norse and Celtic Britain. Let's have a look at another example.

Earendil of the Morning Star

Earendil is one of the legendary characters from the First Age, who together form a backdrop to the events of *The Lord of the Rings* (1954–5). He is chiefly commemorated in a ditty composed by Bilbo at the elvish stronghold of Rivendell. However, in *The Silmarillion* (posthumously, 1977), Earendil performs one of the vital roles that save the world. He is a great mariner, who binds a gleaming 'silmaril' on the prow of his ship to pierce the enchanted mists around Valimar, where the Powers dwell. He wins through, to plead for aid in the struggle against the dark lord, Morgoth. However, having set foot on the blessed land, he is not permitted to return, but is fated to sail for ever in the sky, the silmaril still bound on the prow and seen by men as the Morning Star (the planet Venus).

This tale arose out of some lines in a poem Tolkien read as an undergraduate in Oxford. The poem was the ninth-century Old English poem

Christ (known as *Christ I–III*), which was probably edited and bound by the poet Cynewulf who composed the second of its three parts, *Christ II* (see Chapter 7, p. 212). The relevant lines, a hymn to Christ as the Messiah, depict the dawning light, realised as the Morning Star, as a prophecy for his coming to earth:

> Eala earendel   engla beorhtast,
> ofer middangeard   monnum sended (*Christ I*, lines 104–5)

> Behold Earendel [the Morning Star], brightest of angels,
> over middle earth sent to men.

It would scarcely be going too far to say that the thrill Tolkien experienced on reading these lines marked the beginning of the creation of Middle Earth.

The process by which the legend of Earendil (or Earendel in the earlier versions) grew out of these lines is rather complex, however – but it is a good example of the extent to which Tolkien's imagination was honed towards linguistic inspiration. The focus of Tolkien's attention was clearly on the word *earendel*, meaning (probably) 'Morning Star'. The root of the word, found also in *east*, *Easter* and Latin *Aurora*, apparently means the 'dawning light'; however, as Tolkien recognised, Earendel was also almost certainly seen as a person. If we look to Old Norse, for example, we find stories about Aurvandill, of how, being carried over icy rivers by Þórr, his toe froze, so that the god set it in the heavens as a star in compensation.

Thus brightness was associated with *earendel* from the beginning. But where has Tolkien got the idea of linking him with the sea from? Three possible sources suggest themselves. There is another word in Old English, *ear*, a poetic word which means 'ocean' (on poetic vocabulary per se, see Chapter 10, p. 290). This word is probably unrelated to *earendel* but the similarities of the words were probably suggestive to Tolkien. Moreover, the icy rivers of the Norse tale of Aurvandill suggest a watery element to the tale of Earendil. Finally, strange as it may seem, there is a link with *Hamlet, Prince of Denmark* (1601). Shakespeare's play goes back to a Danish Latin chronicle called *The History of the Danes* (*Gesta Danorum*), written by Saxo Grammaticus in the late twelfth century (see p. 355). In Saxo's chronicle a certain Horwendillus (i.e. Aurvandill/Earendil) is the father of Amlethus (i.e. Hamlet). Amlethus appears originally to have been some sort of personification of the raging ocean, a connection with a shadowy reflection still in Shakespeare's play, whose Hamlet, feigning madness, walks along the sea shore, talking of sand as the meal of the sea.

The association with the sea naturally suggests a ship. Where was Earendel to get his vessel? Tolkien turned to another legend, preserved in just as fragmentary a state: that of Wade, father of the legendary smith Wayland. Wade is mentioned twice by Chaucer, who revealed he had a famous boat (see Chapter 4, p. 109). Wade's ship is cited also in 1598, in Thomas Speght's edition of Chaucer. Speght made the frustrating comment: 'Concerning Wade and his bote called Guingelot, as also his strange exploits in the same, because the matter is long and fabulous, I passe it over.' Guingelot is a Norman French version of an original *Wingelot*, the very name of Earendel's ship in Tolkien. The name is highly unlikely to be original as the name of Wade's ship. It is Celtic in origin and is, in fact, probably a mistake on Speght's part. It is more usually found as the name of Sir Gawain's horse in the Arthurian cycle, including in the English *Sir Gawain and the Green Knight*, which Tolkien edited and translated. This very anomaly may have been the thing that attracted Tolkien. In his world, the anomaly disappears and *Wingelot* becomes 'Foam Flower', a beautiful name, the meaning of which derives in part from the fortuity that *lóte*, clearly derived from *lotus* (a flower with a strong literary tradition going back to the Homeric Odyssey and later including Lord Alfred Tennyson), already meant 'flower' in Elvish, Tolkien's invented language.

In these tales of Wade, there is little sense of pressing purpose, which is so characteristic of the Earendil story in Tolkien. However, this proves to be a later feature of the legend. In the early versions presented in the History of Middle Earth volumes, Earendel arrives too late in Valimar to ask for help. He sets sail in the sky merely in search of his beloved Elwing and his association with brightness comes from the diamond dust he picks up in Eldamar, not from having a silmaril on his prow. All the elements that dignify the legend as we know it from *The Lord of the Rings* are later features.

Conclusion

I started with *The Lord of the Rings* film in order to show how an informed and critical approach may help illuminate what the director, Peter Jackson, has and has not achieved on the basis of Tolkien's novels. Such an approach demands that we move beyond the film to the book Tolkien actually wrote. Yet to understand Tolkien we have, again, to look at him critically to see what he is really doing, what he is concerned with. In a word, we are confronted with the major literary principle of *allusion*. All great literature alludes to other literature, considers it, answers it, manipulates it. Tolkien is no exception. He does, however, allude perhaps more than most to ancient literatures, in particular to Old English and Old Norse, and to understand him presupposes a knowledge of this literature. This chapter aims to show, largely through Tolkien's own words, why he found this literature import-ant enough to bother paying it so much attention. In writing it, I hope I have encouraged readers to think of looking at this literature for themselves. It goes without saying that the same critical and questioning approach I have encouraged from the beginning is all the more necessary when we look at Old English and Old Norse literatures, but I leave this side of things for later chapters.

Many of my points do not relate to Old English. It has been my deliber-ate aim not to divorce Old English from the many other sources of inspira-tion for Tolkien. To achieve any level of understanding, be it of Tolkien or of the Old English and other literatures which inspired him, it is vital to perceive Old English not as an isolated subject, but as part of a truly world-wide web of literature and culture, which crosses time, place and language. Together with the other literary traditions, Old English forms an artistic tradition, a glory of mankind whose majesty shines out to all who wish to see it. As one great poet, thinking of another Dark Age, once said of the glories of his 'Golden Hall':

> lixte se leoma ofer landa fela (*Beowulf*, line 311)
>
> its light shone over many lands.

Translations and texts

Beowulf. Many editions of the original Old English exist; the standard
   remains that of Klaeber, F., 3rd edn (Boston, MA, 1950). More useful
   to beginning students is *Beowulf: A Student Edition*, G. Jack, ed.
   (Oxford, 1994). Seamus Heaney has produced one of the most
   successful translations in modern years: *Beowulf: A New Translation*
   (London, 1999).

Bosworth, J., *An Anglo-Saxon Dictionary*, rev. T. Northcote Toller (Oxford,
   1898), with a *Supplement* (Oxford, 1921).

Christ. A translation is available in *Anglo-Saxon Poetry*, S.A.J. Bradley, trans.
   and ed. (London, 1982).

Dronke, Ursula, ed., comm. and trans., *The Poetic Edda II: Mythological
   Poems* (Oxford, 1997). The poem *Vǫluspá* is edited, translated and

discussed in full in this highly accomplished work (see Chapter 12, p. 357).

Fisher, Peter, trans. and Hilda Ellis Davidson, ed., *Saxo Grammaticus: Gesta Danorum, Books I–IX* (Cambridge, 1979–80). This is where to find the original story of Hamlet.

Gordon, E.V., ed., *Pearl* (Oxford, 1953). There are other editions, but Gordon was Tolkien's colleague and Tolkien contributed to this text.

Kunin, D. and Carl Phelpstead, trans., *A History of Norway and The Passion and Miracles of the Blessed Óláfr* (London, 2001). This is for *Historia Norwegiae*.

Rider Haggard, Henry, *King Solomon's Mines* (London, 1885), available in many editions and as a free e-book.

Tolkien, J.R.R., '*Beowulf*: The Monsters and the Critics' (Oxford, 1936). Originally given as a British Academy lecture in 1936, the standard edition (used for reference here) is now that edited by Christopher Tolkien in *The Monsters and the Critics and Other Essays* (London, 1983), which contains further important literary essays by Tolkien; however, the citations from Old English are not translated, as they are in the version published in *An Anthology of Beowulf Criticism* (L.E. Nicholson, ed., Notre Dame, 1963, pp. 51–103). Two drafts of the piece have now been published, with full explanation of the many references Tolkien makes to other works and with translations of Old English, in *Beowulf and the Critics*, Michael Drout, ed. (Tempe, Arizona, 2002).

Tolkien, J.R.R., *The Lord of the Rings* (London, 1954–5).

Tolkien, J.R.R., 'Tolkien on Tolkien', *The Diplomat* (vol. xviii, no. 197, Oct. 1966); citation on p. 39.

Tolkien, J.R.R., *On Fairy Stories*, in *Essays Presented to Charles Williams* (Oxford, 1947), subsequently issued many times, for example in *Tree and Leaf*.

Tolkien, J.R.R., *The Silmarillion*, Christopher Tolkien, ed. (London, 1977).

Tolkien, J.R.R., trans., *Sir Gawain and the Green Knight, Pearl, Sir Orfeo* (London, 1975). This translation tends to archaise its English and for that reason cannot be called wholly successful.

Tolkien, J.R.R. and E.V. Gordon, eds, *Sir Gawain and the Green Knight* (Oxford, 1925).

The Wanderer. One of the finest short poems in Old English. Translation in
Bradley's anthology.

Acknowledgement

I would like to thank the sixth-form girls of The Queen's School, Chester, on whom I tried out a portion of this chapter.

CHAPTER 3

Beowulf and other battlers: an introduction to *Beowulf*

Andy Orchard

There is no doubt that today's concerned liberals think the epic poem *Beowulf* is about nothing but violence. A would-be student in Woody Allen's 1972 multiple Oscar-winning film *Annie Hall* is given some earnest advice: 'Just don't take any course where they make you read *Beowulf*.' Many modern-day readers seem to have felt the same, including the poet and professional grumpy old git, Philip Larkin, who whinged to the author Kingsley Amis in World War II, in 1942, just after Amis had joined the army (and when his mind might reasonably be supposed to have been focused elsewhere): 'Life is a fanged monster, sonny, that lies in wait for you . . . Sometimes I think of *Beowulf* and *The Wanderer*. Oh boo hoo. You lucky man to be in the army away from it all.' Both Amis and Larkin had taken a course, compulsory at Oxford, in the language of Anglo-Saxon England, which they ruefully called 'Old Anguish', and had apparently come away permanently scarred.

But not all who have read *Beowulf* have been so adversely affected. Among the many nineteenth- and twentieth-century authors and especially poets who have claimed the positive influence of Old English in general, and *Beowulf* in particular, on their work have been J.R.R. Tolkien (as we have just seen), Alfred Lord Tennyson, Ezra Pound, Gerald Manley Hopkins, W.H. Auden and Seamus Heaney. The last, indeed, added several literary prizes to his Nobel Prize for Literature through his strikingly popular translation of *Beowulf*, first published in 2000. Together, Heaney and Tolkien (the latter both through Peter Jackson's phenomenally successful *Lord of the Rings* film trilogy and, of course, through his own writings) can be credited with an ongoing resurgence of public interest. At the time of writing (summer 2006), one live-action feature film of *Beowulf* has recently been released (supplanting a science-fiction version from 1999), another computer-generated animated version is in production and getting the full Hollywood treatment (superseding an earlier animated version from 1998) and an operatic version is due to open soon in New York (again, an earlier rock opera exists). Indeed, the new opera is, in effect, a reworking of a reworking, being based less on the poem itself than on the striking and powerful novel *Grendel*, written in 1971 by John Gardner, and presenting the action of the poem from the monster's point of view. Elsewhere, Beowulf has been remodelled as a D.C. Comics hero, as well as appearing in cartoons and computer games and *Beowulf*-derived storylines have turned up in TV episodes of both *Xena: Warrior Princess* and *Star Trek: Voyager*. Meanwhile, the terms 'Beowulf' and 'Grendel' have been appropriated by cyber-geeks for mighty (and mighty specialised) types of computer clusters. Thus *Beowulf* has expanded beyond its traditional place in studies of English language and literature and history and seems relevant now to the very different disciplines of film and TV studies, music and computer studies. In the future, in this way, it may turn out to be more difficult than Woody Allen supposed to avoid a course where they teach *Beowulf*, at least in some form.

First things first: the *Beowulf* manuscript

Despite the continuing popularisation, repackaging and reinterpretation of *Beowulf*, in versions that to the purist might seem variously dumbed down, screwed up or just far out, it is important to note that the original Old English poem is itself a difficult text. It contains literally thousands of words and forms not found elsewhere in surviving records. *Beowulf*'s sole existing text is found in the Nowell Codex, a manuscript which is more formally known as British Library, Cotton Vitellius A.XV. Set out in verse lines, the poem *Beowulf* is some 3182 lines long, although, like virtually all other Old English poems, it is written in prose set out in 'fitts' or blocks. Two scribes, one taking over from the other about two thirds through, copied this poem out around the year 1000. Viewed as a whole, the codex they copied *Beowulf* into appears to be little more than a kind of 'Big Boys' Bumper Book of Monsters', pictures and all. It also contains an Old English adaptation of *Alexander´s Letter to Aristotle* and another Old English text known as *Marvels of the East*. The scribes (called A and B!) certainly seem to have found it rather amazing, for while they both take great care to correct what they write, it is sometimes clear that even they, as native speakers of 'Old English', cannot quite understand what they are copying. That they copy *Beowulf* at all, and take such pains at attempted correction, may indicate either that it had some status as a text (since neither scribe bothers much correcting the other four texts in the manuscript), that they had difficulty with the language (perhaps because of its antiquity) or both. And that's not all. The task of reading *Beowulf* for modern readers is vitiated not only by the difficult language and the lack of other manuscript witnesses, but also by the damaged nature of what does survive. The *Beowulf* manuscript was one of around 200 manuscripts affected or destroyed by a terrible fire that swept through the collection of Sir Robert Cotton in 1731. Some bright spark had the fatal notion of housing this collection in the fatefully named Ashburnham House, which duly did. The *Beowulf* manuscript has rightly been described as a ruin, albeit a noble and precious one.

Most scholars now accept that the poem is older than the manuscript that contains it, but estimates of the age of *Beowulf* range somewhat unhelpfully from the seventh century to the eleventh, which is to say the entire span of recorded Anglo-Saxon literature. The special poetic register and resolutely antiquarian focus of *Beowulf* make any dating on purely linguistic grounds difficult: we simply have nothing that is really comparable. The Christian focus of the poet, and the Christian subject matter of at least some of the other texts preserved alongside *Beowulf*, may well have helped its survival in an age when the production of manuscripts from laboriously prepared animal skins and specially produced ink was a long and costly process and when the Church had a virtual monopoly on literacy. However, it is also clear that *Beowulf* seems to draw in style and language on a much earlier compositional technique. This was originally oral formulaic, of native Anglo-Saxon rather than learned Latin origins (see later, p. 96). As we shall see in the next chapter, there is relatively little other heroic narrative verse surviving in Old English and *Beowulf*'s precise relationship to the four poems which do survive is therefore impossible to determine. Like the manuscript that contains it, *Beowulf* itself seems a chance survival and a silent witness to a vibrant and ancient world of sound now stilled beyond hope of full recovery. Scholars have, however, worked out that the poem contains enough material to have taken four or more hours for a complete performance. Perhaps, one may speculate, the poem was performed at a feast in a royal banqueting hall.

Next on the menu: the *Beowulf* story

If the language of *Beowulf* is beguilingly, often bafflingly, complex, then we can say the basic plot is simple to the point of bewilderment. Basically, the story gives us three battles in two lands and a hero who is a young champion in the first two and an old king in the third. Between Beowulf's youth and his age the poet puts a gap of more than 50 years. In his youth, the monster-slayer Beowulf fights for one people, the Danes, whereas in his old age he dies for another, his own, the Geats (of 'Geatland' or modern-day Göteland in Sweden). He fights his first battle for King Hrothgar of Denmark in order to liberate Heorot, his great hall, from a half-human half-devil cannibal named Grendel who has haunted it at night for 12 unstoppable years. Having done this, by tearing off Grendel's right arm at the shoulder, Beowulf takes on and destroys Grendel's mother, another fearsome monster who raids Heorot the night after her son's death in revenge for losing him. The poet tells us that the Grendels are of the kin of Cain, who is the first murderer in the Bible and, like Grendel, an outcast. Beowulf kills both mother and son and comes home to his uncle, King Hygelac of Geatland.

After the leap of 50 years following Beowulf's triumphant return, we find him as an aged king who is facing his third monster, a fire-breathing dragon. This creature has set Beowulf's whole country alight in revenge for losing a cup from the hoard of treasure he was guarding in the barrow where he lived (dragons *do* live in barrows). Beowulf is now a king, aged like Hrothgar, yet unlike Hrothgar he is still a capable fighter, one willing to duel with the offending monster himself. He kills the dragon with the help of Wiglaf, a much younger distant relative, but then dies of his terrible wounds, leaving the Geats to a very uncertain future. All this takes place against a spiralling cycle of human feuds and fighting from which Beowulf, young or old, seems curiously detached. More than 70 characters are named in this story, half of them only once. It is questionable whether the poet ever expected his audience to recognise all of these characters, for at the time the manuscript was written, as we have seen, the scribes sometimes struggle and seem to have garbled some names. Part of the problem lies in the strangeness and unfamiliarity of background and plot. With the scene set in Denmark and Geatland, the story takes place both long ago and far away, in Scandinavian homelands with which both the Anglo-Saxons and (by the ninth century at least) their Viking enemies could have identified. There is no reference to England in *Beowulf* neither is there any to any English character at all, bar two possibles. One is in an oblique allusion (in Beowulf's homecoming passage) to the mighty and fearsome fourth-century King Offa of Angeln (see p. 104), one that the poet (or someone else) may have included in homage to his namesake and descendant, the equally mighty and fearsome eighth-century King Offa of Mercia (ruled 757–96; see p. 233). Another possible 'Englishman' is Hengest, who has a role to play in Beowulf's Finnsburh Episode (see p. 100). As we saw in Chapter 1, Hengest or Hengistus, together with his brother Horsa (both men have names that suspiciously mean 'horse'), traditionally sparked off the Anglo-Saxon invasion of Britain in the mid-fifth century. Both Offa of Angeln and Hengest were Germanic heathens, or pagans, just like everyone else in *Beowulf*. Although the poet of *Beowulf* is clearly Christian, spicing up his narrative with talk of 'heathens' and 'hell', and making direct reference to biblical history, nonetheless he chooses to depict a pagan past with far more sympathy than one might have expected.

Indeed, this ability to see more than one side of the picture is perhaps the hallmark of the *Beowulf* poet's perspective. With this latitude, it could be argued, he saves his tale from being a simple catalogue of glorious and gory deeds of yore (although those deeds are certainly told) and actually delineates the human and pagan characters rather subtly. His sympathy for them seems clear especially when (as often) the poem is viewed through the distorting lens of modern translation. Moreover, the monsters that Beowulf fights are also strangely stylised: Grendel is an outcast giant man-shaped monster; his vengeful mother seems more bestial than human; finally, there is a mighty dragon. The same tripartite division of monsters into man-shaped, bestial and serpentine creatures is also found in an eighth-century Anglo-Saxon spotter's guide to around 120 different types of monster called the *Liber monstrorum* ('Book of Monsters'). Intriguingly for our purposes, King Hygelac of the Geats (Beowulf's lord in the poem) is explicitly named in this book, as the second of the human-shaped monsters (the first is given in a brief description of a bisexual male prostitute that Saint Augustine apparently knew personally). In *Beowulf*, only the first of the three monsters Beowulf battles is named, albeit the word 'Grendel' seems both suspicious and unusual as a name. While each monster evokes profound terror for the destruction they bring, each can also stir our pity, if we see things from their point of view. The poet appears to encourage us to do just this.

In Denmark, when Beowulf is young and consolidating his reputation abroad, we are told that Grendel only begins his man-eating marauding (30 men on his first visit to this restaurant) when the Danish King Hrothgar builds his mighty hall called Heorot (the name means 'hart' or 'stag'). Another reason for the attack is perhaps that Hrothgar's proud poet celebrates the building by singing a song of the creation of the world that implicitly compares Hrothgar with the Creator Himself. Outside in the darkness lurks Grendel, excluded from the Danish feast. For these reasons we can view Grendel's ravaging as either an extreme case of retaliation against noisy neighbours, as a reflex of his Cain seed evil upbringing or, more intriguingly, as an instrument of God's wrath against the uppity Danes. The poet leaves the matter nicely poised, as he describes the approach of Beowulf's first great foe to his unwitting encounter with the hero:

> Ða com of more   under misthleoþum
> Grendel gongan,   godes yrre bær;
> mynte se manscaða   manna cynnes
> sumne besyrwan   in sele þam hean. (*Beowulf*, lines 710–13)

> Then there came from the moors, under misty slopes, Grendel striding: he bore God's anger; the wicked destroyer [or 'destroyer of wickedness'] intended to ensnare one of mankind in that high hall.

The phrase 'he bore God's anger' (*godes yrre bær*) is ambiguous: Grendel is potentially both the recipient and the agent of God's wrath. Likewise, the following line links by alliteration two contrasting elements: 'man' (part of 'mankind', *manna cynnes*) and 'wickedness' (part of 'wicked destroyer', *manscaða*), by using a compound word that could, in theory, signal both a 'wicked destroyer' and a 'destroyer of wickedness'; and, of course, Grendel himself is shaped like a man. His human characteristics are highlighted by the third alliterating element in the line, which focuses on the fact that Grendel is not mindless: he intended (*mynte*) what he did, albeit that chillingly the abritrariness of his frenzied intentions is itself signalled in the very next line, where we learn that any 'one' (*sumne*) of mankind will do.

Not that there be any doubt of the intended horror and revulsion for Grendel's devouring of men, described in chilling detail, after Grendel bursts into the Danish hall on his way to a fatal encounter with Beowulf:

> Ne þæt se aglæca   yldan þohte,
> ac he gefeng hraðe   forman siðe
> slæpende rinc,   slat unwearnum,
> bat banlocan,   blod edrum dranc,
> synsnædum swealh;   sona hæfde
> unlyfigendes   eal gefeormod,
> fet ond folma. (*Beowulf*, lines 739–45)

> Nor did that awesome assailant think to delay, but he quickly seized at the first opportunity a sleeping warrior, tore him greedily, bit the joints, drank the blood from the veins, swallowed in sinful gulps [or 'mighty gulps']; he had soon taken full care of the feet and hands of the unliving man.

This gruesome vision is made all the more horrific because it goes against a double biblical injunction not to eat flesh with blood that is widely repeated in Anglo-Saxon texts (and observed today by both Muslims and Jews) and such a bloody feast may have been considered particularly repellent to a Christian Anglo-Saxon audience, given the ancient pagan veneration of blood, as enshrined in our modern English word 'bless' (Old English *bletsian*), which is derived from the Old English word for 'blood' (*blod*), with the same simple vowel change that give us the modern English pairs 'doom/deem', 'goose/geese', which equally come from Old English (*dom-/dem-*, *gos/ges*). The Christian perspective is emphasised by the ambiguous word *synsnædum*, which can mean both 'sinful gulps' and 'mighty gulps': presumably Grendel's are both. But we should also note here the poet's use of the word *aglæca*, translated in this case 'awesome assailant', which in various forms applies not only to Grendel, but to his mother, the dragon, and the water creatures that inhabit Grendel's mere. So far, so simple: earlier translators just use the term 'monster'. Yet, uneasily for us, the poet employs precisely the same word to refer both to Beowulf himself and to another pagan hero of legend, Sigemund, who in *Beowulf* is depicted as a mighty dragon-slayer not unlike Beowulf. Is Beowulf, then, himself a monster? Certainly not from the viewpoint of numerous characters in the poem, although some of the poet's original Christian audience, unwilling to see past the fact that he was a pagan, may have considered that in itself damning enough. But the use in the poem of such a shared term underlines the extent to which the *Beowulf* poet seems to have viewed both the pagan warriors and the monsters they fight as equally outlandish and equally worthy of serious scrutiny, with any final judgement left to God.

Yet if Grendel's motivation for his killing spree is somewhat nebulous, albeit, apparently, not wholly without provocation, given the incursion of the Danes into the fens that he thought were his, the motive of Grendel's mother is entirely clear: vengeance. Unlike Grendel, who for some real or imagined affront carries on killing until he is stopped, Grendel's mother, who is honour bound to extract vengeance in the apparent absence of any surviving male relative, offers a measured and strictly limited response: in return for her dead son she kills a single Dane, namely Æschere, Hrothgar's closest friend. The poet is at pains to describe her trip for vengeance as a 'sorrowful journey', again apparently playing both sides: her sorrow will cause further sorrow for Hrothgar, until Beowulf, arguably extending the feud by his action, puts an end to misery for both her and the Danes. Again, the poet is careful to draw parallels between the attack of Grendel on the hall of Heorot and that of Beowulf himself on the hall of Grendel's mother in the monster Mere. Just as Grendel burst unexpectedly one evening out of the fens into the firelit hall of Heorot and was unwounded by the sword thrusts of Beowulf's men, so Beowulf the following evening bursts into the underwater and mysteriously lit hall of Grendel's mother, unwounded by the sharp tusks of the water monsters in the Mere itself. Likewise, just as Grendel's attacks happen when Hrothgar has ruled Denmark for 50 years, so, too, we are explicitly told that Grendel's mother has governed her own watery domain for precisely the same period of time. So who is the 'awesome assailant' here?

Given this background, an attentive audience might be forgiven for feeling a little nervous when told, after a brisk and sudden 'flash forward' two-thirds of the way through the poem, how back in his homeland Beowulf, now King Beowulf of the Geats, ruled for 50 years before suffering a shocking infestation of worm. The dragon cannot match the infamous biblical ancestry of Grendel and his mother, but is, in Christian terms, nonetheless a clear symbol of evil: there are enough dragon-slaying saints to attest to that, and several of their stories have interesting parallels with that of Beowulf. We are told that the dragon had lain quiet for 300 years, until a thief, perhaps an outcast from Beowulf's own court, in which case under Anglo-Saxon law Beowulf himself would have been held responsible for any crimes committed by one of his men, stole a single golden cup. In terms of motivation, one might say that the dragon has an even clearer case for action than the spatter-happy Grendel or his awesome mum. That the poet intended Beowulf's three monster fights to be read as a sequence seems clear from narrative patterns that connect them all, with Beowulf employing more and more weaponry to fight the three foes and yet experiencing more and more difficulty in achieving success. In this context, the long description of the peeved dragon righteously roused is both memorable and, in its declaration of Beowulf's death nearly 900 lines before the end of the poem, wholly chilling:

> Then the dragon awoke, wrath was renewed, it scoured along the stone, fierce-hearted found the track of the foe; he had stepped forward with cunning craft close by the dragon's head. So may an undoomed man easily survive misery and exile, when he keeps the favour of the Ruler. The guardian of the hoard searched eagerly along the ground; it wished to find the man who had grievously treated him in his sleep. Hot and fierce in heart it often stalked around the mound, all around the outside: there was no one there in the wilderness, yet it exulted in war, deeds of battle. Sometimes it stalked back into the barrow, sought out the precious vessel; it immediately discovered that a man had tampered with the gold, the rich treasures. The guardian of the hoard waited with difficulty until the evening came; then the keeper of the barrow was enraged, the hateful foe wished to pay back with flame for the precious drinking-vessel. Then the day was done, as the dragon wished; no longer would it wait by the wall, but it went with flame, ready with fire. The beginning was terrible for the people in the land, as it was swiftly brought to a dreadful end on their treasure-giver. Then the stranger began to spew flames, to burn the bright

dwellings; the fire-glow remained in malice for men: the hateful flying-creature would not leave anything alive. The dragon's fighting-power was widely visible, the wickedness of the difficult and hostile one both near and far, how that warlike ravager hated and humiliated the people of the Geats; it hastened back to the hoard, the secret noble hall before day. It had encircled the nation's people in flame, with fire and burning: it trusted in its barrow, its fighting-power and fortification; that hope deceived it. Then the terror was made known to Beowulf, swiftly and truly, that his own home, best of buildings, had melted in surges of flames, the gift-throne of the Geats. For that good man there was sorrow in his heart, the greatest of griefs, the wise one reckoned that he had severely offended the Ruler, the eternal Lord, contrary to ancient law; his breast welled up inside with dark thoughts, as was not customary for him. The fire-dragon had destroyed with flame that people's stronghold, the fortress and coastal land beyond; for that the warlike king, the prince of the Weder-Geats planned vengeance.

Whereas the dragon is seen in a frenzy of impatient action, with a clearly developing line of frenzied thought ('I smell man: where? I'll get him. My cup! My precious cup! I'll get them all. I'll wait till night and burn them; they'll never be brave or strong enough to attack me here in my grave-mound hall'), the doomed and ageing Beowulf is depicted as frozen in melancholy contemplation of what he has done to deserve this attack ('What have I done wrong? Why do I feel so miserable? I never used to have such doubts when I was young. But I am the king; I am Beowulf the monster-slayer, however old I am: that dragon is mine'). By contrast, the poet goes out of his way to describe the thief who had stirred the dragon's wrath in the first place as 'undoomed', in a curious comment about how even a thief can be spared in the name of God that makes it seem as if the whole episode, culminating in Beowulf's death, is simply unfolding according to God's will.

The whole sequence of the dragon episode leads inexorably to the funeral of Beowulf that closes the poem, so echoing the funeral, described in detail towards the beginning of the text, of Scyld Scefing, another outsider who once came to aid the Danes in their dire distress. In this last third of this lengthy poem, the poet stresses again and again the fact that Beowulf's time has come. Nonetheless, the long-drawn out and often repetitive account of Beowulf's death is described in such a way that in terms of the wider narrative of the poem's main action it cannot fairly be said that 'it was swiftly brought to a dreadful end'.

But perhaps that is the point: the *Beowulf* poet is working against a much broader canvas of cosmic time, against which the significance of Beowulf's life and death must be assessed. So the poem looks back to biblical events, ranging from Creation, to Cain's killing of Abel, to the Flood and its aftermath, and sweeps through a series of past events from Germanic myth and legend, before focusing on the main action of the poem, which takes place over just a few days on either side of a gaping gap of more than half a century. As Beowulf and his final foe, the dragon, lie dead on the headland, a sombre messenger looks forward to the destruction of Beowulf's people, the Geats, a calamitous event that must have already taken place some time before the poem was composed, whenever that may have been. And yet the poet implicitly insists on the relevance of all this ancient action for his current audience and successive critics, beginning with J.R.R. Tolkien, have argued that the poet treats of such broad and universal themes that it is still relevant to us today. For in its loving contemplation of the thoughts and feelings of characters, both human and monstrous, who are trapped in cycles of terror they can only dimly comprehend, *Beowulf* seems a poem less about action than about reaction, less about conflict than about the aftermath of conflict, less about little victories and tiny triumphs than about the great defeat of death that awaits us all. And so, ultimately, about our place in the world and how we should act – and why. Even in an age when our former heroes are flawed, the Christian poet of *Beowulf* seems to be saying of his pagan protagonists, we can still find much to admire. It is a generous and noble vision and one that those who come to *Beowulf* as a simple celebration of an uncomplicated martial hero will perhaps find hard to share. But it is the same pragmatic spirit that sees both Christian and pagan symbols jostling for prominence on a series of seventh- and eighth-century helmets from Benty Grange (with its boar motif, a pagan protective symbol mentioned in *Beowulf*, alongside a cross on the nosepiece), from York (with a Christian inscription formed crosswise above a traditional eye and nose guard built on Norse pagan models), and at Sutton Hoo (where the traditional pagan Scandinavian patterned helmet is found alongside silver spoons engraved with the biblical conversion symbols 'Saul' and 'Paul'). Modern readers would do well to recall that even after the *Beowulf* manuscript was composed, Anglo-Saxon kings still traced their ancestry back to pagan deities and pagan customs were apparently still observed.

Beowulf: a heathen hero for a Christian time

Beowulf is often rightly heralded as an extraordinarily dense and complex masterpiece, a brooding and thoughtful poem that contemplates the glories of the pagan heroic past from a deeply Christian perspective and still seems to find much to appreciate in a world that is too often simply condemned in the surviving written record. Nonetheless, the poet is careful to distance himself from the world he depicts, beginning with a portentous evocation of a lost world, beginning with the glories of the warlike Danes:

> Hwæt, we Gardena   in geardagum,
> þeodcyninga   þrym gefrunon,
> hu ða æþelingas   ellen fremedon!
> Oft Scyld Scefing   sceaþena þreatum,
> monegum mægþum   meodosetla ofteah,
> egsode eorlas,   syððan ærest wearð
> feasceaft funden;   he þæs frofre gebad,
> weox under wolcnum   weorðmyndum þah,
> oð þæt him æghwylc   ymbsittendra
> ofer hronrade   hyran scolde,
> gomban gyldan;   þæt wæs god cyning! (*Beowulf*, lines 1–11)

> Listen! We have heard of the power of the mighty kings of the Spear-Danes in bygone days, how those princes did bold deeds. Often Scyld Scefing snatched off mead-benches from bands of foes, from many nations, spread awe among warriors since first he was discovered, poor of fortune; he had comfort for that: he grew under the skies, flourished in glorious deeds, until each of the neighbouring peoples there over the whale's riding had to obey, pay tribute. That was a good king!

The poet insists that he is beginning from a background of the martial prowess of the ancient Danish kings that his audience will share: in the Old English, the words 'We' and 'have heard' (*We . . . gefrunon*) are separated, neatly bracketing what it is we are all supposed to know ('the power of the mighty kings of the Spear-Danes in bygone days'). The poet moves swiftly on to mention the first and founding ancestor of the Danish ruling dynasty, namely Scyld Scefing, the boy-king mysteriously sent by God from elsewhere to help the Danes in their time of greatest need; his descendants, the so-called Scyldings, indeed rule Denmark down to the Anglo-Saxon period. From this familiar background, the poet gently draws his audience into much less familiar territory, slowly introducing Grendel and Beowulf, characters otherwise unattested in Germanic lore, and interweaves his story of the pagan Danes (some of whom were still pagan when the *Beowulf* manuscript was written) with clear reference to Christian tales enshrined in the Bible. These opening lines are typical of the poet's style, including a chain of no fewer than eight so-called compounds (in general, single words in Old English are made up of two elements and, therefore, require more than one modern English word to translate them) that clog the verses, forcing a reader or listener to pause and contemplate what is being said: *Gardena*

('Spear-Danes'), *geardagum* ('bygone days'), *þeodcyninga* ('mighty kings'), *meodosetla* ('mead-benches'), *feasceaft* ('poor of fortune'), *weorðmyndum* ('glorious deeds'), *ymbsittendra* ('neighbouring peoples'), *hronrade* ('whale's riding'). Intriguingly, for a poem so often associated with violent and heroic deed, only one of these eight compounds, *Gardena* ('Spear-Danes'), smacks of conflict, and it is also the only compound in this opening passage the usage of which is restricted to *Beowulf*. From the first, then, the poet tells us that this will be a tale of battles and of deeds of derring-do, for sure: but it will also be much more than that.

In a similarly unsettling move, and even before he names the hero of his poem, the poet carefully puts him in his place. After describing how one of Scyld's descendants, Hrothgar, grows powerful and builds himself a mighty hall, Heorot, whereupon it is ravaged by the monster Grendel, who emerges from the fens to wreak havoc on the helpless Danes, Beowulf, at this point unnamed, is introduced for the first time:

Þæt fram ham gefrægn Higelaces þegn,
god mid Geatum, Grendles dæda;
se wæs moncynnes mægenes strengest
on þæm dæge þysses lifes,
æþele ond eacen. (*Beowulf*, lines 194–8)

Hygelac's thegn, a good man among the Geats, learned about Grendel's deeds from home; he was of men the strongest in might on that day of this life, noble and vast.

Beginning with a near-rhyme (*gefrægn . . . þegn*, line 194), these lines emphasise Beowulf's foreignness (he is a Geat, not a Dane), his nobility (we later learn that he is closely related to King Hygelac of the Geats and is likely his sister's son) and his pre-eminence; the use of the term 'vast' (*eacen*, line 198a; the word seems to have the sense 'increased [beyond what is normal]') is particularly relevant, since elsewhere in the poem the term is used only of the giant sword taken by Beowulf from the monster Mere, the monster Mere itself, the dragon and the dragon's cursed treasure. Still more striking, however, is the way in which the poet effectively delimits and indeed undercuts Beowulf's power through alliteration of elements which do not normally carry either stress or alliteration: he was the strongest on *that* day of *this* life. The poet repeats the phrase precisely twice more in the battle between Beowulf and Grendel, using it once of each protagonist, so emphasising its importance for his own view of his hero and of the first monster he fights: both are creatures of their specific time and place. For a sense of the effect of this kind of delimiting phrase, imagine walking up to a certain special someone you would very much like to know better and saying: 'You are the best-looking person that I have seen. In that seat. Today.' Good luck with that. At all events, it is clear how the poet of *Beowulf* viewed his hero; a man, a strong man certainly, but a man not only of 'then' and 'there', but also of 'here': the sublunary world that all mortals share. Strong as he is, Beowulf will die, whenever God wills it, just like us, and it is for us to try to make sense of what he does and for God to decide where he goes.

Beowulf, then, seems a different and more developed kind of hero than is found elsewhere in Old English literature and, indeed, in the heroic literature of other nations, too. In the Greek of Homer's *Iliad*, for example, Achilles is fierce and implacable, with a desire 'always to excel and to be beyond other men': his heroism lies in the recognition of his own unique talents as a killing machine and of his willingness to sacrifice everything for his own fame. The Latin Aeneas, by contrast, is in Vergil's *Aeneid* a good deal more thoughtful and brooding, with a keen sense of destiny that extends far beyond the purely personal: his abilities as a fighting man are matched by his propensity for planning and he is characterised by twin virtues of 'wisdom and strength' (Latin *sapientia et fortitudo*). Beowulf certainly shares both these characteristics, but also has a gift for skilful speech that is rightly celebrated by King Hrothgar, as he bids his nation's saviour farewell:

'Þu eart mægenes strang   ond on mode frod,
wis wordcwida.' (*Beowulf*, lines 1844–5)

'You are strong in might and wise in mind, clever in speeches.'

This particular combination, often described as the 'thought, word and deed' triad, and probably popularised in Anglo-Saxon England through Irish Christian sources, can be found in a number of places elsewhere in the poem, as for example, where Hrothgar mourns the loss of his companion Æschere, ripped apart by Grendel's mother:

   'Dead is Æschere,
Yrmenlafes   yldra broþor,
min runwita   ond min rædbora,
eaxlgestealla,   ðonne we on orlege
hafelan weredon,   þonne hniton feþan,
eoferas cnysedan.' (*Beowulf*, lines 1324–9)

'Æschere is dead, Yrmenlaf's elder brother, my close confidant and my counsel-giver, my shoulder-companion when in battle we protected our heads as footsoldiers clashed, struck boar-helmets.'

The triad 'close confidant . . . counsel-giver . . . shoulder-companion' (*runwita . . . rædbora, eaxlgestealla*) evidently alludes to the same 'thought, word, and deed' triad, in precisely the same order.

The interest of the *Beowulf* poet's evident identification of this triad with worldly and individual heroic endeavour is that it can be traced back to a Christian pattern describing how at Doomsday mankind will be judged for what they have done in 'thought, word and deed', and it became a motif most associated with preaching texts. However, certain Anglo-Saxons writing Latin poetry in the earlier period extend the theme, like the *Beowulf* poet, to praise individuals for their meritorious lives. So, for example, Bede (who died in 735), says in his poetic account of Saint Cuthbert that 'Cuthbert shines brilliant in mind, in hand, and in mouth, and looks after the flocks entrusted to him with prayers and advice'; later in the same poem he reuses the same theme to connect Cuthbert to the Church Fathers: 'For that man was devoted to God in his mind, and pleasant in his mouth, accustomed to recall the holy deeds of the Fathers, he also introduces quite often those of his own, which triumphs he performed with only a heavenly witness.' Towards the end of the eighth century, the theme has evidently become so familiar that Alcuin (who died in 804), a Northumbrian like Bede, and a keen student of the latter's works, can not only use it himself, but play on the theme. Alcuin clearly invokes the triad right at the beginning of his poem on the Anglo-Saxon missionary Willibrord (who just happens to have come from Alcuin's own family), calling him 'wise in mouth and watchful in mind and vigorous in action'. But he also seems to play on the theme in praising his own dead teacher, Ælberht, whom he gushingly describes as:

> A good and just man, generous, kind, and benevolent, a fosterer, advisor, and lover of the catholic faith; a ruler, teacher, defender, student of the Church, a cultivator of justice, a trumpet of law, a preacher of salvation, a hope for the poor, a father to orphans, a comforter of the needy, harsh to the stiff, gentle to the good, hard on the proud; strong in adversity, he was humble in prosperity, clever in mind, not loquacious in speech, but energetic in action.

The whole crescendo of praise evidently builds up to the final flourish, where, however, the taciturn Ælberht evidently doesn't quite live up to full heroic billing: he may be strong and clever, but is not a great speaker. Still, for a quiet and pious man who was likely just a beaky bookworm and all-round swot, two out three aint so bad.

That an Old English poem that purports to memorialise a mighty pagan hero from a distant land in the distant past should apparently employ a pattern that derives from the much closer (in both senses) Latin world of Christian education is no less striking than that the same poem should appear to focus so resolutely on the plight of those adversely affected by the heroic creed the poem recreates. But such an outlook is particularly clear not only in the poet's treatment of the monsters, as we have seen, but also in his depiction of those other marginal and often ignored figures of heroic life, namely the women. There are six major female characters in *Beowulf* and it is striking the extent to which the poet carefully patterns their appearance: three emerge in the earlier part of the poem, set in Denmark, when Beowulf is young, and three more in the second part, set in Geatland, when Beowulf is old. The first three women are the Danish King Hrothgar's queen, Wealhtheow, the hapless Hildeburh of legend and Grendel's mother. All can be described as women of a certain age, defined primarily through their sons. The role of Grendel's mother has already been examined; suffice it to say that she is an unwitting victim of the war game being played and that even if she involves herself in the cycle of revenge, she seems to do so primarily out of sorrow and necessity, and surely does not appear to revel in the task that is laid on her and which brings about her death.

The fact that Wealhtheow's name seems to mean 'foreign slave' is perhaps surprising (not quite the name that doting parents would bestow on a girl they hoped would end up Queen of Denmark!), but less so when it is realised that no one actually addresses her in this way; it seems to be the nickname given her by the Danish court, where she has presumably fetched up after being married off from another land as a so-called 'peace-weaver' (*freoðuwebbe*), a guarantor of settlement who was a hostage in all but name. To the warrior-Danes of Hrothgar's court, she may have seemed just a pawn in the game of politics, for all her posturing. Wealhtheow's role in *Beowulf* is partly decorative, serving drinks at the feast in a ceremonial fashion, but she also attempts to interfere in politics herself, especially when she learns that after Beowulf has defeated Grendel, Hrothgar says that he considers him as a son. Wealhtheow swiftly utters two speeches defending the right to succession of her own two boys, adding for good measure that she knows that Hrothgar's nephew, Hrothulf, will see them right. Significantly, neither of Wealhtheow's speeches is answered, a breach of courtly etiquette that of itself underlines her impotence and, moreover, it seems likely that an Anglo-Saxon audience would know what is confirmed in Scandinavian sources, namely that King Hrothgar is indeed succeeded not by either of his sons, but by Hrothulf (Old Norse Hrólfr, one of the most celebrated of Danish kings). For all her finery, Wealhtheow seems to be a helpless pawn in the power politics of the time.

The same can be said of Hildeburh, whose story is told by a poet (Old English *scop*) celebrating Beowulf's victory over Grendel. Her role seems tangential to the main tale the poet is producing, which we can for once deduce with the help of another witness, the so-called *Finnsburh Fragment*. That this legend concerns a case where the Danes suffer killings in a hall that they seem unable to avenge without the help of a foreign fighter, in this case Hengest (who went on to help conquer Britain, so providing another tenuous link with Anglo-Saxon England), makes it a decorous and highly suitable story to celebrate Beowulf's own similar service, a foreign warrior restoring Danish pride after a setback in their hall. But importantly, the *Beowulf* poet does not attempt to reproduce the song that Hrothgar's poet sings. Instead, he offers a kind of interpretive gloss, focusing on the plight of Hildeburh, who is a Dane married off as a peace weaver to the Frisian lord, Finn. She is named at the beginning and middle of the episode and mentioned again, by this time nameless, right at the end, when she is carted off back to Denmark with the other booty, after a chain of killings in which she loses at least one son, her brother and her husband. The *Beowulf* poet's sympathy for Hildeburh is made plain when she is described at the side of the funeral pyre that will consume both her Danish brother, Hnæf, and the sons (or perhaps son) that she shared with her Frisian husband. Although they fought on different sides, they will burn together and she weeps for them all:

> The pyre was prepared, and splendid (?) gold taken up from the hoard; the best of the battle-warriors of the warlike Scyldings was made ready on the funeral-pile. At that pyre was easily seen the blood-stained corselet, the all-golden swine, the iron-hard boar, many a noble killed by wounds; fine men had fallen in the slaughter. Then Hildeburh ordered her own sons [or 'son'] to be entrusted to the fire at Hnæf's pyre, their bone vessels to burn and be placed on the funeral-pile, wretched, side by side. The lady grieved and sang sorrowful songs. The battle-smoke went up, curled to the clouds, the greatest of slaughter-fires roared before the grave-mound; heads melted, wound-gashes burst; as blood spurted out, the cruel biting of the body. Flame, the greediest of spirits, swallowed all of those that battle took off of both peoples; their flowering had passed away.

In choosing to focus not on the glories of victory (something that surely Hrothgar's poet must have done), but instead on the horrific and painful effect of such conflict on innocents, the *Beowulf* poet offers a powerful critique of the heroic creed.

The three female characters in the second part of *Beowulf* (Hygd, Freawaru and Fremu, who is called Thryth or Modthryth by earlier commentators) are likewise linked by age and status: all seem to be much younger women than their counterparts in the first part of the poem and all are defined primarily not through their sons, but, rather, through their husbands. As with the earler three women, two are characters from the 'real time' of the poem, namely Hygd and Freawaru and the third, Fremu, appears (like Hildeburh) in an aside drawn from legendary history. Hygd is the Queen of Geatland, wife of Beowulf's lord, King Hygelac, and appears as an essentially passive and decorous lady. We are not told if she is a 'peace-weaver', although we know that both Freawaru and Fremu are. In the cases of these last two, we are also told that in one case (drawn from legend), the attempt to settle violence through marriage is successful, as the feisty young woman is herself tamed, but in the other case (drawn from life), the attempt spectacularly fails. Such failure is seen as unexceptional. As Beowulf himself observes: 'The killing-spear seldom stays idle anywhere after a man dies, although the bride is fine.' In choosing to focus on six women in all, none of whom can really be said to escape unscathed (even Fremu has to bow the head to her new lord, Offa), the *Beowulf* poet is offering an alternative vision of the implications of the relentless violence that underlines the heroic ethos, one that takes a colder and more realistic view of the grief and misery implied.

Literary context and aftermath of *Beowulf*: a foretaste

Now, of course, it has often been observed that medieval life was 'nasty, brutish and short': from the stereotypical depiction of early medieval characters in modern films and books, one might suppose that the same goes for medieval people. A recent analysis of DNA from early medieval skeletons throughout mainland Britain suggests that a relatively small number of Germanic invaders effectively suppressed and all but wiped out the native population in comparatively short order. Soon after the first wave of invasions in the mid-fifth century the British population was literally marginalised: swept off to the Celtic fringes of what is now Wales, Scotland and Cornwall by aggressive Anglo-Saxon incomers who took over the land and imposed their own perspective, so that even today the word 'Welsh' can be traced back directly to an Anglo-Saxon word (*wealh*) that means 'foreigner', in a process that smacks uncomfortably of what is now termed 'ethnic cleansing'. The Anglo-Saxons not only took the land, it seems, but the women too. It is notable that even in the often light-hearted Old English *Riddles* there are demeaning references to drunk and promiscuous Welsh slave girls, fit only to assist in the transfer of Germanic DNA to the next generation (see p. 143). But, as we shall see, rape and pillage were not only the preserve of invading Anglo-Saxons and it was not so long until the Anglo-Saxons themselves were invaded, by Vikings who took a similarly casual view of the 'foreigners' whose land and people they took for their own purposes. A thirteenth-century saga author can put the following verse into the mouth of the seven-year-old Icelander and budding Viking, Egill Skalla-Grímsson: 'My mother said that she would buy me a boat with beautiful oars, to go abroad with vikings, stand up in the stern, steer the precious vessel, make for harbour, cut down one man after another.' What more in a heroic society could a young boy want? (see further, p. 401).

But against this background of violence, it is important to remember that the great majority of the literature that has survived from the period is (like *Beowulf*) Christian in outlook and focus. Nonetheless, the influence of older, more martial and heroic verse often shines through; sometimes, indeed we might suspect the influence of *Beowulf* itself, even on the most overtly Christian topics and themes. So, for example, the opening lines of the first poem in an Old English manuscript now preserved in the cathedral in Vercelli, a city in the north of Italy on the pilgrim route to Rome (see p. 213), read as follows:

> Listen! We have heard of twelve glory-blessed heroes under the stars in days gone by, prince's thegns. Their power did not fail in battle-fighting, when banners clashed, after they departed as the Lord himself, the high king of the heavens, directed their lot. They were men famed across the earth, bold war-leaders and battle-brave, daring warriors, when shield and hand defended the helmet on the battlefield, on the plain of fate.

While the general tenor of these verses certainly calls to mind the opening lines of *Beowulf* cited earlier (and indeed the poet here is often held to have been directly influenced by *Beowulf*), there are crucial differences. Part of the portentous nature of this passage stems from its use in these ten-and-a-half lines of no fewer than eight compounds (precisely the same number as in the opening passage of *Beowulf* and used for a similar effect): 'days gone by', 'glory-blessed', 'battle-fighting', 'high king', 'war-leaders', 'battle-brave', 'battlefield' and 'plain of fate'). While half of these compounds are relatively commonplace, half are either unique to this poem or are found in the surviving works of only one or two other poets. At all events, such a clustering of compounds, more than half of which have a martial flavour (recall that in the parallel passage from *Beowulf*, only one such compound had a similar flavour), lends these opening lines a formal and self-conscious quality. It comes, then, as something of a surprise for modern readers to realise that these fearsome warriors are the 12 Apostles, mightily morphed from their traditional depiction as meek men in sandals. The poem as a whole, now called *Andreas* by modern scholars, follows the adventures of the Apostle Andrew, whose Greek name means 'manly', and who vigorously lives up to billing, travelling to rescue his fellow Apostle Matthew from prison in a far-flung land, where he is being held captive by cannibals. Neither is *Andreas* the only Old English poem which seems to take a delight in using the martial and heroic language of the inherited native tradition to describe a Christian heroism that is elsewhere depicted in less aggressive terms.

The same manuscript also contains a superb vision of the Cross now known by the somewhat old-fashioned title of *The Dream of the Rood*, where the Crucifixion itself is portrayed as a heroic conflict willingly entered into by the young warrior Christ (see p. 161). In this poem, Christ strips willingly for the fray in a reversal of the traditional description of the arming of the hero. Here the nails of the Cross are described as arrows that pierce both Christ and his heroic retainer, the Cross, which is made to speak in the poem and describe the scene for itself. In a somewhat similar vein, the final poem in the Vercelli Book, now entitled *Elene* and signed in runes by a poet called Cynewulf, one of the very few Old English poets we can name, gives an account of the adventures of Saint Helena, mother of the Emperor Constantine, as she travels to the Holy Land in search of the True Cross. Early on, the poem's Latin source makes a brief allusion to the decisive battle of the Milvian Bridge in 312, before which Constantine is said to have had his own vision of the Cross, promising victory. The source is crisp and understated:

> And rising up he made an attack against the barbarians, and had the sign [of the Cross] go before, and coming upon the barbarians with his army he began to slaughter them at break of day. And the barbarians were afraid, and fled along the banks of the Danube, and no small multitude was killed. And God gave King Constantine the victory that day through the power of the Cross. But King Constantine, coming into his own city.

On this slim and unpromising foundation, Cynewulf builds one of the most arresting extended battle scenes to have survived in Old English. I will set this out in the following groups of text (but note that the Anglo-Saxons did not use stanzas in their poetry):

> Heht þa onlice   æðelinga hleo,
> beorna beaggifa,   swa he þæt beacen geseah,
> heria hildfruma,   þæt him on heofonum ær
> geiewed wearð,   ofstum myclum,
> Constantinus,   Cristes rode,
> tireadig cyning,   tacen gewyrcan.
>
> Heht þa on uhtan   mid ærdæge
> wigend wreccan,   ond wæpenþræce

hebban heorucumbul,   ond þæt halige treo
him beforan ferian   on feonda gemang,
beran beacen godes.
                        Byman sungon
hlude for hergum.   Hrefn weorces gefeah,
urigfeðra,   earn sið beheold,
wælhreowra wig.   Wulf sang ahof,
holtes gehleða.   Hildegesa stod.

Þær wæs borda gebrec   ond beorna geþrec,
heard handgeswing   ond herga gering,
syððan heo earhfære   ærest metton.
On þæt fæge folc   flana scuras,
garas ofer geolorand   on gramra gemang,
hetend heorugrimme,   hildenædran,
þurh fingra geweald   forð onsendan.

Stopon stiðhidige,   stundum wræcon,
bræcon bordhreðan,   bil in dufan,
þrungon þræchearde.   þa wæs þuf hafen.
segn for sweotum,   sigeleoð galen.
Gylden grima,   garas lixtan
on herefelda.   Hæðene grungon,
feollon friðelease.   Flugon instæpes
Huna leode,   swa þæt halige treo
aræran heht   Romwara cyning,
heaðofremmende.   Wurdon heardingas
wide towrecene.
                        Sume wig fornam.
Sume unsofte   aldor generedon
on þam heresiðe.   Sume healfcwice
flugon on fæsten   ond feore burgon
æfter stanclifum,   stede weardedon
ymb Danubie.   Sume drenc fornam
on lagostreame   lifes æt ende.

Ða wæs modigra   mægen on luste,
ehton elþeoda   oð þæt æfen forð
fram dæges orde.   Daroðæsc flugon,
hildenædran.   Heap wæs gescyrded,
laðra lindwered.   Lythwon becwom
Huna herges   ham eft þanon.
Þa wæs gesyne   þæt sige forgeaf
Constantino   cyning ælmihtig

æt þam dægweorce,   domweorðunga,
rice under roderum,   þurh his rode treo.

Gewat þa heriga helm   ham eft þanon,
huðe hremig,   (hild wæs gesceaden),
wigge geweorðod.   Com þa wigena hleo
þegna þreate   þryðbold secan,
beadurof cyning   burga neosan. (Cynewulf's *Elene*, lines 99–152)

Then he ordered likewise, the protector of princes, ring-giver of warriors, just as he saw that sign, the war-leader of hosts, which had been shown to him in the heavens, with great haste, the glorious king, Constantine, Christ's cross, to be made a symbol.

Then he ordered at dawn, with the break of day, warriors to waken and in that weapon-storm to raise the battle-standard and to carry that holy tree before them into the throng of foes, to bear the sign of God.

Trumpets sang, loudly before the hosts, the raven rejoiced in the deed, the dewy-feathered eagle beheld the foray, the battle of the slaughter-fierce ones; the wolf raised up a song, the wood's companion; battle-terror reared.

There was the clash of shields and the thrash of men; the hard hand-swing and the crash of hosts, after they first found the arrows' flight. Onto that doomed folk showers of darts, spears over the yellow shields into the throng of fierce ones, dire enemies sent forth battle-adders through fingers' force.

Bold-hearted they advanced, at times pressed on, broke through the shield-cover, plunged in the blade, thronged on hard in fray. Then was the banner raised, the sign over the troops, the song of victory sung. The golden helmet and spears shone on the field of war. The heathens perished, fell without peace. All at once they fled, the people of the Huns, as that holy tree the king of the Romans ordered raised, doing battle. The bold ones were widely split asunder.

Some battle took off, some unsoftly saved their lives in that war-fray, some half-dead fled into the fastness and saved their lives along the stone cliffs, took their places around the Danube, some drowning took off in the water-stream at their life's end.

Then was the force of the brave ones in hot spirits; they pursued the foreigners right up the evening from the start of the day: ash-darts flew, battle-adders. The army was destroyed, the shield-troop of foes: few of the force of the Huns reached thence home again. Then it was clear that the almighty king granted victory to Constantine in that day's work, mighty honours, powerful under the heavens, through his rood-tree.

Then the defender of hosts went thence home again, exulting in booty (the battle was settled), made worthy by war. The protector of warriors then went to seek his mighty abode, the battle-brave king, to visit the strongholds, with a band of thegns.

This striking scene, so carefully and lovingly depicted by an artist who at this juncture seems to have considered himself a poet first and a Christian second, evidently exults in the fray and includes a number of what we can only presume were motifs and images that would be still more familiar had more Old English battle poetry survived. The theme of the carrion creatures (wolf, eagle and raven) eagerly awaiting the coming feast on slaughtered men was evidently once widespread: no fewer than 16 examples of the so-called 'Beasts of Battle' motif have been found in existing Old English verse, often introduced in a partial or tenuous fashion that strongly suggests that a poet could expect his audience to recognise it. Cynewulf emphasises the clash and clatter of battle through a number of sound effects, including a repeated set of cracking rhymes in close proximity (lines 114–15 and 121–23: *gebrec . . . geþrec . . . handgeswing . . . herga gring . . . wræcon bræcon . . . þræchearde*). An equally effective technique (because it is unusual in Old English poetry) is Cynewulf's emphasis on verbs in general and his use of what might be called 'clashing verbs', where consecutive verbs are crammed together at the end of one line and the beginning of the next (lines 120–27: *onsendan/stopon; wræcon/bræcon; dufan/þrungon; grungon/feollan*), creating an effect of frantic activity. The grim litany of the terrible fates of the slaughtered ('Some battle took off, some unsoftly saved their lives in that war-fray, some half-dead fled into the fastness and saved their lives along the stone cliffs, took their places around the Danube, some drowning took off in the water-stream at their life's end') is highlighted in Old English, as in the translation, through the repetition of the word 'some' (Old English *sum*) no fewer than four times in succession. However tenuous its connection with its Latin source, this is a vivid and artful scene, one that seems to emphasise the strengths of the short and snappy Old English poetic line in the depiction of brisk action.

That a clearly Latin-trained and Christian poet like Cynewulf could revel in the dramatic and martial possibilitities of the native verse form is emphasised still further in another of his signed poems, this time on Saint Juliana, in a poem by her name found in another of the four major poetic codices, the 'Exeter Book'. Once again, one might think that the sufferings of a Christian martyr who died defending her virginity against the blandishments of a well-placed pagan suitor who wanted her to reject her faith and embrace him and his would offer little scope for the language of war, but the poet sees the saint's whole internal struggle through the lens of what in Christian terms is called a *psychomachia*, a Greek term for the battling of the torn soul. Often, the battle is seen as one between the Virtues and the Vices, with the soul as so much spoil. Anglo-Saxon England was fully familiar with the concept, thanks to the use as a schoolroom text of a poem of the same title by the fourth-century Latin poet, Prudentius. No fewer than ten manuscripts containing Prudentius' *Psychomachia* written or owned in Anglo-Saxon England have survived, most of which are heavily glossed, gruesomely illustrated or otherwise showing signs of heavy use.

Cynewulf was evidently a keen student and, in his poem *Juliana*, he has a devil confess to the imprisoned heroine that he can only be defeated by a truly heroic foe:

> 'If I meet any champion of God fresh in fighting spirit, brave against the force of arrows, one who will not flee from battle far from there, but, wise in mind, lifts his wooden board, his holy shield, his spiritual war-gear, will not betray God, but, bold in prayer, makes a stand, firmly among the foot-soldiers, then I have to turn far from there, wretched at heart, bereft of honours, into the grip of flames, mourn my sorrows, that I was unable by the skill of my strength to carry off the victory, but I sadly have to look for another, less bold under the banner-defence, a slower warrior, whom I can exite with my contamination, hinder in battle. Even though he begins something good spiritually, I am ready straightaway so that I may consider all his inner thought, how his mind is secured within, his defences set up. I open the gate of that wall by means of malice; the tower is pierced, the entrance opened, when first I send forth bitter thoughts into him through a flight of arrows, into his breast through various desires of the mind, so that it seems to himself better to commit sins contrary to the praise of God, the body's lusts.'

The notion of a 'champion of God' emphasises the idea of the 'soldier of Christ' (Latin *miles Christi*) fighting spiritual wars for his or her Christian faith that is again widespread in early medieval literature; its wholesale adoption into Old English literature is yet another example of the way in which the native and inherited secular heroic culture was adopted and adapted for Christian purposes.

But it is important to emphasise that it is not simply Christ and his saints and apostles who in Old English literature evidently warrant rebranding as Germanic warriors keen for the fray. A whole range of Old Testament biblical characters also come in for the full gung-ho treatment in Old English verse, where the language sometimes lingers a little too lovingly on grisly details and imaginary battles. The Junius manuscript, the earliest of the four major poetic manuscripts to have been written, and one that contains only biblical verse, shows a clear concern for martial and heroic imagery in each of its four lengthy poems.

So, for example, the opening lines of *Daniel*, a poem in the Junius Book, can be measured alongside both *Beowulf* and *Andreas* in their perhaps surprising depiction of the Jews fleeing from Egypt under Moses as a triumphant army:

> I have heard that the Hebrews lived blessed in Jerusalem, dealt out treasure, had a kingdom, as was natural for them, since through the might of the Creator an army was given into Moses' hand, a multitude of warriors, and they went out from Egypt, a mighty force. That was a brave nation! As long as they were allowed to govern that realm, to rule in the strongholds, bright was their wealth; as long as that people were willing to keep their father's covenant, God was their shepherd, the guardian of the heavenly kingdom, the holy lord, the ruler of glory. He gave to that troop bravery and might, the Creator of all creatures, so that they often destroyed the lives of many peoples, the protectors of the army of those who were not loyal to Him, until pride entered them at a drinking-feast, drunken thoughts, with wicked deeds.

Likewise, alongside *Beowulf* in its sole surviving manuscript, the Nowell Codex, is a poetic account of how the beautiful Hebrew widow Judith defended her honour when she was summoned to the tent of the invading Assyrian warlord, Holofernes, whose motives were not entirely honorable. Happily, he gets drunk and falls asleep before he can realise his foul intentions and Judith seizes her chance. In the Latin version of the Bible that would have been familiar in Anglo-Saxon England (the so-called Vulgate), we are simply told that 'she struck twice upon his neck, and cut off his head' (*et percussit bis in cervicem eius, et abscidit caput eius*). Well, the girl had a right to be piqued, I suppose. The Old English poet, by contrast to this pithy if shocking account, gives his imagination full rein and describes the scene as follows:

> Then she took the heathen man firmly by his hair, and dragged him shamefully towards her with her hands and carefully arranged the wicked and loathsome man so that she could most easily deal effectively with the wretch. Then that curly-haired [woman] struck the wicked-minded foe with a decorated sword so that she sliced through half his neck, so that he lay in a daze, drunk and maimed. He was not dead yet, not quite lifeless. The brave lady then struck the heathen dog in earnest a second time, so that his head flew off on the floor.

Using a technique of repeated references to the same person or object (usually called 'variation') that is entirely characteristic of Old English verse, the poet progressively dehumanises Holofernes, who is 'the heathen man . . . the wicked and loathsome man . . . the wretch . . . the wicked-minded foe . . . drunk and maimed . . . the heathen dog'. In this way, the poet depicts the man as a beast, ripe for slaughter. By contrast, Judith is only lightly described as 'curly-haired' and 'a brave lady' and instead the focus is on her actions: 'she took . . . dragged . . . arranged . . . struck . . . sliced . . . struck'. The artful repetition of the verb 'struck' (Old English *sloh*), positioned in the original halfway through the line in half-lines with clearly similar rhythm and structure (*sloh ða wundenlocc . . . sloh ða eornoste*) heightens the sense of her double hacking, although in neither line does the verb contribute to the main alliteration of the line; the (as it were) striking detail that the dead man's head 'flew' (Old English *wand*) off at the second blow is likewise cleverly emphasised by placing this vigorous verb at the end of the poetic line (a position which it does not occupy in any of its other appearances in surviving Old English poetry) and placing it opposite the partially rhyming monosyllable *hund* ('dog') that describes Judith's victim.

We cannot put a secure date on the composition of *Judith*, although the *Beowulf* manuscript as a whole was written around the year 1000. But it is tempting to associate this heroic tale of one woman's stand against an invading would-be rapist with the circumstances surroung the successive waves of Viking raiders who scoured and spoiled and eventually settled great swathes of Anglo-Saxon England from 793 until the generation after the *Beowulf* manuscript was written, when indeed Anglo-Saxon England was ruled by the Danish King Cnut. Certainly, the same kind of rage and indignation against imagined and actual sex crimes of this sort is expressed vividly by Archbishop Wulfstan of York (died 1023) at a very similar time to the date when the *Beowulf* manuscript was written, a time, he tells us, 'when the Danes most greatly persecuted the English'. In startling terms, we learn of the Norse invaders that:

> Often ten or twelve men, each after the other, shamefully violates the thegn's wife, and sometimes his daughter or near-kinswoman while he looks on, who thought himself proud and powerful and good enough before that happened.

Earlier in the same powerful speech, evidently so powerful that he seems to have repeated it in various forms on at least three other occasions, Wulfstan lists further the fact that:

> It is shameful to speak about what has happened too widely, and it is a terrible thing to know the disgrace that too many do too often, when they club together and buy a woman for a joint price jointly, and with that one woman they commit filth one after another and each after the other, just like dogs that don't care for the filth, and then they sell off this creature of God, that He had dearly bought for his own price, into the power of foreign enemies.

Wulfstan's description of the perpetrators as 'just like dogs' (*hundum gelicost*) calls to mind the description of the stricken Holofernes as a 'heathen dog' (*hæðenan hund*). In this context, it is interesting the extent to which the author of *Judith* so evidently relished his depiction of the unseemly decapitation of an unarmed and incapacitated enemy: one wonders how many Anglo-Saxon women would have wished to react in the same robust fashion when confronted by a lusty drunken Viking raider and how many hapless husbands, brothers, fathers and sons would have wished their womenfolk to do likewise in similar circumstances. In assessing and appreciating and even sometimes applauding the undeniably violent images that are found widely in Old English literature, it is as well to remember that for long stretches of time throughout the period few Anglo-Saxons lived to see peace or even old age.

With regard to *Judith*, moreover, it is notable the extent to which a scarcely squeamish source has been juiced up in translation. Still more striking, however, as a departure from the biblical source than the unedited cutting off of Holofernes' head is the Old English poet's insertion of an entire battle sequence, where there is in the Vulgate no real trace of direct combat at all. The Bible says merely that after Judith has escaped, carrying off Holofernes' head as a trophy in a sack, the Assyrians, finding their leader dead, simply run away and are cut down by the Jews, who have been greatly encouraged by Judith's triumphant return. All we see in the Vulgate is an account of how the Jewish army looks forward to defeating their enemies: 'And immediately at break of day, they hung up the head of Holofernes upon the walls, and every man took his arms, they went out with a great noise and shouting.' Such an unheroic and oblique account was evidently unsatisfactory to the Anglo-Saxon poet, who offers instead an extraordinary and lengthy description, again beginning with the preparations for conflict, but expanding it in ways which strongly suggest that he had the similarly expanded scene in *Elene* in mind as a direct model:

> Then a troop of eager ones was quickly prepared, keen for battle; the very brave ones advanced, men and retainers, bore victory-banners; they went to the fight, straight ahead, heroes under helmets, from that holy stronghold, at the very break of day. Shields clattered, resounded loud. At that the lean wolf in the wood rejoiced, and the dark raven, carrion-keen bird; they both knew that those mighty men thought to supply them with their fill of the fey; but there flew in their wake an eagle eager for food, dewy-feathered; the dark-coated one sang a war-song, the one with horned beak. The battle-troops advanced, warriors to the fray, protected by bucklers, hollow shields, those who previously had endured the scorn of foreigners, the heathens' contempt. To them that was harshly paid back at the ash-play to all the Assyrians, after the Jews under war-banners had reached the encampment. Then they promptly let fly forth showers of darts, battle-adders from horn bows, firm-fixed arrows. They stormed loud, the fierce

war-fighters, sent spears into the throng of the hard ones. The warriors were angry, the land's inhabitants, with the hostile race; they advanced stern-hearted, resolute in spirit; they woke up unsoftly the ancient enemies, weary from drinking. With their hands the troops drew from their sheaths the brightly decorated swords, trusty of edge, slew the Assyrian warriors, evil-schemers. They spared none of that army, high or low, of living men that they could overcome. So those noble thegns throughout the morning pursued the foreigners the whole time, until that army's body-guards, those who were fierce, perceived that the Jewish men mightily showed them sword-strokes.

Here, the progressive advance of the Hebrew army is emphasised by repetition of the same verb 'advanced' (Old English *stopon*), followed in each case by a compound word in Old English that needs two modern English words to translate it: 'the royally brave ones advanced . . . the battle-warriors advanced . . . the stern-hearted ones advanced'; a very similar technique is used by the *Beowulf* poet elsewhere in the same manuscript to describe the advance of the monster Grendel, attacking the Danish royal hall. Four uniquely shared phrases appear in the same order in the two battle sequences in *Judith* and *Elene*: 'dewy-feathered eagle' (*earn . . . urigfeðera*), 'showers of darts' (*flana scuras*), 'battle-adders' (*hildenædran*, twice in *Elene*), and 'pursued the foreigners' (*ehton elðeoda*). Indeed, these four shared phrases are just part of an extraordinary shared chain of more than 20 individual words in almost identical order best traced through the Old English, where in *Elene* we find *sungon . . . hlude . . . hrefn . . . gefeah urigfeðra earn . . . wulf . . . sang . . . flana scuras garas . . . on gramra gemang . . . hildenædran . . . forð onsendan stopon . . . unsofte . . . ehton elþeoda*, while in *Judith* we find *hlude . . . gefeah wulf . . . hrefn earn . . . urigfeðera . . . sang . . . stopon . . . forð . . . flana scuras hildenædran . . . garas sendon in heardra gemang . . . stopon . . . unsofte . . . ehton elðeoda*. It is hard to resist the notion that the poet of *Judith*, keen to introduce a battle scene sadly missing from his source, turns instead to a similar description, itself massively expanded from its own source, found in another poem celebrating another strong woman's moral rectitude.

But if the battles celebrated in *Judith* and *Elene* smack of literary productions far removed from grim reality, genuine Anglo-Saxon heroism and its stark effects are also carefully commemorated in the literature, for example in an extraordinary and fragmentary poem on what must have seemed the last hoorah for English men in the early eleventh century. At Maldon in Essex in 991, the aged Ealdorman Byrhtnoth had confronted a Viking army and, even though he had them holed up on a tidal island, allowed them to pass over to the mainland for pitched battle that, along with his own life, he was to lose. Byrhtnoth's rash heroism was apparently commemorated by an elaborate embroidery commissioned by his widow, a wall hanging that may even have echoed in scale and theme the Bayeux Tapestry. A fragment of a poem on *The Battle of Maldon* also survives, albeit only in an eighteenth-century transcription. The poem focuses on young lives lost and on the national nature of the catastrophic defeat, of an army of English men drawn not only from Essex, but from Mercia, Wessex and Northumbria, too. Many of the English are carefully named, in contrast to their largely name-less, faceless, almost bestial enemy of 'slaughter-wolves' (*wælwulfas*). The *Anglo-Saxon Chronicle* reminds us of the watershed character of the defeat, after which for the first time the English had to pay a ransom to keep the marauders at peace; and it was to get worse, as Wulfstan described earlier. In *The Battle of Maldon*, after Byrhtnoth has been killed, an aged comrade urges the remaining warriors to fight to the death rather than flee. His words are worth quoting:

> 'Hige sceal þe heardra,   heorte þe cenre,
> mod sceal þe mare,   þe ure mægen lytlað.
> Her lið ure ealdor   eall forheawen,
> god on greote.   A mæg gnornian
> se ðe nu fram þis wigplegan   wendan þenceð.' (*The Battle of Maldon*,
> lines 312–16)

> 'Courage must be the harder, heart the keener, mind must be the greater,
> as our strength wanes. Here lies our leader, entirely cut to pieces, a good man
> in the dirt. Ever may he mourn who thinks to turn now from this warplay.'

We note how the first two lines ('Courage . . . wanes') express a noble and heroic sentiment that stands outside the immediate temporal concerns of the battle at hand and might, indeed, be used to rally troops at any time or place. Such heroic idealism is properly tempered in the next line and a half ('Here . . . dirt'), which in a spirit of grim realism point to the less pretty side of war, as it takes place 'here' and affects 'our leader, entirely cut to pieces, a good man in the dirt'). The final line and a half of the passage attempts to reconcile idealism and realism, by expanding what would have been another heroic sentiment ('Ever may he mourn who thinks to turn from warplay') by the simple insertion of the words 'now' (*nu*) and 'this' (*þis*), crowded into the overly long penultimate half-line. It is war and it is glorious, but it is doomed, the poet seems to be saying. In such ways does the multiple (and multiply sympathetic) perspective of *Beowulf* live on.

The Battle of Maldon celebrates (if that is the right word) an English defeat at the hands of Viking raiders in the reign of Æthelred II ('the unready'; see later, p. 339). It also foreshadows the many humiliations the Anglo-Saxons would suffer in the years ahead, until the Danish King Cnut took over (ruled 1016–35). In closing our consideration of the depiction of violence in Old English literature, we might focus finally on another grim and gruesome description that stems from these vicious times. In *Beowulf*, as we have seen, women played little part in high politics, but in Anglo-Saxon history, especially in the later period, they sometimes certainly exercised a leading role. Consider, for example, Emma of Normandy, one of the most extraordinary and powerful women from Anglo-Saxon times (see further p. 455). Emma was married as a sort of guarantor of peace and good relations to two men. The first husband was Æthelred, the second Cnut. Emma was also mother of two more kings of England in the shape of Harthacnut (her son by Cnut) and Edward the Confessor (her son by Æthelred). She clearly had a good deal of authority, yet Emma's long-lasting influence and careful political positioning did not come without cost. Another of her sons by Æthelred, Alfred the ætheling, paid a heavy price when he evidently mistimed his return from the exile in his mother's ancestral Normandy that he shared with his luckier brother Edward. Earl Godwine, one of Cnut's most powerful followers, who was to have a lasting influence on the politics of his time before and after Cnut, intercepted the young prince on arrival, some said with the connivance of Emma herself. At this point, the *Anglo-Saxon Chronicle* for the year 1036 breaks into rhyming verse:

Ac Godwine hine þa gelette   and hine on hæft sette,
and his geferan he todraf,   and sume mislice ofsloh;
sume hi man wið feo sealde,   sume hreowlice acwealde,
sume hi man bende,   sume hi man blende,
sume hamelode,   sume hættode.
Ne wearð dreorlicre dæd   gedon on þison earde,
syþþan Dene comon   and her frið namon.
Nu is to gelyfenne   to ðan leofan gode,
þæt hi blission   bliðe mid Criste
þe wæron butan scylde   swa earmlice acwealde.

But Godwine then stopped him and set him in fetters, and he drove off his companions and slaughtered some in various ways; some of them were sold for cash, some viciously killed, some were bound, some were blinded, some maimed, some scalped. No more bloody deed was done in this land since the Danes came and made peace here. Now it is to be believed in the beloved God that they rejoice joyously with Christ who were without guilt so wretchedly killed.

The litany of torture and slaughter ('some . . . some . . . some . . . some . . . some . . . some . . . some'; the Old English in each case is *sume*) recalls the same technique found earlier in the battle sequence in *Elene*, but here the violence is real, not imagined. It is hard not to read bitterness into the lines that immediately follow this catalogue of cruelty, commenting ruefully that 'No more bloody deed was done in this land since the Danes came and made peace here'; the peace implied is the silence of the grave. Likewise, there is an archness to the observation in the last line that these poor wretches were killed 'without guilt' (*butan scylde*), since the same Old English phrase can also mean 'without a shield', 'defenceless'. Again, the innocents are seen to suffer. No amount of rhyme, wordplay or careful use of repeated phrasing can cover up the sheer horror and shocking nature of this gruesome piece of politics. We later learn that Earl Godwine died at a feast, choking to death after he swore that he was only acting under orders in the killing of Alfred and that Emma was finally faced down by her son Edward when he became king and sent off to genteel retirement in Winchester. Neither Emma nor Godwine lived to see the violent outcome of their politicking and pulling of family strings, which kicked in when Edward the Confessor died childless, even though Earl Godwine had made him marry one of the earl's own daughters. On 14 October 1066 there faced each other across a field near Hastings, at a place the French victors were to dub 'Senlac' ('the lake of blood'), Harold Godwinsson, Edward's English successor and the son of the disgraced earl, and William of Normandy, soon to be William the Conqueror, who was Emma's own great-nephew. The heirs of the invading Anglo-Saxons, twice invaded by Norsemen, were finally to be conquered by the Normans, themselves heirs of Norsemen who settled in a stretch of Northern France. Thus, in a fittingly bloody manner, Anglo-Saxon England came to an end as a political entity.

Beowulf and other stories

The rest is history. But we should note that neither the five Anglo-Saxon centuries nor the medieval periods after it have to be defined necessarily as the history of violence. It is true that *Beowulf* and the other works are by and large 'heroic literature', products of a society organised along lines for war. But is war something we have lost since then? The promise to 'get medieval on yo'' and other expressions from today's happy culture appear to tell us that violence is the particular state of being of the period before, say, 1500. The snide implication is that violence, by being Beowulfian, has nothing to do with the moderns – as if it was untrue that the literature of the twentieth or twenty-first century is profoundly shaken and shaped by the Great War, World War II, the nuclear bomb etc., etc. By the same token, if you read *Beowulf* and any of the other Old English (Old Norse or later medieval) poems, prose works and annals featured in this book, you will find a literature that faces up to our human problem with courage, style and unblinking honesty.

Translations and texts

Heaney, Seamus, trans., *Beowulf: A New Translation* (New York, 2000).

Kiernan, Kevin S., Andrew Prescott *et al.*, eds, *Electronic Beowulf*, 2 CDs (London, 2000).

Klaeber, Friedrich, ed., *Beowulf*, 3rd edn (Boston, MA, 1950).

Liuzza, Roy M., trans., *Beowulf: A New Verse Translation* (Toronto, 2000).

Further reading

Baker, Peter S., ed., *'Beowulf': Basic Readings*, Basic Readings in Anglo-Saxon England 1 (New York, 1995).

Bjork, Robert E. and John D. Niles, eds, *A 'Beowulf' Handbook* (Lincoln, NA, 1997).

Fry, Donald K., ed., *The 'Beowulf'-Poet: a Collection of Critical Essays* (Englewood Cliffs, NJ, 1968).

Gardner, John, *Grendel* (New York, 1971).

Hermann, John P., *Allegories of War: Language and Violence in Old English Poetry* (Ann Arbor, MI, 1989).

Lapidge, Michael, 'The Archetype of *Beowulf*', *Anglo-Saxon England* 29 (2000), pp. 5–41.

Morrison, Stephen, 'Old English *cempa* in Cynewulf's *Juliana* and the Figure of the *Miles Christi*', *English Language Notes* 17 (1979), pp. 81–4.

Orchard, Andy, *A Critical Companion to 'Beowulf'* (Cambridge, 2005).

Orchard, Andy, *Pride and Prodigies: Studies in the Monsters of the 'Beowulf' Manuscript* (Toronto, 2003).

Orchard, Andy, 'Reading *Beowulf* Now and Then', *SELIM* 12 (2003–4 [2005]), pp. 49–81.

Rauer, Christine, *Beowulf and the Dragon: Parallels and Analogues* (Cambridge, 2000).

Robinson, Fred C., *'Beowulf' and the Appositive Style* (Knoxville, TN, 1985).

Sisam, Kenneth, *The Structure of 'Beowulf'* (Oxford, 1965).

Tolkien, J.R.R., *'Beowulf:* the Monsters and the Critics', *Publications of the British Academy* 22 (1936), pp. 245–95.

Whitelock, Dorothy, *The Audience of 'Beowulf'* (Oxford, 1950).

Wormald, Patrick, 'Bede, *Beowulf,* and the Conversion of the Anglo-Saxon Aristocracy', in *Bede and Anglo-Saxon England,* Farrell, Robert T., ed., *British Archaeological Reports* 46 (Oxford, 1978), pp. 32–95.

CHAPTER 4

Old English minor heroic poems

Richard North

For many people, *Beowulf is* Old English literature and, as the previous chapter has shown, there are good reasons for this. It is, without doubt, an exciting, engaging piece of work. It touches on many of the themes that have illuminated great works of art through the ages: honour and dishonour, cowardice and bravery, mothers and their sons, and, of course, it is riddled with violence. All factors, no doubt, in the recent decisions to film this great Old English legend. But to stop at *Beowulf* is to miss out on a great deal. Although extant manuscripts are few and far between, there is evidence of a very strong tradition of heroic poetry in Old English and Old Norse. This evidence is to be found in some fragments of existing verse, it is to be found in the Exeter Book and it is to be found, as you will see, in the old-fashioned art of reading between the lines.

The other pieces of Old English heroic poetry that have come down to us are *The Finnsburh Fragment*, *Widsith* ('Widely-Travelled'), *Deor* ('Valiant') and *Waldere* ('Walter'). Because each of them is much shorter than *Beowulf*, even the *Finnsburh Fragment* and *Waldere*, which are fragments surviving from longer works, all four are known as 'minor heroic poems'. There are other poems composed in the heroic style, to do with battles fought in England in the tenth centuriy, such as *The Battle of Brunanburh* (in 937) and *The Battle of Maldon* (in 991). But in the sense that a true 'heroic poem' deals with legendary material, we will leave these other works for consideration in a later chapter (see pp. 323, 339). In this chapter I will introduce the background of the four Old English minor heroic poems before moving through each one in turn. They can all be dated very roughly to the ninth century. Along the way I will look at the Scandinavian tales on the margins of the main narrative in *Beowulf*, finishing with the poet's allusion to Sigemund the Dragon-Slayer. I will also show you what heroic poems were like in related traditions. Mainly, however, you will get a tour through the Old English minor heroic poems, with reference to the compassion of poets who believed their heroes were damned.

Poetry in performance, Dark Ages' style

At one time, it seems, there were many heroic poems in Old English, short lays, eulogies and long epics. You can see a plenitude of lost verse of this kind simply from the number of other stories in *Beowulf* – Sigemund the Dragon-Slayer (lines 874–900), Heremod the Bad (lines 901–15 and 1709–22), Finn and Hengest (lines 1068–1159), Hama the necklace stealer and Eormanric the Gothic emperor (lines 1198–1201), Offa of Angeln and his queen (lines 1931–62), Ingeld's marriage (lines 82–5 and 2020–69), Heoroweard's attack on Hrothulf (lines 2160–9) – all of which the poet must expect his audience to know.

In general, the tradition of Old English heroic poems can be divided by material dealing with north and south. Stories from the northern Germanic area, Frisia on the islands and coastline of today's Netherlands as well as in Scandinavia, are told in *Beowulf* and in *The Finnsburh Fragment* and *Widsith*. (see Map 2). The stories in *Deor* and *Waldere* come from further south, from Frankish and Gothic regions which correspond to present-day eastern France, Germany, northern Italy, Austria and the Balkans. Both *Deor* and *Waldere*, the latter consisting two fragments from a long epic, are proof of central European tales which were known in England but which, for the most part, the poet of *Beowulf* saw no reason to include, given that he sets his main story in Denmark and the southern Swedish peninsular. The secular literary culture that gave rise to all five heroic poems, *Beowulf* and the four 'minor' ones, was itself derived from a once prolific circulation of oral-formulaic poems in the North Sea Germanic trading area, one which lasted very roughly from the years 600 to 900.

'Oral formulaic' is a term for poetry that was knocked out line by line by poets who used stock words, epithets and phrases almost like building a poem out of clichés. A preliterate poet was expected to have a reservoir of such 'formulae' with which to generate a long poem at fairly short notice. The larger textual units were 'type scenes', different narrative templates for heroic situations of various kinds. This chapter will show the use of type scenes such as 'the dawn wake-up call', 'the woman laments', 'the goading woman' and 'exchanging insults before battle' or 'flyting'. We already know of this style of composition from the Homeric epics *Odyssey* and *Iliad*, both

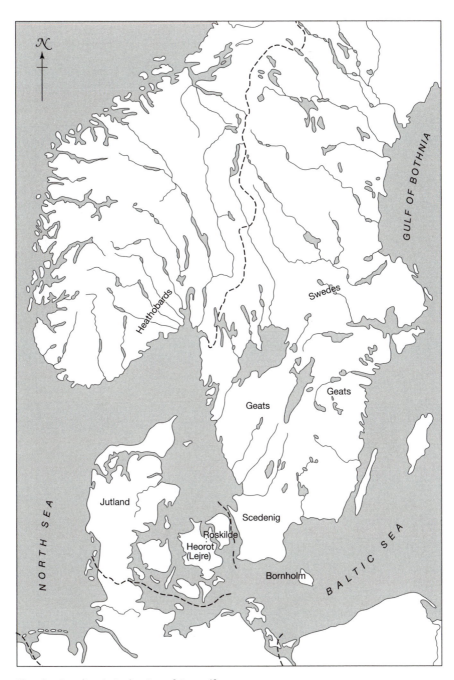

Map 2   Scandinavia in the time of *Beowulf*

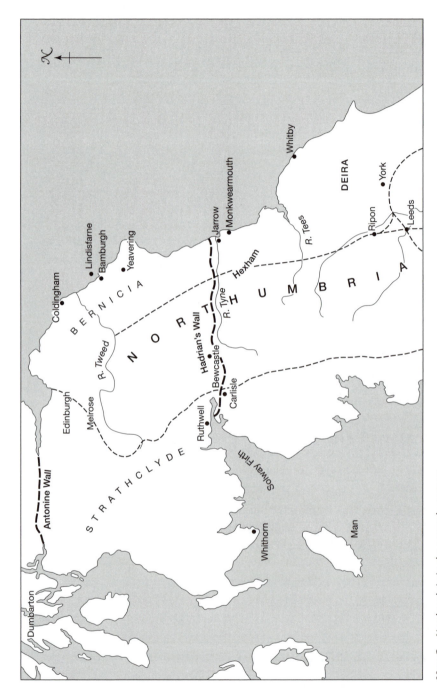

Map 3   Northumbria in the seventh century

of which were composed with oral-formulaic techniques. The poet of *Beowulf* did not know these Greek poems, but it is clear that he thought of ancient Germanic poetry in a similar way, as the spontaneous effusions of epic. We can see this from the preamble to his long passage on the hero Sigemund [/see:yemund/] the Dragon-Slayer. As the Danes ride back from Grendel's Mere, believing Grendel dead and their troubles over, one of them makes up a poem:

> Hwilum cyninges þegn
> guma gilphlæden   gidda gemyndig,
> se ðe ealfela   ealdgesegena
> worn gemunde,   word oþer fand
> soðe gebunden.   Secg eft ongan
> sið Beowulfes   snyttrum styrian
> ond on sped wrecan   spel gerade,
> wordum wrixlan;   (*Beowulf*, lines 867–74)

Sometimes a king's thane,
a man honoured for his brag, mindful of elegies,
who remembered an encyclopaedic number
of old sayings, found other words
bound together by truth. After that, this man began
cleverly to stir up Beowulf's adventure,
successfully to recite a fitting story,
to vary his words.

These lines are an allusion to oral-formulaic verse technique in the antique Old English tradition. It is rare enough to hear from the Anglo-Saxons how they thought preliterate heathens composed. The poet of *Beowulf* was an educated Christian, so it is unlikely that *Beowulf* was composed in quite this way. And yet his words above do show us the extent to which memory, not writing, remained important to the poets of a warlike society even in Christian times. To have written something as complex as *Beowulf*, he would have had to know poems that were either unwritten heroic works produced in oral-formulaic style, as above; or written texts transcribed from these; or poems, like his, composed with the aid of writing. This is just as true for the poets of *The Finnsburh Fragment*, *Widsith*, *Deor* and *Waldere*.

The fight at Finnsburh in *Fragment* and 'Episode'

The story of Finnsburh, covering a battle, peace deal and renewed battle, is set in the mid-fifth century in Frisia not long before the first Germanic settlements in Britain. King Finn of the Frisians has a bodyguard made up of foreigners known as 'Half-Danes' because around half of them are Scylding tribesmen from Denmark. Early one morning he attacks his own bodyguard in their hall and eventually kills their leader, his wife's brother Hnæf. The Half-Dane survivors regroup under a lieutenant named Hengest, who agrees to a peace with Finn whereby nobody on either side is allowed to mention the battle that has just taken place. They stay together over winter, but in spring the treaty is broken when the Half-Danes rise up and kill Finn in revenge for Hnæf.

The following section will show how that treaty fails. *The Finnsburh Fragment*, all 48 extant lines of it, tells the first part of the story. The second, dealing with the treaty and aftermath, is reported to us in the 'Finnsburh Episode', *Beowulf*, lines 1068–1159. Taken together, the *Fragment* and 'Episode' have a story like a Jacobean revenge tragedy. To start with *The Fragment*. This is a text copied rather awkwardly in 1705 from a single manuscript folio which is now lost. It opens at dawn with a young captain rousing his troops in response to the cry of a watchman. The young man is Hnæf [/hnaf/], Danish on his mother's side. Hnæf is captain of the mongrel band known as 'Half-Danes'. Some time ago he brought them to Frisia to serve in the king's bodyguard. Lately there has been bad feeling between the in-laws, something to do with a despot's paranoia. Now, although it appears Finn wants to wipe him out, Hnæf is calm and purposeful:

> 'Ne ðis ne dagað eastan,   ne her draca ne fleogeð
> ne her ðisse healle   hornas ne byrnað.
> Ac her forð berað,   fugelas singað,
> gylleð græghama,   guðwudu hlynneð,
> scyld scefte oncwyð.   Nu scyneð þes mona
> waðol under wolcnum;   nu arisað weadæda
> ðe ðisne folces nið   fremmað willað.
> Ac onwacnigeað nu,   wigend mine,
> habbað eowre linda,   hicgeaþ on ellen,
> windað on orde,   wesað onmode.' (*Fragment*, lines 3–12)

> 'This light is not eastern daybreak, nor does a dragon fly here,
> nor is it a burning of the gables of this hall,
> but here men march towards us, birds are singing,
> the greycoat howls, the battle-board thunders,
> shield gives back word to spearshaft. Now shines this moon,
> wandering behind the clouds, now arise deeds of woe
> which will further this hostility in the nation.
> So awake now, my warriors,

take your linden-shields, think of valour,
fall into line, be of one mind!'

The style has the lyricism of a warlike tradition. There is a wolf ('grey-coat', *græghama*) and a raven ('birds', *fugelas*), traditional portents of battle, while Hnæf's speech itself is built out of a type scene that we can name 'the dawn wake-up call'. There is another example of this type scene in an Old Norse poem from the tenth or eleventh century, *The Lay of Bjarki* (*Bjarkamál*), which has a young hero rousing some troops in a similar way:

'Dagr es upp kominn,   dynja hana fjaðrar,
mál es vílmǫgum   at vinna erfiði.
Vaki æ ok vaki   vina hǫfuð,
allir enir œztu   Aðils of sinnar.
'Hár enn harðgreipi,   Hrólfr skjótandi,
ættum góðir menn,   þeirs ekki flýja,
vekka yðr at víni   né at vífs rúnum,
heldr vekk yðr at hǫrðum   Hildar leiki.'

'Day has come up, the cocks shake their feathers,
it is time for serving-men to carry out their tasks.
Let the friends' main man [Hrólfr] wake for all time,
and let them wake, all the best companions of Aðils.

'Hoary the hard-gripper, Hrólfr the shooter,
men of good family who do not flee,
I wake you not to wine nor to the mysteries of a woman,
rather I wake you into the hard play of Hildr [battle]!'

The sleeping warriors in *The Lay of Bjarki* serve King Hrólfr, whose hall in Lejre, Denmark, has just been attacked by King Hjǫrvarðr. This is actually the same story as the destruction of King Hrothulf by (his cousin) Heoroweard, to which the poet of *Beowulf* alludes as a future event in lines 2160–69. In their own way the lines of *The Lay of Bjarki* are more ironic, more detached, than Hnæf's speech in *The Finnsburh Fragment*. They present battle as a form of love play. Hildr, 'Battle', is one of the 'Valkyries', who choose warriors for Óðinn, the war god (see p. 357). Hnæf in his speech is less flippant, a man looking fate in the eye. The *Fragment* goes on with a parley between combatants, before battle erupts and the Half-Danes hold the door against Finn and the Frisians for five fierce days. Around here the *Fragment* runs out and the 'Finnsburh Episode' in *Beowulf* takes over.

The 'Episode' is a name for the public performance of a Finnsburh epic in Heorot on the day the Danes ride back from the Mere. At this point they are euphoric, celebrating Beowulf's victory as if it were their own. The poet of *Beowulf*, however, reports this to us more sombrely by opening with the grieving woman, Finn's queen who has lost her son and brother. Hnæf is now dead and yet everything goes on as before, with the Half-Danes back in the Frisian army, although no one on either side, Hengest's or Finn's, must mention the war. Finn suspected his brother-in-law and got him out of the way, but the others can stay. Of course Hnæf's Danish kinsmen have some unfinished business. It is no surprise that these members of the Half-Danes want Finn dead in revenge for Hnæf. But Finn, seeing this, has drawn up the treaty so that Hengest must join him in liquidating the Danish core of the Half-Danes should they so much as say a word out of place. As a Jute, Hengest has no duty to avenge Hnæf. For his own part, Finn will kill any malcontents on the Frisian side. This is how the Danes are locked into a peace shameful to them.

The treaty is sealed with oaths and the dead are cremated on a funeral pyre. Hnæf's body is laid next to that of Finn's son. Here the poet returns to the grieving queen, with a type scene we can call 'the woman laments':

> Ides gnornode,
> geomrode giddum.   Guðrinc astah.
> Wand to wolcnum   wælfyra mæst,
> hlynode for hlawe;   hafelan multon,
> bengeato burston   ðonne blod ætspranc,
> laðbite liges.   Lig ealle forswealg,
> gæsta gifrost,   þara ðe þær guð fornam
> bega folces;   wæs hira blæd scacen. (*Beowulf*, lines 1117–24)

> The lady mourned,
> lamented in song. The man of battle ascended.
> The biggest flames of any war-dead twisted up to the clouds,
> roared over the pyre; heads melted,
> wound openings burst, as blood sprang out of them,
> hateful bites on bodies. Fire, greediest of demons,
> swallowed all the men whom battle had taken there,
> from both sides of the army; their glory was gone.

After this, Finn's Frisian thanes disperse to their low-lying homes, leaving their king safe with his cleansed Half-Dane bodyguard. The poet now dwells on Hengest's state of mind. Having focused on the queen, whose name is Hildeburh [/hi:ldeboorhh/], he makes us wonder at Hengest's reasons for staying in Finnsburh. Why delay the act of vengeance? Does he want to be Hamlet? The nights draw in; Hengest, though he wants to leave, stays on with the Half-Danes. Autumn leads to an ice-bound winter and in spring, when the ice melts, Hengest still wants to leave (when it was over, so the story goes, he did, and took service in Britain with King Vortigern):

> fundode wrecca,
> gist of geardum;   he to gyrnwræce
> swiðor þohte   þonne to sælade,
> gif he torngemot   þurhteon mihte,
> þæt he Eotena bearn   inne gemunde.
> Swa he ne forwyrnde   woroldrædenne
> þonne him Hunlafing   hildeleoman
> billa selest   on bearm dyde;
> þæs wæron mid Eotenum   ecge cuðe. (*Beowulf*, lines 1137–44)

> The exile strove to go,
> the guest, from the settlements; he thought more strongly
> of vengeance for injury than of taking the sea-road,
> to see if he could bring about an angry encounter
> in such a way as to remember the sons of Jutes in this country.
> So it was that he did not refuse the counsel of the world
> when the son of Hunlaf [a Scylding] placed
> a battle-flash, best of blades, in his lap:
> its edges were famous among the Jutes.

His 'injury' (*gyrn-*) is not the death of Hnæf, but rather something to do with his identity as a 'Jute'. The Jutes are an ancient uncanny crowd living in various lands, some of them in Frisia (*eoten*, which means 'Jute' here, also means 'giant'). In short, there are Jutes on both sides. Finn got his Frisian Jutes to lead the attack on Hnæf, as a test of their loyalty to Frisia (lines 1171–2). Hengest has been thinking of these traitors all winter long, looking to kill them in revenge. To do this, he attempts to draw out various people on Finn's side, in order to get them, not him, to break the oath. He can't break the oath himself, having been forced to swear it on his god. Circumventing the oath in this way is Hengest's strategy to get his 'vengeance for injury' (*gyrnwræce*). He fails, however, because Finn, as we have seen, has promised death to any of his men who break the treaty first.

Sizing this up are the Scyldings. Unconcerned about perjury, they come to Hengest with a deal: we take over the oath, so you can carry out your own vengeance; you kill Finn for us. Hengest gives them command of the Half-Danes by taking their sword (the 'battle-flash', *hildeleoma*). The poet dwells on this ritual moment more on the carnage that follows; but when the Scyldings speak the first angry words, and Hengest, sitting next to Finn at the banquet, runs him through with the Danish sword, Queen Hildeburh ends up widowed as well as bereaved of brother and son. Hrothgar's bard revels in all this as a past Danish triumph, but the poet of *Beowulf* grieves with the woman. She is the victim of Hengest's 'counsel of the world' (*woroldrædenne*), undergoing bereavement as she did before when she saw her brother and son, her one-time 'joys of the world' (*worolde wynne*, line 1080), sprawled dead before her. Now she is part of the loot which the Scyldings, her remaining family, ship home to Denmark.

Widsith

The Scyldings are also mentioned in *Widsith*, a verse catalogue of famous kings and tribes which is found in a late tenth-century book of poems known as the Exeter Book (because preserved in Exeter Cathedral). This poem of 143 lines looks like a template for poets who wished to make epic lays of their own. 'Widsith' [/wee:dseeth/], or 'Widely-Travelled', is the name of the persona whom the poet introduces to us as the speaker in lines 1–9. As a travelling bard, he is now staying in the court of King Eormanric of the Ostrogoths, and he comes from 'Angeln' (*Ongle*, line 8), the same region in the far north of Germany from where the 'Angles' crossed to Britain. Widsith delivers his catalogue on the pretext of telling us the names of tribes through which he has passed.

Although *Widsith* has little merit of its own, it does give us the essentials, the names of kings and nations which had to be mastered by Anglo-Saxon poets if they wanted to compose heroic verse. The first longer passage dwells on King Offa of Angeln, which is Widsith's homeland. To sketch out his story from the other sources (Garmonsway and Simpson 1968), Offa had an unusual childhood. He is said to have been blind until 7 and dumb until 30, speaking his first words only when calling God to witness that he would defend his father's kingdom against a foreign usurper. To everyone's surprise he does, killing two of the latter's champions in a fight by a river boundary:

Offa weold Ongle,   Alewih Denum;
se wæs þara manna   modgast ealra,
no hwæþre he ofer Offan   eorlscype fremede
ac Offa geslog   ærest monna
cnihtwesende   cynerica mæst;
nænig efeneald him   eorlscipe maran
on orette;   ane sweorde
merce gemærde   wið Myrgingum
bi Fifeldore.   Heoldon forð siþþan
Engle ond Swæfe   swa hit Offa geslog. (*Wid* 35–44)

> Offa ruled the Angles, Alewih the Danes;
> he was of all these men the bravest,
> yet he did not perform deeds of courage greater than Offa did.
> For Offa, first among men, fought for and won
> the greatest of kingdoms even while he was a youth;
> no one of the same age was warrior enough
> to achieve greater deeds of courage; with one special sword
> he fixed a boundary against the Myrgings
> at the river Eider. From that time forth
> Angles and Swabians kept to the line Offa won by fighting.

The poet of *Beowulf* alludes to Offa's later career when he glorifies his marriage to a princess (sometimes known as 'Thryth') whose sole foible is that she kills any man who looks at her. Offa calms her down and the poet goes on to praise him apropos of nothing in *Beowulf*, as:

> ealles moncynnes   mine gefræge
> þæs selestan   bi sæm tweonum
> eormencynnes;   forðam Offa wæs
> geofum ond guðum   garcene man
> wide geweorðod,   wisdome heold
> eðel sinne,   þonon Eomer woc
> hæleðum to helpe,   Hem[m]inges mæg
> nefa Garmundes   niða cræftig. (*Beowulf*, lines 1955–62)

> according to what I have heard, the best man
> in all the world between the seas,
> of the vast human race; for Offa was
> widely honoured in his gifts and battles,
> a spear-keen man, guarded with wisdom
> his inherited land; from whom arose Eomer
> in aid of men, kinsman of Hemming,
> nephew of Garmund, skilled in war.

Offa's tale was important to his namesake, King Offa of Mercia, who ruled the middle of England and dominated the rest from 757 to 796 (see later p. 233). There is a royal deed to property from Worcester in around 757 in which this Offa says that at one time he was 'an inactive boy' (*puer indolis*). In his own genealogy he looks back to King Offa of Angeln as an ancestor. Some people think the allusion to this Offa in *Beowulf* is a sign that the poet was composing his work for King Offa of Mercia. Of course the same, for the same reasons, could be said of *Widsith*.

The poet of *Widsith* knows nothing of *Beowulf*. If he did, surely, he would have included Beowulf, or at least his uncle Hygelac, as a king of the Geats, who are cited without a king on line 58. For his own part the poet of *Beowulf* seems too experienced to have needed *Widsith*, a poem which reads like a digest for beginners. Other discrepancies show that both *Beowulf* and *Widsith* were composed with knowledge of a heroic poem that had been famous in its day, but which is now lost. This was a big poem on Ingeld, king of the Heathobards. Ingeld is famous in legend for repudiating his Danish bride, King Hrothgar's daughter, then burning down Heorot in an attempted invasion of Denmark. The poet of *Widsith* cites Ingeld in the vanguard of his attack on King Hrothgar:

> Hroþwulf ond Hroðgar   heoldon lengest
> sibbe ætsomne   suhtorfædran,
> siþþan hy forwræcon   wicinga cynn
> ond Ingeldes   ord forbigdan,
> forheowan æt Heorote   Heaðobeardna þrym. (*Widsith*, lines 45–9)

> Hrothulf and Hrothgar for the longest time,
> uncle and nephew, had kept their family united
> when they drove off a tribe of pirates,
> and crushed Ingeld's front line,
> cut down the glory of the Heathobards at Heorot.

Ingeld's story was even more important to the poet of *Beowulf*, who gives us a foretaste of the attack at the moment he describes the building of Heorot as finished:

> Sele hlifade
> heah ond horngeap,   heaðowylma bad
> laðan liges;   ne wæs hit lenge þa gen
> þæt se ecghete   aþumsweorum
> æfter wælniðe   wæcnan scolde. (*Beowulf*, lines 81–5)

> The hall towered,
> high and horn-gabled, awaited the hostile flame
> of battle-surges; nor was it then yet at hand
> that sword-hate after murderous enmity
> should awake between father- and son-in-law.

Amazingly, Beowulf sees this attack coming. We know this because he predicts it to his own people when he comes home. King Hrothgar, he says, has been planning a marriage between his daughter and Ingeld of the Heathobards. The marriage is meant to heal an old feud, but when the princess comes to Norway with her Danish bodyguards, he says, some old wounds will break open. Out of nowhere an 'old spear-fighter' (*eald æscwiga*, line 2042) will begin to goad a young local into attacking the Danish visitors. Norse analogues tell us that this was indeed what came to pass (Garmonsway and Simpson 1968). In Old Norse, the old stirrer was known as 'Starkaðr' ('toughened one'), a giant-descended devotee of Óðinn who enjoys his malign role. The main Norse versions of Ingeld's story are *The Saga of the Skjǫldungs* (*Skjǫldunga saga*), which was written around 1200 but now survives only in a Latin paraphrase made in 1596; and *The History of the Danes* (*Gesta Danorum*), written also *c.* 1200 by the Danish historian Saxo Grammaticus ('the grammarian'). In *Beowulf,* the poet's allusion to this story serves a deeper purpose, allowing us to see Beowulf as a young blood who had wanted Hrothgar's daughter for himself:

'Þonne bioð gebrocene   on ba healfe
aðsweord eorla;   syððan Ingelde
weallað wælniðas   ond him wiflufan
æfter cearwælmum   colran weorðað.
Þy ic Heaðo-Bear[d]na   hyldo ne telge,
dryhtsibbe dæl   Denum unfæcne,
freondscipe fæstne.'   (*Beowulf,* lines 2063–9)

'Then will be broken on both sides
the oath-pledges of noblemen; in Ingeld thereafter
murderous enmities will surge and in him the love of his wife,
after waves of grief, will grow cool.
For this reason I do not reckon the loyalty of the Heathobards,
their alliance with the Danes, to be free of deceit,
their pact of friendship firm.'

The story of Ingeld was well known. In 797, Alcuin of York, courtier theologian of Emperor Charlemagne of the Franks (see p. 233), refers to a performance on a poem on this theme in a reproachful letter to 'Speratus', a bishop probably in Mercia:

Verba Dei legantur in sacerdotali convivio. Ibi decet lectorem audiri, non citharistam: sermones patrum, non carmina gentilium. Quid Hinieldus cum Christo? Angusta est domus: utrosque tenere non poterit. Non vult rex celestis cum paganis et perditis nominetenus regibus communionem habere; quia rex ille aeternus regnat in caelis, ille paganus perditus plangit in inferno. (Bullough 1993: 124)

Let God's word be read at the episcopal dinner-table. There it is fitting for a reader to be heard, not a harper: sermons of the Fathers, not the songs of heathens. What has Ingeld to do with Christ? The house is narrow: it will not be able to hold them both. The Heavenly King will have no communion with so-called kings who are pagan and damned; for the One King rules in Heaven, while the other, a pagan, is damned and wails in hell.

Alcuin's unkind words show what fun the Anglo-Saxon clergy in general, and his bishop friend in particular, were having with heroic poems in the eighth and ninth centuries.

Widsith is a touchstone for all kinds of other heroic legends which the Anglo-Saxons knew. As tribes go in *Beowulf, The Finnsburh Fragment* and *Widsith,* so far we have seen Danes and Geats, Frisians, Jutes, continental Angles and Heathobards. There are many others from northern lands. We know of these in many cases from the Old Icelandic 'sagas of ancient times' (*fornaldar sögur*), which are about 20 to 30 heroic stories in prose dealing with the adventures of heroes such as the Danish Hrólfr kraki (i.e. Hrothulf in *Beowulf*), Bǫðvarr bjarki (i.e. Beowulf himself) and the Norwegian Starkaðr the Old (unnamed but in *Beowulf* too, as it happens). In *Widsith,* however, we also see references to kings from further south, from the German Rhineland and central and eastern Europe. The common Germanic legendary tradition made these kings contemporaries without regard for history. Thus the poet of *Widsith* puts Attila the Hun, who died in 454, together with Ermanaric the Goth, who died in around 376, and King Gibicha of Burgundy, who died in around 412 far away in France (Dronke 1969: 29–34):

> Ætla weold Hunum,   Eormanric Gotum,
> Becca Baningum,   Burgendum Gifica. (*Widsith*, lines 18–19)
> Attila ruled the Huns, Eormanric the Goths,
> Becca the Banings, Gifica the Burgundians.

This is the rogues' gallery of *Widsith*. As 'Ætla', Attila the Hun was no less a byword to the Anglo-Saxons than he is to us. As 'Eormanric', the Gothic Ermanaric was an even greater villain. 'Becca' was remembered in the Old Norse tradition as 'Bikki', Ermanaric's evil counsellor (*The Saga of the Vǫlsungs,* Chapter 42). Knowledge of this tradition is reflected in *Deor,* which makes King Eormanric a shining example of tyranny; and in *Waldere,* whose story could not have been told without the presumption that its audience was well acquainted with King Ætla as the overlord of Huns and Burgundians. To go on with *Deor.*

Deor

The narrator of this poem is another bard, a persona named 'Deor' ('Valiant'), who tells five stories of misfortune, ending each one with a refrain: 'That passed over, so can this.' Eventually he tells of his own sadness, that his family lands were taken back by the king. He consoles himself with the refrain he has used five times before. *Deor*, a poem of 42 lines, is found like *Widsith* in the Exeter Book. Unlike *Widsith* and all other poems in the Exeter Book, however, *Deor* is copied out in blocks of text approximating to stanzas. There are six blocks, five for the past stories and one for Deor's, each ending with the same refrain. This unique style of manuscript layout may show that in its own time *Deor* was regarded as a more literary poem than the usual heroic lays.

All Deor's stories bar his own are related in some way to the Goths, who have lent their name to many things over the last thousand years: art and architecture, romantic novels, modern lifestyle choice. Before 'England' existed the Goths were known as a tribe that came from the isle of Gotland in the Baltic, which had settled in barbarian hinterlands east of the Roman Empire, but which then migrated west when the Huns arrived behind them, spilling over the Danube into northern Greece in 376 AD. They and some other tribes, the Vandals, Alans and Suevi, spread further west anticlockwise around the Mediterranean shoreline, taking in what we call the former Yugoslavia, northern and southern Italy, Toulouse in southern France and a new 'Visigothic' kingdom based on Toledo in central Spain; the Vandals moved either west into Portugal or south out of '[W]andalusia', acoss the straits and east along the North African coast as far as Tunisia, where they were still a menace for civilised life in the sixth century. For a while the Mediterranean Sea was named the 'Vandal Sea' after them (*Wendelsæ* in Old English).

The Gothic theme starts unobtrusively in *Deor* with 'Weland', a vengeful Lapp, shaman and renowned craftsman whom today's culture sometimes remembers as 'Wayland the Smith'. Weland's first tragedy is to be abandoned by his wife. Not long after, he is hamstrung by King Nithad of Sweden so he can make trinkets for him and his queen. The poet of *Deor* portrays this and his desire for vengeance in lines 1–6. The poem's second story concerns Beadohild [/bay:adohild/], the daughter of Weland's captors, whom Weland makes pregnant after secretly doing away with her brothers. As the poet says, with the focus on her mental distraction:

Beadohilde ne wæs   hyre broþra deaþ
on sefan swa sar   swa hyre sylfre þing,
þæt heo gearolice   ongieten hæfde
þæt heo eacen wæs;   æfre ne meahte
þriste geþencan   hu ymb þæt sceolde.
Þæs ofereode,   þisses swa mæg. (*Deor*, lines 8–13)

To Beadohild the death of her brothers
was not so grievous in mind as her own condition,

that she had suddenly perceived
that she was pregnant; never could she
think with any boldness how it would turn out afterwards.
That passed over, so can this.

A fuller version of Weland's rape of Beadohild is known from a poem in the *Edda*, *The Lay of Wayland* (*Vǫlundarkviða*), which tells us that he seduces her with drink. As the shaman says in the Norse lay, laughing at the girl's father from the sky into which his powers have shot him:

'Nú gengr Bǫðvildr   barni aukin,
eingadóttir   ykkor beggia.' (*The Lay of Wayland*, stanza 36)

'Now Bǫðvildr goes made big with child,
that only daughter of the two of you!'

Questioned by her father here, 'Bǫðvildr' is aware that her one-time love for 'Vǫlundr' will lead to a big change:

'Satt er þat, Níðaðr,   er sagði þér:
sáto vit Vǫlundr   saman í hólmi
– eina Qgurstund –   æva skyldi!
Ek vætr hánom   [vinna] kunnak,
ek vætr hánom   vinna máttak.' (stanza 41, the last)

'It is true, Níðaðr, what he said to you:
Vǫlundr and I sat together on the island,
– just for the turning of the tide – would it had never happened!
I didn't know how to prevent him,
I had no power to prevent him at all.'

The Lay of Wayland is a mentally sharp poem but one rather battered in transmission, possibly from early tenth-century Norway, but with English connections (nowhere else is the Norse word *aukin* used for 'pregnant', the meaning of Old English *eacen* [/ay:aken/]). Like lines 1–13 of *Deor*, however, it appears to end by looking into the future. The event that will follow is the birth of a Gothic hero.

The Goths named this hero Vidigoia. In Old English Weland's son was variously called 'Wudga' in *Widsith*, line 124 and 'Widia' in *Waldere*, I, lines 4 and 9. In *Widsith*, Wudga is also known as the friend of another hero named 'Hama' [/hah:ma/]. More on their friendship is given in the adventures of 'Witege' and 'Heime' in medieval German Romance. In *Beowulf*, Hama is famous for dumping an evil necklace in favour of higher rewards, possibly conversion to Christianity. There is no doubt that spiritual values meant more than material wealth to the poet of *Beowulf*. He says that

Hama's necklace was even greater than the one Beowulf received for killing Grendel. Never, he says, did he hear of a necklace greater than Beowulf's, at least not:

> syÞðan Hama ætwæg
> to *þære* byrhtan byrig   Brosinga mene,
> sigle ond sincfæt;   searoniðas fl*eah*
> Eormanrices,   geceas ecne ræd. (*Beowulf*, lines 1198–1201)

> since Hama carried off
> to the bright city the necklace of the Brosings,
> its jewels and their precious setting; he fled the cunning enmities
> of Eormanric, chose an eternal reward.

A fuller version of this story can be found in *The Saga of Þiðrekr of Verona* (*Þiðreks saga af Bern*), a prose romance that was translated into Norwegian from a north German original in the late thirteenth century. This saga is valuable for preserving some German stories from the tenth to eleven centuries which perished in contemporary form. In this late Norse version of the Beowulfian tale, we see the knight 'Heimir' taking some treasure from King 'Erminríkr' which he then bequeaths to a monastery in order to become a monk. In *Beowulf* it seems that Hama does likewise, fleeing to a Roman city where he can become a Christian. Some of Hama's virtue rubbed off on his friend Wudga or Widia, whose excellence, indeed, may explain why the Frank's Casket, an English whale-bone sewing box from around 700, has one side with a picture of his father's, Weland's, encounter with his mother Beadohild just next to a picture of the three Magi visiting Mary in Bethlehem after the birth of Christ (see plate 4).

After Beadohild comes a story which might be explained as a botched attempt by the founding father of the Goths to father a child on a Frankish lady who strings him contemptuously along for one unsatisfied night:

> We þæt Mæðhilde   monge gefrugnon
> (wurdon grundlease   Geates frige)
> þæt hi[m] seo sorglufu   slæp ealle binom.
> Þæs ofereode,   þisses swa mæg. (*Deor*, lines 14–17)

> We heard this about Mæthild's transaction
> (Geat's lust went without fulfilment)
> that the sorrowful love deprived him of sleep completely.
> That passed over, so can this.

'Geat', the first ever Gothic hero, was claimed as an ancestor by King Æthelwulf of Wessex (ruled 839–58), father of King Alfred the Great.

'Mæthild' is Old English for 'Matilda', a name popular among the Franks. That the story in this part of *Deor* is not flattering to Geat, here a type known as the *senex amans* ('old man lover'), shows that not all this poem has to be sad.

The fourth story in *Deor* is shorter, just two lines which allude to 'Theodric', the Old English name for Prefect Theodoric the Ostrogoth (eastern Goth), who ruled the Byzantine kingdom of Italy from 493 to 526. History remembered Theodoric as a villain, for reasons which will become clear. Legend, by way of contrast, said that he was driven out of his kingdom by a usurper named Odoacar, into an exile which lasted 30 years. The poet of *Deor* seems to have this in mind:

> Ðeodric ahte   þritig wintra
> Mæringa burg;   þæt was monegum cuþ.
> Þæs ofereode,   þisses swa mæg. (*Deor*, lines 28–30)

> Theodric ruled for thirty winters [i.e. years]
> the city of the Mærings; that was well known to many.
> That passed over, so can this.

If we retranslate the phrase *mæringa burg* as 'the city of famous men', which is what it literally means, these lines refer to the legend of Theodric's 30-year exile. A city of warriors is a band of retainers protecting their lord.

The story of Theodoric's exile is the backdrop to another poem, *The Lay of Hildebrand* (*Das Hildebrandslied*), which was composed in Germany some time before 800. This poem was probably one of the 'barbarian and most ancient lays' (*barbara et antiquissima carmina*) which the Emperor Charlemagne (died 814) is said to have had ordered his clerks to transcribe, about 15 years before his son, Louis the Pious, living up to his name, had them all burned – all but *The Lay of Hildebrand*. In its extant form, a couple of fragments, this German poem tells us that when King 'Detrih' (i.e. Theodoric) the Goth is driven out of his kingdom in Italy, Hildebrand and other warriors go into exile with him; all join the service of King Attila the Hun. Thirty years later Detrih is back with an army to get his throne. Hildebrand, challenging Odoacar's champion to single combat, finds out this bruiser is his son Hadubrand, whom he left behind in Italy. The tragedy is that 30 years of service to the new order have brainwashed the boy, who doggedly refuses to believe that Hildebrand is his father:

> 'du bist der alter Hun   ummet spaher,
> spenis mih mit dinem wortun,   wili mih dinu speru werpan,
> pist also gialte man   so du ewin inwit fortos.
> Dat sagetun mi   seolidante

westar ubar Wentilseo   dat inan wic furnam:
tot ist Hiltibrant   Heribrantes suno.' (*The Lay of Hildebrand*, lines 40–4)

'You are extremely sly, old Hun,
would trap me with your words, then spear me through,
have lived to old age just so, by always deceiving in this way.
Seafarers told me, those who went west
across the Vandal Sea, that battle took him:
Hildebrand, son of Herebrand, is dead!'

The type scene is 'exchanging insults before battle', better known as a 'flyting' (from similar scenarios in Middle Scots poetry). In *The Lay of Hildebrand* we see a tragic flyting, in which the son, believing what he wants to, perhaps afraid of the truth before his eyes, rejects his father's offer of a separate peace. In grief, the old man cries out:

'Welaga nu Waltant Got,' quad Hiltibrant,   'wewurt skihit.
Ih wallota sumaro enti wintro   sehstic ur lante,
dar man mih eo scerita   in folc sceotantero:
so man mir at burc enigeru   banun ni gifasta,
nu scal mih suasat chind   suertu hauwan,
breton mit sinu billiu,   eddo ih imo ti banin werdan.' (lines 49–54)

'Woe now O Ruling God', said Hildebrand, 'the fate which is awful.
I wandered sixty seasons [30 years] away from home,
places where they always sent me into the advance guard:
no man before any walled city could slay me.
But now either my sweet child will cut me down with his sword,
kill me with his blade, or I will become his slayer!'

Hildebrand accepts the situation and prepares to fight the duel. Beyond the end of this fragment, the story ends with a father killing his son.

That heroic agony is the price of Theodric's restoration to his throne in Italy, but the poet of *Deor* does not show it. He does, however, reveal knowledge of a more learned kind. Prefect Theodoric, the historical figure on which his Theodric is based, became infamous in 524 for executing the philosopher Boethius, who wrote *On the Consolation of Philosophy* (*De consolatione Philosophiae*) while he sat on death row. In this consolatory treatise, Boethius personifies his education as Lady Philosophy, a Neo-Platonist divinity who argues his renunciation of all worldly values in favour of accepting whatever divine providence, unbeknown but in the best interest of all, might have to offer him. As you can see in another chapter, versions of the *Consolation* were put into West Saxon on King Alfred's orders in the 890s (see p. 256). The poet of *Deor* prefaces his own story at the end

of the poem with a reflection on a solitary man who sits sorrowfully thinking his misfortune to be endless (lines 28–30). This imagined figure looks
a lot like Boethius at the beginning of the *Consolation*. Otherwise *The Lay
of Hildebrand* shows us a belief, widely held in Germanic Europe, that
Theodric's change of fortune was paid for by a father killing his son.

To go back to Eormanric, this Gothic tyrant is the subject of Deor's fifth
story, in lines 21–7. In Germanic legend, the reflex of old Ermanaric the
Goth is nothing but bad. In *Widsith* Eormanric is not only a practicioner of
the black arts (a 'mad warlock', *wraþ wærloga*, in line 9), but also an old man
who married a young princess (Ealhhild in lines 5 and 97). Old Norse poems
tell us that he had horses trample her to death after suspecting her of
adultery with the son of his first marriage, whom he had hanged. In one of
these other poems, the eleventh-century *Guðrún's Goading* (*Guðrúnarhvǫt*),
we hear Guðrún, the bride's mother, recalling her daughter as she once was:

'Svá var Svanhildr   í sal mínom
sem væri sœmleitr   sólar geisli.

'Gœdda ek gulli   ok guðvefiom,
áðr ek gæfak   Gotþióðar til.
Þat er mér harð*ast*   harma minna
of þann inn hvíta hadd Svanhildar
– auri troddo   und ióa fótom.' (stanzas 15–16)

'Svanhildr [i.e. Ealhhild] seemed in my chamber
to be a glorious gleam of the sun.

'I adorned her with gold and gorgeous robes
before I gave her to the Gothic race.
To me the cruellest of my griefs
is for the flaxen locks of Svanhildr
– they trod them with the mud under their chargers' hooves.'
(Dronke 1969: 149)

In the Norse poem, this type scene, 'the woman laments', comes before
Guðrún goads her two sons into avengeing their sister. They ride off but
turn out to be mad themselves, killing a cleverer half-brother on the way
who had offered to help. Later they miss his input when failing to carve
up King 'Jǫrmunrekkr' (i.e. Eormanric) properly, when they start with his
limbs, rather than his head (but that's another story). It is clear that all this
was known to the Anglo-Saxons in their own version of the common
Germanic tradition. The poet of *Deor* makes Eormanric both the subject of
his fifth story and his exemplary climax:

We geascodan Eormanrices
wylfenne geþoht;   ahte wide folc
Gotena rices.   Þæt wæs grim cyning.
Sæt secg monig   sorgum gebunden
wean on wenan,   wyscte geneahhe
þæt þæs cynerices   ofercumen wære.
Þæs ofereode,   þisses swa mæg. (*Deor*, lines 21–7)

We have heard about Eormanric's
wolvish intention; he had power over the wide nation
of the kingdom of the Goths. That was a fierce king!
Many a man sat bound up with sorrows,
with woe all he could hope for, constantly wished
that this man's kingdom might be overcome.
That passed over, so can this.

The prospect of this Goth's senile marriage with a young woman seems
to to lurk behind Eormanric's 'wolvish intention' displayed on line 22. The
poet takes the story as known.

Hereafter Deor reflects on the inscrutable but benign providence of
God (lines 28–34), before revealing his own misfortune: he was once 'court
poet of the Heodenings' (*Heodeninga scop*, line 35), but his king, before firing
him, gave his lands to a rival poet named Heorrenda. Why King Heoden
needed Heorrenda is known from later romance, from the Middle High
German *Kudrun*, composed around 1230–40. *Kudrun* presents 'Hôrant' (i.e.
Heorrenda) as the Frank Sinatra of early Germanic verse composition. When
King 'Hetele' (i.e. Heoden) falls in love with Kudrun, he enlists his crooner's
help to get her away from her father. Hôrant obliges:

Dô sich diu naht verendet   und ez begunde tagen,
Hôránt begunde singen,   daz dâ bî in den hagen
geswigen alle vogele   von sînem süezen sange.
Die liute, die dâ sliefen,   die [en]lâgen dô niht [se] lange.
(*Kudrun* VI, lines 379–82)

When night came to an end and it began to dawn,
Hôrant began to sing so well that in the hedgerows
all the birds fell silent at his sweet song.
The people sleeping didn't lie down too long!

Hôrant charms the girl's mother (the father is absent), allowing Hetele to
elope with her into a get-away boat steered by another friend named Wâte.
This is also the story behind Heoden and Heorrenda in the Old English
poem *Deor*. It survived in England longer than *Deor*. Geoffrey Chaucer knew

it. In his *Troilus and Criseyde* III, line 614, Pandarus 'tolde tale of Wade' to Criseyde, shortly before she is joined in bed by his friend Troilus; and in *The Merchant's Tale*, lines 1423–4, the aged January, looking for marriage with a young beauty, disdains 'thise olde wydwes' who, as if staging their own elopements, 'konne so muchel crafte on Wades boot'. In the *Deor* version, it is clear that King Heoden's elopement has yet to occur. If 'Deor' in this way alludes only to the prospect of Heorrenda helping his king, it becomes possible to interpret the poem as a satire: one written for Prince Æthelbald of Wessex against his (and Alfred's) father, King Æthelwulf, who, in 856, at more than 60 years of age, put his wife aside in order to marry the 12-year-old daughter of King Charles the Bald of France.

Waldere

In *Waldere*, a fragmentary Old English poem possibly from the mid-ninth century, a woman encourages her lover to fight their way out of an ambush; a little later this man parleys with his attackers, reaffirming his friendship with one and mocking the other. The hero, Waldere (i.e. Walter), gives the poem its modern name; his lover is Hildegyth, his old friend Hagena [/ha:yena/] and enemy Guthere [/goo:thereh/]. Their story comes from a legend concerning Attila the Hun. We have seen that *Widsith* hints at a network of such poems once in England which dealt with southern and eastern Europe. The southern Germanic tradition is still extant in the Norse poetic *Edda*, in a comprehensive prose redaction in *The Saga of the Vǫlsungs* and in Middle High German romances such as *The Lay of the Nibelungs*. The Old English *Waldere* was discovered in 1860 when the Chief Librarian of the Royal Library in Copenhagen chanced on two vellum folds in a pile of old papers and parchments (Ny kongelig Samling 167b). Both were written by the same hand, a rather poor one, and appeared to have been taken out of the same or two different gatherings of vellum pages in a larger manuscript. No one knows where each fold was once bound in relation to the other, but the texts that survive, amounting to four of our pages in all, showed that they came from the same poem. This poem has been named *Waldere* (parts I and II).

Waldere has been explained largely with the help of a ninth- or tenth-century German Latin epic called *Waltharius* (the Latin for 'Walter'). There are some six other, later, versions of the story, but only *Waltharius* gives us an idea of what happened in the complete Old English poem, which scholars think may have run to about 1000 lines (one-third the length of *Beowulf*). The larger story opens in France, in the adjoining kingdoms of

Aquitaine and Burgundy. Waldere is the son of Ælfhere, king of Aquitaine, who engages him as a child to the girl Hildegyth, a Burgundian princess (her name is not recorded, but is here reconstructed from 'Hiltgunt', Waltharius' lover in the *Waltharius*). As we have seen in *Widsith*, line 19, the Burgundians' king is called Gifica. When both kingdoms surrender to the Huns after losing a war against King Ætla (i.e. Attila), Waldere and Hildegyth are sent to live in the east as hostages at his court. Waldere grows up to become a champion in the Hunnish army. There he befriends Hagena, another Burgundian hostage, whom the Huns later allow to go home. All is well until Waldere and Hildegyth make their own break for freedom, Waldere to avoid a Hunnish marriage, Hildegyth to accompany her lover. They take a few caskets of Ætla's treasure with them, Hildegyth having drugged the Huns with liquor. Although Ætla later sends men to catch them, no attempt is made, given Waldere's record as a fighter. But on the west side of the Rhine things are different, for there King Guthere of the Burgundians, son of Gifica and a new vassal to King Ætla, makes ready to ambush the loving couple in the Vosges Mountains. Guthere takes with him a platoon including a reluctant Hagena, who does his best to talk them all out of it. One complication for Hagena is his friendship with Waldere; another is his kinship not only with Guthere, but with Hildegyth as well. Clashing wills, conflicting loyalties, love against honour: the best heroic poems are driven by this.

The Old English poem, as we have it, begins some way into the ambush with Hildegyth preparing to put some backbone into Waldere. He is carrying Mimming, a famous sword made by Weland. It seems that Waldere has already offered this sword to Guthere as an incentive not to fight. Here the poet varies the type scene known as 'the goading woman':

> *** hyrde hyne georne:
> 'Huru Weland[es]   worc ne geswiceð
> monna ænigum   ðara ðe Mimming can
> hear[d]ne gehealdan.   Oft æt hilde gedreas
> swatfag ond sweordwund   sec[g] æfter oðrum.
> Ætlan ordwyga,   ne læt ðin ellen nu gy[t]
> gedreosan to dæge,   dryhtscipe **
> ********   [Nu] is se dæg cumen,
> þæt ðu scealt aninga   oðer twega,
> lif forleosan   oððe l[an]gne dom
> agan mid eldum,   Ælfheres sunu.' (*Waldere* I, lines 1–11)

>   [she] eagerly hardened his resolve:
> 'At least Weland's work will not fail

any man who knows how to hold
the cruel Mimming. Often in battle there fell down
one man after another, blood-bespattered and wounded by that sword.
Frontline man of Ætla, don't now let your courage
or your discipline themselves fall down on this day.
********. [Now] the day has come
when you must do one of two things,
either lose your life or take possession,
son of Ælfhere, of lasting fame among men.'

Hildegyth's words show that the fight is half over, with most of Guthere's
warriors dead. It is Waldere who has killed them (11 attackers according to
the *Waltharius*). So why does he hold back now? The context tells us that he
feels loyal to Hagena, who has stayed out of it. Not that their friendship cuts
any ice with Hildegyth. To go on with what she says:

'Nalles ic ðe, wine min,   wordum cide
ðy ic ðe gesawe   æt ðam sweordplegan
ðurh edwitscype   æniges monnes
wig forbugan   oððe on weal fleon
lice beorgan   ðeah þe laðra fela
ðinne byrnhomon   billum heowun.
Ac ðu symle   furðor feohtan sohtest,
mæl ofer mearce;   ðy ic ðe metod ondred
þæt ðu to fyrenlice   feohtan sohtest
æt ðam ætstealle   oðres monnes wigrædenne.' (*Waldere* I, lines 12–22)

'Not at all with these words, my love, do I chide you
as if I had seen you shame yourself in that sword-play
by shirking battle with any man or fleeing that slaughter,
saving your body, though a lot of enemies
were hacking with blades at your coat of mail.
But you were always seeking to fight more,
looking for business on their side of the boundary.
I have been dreading the fate that would see you seeking to fight
too rashly, out of position, to the place your opponent wanted.'

Not since Eve with Adam was there such tender loving care. Hildegyth
has observed the earlier battle. She is a woman who can stand by her man,
unlike Hiltgunt of the *Waltharius*, whose heart flutters when the leaves
rustle and who begs her lover to run off. In contrast to her vapid German
analogue, Hildegyth is all too keen to send Waldere back into battle, telling
him how best to fight and at the same time massaging his pride. And she
is right: as long as they are holed up in a defile with no exit, his steady

elimination of opponents is the only option. Hagena is the big problem. Ignoring him, Hildegyth tells Waldere to cover himself in glory as long as God permits it, not to worry about losing or breaking his sword, but rather to make Guthere pay for his vow to King Ætla to stop them getting home. It was Guthere who started this by refusing Mimming or the Hunnish treasures they offered. Now, she curses, the only choice for Guthere will be to leave the battle 'without rings' (*beaga leas*, line 29), or 'sooner sleep here' (*her ær swefan*, line 31). At this point the first fragment runs out.

Waldere II begins a little later, towards the end of a speech that scholars have variously assigned to Guthere, Hagena and Waldere himself. The tightest case is for Hagena. From what Waldere says afterwards, it appears Guthere had hoped he would do the fighting for him. Hagena steps forward, Waldere tries to buy him off with Mimming, his sword, sheathed in its scabbard; but then, instead of rejecting him, like Guthere did, Hagena declares himself out of the battle. Saving his own face as well as Waldere's feelings about their friendship, Hagena turns down the offer of Mimming on the pretext that his own sword is better:

'[nat ic mid mannum   me]ce bæteran
buton ðam anum   ðe ic eac hafa
on stanfate   stille gehided.
Ic wat þæt [h]i*t* ðohte   Ðeodric Widian
selfum onsendon   ond eac sinc micel
maðma mid ði mece,   monig oðres mid him
golde gegirwan;   iulean genam
þæs ðe hine of nearwum   Niðhades mæg,
Welandes bearn,   Widia ut forlet;
ðurh fifela ge[wea]ld   forð onette.' (*Waldere* II, lines 1–10)

'[I don't know of any sword among men] that is better,
but for the one that I, too, have
hidden quiet in its jewelled housing.
I know that Theodric thought of sending it to Widia
himself, and also much treasure with that sword,
great riches, and thought of adorning much beside it
with gold; this was a reward Widia,
Nithad's grandson, Weland's child, received
for a past service, for having released Theodric from captivity.
He hurried him right out of the clutches of giants.'

There is more in these words than diplomacy. There is a hint of irony in Hagena's account of his sword as one which Widia was promised by a man he helped out of a tight spot. However the sword came into Hagena's possession (no one knows how), it seems he means to do the same by Waldere, his friend.

Waldere is relieved, even rejuvenated, to hear this. Holding Mimming in his hand, his 'battle-solace, catcher of war-blades' (*hildefro[f]re, guðbilla gripe, Waldere* II, lines 12–13), he turns to Guthere, the king lurking out of view, and begins to mock him:

'Hwæt, ðu huru wendest,   wine Burgenda,
þæt me Hagenan hand   hilde gefremede
ond getwæmde [fe]ðewigges?   Feta, gyf ðu dyrre,
æt ðus heaðuwerigan   hare byrnan.
Standað me her on eaxelum   Ælfheres laf
god ond geapneb   golde geweorðod
ealles unscende   æðelinges reaf
to habbanne   þonne ha[n]d wereð
feorhhord feondum;   *ne* bið fah wið me
þonne [..] unmægas   eft ongynnað,
mecum gemetað   swa ge me dydon.' (*Waldere* II, lines 14–24)

'So, gracious lord of the Burgundians, were you really expecting
the hand of Hagena to do battle with me
and stop the foot-combat? Fetch, if you dare,
the grey coat of mail from a man so weary with battle!
It stands ready for me on my back, left me by Ælfhere,
good and well-bossed, ornamented in gold,
the all-unblemished war-gear that a prince
should have when his arm defends
his lifehoard from enemies. It won't turn on me
when *** false kinsmen begin on me once more
or meet me with swords as you lot have done.'

Let us look at Guthere. The Anglo-Saxons probably knew him as the son of the same King Gifica who is mentioned in company with Ætla, Eormanric and Becca in *Widsith*, lines 18–19. Although Guthere is in no other extant Old English poem, there is much that survives about the same figure in Old Norse literature. His Norse version is named 'Gunnarr', called 'gracious lord of the Burgundians' (*vin Borgunda*) in *The Lay of Atli* (*Atlakviða*, stanza 18) of the poetic *Edda*: just as Guthere is called *wine Burgenda* in *Waldere* II, line 14. Guthere's Bavarian version is 'Günther' in *The Lay of the Nibelungs* (*c.* 1200). The historical person on whom these heroes are based was King Gundaharius of the Burgundians, famous for being annihilated by the Huns with his people west of the Rhine in 437. As *Widsith* shows, legend put Gundaharius together with Attila, who died far to the east in 454, along with a number of other people who had never been connected or even contemporaries.

The Norse Gunnarr gives us the best notion of Guthere's now-lost story. Gunnarr has two great roles to play. One of these is to become blood brother to the hero Sigurðr, who slays the dragon Fáfnir, wins the dragon's treasure and goes on to marry Guðrún, Gunnarr's sister. The tragedy of all this is that, a few years later, Gunnarr is forced to kill his new brother-in-law. This is to save his face when Brynhildr, his own wife, having discovered that Sigurðr wooed her in Gunnarr's shape, tells him that Sigurðr first consummated their marriage. Gunnarr is aided in this killing by his brother Hǫgni [/höːgni/] and in other versions by another brother as well. These two are the Norse names for Guthere and Hagena, whose past crime against an in-law may be what Waldere refers to when he calls them 'false kinsmen' (*unmægas*) in *Waldere* II, line 23.

Gunnarr's other great role is to turn his own death into a work of art, when Atli, Guðrún's second husband, invites him to Hunland on a one-way ticket. This story is told in royal courtly style in *The Lay of Atli*, in versified saga-style in *The Greenland Lay of Atli* (*Atlamál in Grœnlenzku*, because written in the Norse colony in Greenland in the thirteenth century), and in prose in *The Saga of the Vǫlsungs*. In *The Lay of Atli* we see a Hunnish messenger come to Worms, Gunnarr's royal seat, with a summons from his master for both Gunnarr and Hǫgni. Treasures beyond imagining will be theirs – also a resettlement for Burgundians along the river Dnieper in Ukraine. Gunnarr turns to his brother and makes it clear they are rich enough already. For one thing he has an even bigger treasure, Sigurðr's dragon hoard, which is doubtless the reason for Atli's summons: Atli would like to know where it is. And Guðrún, says Hǫgni, has sent them a warning, a ring twisted with a wolf's hair, wrapped inside a wolfskin. Not the best omen for a trip to eastern Europe. Later, when her brothers have duly been killed by the gold-hungry Hun, Guðrún feeds her children to Atli, their father, as a stew, telling him thereafter so as to give him an idea of the enormity of what he did to her brothers. This part of *The Lay of Atli* reads like a Norse *Titus Andronicus*.

Earlier on the Burgundians all beg Gunnarr not to go, for he is their king. What would they do without him?, is a question that accompanies us through the next surprise, Gunnarr's cheerful acceptance, both of Atli's invitation and the tribal doom that follows:

'Úlfr mun ráða   arfi Niflunga,
gamlar gránferðir,   ef Gunnars missir,
birnir blakfialler   bíta þreftǫnnum,
gamna greystóði,   ef Gunnarr né kømrat.' (stanza 11)

'The wolf will rule the inheritance of the Nibelungs,
the old packs of grey ones, if Gunnarr is lost.
Black-pelted bears shall bite with wrangling teeth,
bring sport to the stud of curs, if Gunnarr does not come back.'

That is to say, the Huns will be the dogs in a double bear-baiting in which Gunnarr and Hǫgni play the starring role (there is a bear guardian spirit in the Icelandic Gunnarr's family). Bear baitings only end one way. Setting off while their family weep, the brothers gallop across 'untracked Mirkwood' (*Myrkvið inn ókunnna*, stanza 13), through the green plains beyond and into Atli's hall. Brushing aside their sister, who wants them to get out, they wait for the Huns to arrest them. Gunnarr even holds out his hands for the cuffs. Hǫgni, however, kills seven before the Huns get a chain on him. What is Gunnarr doing? The Huns offer him his life for knowledge of the whereabouts of the Nibelung hoard which they wanted all along. First, says Gunnarr, I must see my brother's heart on a plate. Suspecting trickery, the Huns give him someone else's, but Gunnarr knows his brother's heart when he sees it and this one quivers too much to be Hǫgni's. So the Huns perform the same surgery on Gunnarr's brother. What does Hǫgni believe in?, we might ask when we see his last moments:

Hló þá Hǫgni   er til hiarta skáro
kvikvan kumblasmið,   kløkkva hann sízt hugði. (stanza 24)

Hǫgni laughed then as they cut to the heart
the living sculptor of scars – to cry out never entered his thoughts.

At this point Gunnarr decides to put his brother-in-law out of his misery concerning the treasure. Having seen his brother's firm heart on the plate, Gunnarr knows that now only he knows the whereabouts of the Nibelung hoard. Of course, there is no way he will divulge this:

'Ey var mér týia   meðan vit tveir lifðom,
nú er mér engi   er ek einn lifik.
Rín skal ráða   rógmálmi skatna,
[á] sú in áskunna,   arfi Niflunga.
Í veltanda vatni   lýsaz valbaugar
heldr en á hǫndum   gull skíni Húna bǫrnum.' (stanza 27)

'A doubt was always with me while both of us lived,
now there is none, when alone I am alive.
The Rhine shall rule the metal of men's strife,
the god-sprung river rule the Nibelungs' inheritance.
In rolling waters rather shall the foreign rings glint
than that gold should shine on the Huns' children's hands!'

Although Gunnarr is finished, at least Atli is defeated. There is nothing he can do but say 'Wheel out the chariot! Now the prisoner is in bonds!' (*Ýkvið ér hvélvǫgnum, haptr er nú í bǫndum!*, stanza 28). These are his only words in *The Lay of Atli*. In slo-mo cinematic style, Gunnarr's tumbril heads for the snake pit where he dies plucking the strings of a lyre. So should a king keep his gold from men, the poet muses, sardonically reversing the dictum that a king should be generous. In true existentialist, one might say 'pure heroic', style, Gunnarr has made his death into a poem, so why shouldn't he sing himself into oblivion? If we wonder what Gunnarr believes in, it is not in God, providence or any other divine power, for in this poem there is none. Believing in himself alone, Gunnarr walks into the abyss with both eyes open.

In contrast with this Norse image of godless self-sufficiency in *The Lay of Atli*, it must be said that not only the style but also the basis of *Waldere* and other Old English heroic poems is Christian religious. In Old English heroic poetry, a hero will always conceive of his actions in relation to God. As Waldere says to Guthere, before the second fragment runs out:

'Ðeah mæg sige syllan   Se ðe symle byð
recon ond rædfest   ryh[t]a gehwilces;
se ðe him to ðam Halgan   helpe gelifeð
to Gode gioce   he þær gearo findeð,
gif þa earnunga   ær geðenceð.
Þonne moten wlance   welan britnian,
æhtum wealdan,   þæt is [ ]' (*Waldere* II, lines 25–31)

'And yet He can give victory, He Who is ever
prompt and resolute in all judgements.
That man who believes in help from the Holy One,
aid from God, will get this straightaway,
if only he thinks of the means of earning that reward.
Only then may proud warriors distribute treasure,
dispose of their wealth, that is [ ]'

The *Waltharius* tells us that the full version of *Waldere* stopped short of death. To reconstruct the lost outcome of *Waldere*, Guthere responds to Waldere's speech by stepping into the light and thus drawing him out of the defile. Although Waldere gains the upper hand, severely wounds Guthere and is about to finish him off, Hagena intervenes to save his kinsman. Mimming breaks on Hagena's helmet, Hagena chops off Waldere's hand but with a second sword in the other Waldere puts out one of Hagena's eyes (for ever giving him the appearance of Woden, the one-eyed god: see p. 357).

Hildegyth takes care of the wounds and all combatants go home, with Waldere and Hildegyth living happily married in Aquitaine for as many as 30 years. It is in the surviving lines above, however, that Waldere was willing to make peace; his faith averted a tragedy; and that, perhaps, was the theme of this poem.

The Christianisation of heroic poems

If the dilution of Germanic heroes into moral figures was the price to be paid not only in England, but also in continental Europe, for the continuance of heroic poetry after the end of paganism into the tenth century and beyond, then this was a price worth paying. A long-established integration of religion in *Beowulf*, *Deor* and *Waldere* (fitting the heathens to the Judaic role of pre-Christian monotheists) accounts for the beautiful melancholy in these Old English poems, the gloom which is periodically illuminated by flashes of hope, humour or sublime compassion. *Beowulf* is our greatest Old English poem perhaps not only because *Beowulf* is the only heroic poem of any length that survives. *Beowulf*, a religious poem through and through, is also one in which old heroic legends have been adapted and transformed. In this poem there is both a moral vision and a willingness to change the story.

As we saw, the Danish bard, changing what he needed to, 'began cleverly to stir up Beowulf's adventure' (*ongan sið Beowulfes snyttrum styrian*, lines 871–2). Rearranging the story is what all great authors have done, Anglo-Saxons no less than others. Much has been written on the 'anxiety of influence' which a new author, such as Milton, feels about an old one, such as Virgil. In the words of one critic: 'The rebellions of these great figures against their predecessors are not patriarchal gigantomachies, as a poet-hero struggles for mastery over a Great Name from the past. They are revolutions of discourse' (Burrow 1993: 5). This influence proved to be less anxious among poets who worked with unwritten material. Legendary tradition was fluid, never fixed, despite the inevitable claims of authenticity. In *Beowulf*, just after the allusion to his 'encyclopaedic number of old sayings' (*eald-segena worn*, lines 869–70), the Danish bard is said to say nearly everything that he knows about Sigemund's brave deeds, such things as most men didn't know, the crimes and feuds of which Sigemund told only Fitela, his sister's son and close companion in battle. With an old poem on Sigemund he makes a new one on Beowulf.

The same might be said of the poet of *Beowulf* himself. Sigemund's story was presumably known to the audience for which he composed, but is not always clear to us, who know nothing of *Beowulf*'s date and little of the literary culture from which it sprang. The story in *The Saga of the Vǫlsungs* (Chapters 2–8) is that Sigmundr avenged his father Vǫlsungr on the man who killed him, with the aid of his sister Signý, married to the perpetrator. She visits her brother in another woman's shape, conceiving his child whom she later gives back to Sigmundr for training in the arts of vengeance. Signý does not tell Sigmundr or Sinfjǫtli, the boy, of their relation until they achieve this. By then the two of them have turned into werewolves. This frightful Norse tale allows us to see what lay behind *Beowulf*'s passage on Sigemund. If this passage is an allusion to Sigemund's vengeance for Wæls with the aid of Fitela, then it appears that the poet of *Beowulf* knew that Fitela was Sigemund's son as well as his nephew. Strong stuff for a Christian poet. It is no wonder that he has nothing on the incest or lycanthropy, although he mentions battles with giants in the wild places through which uncle and nephew prowl. Why the poet should include this heroic duo at all, monsters as they are, becomes clear in the culmination of Sigemund's glory:

> Sigemunde gesprong
> æfter deaðdæge   dom unlytel
> syþðan wiges heard   wyrm acwealde
> hordes hyrde;   he under harne stan
> æþelinges bearn   ana geneðde
> frecne dæde   ne wæs him Fitela mid;
> hwæþre him gesealde,   ðæt þæt swurd þurhwod
> wrætlicne wyrm   þæt hit on wealle ætstod
> dryhtlic iren;   draca <u>morðre</u> swealt.
> Hæfde <u>aglæca</u>   elne gegongen,
> þæt he beahhordes   brucan moste
> selfes dome: sæbat gehleod,
> bær on bearm scipes   beorhte frætwa,
> Wælses eafera;   wyrm hat gemealt. (*Beowulf*, lines 884–97)

> For Sigemund after his dying day
> there sprang up no small measure of renown,
> when the combat-hardened man killed the serpent,
> guardian of the hoard. Beneath the hoary rock
> and alone he braved a daring deed,
> did that prince's son, nor was Fitela with him.
> Yet it was granted to him that the sword impaled
> the wondrous serpent until the point, the noble iron,
> stood fixed in the wall. From this <u>assault</u> the dragon died.
> The <u>hero</u> had brought off a deed of courage
> by which he might make use of the ring-hoard
> on his own terms. So it was that Wæls' progeny

loaded up his boat on sea, carried bright treasures
into the bosom of his ship; the hot serpent melted.

This is the feat that the Scandinavians, in their later versions ('sagas of ancient times', *fornaldar sögur*), gave to Sigurðr; the Germans, in theirs (*The Lay of the Nibelungs*), to Siegfried: in each case to the son of 'Sigmund', the man to whom the common Germanic story belonged at an earlier stage. In their own ways, the *Edda* and *Lay of the Nibelungs* show us that Sigemund's hoard brings him and his friends and new family nothing but misery. This is not the message of the Danish bard who builds Beowulf a new epic out of one on Sigemund, for the Danes have no doubts about Sigemund. But there is no doubt that Sigemund is problematic for the poet of *Beowulf*. The poet's view of this hero is expressed on lines 892–3 (see above for the underlined words), in the ambiguity of his terms *morðor*, which means 'crime' more than 'assault'; and *aglæca*, which means 'monster' as well as 'hero' (Grendel, for example, on line 159). The Norse analogues tell us that it is a cursed treasure that Sigemund brings home.

At the end of his life Beowulf fights another dragon for its hoard in almost the same way. Here the gap between the poet and the old culture he represents widens even further. The poet cannot resist treating this dragon's treasure as a metaphor for the damnation of all heathens in general. He starts off innocently enough:

> Wundur hwar þonne
> eorl ellenrof   ende gefere
> lifgesceafta   þonne leng ne mæg
> mon mid his magum   meduseld buan. (*Beowulf*, lines 3062–5)

> It is a wonder where
> a courageous warrior may reach the end
> of his predestined life when he, a man, can no longer
> inhabit the mead-building with his kinsmen.

True for anyone, you might say, heathen or Christian. But there is a difference. Heroes love winning treasure, which they can distribute to others; kings even more so. But some treasures have a history. As a heathen, Beowulf has no idea of the dangers of this one:

> Swa wæs Biowulfe   þa he biorges weard
> sohte searoniðas,   seolfa ne cuðe
> þurh hwæt his worulde gedal   weorðan sceolde.
> Swa hit oð domes dæg   diope benemdon
> þeodnas mære,   þa ðæt þær dydon,
> þæt se secg wære   synnum scildig

hergum geheaðerod   hellbendum fæst
wommum gewitnad   se ðone wong strude;
næs he goldhwæte   gearwor hæfde
agendes est   ær gesceawod. (lines 3066–75)

So it was with Beowulf, when he sought the barrow's guardian,
cunning enmities, he himself did not know
by what means his departure from the world should come about.
So it was that the renowned princes who put it there
solemnly declared that until the Day of Judgement
the man who plundered that place would be guilty of crimes,
closed up in heathen shrines, firmly bound
in the bonds of hell, punished with defilements;
never before this time had he been
more ready to see an owner's gold-bestowing favour.

In these lines, the poet comes as near as he can to defining Beowulf, our hero, as damned. He has already redefined heroic epic as an essentially tragic genre. This is rather a prominent example of the variance between the Anglo-Saxons who created heroic literature and the status of the heroes on which they improvised, composed or wrote.

At the same time, it is clear that the poet of *Beowulf* felt free to change his story. Heroic legends were never fixed. According to the Norse versions of Beowulf's tale, the hero ends his life not with a dragon but with a band of other champions defending their king in Denmark. That is to say, Bǫðvarr bjarki ('little bear', like Beowulf = 'bee-wolf' = 'bear') dies with other champions defending his master King Hrólfr (i.e. Hrothulf). This story is known from the 'saga of ancient times', *The Saga of King Hrólfr Pole-Ladder* (*Hrólfs saga kraka*), and other sources. Not one of the Norse tales has a dragon fight at the end of Bjarki's career. Consequently we can suppose that 'King Hrothulf's last stand' was essentially the finale of Beowulf's story as it reached the poet of *Beowulf*. What did he do with this story? Just like his bard on the ride back from the Mere, he modelled his hero on Sigemund the Dragon-Slayer. He makes Beowulf end his career not as a servant of King Hrothulf in Denmark, but as a king in his own right. Possibly this innovation could lead us to seeing why or for whom the poet was writing *Beowulf* in the first place (North, 2006). More generally, however, these changes might show us what was possible in all Old English heroic poems. Stories on Beowulf and other heroes could be revised and they frequently were.

The four Old English minor heroic poems in this chapter are all that survive of such poetry outside *Beowulf*, but the approaches they offer to heroic legend are as various as they are. Perhaps, guessing at their order of composition, we could say that *The Finnsburh Fragment* offers a straight-up epic lay, *Waldere* a meditation on friendships, *Deor* a satirical distillation and *Widsith* a workaday manual of heroic themes. As part of a much larger tradition, which lasted more than four centuries, *Beowulf* and the other poems show that Old English poetry changed over time no less than the rest of 'English literature'. And yet we must never forget that the other heroic poems disappeared. Unless we are careful, the same will happen with these poems as well.

Translations and texts

Bullough, Donald A., 'What has Ingeld to do with Lindisfarne?', *Anglo-Saxon England* 22 (1993), pp. 93–125.

Byock, Jesse L., trans. and intro., *The Saga of Hrolf Kraki* (Harmondsworth, 1998).

Byock, Jesse L., trans. and intro., *The Saga of the Volsungs: The Norse Epic of Sigurd the Dragonslayer* (Los Angeles and London, 1990).

Crossley-Holland, Kevin, trans., *The Anglo-Saxon World: An Anthology* (Woodbridge, 1982, repr. Oxford, 1984). He offers interpretations which are usually the most pragmatic.

Dronke, Ursula, ed. and trans., *The Poetic Edda*, Vol. I, *Heroic Poems* (Oxford, 1969). Her translations, on which I base mine in this chapter, are really the best, although the books are priced rather high.

Dronke, Ursula, ed. and trans., *The Poetic Edda*, Vol. II, *Mythological Poems* (Oxford, 1997). Ditto.

Garmonsway, G.N. and Jacqueline Simpson, trans., with Hilda Ellis Davidson, *Beowulf and its Analogues* (London, 1968).

Larrington, Carolyne, trans., with an introduction and notes, *The Poetic Edda*, World's Classics (Oxford and New York, 1996). Accessible and up-to-date rendering of some of the most difficult-to-translate Norse poems.

Mitchell, Bruce and Fred C. Robinson, eds, *Beowulf: An Edition with Relevant Shorter Texts* (Oxford, 1998). With a few changes, texts for all OE works in this chapter come from here.

Further reading

Burrow, Colin, *Epic Romance: Homer to Milton* (Oxford, 1993). A useful guide to questions of authors and imitators in the English Renaissance.

Davis, Craig R., *Beowulf and the Demise of Germanic Legend in England* (New York and London, 1996). Overplays the idea that heroic lays disappeared by diminishing into entertainments, but has a readable survey at greater length than this chapter can provide.

Hill, Joyce, ed., *Old English Minor Heroic Poems*, Durham and St Andrews Medieval Texts, 4 (Durham, 1983). Although to be found in libraries rather than bookshops, this book provides a convenient text and commentary, with general introduction and glossary, for *Widsith*, *Deor*, *Waldere* and *The Finnsburh Fragment*.

Norman, Frederick, ed., *Waldere* (London, 1933). Useful for the detail on related traditions.

North, Richard, *Heathen Gods in Old English Literature*, Cambridge Studies in Anglo-Saxon England, 22 (Cambridge, 1997).

North, Richard, *The Origins of Beowulf: From Vergil to Wiglaf* (Oxford, 2006).

CHAPTER 5

Joyous play and bitter tears: the *Riddles* and the Elegies

Jennifer Neville

Poets or not, the Anglo-Saxons lived in another world. Most of them wore themselves out simply trying to produce food to eat. A few lived in constant fear of the end of the world and occupied themselves trying to convince everyone else to do the same. A few others focused their entire being on killing like-minded others as gloriously as possible. Few of us do anything similar today. Few of us would want to (although there are always a few). Yet the gulf between us and them is deceptive. I do not want to magic those differences away, since they are fascinating and worth knowing about. For this chapter, however, I want to introduce you to some of the literature written in Old English which reveals that the Anglo-Saxons, like many of us, enjoyed a joke, were obsessed with sex and sometimes felt lonely, alienated and depressed.

Jokes

It is not usual to think of the Anglo-Saxons as light hearted, but we're lucky to have the Exeter Book not only because of *Widsith* and *Deor* (see pp. 104, 108), but also because it preserves, among other things, a collection of riddles. Some of these are very serious indeed, addressing unfunny topics such as life and death, ravaging storms and religious objects. Some of them, however, are not so different from the kinds of riddle that amuse us today and, at the same time, they give us a peek at ordinary life 1000 years ago. The best (and worst!) thing about them, however, is that we don't know the answers: the solutions are not included in the manuscript. I can tell you what I think, but, really, your guess is as good as mine. Don't just take my word for any of these: have a go for yourself!

Riddle 5 seems to describe the world of warriors made familiar by *Beowulf,* although from much more pessimistic perspective:

Ic eom anhaga   iserne wund,
bille gebennad,   beadoweorca sæd,
ecgum werig.   Oft ic wig seo,
frecne feohtan.   Frofre ne wene,
þæt me geoc cyme   guðgewinnes,
ær ic mid ældum   eal forwurðe,
ac mec hnossiað   homera lafe,
heardecg heoroscearp,   hondweorc smiþa,
bitað in burgum;   ic abidan sceal
laþran gemotes.   Næfre læcecynn
on folcstede   findan meahte,
þara þe mid wyrtum   wunde gehælde,
ac me ecga dolg   eacen weorðað
þurh deaðslege   dagum ond nihtum. (*Riddle* 5)

I'm a loner.
I've been wounded by iron,
        I've been injured by blades.
I'm tired of battle-work;
        I'm weary of swords.
I often see battle and fight danger.
I have no hope of relief,
no hope that rescue from war-struggle
will come to me before I entirely perish among men.
Instead, the leavings of hammers,
        the work of smiths,
                hard-edged and battle sharp,
will bite me in the enclosures,
and I'm forced to await an even harder conflict.
In the settlement I could never find
one of the race of doctors
who could heal my wounds with herbs.
Instead, day and night the scars from swords
become greater with every deadly stroke.

Obviously, this isn't *funny.* This is the other side of war, the side you don't hear much about in *Beowulf* (unless you are listening very carefully): all the boasts and talk of glory are long gone and we have here the battered veteran of battle, bearing unhealable scars and wounds, with nothing to hope for except worse and worse, until the inevitable end finally comes to put him out of his misery. It is all tragic, really . . . but there's something not quite right.

First of all, why is he a loner (*anhaga*)? Anglo-Saxon armies weren't large (one law code defines any group of more than 35 men as an army), but still, you aren't really alone if you have 34 men for company. Beowulf often fights alone, but he comes home afterward to tell everyone about it; even the singular hero is not a loner. In other poems, such as *The Wanderer* (which I'll come to later in this chapter), we hear of the loneliness of those who used to have company but now live alone, but that's not the case here. The lone warrior of *Riddle* 5 is not an exile who's lost his home or been driven out, for he lives 'among people' (*mid ældum*), within the 'fortifications' (*burgum*) that enclose a typical Anglo-Saxon 'settlement' (*folcstede*).

Second, in the Anglo-Saxon period you don't survive when you've been hacked up by a sword. The medical texts show that the doctors (known as 'leeches', because they used them) did try: they knew how to do amputations to deal with gangrene, for example, and they knew about herbs, but they had no idea about antibiotics, antiseptics or anaesthetics. Thus, although some people have thought that the Anglo-Saxons poisoned their sword blades (*Beowulf* refers to a sword with 'poison twigs' (*atertanum*) on the blade), there was probably no need: most people cut by a sword who didn't die immediately from blood loss probably died soon afterward from infection. The lone warrior's ability to survive repeated wounds is superhuman.

Third, as a general rule, you don't fight battles 'inside a settlement' (*in burgum*) if you can possibly avoid it. That's what battlefields are for. Once an army gets inside a settlement, the fighting is over, and looting, pillaging, raping, etc. begin. But this lone warrior expects sword bites *inside* the enclosures.

Fourth, what could possibly be harder than what he's already experienced?

So, despite the moving picture of the beleaguered Anglo-Saxon warrior, that's not the answer to the riddle. Perhaps you have already come up with an alternative? Most people choose 'shield', which makes a lot of sense. A shield goes to battle and is 'bitten' repeatedly by swords; its whole purpose is to receive sword bites until it is utterly destroyed. The worse fate that it can expect could be being burnt up in a fire: the Anglo-Saxons made their shields out of wood and it is possible to translate *mid ældum eal forwurðe* not as 'entirely perish among men' as I did before but rather as 'entirely perish among flames'. And, obviously a doctor could never heal a shield, even with the best herbs in the world.

Most people accept 'shield' as the answer and you may be happy with it, but I still think that there is a problem with having the fighting going on inside the enclosures: it might have happened occasionally in real life, but this fighting seems to be envisaged as going on habitually *in burgum*. More important, there is a problem with the fighting going on 'day and night' (*dagum ond nihtum*). Old English poetry notes again and again that battles start at dawn and end at sunset, for obvious reasons: if you swing a sword around in the dark, you are more likely to hurt yourself and the people next to you than the enemy. This warrior sees his future and it involves blows day and night. So what kind of warrior is he?

I think that *Riddle* 5 is a joke and the joke is that this speaker doesn't belong to the heroic world of Anglo-Saxon battles at all. He's a lowly chopping board, used for domestic chores – probably by women – indoors, within the enclosures, not outside in the man's world. Those high-sounding 'swords', those 'leavings of hammers, hard-edged and battle sharp, the work of smiths' (*homera lafe, heardecg heoroscearp, hondweorc smiþa*) are merely ordinary knives, which everyone in Anglo-Saxon England, men, women and children, seem to have carried for personal use, rather than the great, lordly, expensive heirlooms that get passed around by kings and heroes in *Beowulf* or buried with kings, as at Sutton Hoo. The 'battle-work' (*beadoweorca*), 'war' (*wig*), and 'war-struggle' (*guðgewinnes*) that he experiences day and night are the ordinary, mundane, distinctly unglorious processes of pre-paring meals every day. He may well have herbs applied to his wounds, but not by a doctor and, of course, a bit of parsley won't cure him. It still may seem rather sad that he is wounded and that he probably will get thrown in the fire when he's no good any more, but the exaggerated, lofty language and high seriousness devoted to this trivial, domestic object ultimately makes this text funny, not tragic.

Yet that's not to say that it is not important. It is still social commentary. It is important to see this negative view of warfare, because in most of the Old English poetry that we read war is absolutely glorious. We never see the wounded and we rarely hear any hint that Anglo-Saxon warriors questioned the value of war or thought about it as anything other than the best way to live and die. And, of course, it is good to know that they liked a good joke.

Riddle 17 plays a similar trick on us, with a better punch-line:

Ic eom mundbora minre heorde,
eodorwirum fæst, innan gefylled
dryhtgestreona. Dægtidum oft
spæte sperebrogan; sped biþ þy mare
fylle minre. Frea þæt bihealdeð,
hu me of hrife fleogað hyldepilas.
Hwilum ic sweartum swelgan onginne
brunum beadowæpnum, bitrum ordum,
eglum attorsperum. Is min innað til,

wombhord wlitig,   wloncum deore;
men gemunan   þæt me þurh muþ fareð. (*Riddle* 17)

I am the protector of my herd.
I'm securely enclosed in wires.
I'm filled inside with noble treasures.
During the day I often spit out spear-terror.
       The fuller I am, the greater my success.
My lord observes the battle-darts
flying out of my belly.
Sometimes I begin to swallow
       dark, glinting battle-weapons,
       sharp points,
       painful poison-spears.
Yet my inner womb-hoard is excellent,
       radiant,
       precious to the powerful.
Men remember what comes through my mouth.

To answer this riddle, scholars have spent a lot of time combing the records and making unfounded assertions about the Anglo-Saxons' knowledge of siege equipment like the ballista or *trebuchet*. If they're right, the 'herd' enclosed inside the object consists of the projectiles, which the text describes in various ways – far too explicitly, I think, for that to be the answer. Plus, although the Romans and later medieval people did use such equipment, they did so because they had large-scale fortifications – castles and the like. The Anglo-Saxons didn't. It is possible, as some have argued, that they read about siege engines in books, but this text seems to betray real knowledge of something. What is it?

No one is absolutely sure. A quiver for arrows is a much better idea, but the arrows just seem too obvious; what kind of a riddle simply asks, 'What do you keep arrows in?' I prefer to think of it as a beehive. A beehive protects its 'herd' (*heorde*), its colony of bees, which are very much like flying 'battle-darts' (*hyldepilas*), and which carry 'spears' which are 'painful' and 'poisonous' (*eglum attorsperum*), especially if you happen to be allergic to their stings. The radiant treasure, precious to the powerful (kings, warriors and the like) is honey, which was not only the best sweetener available before the discovery of sugarcane in the New World, but also the raw material for making mead, a favourite alcoholic beverage consumed, of course, in the 'mead hall' (*meadoseld*: Meduseld is the name of King Théoden's hall in *The Lord of the Rings*). Honey was important: we still have Old English manuscripts with laws and magic charms designed to protect beekeepers from losing their important property. People thus remember the honey that comes out of the hive . . . but they are even more likely to remember bees pursuing them out the hive's 'mouth' (*muþ*), especially if the swarm catches them.

This isn't the only riddle that opens up Anglo-Saxon society for us. *Riddle* 27 describes some of the activities that might go on inside the mead hall:

Ic eom weorð werum,   wide funden,
brungen of bearwum   ond of burghleoþum,
of denum ond of dunum.   Dæges mec wægun
feþre on lifte,   feredon mid liste
under hrofes hleo.   Hæleð mec siþþan
baþedan in bydene.   Nu ic eom bindere
ond swingere,   sona weorpe
esne to eorþan,   hwilum ealdne ceorl.
Sona þæt onfindeð,   se þe mec fehð ongean,
ond wið mægenþisan   minre genæsteð,
þæt he hrycge sceal   hrusan secan,
gif he unrædes   ær ne geswiceð,
strengo bistolen,   strong on spræce,
mægene binumen;   nah his modes geweald,
fota ne folma.   Frige hwæt ic hatte,
ðe on eorþan swa   esnas binde,
dole æfter dyntum   be dæges leohte. (*Riddle* 27)

I am valuable to men,
widely found,
brought from groves and mountain slopes,
        from valleys and hills.
By day wings carried me skilfully
in wagons in the air,
under a roof's protection.
Afterwards a man bathed me in a barrel.
Now I am a binder and scourger;
I swiftly throw a youth to the earth,
        sometimes an old man.
Anyone who takes me on
and tries his force against me
will quickly discover that,
if he doesn't stop his stupidity,
he'll be flat on his back on the ground,
        his strength stolen away.
Strong in speech but deprived of force,
he'll have no power over his mind, feet, and hands.

Find out what I am called,
who thus bind men, foolish from blows,
to the ground, at the light of day.

Although it might seem that some kind of monster has been let loose in the enclosures, this is actually a description of the process of making mead and the results of drinking it. First pollen, carried by winged bees, is carried into their hive, under their roof; then the honey is brought from the groves, hills and valleys and put into a vat for fermentation. If you dare to take it on, you'll suffer the consequences, for what seems like a pub brawl, with young and old men being thrown to the ground, is what happens if you drink too much alcohol: you lose control over your limbs, mind and mouth. So, beware.

Again, what we have here is a text making fun of the heroic world. Drinking is a big part of the heroic ideal. In *Beowulf*, for example, there are lots of feasts to celebrate the hero, which include beer, wine and mead (but, funnily enough, no food). The drinking is important, not only because it helps to ensure an enjoyable evening, but because it is part of the social exchanges and rituals that ensure that everyone knows his place. In *Riddle* 27, however, the drinking is neither enjoyable nor social. It may seem that brave men are taking on a powerful enemy, but these men aren't heroes. They are common men, 'servants' (*esnas*) and the courage of those who dare to take on this creature is not even 'Dutch courage', for the real enemy is not the mead itself but their own lack of self-control. So we end with drunken men sprawled on the floor, shouting incomprehensibly, unable to think and unable to get up in the morning. So much for glory.

Most Old English literature takes the heroic life very seriously, so it is interesting to see a text that undercuts it, even if the butt of the joke is the lower classes rather than the lords themselves. Normally, Old English literature takes itself very seriously. Yet *Riddle* 46 shows us that even so serious a text as the Bible can provide a good joke, if you know where to look:

Wer sæt æt wine   mid his wifum twam
ond his twegen suno   ond his twa dohtor,
swase gesweostor,   ond hyra suno twegen,
freolico frumbearn;   fæder wæs þær inne
þara æþelinga   æghwæðres mid,
eam ond nefa.   Ealra wæron fife
eorla ond idesa   insittendra. (*Riddle* 46)

A man sat at wine
        with his two wives
        and his two sons

and his two daughters – dear sisters –
and their two sons, their noble firstborn.
Also there with them were
the father of the two nobles,
and their uncle
and his nephews.
In all there were five men and women sitting inside.

Start counting: one man, two wives, two sons, two daughters, two grand-sons, the grandsons' father(s), one uncle, and an unspecified number of nephews. That should be at least twelve people. The text tells us there were five. How is that possible?

The crucial clue is in the first line. Anglo-Saxon men weren't supposed to have more than one wife. The setting thus is somewhere where polygamy was allowed: the Old Testament. Even with that clue, however, you need to be well versed in Bible trivia to solve this one. You may remember the story of Sodom and Gomorrah – when those two cities were utterly wiped out by fire and brimstone because the inhabitants had disgusted God for too long (Genesis 19). You may even remember that Lot was saved, along with his wife and daughters, but that his wife made the mistake of looking back and thus was turned into a pillar of salt. Not everyone remembers what hap-pened next, however; it is not one of the most popular or edifying stories from the Old Testament. After the disaster, Lot and his two daughters went up into a cave on their own. The two daughters decided that the only way they'd ever have children would be by having sex with their father. So they got him drunk and both conceived boys. And thus we have this cosy table, complete with the wine that made it all possible, around which is sitting Lot and his two daughters, who are also his 'wives', and his sons, their firstborn, who are also his grandsons. The two boys are both brothers (by the same father) and cousins (by different mothers) of each other. As the father of a cousin is an uncle, the uncle is Lot again, and the nephews are the grand-sons, looked at another way. Don't think about it too long.

So the Anglo-Saxons liked number games. Perhaps more surprisingly, they liked incest jokes. This isn't what most people expect. But the riddles have yet more surprises to offer.

Sex

There is a long-running belief that the Anglo-Saxons didn't like sex. In the riddles, we have proof that this isn't so. Obviously, it is silly to have to prove such a thing. But one of the clearest statements of an Anglo-Saxon attitude toward sex comes from a riddle which should have nothing to do with sex. In *Riddle* 20, a lightly disguised sword movingly laments his inability to make love. He has everything that a noble Anglo-Saxon warrior could want – treasure, respect, and fame – but the 'joyous play' of 'sex' (*hyhtplegan, hæmed*) is denied to him, and there can be no doubt that he feels his deprivation keenly. It is worth noting that what he misses is the experience itself, the pleasure of intercourse; although he regrets not having children, too, sex here is clearly seen as something worth having – whatever the priests might have said – and sorely missed.

Other riddles hint that not everyone was so deprived. *Riddle* 44 describes something stiff and hard, with a hole at the front, which hangs by a man's thigh and often fills up a hole just the right size for it. It is, of course, a key, but that's probably not the first thing that an Anglo-Saxon audience thought of, either. There are a fair number of these riddles, which describe sex in a very open and straightforward fashion but actually have an 'innocent' answer as well. Although the final answer is 'innocent', however, the sex doesn't disappear. I don't think we can ever entirely forget about that other 'wonderful thing' (*wrætlic*) hanging by the man's thigh, even if we know the 'real' answer, just as the basic truth that sex is wonderful isn't denied just because the 'person' missing it is actually a sword. Of course, swords are pretty phallic in any case.

Considering how prudish most scholars assume the Anglo-Saxons to have been, the riddles can appear shockingly direct, even from a modern point of view. *Riddle* 54, for example, tells us the whole story of a sexual encounter from start to finish:

> Hyse cwom gangan,   þær he hie wisse
> stondan in wincsele,   stop feorran to,
> hror hægstealdmon,   hof his agen
> hrægl hondum up,   hrand under gyrdels
> hyre stondendre   stiþes nathwæt,
> worhte his willan;   wagedan buta.
> Þegn onnette,   wæs þragum nyt
> tillic esne,   teorode hwæþre
> æt stunda gehwam   strong ær þon hio,
> werig þæs weorces.   Hyre weaxan ongon
> under gyrdelse . . . (*Riddle* 54)

> A young man came walking –
>   he knew she was waiting there in the corner.
> Marching to her from afar,
> that bold bachelor heaved up his garment with his hands

and thrust something stiff
under her girdle as she stood there.
>   And then he had his pleasure.
>   Both of them shook.
The man moved quickly,
and that good servant was useful for awhile,
but, although previously stronger than she,
he grew tired and weary from his work.
Under her girdle, something began to grow . . .

There's no courtship and no foreplay here, but there is also no coyness about thrusting or about the fact that even a 'good servant' gets tired after performing such heroic exertions; after all, he is doing it all standing up in the corner. There's no birth control, either, of course, so it is inevitable that offspring will result. This offspring, however, is probably butter, since that's what you get from working with a churn.

And maybe there was birth control, after all. The answer to *Riddle* 61 is not entirely certain. In fact, like *Riddle* 44 and *Riddle* 54, it has two answers, one innocent and one not and we're not sure about either of them, although we can get the general idea:

Oft mec fæste bileac   freolicu meowle,
ides on earce,   hwilum up ateah
folmum sinum   ond frean sealde,
holdum þeodne,   swa hio haten wæs.
Siðþan me on hreþre   heafod sticade,
nioþan upweardne,   on nearo fegde.
Gif þæs ondfengan   ellen dohte,
mec frætwedne   fyllan sceolde
ruwes nathwæt.   Ræd hwæt ic mæne. (*Riddle* 61)

Often a noble maiden, a lady,
locked me firmly in a chest.
Other times she drew me out with her own hands
and gave me to her lord, her loyal prince,
as she was commanded.
>   Then he stuck his head inside me,
>   upwards from below,
>   and confined it in my narrowness.
If the courage of the one receiving me was strong,
something rough –
>   I don't know what –
filled me, adorned.
Explain what I mean.

Do I *dare* explain what this means? The 'lord and master' (*frean*) of the house is probably this noble woman's husband, and – *probably* – she's helping him to put his helmet on, as he's requested. After all, if he's going to go out and show his 'courage' (*ellen*) on the battlefield, he needs to wear a good helmet, preferably a nice 'ornamented' one (*frætwedne*) like the Sutton Hoo helmet, a very expensive object, which is why it is normally locked up in a 'chest' (*earce*). Or it could be a chain-mail shirt, since he'd have to push his hairy head up through that to put it on, too, and would appreciate a 'hand' (*folmum*) from his wife with that. So it is all perfectly innocent and it is quite a nice image of domestic bliss, with the great warrior enjoying a little tender loving care from his wife. Or maybe not . . .

There's just no way of avoiding the fact that sticking a 'head' (*heafod*) up inside something else, especially when there's a lady present, suggests something other than merely getting dressed. What makes it even more suggestive is the fact that the poet refuses to tell us *what* exactly is filling the mystery object. It is a *nathwæt*, an 'I don't know what', which, of course, means that the poet knows very well what it is but isn't going to tell us. So what *are* they doing? If you try to spell it out clearly, it all gets terribly explicit very quickly, but it is worth going through it in detail, because I think that there are two, equally sexy, possibilities here.

The first one is that the mystery object is the woman's vagina, normally private and off-limits, locked in a chest. Maybe that's a metaphorical chest – a sense of general propriety that means you don't go around with your genitals exposed – or maybe it is some kind of chastity belt (although these are not known from the Anglo-Saxon period, as far as I know). On particular occasions, however, when her man wants it, she gives it to him 'with her own hands' (*folmum sinum* – is she guiding him in with her hands?). It is a 'tight spot' (*nearo*), but, 'if he's man enough' (*gif ellen dohte*), his hairy thing will fill it up. There: I've explained what the poet meant.

The only problem with this explanation is one little word: *frætwedne*. It means 'adorned' or 'decorated', and it is a perfectly good way of describing a helmet or chain-mail shirt, but it doesn't work all that well for vagina. Although one *can* imagine ways in which a vagina might be adorned, maybe there's another possibility. That brings me back to the idea of birth control.

There's some evidence that people made condoms out of leather or animal bladders long before the Anglo-Saxon period and it seems to me that it would be perfectly possible that one might keep one's condom locked up in a chest until needed. The woman might then use her hands to help her husband put it on, if he asked her nicely. To work properly, he would have to stick his head up into it and it would have to be a tight fit. And maybe it was decorated. Who knows? Certainly we would know nothing about Anglo-Saxon condoms without this riddle and maybe we still don't, but it is worth considering.

Sex isn't just about men mounting receptive women, either. Sometimes the women take the lead. For example, in *Riddle* 45 it is the woman who goes looking in the corner:

> Ic on wincle gefrægn   weaxan nathwæt,
> þindan ond þunian,   þecene hebban;
> on þæt banlease   bryd grapode,
> hygewlonc hondum,   hrægle þeahte
> þrindende þing   þeodnes dohtor. (*Riddle* 45)

> I heard about an 'I don't know what' growing in a corner.
>   It swelled up,
>   stood proud,
>   and lifted up its covering.
> With her hands a lusty bride
> grabbed that boneless thing.
> With her clothing the prince's daughter
> covered the swelling thing.

Here we find that dead give-away of something interesting going on: another something or other that I'm not going to name (nudge, nudge, wink, wink) – our friend the *nathwæt* again. Whatever it is, it is growing, so much that you can see it lifting up underneath the cloth that covers it. In this case, this something is not locked in a chest, but it is in a 'corner' (*wincle*), and it is 'boneless' (*banlease*). When it grows, a woman with something in particular on her mind grabs it with her hands and tucks that 'swelling thing' (*þrindende þing*) under her clothing. Whatever are you thinking? It is dough, of course!

In *Riddle* 25 the woman appears very eager indeed (and who can blame her?):

> Ic eom wunderlicu wiht,   wifum on hyhte,
> neahbuendum nyt;   nængum sceþþe
> burgsittendra,   nymþe bonan anum.
> Staþol min is steapheah,   stonde ic on bedde,
> neoþan ruh nathwær.   Neþeð hwilum
> ful cyrtenu   ceorles dohtor,
> modwlonc meowle,   þæt heo on mec gripeð,
> ræseð mec on reodne,   reafað min heafod,
> fegeð mec on fæsten.   Feleþ sona

mines gemotes,   seo þe mec nearwað,
wif wundenlocc.   Wæt bið þæt eage. (*Riddle* 25)

I am a wonderful creature;
        I am the desire of women
        and useful to the neighbours.
I don't harm anyone in town,
        except my slayer alone.
I'm steep and high by nature,
I stand in a bed, shaggy below –
        I won't say where!
Sometimes a very beautiful farmer's daughter,
a proud-minded maiden,
        dares to grip me,
        rush upon me in my redness,
        plunder my head,
        fix me in a tight spot.
The one who afflicts me,
this woman with braided locks,
will immediately feel
the effect of our meeting:
        an eye will be wet.

This is starting to sound familiar. Here's another 'wonderful thing' (*wunderlicu wiht*), which lives 'somewhere or other' the poet won't say (*nathwær*) – you know what I mean! And this lovely girl can't wait to get her hands on it. It is, after all, what women want (*wifum on hyhte*). So, when it stands up steep and high in bed, she grabs it and sticks it in a tight spot. She feels something. It was such a moving experience that she cries . . . or maybe it is a different kind of fluid, from an eye lower down.

Shocking. We don't talk about such things in polite company – certainly not in monasteries. But why not? What's wrong with a farmer's daughter picking an onion? Ah, now we understand why it was so useful to the neighbours! Now it makes perfect sense that it harms no one except the one who kills it: an onion doesn't 'bite' you unless you bite it. And, of course, your eyes water afterward. It was clear all along . . . Of course it was.

This is all wholesome, straightforward stuff: men and women doing what comes naturally (picking onions and so on). Sometimes, however, people need to 'work' on their own. Monks are very much against this kind of behaviour, even the kind of monk who wrote out the Exeter Book *Riddles*, who, as we have seen, seems fairly down to earth and open to what comes naturally. In *Riddle* 12, however, there's a strong sense of disapproval:

Fotum ic fere,   foldan slite,
grene wongas,   þenden ic gæst bere.
Gif me feorh losað,   fæste binde
swearte Wealas,   hwilum sellan men.
Hwilum ic deorum   drincan selle
beorne of bosme,   hwilum mec bryd triedeð
felawlonc fotum,   hwilum feorran broht
wonfeax Wale   wegeð ond þyð,
dol druncmennen   deorcum nihtum,
wæteð in wætre,   wyrmeð hwilum
fægre to fyre;   me on fæðme sticaþ
hygegalan hond,   hwyrfeð geneahhe,
swifeð me geond sweartne.   Saga hwæt ic hatte,
þe ic lifgende   lond reafige
ond æfter deaþe   dryhtum þeowige. (*Riddle* 12)

I travel on foot,
slice the earth and its green fields,
as long as I'm alive.
If I lose my life, I firmly bind the dark Welsh –
        and sometimes better men.
Sometimes I give drink to brave men from my belly;
sometimes a very proud bride treads on me with her feet;
sometimes during dark nights
        a dark-haired Welsh woman,
        a foolish drunken slave-girl,
        brought from afar,
        moves me,
        presses me,
        wets me in water,
        warms me well by the fire
The lustful one's hand sticks me
                in her enclosure,
        turns me frequently,
        sweeps me through that dark thing.
Say what I am called,
I who living ravage the land
and after death serve the lordly multitude.

This is an easy riddle. The creature ripping up the land is an ox ploughing, and, once it is dead, its hide 'serves the band of warriors' (*dryhtum þeowige*) in various ways. That is, it is made into useful leather objects: fetters for slaves, belts for 'better men' (*sellan men*), drinking bottles, shoes for a bride

. . . and something else. Early scholars refused to discuss what that Welsh slave girl was doing. Later scholars said it was 'obvious' but wouldn't say what it was. Recently there's been a lot more work done on the issue, but there is still no absolute agreement. But that seems to be the point. The riddle is deliberately vague. It teases us with its ambiguity and leads us into thinking all kinds of naughty things; we can get so wrapped up with the grammar (it doesn't work right) and the vocabulary (it doesn't work, either) that we utterly forget that all we're supposed to do is 'say what I am called' (*saga hwæt ic hatte*). Looking back at *The Lord of the Rings*, for a moment, you could say we are like Gandalf before the gate of Moria: the question is too easy ('Say "Friend" and enter') and we are utterly distracted by all the tricky matters before us. Just say 'ox' and you're done. That's it.

But we can't leave it at that, can we? There are too many issues crying out for attention. The first one is the racism: the utterly blatant negative stereotyping of the Welsh. The Welsh are dark, low class, not as good as the English; they're drunks; they're lewd. Why did the Anglo-Saxons look down on the Welsh? There is evidence that many of the indigenous Celtic people were enslaved by the Anglo-Saxons; there is also evidence that Anglo-Saxons sent raiding parties into Wales to capture more. In the Old English word *wealh*, which has both meanings, 'Welsh' itself was almost synonymous with 'slave', and this term for the lowest of the low possessed all the negative connotations found here in this riddle and more: the Welsh were seen as lazy, cowardly, stupid and shameless.

As for what she's doing . . . One of the more recent guesses is that she's making a leather bottle, using a particular process called *cuir bouilli*, which involves stretching, wetting, heating, rubbing and perhaps embossing leather. It is hard work, requiring considerable skill and results in very useful objects. Another guess is that she's washing up the dishes with a leather rag, maybe after one of those feasts with lots of drink and not so much food. Again, however, as with the Key, Dough, Helmet and Onion, there's clearly sexual innuendo here. You can't 'stick' something 'in an enclosure' (*fæðme sticaþ*) or a 'dark thing' (*sweartne* – another something or other that the poet won't name?) without raising eyebrows, especially if you've been labelled 'lustful' (*hygegalan*). This time, however, it is not good clean sex between consenting heterosexual adults; it is a drunk woman masturbating late at night next to a fire with a dildo (made of leather, of course). Maybe. As I said before, there are no answers in the manuscript and the grammar and vocabulary here are very confusing – deliberately so. As far as we know, *sticaþ* and *swifeð* just can't be used that way. Perhaps what we have here are some rude, colloquial expressions that haven't survived anywhere else. Certainly *swifan* has an interesting later life in Chaucerian English, where a young man 'swyved' a young woman, even in a pear tree (see *The Merchant's Tale*, line 2378).

Depression

Of course, life isn't all fun and games. It wasn't for the Anglo-Saxons, either, and so, alongside the *Riddles*, in the same manuscript, we find texts of a very different mood: the 'Elegies'. We tend to think of alienation and depression as our own, particularly modern hardship, but songs like The Police's 'Message in a Bottle' and Nirvana's 'Smells Like Teen Spirit' are matched by Old English poems. Sometimes the weather got them down, too. However, when Travis complained, 'Why does it always rain on me?', he wasn't only talking about the weather and, in the same way, when the unknown speaker of *The Seafarer* tells us about the misery of winter days on a ship, the real problem is inside, not outside:

Mæg ic be me sylfum   soðgied wrecan,
siþas secgan,   hu ic geswincdagum
earfoðhwile   oft þrowade,
bitre breostceare   gebiden hæbbe,
gecunnad in ceole   cearselda fela,
atol yþa gewealc,   þær mec oft bigeat
nearo nihtwaco   æt nacan stefnan,
þonne he be clifum cnossað.   Calde geþrungen
wæron mine fet,   forste gebunden,
caldum clommum,   þær þa ceare seofedun
hat ymb heortan;   hungor innan slat
merewerges mod.   Þæt se mon ne wat
þe him on foldan   fægrost limpeð,
hu ic earmcearig   iscealdne sæ
winter wunade   wræccan lastum,
winemægum bidroren,
bihongen hrimgicelum;   hægl scurum fleag.
Þær ic ne gehyrde   butan hlimman sæ,
iscaldne wæg.   Hwilum ylfete song
dyde ic me to gomene,   ganetes hleoþor
ond huilpan sweg   fore hleahtor wera,
mæw singende   fore medodrince.
Stormas þær stanclifu beotan,   þær him stearn oncwæð
isigfeþera;   ful oft þæt earn bigeal,
urigfeþra;   ne ænig hleomæga
feasceaftig ferð   frefran meahte . . . (*The Seafarer*, lines 1–26)

I can sing the truth about myself –
tell you about my journey
and how often I've suffered
> long days of pain,
> long times of trouble,
> biting heartache.
I've tried out many a house of pain on a ship,
lived through terrifying, heaving seas,
found myself keeping watch at the ship's prow
when it ground against cliffs.
Freezing chains of frost bound my feet,
but searing hunger burned my heart,
sliced open a mind weary of the sea.
Other people live happily on land:
they don't know how wretchedly
I spent the winter on an ice-cold sea,
how I lived in exile –
> stripped of friends,
> decked with icicles,
> showered with hail-stones.
There I heard nothing but the roaring, ice-cold waves,
so I had to take the sound of birds for company –
> the song of the wild swan
> the voice of the gannet
> the cries of the curlew
> the singing of the gull
instead of music, men's laughter, and mead drinking.
Storms thrashed the stony cliffs
and the tern, its feathers frosted, called out.
The sharp-beaked eagle screamed.
No friend could comfort my desolate heart . . .

And so on . . . The Seafarer probably wasn't the only person on his ship, but, as far as he was concerned, he was utterly deserted, left freezing and alone while the weather heaped insult on injury by adding hailstones to his icicles and frozen feet. Romantic poets, such as Wordsworth, took comfort in the beauty and peace of the natural world, but for the Seafarer the roaring sea brings no comfort and the sound of seabirds here only makes him feel worse: their cries are a pathetic, even mocking reminder of the sounds he is missing, the sounds of human community, of people laughing and drinking together. It is not simply that times are tough at the present, either: even if there had been someone there, 'no friend could comfort my desolate heart' (*ne ænig hleomæga feasceaftig ferð frefran meahte*). We don't need to have been on an Anglo-Saxon ship in the winter to feel what's going on here, for the physical circumstances are merely details, reflections of his inner isolation and alienation from other people – those who know how to be happy. The Seafarer doesn't. For him this world is utterly bleak and an improvement in the weather or being able to enjoy wine, women, and song, would only make his depression worse. He needs counselling . . . or something.

As it turns out, he finds religion. Faced with a world in which everything is bad and getting worse, a world which itself seems to be getting old and grey, crumbling and deteriorating like an old man who can no longer even 'taste sweetness' (*swete forswelgan*), his heart transforms itself into something like a bird itself (*anfloga*), burning to fly away to another world, where he is not faced with the absolute certainty of 'sickness', 'old age' and the violence of 'sword-hate' (*adl oþþe yldo oþþe ecghete*). Everything on earth is transitory and passes away, so he rejects this cold, 'dead life' (*deade life*) for the 'Lord's joys' (*Dryhtnes dreamas*), which are 'hotter' (*hatran*).

Another poem, *The Wanderer*, shows us the longing and the deep emotional anguish caused by the separation of loved ones – not of man and woman, however, but of man and man. When we read Old English poetry, we tend to focus on heroism and loyalty; we don't think too much about how a warrior might have *felt* about his lord. In *The Wanderer* it is clear that this relationship was close and affectionate. Having buried his 'gold-friend' (*goldwine*), the Wanderer is 'winter-desolate' (*wintercearig*), 'friendless' (*freondlease*), and 'hall-dreary' (*seledreorig*). His sorrow transforms his heart into a coffin, a locked box (*ferðlocan, hordcofan, breostcofan*), from which he can escape only in dreams:

> Forþon wat se þe sceal   his winedryhtnes
> leofes larcwidum   longe forþolian,
> ðonne sorg ond slæp   somod ætgædre
> earmne anhogan   oft gebindað.
> Þinceð him on mode   þæt he his mondryhten
> clyppe ond cysse,   ond on cneo lecge
> honda ond heafod,   swa he hwilum ær
> in geardagum   giefstolas breac.
> Ðonne onwæcneð eft   wineleas guma,
> gesihð him biforan   fealwe wegas,
> baþian brimfuglas,   brædan feþra,
> hreosan hrim ond snaw,   hagle gemenged.
> Þonne beoð þy hefigran   heortan benne,
> sare æfter swæsne.   Sorg bið geniwad,
> þonne maga gemynd   mod geondhweorfeð;
> greteð gliwstafum,   georne geondsceawað

secga geseldan.   Swimmað eft on weg!
Fleotendra ferð   no þær fela bringeð
cuðra cwidegiedda.   Cearo bið geniwad
þam þe sendan sceal   swiþe geneahhe
ofer waþema gebind   werigne sefan. (*The Wanderer*, lines 37–57)

The one who is forced to go a long time
without the counsel of his beloved lord-friend
knows this:
>   When sorrow and sleep together
>   bind the wretched loner again and again,
>   he imagines in his mind
>   that he embraces and kisses his lord,
>   lays his hands and head on his knee,
>   just as he did before
>   when he enjoyed the gift-giving
>   in days gone by.

But then he awakes again.
The friendless man sees before him dark waves,
sees the seabirds bathing, spreading their feathers,
sees the frost and snow falling, mingled with hail.
Then the heart's wound, aching for his beloved,
is even heavier. And sorrow is renewed
when the memory of his family
turns through his mind:
>   He greets them joyfully
>   eagerly scans through the men's companions . . .

But they swim away again –
the heart of those floating ones
does not bring many songs of his dear ones.
Sorrow is renewed for the one
who must again and again
send his weary heart over the tossing waves.

The seabirds come again. This time, however, the birds melt before our very eyes, transforming themselves from birds to visions of the past and back into birds again. Somewhere between sleeping and waking, the wanderer relives those happy days when he was not alone, locked inside his wintry heart. Then he could be close to his lord and express his love physically as well as participate in the social rituals of gift giving. Now, in contrast, he has seabirds, and, like the seafarer, he is not comforted. As we watch them bathing themselves, we notice that the weather – frost and snow mingled with hail – is as cold as the wanderer's heart. Remembering his family only makes the pain worse and he slips again into a vision. He seems to see his relatives there before him, until they resolve themselves once again into birds, birds swimming away, birds floating on the water, birds whose cries are a wretchedly inadequate replacement for those sung by the people he knew and loved. Once again the pain is worse and worse again and again, as the process repeats.

Turning from his personal loss to the world at large makes the wanderer even bleaker:

> Hwær cwom mearg? Hwær cwom mago?   Hwær cwom maþþumgyfa?
> Hwær cwom symbla gesetu?   Hwær sindon seledreamas?
> Eala beorht bune!   Eala byrnwiga!
> Eala þeodnes þrym!   Hu seo þrag gewat,
> genap under nihthelm,   swa heo no wære.
> Stondeð nu on laste   leofre duguþe
> weal wundrum heah,   wyrmlicum fah.
> Eorlas fornoman   asca þryþe,
> wæpen wælgifru,   wyrd seo mære,
> ond þas stanhleoþu   stormas cnyssað,
> hrið hreosende   hrusan bindeð,
> wintres woma,   þonne won cymeð,
> nipeð nihtscua,   norþan onsendeð
> hreo hæglfare   hæleþum on andan.
> Eall is earfoðlic   eorþan rice,
> onwendeð wyrda gesceaft   weoruld under heofonum.
> Her bið feoh læne,   her bið freond læne,
> her bið mon læne,   her bið mæg læne,
> eal þis eorþan gesteal   idel weorþeð! (*The Wanderer*, lines 92–110)

> Where has the horse gone?
> Where has the young man gone?
> Where has the treasure-giver gone?
> Where has the feast-seat gone?
> Where are the joys of the hall?
>   Alas, bright goblet!
>   Alas, armed warrior!
>   Alas, glory of the prince!
>   How that time has passed,
>   grown dark under night's covering,
>   as if it never were.
> Left behind after the beloved troop
> a wondrously tall wall stands alone,
> decorated with snake-like images.

The power of spears,
slaughter-greedy weapons,
and mighty fate destroyed the warriors.
Storms strike against the rocky cliffs;
howling winter, an attacking snowstorm,
binds the earth. Then the darkness comes:
the night-shade grows dark
and sends a fierce hailstorm from the north
in hatred against men.
> All is full of hardship in the kingdom of the earth;
> fate changes the world for the worse under the heavens.
> > Here wealth is only loaned;
> > here the friend is loaned;
> > here the man is loaned;
> > here the kinsmen is loaned.
This place on the earth will become completely empty!

Tolkien famously used this passage to characterise the melancholic poetry of his fictional (but strikingly Anglo-Saxon) Rohirrim; Peter Jackson used it in his film to indicate Théoden's utter despair when facing Saruman's immense army of orcs at the Battle of Helm's Deep. Looking simultaneously back to all the good that's been lost and forward to all the bad that's coming, it is a vision without hope. What can you say to cheer someone up in this state? The Old English poem offers only this:

Til biþ se þe his treowe gehealdeþ,   ne sceal næfre his torn to rycene
beorn of his breostum acyþan,   nemþe he ær þa bote cunne,
eorl mid elne gefremman.   Wel bið þam þe him are seceð,
frofre to fæder on heofonum,   þær us eal seo fæstnung stondeð.

(The Wanderer, lines 112–15)

It is good for a man to keep his promises,
and he should never be too quick
to proclaim his heart's grief
unless he already knows a cure
and can bring it about with courage.
He'll do well to seek reward
and comfort from the Father in heaven,
where security stands for us all.

You can't argue with this – obviously it is a good thing to keep your promises, and so on – but not many modern readers have found it entirely satisfying. It is probably fair to assume that Anglo-Saxons contemplating the death of all their loved ones and a world that seemed to hate humanity would have had a hard time feeling cheered by the prospect of heaven, too, however strong their belief.

In other texts, even this consolation is lacking and it is interesting to find that, however bad the men had it, the women probably had it even worse. For example, while the wanderer at least has some happy memories, the speaker in *The Wife's Lament* looks back to a frustratingly vague but fascinating past full of love, betrayal, evil in-laws, and heartache:

> Ic þis giedd wrece   bi me ful geomorre,
> minre sylfre sið.   Ic þæt secgan mæg,
> hwæt ic yrmþa gebad,   siþþan ic up weox,
> niwes oþþe ealdes,   no ma þonne nu.
> A ic wite wonn   minra wræcsiþa.
> Ærest min hlaford gewat   heonan of leodum
> ofer yþa gelac;   hæfde ic uhtceare
> hwær min leodfruma   londes wære.
> Ða ic me feran gewat   folgað secan,
> wineleas wrècca,   for minre weaþearfe.
> Ongunnon þæt þæs monnes   magas hycgan
> þurh dyrne geþoht,   þæt hy todælden unc,
> þæt wit gewidost   in woruldrice
> lifdon laðlicost,   ond mec longade. (*The Wife's Lament*, lines 1–14)

> I make this song:
>> it is about me,
>> miserable me,
>> my own journey.
> I can tell you what troubles I've experienced
> since I grew up, both early and late,
> but never more than now!
> I have struggled always
> with the torment of my journeys into exile.
> First my lord departed from here, from his people,
> over the tossing waves.
> At every dawn I grieved:
> where could my lord be?
> Then I went to seek his following,
> a friendless exile in woeful need.
> Then the man's kin began to plot secretly
> that they would divide us
> so that we two should live most hatefully,
> at opposite ends of the world,
> and longing pained me.

It is hard to know what went wrong. Why did her lord – her husband –
leave? Perhaps he went off to war. Why did she go after him? Did she ever
find him? Why did his family start to plot to separate them? Like many,
many scholars, we can try to guess, but the poem refuses to tell us anything
specific. Only one thing is perfectly clear: how the speaker feels about it.
This is not a story; it is a lyric about sorrow. And it goes on:

Ða ic me ful gemæcne   monnan funde,
heardsæligne,   hygegeomorne,
mod miþendne,   morþor hycgendne.
Bliþe gebæro   ful oft wit beotedan
þæt unc ne gedælde   nemne deað ana
owiht elles;   eft is þæt onhworfen,
is nu   swa hit no wære
freondscipe uncer.   Sceal ic feor ge neah
mines felaleofan   fæhðu dreogan. (*The Wife's Lament*, lines 18–26)

Then I found a man fully matched to me:
        unfortunate,
        mournful,
        duplicitous,
        plotting murder.
With happy faces we two often vowed
that nothing but death itself should divide us.
That has been reversed;
now our love is as if it had never been.
Far and near I must endure my beloved's feud.

Who's this, then? Is this a memory of her first meeting with her husband
or is this some other man, another lover who's let her down? And who let
whom down? And what exactly is going on here? There's a brief hint of
a happy past when romantic promises were made, but even then, things
weren't right: they may have had happy faces (*bliþe gebæro*), but at least one,
and maybe both of them, were 'plotting murder' (*morþor hycgende*). The only
trace of their relationship now is the continuing feud. Feud generally
involves revenge for the death of family members. What happened to this
relationship? We will never know.

Elsewhere, we are told, lovers share a bed, but here the speaker sits alone,
weeping, exiled in a cave, unable ever to find peace. The poem ends with
bitterness and what sounds very much like a curse:

A scyle geong mon   wesan geomormod,
heard heortan geþoht,   swylce habban sceal

bliþe gebæro,   eac þon breostceare,
sinsorgna gedreag,   sy æt him sylfum gelong
eal his worulde wyn,   sy ful wide fah
feorres folclondes,   þæt min freond siteð
under stanhliþe   storme behrimed,
wine werigmod,   wætre beflowen
on dreorsele.   Dreogeð se min wine
micle modceare;   he gemon to oft
wynlicran wic.   Wa bið þam þe sceal
of langoþe   leofes abidan. (*The Wife's Lament*, lines 42–53)

Let that young man
cruel in his heart's thoughts,
be for ever mournful.
He must have a happy face,
          but also heartache,
          a throng of immense sorrows.
Let all his worldly joy
be dependent on himself alone.
Let him be exiled
to the farthest of far-away lands,
so that my lover,
my sad-minded companion,
will sit in a dreary hall
          under a stony cliff,
          frosted by storm
          flooded by water.
My lover will endure great anguish,
as he too often reminds himself
of a more joyful dwelling.
There is always woe for one
who must wait for love to come out of longing.

Throughout the poem the speaker has emphasised her alienation – how she is cut off not only from her husband but from everyone else as well. Here she wishes that same alienation on her lover (who may or may not be the same man as the husband mentioned earlier). She hopes that, if he's with other people, he'll be unable to share his true feelings with them, that he'll have to hide his heartache. She hopes that he'll be unable to count on anyone to help him. More, she wishes him exiled, like she is, away from all human company, exposed to the ravages of the weather and bitterly remembering better times – or perhaps even dead, his corpse washed up by the sea at the foot of a 'cliff' (*stanhliþe*), or buried underground in a barrow, a 'dreary hall' (*dreorsele*). Life seems worse than death for those who wait, longing for love that never comes.

Another poem with a female speaker, *Wulf and Eadwacer*, demonstrates the same depth of feeling and the same mysteriousness:

> Leodum is minum   swylce him mon lac gife;
> willað hy hine aþecgan,   gif he on þreat cymeð.
> Ungelic is us.
>
> Wulf is on iege,   ic on oþerre.
> Fæst is þæt eglond,   fenne biworpen.
> Sindon wælreowe   weras þær on ige;
> willað hy hine aþecgan,   gif he on þreat cymeð.
> Ungelice is us.
>
> Wulfes ic mines widlastum   wenum dogode;
> þonne hit wæs renig weder   ond ic reotugu sæt,
> þonne mec se beaducafa   bogum bilegde,
> wæs me wyn to þon,   wæs me hwæþre eac lað.
>
> Wulf, min Wulf,   wena me þine
> seoce gedydon,   þine seldcymas,
> murnende mod,   nales meteliste.
>
> Gehyrest þu, Eadwacer?   Uncerne earne hwelp
> bireð wulf to wuda.
>
> Þæt mon eaþe tosliteð   þætte næfre gesomnad wæs,
> uncer giedd geador. (*Wulf and Eadwacer*)

For my people it is as if someone gave them a gift.
They will take care of him if he comes under threat.
    It is different for us.

Wulf is on one island, I on another.
Secure is that island, surrounded by fens.
The men there on that island are mad for slaughter.
They will take care of him, if he comes under their threat.
    It is different for us.

I suffered because of the wanderings of my Wulf,
    because of my hopes;
when it was rainy weather and I sat weeping –
when the brave warrior laid his arms around me –
there was some pleasure for me in it, but there was also hate.

Wulf, my Wulf, longing for you,
the lack of your visits, has made me sick –
my mourning heart, not lack of food.

Eadwacer, do you hear?
the wolf bears our wretched whelp
to the woods.

One can easily slice apart what was never united:
our song together.

Where do you start with a text like this? You can try to guess who the people are, perhaps. But as with all Old English poems, the title is a guess. There is no title in the manuscript. We don't know what the speaker's name is and we don't actually *know* that either *Wulf* or *Eadwacer* is a real name: the first could be a nickname or a short form (for Wulfstan, for example) and the second could be a title or job description (it literally means 'wealth-watcher'). What about the setting? The geography described in the poem (two islands) is vague enough that the story could take place almost anywhere. Even the words are hard to pin down. As in *Riddle* 12, some of the vocabulary is unique and uncertain. For example, we don't really understand what *apecgan* (in the second and seventh line) means in this context. It is been translated both as 'receive' and as 'devour'. I have tried to retain that ambiguity by using a modern expression that can cover both extremes of its possible meaning: to take care of someone can mean to welcome him, but it can also mean to finish him off – to kill him. The difference is obviously significant, but we really can't know for sure.

My translation tries to make sense of the story as follows: the speaker is longing for a man named Wulf, who previously was her lover (or maybe her husband). He used to come and visit, but not very often and, although she had enough food, she was lovesick for him and the weather seemed to weep in sympathy for her. The reason he doesn't come to visit is that her people would kill him if they could catch him. Perhaps Wulf is an outlaw, a criminal. Or perhaps he comes from a neighbouring tribe or family with which her own people are at war. Maybe it is something like *Romeo and Juliet*, with Anglo-Saxon Montagues and Capulets.

But there is more. While she is pining for Wulf, someone else has put his arms around her: a 'brave warrior' (*beaducafa*). Has she been forced to marry someone else? Her feelings about her situation are strongly ambivalent: although she hates it, she loves it, too. Does she hate the warrior but enjoy his embrace and is this warrior named Eadwacer? Perhaps his embrace has resulted in a child, a 'whelp' (*hwelp*), which the speaker, in her hatred for the man who's been forced (or has forced himself) on her, has abandoned in the forest, to be taken by wolves . . . or by a man named Wulf.

The final two lines, unlike the rest of the poem, seem reasonably easy to understand: you can easily divide people who were never together – people whose lives were never in tune, who never sang from the same song sheet. Once you start thinking about them, however, you realise that these lines are ambiguous, too: they could refer to the speaker's relationship with Eadwacer or to her relationship with Wulf or to her relationship with the child or to all three. Nothing is certain about this little poem. Even the love triangle I've described is not accepted by all scholars. It is been argued, for example, that Wulf is the speaker's son; that the poem is actually about dogs; that it is about mixing up pages in a manuscript; that it is a riddle whose solution is a man's name; and that it is a medical charm to cure tumours. Some of these are a bit far fetched, of course, but the point is that the text is so elliptical that we can't be sure. Maybe it was a kind of riddle for the Anglo-Saxons, too. It is possible, however, that the story was so familiar to the Anglo-Saxons that they would have immediately recognised the speaker and her situation. From where we stand, however, the only thing that's really clear is the feeling behind the poem, the sense of longing and alienation.

It is tempting to think that there is a reply to such a cry of anguish and a happy ending, in the form of another poem in this manuscript, a text that we now call *The Husband's Message*. Like many of the riddles, this is a poem spoken by an inanimate object – in this case, it is a piece of wood on which a message has been inscribed in runic letters. Like the Wanderer and Seafarer, this messenger has been obliged to leave its homeland and cross the 'salty streams' (*sealte streamas*); unlike the Wanderer and Seafarer, however, this travel is for joyful purposes. Like *The Wife's Lament* and *Wulf and Eadwacer*, this poem is about a romantic relationship between a man and a woman; very unlike those poems, however, this relationship, although it is been through some hard times, seems destined for a 'happily ever after' ending:

> Hwæt, þec þonne biddan het   se þisne beam agrof
> þæt þu sinchroden   sylf gemunde
> on gewitlocan   wordbeotunga,
> þe git on ærdagum   oft gespræcon,
> þenden git moston   on meoduburgum
> eard weardigan,   an lond bugan,
> freondscype fremman.   Hine fæhþo adraf
> of sigeþeode;   heht nu sylfa þe
> lustum læran,   þæt þu lagu drefde,
> siþþan þu gehyrde   on hliþes oran
> galan geomorne   geac on bearwe.
> Ne læt þu þec siþþan   siþes getwæfan,
> lade gelettan   lifgendne monn.

Ongin mere secan,   mæwes eþel,
onsite sænacan,   þæt þu suð heonan
ofer merelade   monnan findest,
þær se þeoden is   þin on wenum. (*The Husband's Message*, lines 13–29)

Listen, woman adorned with treasure:
the one who carved this wood commanded me
to tell you to remember in your own heart
the vows which you two often spoke in former days
when you were able to be together
      to possess your homeland,
      to occupy one land,
      to express your love.
Feud drove him away from this glorious people,
but now he himself commands
that I teach you joyfully to drive through the sea
as soon as you have heard the mournful cuckoo singing
in the grove or near the edge of the hill.
Then let no living man hinder your passage
or turn you from the journey.
Seek the sea, the gull's homeland –
board a sea-vessel, so that you can find
this man south from here over the water,
where your prince waits in hope of you.

The wooden messenger goes on to assure that this prince has treasures, horses, men, a new land to rule, and everything he could possibly desire except one thing only: his one true love. Thus sunshine comes after rain and joyous play returns after bitter tears. What princess could refuse?

Conclusion

There are a lot of things in Old English poetry that are difficult for us to empathise with. These are things like the importance of honour, the glory of killing, the warrior's love for his lord, the idea of sin and fear of Doomsday and so on. Yet this poetry can still touch us, given half a chance. Through the Elegies and *Riddles* presented in this chapter Old English literature will show you the warmth, vulnerability, eroticism, loving kindness and pathos of a society in which life was often exhilarating, but, usually, painfully short. Remember, the next time you get caught in the freezing rain, the Anglo-Saxons were there as well. If you ever need a good party trick, the onion riddle works every time.

Translations and texts

Bradley, S.A.J., *Anglo-Saxon Poetry: An Anthology of Old English Poems in Prose Translation with Introduction and Headnotes* (London, 1982). This is a collection of prose translations from Old English poetry. It includes most of the existing Old English poems, so gives a good sense of what's available. It is not a great choice for getting a sense of the poetry, however.

Crossley-Holland, Kevin and Lawrence Sail, *The New Exeter Book of Riddles* (London, 1999). This isn't really a translation but a collection of new riddles made in imitation of the Old English collection. Highly interesting.

Hamer, Richard, *A Choice of Anglo-Saxon Verse* (London, 1970, repr. 2006). Includes verse translations of a few riddles, plus *The Wanderer, The Seafarer, The Wife's Lament, Wulf and Eadwacer,* and *The Husband's Message,* among many other important Old English poems. This book has the great advantage of having the original Old English text across the page from the translation.

Raffel, Burton, *Poems from the Old English*, 2nd edn (Lincoln, 1964). Raffel is primarily a poet rather than a scholar, so his translations are a bit freer and more poetic than some.

Further reading

Banham, Debbie, 'Anglo-Saxon Attitudes: In Search of the Origins of English Racism', *European Review of History* 1 (1994), pp. 143–57. An overview of Anglo-Saxon views of the Welsh.

Cameron, M.L., *Anglo-Saxon Medicine* (Cambridge, 1993). This is an advanced book, written by a doctor, but skimming parts of it will give a good idea of what medical knowledge the Anglo-Saxons had.

Higley, Sarah L., 'The Wanton Hand: Reading and Reaching into Grammars and Bodies in Old English Riddle 12', in *Naked Before God: Uncovering the Body in Anglo-Saxon England*, Withers Benjamin C. and Jonathan Wilcox, eds (Morgantown, WI, 2003), pp. 29–59. This explains why it is so hard to be sure about anything in *Riddle* 12.

Irving, Edward B., Jr, 'Heroic Experience in the Old English Riddles', in *Old English Shorter Poems: Basic Readings*, O'Keeffe, Katherine O'Brien, ed. (New York, 1994), pp. 199–212. This is a very evocative reading of the image of the tragic warrior in *Riddle* 5.

Johnson, David and Elaine Treharne, *Readings in Medieval Texts: Interpreting Old and Middle English Literature* (Oxford, 2005). Includes nice, short, introductory chapters on the *Riddles* and the Elegies.

Osborn, Marijane, ' "Skep" ("Bienenkorb, *beoleap*") as a Culture-Specific Solution to "Exeter Book" Riddle 17', *American Notes and Queries* 18 (2005), pp. 7–18. An explanation of *Riddle* 17 as a beehive.

Rulon-Miller, Nina, 'Sexual Humor and Fettered Desire in Exeter Book Riddle 12', in *Humour in Anglo-Saxon Literature*, Wilcox, Jonathan, ed. (Cambridge, 2000), pp. 99–126. This article explores both the leather working apparently being done by the Welsh slave woman and the disturbing undertones in *Riddle* 12.

Wilcox, Jonathan, 'New Solutions to the Old English Riddles: Riddles 17 and 53,' *Philological Quarterly* 69 (1990), pp. 393–408. For the interpretation of *Riddle* 17 as a quiver of arrows.

CHAPTER 6

The Dream of the Rood and Anglo-Saxon Northumbria

Éamonn Ó Carragáin and Richard North

C hristianity was the driving force of Old English literature. If we haven't looked at this force until now, it is probably because much of today's western society is too secular for any but a gradual introduction. For many, but by no means all of our potential readers in the English-speaking world, religion lies a few steps back in cultural history. So prepare for a change. From this chapter forward we will be revisiting Christianity, in its Roman and Irish Christian forms, for the purpose of reading Old English literature in the depth it deserves. It is true, the people whose feelings you saw displayed through the imaginative craftsmanship of the *Riddles* and Elegies of the last chapter were people like us. But they were also different from many of us now. The imagination of their poets in seventh- to eleventh-century England was fixated on the symbolism of the Christian mystery, which they presented in an often uncompromising heroic form. We know now what 'the heroic' is from seeing it celebrated in Tolkien, *Beowulf* and the minor heroic poems in Chapters 2–4. We have also seen heroic ideology undermined and questioned to much comic and melancholy effect in the literature of Chapter 5. But not until now have we seen it as the expression of Christian devotion. Jesus and the disciples? That's a warlord with his bodyguards. The Crucifixion? Christ's battle with Satan, his sacrifice on the world tree or both ideas and more all rolled into one. The Acts of the Apostles? The lonely deeds of exiles when their leader is killed, the war band dispersed. And the Cross? Among a profusion of other conceits, the Cross was pitied as the lieutenant suddenly ordered to kill his captain – by the victim himself. Such conflicts as this were the staple of the best heroic poems. In this chapter, we will show you a similar collision of love and duty in a poetic masterpiece from Northumbria which was probably composed ten years or so before 700. This poem tells the story of Christ's Crucifixion. It is now known as *The Dream of the Rood*.

The Dream of the Rood

The Dream of the Rood is an odd title. It was invented by the scholars who first published and studied the poem in the early nineteenth century, so no Anglo-Saxon could have known it. In the manuscript the late tenth-century Vercelli Book, the poem has no title at all. It begins abruptly near the top of a manuscript page, the second side, or verso, of folio 104:

Hwæt ic swefna cyst   secgan wylle
       So: I want to tell the best of dreams
h[w]æt me gemætte   to midre nihte
       which came to me about midnight
syðþan reord berend   reste wunedon.
       after voice-bearers took their rest.
þuhte me þæt ic gesawe   syllicre <u>treow</u>
       It seemed to me that I saw a most splendid <u>tree</u>
on lyft lædan   leohte bewunden
       towering aloft suffused with light
beama beorhtost   eall þæt beacen wæs
       – the brightest of beams. That beacon was all
begoten mid golde   gimmas stodon
       encrusted with gold: gems stood out
fægere æt foldan sceatum   swylce þær fife wæron
       beautiful at the surfaces of the earth: also there were five
uppe on þam eaxle ge spanne   beheoldon þær engel dryhtnes
       up on the shoulder-span. All fair beings throughout time and
       creation
ealle fægere þurh forð ge sceaft   ne wæs ðær huru fracodes gealga.
       looked on the lord's messenger [i.e. angel] there. Indeed that was
       no criminal's gallows:
Ac hine þær beheoldon   halige gastas
       But holy spirits looked upon it there
men ofer moldan   ond eall þeos mære ge sceaft:
       men throughout the earth and all this glorious creation.
                  (*The Dream of the Rood*, lines 1–12)

We have set out our texts here and elsewhere in this chapter with a view to showing the likeness between Old and modern English at many points.

Go back and read the Old English if you like. Once you have done this, you will find the corresponding lines in the facsimile of the manuscript page also surprisingly easy to read. The poem is spoken by a man who dreams of the Cross. More exactly, the dream comes to him as he lies there. The first part, much of it just quoted, is the man's description of the Cross. The second, a speech made by the Cross in which it (a) tells of the Crucifixion from its own unique point of view and (b) gives us its take on the meaning of this event in relation to the event that follows, the Harrowing of Hell (in which Jesus takes out, or 'redeems', all the noble pagans, Adam and Eve, the patriarchs, who languished in hell simply because until his self-sacrifice there was no means of getting them into heaven). In the third part of this poem, the Dreamer declares his intention to live a more spiritual life.

In its manuscript *The Dream of the Rood* (we'll call it *The Dream* mostly from now on) is like almost all Old English poetry in being laid out like prose, not verse. As we have seen, Anglo-Saxon scribes generally set out Latin verse in separate lines, but set out their own poetry as continuous text, like prose. They seem to have understood their own poetry as sung or chanted speech and as having the immediacy of speech. This poem immediately grabs the reader's urgent attention: it begins with *Hwæt*! Compare the modern word 'what'. *Hwæt* implied that someone was beginning to recite a poem and that people should stop talking and listen. We do not have a similar convention in modern printed English and so the '*Hwæt*' is difficult to translate: 'Lo!' is far too old fashioned, and 'Listen' is over-bossy and overloud. In his translation of *Beowulf*, Seamus Heaney had the brilliant idea of translating the *Hwæt* that opens that poem as 'So': the word a story-teller in Ireland would use to create a moment of pause for the audience to get themselves comfortable and quiet and to give himself time to recall the essential details of the narrative he was going to tell.

An Anglo-Saxon reader working his way through the texts in the Vercelli Book certainly needed to hear something cheerful at this point of the manuscript. As they lack titles, the poems in the manuscript seem to follow on from each other naturally, like a series of connected readings that can be read as stages in a dialogue or conversation. Individual sections appear, when read in sequence in the manuscript, to answer problems raised in the section which the reader has just worked his or her way through. Some of these sections have been worked out by modern editors to be separate poems, composed a long time before the manuscript was compiled: it may have been the compiler of the Vercelli Book who first brought them together in the sequence in which we have them. The poems that the Anglo-Saxon reader would have just read here in the Vercelli Book before coming to *The Dream* were, on the whole, highly depressing and, indeed, frightening. The first poem is set at midnight, a time at which *The Dream* will also be set, and this first poem is called *Soul and Body I*. It starts by proclaiming that everyone should imagine how terrible it will be when, at death, soul and body are parted (*Soul and Body I*, lines 1–5). In the first manuscript section of this poem, a damned soul comes back to its body, lying in the grave, one night each week and until dawn berates its body for the bad actions (including gluttony and sex) that caused the soul to be damned. The second section is equally simplistic but perhaps more cheerful: a saved soul comes back each week to congratulate its body, which has not been so fond of food or sex, for ensuring the soul's happiness after death. The third manuscript section is the one immediately before the start of *The Dream*. This section (now called *Homiletic Fragment I*) is as gloomy as the first verse section of the sequence and proclaims that now, at the end of the world, you can trust no one: everyone will let you down and injure you by calumny and backbiting. It is clear that the compiler of the manuscript wanted to have each gloomy reading followed by one that cheered you up. Any Anglo-Saxon reader would certainly have come to the fourth reading in the sequence, *The Dream*, with a sense of relief. It provides the reassurance which, by then, any reader of the Vercelli Book would have badly needed: 'the best of dreams' (*swefna cyst*), in which the Dreamer sees 'a most splendid tree' (*syllicre treow*).

Of course, this tree is really the Cross, but it is worth saying that the poet does not come out and say it is the Cross until line 44, much further into the poem. His indirection here amounts to a riddling technique such as that we have already seen in the *Riddles* of the Exeter Book, even if, as you can imagine, the aims are radically different. Like some riddles, this one uses puns in order to mislead and then add one meaning to another. The poet's word *treow* here ('tree', line 4) recalls another word, almost a homophone, the reassuring word *treowe*, 'pledge', 'assurance', 'something you can rely on'. But the image of the tree brought with it other complex associations as well as 'pledge'. One of these was to do with the Tree of Life. This image, of life and fruitfulness, was a primary one. The Tree of Life was an important religious symbol, not only in the Mediterranean world from which early Christianity came, but also in the old world of Anglo-Saxon paganism. What we call a 'cross' the French call 'croix', the Spanish 'cruz' and the Germans 'Kreuz'. These words all come from Latin *crux*. But the Anglo-Saxons called the Cross (to give length marks) either a *rōd* ('rood') or a *trēow* ('tree') or a *gealga* ('gallows') or a *bēam* ('beam'). The fact that they used these words, rather than the one they got from Latin, *crūc* ('crouch', the 'sign of the cross'), is probably evidence that *rōd*, *trēow*, *gealga* and *bēam* were thought to be adequate to render 'cross' on their own. In other words, there was a tree persona in Anglo-Saxon paganism with which the heathens, or the missionaries staying with them in the sixth and seventh centuries, portrayed the Cross around the time they were converted to Christianity. Their heathen cousins in Scandinavia kept this tree persona right into the eleventh century, where it survives, in Old Norse mythology, under various names for 'the World Tree' (see Chapter 12, p. 367). The Northumbrian English 'World Tree' persona was a perfect opportunity for importing, or inculturating, the Christian image of the 'Tree of Life' (Latin *arbor vitae*) into a heathen culture. In *The Dream*, in some ways, we can see the inculturation still taking place.

The greatest image of the Tree of Life surviving from southern Europe is the twelfth-century mosaic in San Clemente in Rome. In this mosaic, animals and humans of both clergy and laypeople all live embraced by the Tree of Life, which itself grows from the Cross of Christ. The tree in *The Dream* is even more exciting. The scale of this vision is panoramic. At the centre of the universe is the tree, which is covered in gold and shining with light (*leohte bewunden*: literally, 'wound round with light'). In this way the tree is 'a beacon' (*beacen*), 'the brightest of beams' (*beama beorhtost*). Just as in modern English, the Anglo-Saxon word *bēam* could mean a 'beam of light' as well as a 'beam of wood'. And yet, from the opening lines, this glorious tree spanning the heavens has grimmer associations. These first appear through statements of what the tree is not. When the poet says 'that was not a criminal's gallows' the paradoxical effect is precisely to bring thoughts of death and execution into the poem. When we hear that 'there were five [gems] up on the shoulder-span' of the tree (the word *eaxle-*, which gives the modern word 'axle', means 'shoulder'), we begin to see that the tree has a crossing, that it is cross-shaped. The five gems recall the body of Christ who, on the Cross, received five wounds, the wounds of nails in his feet and his hands and, at the point of death, a spear wound on his side. At one monastery in Ireland, Ahenny, monastic sculptors provided five gems around the crossing of their great stone high cross precisely in order to recall the five wounds and so to associate their cross with the body of Christ. Note that the late eighth-century Ahenny stone high cross is covered with complicated interlace patterns, of the sort we find in early metalwork. We can therefore be certain that the Ahenny cross was originally painted in bright colours, so as to look as if it were made of gold and covered with jewels. Ahenny, in other words, created a 'most splendid tree' (*syllicre treow*) like that imagined, perhaps a century earlier, by the Northumbrian poet of *The Dream of the Rood*.

This Tree of Life, however, recalls Christ's own body as well as the Cross on which Christ died. When the poet says that 'all fair creatures throughout time and creation looked on the messenger [i.e. angel] of the lord there', monastic readers would have remembered that each Christmas morning, at the beginning of the community Mass, they sang a Latin chant which proclaimed: 'A child is born to us, and a son is given to us: whose power is on his shoulder, and his name shall be called, the messenger [angel] of great counsel.' The chant was based on The Book of Isaiah, chapter 9, verse 6, in whose Latin the last phase is *magni consilii Angelus*. In *The Dream*, the Tree of Life, spanning the universe, is looked on by 'holy spirits, men on earth and all this glorious creation'. Now this phase is a clear reminiscence of a New Testament text, St Paul's Letter to the Philippians, chapter 2, verse 10, which says that, when God exalted Christ who had been obedient unto death, 'at the name of Jesus every knee should bend, on heaven and on earth and under the earth'. But that verse comes from a liturgical reading, the Epistle chanted at Mass on Palm Sunday, the Sunday before Good Friday (Philippians chapter 2, verses 5–11). As we shall see, that Epistle was centrally important to the way in which Christ's life and death was understood by the early Christian churches. The poet's use of these two biblical texts, from the Old and New Testaments respectively, one chanted on Christmas Day and the other on the Sunday before Good Friday, shows that his poem is about more than gold and glory. Among other things, the poem dramatises the dreamer's choked-up emotional response to the vision:

Syllic wæs se sigebeam   and ic synnum fah,
    Splendid was the victory-tree and I, stained (made hateful) with sins,
forwundod mid wommum.   Geseah ic wuldres treow
    wounded with wickednesses. I saw the tree of glory
              (*The Dream of the Rood*, lines 13–14)

Again, the poem works through puns: 'fah' can, depending on the context, mean 'brightly coloured' or 'hated, hateful'; 'wommum' means 'stains, blemishes'. The contrast between cross and dreamer could be called *chiaroscuro*, after the 'light-dark' effect of seventeenth-century Italian paintings. Light for the tree, which is like a legion's golden standard raised in victory. Dark for the physical and moral blemish which the dreamer feels is his, given that he has wounded himself with all the misdeeds of a lifetime. The contrast is weighted in the syntax of the line. On line 13 is a word order that goes:

ADJECTIVE – NOUN SUBJECT – PRONOUN SUBJECT – ADJECTIVES

This pattern is called *chiasmus*, like A-B-B-A, and it presents a contrast in the sharpest form. As A-B-B-A is a cross-pattern in words, you will be able to find a number of examples of *chiasmus* in this poem about the Cross. The dreamer is pretty cut up. He thinks of all the rotten things he did. He can't tell why he feels this way unless it comes from looking at a dazzling tree in a dream. To go on:

> Geseah ic wuldres treow
> > I saw the tree of glory
> wædum geweorðod   wynnum scinan,
> > venerated with vestments, shining with joys,
> gegyred mid golde;   gimmas hæfdon
> > girt with gold; gems had
> bewrigen weorðlice   Wealdendes treow.
> > covered worthily the Ruler's tree. (*The Dream of the Rood*, lines 14–17)

These lines appear truly visionary, as do some lines following, lines 21–23, in which the 'beacon' alternates from garments and colours to blood-soaked wood to treasure-encrusted reliquary (a container for relics). To the untrained eye the effect is pure psychedelia, but we should note that the meaning can all be explained in terms of biblical symbolism.

The dreamer's vision is implicitly disturbing rather than aimlessly hallu-cinogenic. Every image in this poem has its own story. The next image con-tains another reminiscence of what happened to Christ's body on the Cross:

> Hwæðere ic þurh þæt gold   ongytan meahte
> > But through that gold I could perceive
> earmra ærgewin   þæt hit ærest ongan
> > the former struggle of wretched people, when it first began
> swætan on þa swiðran healfe   eall ic wæs mid sorgum gedrefed.
> > to sweat on the right side. I was completely depressed by sorrow;
> Forht ic wæs for þære fægran ge syhðe
> > I was frightened by that fair sight. (*The Dream of the Rood*, lines 18–21)

At the opening of the vision 'all fair beings throughout time and cre-ation' had looked on the Tree of Life; the poet's word *forðgesceaft* (line 10) combined 'creation' (*gesceaft*, a physical concept) with a suggestion of move-ment and change in time, especially in future time (*forð*: compare modern English 'forth', 'forward'). Now, in lines 18–21, we hear not of the future but of the past. The word *ærgewin* ('former struggle') implies that the Crucifixion was 'ancient' (for OE *ær-* ('former'), compare the expression 'ere long'). This ancient war is recalled, paradoxically, by a beautiful and surreal image: the tree begins to 'sweat' on its right side. At Easter, a chant was sung which saw Christ's body as the new temple, with baptism as a saving stream springing from the wound in his side. The Latin chant began with the words *Vidi aquam*: '*I saw water* coming from the temple, from its right side, Alleluia. And all those to whom that water came were saved, and say Alleluia, allelluia.' When on the Cross the dead body of Christ was wounded by the spear, 'at once blood and water came out' (John's Gospel, chapter 19, verse 34). This was an important image: the blood was seen as an image of the wine of the Eucharist, Jesus' own 'blood' in the Last Supper; and the water is an image of baptism. In this way, the essentials of what Christianity had to offer were seen to flow from Christ's death on the Cross.

Blood in Old English poetry was sometimes called 'battle-sweat' (*hilde-swat*), as if fighting was a grim athletics, as if blood was produced naturally by such strenuous activity. In *The Dream*, line 20, the phrase *swætan on þa swiðran healfe* ('to sweat on the right side') could be translated 'to bleed' as well as 'to sweat', for the riddling image refers to both primary images of salvation, Eucharist as well as baptism, in the liquid which flows out of Christ's side on the Cross. In Christian art, as in *The Dream*, Christ is usually seen as wounded on his right side. This is because Christ's body was seen as replacing, for Christians, the Old Testament Temple of Jerusalem: in a vision told by the prophet Ezekiel (chapter 47, verse 2), of the wonderful Temple that would some day be built in Jerusalem when the Jews got back from exile by the river of Babylon, Ezekiel saw a stream of saving water flowed from the Temple's right side. As we have seen, this passage was made into a Christian chant, *Vidi aquam*, sung each day during Easter week to celebrate how Christ's death on Good Friday had brought salvation and baptism. The Old English poetic technique is essentially that of a riddle which invites us to find the right answer, i.e. the truth, through various layers of imagery. For poets such as that of *The Dream*, this technique became a perfect means of presenting some complex Christian symbolism to an audience who regularly sang chants like *Vidi aquam*.

The dreamer in the poem, however, is imagined as being far less educated than the people who heard or read this poem. We could think of the dreamer as an untutored Everyman. As yet he doesn't understand this vivid riddling image, of salvation flowing from the visionary Tree. So, even though the tree is 'fair' to him, he says it causes him 'fear'. It is only when the Tree speaks, thereby truly becoming a messenger (or 'angel'), that the riddle is resolved for the dreamer: and his life is transformed by the message. Indeed, the Cross later will explicitly urge the dreamer to become a 'messenger' in his turn for other listeners (line 95). In solving the riddle for the dreamer, that of the opening vision, the Cross gives an account of its own experience at the Crucifixion. This narrative perspective, a normally lifeless object telling its own story, is called *prosopopoeia*. Here, and in some Cross *Riddles*, Old English literature is the only place where this is found. It looks as if many Anglo-Saxons still believed trees could talk.

Not only that, but the Tree's account of the Crucifixion is itself highly unusual. The story the Cross tells us contradicts, in important ways, the narratives of the four gospels by Matthew, Mark, Luke and John. In the gospels, the Cross reaches Mount Calvary together with Christ: either carried by Christ himself (John's gospel); or carried, in Christ's company, by Simon of Cyrene (Matthew, Mark and Luke). In *The Dream*, however, there is no mention of Jesus carrying the Cross or of Simon of Cyrene. Instead, the Cross tells how, while still a living tree, it was 'torn up from its roots' by its enemies where it had stood at the edge of a wood. To be torn up by your roots is to be forced into exile and to be an exile was an important and moving image in Anglo-Saxon poetry (p. 145). In one of the gospels, Christ on the way to Calvary refers to himself as a green tree cut down and this image of the green tree may have inspired the poet: 'For if they do this to the green tree, what shall be done when the wood is dry?' (Luke 23: 31).

Its enemies carry the exiled tree, by force, to 'a hill' (*on beorg*, line 32). Literally, Old English *beorg* means 'mound of death', a 'barrow', and thus the poet alludes to the place as a killing ground, Calvary or Golgotha ('the hill of skulls'). The tree is thus standing on the mound when it sees Christ 'hastening with great courage' (*efstan elne mycle*, line 34) to choose his death on it. Christ is here no lamb led to the slaughter. The poet has deliberately altered the gospel narratives so as to bring about a confrontation between Christ, heroically choosing his own death, and the horrified Cross. Anglo-Saxon warriors were supposed to defend their lord to the death, to kill his enemies. In this case the Cross, a loyal lieutenant, is being asked to break the fundamental rule of Anglo-Saxon heroic society and to become, not the defender of its lord, but his killer. The Cross still remembers, with agonised vividness, that it could have taken vengeance on its lord's killers but that, in obedience to 'the Lord's word', it stood fast and bore him to his death:

> þær ic þa ne dorste   ofer dryhtnes word
> > There and then I dared not, against the lord's word
> bugan oððe berstan   þa ic bifian geseah
> > bow down or break, although I saw quaking
> eorðan sceatas   ealle ic mihte
> > the surfaces of the earth: I could have
> feondas gefyllan   hwæðere ic fæste stod.
> > felled all the fiends [i.e. enemies]: but I stood fast. (*The Dream of the Rood*, lines 35–8)

Where did the poet get the courage to retell the story of Christ's death in such a disturbing way? In the poem, the Tree–Cross emphasises that it was its lord's killer. It dramatises its fears that doing this to Christ would be to betray him. It repeats its amazement that its own lord prevented the natural reactions of his follower, to avenge him on his enemies. This poem emphasises, in a way no other Christian poem does, past or present, English or other, the ambiguity of the role of the Cross and its complicity in Christ's death. *The Dream* makes the Cross uniquely an anti-hero rather than a hero. By doing this the poem draws attention also to the strangeness of Christ's choice of death on the Cross. For the Anglo-Saxons, Christ also was a new and strange kind of hero: one who took no vengeance on his enemies, who forbids his follower to avenge him on them, but who permits himself to be mocked by them, together with the Cross:

> bysmeredon hie unc butu ætgædere,   eall ic wæs mid blode gestemed.
>> they mocked the pair of us, both together; I was all drenched with blood
>
> begoten of þæs guman sidan   siððan he hæfde his gast onsended.
>> poured from the man's side, after he had sent forth his spirit.
>> (*The Dream of the Rood*, lines 48–9)

Here, at the moment of Christ's death, the union between the Cross and Christ becomes particularly intense. OE *unc* in the phrase *unc butu ætgædere* is the dual form of *us* ('us'), one that says there were just two of them and no one else. This is reinforced not only with *butu* ('both') but also with *ætgædere* ('together'). It would be difficult to imagine a stronger way of emphasising the close union between two people. The Cross is united to Christ in apparent defeat: by their enemies mocking them and by the blood that, just after his death, flowed from the spear wound of Christ's side. We have already seen the ambiguity of this wound: it made it clear that Christ had really died and was not just unconscious; but it was seen also as the moment when baptism and the Eucharist sprang from his body.

So the heroic ethic is taken into another dimension. Christ, this strange hero who forbids the Cross to avenge him, embraces the Cross as his fate. For its own part, the Cross, agonised and uncomprehending, loyally becomes his slayer. It says 'I trembled when the warrior embraced me' (*bifode ic þa me se beorn ymbclypte*, in *The Dream of the Rood*, line 42). The battle that follows is not of this world. It embraces the cosmos and in it the cosmic powers of evil and darkness seem to win:

> þystro hæfdon
> The darknesses had

> bewrigen mid wolcnum   wealdendes hræw
> > wrapped in clouds the ruler's body,
> scirne sciman   sceadu forð eode
> > the bright shining one. Shadow went forth,
> <u>wann</u> under wolcnum   weop eal gesceaft
> > <u>struggled</u> under the clouds. All creation wept,
> cwiðdon cyninges fyll   crist wæs on rode
> > lamented the killing of the king. Christ was on the Rood.
> > > (*The Dream of the Rood*, lines 52–6)

The translation just given follows the word order and the word divisions in the manuscript, ignoring the manuscript punctuation. But medieval readers read slowly; chewing over each text until they got it by heart. Medieval readers got to know a lot fewer books than we do, but they 'made their own' of them, got them by heart, in a way which is quite unfamiliar to us. As we will see in the next chapter, the Venerable Bede shows that readers 'tasted' a text, when he says that Cædmon, the first named English poet, learned biblical stories 'like a clean beast ruminating' (see p. 192). Readers of *The Dream* would have naturally 'tasted', as it were, 'repunctuated', this poem by putting their pauses in different places as they chewed the text over. The manuscript punctuation suggests that one could pause after *hræw*, and again after *eode*. This style of punctuation allows for a flexibility of meaning which cannot be rendered easily in modern English translation. So, for example, the line between the punctuation marks could be taken as follows. Not as 'the bright shining one. Shadow went forth' (*scirne sciman. Sceadu forð eode*); but as:

> . scirne sciman   sceadu forðeode .
> > The shadow oppressed [*þeow*, a slave: *for-ðeo[w]de*
> > literally 'made a slave of'] the bright shining one.
> > > (*The Dream of the Rood*, line 54)

On the next line, the word *wann* has been translated in the longer earlier passage as 'struggled', i.e. as the past tense of the verb *winnan* 'to struggle', like modern English *won* (from *win*). But *wann* here could also be taken as the adjective *wann*, which means 'dark' (modern English *wan*). Thus the phrase *wann under wolcnum*, taken as 'dark under the clouds' could be interpreted either with *sceadu* ('the shadow, dark under the clouds') or with *eal gesceaft* ('dark under the clouds, all creation wept'). The climax of the passage, on line 56, *Crist wæs on rode*, uses the word *rod* (rood'). This word was first used a little earlier in the poem, in 'as a rood I was reared up' (*rod wæs ic aræred*, line 44). So, at the moment when it bears Christ, the Tree of Life finally becomes the *rod*, the Cross. The nineteenth-century scholars who gave the

poem the title *The Dream of the Rood* sensed, and highlighted, the importance of the word in the poem's narrative. The poem dramatises the precise
moment when the old Anglian World-Tree became the Christian Rood.

The poet has retold the gospel accounts of Christ's death so as to present
it as a struggle between 'the bright shining one' and the powers of darkness
and at the same time an encounter between Christ, 'brave in the sight of
many' and the startled Cross. It was not usual to see Christ's death in such
terms; rather, the image of the struggle between an heroic Christ and the
powers of darknesss was traditionally used of Christ's original decision, as
Son of God, 'born from the Father before all ages' (as the Christian creeds
put it) to descend from heaven and become human. The Gospel of Luke tells
us about the 'Annunciation': that the Angel Gabriel was sent to Nazareth
to announce to the Virgin Mary that, in her womb, the Messiah should
take on human flesh and a human nature (Luke 1: 28–37), and to ask for her
agreement to this. Gabriel's (Hebrew) name was interpreted as 'the courage
[or strength] of God' (Latin *fortitudo Dei*). Here is how the Annunciation was
imagined by Gregory the Great, in a passage which was to be paraphrased
repeatedly by Anglo-Saxon writers, from Bede in the early eighth century
down to Ælfric in the late tenth century, whenever they retold the story of
the Annunciation:

> Therefore to the virgin Mary is sent Gabriel, who is called 'the courage [or
> strength] of God' (*Dei fortitudo*): for he came to announce Him who deigned to
> appear, humble, in order to defeat the powers of the air (*aereas potestates*). About
> him it is said by the Psalmist: Lift up your gates, o ye princes, and be ye lifted
> up, O eternal gates: and the King of Glory shall enter in. Who is this king of
> glory? [Psalm 23 (24): 7–8a] The Lord who is strong and mighty: the Lord
> mighty in battle' [Ps. 23 (24): 8b]: and again, 'The Lord of hosts, he is the King
> of Glory' [Ps. 23 (24): 10]. He was therefore to be announced by The Courage
> [or Strength] of God who, Lord of Hosts and powerful in battle, came to make
> war against the powers of the air.

Gregory the Great, who had written this account of the Annunciation
as the first stage in Christ's battle against Satan (a battle which would be
decisively won by Christ's heroic death), was particularly important for
Anglo-Saxon writers, because it was he who in 597 sent the Roman monk
Augustine to Canterbury, to organise the conversion of Kent.

Thanks to Gregory, it was natural for an Anglo-Saxon poet to imagine
the Annunciation and Crucifixion as stages in the same cosmic battle. *The
Dream*, too, imagines the situation of the startled Cross at the Crucifixion
in terms which recall Mary's dilemma at the Annunciation: how could she,
a virgin who (early medieval writers believed) had taken a vow to remain

a virgin, become a mother and bear Christ into life? She needed Gabriel to reassure her and resolve her dilemma (on Calvary, of course, the Cross would get no such reassurance in its terrible dilemma that it was required to bear its lord to his death). As it happens, both the Annunciation and the Crucifixion were believed to have happened on the same day in the calendar year. That day was 25 March, which is also the original date in the Roman calendar of the Spring Equinox, when the sun's light begins to get the upper hand over the winter darkness. Similar cosmic imagery lies behind the celebration of Christmas on 25 December, the Winter Solstice in the Roman calendar and the ancient Mithradatic Roman feast of Sol Invictus, the unconquered Sun: at the darkest time of the year, Christ the 'Light of the World' was seen to make a triumphal entry into the world where darkness had reigned up to then. In its paragraph on 25 March, *The Old English Martyrology*, a work from the ninth century, beautifully relates the coincidence of Annunciation and Crucifixion to the blossoming of plants in the breezes of Spring:

> On the twenty-fifth day of [March] the angel Gabriel came to St Mary the first time with God's errand, and on this day St Mary became pregnant in the town of Nazareth by the angel's word and by the hearing of her ears, like the trees when they blossom under the breeze of the wind (*swa þas treowa ðonne hie blostmiað þurh þæs windes blæd*) [. . .] After two and thirty years and three months Christ was crucified on the same day, and when he was on the cross, the creation immediately proved that he was the true God.

In *The Dream*, lines 52–4, as we have seen, the darkness seems to defeat the 'bright shining one'. Paradoxically, it is just after his death that phrases asserting his power and divinity begin to flood into the poem: the Cross bows down to give Christ's dead body to his followers, and they 'seized there Almighty God' (*genamon hie þær ælmihtigne God*, line 60); as they contemplate his dead body, we are told that 'there they beheld the Lord of Heaven' (*beheoldon hie ðær heofenes Dryhten*, line 64). Educated Anglo-Saxon Christians would have been aware that *fortitudo Dei*, the 'courage of' or 'strength of God', was made manifest at the Annunciation, when God the Son took on human nature. As the Epistle for Palm Sunday put it each year, the Lord then 'emptied himself, taking the form of a slave, being born in human likeness and being found in human form' (Philippians 2: 7). The Northumbrian poet of *The Dream* now retold the Crucifixion to make it clear that the courage of God and his war against the powers of darkness, central to the Annunciation, was equally central to the Crucifixion, when Christ 'humbled himself and became obedient to the point of death – even death on a cross' (Philippians 2: 8). The Cross thus emphasises that the Lord has honoured the Cross above all trees in the same way that he honoured his mother, Mary, above all women (lines 90–94).

The Dream, centred on a narrative that sees Christ's death in terms of his incarnation and birth, ends by placing the Crucifixion in the perspective of human history (as the poet understood it), from the fall of Adam to the last Judgement. The Tree tells the dreamer to tell people that it is the Cross, the selfsame 'tree of glory' (*wuldres beam*, line 97) on which Christ suffered:

> for mancynnes   manegum synnum
>> for mankind's many sins
> ond Adomes   ealdgewyhrtum
>> and Adam's ancient actions
> deað he þær <u>byrigde</u>   hwæðere eft dryhten aras
>> he <u>tasted</u> death there, but the Lord rose again
>>> (*The Dream of the Rood*, lines 99–101)

Line 101 turns on a pun: the word *byrigde* means not only 'he tasted' but also 'he buried', i.e. Adam tasted death in the apple at the beginning of human history, Christ at the end of it buried death by rising again from the dead. Christ was known as the 'second Adam' for this reason. The poem moves from Adam to the Last Judgement within six lines (100–105). On that day, fear will reduce all to silence: at the moment of Judgement, human beings will no longer be *reordberend*, 'voice-bearers' as at the beginning of the poem (line 3), but rather 'bearers of the rood' to the extent that during their lives they have borne a symbol of the rood. None of these people needs be afraid:

> Ne þearf ðær þonne ænig   unforht wesan
>> Then no one need be very much afraid
> þe him ær in breostum bereð   beacna selest
>> who previously has borne the best of symbols on his breast.
>>> (*The Dream of the Rood*, lines 117–18)

The first moment that the startled Cross saw Christ, it described him as 'hastening with great courage' (*efstan elne mycle*, line 34). The end of the poem puts this image in a cosmic perspective. Christ is hastening, like a warrior into a duel, because he has a great expedition to perform. It will lead him to raid hell and take from the devil the souls previously held in darkness, in the devil's power: 'joy was renewed, with happiness and bliss, for those who had previously suffered burning' (lines 148–9). Christ's expedition is completed when, in the final line of the poem, he leads the souls he has saved to heaven, 'where his homeland was' (*þær his eðel wæs*, line 156).

The poet implies that Christ's victory over the powers of darkness has been as wide ranging as the sun's own course, by punning again, this time between *se sunu* ('the son [of God]') and *seo sunne* ('the sun'):

> se <u>sunu</u> wæs sigorfæst   on þam siðfate
>> The <u>Son (/sun)</u> was victorious on the expedition,
> mihtig ond spedig
>> mighty and successful. (*The Dream of the Rood*, lines 150–51)

This is how the poet of *The Dream*, among many other subtleties, transforms Christ the warrior into a solar hero and the Cross into his agonised friend and lieutenant. More importantly for the poet's audience, perhaps, he also seems to make his English ancestors, heathens the lot of them, into people as worthy of redemption as the souls Jesus rescued from hell.

Christianity in Northumbria: the first 70 years

The Vercelli Book, like the other three major manuscripts of Anglo-Saxon poetry that have survived (Nowell Codex, Junius Book, Exeter Book), was written towards the end of the Anglo-Saxon period near the end of the tenth century. But versions of *The Dream* must have existed, perhaps simply as songs passed on orally from singer to singer, for some three centuries before that. There are various reasons to believe that *The Dream* was originally a Northumbrian poem and that it was composed early, perhaps in the 680s or 690s. So the poem is probably ancient, but, as we have seen, it is sophisticated. A sketch of the first 70 years of Christianity in Northumbria, from 619 to 689, will make the poet's cosmopolitan background clearer.

We could say that 619 was the year Christianity began in Northumbria. This is when the daughter of King Æthelberht of Kent travelled north to become the queen of King Edwin of Deira (present-day Yorkshire). Edwin (ruled 616–33) was still heathen and so his Christian princess, whose name was Æthelburh, took a chaplain with her to convert him. He was an Italian called Paulinus who had been working in Kent as a missionary for 18 years. But the fact that Paulinus spoke the language made little difference to the Northumbrians. At this time, it has been argued, they worshipped gods called *uani* including the main devil whose name was variously Ingui, Ing or 'god of the world' (North 1997: 176–9, 323–6). Paulinus would change these people to his new ways and then they would slide back into their old ones. This game of cat and mouse went on for six years. Furthermore, there was another missionary in Edwin's court. This was a prince named Rhun ab Urbgen from a Welsh kingdom in Cumbria, who was hoping to claim Edwin for the Welsh, not the Roman, church. The Pope saw to it accordingly that Paulinus was consecrated bishop of York on 21 July 625.

Paulinus, in turn, saw to it that Edwin became Christian, according to Bede who tells the story (*History of the English Church and People*, Book II, Chapters 9–14). How this happened is not so clear, although Edwin did promise (for a while) to become Christian after surviving an attempt on his life on Easter Sunday 626. Nearly a year later the king, still mulling it over, was in council not far from Goodmanham, a cultic centre near Market Weighton in eastern Yorkshire. Suddenly his high priest, Coifi, announced that serving their religion had brought him no tangible rewards and he was ready to trade in his old faith for the new one. At this point, according to Bede, an unnamed thane spoke up comparing the life of man to the swift flight of a sparrow through the fire-lit hall on a winter's night, in through one gable and out the other. Darkness – a brief light – darkness: 'So it is that of what went before this life or of what follows, we know nothing.' Edwin was so impressed that he publicly renounced his idols and asked Coifi which of his heathen priests would destroy them. Coifi volunteered. On the king's stallion and armed with a spear, Coifi rode out against his own shrine in Goodmanham, cast the spear inside and set fire to the place as well. Paulinus' role in this is unknown, although one scholar thinks it was he who did this under the name of 'Coifi' (North 1997: 330–40). Hereupon Edwin had a church built in York and Paulinus baptised him and then thousands of his people in the interior of Deira and Bernicia (Northumberland).

Alas, it all went wrong. Six years later, in 633, Edwin was killed in battle by Penda, the heathen king of Mercia, and the Christian king Caedwalla of Wales. Paulinus fled back to Kent with Queen Æthelburh, leaving Northumbria in the sole care of a deacon in York. There was a wild relapse in the kingdom for two years until Oswald became king (ruled 634–42). Oswald's father had driven Edwin into exile where he tried to kill him, so we know that the life–death decisions of heroic poetry all happened for real in the politics of Northumbria at this time. During Edwin's reign Oswald had lived in exile in the Irish monastery of Iona in Western Scotland. So it was no surprise that when he took over Northumbria in 634, he brought Irish missionaries who set about converting the local heathens rather more successfully than Paulinus had done. The best of these was Bishop Aidan of Lindisfarne. Aidan arrived from Iona in 635 and by the time he died in 651, he had made Northumbria into a Christian country.

But the Roman connection with Northumbria was by no means dead. Oswiu (ruled 642–70) took over the kingdom after his brother Oswald, keeping the Irish clergy on station. While in exile with his brother, he had lived with a Gaelic princess of the clan Uí Níaill (guess how we spell that now). As king, Oswiu continued to observe Irish Christian practices even while Eanfled Edwin's daughter, his wife in Northumbria, followed Roman ones. Oswiu later married a Welsh princess, Riemmelth, which allows for a certain admixture of Welsh Christianity as well (on the Welsh here, see Cædmon in the next chapter). The fact that Oswiu was also connected to the Strathclyde Welsh and the Picts of western Scotland goes to show that Northumbria was then swirling with peoples of diverse origins whose customs caused the Roman Church the utmost concern. The Roman Church calculated Easter Sunday differently from the Irish and Welsh and there were other doctrinal differences. To settle the growing disputes, Oswiu called a church council, the famous 'Synod', that was held in the monastery of Whitby in 664. After many heated debates, the council opted to follow the Roman Catholic model, but many Irish and Welsh Christians carried on regardless until the end of the seventh century.

In Oswiu's court in the early years was a young thane by the name of Biscop son of Baduca [/bah:duca/]. Biscop was probably christened by Paulinus as a baby in the late 620s. The meaning 'bishop' suggests that his parents gave him his name from the Italian's official title. As a young man Biscop went down to Rome in 652, the first of six visits. In Kent, on the way, he picked up the even younger Wilfrid (634–709), a fellow Northumbrian, whose future in the church of their land was to be equally glorious, if rather more controversial. Following his second trip to Rome, Biscop became a monk in Lérins in southern France in 666 when he became known as Benedict Biscop after St Benedict of Nursia (*c.* 480–543), the great Italian monastic reformer. Benedict (we will call him) rose through the church hierarchy, becoming abbot of a monastery in Canterbury after his third visit to Rome, from where he had escorted the Greek Archbishop Theodore (602–90) to Canterbury. But Benedict wanted to go back home. He went to Rome for the fourth time and bought lots of books for a new monastery in Northumbria, (Monk)wearmouth, which he dedicated to St Peter (like St Peter's on the Vatican hill in Rome) in 674. The church there was finished about two years later with the aid of Frankish stonemasons and glaziers who had learned their trade from Italians. But that wasn't enough. Benedict went back to Rome again and bought more books, as well as icons of Mary and the Apostles, with which he adorned his new monastery in Wearmouth. In about 681 he persuaded King Ecgfrith [/e:dge-frith/] of Northumbria (670–85, son of Oswiu), to build a new monastery nearby in Jarrow. In 685 Benedict went back to Rome for more books, which he put in Jarrow, along with a new abbot named Ceolfrith [/chay:ol-frith/]. Benedict died in 689, one of the most energetic new Christians there ever was. One reason for all this potted biography is to introduce Benedict Biscop: in his monasteries at Wearmouth and Jarrow, the Venerable Bede (673–735) lived and worked and we shall see more of him in the next chapter.

Coming back to Wearmouth from Rome in 679, Benedict brought with him a man from Italy called John the Archcantor. The title 'Archcantor' tells us that he was in charge of the liturgy, that is, of all the public religious ceremonies, at St Peter's in Rome. It was clearly a great coup for Benedict Biscop to make a friend of such a distinguished singer and to persuade him to come to teach the monks of St Peter's new monastery at Wearmouth just how ceremonies were carried out at St Peter's own tomb in St Peter's on the Vatican. Monks flocked to Wearmouth from all over Northumbria to learn the latest chants 'viva voce' from John. The monks of St Peter's in Rome had just recently composed a unique set of prayers for Mass on 25 March (the author was very likely John himself: he was, after all, their liturgical expert and their abbot). The title of the Vatican Mass for that day was 'The Annunciation of the Lord and his Passion' and the prayers said during the Mass explicitly linked the Annunciation to the Passion. In this way St Peter's produced a rationale for celebrating the Annunciation, the joyful feast which celebrated how God became human in Christ, during the penitential season of Lent, which led up to the commemoration of Christ's Passion and death: no other basilica found such a solution. Because 25 March, which nearly always falls during Lent or Holy Week, was the anniversary both of the Annunciation and of the Crucifixion, the conception and death of Christ could be celebrated together and thus seen as closely linked. But John had another important job to do in England. He acted as the representative of the pope at a church council held at Hatfield, at which English clerics (who included the Greek Theodore of Canterbury, Bishop Wilfrid of York, Benedict Biscop and Ceolfrith) solemnly declared their belief that Christ had a real human will of his own: in effect, that he had human courage. Some emperors at Constantinople and their court theologians had specu-lated that Christ had no distinct human will: that it was, as it were, sub-merged in the divine will. But the western Church and English theologians held instead that Christ's human will was vital to his humanity. The declara-tion at Hatfield implied that to be fully human you had to have human courage, a will of your own. This idea must have strongly appealed to the English, because, as we have seen, courage (*mōd*: compare modern English *mood* and modern German *Mut*) was the central human quality celebrated in their heroic poetry. That Christ was 'modig', courageous, in choosing his death on the Cross is, of course, a major theme in *The Dream of the Rood*. The western Church and Rome held that Christ's will was uniquely incorruptible because he had been born from the Virgin Mary; thus, when he returned to Wearmouth with John the Archantor in 679 Benedict brought back from Rome an icon of the Virgin Mary and hung it (flanked by icons of the 12 apostles) over the altar at St Peter's Wearmouth. Henceforth Benedict's monks, each time that they recalled Christ's Passion and death at Mass, would also recall his incarnation by means of the icon of the Virgin just over the altar. Anglo-Saxons were facing the most important theological issue then facing the Christian Church in east and west when they emphasised the courage or strength (*fortitudo*) which united the Annunciation and the Passion of Christ. The British and Irish churches agreed with the English and Romans that 25 March was the anniversary of the first Good Friday, as well as of the Annunciation: thus, to emphasise that Mary at the Annunciation and the Cross at the Passion had both encountered *fortitudo Dei* was a way of getting over the disputes, about how to calculate Easter, which had earlier caused tension between the English and the Irish clerics. To emphasise that Christ was conceived and died near the Spring Equinox, and that he had been born near the Winter Solstice, days on which the sun triumphed over winter darkness, enabled Christians to characterise Christ as the solar hero, the 'Light of the World' who defeats the powers of darkness. As we have seen, with the poet's likely pun on *sunu* and *sunne*, this is also an attribute of Christ in *The Dream of the Rood*. We know that the poem goes back at least to the lifetime of Bede, that is, to the early eighth century. The main reason we know this is that another version of *The Dream*, much older than its text in the Vercelli Book, is found on the sides of a stone cross which was carved on the far west side of Northumbria.

The Dream on the Ruthwell Cross

Ruthwell is now in Scotland, in Dumfriesshire, on the Solway Firth, some 20 miles west of Carlisle. The cross was erected about 730–40. It may have been commissioned by Bishop Acca of Hexham (died 740) or by Bishop Pehthelm of Whithorn (also on Solway Firth, to the west of Ruthwell) who died in 731. Both bishops were friends of Bede and both would have been fully in touch with the major theological issues of the previous 50 years, including the Council of Hatfield. Ruthwell was at the north-western borders of Anglian territory, on land which a generation before had been part of the British kingdom of Rheged. The parish church in Ruthwell still has its amazing tall stone high cross (about six metres high). No thanks to the Scottish Reformation, whose agents smashed it up in 1642. It had to be pieced together again and is still missing its cross-piece (the present cross-piece or transom is a nineteenth-century reconstruction). In order to increase the height of the cross, the designer used two separate blocks of stone, one atop the other. The two broad sides of the cross display a carefully conceived and executed theological programme of panels representing scenes from the gospels, along with Latin inscriptions called *incipits* or 'cues': prompts, effectively, for liturgical readings and chants. The side with St John the Baptist at the top (the so-called 'north side') was probably meant to face west, allowing an observer to sight the sun as it rose behind the cross. That the upper stone should lay great emphasis on St John the Baptist is particularly interesting. John, the cousin of Jesus, was also the forerunner or 'messenger' ('angelus': Mark 1: 2) of Jesus' teaching. The Gospel of John says that 'he was not the light, but was to give testimony to the light' (1: 8). Thus the early medieval church, which celebrated Christ's birth and death on the 'growing days', near the Spring Solstice and Winter Equinox when the sun conquered the winter darkness, celebrated John on the 'lessening days' (conception on 24 September, near the Autumn Equinox; birth on 24 June, near the Summer Solstice), the times of the year when the sun became less powerful: because, as John the Baptist says later in the Gospel of John, 'he [Christ] must grow greater, but I must grow less' (3: 30).

If we remember that it was usual to see crosses as symbols of Christ, the narrow sides of the Ruthwell are the symbolic centre of the monument: after all, we have seen the symbolic importance of the wound on Christ's right side. At Ruthwell, each narrow side is covered by the largest and most imposing visual image on the cross: great inhabited vine scrolls. The vine scrolls were clearly designed as images of the Tree of Life: Christianized versions, in the sophisticated new visual language of relief sculpture, of the ancient Germanic World Tree. The Vercelli 'Dream of the Rood' begins, as we have seen, with vivid images of the Tree of Life. The Ruthwell designer may have been inspired by early sung versions of the 'Dream' in the brilliant decision to provide captions for these two great Tree of Life images: these captions explain the new Christian significance of that Tree: that it has become the rood on which Christ, dying heroically, brought life to the world.

These captions are carved in runes, the ancient alphabet which the Germanic peoples developed, for inscriptions on wood, stone and ivory. The narrative runs across the top margin of the lower of the two stones of which the Ruthwell Cross is built and then proceeds in a great column of runes down the right side of the Tree of Life. No doubt the vine scroll, and the whole Cross, was originally as brightly painted as the Ahenny Cross must have been: perhaps in brilliant blues, golds and reds that would recall the gems and gold of the beginning of *The Dream*. Damage to the cross has deprived us not only of the colours but also of the end of each column of runes. The Ruthwell editor reduced the narrative to its essentials. He starts with the dilemma of the Cross, which must kill its own lord, 'Almighty God':

> [+ ond]geredæ hinæ god almehttig   þa he walde on galgu gistiga
>> Almighty God stripped himself. When he willed to mount the gallows,
> modig f[ore allæ] men
>> Courageous before all men
> b[uga] {ic ni dorstæ} [. . .]
>> I dared not bow [. . .] (Ruthwell Cross poem, lines 1–3)

This is a revelation of God Himself, for it is 'Almighty God' who strips himself here, 'brave before all men' (which can mean both 'brave in the sight of all humans' and 'braver than all humans'). The human will and courage of Christ, the central issue at the Council of Hatfield, is also clearly the central issue in this narrative, as is the human predicament of the Cross which sees that it must bear Christ to his death. The second column of runes, to the left of the Tree of Life, further emphasises the Cross's dilemma, and brings the narrative precisely to the moment when, just after Christ's death, the Cross is drenched by the blood from Christ's pierced side. Cross and Christ, mocked by their enemies, are, as in the later poem, unified as closely as language can express it: note that the Anglo-Saxon dual number (here, *ungket*, 'the two of us') again appears, and is again reinforced by *ba* ('both') and *ætgadre* ('together'):

> [Ahof] ic riicnæ kyningc [.]
>> I [lifted up] a powerful king
> hêafunæs h[l]afard   hælda ic ni dorstæ
>> the Lord of Heaven I dared not tilt
> [b]ismæra[d]u ungket men ba æt[g]ad[re   i]c [wæs m]iþ blodi bist[e]mi[d]
>> men insulted the pair of us together; I was drenched with blood
> bi{goten of þæs gumu sida}
>> po{ured from the man's side} [. . .] (Ruthwell Cross poem, lines 5–8)

To read the two runic columns in the order in which the designer has placed them, people have to move from right to left, around the cross in the same direction of the sun: sunwise. When they continue around the monument, they come to the column of sculpted scenes on the broad side (which would originally have faced east). On the shaft of the cross, the first panel is a moving scene of the Annunciation.

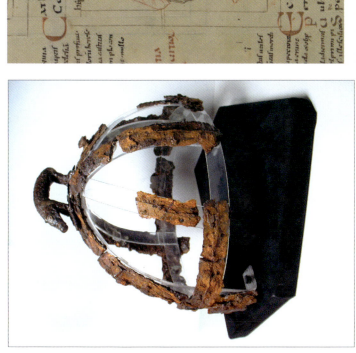

Plate 1 The pagan protective boar figure on the Benty Grange helmet – its back has holes to accommodate bristles (courtesy of Sheffield Galleries and Museums Trust)

Plate 2 An Anglo-Saxon manuscript of Prudentius' *Psychomachia* (courtesy of the Master and Fellows of Corpus Christi College, Cambridge)

Plate 3   The York helmet, with a Christian inscription cross-wise over the top (courtesy of York Archaeological Trust)

Plate 4 The Franks Casket (courtesy of the British Museum)

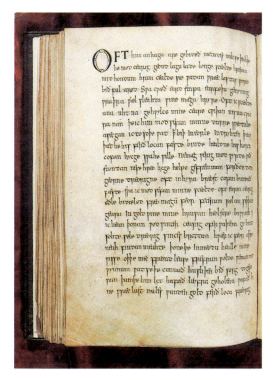

Plate 5 The Exeter Book of Anglo-Saxon poetry: first page of *The Wanderer* (by permission of the Dean and Chapter of Exeter)

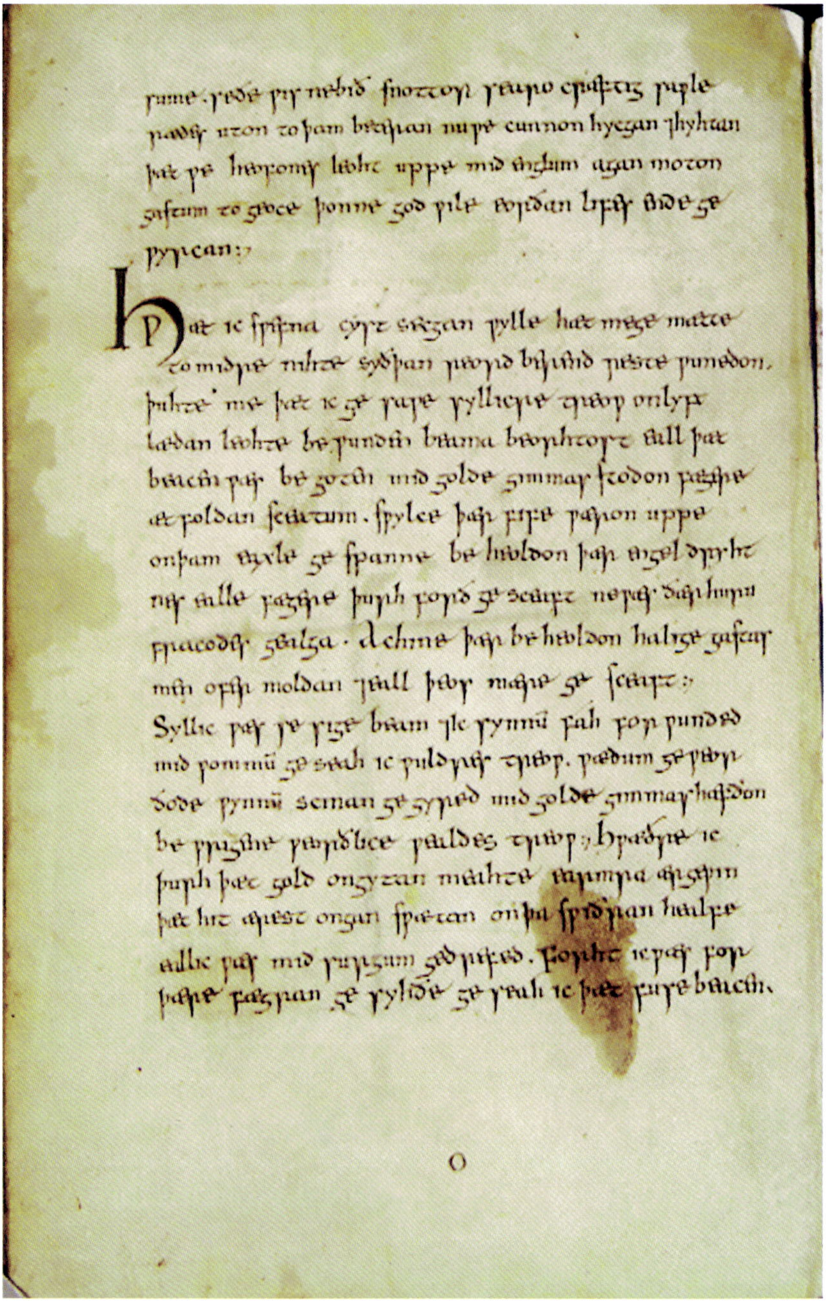

Plate 6 The Vercelli Book, opening of *The Dream of the Rood* (courtesy of the Cathedral Library, Vercelli)

Plate 7 Twelfth-century mosaic in San Clemente Church, Rome

Plate 8 The five gems of the Ahenny Stone High Cross (photograph by P. Belzeaux, published by Zochiaque)

Plate 9 The Ruthwell High Cross (courtesy of Ross Trench–Jellicoe)

Plate 10 Gabriel with Mary: Annunciation panel on the Ruthwell Cross (copyright the Department of Archaeology, Durham University, photographer: T. Middlemass)

Here the Angel Gabriel (*fortitudo Dei*, 'the courage or strength of God') advances from the left, towards the Virgin Mary on the right. He advances, and she, startled, draws back: his halo is four centimetres in from the left of the panel, while Mary's halo touches the right side of the panel. Mary's right hand, pointing at her own body just under her chin, expresses how surprised she is (as though she is saying 'Who, me? How can it happen that I, a virgin, can bear the Messiah into life?'). Her left hand clutches her garment in front of her body, as though she were alarmed. The lower hem of the garment swings back so that invades the lower right margin of the panel. The designer of the Ruthwell Cross provided a visual commentary on the dilemma of the startled Cross in the runic caption to the Tree of Life: here Mary encounters 'the courage or strength of God' in the Angel Gabriel, as the Cross will encounter 'Almighty God [. . .] brave before all men' in Christ's advance to his death. A later sculptor provided a Crucifixion scene, on the base just below the Annunciation panel, as though to confirm the similarity between the two narratives.

The caption to the second image of the Tree of Life, the opposite narrow side of the cross, proclaims that the tree has become a rood, a liturgical cross:

> [+] kris[t] wæs on rodi.
>> Christ was on the Rood.
> hweþræ þer fus[æ] fêârran kw[o]mu
>> However, eager ones came thither from afar,
> [æ]þþilæ til anum   ic þæt al bi[hêâld]
>> The noble ones came together: I beheld all that.
> sa[ræ] ic w[æ]s mi[þ] s[or]gu[m] gidrœ[fi]d   h[n]ag {ic þam secgum til handa}
>> I was terribly afflicted with sorrows: I bowed {to the hands of the men}.
>> (Ruthwell Cross poem, lines 9–12)

Now everything in the narrative is transformed. In the first caption, the Cross was surrounded by enemies who mock 'the pair of us both together'; now, in the second caption, noble and eager followers come from afar to gather 'together', 'into one' (*til anum*) at the rood. The two captions were carefully edited so as to contrast the two possible human reactions to Christ's death: mockery (in the first half of the Ruthwell edition) or faith (in the second half). In the first caption, the dramatic tension of the narrative stemmed from the dilemma of the Cross, which could not bend, but had to stand fast; but now that Christ is dead, it can bow down to hand on Christ's dead body to his followers. The idea that the Cross should bow down, to present the body of Christ to his followers, is found neither in the gospels nor in any other text, but is an essential part of the unique Anglo-Saxon narrative. The second column of runes, to the left of the vine scroll, tells how they received the body of Christ:

> [m]iþ s[t]re[l]um giwundad
>   wounded with arrows
> alegdun hiæ hinæ limwœrignæ   gistoddu[n] him [æt his li]cæs [hêâ]f[du]m
>   They laid him down limb-weary. They took their stand at his
>   head and feet
> [bih]êâ[ld]u[n] [h]iæ [þ]e[r] {*hêâfunæs dryctin*} [. . .]
>   there they looked on {*the Lord of heaven*}. (Ruthwell Cross
>   poem, lines 13–15)

Christ is 'wounded with arrows', a phrase from the poetry of battle that here can act as a metaphor both for the four nails that wounded his hands and feet and, because an arrow is a kind of spear 'thrown' by a bow, for the spear which wounded his side just after his death. This emphasis on Christ's wounds prepares us for the vivid metaphor *limwœrig*, 'limb-weary'. Old English poets were fond of grim understatement: for them, to be *guðwerig*, 'battle-weary' was to be dead, killed by the fighting that 'tired' you out. In an original variant of this grim understatement, the poet states that Christ, wounded by the 'arrows' is 'tired out by his limbs' because the limbs were pierced by the nails. So, in the Ruthwell poem, there is a close link between the idea that Christ is 'wounded with arrows' and the idea that he is 'limb-weary'. In the later manuscript version of the poem, this early link was lost: in *The Dream*, the Cross tells us that it itself was wounded with arrows, although in that version Christ is still 'the limb-weary one', an image which the 'Dream' expands into cosmic terms: Christ is 'tired out after the great struggle' (that is, the cosmic battle with 'the powers of the air'):

> eall ic wæs mid strælum forwundod.
>   I was all terribly wounded with arrows
> Aledon hie ðær limwerigne   gestodun him æt his lices heafdum
>   There they laid him down limb-weary: they took their stand at his
>   head and feet
> beheoldon hie ðær heofenes dryhten,   ond he hine ðær hwile reste,
>   There they looked on the Lord of Heaven, and he rested himself
>   there for a while
> meðe æfter ðam miclan gewinne.
>   tired out after the great struggle. (*The Dream of the Rood*, lines 62–5)

But the Ruthwell poem ends with the image of Christ's followers 'looking on the Lord of Heaven'. That final image of the Ruthwell edition confronted any early members of the Ruthwell Community who read the runes, or who heard them sung or chanted, with an urgent challenge: how do we, how do I, look on the Lord of Heaven? How do I see him? The second broad side of the Ruthwell Cross provides a wonderful answer to that question. It gives us a uniquely rich sequence of images of Christ: some of them presenting him in human form, some in symbolic form. In them (reading upwards from the base of the shaft) Christ is shown as a child, crossing the Egyptian desert with Mary and Joseph when they fled from Herod; he is to be known in the Eucharistic bread, broken by two priestly figures in imitation of the two early monks, Saints Paul and Anthony; he is acclaimed in majestic human form by the beasts of the desert. Just above that panel, in an image what each morning would have been silhouetted against the rising sun, John the Baptist, 'who was not the light but gave testimony to the light', acclaims him as the Lamb of God.

The 'Agnus Dei' chant, based on John the Baptist's greeting of Christ in the gospel of John chapter 1, verses 29 and 36 ('Lamb of God who takes away the sins of the world, have mercy on us') had recently been introduced into the Roman rite of the Mass to accompany the breaking of bread for communion. The Ruthwell Crosshead was badly damaged when the iconoclasts tore down the upper stone in 1642 and the crosspiece or transom is a nineteenth-century reconstruction; but it seems likely that it, too, had an image of Christ, surrounded by the four beasts (lion, ox, eagle, angel) of the Apocalypse, who were identified with the four Evangelists. This great Cross reaches out to Irish and British traditions as well as to Anglo-Saxon and Roman. While the 'Agnus Dei' chant had recently been introduced from Rome, 'Paul and Anthony' panels are found nowhere else in Anglo-Saxon England, but are common in the early sculpture of Scotland and Ireland: the image seems to have been important in the Irish Columban tradition. At the monastery on Iona, from the time of St Columba (St Columcille of Derry), the monastic community welcomed visiting priests by inviting them to break the bread for communion together with the abbot, in imitation of the first monks, Saints Paul and Anthony of Egypt, who had broken bread together in the desert. The Ruthwell Cross is a monument that celebrates Celtic as well as Roman traditions: St Aidan would have understood it, as would St Cuthbert (635–87), Bishop of Lindisfarne in 685, who was familiar with Celtic as well as Roman traditions and became an ascetic bishop in Irish style on the lonely island of Farne. On the Ruthwell Cross, the vine scrolls and their runic captions (the Old English poem) provide the central image of the whole monument, an image which is at once visual (the vine scroll) and verbal (the poem). The new English Crucifixion narrative places the ancient pagan image of the Tree of Life (an image common to the Roman world as well as to Germanic tribes) in an explicitly Christian setting. The captioned Tree of Life image provides the single unifying metaphor behind the many images of the broad sides. The logic behind these rich sequences of carved images can only be understood by continual reference to that single past event: the shedding of Christ's blood on the Cross when the sun, darkened for a time, triumphed over winter darkness; and the Son, the Courage of God, divested himself to defeat the powers of the air.

The Dream in the Vercelli Book

As we have seen, the full text of *The Dream* is preserved in a late tenth-century form of Old English (West Saxon) in the Vercelli Book. The book gets its name because it has survived in the cathedral library at Vercelli, an Italian city on the plains of Lombardy, halfway between Milan and Turin. There is a piece of northern Italian chant, scribbled on to a page of the manuscript, which shows that the book was already at Vercelli by, say, 1000–1100 AD. How did it get there? The answer is that Vercelli was on one of the important pilgrimage routes which led over the Alps and south across the Lombard plains on the way to Rome. The book, which is entirely full of religious texts in prose and verse, may have been used for reading out to a group of pilgrims on their way to Rome. But there may be a more specific reason why the book ended up in Vercelli. As we have seen, it is a personal collection, reflecting the interests, and indeed the obsessions, of the person who collected the homilies and poems of the manuscript. We have seen a little of that person's preoccupation with death and the Last Judgement. The lack of titles for most of the texts, including all the poems, made it very difficult for anyone, except for the original compiler, to find their way around the book. But from 970 AD onwards the great monasteries of England had been reformed and reorganised by order of King Edgar the Peace-maker. This was the full flush of the Benedictine Reform, of which we will see more in Chapter 14. An essential feature of this monastic reform was that personal property for monks was bad. All possessions, including books, now had to be held in common. So personal manuscripts were out of fashion. Before the reform, ancient churches (such as, for example, St Augustine's, Canterbury) used to be run by clerics who lived in much less highly organised communities. Now these clerics, known as canons, were thrown out and replaced by highly organised communities of reformed monks. Vercelli was famous for its cathedral, which held the relics of a fourth-century bishop, St Eusebius, who had encouraged his priests not to become monks, but to live in informal communities as canons. As Eusebius planned it, although these canons lived in the same house, they could still have personal possessions such as their own books. In short, St Eusebius of Vercelli was famous as the patron saint of canons. So it is possible that the Vercelli Book was brought over the Alps by a group of pilgrims led by a canon: the sort of old-fashioned cleric, now more or less an outlaw, who appreciated the sort of old-fashioned personal anthology no longer welcome in the communal libraries of reformed English monasteries.

The Dream on the Brussels Cross

At the end of the Anglo-Saxon period, an artist incorporated a version of the Old English Crucifixion narrative, possibly even from *The Dream* itself, into another cross. This metalwork cross was designed to be carried in procession, and was made in the south of England in the early eleventh century: it was indeed the sort of lavish work of art much loved by the aristocrats who sponsored the monastic reform we have just spoken about. This processional cross was made of wood, originally covered by gilded silver: seventeenth-century accounts of the cross tell us that its front was then studded with 24 rubies and 14 diamonds. It was taken to the continent in the Middle Ages, and the jewels, as well as the precious metal covering the front of the cross, were looted at Brussels by soldiers of the French army which invaded Belgium in 1793. The wooden core of the cross had in it a small hollow, to hold a little piece of wood, a piece or relic of the True Cross, on which Christ had died. As such, the Brussels Cross is called a reliquary.

The Brussels Cross gets its name because it can now be seen displayed in the treasury of the Cathedral of Saints Michael and Gudule at Brussels. The metalworker who designed the cross left his name on the gilded silver that still survives on the back of the cross: 'Drahmal wrought [i.e. made] me' (DRAHMAL ME WORHTE). Drahmal imagines the cross as speaking to us, to tell us the name of its designer. As the cross was carried in procession, this cross must have seemed to come alive when the light of candles glinted, first on the massed rubies and diamonds on the front of the cross and, then, as the procession passed, on the gleaming gilded silver that still survives on the back of the cross. As they saw the cross reliquary carried at the head of a procession, people who knew *The Dream* by heart may well have recalled its image of 'an eager, restless symbol' (*þæt fuse beacen*, line 22).

The Brussels Cross is only a little more than one centimetre thick. To cover the narrow surface of the thickness, Drahmal nailed five narrow strips of silver: he carefully cut the strips to the proper lengths and inscribed them with ornament and with writing. The writing could not be read by ordinary onlookers when the cross was carried in procession; but it could easily be read by any cleric when the cross was brought back to the sacristy where it would have been stored in safety. To read the inscription, the cross needs to be held bowed forward, if not 'to the hands of the men' (as in the Ruthwell poem and in *The Dream of the Rood*, line 59), at least to their eyes. When the cross is bowed forward, all the letters on the silver strips appear the right way up, and it is easy to read the inscription. It tells us the names of the Anglo-Saxon noblemen who commissioned Drahmal to make the cross in memory of their dead brother: 'Æthelmær ordered this cross to be made, and Æthelwold his brother: in Christ's honour, for the soul of Ælfric their brother'. But before the cleric got to this information, he would first have read two lines of verse in which this cross speaks of itself:

+ ROD IS MIN NAMA   GEO IC RICNE CYNING
    'Rood' is my name; long ago a powerful king
BÆR BYFIGYNDE   BLODE BESTEMED.
    I bore, trembling, drenched with blood.

For his masterpiece, Drahmal created a new version of the ancient Old English narrative. This heroic action takes place 'long ago' ('GEO': compare modern English 'yore' and the phrase 'aer gewin' 'former struggle' in line 19 of *The Dream*, p. 166). Once more, a poem dramatises the moment when the Tree of Life became a 'rood'. This 'rood' 'bore' Christ to his death: only this Brussels poem, and neither the Ruthwell poem nor the Vercelli 'Dream', makes the Cross 'bear' Christ. But this brief but powerful narrative centres on the moment just after Christ's death, when the cross was 'drenched by the blood' (*blode bestemed*) which poured from Christ's right side: the moment when baptism and the Eucharist, the sacraments of the Church, were 'born' from the wound in Christ's side. This terrible moment can there-fore carry associations of birth as well as death. Indeed, if we think of the Brusssels Cross as a symbol of Christ's own body (like the Cross in the open-ing vision of *The Dream* or the Ruthwell Cross), in which the surviving silver is on the 'back' and the looted jewels were on the 'front', the two-line Old English poem reads upwards along the 'right' side of the Cross, the side drenched by the wound in Christ's side. Drahmal knew that Christ was wounded on the right side (*on þa swiðran healfe*, *The Dream of the Rood*, line 20). Indeed, it is clear that Drahmal had a deep understanding of whatever version of *The Dream* he knew, presumably by singing it or hearing it sung. Those who saw Drahmal's cross would first have been dazzled and delighted by the rubies and diamonds and by the graceful figures of the four evange-list beasts who surround the 'Agnus Dei' (Lamb of God) on the back of the cross. This is just as those who read *The Dream* are initially delighted by the rich images of the opening vision. But those who enquired further would learn, through this new two-line epitome of *The Dream*, that the most precious thing in this object is not its jewels, but its sliver of the original Cross – the very same that had once, long ago ('GEO'), borne Christ to his death.

With startling immediacy, Drahmal's short poem makes the cross speak, makes it reveal the relic beneath its jewels. In Old English poetry, as in ancient heroic literature generally, names were not lightly given out. Beowulf does not give his name to the coastguard, the first person he meets when he and his companions land in Denmark on their way to defend Heorot against Grendel (*Beowulf*, lines 260–85). Beowulf names himself only when he meets Wulfgar, a noble young warrior of similar social rank, who, like himself, had come to Denmark from far off: 'Beowulf is my name' (*Beowulf is min nama*, line 343). Similarly, the Brussels Cross reveals its name, *Rod is min nama*, only to the person who examines it closely. But the Brussels Cross, like the Ruthwell Cross centuries before and the long version of the narrative in *The Dream*, reveals its depth and richness the closer it is studied.

Conclusion: how Christian indeed?

In its various forms, *The Dream* shows that Old English literature was driven by Christianity from beginning to end of Anglo-Saxon history. But this poem also shows that the earliest form of that Christianity was unusual for being of a breathtakingly symbolic and fiercely imaginative kind. In all this there is the zeal of new converts hungry to learn Latin, the Bible, the new chants of the liturgy, Italian sculpture and painting, even while they proudly look back to the glitter of their warlike barbaric past and the ancient chants of their heroic poetry. In no other literature will we find such a heroic cast to Christ and his sacrifice on Calvary or to the Cross as the unwilling agent of Christ's death. The very style of heroic poetry that we have seen in *Beowulf* and other diverse works, in Chapters 3–5, was here used to accom-modate the ideology of peace to a culture which celebrated war. Old English heroism was redefined. As the church spread ever outwards, illuminating dark tracts of heathen English countryside, so the heroic infiltrated inwards, transforming the imported Christian idiom until it allowed the production of a new poetry in old form. In the following chapter, through Bede's story of Cædmon, we shall see something of the way this happened.

Translations and texts

Crossley-Holland, Kevin, trans., *The Anglo-Saxon World: An Anthology* (Woodbridge, 1982, repr. Oxford, 1984).

Hamer, Richard, *A Choice of Anglo-Saxon Verse* (London, 1970, repr. 2006).

Swanton, Michael, ed., *The Dream of the Rood* (Exeter, 1987).

Further reading

Backhouse, Janet, D.H. Turner and Leslie Webster, eds, *The Golden Age of Anglo-Saxon Art 966–1066* (London, 1984).

Cassidy, Brendan, ed., *The Ruthwell Cross: Papers from the Colloquium Sponsored by the Index of Christian Art, Princeton University, 8 December 1989*, Index of Christian Art, Occasional Papers 1 (Princeton, New Jersey, 1992).

Cramp, Rosemary, 'The Anglian Sculptured Crosses of Dumfriesshire', *Transactions of the Dumfries and Galloway Antiquarian Society* 38 (1959–60), pp. 9–20.

Cramp, Rosemary, 'Anglo-Saxon and Italian Sculpture', in *Angli e sassoni al di qua e al di là del mare*, Settimane di Spoleto 32 (Rome, 1986), pp. 125–40.

North, Richard, *Heathen Gods in Old English Literature*, Cambridge Studies in Anglo-Saxon England 22 (Cambridge, 1997).

Ó Carragáin, Éamonn, *Ritual and the Rood: Liturgical Images and the Old English Poems of the 'Dream of the Rood' Tradition* (Toronto and London, 2005).

CHAPTER 7

Cædmon the cowherd and Old English biblical verse

Bryan Weston Wyly

Old English literature starts with Cædmon, who is said to have lived to old age as a cowherd in the monastery of Whitby, when, suddenly one night in his cow byre, having returned from a communal revel, he composed an Old English poem on creation – despite the fact that he had never learned to sing or compose in his own language. This miracle near a manger took place some time between 657 and 680, when the house at Whitby (in Deira, southern Northumbria) was ruled by Abbess Hild. It was she, maybe the next day, who ascribed this miracle to God when Cædmon's boss brought him forward to recite his new poem to her. Hild then asked Cædmon to join the monastic life and he did, composing many other poems on the books of Genesis and Exodus, the Gospels and Acts of the Apostles and Revelation and on other biblical themes as well. All this pre-dates or nearly matches the time in which another great poet, a Northumbrian like Cædmon, composed *The Dream of the Rood* (see pp. 161–74).

All that survives from Cædmon's huge output, unfortunately, is the first nine lines of his first poem, a work now known as Cædmon's *Hymn*. A modern rendering of this 'first English poem' might go as follows:

Now may the works of the Father of Splendour [i.e. creation]
praise the Guardian of the Kingdom of Heaven,
the powers of the Measurer and the thought of His Spirit,
since He, Eternal Lord, established the origin of every miracle.
He ordained resurrection for the sons of men [or: earth].
With living creatures the Holy Creator,
Guardian of mankind, Eternal Lord,
Almighty Luminary, thereafter ornamented
the heavens for a roof and then the Middle Earth.

Although it amounts to a fragment, no more, this poem gives Cædmon his subsequent fame as the first named English poet whose work survives. In other words, he was the first named poet, whose work survives, to express his Christian faith through the English language. The blank anonymity of all other extant Old English poetry, *The Dream of the Rood* included, is offset by the fact that in Cædmon's case we have a name and some knowledge of the life behind it. As an illiterate, but supposedly divinely inspired poet, Cædmon lives forever in the story as it is told by the Venerable Bede (*c.* 673–735).

Bede was a Northumbrian monk, like Cædmon, but at the same time we know that he was almost everything Cædmon was not: historian, biblical commentator, rhetorician, calendrical computician, in short the most formidable writer of Latin poetry and prose. To historians, at least, Bede's histories, biblical commentaries and rhetorical treatises make him the most famous English writer of the Anglo-Saxon period, not only in Britain but throughout western Europe. Bede was committed to Benedict Biscop's new monastery of Wearmouth in Bernicia (northern Northumbria) in around 680, at the age of 7, where he lived the rest of his life as a sort of colonial within his own native land (on Benedict, see pp. 176–8). Cloistered within his adoptive monastic community, he became a clerical prodigy. Whereas no man usually became a deacon before the age of 25, Bede was already ordained as a deacon by 19 years and he became a priest at 30. His large number of Latin religious treatises rank him among the *doctores* (something like 'teachers' or 'masters') of the Roman Catholic Church. In around 734, when he was over 60 years old, Bede finished his great Ecclesiastical History of the English People (*Historia ecclesiastica gentis Anglorum*). This work put the still young, formerly immigrant, Anglo-Saxon nation on the European map, while stimulating the formation of an 'English' cultural identity out of the political and linguistic fragmentation that characterised post-Roman Britain. Yet for all the volumes that survive of Bede's Latin works, only an epigram, five lines of Old English verse, has been passed down to us under Bede's name. This is even shorter than the sole snippet, nine lines, which survives of Cædmon's poetry.

Bede gave Cædmon's story a whole chapter (Book IV, Chapter 24) in his *Ecclesiastical History* (Colgrave and Mynors 1969: 414–21). Without this generous coverage it is fair to say we would know nothing of Cædmon at all. And yet Bede himself did not preserve the text of Cædmon's *Hymn*: he gave only his Latin paraphrase, while apologising for the inferiority of this to the Old English original. Luckily for us, later copyists of Bede's *History* added Old English versions in the margins to the Latin text. Along with

Cædmon's original text, Bede seems to leave out many things from his story. His inevitably partial write-up has allowed a number of assumptions about Cædmon's career to take on a gospel status in English literary histories. That is inevitable. In what follows, I shall discuss the text of his *Hymn* in more detail, present an alternative interpretation of Cædmon to add to the received view of his career, then lay out a summary of the many surviving Old English biblical poems which were once treated as Cædmon's works.

Cædmon's dream and the nature of poetic inspiration

This is the story of an Anglo-Saxon 'poet', a *scop*. Bede starts his narrative in Cædmon's heyday, introducing him to us as the monk from *Streonaeshalch* (modern-day Whitby) famed for the God-given skill of transforming any biblical story into Old English verse (Book IV, Chapter 24). Naturally, Bede says, interpreters were first required to translate the stories from their biblical Latin. Neither could Cædmon compose any 'trivial poems' (*poemata supervacua*). With this phrase, presumably, Bede means the more secular pieces such as poems of the kind we have seen so far in Chapters 4 and 5 of this book. What was remarkable about Cædmon was that he had never composed a line until the miracle which forms the centre of his story. Whenever the lyre came near him at the celebrations held at Whitby's secular domains, Cædmon would rise up, go out and return 'to his home' (*ad suam domum*).

   On one such occasion, as he went back to the cattle byre to begin work on his shift, a voice came to Cædmon in a dream. Stretching out on the straw, he fell asleep, when suddenly a voice addressed him by name and asked him to sing. Cædmon said he couldn't. 'Sing to me anyway', the voice said. 'What must I sing?' asked Cædmon. 'Sing to me of creation!', the voice said. More specifically, this request was for 'the beginning of created things' (*principium creaturarum*). And so the old farm labourer entered into his new beginning, singing verses he had never heard, in praise of God the Creator. Bede leaves out the Old English, giving instead a Latin version which he calls 'the general sense' (*sensus*). I will set this out with a translation in eight lines:

> Nunc laudare debemus auctorem regni caelestis, potentiam creatoris et consilium illius, facta patris gloriae, quomodo ille, cum sit eternus Deus, omnium miraculorum auctor exstitit, qui primo filiis hominum caelum pro culmine tecti dehinc terram custos humani generis omnipotens creavit.

> Now we ought to praise the Maker of the Heavenly Kingdom,
> the power of the Creator and His counsel,

the deeds of the Father of Glory,
how He, as God is eternal,
was the Maker of all miracles,
the Almighty Guardian of the human race
Who for the sons of men created first heaven
as a roof and thence the earth.

When Cædmon awoke, Bede says, he remembered everything he had sung while asleep and went on to compose more. His boss, the 'reeve' (*vilicus*), took him to see the abbess later the same morning. Hearing the poem, Abbess Hild and her advisors agreed that this was a miracle from God. They read out in English a passage from the Bible and the next day, when Cædmon repeated this successfully in Old English poetic form, Hild asked him if he would like to take his vows as a monk. In the days that followed, like a clean animal chewing the cud and yielding milk, Cædmon demonstrated himself capable of 'composing exceptionally sweet and highly moving songs' for Christian audiences (*verba poetica maxima suavitate et compunctione composita*). He produced poem after poem on the creation of the world, the origin of mankind, the history of Genesis and the flight of the 12 tribes of Israel from Egypt to the promised land, the incarnation, life and works of Jesus Christ, his passion and resurrection and ascension, the acts of the apostles and the day of judgement: in short, most of the Bible. The rest of Cædmon's life takes on the form of a saint's life, with ideal monastic conduct, his foreknowledge of his own death a fortnight before this happened and an exemplary passing into God's hands.

Bede never explicitly passes judgement as to whether or not Cædmon's dream was a miracle. His historical claim is simply that Cædmon had never sung before, whereas afterwards, in the presence of his reeve, and later at Whitby, he composed poetry of the highest quality. From Bede's account it appears that Cædmon remained illiterate all his life, so he composed entirely from memory throughout his career, despite his having entered Hild's monastery at her request. While he does not appear to have completely extemporised on the spot, Bede tells that, on being read some passage, Cædmon could demonstrate his abilities by being able to present this in a versified form after a short while.

Following Hild's verdict of Cædmon's having received divine grace (*caelesta ei a Domino concessa gratia*), Bede interprets Cædmon's overnight success as being due to his having freely received a 'gift' for singing through divine agency (*divinitus adiutus gratis canendi donum accepit*), rather than having been instructed in singing by men or at the behest of any human being (*non ab hominibus neque per hominem institutus canendi artem didicit*).

The psychological plausibility of the story depends on several considerations as to the nature of Cædmon's compositional techniques.

As a remarkable historical event, the story of Cædmon's ability is believable. Although the number of functionally illiterate cultures has today dwindled to the point at which no society is completely without writing, attempts have been made for over a century now to record poetic performers employing such techniques in real time. Similar to warrior training, oral performance can be described as radically a physical performance, focusing on the single, present moment of production which can never be fully repeated. Written composition is, in many ways, the attempt to disembody discourse to thereby transcend the context of any particular occasion.

When looking more into this story, we must take into consideration our current ignorance into the psychology of general language use before we attempt to assess the credibility of Cædmon's taking up poetic composition overnight. In traditional societies, poetic composition is an extension of daily language use, which may be thought of as having its own 'grammar' and 'vocabulary'. In preliterate society, versification serves to enhance memory and thereby extend the mind's analytical potential. Lacking written documents to function as external memory, poetic formulation helps to optimise both the capacity to store and recall important information in internal memory. As a result, versification becomes an imminently practical ability and remains so as long as external memory, i.e. written or illustrative record is limited, costly or difficult to access. There is every reason to think that memory skills were highly valued and expected, if not indeed inculcated, among Anglo-Saxon war bands even before this society entered its monastic phase.

Children can pick up their native language with minimal linguistic instruction, so that most people take for granted a person's ability to improvise sequences of grammatically complex sentences without consciously concentrating on the grammar of their speech. Psycholinguistic studies have shown that the acquisition of one's primary language can potentially continue throughout one's life, with successive developmental stages being characterised by qualitative restructuring of the encyclopaedic mental lexicon. Such restructuring can at times become manifest in quite abrupt behavioural change. It could well be, therefore, that the integration of external memory which comes through literacy might suppress the development of a poetic grammar that would otherwise take place at a more mature developmental phase. For us, as already for Bede perhaps, the artifice of literacy may thus have become so engrained that we can no longer recognise the naturalness of Cædmon's breakthrough. As Cædmon was a native speaker of Old English in an essentially preliterate society, the question of Bede's credibility must be approached through imagining what it was like to compose poetry fluently in oral-formulaic style.

To put it another way, were someone to tell a story of a person who, having never seen a trumpet before, suddenly picked one up and began to improvise a remarkably personalised jazz solo, the story would sound like a miracle to anyone who appreciated how much physical coordination is needed just to get a clear sound out of such an instrument. Yet if the same story were told about someone trained in bugling complex sequences of signals as a practical means of battlefield communication, who had for years been eavesdropping on Miles Davis's jam sessions, suddenly walking into a jazz club and auditioning with a breathtakingly original solo, this story might sound at least possible.

How does one teach creativity and where does genius stem from? These are issues we have hardly answered for ourselves. Not only is Cædmon's story a mystery to us, but also the question of how poets were trained in Anglo-Saxon culture: were the would-be poets selected and explicitly taught to compose, for example? Or was the acquisition of poetic skills, like the acquisition of one's native language, left to intuitive learning, with those demonstrating the greatest native aptitude then being encouraged though practical opportunities to further develop their talent?

Bede composes his narrative as though the art of the Anglo-Saxon *scop* ('poet') were explicitly taught, just as the art of intoning the Latin hymns of the liturgy after the Roman manner had been taught in his monastery at Wearmouth–Jarrow employing 'contemporaneously the human voice and written text' (Hunter Blair 1990: 170–71). At the same time Bede models his analysis of Cædmon's illiterate compositional technique on a story that was well known in his day, that of a blind scholar in Alexandria called Didymus, who lost his sight in early childhood before he had time to learn to read. Didymus nonetheless managed to re-elaborate any information that was read to him, so well indeed that he liberated himself from the need to have the same material read to him again (Pizarro 2005). Bede rationalises Cædmon's development as a divine 'gift' because Cædmon, without waiting to be taught to sing, acquired his poetic skill in a seemingly effortless way. Bede is clearly astonished at Cædmon's initiative in doing this on his own account without being trained.

There is some evidence that Bede's 'God-given talent' explanation is based on Anglo-Saxon folk psychology. In a wisdom poem from the Exeter Book, *Maxims I*, we find the statement that anyone who knows many songs and can play the harp 'has for himself the gift of brilliance which God gave him' (*hafaþ him his gliwes giefe þe him god sealde*, line 171). *Maxims I* represents the proverbial lore of the Anglo-Saxons, yet these words could just as well be the product of imported monastic learning, involving an originally Greek trope that a poet is inspired by his Muse. Even if this Classical notion had long been deeply engrained within Anglo-Saxon ideas about the nature of poetic ability, it poses several problems for Bede's explanation of Cædmon's dream. First of all, Cædmon could have done this without divine inspiration. His self-taught case may be more typical than Bede would have us believe. Second, it was common for the medieval mind to attribute divine will to unpredictable events. Yet if the ability to sing and play were considered as regularly a product of divine will, Anglo-Saxon training methods in poetry and music would have had no incentive to develop.

Another Old English wisdom poem, *The Fortunes of Men*, also from the Exeter Book, refers to a poet as one who 'is a bearer of poetic inspiration, steady in the giving of songs' (*sum biþ woðbera giedda giffæst*, lines 35–6). Here, the concept of 'giving (a performance)', may be based on a much older idea, in which poetic compositions act as a sort of intellectual property which can be exchanged. This exchange may be for similar intellectual property, as in *Maxims I* again: 'wise men are said to exchange songs' (*gleawe men sceolon gieddum wrixlan*, line 4). Or it may be for material goods, as in *The Fortunes of Men*, where 'one man is said to sit with a lyre, to receive money, at his lord's feet' (*sum sceal mid hearpan æt his hlafordes fotum sittan, feoh þicgan*, lines 80–1). The idea of poetics as a sort of intellectual capital within warrior society appears to be quite ancient. You can see this in *Widsith* (cf. pp. 104–8), where 'Widsith', the poet speaking, presents himself as the prototypical poet-for-hire of a Germanic war band, gleefully receiving 'gladdening treasures as song's reward' (*glædlicne maþþum songes to leane*, lines 66–7).

Of course, cash for songs is a model for musicians in real life. If it worked in Anglo-Saxon times for prince and poet, couldn't it work also for a god and his religiously minded poet? So it may have been even earlier, in the heathen age: a god gives poetic skill, the poet gives him back a song (compare the Viking cult of Óðinn, pp. 357–9). This was also a judgement in Christian times, for Abbess Hild saw Cædmon's poem as resulting from 'divine grace in the man' (*gratia Dei in viro*). Bede reports this, yet appears to be struggling against this essentially mercenary idea when he later says that Cædmon's divine gift was given 'as a favour' (Latin *gratis*), i.e. for free, without God's thought of Cædmon repaying Him. In principle with his new gift, therefore, Cædmon could have turned his talent to poetry which was utterly secular. In his emphasis on the liberality of this type of Christian poetic inspiration, Bede echoes the thoughts of another Anglo-Saxon monastic poet, Bishop Aldhelm of Sherborne in Wessex (c. 639–c. 709). Aldhelm was Bede's most significant Anglo-Saxon predecessor in the composition of Latin verse. In this way the idea of a 'mercenary muse' may have been used by Christians to stigmatise a particularly pagan type of poetic inspiration, from which Bede may have wished to distance Cædmon.

Most Anglo-Saxon comments on poetic practice treat their subject rather statically. Songs there are things which are remembered and reproduced rather than considered as original creations. This is only in keeping with the monastic culture of the period, which aimed to compile and transmit Latinate learning from the past rather than to generate new personal ideas. The great poem *Beowulf*, in its characteristically exceptional way, gives us the best vernacular description of how new songs were created (lines 867–74). The technique here is broken down, as we have seen (pp. 96–9), into a series of steps. First a king's thane 'who remembered an encyclopaedic number of old sayings' (*se þe ealfela ealdgesegena worn gemunde*, lines 869–70) proceeds to apply his art as though mixing a cocktail: 'he found other words bound together in truth' (*word oþer fand soðe gebunden*, lines 870–71) before beginning 'cleverly to stir up Beowulf's adventure, successfully to recite a fitting story, to vary his words' (*secg eft ongan sið Beowulfes snyttrum styrian ond on sped wrecan spel gerad wordum wrixlan*, lines 871–4). Today we call this an 'oral-formulaic' style of composition.

Cædmon's *Hymn* and the oral-formulaic style

As we have seen, versions of the Old English text of Cædmon's *Hymn* are found not in Bede's writing, but in other forms. Two of the oldest manuscripts of Bede's *History of the English Church and People*, from the eighth century, are called the 'Leningrad Bede' (St Petersburg, Saltykov-Shchedrin Public Library, Q.v.I.18) and the 'Moore Bede' (Cambridge, University Library, Kk.5.16). The Leningrad Bede has Cædmon's *Hymn* written in the margin of Bede's Latin as a kind of Old English gloss. The Moore Bede has it at the end of the manuscript written as a kind of addendum. Both texts are written in Northumbrian Old English, which looks quite different from West Saxon (the commonest version of Old English; see p. 17), although it is the ancestor of Lowland Scots. Robbie Burns isn't far away from the language of Cædmon. In addition, there are some later West Saxon texts of Cædmon's *Hymn*, which represent the poem as it was passed down through the generations in the southern Anglo-Saxon kingdoms. Although Bede professes to be unable to capture the essence of Cædmon's opening in his Latin paraphrasis, today you will find most readers following his crib in translating Cædmon's Northumbrian lines. The most recent text for these has been established as follows (O'Donnell 2005: 205):

Nu scylun hergan   hefaenricaes uard
medudæs maecti   end his modgidanc
uerc uuldurfadur   sue he uundra gihuaes
eci dryhtin   or astelidæ.
He ærist scop   eordu barnum.
Heben til hrofe   haleg sceppend
tha middungeard   moncynnæs uard
eci dryhtin   æfter tiadæ
firum foldu   frea all-mectig.

Inevitably, Bede's Latin paraphrase represents considerable impoverishment of the structure and content of these nine lines. Some have even questioned the Old English text to the extent of asking whether it is really nothing more than an attempt to reconstruct the original from the Latin paraphrase (Kiernan 1990). But this kind of exercise would be rather pointless unless the forger of the Old English version was himself a teacher, like Kiernan, me and many other people in the Anglo-Saxon field. To repeat the translation given at the head of this chapter:

Now may the works of the Father of Splendour
praise the Guardian of the Kingdom of Heaven,
the powers of the Measurer and the thought of His Spirit,
since He, Eternal Lord, established the origin of every miracle.
He ordained resurrection for the sons of men.
With living creatures the Holy Creator,
Guardian of mankind, Eternal Lord,
Almighty Luminary, thereafter ornamented
the heavens for a roof and then the Middle Earth.

There will be many other ways of translating these lines. No one can be really sure of their exact meaning. That goes for translating poetry from any language, of course. While very short, Cædmon's *Hymn* is virtually the oldest piece of continuous verse we have from any Germanic language, so it is usually read looking backwards from a perspective conditioned by subsequent English tradition. And yet Bede specifies that Cædmon's superior artistic ability set him apart from those who tried to imitate him. So one may wonder whether the later Old English tradition gives us the right context for appreciating Cædmon's poetic achievement. The fact that Abbess Hild had Cædmon's poetic ability subjected to rigorous doctrinal inquisition, before she offered him a place in her monastery, tells us that she knew Old English verse could be fluid. A poet in Cædmon's day could make use of ambiguities in case endings, compounding, poetic word order and metrical correspondences to construct a single expression which permitted multiple interpretations. This is the enigmatic, if not esoteric, technique behind the composition of 'oral-formulaic' verse.

What we can say, however, is Cædmon sees all of us as God's creation with the job of praising the Creator. There is the idea of the Trinity in his *Hymn* as well: God the Father (*hefaenricaes uard, uuldurfadur*), the Son (*medudæs maecti*) and Holy Ghost (*his modgidanc*). While these concepts are fundamental to many Christian credoes, one would be hard pressed to find an Anglo-Saxon author who succeeded in expressing such mysteries with Cædmon's poetic fluency and economy. Third, with the word *ærist* on line 5, Cædmon strikes home with the evangelical message of resurrection. The interpretations I offer here are not accepted by all and it is fair to say that the ideas of Trinity and Resurrection are not presented in this poem as clearly as they later were in prose. Indeed Cædmon's half-line *He ærist scop* could mean 'He first created' as well as or apart from 'He ordained resurrection', depending on whether we want to add the Christian idea of redemption to the theme of creation in this poem.

At any rate, it could be argued that Cædmon balances the four verse lines which precede his focal 'resurrection' statement with four more on God's creation itself (lines 6–9). Again, his poem, for all its brevity, represents a masterwork of balance and economy, structured around a parallelism between heaven and earth according to the biblical order of precedence. The phrase 'adorned with living creatures' (*tiadae firum*, lines 8–9) ties together the temporal sequence of 'heaven' (*heben*, line 6) and 'then Middle Earth' (*þa middangard*, line 7). The Book of Genesis has the creation of the environments (Gen 1: 7–10) swiftly followed by that of their inhabitants (Gen 1: 11–27). This compression allows Cædmon to again focus on the biblical cosmology without upsetting the careful formal balance of the text. The composite nature of the Christian divinity is signalled though the apposition between God the Father 'the Holy Creator' (*haleg sceppend*, line 6) and the 'Almighty Luminary of the world' (*foldu frea almihteg*, line 9; see Wyly 1999: 235–52). Cædmon thus refers to Jesus' naming of himself as 'the light of the world' in the Gospel of John 8: 12.

Read in this way, Cædmon's brief poem imparts a sense of wonder, together with the freshness which perhaps comes from the novelty of his putting the vocabulary of warlike bombast into the service of devotional poetry for God. That is to say, he followed the same procedure for composing verse as is described in *Beowulf*: he neither invented words nor borrowed terms from foreign languages, but discovered a means of reformulating existing phraseology so as to convey a sense appropriate to his immediate context. In short, he was using the techniques of a warlike, formerly heathen, tradition.

Cædmon: the Christian background

Bede set out in his *History* to describe a history of an English church, not of the English Christian faith. His focus was on a social structure rather than a set of ideas. Perhaps this was because he thought the English should not have any ideas of their own such as could be identified as aberrant within a universal 'catholic' religion. In Bede's day, no less than earlier, northern Britain was a multicultural, multiethnic world, where the question of just who could call himself a 'Christian' was as difficult and contentious as it is in any corner of 'western' society today. Yet since around 180 AD, when Bishop Irenaeus of Lyon wrote his *Against Sectarianism*, a movement had been growing in Christian communities regarding itself as the arbiter of a privileged, universalist definition of Christianity. This consortium was exclusionary in ideology and monopolistic in matters of cult practice and it succeeded in advancing its political and social power when its interpretation of Christianity was legalised by the Roman Emperor Constantine in 313 AD. Hereafter the organisers of this hierarchical faction were in a key position to define what 'Christianity' was. It was no surprise that theirs became the version adopted as official in around 380. Their headquarters, at least as far as the western empire was concerned, were set up in the ancient imperial capital at Rome. In due course an adherence to the principles of Catholicism went on to give this corporation the tenacity to survive the military collapse of the empire that had once fostered it.

Pope Gregory's and Augustine's mission to Britain represents a landmark in the colonisation of northern Europe by Catholic Christianity. By the time Augustine landed on Thanet, in Kent, in 597 (see p. 17), Christian culture had been known in Britain for centuries. While those adhering to groups whose cultural identity was Celtic were most likely to have regarded their lifestyles as predominantly Christian in outlook, even the most recently arrived Germanic barbarian family would have experienced generations of contact with self-professed Christians. The papal embassy came not merely to inform the populace of Britain, but to actively recruit members into its organisation on the condition of their opting into its ideology of Catholicism. For many in Germanic Britain, adherence to the monk

Augustine's canons of religious orthodoxy offered a chance to make new contacts and open new horizons towards a European panorama. This was the Anglo-Saxon 'conversion' and it was now underway.

We have seen a sketch of Northumbria's first 70 Christian years in the previous chapter (pp. 174–8). Much later, however, we see Bede as a leading proponent of Catholicism. This was in the 730s, some 130 years after the beginning of the Roman mission to England. In Bede's day there was an abysmal, but ever widening, gap between the lifestyles of the country's most advantaged and the most disadvantaged inhabitants. As we shall see, the pressures of money and wavering social status may have played a key role in Cædmon's decision to become a monk. Bede conceived his *History* (*c.* 734) to fit English secular and religious society into a purely Catholic world, after the unifying doctrine which the organisers of the Roman Church had long since furnished. Bede's use for dissident religious ideas in all this was to hope that the convictions of his flock could be strengthened by opposing them. It was not, however, the aim in his work to expose any English doctrinal quarrels to the Christian public outside England – that would have courted some unwelcome interest from the church in Rome.

Bede says that Cædmon was already of advanced age by the beginning of his tale. His account of Cædmon's life falls neatly into two halves, whose pivot has Cædmon taking monastic vows at Whitby. There he remained for an undisclosed number of years until succumbing to a pious death. Bede devotes more space to this death than to describing what we might find exceptional in Cædmon's life: his meteoric career as a poet. Bede's clearest indication as to when this happens comes from his mention of the abbess. Abbess Hild, who ruled Whitby from about 657 to 680 (see Map 3, page 98), was the prime instigator of Cædmon's decision to become a monk. Bede's reticence about Cædmon's life prior to this moment has been taken to mean 'that he may have worked on one of the Whitby estates' (Hunter Blair 1990: 149). This view of Cædmon presumes that merely his illiteracy must have made him a farmhand before God graced him with his talent for song.

Thus far the received view, according to which Cædmon was hardly more than a shame-faced menial, fit for little better than dunging fields with the cows, until a dream vision miraculously catapulted him to poetic fame and social distinction for the sake of his religious inspiration. This story reads like an artifice and, to a large extent, it is. What really happened? we may well ask. A careful look at Bede's *History*, both at his text and omissions, could tell a different story. My following case will show you how powerful Bede's story of Cædmon is. As a story which can sustain more than one interpretation, it can inspire you, too, to have your own ideas about

Anglo-Saxon culture and even – who knows? – to take up the study of its language and literature for yourself.

A different view of Cædmon

Whitby was unlike other major Northumbrian monasteries in being ruled by an abbess. As a woman, Hild would not have been allowed to travel to Italy like her male colleagues, her fellow Northumbrians Bishop Wilfrid (634–709) and Benedict Biscop (?628–89). These men brought books back home with them, wishing to emulate in Northumbria what they had seen abroad in Italy and France. The only Latin work to have survived from the monastery at Whitby is the anonymous *Life of Gregory the Great* (*Vita Gregorii Magni*). This is a biography of the Pope who instigated the Roman mission to save Anglo-Saxon souls. The Latin of this *Life*, which was written some time between 709 and 714, is considerably less fluent than that of Bede (Colgrave 1968: 55–6). The odd thing about this *Life*, which presents much local Northumbrian history, is that it says nothing of Cædmon, neither the man nor his miraculous poem.

As we have seen, the only place Cædmon is mentioned is in Book IV, Chapter 24, of Bede's *History* (McClure and Collins 1999: 215–18). We have no way of knowing, but Cædmon looks less likely to have been a farmhand the more one considers the few circumstances Bede does choose to divulge. At the beginning of the Cædmon story proper, Bede states that Cædmon took part in communal 'feasts' (Latin *convivia*), but would retire 'to his own home' (*ad suam domum*) whenever he saw that he would be asked to sing and play the lyre before the others. Having one's own dwelling is hardly the mark of a domestic servant in north-eastern Britain in the late seventh century. Among his drinking companions, Cædmon's seniority might have been in his status as well as his age. Bede says, furthermore, that on the night of his fateful vision, Cædmon was assigned to watch over the 'stables of draught animals' (*stabula iumentorum*) attached to the 'house of feasting' (*domus convivii*). While they could be horses, the 'draught animals' (*iumenta*) most likely to be stabled in Northumbria at this time would have been oxen. In either case, Cædmon would have been watching over the preferred species fit for convivial sacrifice when his vision occurred. Besides rousing suspicions as to just what this structure employed in the communal revelry might have been, Bede's narrative prompts one to ask what role Cædmon was expected to have played at the feast.

In the breakdown in social order which followed the withdrawal of the Roman legions in the early fifth century (see pp. 9–11), Britain came to be dominated by bands of armed men. The Old English termed these *gedryhte* [/ye-drü:hhtə/] 'military retinues'. Another name for them was *hergas* [/he:rrghas/] a word related to the verb 'harry', as in 'plunder'. Only the most successful leaders could afford to maintain these groups, which had clear affinities with analogous social units among the Scandinavians (Old Icelandic *drótt*) and the Irish (Old Irish *fían*), as well as with similar institutions current in the 'heroic' ages of cultures from all around the world. Such companies are formed when the economy produces enough wealth so as to provide something to steal, and when weapons technology has advanced to the point that training in the use of such weapons becomes a specialised business (Veblen 1899). Under such conditions a professional warrior class can prosper, as it came to do among both the formerly Roman-dominated, Celtic inhabitants of Britain and the immigrant groups which arrived in the wake of the Roman withdrawal in 410 AD.

For his own part, the author of *Beowulf* aims at portraying the pinnacle of such a system, in which even the lowest ranking member of Hrothgar's household should himself be seen as commanding homage from vassals further down the Danes' pyramid of suzerainty. But the vast majority of historical *gedryhte* would have operated at modest levels on quite a small scale. The portrayal of warrior life in *Beowulf* can distort our view as to the social status of the historical warrior class among the Anglo-Saxons. One way this happens is when the poet of *Beowulf* promotes artefacts of gold as the principal medium of economic exchange. In Heorot, the only domestic animals permitted on stage are prize war chargers, just as no servant comes clearly into focus, unless one sees Queen Wealhtheow or her daughter Freawaru in that light. Outside *Beowulf*, however, laws and other historical records show that cattle were both a prime source of wealth and medium of exchange, so that cattle raiding and theft were common war band pursuits, just as a heroic cattle raid (Old Irish *táin*) forms the core of the most important Old Irish saga, the *Táin Bo Cuailnge* ('Cooley's cattle raid'). Yet only scant hints at such activity remain in the most archaic Old English heroic poetry (Wyly 1999: 127–33).

Bede avoids any clear indication of who ordered Cædmon to watch the cattle, just as he never clearly indicates who directs the festivities which Cædmon habitually abandons. All we are allowed to know about his social status is that the next day he presents himself to a superior, who directs him to Abbess Hild. While Bede's Latin term for this superior, a 'reeve' (*vilicus*), could refer to some sort of royal administrative official, it is more likely that Bede refers to the lord of the land-holding unit known as a 'hide' (OE *hīd*) [/heed/], who was known as a 'churl' (OE *ceorl*) [/churrl/] in the laws from the southern Anglo-Saxon kingdoms. In due course, as the modern semantics of 'churl' attest, these minor lords underwent a depreciation of status (Charles Edwards 1972). In Cædmon's day, however, members of this class should be seen as exercising control over an extended family along with their retainers and slaves. Their economic power lay in the intensified agricultural production for which plough teams were essential. Possessing his own home, Cædmon would have been among the 'senior retinue' (OE *dugoð*) [/doo:ghoth/] of such a petty lord. While the rest of his men were drinking the night away and so maximally exposed to ambush, what strategic considerations would warrant Cædmon's lord placing a single unarmed, untrained old man in charge of his major capital investment? In terms of today's attitudes towards agrarian occupations, would we be closer to the mark imagining Cædmon as a cowherd or a cowboy?

Another unwarranted assumption lies in Cædmon having come from the Whitby vicinity. When one considers the historical situation in Britain at that time, Hild's monastery may have been the best equipped site in Britain for the examination of Cædmon's experience, especially if the event took place in the early part of Hild's abbacy. By the middle of the seventh century, the Christian mission to England had suffered significant setbacks (Hunter Blair 1992). Of these, the most relevant to Cædmon's story was the inability to generate native bishops from within the ranks of newly initiated Northumbrians and so extend to the influence of the Roman Church beyond its stronghold in the extreme southeast. In the north, the Irish bishops at Lindisfarne and its subordinate centres dominated the ecclesiastical hierarchy until they were eventually superseded by Anglo-Saxon bishops, the majority of whom were trained under Abbess Hild. Cædmon's case of inspired English poetry required inquisitors who were trained not only in orthodox Catholic doctrine, but further had a command of the English language, especially the niceties of vernacular poetry. That the oldest versions of Cædmon's *Hymn* are Northumbrian texts could say more about the dialect of the earliest copyists than about Cædmon's own speech.

The pre-eminence of Whitby as a monastic foundation is signalled by its hosting a famous church council, the 'Synod of Whitby', in 664. This was only seven years after the monastery was founded. In many respects, Hild's monastery was the mirror image of a warrior society. Both *gedryht* and monastery or 'minster' (Old English *mynster*) were structured after an idealised model of the extended patriarchal family. Here a social fiction of brotherhood was inculcated so as to promote social cohesion; and one of fatherhood, so as to command discipline through obedience. Yet whereas the *gedryht* was a male-dominated group, whose highest ranking female served ale to the retinue in one of its most exalted rituals of communal bonding, Whitby was presided over by a matriarch, whose highest ranked male subordinates served God in their most sacred ritual of communal bonding. Had Cædmon come from a warrior background, the social organisation of Hild's monastery may have appeared to him as a strangely familiar community in which to live, for all its differences.

The author of *Beowulf* elegantly, if cryptically, evokes the dark side of the heroic ethos which drove the warrior band. If the *gedryht* modelled itself on a patriarchal family, the sibling rivalry and intergenerational antagonism within such a household could become stifling. A relentless competition for rank and dominion within the group could either compel its members to accomplish new heights of daring or trigger them into devouring its collective assets. Only long after we have come to know Beowulf through the direct presentation of his shrewdness and courage are we told that, prior to leaving for Hrothgar's court, Beowulf was held in little esteem among his uncle's war band for being a 'slouch' (*sleac*) and anything but impetuous (lines 2183–8). The passage implies that his comrades had concluded thus from Beowulf's lack of a 'rough heart' (*hreoh sefa*) and for his almost turn-the-other-cheek restraint in 'on no account striking his drunken comrades in arms' (*nealles druncne slog heorðgeneatas*, lines 2179–80). The upshot of all this is an environment in which some degree of sadistic 'play' with one's companions was counted an integral part of attaining respect. Beowulf lacked not the strength, but the inclination to take part in such sport, making him all the more susceptible to derision and scorn from fellow warriors.

Monastic communities were not immune to inbred jealousy and bullying, but the evolution of monastic regulations aimed at developing strategies for alleviating, if not overcoming, such divisiveness. Although we do not know the details of the Whitby rule which Hild implemented on the model of Bishop Aidan's Irish community at Lindisfarne, Bede tells us that she privileged peace and Christian charity above all; she also forbade personal property within the monastic community (Colgrave and Mynors 1969: 406–409). By Hild's lifetime, the monastic rule of St Benedict of Nursia (*c.* 480–543), would surely have been available for consultation in Northumbria. The Benedictine Rule would eventually come to dominate Roman Catholic monastic life, in part because it aimed at eliminating any link between the determination of status and the disposition of material goods. Thus a Benedictine monastery could become a melting pot of people from both rich backgrounds and poor.

Material goods have to be passed around to keep an economy flowing. These can be had by taking them off others or by trade or manufacture, but the main thing is that some people end up richer than others. This shouldn't matter in a monastery, where private property is supposed to be forbidden. Here the tokens of distinction, like praise and attention, are intangible. Praise is less contentious than money, but even in monasteries there were rivalries, which St Benedict sought to suppress by tying the community's internal politics to length of service. Hierarchical standing in monastic communities was to be determined solely by the length of time one had been a member (Mayr-Harting 1976: 3–5). In this way the monastic rule succeeded in hobbling the psychological drive for wealth and status which elsewhere led men to privilege the life of constant risk and perpetual struggle that lay at the heart of the heroic ethos.

Cædmon's story contrasts two social contexts, one – the secular world – which frustrates his effective participation and another – the religious world – which stimulates it. At the same time his dream vision forms a private interview straddling both worlds. Cædmon himself appears to have been something of an ethnic blend: the *caed*-prefix in his name is name of British Celtic or Welsh origin, but Bede states that his language was English. In northern Britain many people still sprang from Celtic stock and these peoples especially had been in contact with Christianity for centuries, even if their communities were not subordinated into any organised church hierarchy. Whether such people would have labelled themselves as Christians is impossible for us to say, but they could hardly have ignored the growing political influence of the Germanic-speaking enclaves which had taken root in Northumbria. Like so much of the world that lay outside the walls of a monastery in those days, we know nothing of Cædmon's upbringing. Was he even Christian? If he wasn't, it is easy to see how easily the evangelising logic of Bede's narrative could be upset by the need, say, to baptise Cædmon as a Christian convert after he had his vision. Cædmon's dream visitor provides him with an audience for his singing, but Bede does not call this disembodied voice a saint or an angel and while the voice dictates the theme of Cædmon's song, it does not provide him with the words.

Bede's reticence about the nature of this dream visitor is matched by his lack of any description of the revel in which Cædmon refused to sing in turn, except to say that this party took place 'for the sake of merriment' (*laetitiae causa*). Humour is highly subjective: some may laugh where others may be sickened. No sooner has Hrothgar, for example, welcomed Beowulf to Heorot than the musical accompaniment by his royal bard (Old English *scop*) cues Hrothgar's 'orator' (*þyle*), whose name is Unferth, to subject Beowulf to a round of highly rhetorical insults in elaborate verse. This looks to be a stylised ceremonial exchange designed to test a warrior's mental dexterity before drawing a conclusion about his fighting prowess (Enright 1998: 309–11, 327–9). The poet does not tell us about Unferth's competitive animus towards Beowulf, but with his characteristic discretion he does leave his audience to imagine the 'laughter of warriors' (*hæleþa hleahtor*, line 611) which is occasioned by the flyting between these two warriors. Does the war band look on with baited breath throughout the contest or does the ordeal provoke the spectators into raucous jeers and heckling as the verbal duelling proceeds? Either reaction could serve only to heighten the tension in the hall, to raise the stakes in this 'game'.

Any great athlete or musician can vouch for the need to transcend his or her limits in the pursuit of excellence, to attain a mystical state in which there is no place for distraction or feeling self-conscious. This degree of focus needs a lot of preparation. Athletes may spend years in achieving such transcendence. If the warrior's sole prerogative is to train himself to a point where he can reach this state, then the true purpose of the war band's entertainments must be to contribute to his preparation in some way (Enright 1998: 306, 334–5). It is unlikely Bede ever saw a battle, cloistered as he was among 'spiritual warriors', i.e. monks. It is even less likely Bede had any clear understanding of what mental conditioning a real warrior had to have. In monastic meditation or mortification, the soldier in Christ differed from his military counterpart and sought radically different objectives. The highest achievement for a saint, the soldier of the contemplative life, was an introspection so intense as to extinguish the experiential world altogether. Rather than fully participate in the present moment, the objective was to glimpse eternity by escaping metaphysical time altogether (DeGregorio 1999: 26–34). The warrior strove bodily to bring death down on others, but the saint sought to overtake his own mortality through a regimented physical inertia. Cædmon seems to have wished to leave the warrior's world and enter the monk's.

Bede states that Cædmon would leave the feasting when he saw that the lyre was about to come his way. On this point, Bede's conception of feasting may again be based more on Mediterranean learning than on any reports of carousing in English history (Fritz 1969: 336). Two scenarios can be imagined on the basis of Bede's story: depending on his companions' motives for offering the lyre, either they thought Cædmon able to play and sing or they considered him unable to do so. In either case, Cædmon, on account of his experience and rank, may have been expected to sing as part of contributing his due share to the event. Not being able to do so would have put him at risk of losing status. The demand that the poetry be recited to the accompaniment of a lyre only raised the stakes, insofar as the lyre or harp is a musical instrument which necessarily required explicit training and as such was a mark of aristocratic upbringing among the Germanic peoples, much as it had been among the archaic Greeks.

There is a potential comparison here between Cædmon and King David, who played the harp as the author of the psalms. Having said that, the harp plays no part in Cædmon's vision, neither is it mentioned further in Cædmon's career, where the pressures to perform are very different. In this way the secular revel Cædmon attended may have been of higher social status than the world he subsequently entered as a monk. For all their book learning, stone architecture, and pictorial iconography, even the monks at Wearmouth–Jarrow, Romanised as they were, could not keep up pretensions to aristocratic class (Hunter Blair 1990: 257). Warrior societies are different. Unlike the fixed, but leisurely progression of the monastic order, they offer a man mobility both upward and downward according to the unforeseeables of no-holds-barred competition. Any weakness which could lead to defeat on the battlefield is better sounded out first in the hall. What an occasion for public humiliation!

Cædmon would have wished to escape all this. He appears to have reached a rank high enough in worldly society to have something to lose, yet perhaps too high to afford publicly dabbling in experimental improvisation. For Anglo-Saxon farmers, princes and warriors it made as much sense to recite oral poetry in solitude as it did to talk to oneself. For monks, by way of contrast, there was a lot of sense in it. Here was Cædmon's chance. Having a miraculous dream, with its command performance to a mysterious auditor played out within the privacy of his own mind, would have offered Cædmon, as an aspiring retainer, an escape from secular pressures into the safer, more regulated, world of the monastery.

Northumbrian poetry: Bede versus Cædmon

Fifty years after Cædmon's poetic debut, the immensely learned Bede resorted to some Old English verse composition on his own account. His only surviving Old English poem is a five-line epigram which he is said to have composed just before dying. Wistfully, this is known as 'Bede's Death Song' (text after Schopf 1996):

> Fore thaem neidfarae   naenig uuiurthit
> thoncsnotturra   than him tharf sie
> to ymbhycggannae   aer his hinongae
> huat his gastae   godaes aeththa yflaes
> aefter deothdaege   doemid uueorthae.

No man, before making that forced journey, proves
wiser in thought than he needs to be,
to consider, before his going hence,
just what, after his dying day, for good or ill
the judgement on his soul may be.

In this grim poem Bede appears to claim not only that people know nothing of the Judgement that awaits them, but also that they generally don't think of improving their lives until death forces them to do so. This is a Christian use of 'judgement' (Old English *dom*) in opposition to the ancient heroic claim that a man's 'reputation' (also Old English *dōm*) lives eternal (compare the sentiment in *Beowulf*, lines 1386–9). But Bede may be the inferior poet. Whereas Cædmon uses the meanings of his words to generate structure, so as to reduce the amount of purely grammatical signalling to a minimum, Bede swamps his salutary message in a quagmire of adverbs, pronouns, prepositions, auxiliary verbs and conjunctions. From the little this poem gives us of his vernacular work, it appears that Bede has modelled his Old English syntax on the devices of Latin rhetoric (for the structure, see: Schopf 1996: 15). Whereas Cædmon demands that the listener activate his prior knowledge so as to convey meaning to his poem from among a multitude of possibilities, the only thing that makes Bede's composition 'verse' at all is the alliteration (see Introduction, p. 23).

The context for Bede's 'Death Song' is *The Life of Bede* which was written by a student of his named Cuthbert. Claiming that Bede, his teacher, was learned in Old English verse (*erat doctus in nostris carminibus*), Cuthbert reports that Bede rehearsed these verses shortly before that big moment in any saintly life, his departure for the next world (Schopf 1996: 28). As Bede was at work dictating a biblical commentary during his last days, scribes were on hand to record his performance on the spot. Such circumstances may have been the only ones which could have ensured the faithful transmission of Bede's poem to posterity. Cædmon's song, contrariwise, is the Old English poem whose oral transmission we can be most sure about. Despite Bede's decision to leave out the Old English, Cædmon's original text made its way into Bede's *History*, so today we can judge something of his poetic talent for ourselves.

And yet Cuthbert's praise for Bede's poetic abilities need not be taken as insincere or fulsome flattery. Within the colonial context of Wearmouth–Jarrow, Bede's 'Death Song' could well have been beyond the creative abilities of his peers. While Bede's epigram represents a precocious leap in the development of Old English versification away from oral tradition, several of Cædmon's verse techniques are not only unmatched by Bede but unparalleled elsewhere in Old English poetry. For example, the syntactic enjambment which straddles the caesura in lines eight and nine of Cædmon's hymn would be unremarkable in terms of Norse occasional verse, yet have no parallel in Old English. Was Cædmon's poetic licence the product of divine inspiration, consumate individual genius or simply the genuine oral practice handed down from Germanic times?

Remarkably, post-Cædmonian composition practice follows the conventions of Latin poetry in aligning sense with metre. One of Bede's earliest works was a treatise on Latin metrics, *De arte metrica*. Latin metrics played an important function in early medieval language teaching, because an analysis of the verse structure could be used to compensate for the virtual absence of any means for explicitly analysing syntax (Ruff 2005: 149–53). Within 50 years, the monastic audience of Old English poetry had come to be conditioned by Latinate standards of composition. No matter how memorable in itself, any composition in Old English would have had to be written down for it to survive and only within a monastery could this have taken place for virtually the entire Anglo-Saxon period (Fulk 1992: 342–7). This means virtually all of the Old English poetry composed before the eleventh century comes to us through monastic poets or scribes who were trained in Latin.

Cædmon's legacy: the Old English biblical poems

In abandoning material incentives and competitive rankings, such as in the secular world, a monastic community such as Whitby could rely on good deeds as being performed for their own sake. Either that or it could look for other ways of motivating people to live moral lives. Cædmon motivated people, according to Bede. Just as in the war band, where the poet's job is to praise and to blame (Enright 1998: 306–307), so Cædmon inspired people with his songs. Bede says that through his poetry:

> cunctis homines ab amore scelerum abstrahere, ad dilectionem vero et solertiam bonae actionis excitare curabat. Erat enim vir multum religiosus, et regularibus disciplinis humiliter subditus; adversum vero illos, qui aliter facere volebant, zelo magni fervoris accensus.

> he attempted to turn all men away from the love of vice and towards the true delight in, and application to, good works. For he was a very religious man and had submitted humbly to monastic rule, but was incensed with fervent zeal against any who would do otherwise.

Working as it does on the imagination, the threat of punishment is often more persuasive than its physical application. Neither is there any need in monasteries for rewards to stimulate obedience. In his role as monastic monitor, Bede claims that Cædmon:

> de terrore futuri iudicii et horrore poenae gehennalis ac dulcedine regni caelestis multa carmina faciebat, sed et alia perplura de beneficiis et iudiciis divinis.

> would sing of the terror of future judgement, the horror of hellish punishment, and the delights of heavenly kingdom, besides much else concerning divine benefits and judgements.

The anonymous Whitby *Life of Gregory the Great* (c. 704–14) has stories which use the supernatural as a means of policing Christian behaviour. While still alive, the saintly Pope Gregory (c. 540–c. 604) is said there to have condemned a physician to 30 days of punishment in Hell for laying aside three coins. After his death, furthermore, Gregory appeared to his papal successor in a dream when it became clear the latter would no longer maintain Gregory's still-living friends; for this obstinacy, Gregory's apparition kicked the sleeping pope in the head with such violence that he died a few days later (Colgrave 1968: 124–8). Were it not for the positive evangelism we have seen in Cædmon's *Hymn*, one might conclude that fiery appeals to such motivators as hell or heaven may have been Cædmon's only rhetorical means of achieving his social impact: 'through his songs the minds of many were often moved to despise the world and aspire to heavenly life' (*Cuius carminibus multorum saepe animi ad contemptum saeculi et appetitum sunt vitae caelestis accensi*).

Ministering to souls is pastoral work. If the Anglo-Saxon conversion (597–c. 690) were to go forward, the future bishops who were being trained in Hild's monasteries would need to find a practical means of applying such skills. Any speaker of Old English interested in the Christian message would have found Cædmon's presence at Whitby a useful way of learning doctrine without Latin. Indeed, memorising a rigorously organised knowledge of Christian doctrine would lighten the financial burden of keeping a library. As an instrument in developing such a repository in memory, traditional verse compositions on historical or mythological subjects could have been created and passed down orally within monasteries just as outside them. In the same way the writing down of profane classical poetry could be justified as being for didactic purposes, even though in this case some manuscript costs were involved.

At Whitby, Cædmon's initial tests concerned the versification of 'discourse relating to sacred history or doctrine' (*quaedam sacrae historiae sive doctinae sermo*). Entering the monastery, Hild had Cædmon instructed in the cycle of sacred history (*iussutque illum seriem sacrae historiae doceri*), from Creation to Judgement. This was mediated to Cædmon by 'exegetes' or interpreters (*interpretes*), who could hardly have one this without doctrinally conditioning Cædmon as well. The resulting list of topics which Cædmon was supposed to have treated is remarkably like the surviving list of Old English biblical poems.

So, of the 30,000 lines of Old English poetry surviving, we have a long poem now called *Genesis*, which tells of the creation of the world, the origin of the human race and the entire history of the Book of Genesis in the Bible. The Old English *Genesis* is preserved in a manuscript called the Junius Book, which was put together towards the end of the tenth century. It is the first poem in the book and has some textual gaps, as well as another poem inserted into the middle of its text in a position answering to lines 235–851. To distinguish them the larger poem is called *Genesis A*, the smaller inserted poem *Genesis B*. The latter is a better piece of work and tells of Lucifer's fall from heaven, his confinement as Satan in Hell and his decision to send a junior devil to tempt Adam and Eve in the Garden of Eden. The story is here changed so that the devil first tempts Adam, not Eve, telling him that the Lord now wants them to eat the forbidden fruit. When Adam rejects him for his having no means of identification, the devil tries his luck with Eve, now with the ineluctible logic that God will be angry with both of them unless she persuades Adam to change his mind. Eve in this version is presented as a victim of circumstance, of her ignorance, but no less intelligent than Adam her husband. There are also two trees in the garden, with the forbidden fruit being ugly to behold. Unlike *Genesis A*, this smaller poem is thought to have been composed originally in Old Saxon (the ancestor of modern northern German dialects known as *Plattdeutsch*), then transposed into West Saxon probably in the 890s in the reign of Alfred the Great (871–99).

As well as this poem, we have the Old English *Exodus*, which follows it in the Junius Book (Bradley 1982: 49–65). This is a much higher class work, as good in its own way as *Beowulf*, yet with a text which has been messed up by the various scribes who copied it before the final sole-surviving version we have now. Like the book in the Bible by that name, *Exodus* describes the flight of the people of Israel out of Egypt and their crossing of the Red Sea. Unlike the Book of Exodus, however, the poem introduces elements from other parts of the Bible, from Genesis, Numbers, the Psalms and Wisdom. It seems to draw to its conclusion with an injunction to unlock the meaning 'with the keys of the spirit' (*gæstes cægon*, line 525). It compresses some incidents, expands on others and plays with temporal unities by digressing into the story of Noah's Flood and Abraham's near-sacrifice of Isaac – all to show the maintenance of the pledge or covenant which unites the chosen people to God. The chosen people, in this context, are the Northumbrians themselves, one of whom probably produced this poem in emulation of Cædmon. Indeed many people used to believe that not only *Genesis* and *Exodus*, but also *Daniel*, were the work of Cædmon himself, although this idea has long since been laid to rest.

Daniel is the Old English poem which comes after *Exodus* in the Junius Book (Bradley 1982: 66–86). Like the Old English *Genesis*, Daniel is really two poems: *Daniel A*, which tells of King Nebuchadnezzar of Babylon and his feud with the prophet Daniel, who converts him eventually after the miracle of the three children surviving the fiery furnace; and *Daniel B*, which is interpolated into the larger poem, in lines 279–408. To complicate things, *Daniel B* is found in the Exeter Book in a slightly different version which is known as *Azarias*, after one of the children who, in this poem, prays to God for deliverance. It was perhaps the compiler of the Junius Book who blended the two *Genesis* poems as well as the two *Daniel* poems in this way.

There is also a poem called *Judith*, a vigorous work based on the apocryphal Book of Judith, the lady who saved the town of Bethulia from Assyrian invasion by cutting off the head of Holofernes, the general (and in the Old English *Judith*, the king) whose army threatens them. This poem was preserved alongside *Beowulf* in the Nowell Codex (British Library, Cotton Vitellius A.XV), possibly because the compiler wished to collect Holofernes as a monster (see pp. 64–5, 86–7). The poets of *Daniel A* and *B*, *Azarias* and *Judith*, working perhaps in the ninth and tenth centuries, all focus on the 'Babylonian Captivity', an episode in which God was said to punish the Israelites with displacement to Babylon for breaking His laws. As with Cædmon's encouragements to his community to live the good life, this theme is one of divine punishment for sins. But it is worth adding that each time an Anglo-Saxon poet set up a biblical story in heroic dress, he or she changed it so that the characters become recognisable as warriors and heroes all.

Besides these 'Cædmonian' poems, we have some more poems representing verse translations of lyrical portions of the Bible: the psalms in *The Paris Psalter*, *Fragments of Psalms*, *The Kentish Psalm* and *Psalm 50*; and biblical canticles, such as *Azarias* again and *The Gloria I* and *II*; and prayers, in *The Lord's Prayer I, II* and *III*. Other surviving poems celebrate the New Testament: not only *The Dream of the Rood*, the highly imaginative work discussed in the last chapter, a poem probably of before *c.* 700; but also three poems joined together in the Exeter Book: *Christ I* (or *A*) on the incarnation of the Lord, otherwise known as the *Advent Lyrics; Christ II* (or *B*) another poem on Jesus' passion, resurrection and ascension into heaven; and *Christ III* (or C), on the Day of Judgement. A signature presented in runic letters towards the end of *Christ II* identifies the poet of this work as one 'Cynewulf', a man who is thought to have been a Mercian in the ninth century. There are three other poems similarly identified as Cynewulf's, although *Christ II* is usually regarded as his finest work. These are *The Fates of the Apostles*, based on Acts; *Elene*, on the discovery (the word used is 'Invention') of the True Cross in Jerusalem (in 326) by the Roman Empress Helena, mother of Emperor Constantine; and *Juliana*, on the life and death of a Roman virgin martyr who is said to have been executed in an anti-Christian purge in Rome. There is *The Descent into Hell*, in which Christ harrows Hell of all the noble pagans in the same story as we see encapsulated at the end of *The Dream of the Rood*; another poem with this theme is *Christ and Satan*, which features a flyting between these protagonists such as we see later in the medieval mystery plays of the fourteenth and fifteenth centuries, but which also includes a lament of the fallen angels, the Harrowing of Hell, and Christ's ascension. *Christ and Satan* is the last poem to be included in the Junius Book. Where the apostles are concerned, we also have *Andreas*, the Old English poetic rendering of a Latin translation of a Greek romance, based on the life and works of Saints Andrew and Matthew. There is the splendid poem *The Phoenix* in the Exeter Book, an allegorical adaptation of a sixth-century poem on this mythical bird, one which celebrates the resurrection of Christ (Bradley 1982: 284–300). Not to forget Bede, we have two versions of a poem called *Judgement Day* (I and II). Each of these represents an adaptation of a poem called *De die iudicii* which Bede composed, naturally, in Latin.

What about the dates of all these works? All of them have been regarded, with some justification, as poetry inspired by the example of Cædmon in Whitby in 657–80. In the same way that a seasonal ritual is about time and again reliving an experience anew, so a traditional poetic performance involves a sequence of occasions, each one individual yet enhanced by memories of those that have gone before. It is tempting to think of Cædmon as having inaugurated at Whitby a poetic curriculum which he bequeathed to his listeners to take up and make their own: be fruitful and multiply! The extant copies of the Old English biblical poems cited earlier could thus be likened to fossilised exemplars of the various genres of poem Cædmon originated. While the four major poetic codices (the Exeter Book, the Junius Book, the Vercelli Book and the Nowell Codex) all derive from *c.* 975–*c.* 1025, rather late in the Anglo-Saxon period, most of the biblical poems can be dated on formal grounds as having become relatively fixed in their recorded forms prior to the Alfredian 880s. With only the hymns being clearly post-Alfredian in metrical form, much of the biblical poetry may have already been of primarily antiquarian interest by the tenth century. The earliest poems to reach their attested form were those based primarily on the Hebrew Bible: *Genesis A*, *Exodus* and *Daniel* are among the most archaic poems which survive and any of their attested forms may have been current in Bede's Day. While *Azarias* and its corresponding section within Daniel (lines 279–361) may trace back to one of the earliest attempts at paraphrasing a key liturgical text, the metrical translations of the psalms are attested in relatively late forms, probably in response to the Benedictine reform. The only other text dealing with the pre-Christian era, *Judith*, has given up any apocryphal pretence to Jewish relevance: the heroine is fully enmeshed in a warrior ethos of Christian fortitude. Its dating remains controversial, although it is possible to see it as reflecting an Anglo-Saxon reconquest of the Danelaw in the early tenth century (see pp. 320–2), one which was carried out by Æthelflæd, Lady of the Mercians, the daughter of King Alfred. Similarly, the portion of *Genesis* pertaining to the Fall of Man, *Genesis B* (lines 235–851), retains only the most tenuous ties to the corresponding events related in the Hebraic Bible.

Among the texts relating to the New Testament, the so-called *Christ III* is probably the oldest attested form, perhaps contemporary with the *Genesis A*, *Exodus* and *Daniel*. Next in chronological order may be placed *Andreas*, which shows signs of being composed somewhat earlier than the two biblical poems signed by Cynewulf: *The Fates of the Apostles* and *Christ II*. Cynewulf appears to have composed his poems sometime between 750 and 850. He refers to his poetic voice as having been 'unbound' at night though internal intervention (*Elene*, lines 1236–50) and of poetic craft being a divine gift (*Christ II*, lines 664–85) in a way strongly reminiscent of Bede's description of Cædmon. Cynewulf's style is probably the most amenable to comparison with the continental Germanic religious poetry, with which it is roughly contemporary. *Christ I* and *Christ and Satan* are difficult to date on formal criteria, but they probably do not antedate Cynewulf. The remaining poems are too short to be dated on formal grounds, but are probably no older than the late eighth century at the earliest.

Where Cædmon's lost *œuvre* is concerned, as we can judge it from Bede's chapter in the *History*, this has been likened to the basic historical curriculum which Augustine prescribed for catechumens, people becoming Christians. It has been argued 'that Bede regards Cædmon as Christ's apostle to the English in the matter of vernacular sacred song'. Were that the case, however, Cædmon appears to have left out the liturgical texts essential to Christians who were preparing to go out and evangelise: Jesus' teaching from the Gospels. Further missing from Cædmon's canon are the essential liturgical texts: the Psalms and Canticles. The teaching of Jesus was, paradoxically, the most sacred and the most problematic phase in sacred history for the Catholic establishment: the Gospels of Thomas or of Mary Magdalene; the Secret Book of John or the recently rediscovered Gospel of Judas Iscariot were most fervently condemned as the breeding grounds of heresy. There may well have been ideological reasons not to translate the Gospels into languages which could be easily verified by the Roman establishment.

In this, the Old English tradition contrasts markedly with those of the continental Germanic peoples: the *Heliand*, a life of Jesus the 'Healer' in long Old Saxon verse epic, and Otfrid of Weissenburg's *Evangelienbuch*, composed in Old High German (ancestor of standard modern German as spoken today) both attempt to give coherent, encyclopaedic accounts. If Cædmon's repertoire were meant to lay out a programme, it contributed to a hybrid curriculum of texts, in which the verse translations served to focus the scope of Latin learning on the core Christian texts. As in the strict seniority system of Benedict's Rule, the Old English vernacular would have had to submit to Latin in the promulgation of monastic culture.

Working far north of Whitby at the combined monasteries of Wearmouth–Jarrow, Bede immersed himself in Latin culture. For all his dedication as a teacher, however, Bede does not appear to have given top priority to communicating to the majority of his Anglo-Saxon contemporaries. By writing texts all in Latin, he limited his English audience to an elite colony of those with the means to acquire his foreign language. At best, he could be seen as helping the common people indirectly, through establishing cultural diplomatic ties with the Mediterranean and Merovingian intellectual elites in Italy and France respectively. He may also have looked ahead to a day when the entire English nation would have shared his command of Latin. That is something King Alfred must have hoped to achieve with his programme of rebuilding education one and a half centuries later, in Wessex in the 880s (see pp. 252–8). Even in Bede's time, however, when Christianity was firmly ensconced among the highest Anglo-Saxon elites, reaching the greater mass of the English nation was little more than a dream for any writer of Latin.

The official conversion of the Anglo-Saxon kingdoms to Catholicism was a question of language and culture as much as of religion. To what extent could Old English accommodate new concepts and new patterns of thought and still be English? Unlike all the other Germanic peoples to invade areas of the western Roman Empire, the Anglo-Saxons appear to have encountered no significant population who spoke Latin as a native language. Neither does it appear that there were ever the resources, in terms of either teaching materials or didactic know-how, to convert the English into a Romance-speaking people. Among the monastic elite, however, Latinate learning overtook native lore in the competition to claim whatever educational resources were available, just as French did for several centuries after the Norman Conquest (see pp. 480–2).

In the long run, by acculturating himself to the privileged Latinate world, Bede became the giant of English literary history – Cædmon the footnote. It may seem there are many Old English biblical poems, from the list of them above. But writing salvaged relatively little Old English from the period, in relation to the quantity of Latin. Where most Old English poetry was concerned, delivered through oral formulae to audiences in halls or cloisters, there was nothing beyond the moment of performance itself. It may well be, that in their rush to become Catholic at home as well as welcome guests in the civilised outposts of Mediterranean Christiandom, some Anglo-Saxon clerics condoned the loss of this part of their native heritage. But Cædmon's evocative fragment gives us a glimpse of what other scholars were doing. The strength of Cædmon's song lies not simply in its rhetorical elegance; its rhetorical elegance is the reason why it was retained. Important work remains to be done in relating the other Old English biblical poems to the matrix of texts and doctrine derived from the medieval Bible. Even those Old English compositions most tightly bound to the form and expression of their biblical sources can potentially supply a great deal of information about the inner nature of Anglo-Saxon poetry. Where once these biblical poems served to mediate between traditional ideas and exotic information, to bring into focus an unfamiliar Latinate culture, the challenge for us lies in reversing this process in order to glimpse the otherness of the ancient English mentality.

Translations and texts

Bradley, S.A.J., trans., *Anglo-Saxon Poetry: An Anthology of Old English Poems in Prose Translation with Introduction and Headnotes* (London, 1982).

Colgrave, Bertram, ed., *The Earliest Life of Gregory the Great: by an Anonymous Monk of Whitby* (Lawrence, KS, 1968).

Colgrave, Bertram and R.A.B. Mynors, eds, *Bede's Ecclesiastical History of the English People* (Oxford, 1969).

McClure, Judith and Roger Collins, trans. and eds, *Bede: The Ecclesiastical History of the English People* (Oxford, 1999).

Further reading

Brooks, Kenneth, ed., *Andreas and The Fates of the Apostles* (Oxford, 1961).

Brown, George Hardin, 'The Meaning of *Interpres* in Aldhelm and Bede', in *Interpretation Medieval and Modern: The J.A.W. Bennett Memorial Lectures*, 8th Series (Perugia, 1992), pp. 43–65.

Campbell, Jackson J., ed., *The Advent Lyrics of the Exeter Book* (Princeton, 1959).

Charles Edwards, T.M., 'Kinship, Status and the Origins of the Hide', *Past and Present* 56 (1972), pp. 3–33.

DeGregorio, Scott, 'The Venerable Bede on Prayer and Contemplation', *Traditio* 54 (1999), pp. 1–39.

Dekker, Kees, 'Pentecost and Linguistic Self-Consciousness in Anglo-Saxon England: Bede and Ælfric', *Journal of English and Germanic Philology* 104 (2005), pp. 345–72.

Doane, A.N., ed., *Genesis A: A New Edition* (Madison, WI, 1978).

Doane, A.N., ed., *The Saxon Genesis: An Edition of the West Saxon Genesis B and the Old Saxon Vatican Genesis* (Madison, WI, 1991).

Enright, Michael J., 'The Warband Context of the Unferth Episode', *Speculum* 73 (1998), pp. 297–337.

Farrell, Robert, ed., *Daniel and Azarias* (London, 1974).

Finnegan, R.E., ed., *Christ and Satan* (Waterloo, ON, 1977).

Fritz, Donald W., 'Cædmon: A Traditional Christian Poet', *Mediaeval Studies* 31 (1969), pp. 334–7.

Fulk, R.D., *A History of Old English Meter* (Philadelphia, PA, 1992)

Griffith, Mark, ed., *Judith* (Exeter, 1997).

Howe, Nicholas, 'Rome: Capital of Anglo-Saxon England', *Journal of Medieval and Early Modern Studies* 34 (2004), pp. 147–72.

Hunter Blair, Peter, 'Whitby as a Centre of Learning in the Seventh Century', in *Learning and Literature in Anglo-Saxon England*, Lapidge Michael, and Helmut Gneuss, eds (Cambridge, 1992), pp. 3–32.

Hunter Blair, Peter, *The World of Bede* (Cambridge, 1990).

Kiernan, Kevin, 'Reading Cædmon's *Hymn* with Someone Else's Glosses', *Representations* 32 (1990), pp. 157–74.

Lees, Clare A. and Gillian R. Overing, 'Birthing Bishops and Fathering Poets: Bede, Hild and Relations of Cultural Production', *Exemplaria* 6 (1994), pp. 35–65.

Lucas, Peter J., ed., *Exodus* (London, 1977).

Mayr-Harting, Henry M.R.E., *The Venerable Bede, the Rule of St Benedict, and Social Class* (Jarrow, 1976).

Mitchell, Bruce, 'Cædmon's Hymn, line 1: What is the Subject of "scylun" or its Variants?', *Leeds Studies in English*, New Series 16 (1985), pp. 190–97.

Muir, Bernard J., ed., *The Exeter Anthology of Old English Poetry: An Edition of Exeter Dean and Chapter MS 3501* (Exeter, 1994).

O'Donnell, Daniel P., *Cædmon's Hymn: A Multimedia Study, Archive and Edition* (Cambridge, 2005).

Orchard, Andy, 'Poetic inspiration and prosaic translation: the making of *Cædmon's Hymn*', in *Studies in English Language and Literature: 'Doubt wisely', Papers in Honour of E.G. Stanley*, Toswell, Mary J., and Elizabeth M. Tyler, eds (London, 1996), pp. 402–22.

Pizarro, Joaquín Martinez, 'Poetry as Rumination: the Model for Bede's Cædmon', *Neophilologus* 89 (2005), pp. 469–72.

Ruff, Carin, 'The Place of Metrics in Anglo-Saxon Latin Education: Aldhelm and Bede', *Journal of English and Germanic Philology* 104 (2005), pp. 149–70.

Schopf, Alfred, 'Bedas Sterblied', *Literaturwissenschaftliches Jahrbuch* 73 (1996), pp. 9–30.

Veblen, Thorstein, *The Theory of the Leisure Class: An Economic Study in the Evolution of Institutions* (London and New York, 1899).

Wyly, Bryan W., *Figures of Authority in the Old English 'Exodus'* (Heidelberg, 1999).

Wyly, Bryan W., *On the Key to 'Exodus'* (Milan, 2004).

CHAPTER 8

Monasteries and courts: Alcuin and Offa

Andy Orchard

Not all the poets were monks, but it helped. There again, not all the monks were very monastic. To add to Cædmon's *Hymn* is another ancient English poem, one which is perhaps the earliest Old English poem to survive without any clearly Christian content. This can be found preserved in a Latin letter written by an anonymous Anglo-Saxon missionary in the early eighth century, who was encouraging another unknown colleague not to hesitate about a trip he was planning. In somewhat shaky Latin, the missionary asks his correspondent to 'remember the Saxon proverb', and then switches to Old English, quoting two lines of poetry that make his point perfectly:

> Oft daedlata domæ forę̧ldit,
> sigisitha gahuem, suuyltit thi ana.

> Often a deed-slack man puts off glory,
> every chance of winning: for that, he dies alone.

The individualism of this sentiment seems worldly and heroic. Indeed it wouldn't be out of place among those expressed by the pagan characters in *Beowulf*. Beowulf himself says that 'Fate often spares an undoomed man, when his courage has held' (*Wyrd oft nereð unfægne eorl þonne his ellen deah*, lines 572–3), while King Hrothgar of the Danes congratulates the monster-slaying hero by saying that 'you yourself have caused by your deeds your glory to live for ever' (*Þu þe self hafast dædum gefremed þæt þin dom lyfað awa to aldre*, lines 953–5). According to the Saxon proverb quoted, success brings fame; lack of success, a lonely death. At a time more sensitive to advertising, this missionary might as well have said 'just do it'.

Whoever coined this Saxon proverb certainly shared not only the world-view of the heathens in *Beowulf*, but also the *Beowulf* poet's gift for com-pressed and innovative expression. The proverb's two short lines contain two poetic compounds (here translated as 'a deed-slack man' (*daedlata*) and 'chance of winning' (*sigisitha*)) that are not found anywhere else in surviv-ing Old English verse. In somewhat the same way, these lines share with *Beowulf* an apparently traditional pairing of the Old English word for 'deeds' (*daed-*) and that for 'glory' (*dom-*), highlighted by alliteration, that emphas-ises the connection between acts and fame. The same pairing is also found in clearly Christian poetry, where, however, the term translated here as 'glory' (Old English *dom*) has its other sense of 'judgement'. Specifically this refers to 'Judgement Day' or 'Doomsday' (*domesdæg*), when the deeds done in this world are a measure of rewards in the next. It was in ways like this that the traditional values of an inherited, native, spoken, and Germanic pre-Christian past were transformed through the influence of the new, imported, literate and Latinate Christian culture. We have seen something of this with Cædmon in the previous chapter (see pp. 198–9). These days we are perhaps too used to thinking of Latin and Old English as quite distinct languages in Anglo-Saxon England: the one the language of the Anglo-Saxon church and the other that of the mead hall. But it is clear throughout the period that significant interaction took place and that there was much contact between cloister and court, between monastery and mead hall.

Books and bookmen

Like the Saxon proverb, most of the literature that survives from Anglo-Saxon has only done so thanks to the efforts of Christian scribes whose main task was to transmit Latin. That is why the overwhelming majority of Old English texts that have survived, whether in prose or verse, are deeply indebted to Latin models, Latin sources or to the fact that they appear (often in the margins or stray spaces at the beginning and end of other texts) in mainly Latin manuscripts. Indeed, when we think of it, Old English poetry is a form that is highly traditional in style and language, with roots extend-ing back into a pre-Christian, preliterate Germanic past. Considering the Christian view of this background we are lucky to have any Old English poetry at all. Only about 30,000 lines and 175,000 words of this survive, equating to about six times as many words as there are in Shakespeare's *Hamlet*. Mostly the poems are found in just four manuscripts, all from around the year 1000, which are all in various ways damaged, botched or incomplete (the Exeter Book, the Junius Book, the Vercelli Book, the Nowell Codex). All four survive thanks to their perceived value as Christian artefacts and our view of Old English literature would certainly be quite different if we had been less lucky and different again if we had been more.

As it is, we may only have *Beowulf* thanks to a compiler's interest in monsters, rather than the heroes who slay them, while all that survives of such thrilling Old English battle poems as *The Fight at Finnsburh* (pp. 99–101) or *The Battle of Maldon* (pp. 339–44) are versions copied at least 600 years after the original manuscripts, which are now lost. In the case of *The Fight at Finnsburh*, indeed, it seems likely that the now-lost manuscript fragment survived long enough to be copied only because it was preserved not for its content, but merely as a piece of stiffening material for another volume in the library at Lambeth Palace, the residence of the Archbishop of Canterbury. Alongside *Beowulf* in the sole fire-damaged manuscript that contains it, are some other texts. Not only are there two prose accounts of exotic marvels catalogued in *The Wonders of the East* and *Alexander's Letter to Aristotle*, but also a prose *Life of Saint Christopher* (in this case not the traveller's friend, but a giant with the head of a dog) and *Judith*, which, as we have seen, is a poem celebrating the biblical Bethulian heroine who gruesomely decapitates her would-be rapist (see pp. 86–9). Given *Beowulf*'s sometimes celebrated status as one of the finest and most important pieces of English poetry, this other material seems strange company for our greatest Old English poem to keep. It may indicate that the manuscript's compiler had a less elevated view of the poem's merits than some modern readers.

Equally unimpressively, another manuscript, the Junius Book, preserves just four lengthy poems. This is probably the earliest of the four main manuscripts containing poetry. As we have seen in the last chapter, the modern titles of its poems (*Genesis*, *Exodus*, *Daniel* and *Christ and Satan*) betray their religious concerns. The beginning of that manuscript is lavishly illustrated, but it seems that the illustrator lost interest or was called away for a more pressing project as the manuscript wears on: at all events, there are spaces for pictures, but none has been drawn. A third manuscript, the Vercelli Book, gets its name from being found in the northern Italian city of Vercelli, which lies on the route to Rome. Presumably the book was brought there from England by a passing Anglo-Saxon pilgrim (see pp. 184–5). Certainly, the six poems that this manuscript contains, alongside 33 sermons and saints' lives in prose, all have strongly religious themes. One of the poems, that moving and brilliant vision of the Cross known as *The Dream of the Rood*, is also found carved in runes on a standing cross at Ruthwell in Dumfriesshire that may have been created more than two-and-a-half centuries before the manuscript was written (p. 178). Some Old English poems at least seem to have been remembered, recorded recycled and recited over a long period of time, even if the manner of their transmission and performance remains obscure.

Even, lastly, the Exeter Book, only survives because it was donated by Bishop Leofric to Exeter Cathedral some time before 1072, when the gift of a manuscript of Old English poems in a country then dominated by the conquering Normans may have seemed a nationalistic and backward-looking act. This book contains the greatest variety of Old English verse, including more than 120 separate poems (the exact number is disputed). Although the collection begins with a conventionally Christian set of poems (the first three are now known as *Christ I*, *Christ II* and *Christ III* (or *Christ A, B, C*) for example), there are also a significant number of poems which either have no explicitly Christian message (including nearly 100 *Riddles*) or which (like the poems *Widsith* or *Deor*) evidently allude to the pre-Christian Germanic past. More than that, some of the riddles seem at first glance distinctly out of place in a compilation that at the beginning at least seems so resolutely pious. Often there is an obvious if rather rude solution, which masks the real answer, such as in the 'onion' (*Riddle* 25). Jenny Neville has discussed this in her chapter (pp. 141–2) and here I will offer my own translation in prose. Everyone can translate this if they want to:

> I am a curious creature: what a woman wants, at the service of neighbours,
> and harmful to none of those at home except the one who hurts me. My base
> is straight up, I stand in a bed, rather hairy beneath. Sometimes the very lovely
> daughter of a churl takes a risk, haughty girl, so that she grasps me, rubs me
> to redness, ravages my head, stuffs me somewhere safe; she soon feels it, her
> encounter with me, the one who confines me, the curly-locked lady: that eye
> is wet.

It is only from a Latin parallel that we can deduce that the true solution is 'onion', although of course it is true that a more obvious (and more obscene) possibility also presents itself. At all events, it is certain that the Exeter Book was not treated well in the centuries that followed. The last few pages are damaged by a large diagonal burn and the last page bears scars that suggest that the book was used both as a chopping board and as a coaster, with what looks very like the stain of a beer mug to indicate a certain lack of care. Likewise, although the Exeter Book is often trumpeted as a triumph of native tradition, it is worth remembering that not only does it contain a so-far unsolved Latin riddle nestling among more than 90 in Old English, but also a poem on the mythical phoenix (*The Phoenix*) half of which is translated from Latin and the last few lines of which are a careful mixture of both Latin and Old English. Indeed, the closest parallel for an Anglo-Saxon manuscript containing a similar mixture of lofty Christian epic poems, riddles and shorter poems of dubious morality and unclear religious function is an equally assorted Latin compilation which, it has been argued, was intended for classroom use. Perhaps the Exeter Book at one time had a similar function. It is hard to say.

But just as Latin and Old English lived side by side throughout the entire period of the Anglo-Saxon written record, so too at the same time the worldly and the spiritual life were often intertwined and the court and the cloister could scarcely be called strangers. Not for nothing did Augustine of Canterbury, sent in 597 by Pope Gregory to convert the heathen English, deliberately target the royal court of Kent in his mission. All over England it was the noble families that were the first to see the educational advantages of the new religion of the Book. For a start, the new technology of writing a Roman alphabet was at once more flexible and more international than the native and highly restricted tradition of using runes. Indeed, a feature of early Anglo-Saxon England was the number of 'private churches' owned and run by the well born, not to mention a notable propensity for noble men and women to escape from worldly concerns into the comfort of the cloister. Here, in an environment where divorce was not an option, monasteries and nunneries (and even mixed houses) obviously offered a safe haven for the abandoned and the abandoning alike.

Likewise, the upper echelons of the church were filled with aristocratic Anglo-Saxon stock. But the relationship between bishops and kings, although necessarily close, was not always cosy. The first 'English man of letters' was Bishop Aldhelm of Sherborne (c. 639–c. 709). Born little more than a generation after Augustine first set foot in Kent, Aldhelm came from the other side of the country. He was a member of the West Saxon royal family and stood sponsor at baptism to the learned and pious King Aldfrith of Northumbria (ruled 686–705), a man who had been trained, like Aldhelm himself, by Irish scholars. Not only this, but Aldhelm felt able to write a damning letter to King Geraint of Dumnonia (roughly modern Devon), putting him straight on the thorny issue of dating Easter that at that time divided the Celtic Church from that of continental Europe (see p. 174). According to much later legend, Aldhelm was the favourite reading of King Alfred the Great (who ruled 871–99), who may even have regarded him as a distant relative. The same source tells us that Aldhelm composed biblical verse in Old English, although none seems to have survived. Aldhelm is best known today (insofar as he is known at all) for becoming bishop of Sherborne and for composing an extraordinary and lengthy work in both prose and verse, in highly ornate Latin, in praise of virginity. This work was directed to the well-born nuns of Barking in Essex, many of whom had fetched up there to escape their husbands or who had been thoughtfully placed there by husbands who had tired of their pleasures. Aldhelm thus takes a suitably broad and practical view of the merits of virginity. Since this was no longer an option to many in his audience, in Aldhelm's eyes both abstinence and chastity were also to be encouraged (see Map 4).

And Bede? In the next generation, and further north, the Venerable Bede (c. 673–735) seems to have largely shunned any regal connections in Northumbria. He took the narrower line available to one who apparently went into the monastery of Wearmouth–Jarrow at the age of 7 and never left. His near-contemporary, however, another apparently well-born Anglo-Saxon named Wynfrith, took a whole troop of noble men and (more interestingly) women with him when he left Anglo-Saxon England to convert the Germans at the instigation of a pope who renamed him *Bonifatius* or 'Boniface' ('good features', a translation of Old English *Wynfrith*). Indeed, a number of surviving letters and poems to and from Boniface (c. 675–754) offer intriguing evidence for the high standard of women's education in Anglo-Saxon England (in Latin at least) at a time when women in Europe left comparatively few traces in the written record. From his lonely isolation, and with papal blessing, Boniface felt able among other things to write a withering letter to the mighty and influential King Æthelbald of Mercia (ruled 716–57), asking him please to leave his frequent fornication aside, especially insofar as it included nuns.

After many such letters of instruction and advice to kings and bishops and even a succession of popes, it is perhaps unsurprising that Boniface should have been cut down in cold blood. The surprising thing is that the deed was done not by royal, episcopal or papal agents, but by wandering pirates at Dokkum (now in the Netherlands) in 755, when Boniface seems to have been in his 80s. Like pirates everywhere and at all times, Boniface's attackers were appropriately disgusted to break open the locked chests that Boniface and his followers were carrying and find not the treasure they expected, but only books. The story goes that Boniface died attempting to defend himself with just such a volume. To this day there survives in Fulda Cathedral in Germany a gruesome set of relics, including sliced-up bones of several Anglo-Saxon missionaries and an authentic eighth-century Anglo-Saxon manuscript, suitably scarred. The deep gashes that mark the top and bottom margins of this book are striking indeed and to some at least have prompted speculation about the extraordinary octogenarian Ninja move that might have allowed a marauder to mark the manuscript so neatly

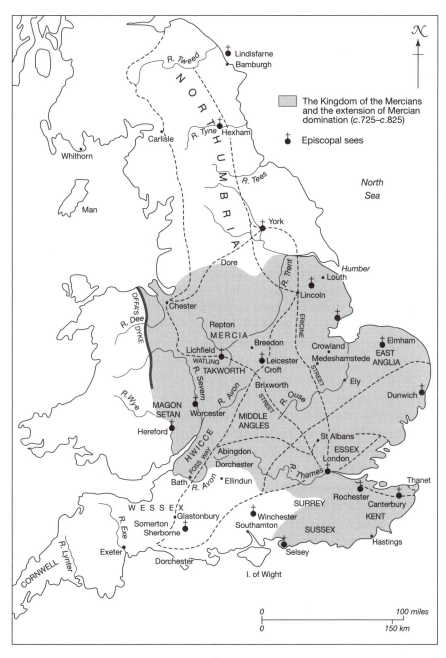

Map 4 The Mercian supremacy (courtesy of Professor Simon Keynes)

in such a way, miraculously avoiding any damage to the written text. Whether the aged Boniface did indeed defend himself with this volume is a matter of faith, but sometimes, it seems, for the Anglo-Saxons the sword was mightier than the pen.

Alcuin of York

While Boniface was still alive and still giving authority figures both at home and on the continent the benefit of his severe advice, there was growing up back in Northumbria a man who was to have an equally decisive impact in Europe. This was Alcuin of York (*c.* 740–804). Alcuin was evidently from another noble family or at least from one wealthy enough to have owned a church at a place (so far unidentified) called Steeple. He was also related to the aristocratic Willibrord (658–739), who had tried to convert the Germans even before Boniface started his own mission. In a spirit of family piety Alcuin was himself to celebrate his relation in both prose and verse. We can gather that Alcuin was raised at York Minster, to which he was presumably given as a child, and became a deacon at the age of about 35, but doesn't seem to have been either a priest or a monk. In spite of this, however, he took over both the school and the library at York Minster when his beloved teacher Ælberht became archbishop of York in 778. Alcuin's close relationship with his mentor appears to have been the key one in his life. He evidently yearned for the same unswerving love and devotion from his own students that he felt towards Ælberht, and it was apparently the death of his dear mentor that led directly to Alcuin's trip to Rome and a fateful meeting with Charlemagne at Parma in 780 or 781, when the Frankish emperor invited the Englishman to join the growing palace school at Aachen.

Alcuin spent almost all his remaining years among the Franks, eventually ruling a succession of important monasteries and dying at the Abbey of Tours in 804. His scholarly achievements in a staggering range of areas made him perhaps the key figure in the extraordinarily impressive renaissance of learning that took place under Charlemagne. This movement itself seems to have proven a key inspiration for King Alfred when he attempted something similar (if more modest in scale) in Anglo-Saxon England a century later. Important as Alcuin's achievements were, however, it is perhaps in his more private capacity as the author of literally hundreds of surviving letters and poems that offer an often poignant picture of a highly sensitive man. Certainly he was often lonely and passed much of his life apart from people and places he clearly loved much. Of Alcuin's predecessors, Bede's private life is a mystery, as he doubtless intended, and Aldhelm left a modest correspondence chiefly notable for its self-consciously stylish diction. Boni-face wrote just over 40 letters that have survived, as have around the same number addressed to him, including several written both by and to women, which generally contain Boniface's most personal advice and reflections. By contrast, Alcuin has left us more than 120 poems, as well as close to 300 letters, almost all of which date from only the last decade or so of his life. From this rich and fascinating archive we can create a detailed and nuanced picture, making Alcuin perhaps the most accessible and human of all the Anglo-Saxons we can name.

One such letter is composed to a former student, in this case the eminent and powerful Bishop Arno of Salzburg. This letter illustrates the tone and depth and style of Alcuin's writings, as well as demonstrating the intensely personal nature of so much of his work that survives (see Map 5). In the let-ter Alcuin offers spiritual advice and an insistent request to be both replied to and remembered. In translation, he starts like this:

> To the beloved Father, Bishop 'Eagle', Albinus [sends] greetings. It is with sweet enough memory, Most Holy Father, that I recall your love and friendship, hoping that when a happy opportunity comes to me I might embrace the neck of your love with the little fingers of my wishes. Oh, if I were suddenly granted the transformation of Habakkuk, with what urgent hands would I rush to your embrace, Father, and with what pressed lips would I kiss not only your eyes and ears and mouth, but also every single joint of your fingers and toes not once but many times. But in truth, since I do not deserve to come to you that way, I shall send you quite often some little messages from my uneducated self, so that they may speak for me in place of my words and say:
>> Always and forever, most holy bishop, greetings;
>> And I ask that all your friends always prosper.

So much for the celebrated English reserve. To modern ears such elabor-ately passionate, almost frenzied, protestations of love and friendship may sound queasily disturbing, but may, in fact, reflect contemporary custom, where, as in many societies today, men could certainly kiss each other in greeting. Alcuin's letter also offers as a parade of somewhat subtler learning that belies the stock false modesty of the author's supposed lack of educa-tion. So, for example, in calling his favoured former student by the familiar nickname 'Eagle' (*Aquilo*), Alcuin is nodding at once toward a Latinisation of Arno's Germanic name (which does indeed mean 'eagle'), as well as towards a characterisation of several of his other students elsewhere as birds who have flown Alcuin's own scholarly nest: we have poems and letters for ex-students named 'Cuckoo' and 'Nightingale', for example, as well as another student whose real name means 'Raven'. A similar kind of punning

Map 5   Carolingian France

on names is evident in Alcuin's expressed desire to be granted the transformation of Habbakuk, since not only was this Old Testament prophet best known for a vision in which he seemed to fly and travel great distances in an instant, but (as Alcuin evidently expected his hapless ex-student to recognise), the standard Latin interpretation of the Hebrew name *Habbakuk* was 'embrace' (*amplexus*). Like many a tediously keen teacher before and since, Alcuin nudges his correspondent towards the solution by repeating the keyword 'embrace'.

In this letter, as commonly elsewhere, Alcuin uses a Latinate form of his own name, 'Albinus', which must have called to mind for Latin speakers images of an almost albino-like pastiness. Certainly one contemporary, the dashing and presumably swarthier Spaniard Theodulf of Orléans, seems to deride Alcuin for his complexion, perhaps suggesting that the Englishman resembled what was apparently one of his favourite foods, namely porridge. To add his own spice, Theodulf was at one time said to be the lover of one of Charlemagne's daughters, presumably a liaison of which Alcuin would have disapproved. Theodulf speaks in horror in a poem describing the court when he says: 'Begone, mass of coagulated milk! Bring on some spicy sausage!', in what seems a less-than-veiled contrast between the racier quality of Theodulf's superior verse and Alcuin's often plodding and repetitive efforts. It is perhaps easy to estimate what Theodulf would have thought of Alcuin's fondness for giving others and himself nicknames drawn from the classical poets: Alcuin styles himself 'Flaccus' after the Roman poet Horace (whose full name was Quintus Horatius Flaccus), while others of his friends are addressed as 'Homer' and 'Naso', after the Roman poet Ovid. Ovid's full name was actually 'Publius Ovidius Naso', although it may be Alcuin's friend in question was distinctive in another way, since the Latin word *Naso* also means 'big nose'. Certainly, Theodulf seems to pun on Alcuin's nickname, Flaccus, and on the Latin term *flaccidus* ('flabby'), and when in the same poem he teases Alcuin for his weakness for drinking both wine and beer (apparently together), it is hard to resist the rather endearing image of a pale and tubby ex-pat Englishman spouting doubtful doggerel and sticking to his beer and porridge despite the spicier delights of the imperial court.

But Alcuin was a rather more significant figure than his role as the butt of Theodulf's rough tongue might suggest. Even Theodulf has to acknowledge Alcuin's intellectual stature and his key role as a teacher. Perhaps the most charming of Alcuin's works are those produced for his students, past and present, inside and outside the classroom. These include an intriguing work which from its title is intended 'To Sharpen Up Young Men'. The work is aimed at making mathematics fun, a perennial challenge even today.

Alcuin's solution is to dress it all up in outlandish problems, starting with one in which he describes how a snail has been invited to supper with a swallow who lives a league away, but who can only travel an inch a day: how long will it take the guest to arrive? Alcuin defines a league as 7500 feet or 90,000 inches and gives the answer as 246 years and 210 days. One wonders how comical the poor kids working the thing out in Roman numerals on wax tablets (not to mention the snail) would have found the puzzle. A similar combination of frustration and delight would likewise presumably have been the result of the question as to how 300 pigs can be slaughtered in three days, with an odd number of pigs being slaughtered each day. The attached solution frankly admits that it is impossible: 'This nonsense is only to tease the boys.' Another puzzle offers an intriguing twist on a familiar challenge by describing how three brothers, each with a strikingly beautiful sister, have to get everyone across a river in a small boat that only seats two, without at any time putting any of the brothers in danger of being alone with a gorgeous girl to whom he was not related. The problem can be solved in eleven trips, if one has the patience to attempt the solution. It is hard to guess what students would have felt about being asked to solve such frustrating and eminently impractical problems, but at least we can glimpse Alcuin trying hard, perhaps a little too hard, to bring humour of a kind into his classroom. Despite his well-established reputation as a scholar, Alcuin was first and foremost a teacher. His epitaph is, perhaps most fittingly, the one he wrote in verse for his own teacher, Ælberht: 'Whenever he saw young men of outstanding character, he took them to him, he taught them, he nourished them, he loved them.'

Of course Alcuin's international standing as a scholar was based on the fact that Latin was the international language of the Christian church, and at that time of all serious scholarship in western Europe. Alcuin was talented and lucky enough to have inherited a fabulous library from his beloved teacher, as well as to gain the imperial support of Charlemagne, who brought to his court a truly international band of scholars. Perhaps inevitably, there were national tensions, such as that between the Anglo-Saxon Alcuin and the Spanish Theodulf, especially as successive waves of clever foreigners tried to make their mark. From this period we also have what might be called the first Irish joke. A continental scholar sitting opposite an Irishman, and playing on the Latin terms, asked aloud 'What is the difference between an Irishman (Latin *Scottus*) and a drunkard (Latin *sottus*)?' Unfortunately for the continental scholar, the Latin question could also be understood as 'What stands between an Irishman and a drunkard?', thus allowing the quick-witted Irishman to look at his mocker and answer 'the table'.

But how did Anglo-Saxons learn Latin? In a time where books were both precious and scarce, the emphasis was inevitably on memorisation of texts perhaps first copied onto wax tablets. The best evidence we have is from monastic contexts, where we know that the psalms were quite literally beaten into children as young as seven. Both Bede and Alcuin would both likely have been the products of this kind of tough love. After that, the kids were made to memorise large quantities of Christian Latin poetry. Verse was chosen in this case precisely because its repeated rhythms evidently made it easier to remember. Neither was the memorisation of great chunks of poetry a teaching technique restricted to Latin. Although King Alfred (ruled 871–99) famously complained how, in his own day, as a result of the raids of the Vikings, the standard of Latin learning had fallen off almost entirely (see pp. 253–5), we are still told how as a boy he had won in a bet a book of Old English poetry from his mother by memorising its contents. The tale is told in a biography of Alfred composed by the Welsh cleric Asser, whom Alfred had invited to his court in the 880s along with other scholars from beyond his borders such as Wærferth the Mercian, John the Old Saxon and Grimbald the Frank in a deliberate (if pale) imitation of Charlemagne's international band of scholarly brothers a century earlier. Interestingly enough, the fact that Asser wrote his *Life of Alfred* in Latin shows that he was aiming it, at least in part, at a Welsh audience. The English had almost lost their Latin by this time. Alfred's attempt to revive it is perhaps a sorry signal of the damage that could be done by pagan Norsemen whose own culture did not rely on the Roman alphabet. Even sorrier may be the very fact Alfred had to bring in foreign scholars to help him do this, namely in his inventive programme to translate from Latin into English what he himself described as 'the books most needful for all men to know'. And yet the success of that programme is a further sign of the esteem in which Latin was held and of the keenness with which it was studied, translated, and assimilated.

From the later period, we have both a grammar and a glossary for Latin written by Ælfric (*c.* 950–*c.* 1010), as well as a series of practice conversations in Latin by both Aelfric and one of his students that are full of lots of different ways of saying the same thing, presumably to increase vocabulary and drum home the point. A sample conversation, which the students were presumably expected to memorise, and which preserves some sense of Latin as a spoken language, can be translated as follows:

'My boy, have you any good undamaged shoes?' 'No way, nor any good leggings. I don't even have a cap, as my friends totally know. I don't even have a coat, and no trousers except the bloodstained ones from when I was beaten with canes a little while back. I don't have any shorts, and God knows there's hardly a thread undamaged in all my clothes. I need a whole new set of clothes, as do most of my friends, like a fur cloak, a shirt, a good hood, leggings, socks, vest, towel, gloves, belt, knife, penknife, various dishes: cup, jug, bowl, and plate; writing-tablet, stylus, and cushion for my seat. Those are the things I need, if I can get them.'

Another conversation, in the same repetitive style, deals intriguingly with the theme of writing itself, and introduces all of the necessary technical vocabulary:

'Who wrote this? Who wrote this writing? Who wrote this book? Who wrote this volume? Who wrote this page or this line or this alphabet or these words or these letters? Is the man who wrote all this still alive? The one who wrote all these things was a fine scribe, and had a splendid hand.' 'Yes, he's still alive, but he's old now, and can't write anything now because his eyes are weak and he's getting on.'

Like Alcuin and the poets of some of the more outrageous Old English *Riddles*, the authors of these conversations knew that to attract the attention of young boys (and most of these conversations seem to be addressed only to boys), it is as well to attract their interest. Even through the use of toilet humour. One conversation, in this way, has one apparently rather childish pupil insult another by comparing him to various kinds of animal dung:

'You idiot! You goat-poo! Sheep-poo! Horse-poo! Cow-dung! Pig-plop! Human-plop! Dog-poo! Cat-plop! Chicken-plop! Donkey-poo! Fox-cub of all fox-cubs! Fox-tail! Fox-beard! Skin of a fox-cub! You dumbo and halfwit! You loony! What do want from me? Nothing good, I reckon!'

This is hardly high literature. Presumably, however, at least part of the point of this remarkable outburst was to fix forever in the minds of students the Latin words for various kinds of animal. One can certainly imagine young Anglo-Saxons gleefully reciting it to themselves, to their teachers and to each other.

Such a need to focus on Latin as the language of medieval Christianity and culture for the western European tradition seems inevitably to have led to tensions with native traditions. So, for example, a prohibition against performing secular (presumably Old English) songs in church is codified in a famous decree at a church Council at *Clofesho* (some think this is Brixworth) that took place as early as 746 or 747. The very fact that such an edict was felt to be necessary suggests that this was not an uncommon practice. Indeed, more than 250 years later, Archbishop Wulfstan of York (died 1023) is still stressing very similar concerns in a series of codes that set down penalties for any priest who is 'too fond of drinking' (*oferdruncen*), or an 'entertainer' (*gliman*), or has become what is called an 'ale poet' (*ealascop*) – presumably someone who performs poetry in a place where people are drinking, an admonition that echoes that of the earlier council. In this context, it is fascinating to see how Alcuin, writing from the continent to 'Speratus', a bishop in Mercia in 797 (i.e. some 50 years after that strict Council at *Clofesho*), should say the following about the hero King Ingeld of the Heathobards (see earlier, pp. 106–8). I offer this in my own translation:

> The words of God should be read at a bishop's feast: it is proper there for a
> reader to be heard, not a harp-player, the words of the Church Fathers, not the
> songs of heathens. What has Ingeld got to do with Christ? The house is narrow:
> it cannot hold both. The king of heaven does not want to hold communion
> with kings who are pagan and damned by their very name: that eternal king
> rules in heaven, but that pagan king rues in hell. It is proper to listen to the
> voices of readers in your buildings, not of those making fun of the crowd in
> the courtyards.

There are a number of things that are striking about this passage. Not the least of these is the insistent contrast between sober reading (the Latin terms corresponding to 'read . . . reader . . . readers' are *legantur . . . lectorem . . . legentium* and are equally repetitive) and lighter and likely more performative modes of entertainment, such as harping, singing and making fun. Ingeld (*Hinieldus*) seems singled out here as a pagan king condemned for being celebrated in such dubious ways presumably precisely because he is one of many heathen 'kings damned by [their] very name' (*perditis nominetenus regibus*). Here it is worth noting that the first element of Ingeld's name recalls a pagan fertility god, Ing or Ingui, who appears as a shadowy figure elsewhere in the written record (see later p. 174). Alcuin had enough on his plate with living Christian kings, let alone the heathen kings that the aristocrats of his time so loved to celebrate in their heroic poems.

Alcuin and Offa of Mercia

This letter from Alcuin contains an obliquely damning assessment of the efforts of King Offa of Mercia (ruled 757–96), who had died the previous year, to secure the succession for his son. Historians have concluded that Offa set about liquidating his boy's rivals for the succession, i.e. all his cousins, in the last ten years of his life. Offa's son was called Ecgfrith [/e:dge-frith/] and perhaps it is a surprise that he outlasted his father by as many as 141 days. Such comment as Alcuin provides in his letter to Speratus is the more intriguing given that Offa was the dominant figure in Anglo-Saxon politics for much of Alcuin's life. As it is, Alcuin still calls him 'that most famous king' (*rex ille clarissimus*). Yet in another letter, to a high-ranking Mercian nobleman, Alcuin is blunter still about the ruthlessly bloody way in which Offa had cleared the path to Ecgfrith's succession: 'That most noble young man did not die through his own sins, I reckon; it was the vengeance for the blood of the father that was shed on the son; for you know full well how much blood the father shed to secure the kingdom for his son.' Here one might also note that, for all his apparent distaste for native songs of bloodshed and vengeance, Alcuin was himself far from squeamish in such matters when it suited him. In a letter dating around 801, for example, Alcuin recommends a number of English travellers to Emperor Charlemagne in France, including a Northumbrian thane called Torhtmund who 'boldly avenged the blood of his lord'. Nonetheless it was only with Offa dead and his dynasty disinherited that Alcuin felt he could safely offer his views on the man.

For almost 40 years, however, Offa had exercised a decisive influence over Anglo-Saxon England; and while Offa was alive Alcuin happily heaped him with praise, describing him as 'the glory of Britain, the trumpet of proclamation, the sword against enemies, the shield against foes', a form of flattery matched in a Kentish charter dating from towards the end of Offa's reign, which calls him 'king and glory of Britain'. Offa is now famed chiefly for building the 74-mile long (103 km) and still largely surviving Offa's Dyke. This was to keep Welsh raiders at bay. Offa was also responsible for establishing a new currency based on the silver penny that was to remain the standard for centuries after his death. Offa's fame extended far beyond his own borders, however, for he was addressed as a brother (and evidently expected to be so treated) by Emperor Charlemagne himself. Offa's still broader international pretensions may be further indicated by an extraordinary (and unique) gold coin that survives bearing his name, which is clearly based on an Arabic dinar and, remarkably, also carries a slightly botched version of a prayer to Allah in the stylised and angular script known as Kufic.

In terms of Offa's lasting fame, then, it is ironic that the modern term 'dyke' by which Offa's mighty fortification is now known is not itself English but rather derived from the language of their Viking invaders (Old Icelandic *dík*). This is as fitting as the fact that the word *Wales* is not a Welsh word either, but derives from the language of the Anglo-Saxon invaders, from *Wēalas* meaning 'foreigners'. Offa's was a turbulent period and superiority was a transient thing.

Offa's path to the throne had been indeed a bloody one. His disreputable predecessor was the same King Æthelbald (ruled 716–57) whose reprehensible behaviour caused Boniface to write so forcefully back in the 740s. Æthelbald's philandering led to his murder at the hands of his own bodyguard in 757. He was briefly succeeded by one Beornred, a kinsman of some kind, against whom Offa launched an immediate set of attacks: an early source notes drily that in 757 Offa 'put Beornred to flight and tried to conquer the Mercian kingdom with sword and bloodshed'. Offa's own family connection to Æthelbald, as that of first cousin twice removed, was a distant one. But Offa went on to reign with an iron fist for 39 years and so was presumably a young man when he seized his chance. He certainly made his name. One version of *The Anglo-Saxon Chronicle* for the year 757 gives Offa a resounding genealogy that extends right back to the heathen god Woden (still recalled these days every Woden's day, *Wōdnes-dæg*), and includes his illustrious namesake, the fourth-century King Offa of Angeln, who in this list is said to be the great-grandson of Woden:

> Offa was the son of Thingferth, Thingferth of Eanwulf, Eanwulf of Osmod, Osmod of Eawa, Eawa of Pybba, Pybba of Creoda, Creoda of Cynewald, Cynewald of Cnebba, Cnebba of Icel, Icel of Eomer, Eomer of Angeltheow, Angeltheow of Offa, Offa of Wermund, Wermund of Wihtlaeg, Wihtlaeg of Woden.

This tally is nearly as impressive as the greatest tally of them all, a genealogy in the *Anglo-Saxon Chronicle* which is that of Alfred the Great himself (ruled 871–99). And we must recall that the *Chronicle* was created in Alfred's reign, to a large extent with the express purpose of extolling his line. Almost exactly 100 years after it registers Offa's ancestry, the *Chronicle* traces Alfred's lineage through his father, Æthelwulf (ruled 839–58). Æthelwulf's list of ancestors is three times as long as Offa's:

> Æthelwulf was the son of Ecgberht, Ecgberht of Ealmund, Ealhmund of Eafa, Eafa of Eoppa, Eoppa of Ingild. Ingild was the brother of Ine, the West Saxon king, who afterwards went to Saint Peter's [in Rome] and gave up his life there. And they were the sons of Cenred, and Cenred was the son of Ceolwald, Ceolwald of Cutha, Cutha of Cuthwine, Cuthwine of Ceawlin, Ceawlin of Cynric, Cynric of Cerdic, Cerdic of Elesa, Elesa of Esla, Esla of Giwis, Giwis of Wig, Wig of Freawine, Freawine of Frithogar, Frithogar of Brond, Brond of Baeldaeg, Baeldaeg of Woden, Woden of Frithowald, Frithowald of Freawine, [Freawine of Frealaf], Frealaf of Frithowulf, Frithowulf of Finn, Finn of Godwulf, Godwulf of Geat [see p. 111], Geat of Taetwa, Taetwa of Beaw, Beaw of Sceldwa, Sceldwa of Heremod, Heremod of Itermon, Itermon of Hrathra, who was born in the ark; Noah, Lamech, Methuselah, Enoch, Jared, Malael, Cainan, Enos, Seth, Adam.

Roll on Wessex! Rolling as it is, however, this genealogy is a carefully constructed piece of work. It emphasises Alfred's family's Christian connections through Ingild (a Christian prince not to be confused with the damned Ingeld), the brother of the saintly West Saxon King Ine, who abandoned his crown to go on a pilgrimage to Rome and who died there. If we go back to Offa, by contrast, we see that his ancestor Eawa was the brother of King Penda (ruled c. 632–55) of Mercia, a pagan diehard who killed the Christian King (later Saint) Oswald of Northumbria in battle in 642 (see p. 175). The only intersection of Alfred's line and Offa's, if you go back far enough, is the heathen god Woden. While Offa's line goes no further back than Woden, however, Alfred's pointedly extends back still further to the point where it is grafted on to a familiar biblical genealogy going even further back to Adam himself. For ancestors no king can do better than that. This connection was made by giving Noah a son who is never mentioned in the Bible but who is said to have been born on the Ark. The presence of both of these formidable genealogies in *The Anglo-Saxon Chronicle* offers further testimony to Offa's fame. They show the extent to which Offa remained a mark for later kings to emulate.

Having won his kingdom by force of arms, the youthful and energetic Offa expanded his dominion into Kent and Sussex by the same method, held it by sheer force of personality, on the one hand, and (again) sheer force, on the other, and left a formidable reputation for later Anglo-Saxons. A descendant of Alfred named Æthelweard (died c. 998), a nobleman who wrote a Latin translation of the *Chronicle*, described Offa in Latin as 'an amazing man' (*uir mirabilis*). Not many years later Offa is mentioned in a legacy from one royal brother to another, both sons of King Æthelred the Unready (ruled 978–1016; another descendant of Alfred). This was when Æthelstan (died 1014) bequeathed to his younger brother Edmund Ironside (reigned briefly 1016) 'the sword which belonged to King Offa'. (This period will be discussed in more detail later in Chapter 11.) It was a sword that had seen much action: as we have seen, Offa himself mercilessly promoted the interests of his own son and heir, Ecgfrith, through the ruthless suppression and elimination of potential rivals.

The reason for Alcuin's apparent change in heart about the relative merits of secular aggression and religious devotion was likely to have been intensely personal, the developing view of an exile abroad. Towards the end of his life, Alcuin was made forcefully aware of the Viking raids that had commenced in earnest when he had left England. One version of *The Anglo-Saxon Chronicle* for the year 793 outlines the portents that preceded the first and cataclysmic attack on the monastery at Lindisfarne:

In this year there were signs over Northumbria, and they terrified the wretched people; there was excessive thunder and lightning, and fiery dragons were seen flying in the sky. A great famine soon followed those signs, and a little after that in the same year on the 8th of January a wretched ravaging of heathen men devastated God's church on the island of Lindisfarne with plunder and slaughter.

A surviving tombstone from Lindisfarne seems to depict the very moment of Viking attack and when it is considered that on the other side is carved a Last Judgement scene, one gets a sense of how this pagan attack must have seemed God's judgement on the sins of the English.

The fact that the extraordinarily supple and efficient longships that underpinned the Viking raid were themselves known as 'dragons' only heightened the parallel implied by the End of Times and hinted at by the reported portents in the sky. It was, however, Alcuin, from his continental vantage point, who drew a direct comparison between the Viking raids suffered by the English and the plight of the native Britons they had themselves supplanted almost 350 years earlier. Alcuin points to a text written at the time of first Saxon incursions by the sixth-century British cleric, Gildas, who directly ascribes the invasions to God's wrath on the sinful British; Alcuin argues that this time it is the Vikings who are the instruments of God's wrath against the English. More than two centuries later another Anglo-Saxon, Archbishop Wulfstan of York (died 1023), using Alcuin's own arguments, made the same case at a time 'when the Danes most greatly persecuted the English' (see p. 432).

It is instructive to consider the parallel careers of Offa and Alcuin, since they both represent the ways in which eighth-century Anglo-Saxons were able to conceive of themselves as major players on the international stage. Both had quite different relationships with Charlemagne, the truly dominant figure of the age. While Alcuin, however, was more obviously in the position of a client and dependant, he certainly had the emperor's ear and seems to have exerted a quiet authority over his lord. King Offa, by the same token, seems to have seen Charlemagne as a ruler to emulate and to attempt to surpass. This is witnessed among other things by Offa's attempts to lure Alcuin back to his own court: Alcuin declined and sent one of his students instead. In another attempt to assert his equality, the stubborn and self-made Offa is said to have turned down a proposed marriage alliance between his daughter and the Frankish prince Charles, since his own counter proposal was snubbed – namely that Charlemagne send one of his own daughters to be married to the precious Ecgfrith. Charlemagne, lord of all he surveyed, must have wondered at the self-confidence of the man.

To this end we have a letter that survives from Charlemagne to Offa, one that casts considerable light on the relationship between these two extraordinary men. It is worth quoting this extensively. Naturally, it is in Latin, but a translation reads as follows:

> Charles, king of the Franks and Lombards by the grace of God, [sends greetings] to his most dear brother Offa, king of the Mercians. We have read your brotherly letter, and first thank God for the sincerity of your Catholic faith that is clear in your pages; we can see that you are not only a very strong protector of your lands in this world, but also a very devout defender of the holy faith . . . With regard to the pilgrims who want to visit the buildings of the blessed Apostles, they can go in peace. But we have found out that some people deceitfully travel with them to engage in business, and those people have to pay the proper taxes at the appropriate places . . . You also wrote about traders, and we grant that they shall have protection in our kingdom, and that if they are unlawfully attacked, they can appeal to us. Likewise, our own folk will appeal to the judgement of your fairness . . . With regard to the priest Odberht, who wants to live abroad, we have sent him to Rome with the other exiles who from fear of death have taken refuge under our protection . . . With regard to the black stones which your revered majesty requested to be sent, we will happily order them granted. But just as you indicated your wishes about the size of the stones, likewise our own people make a demand about the size of cloaks, that you order that they be like the ones that used to come to us . . . We have sent a gift to the various bishoprics of both your kingdom and of Æthelred's [see later], as alms for the apostolic lord, [Pope] Hadrian, our father and your friend. Also to you, dear sir, we have sent a belt and a Hunnish sword . . . May Almighty God keep the excellence of your worthiness for the protection of his Holy Church.

This is one of only a small handful of surviving letters in which Charlemagne deigned to address another western king as 'brother'. It is interesting that it focuses so sharply and resolutely on issues of trade. While the letter is quite rightly often cited as evidence for the esteem in which Offa was held beyond his own borders, it is equally clear that Charlemagne very definitely reckoned to have the upper hand here: while he will acquiesce to Offa's requests, he insists that his own rights be upheld in return; and in the matter of the 'black stones' (presumably grindstones of one kind or another), he points to a parallel drop in the quality of English trade goods, here, cloaks. One gets the sense of two stubborn and wily men negotiating hard, but with Charlemagne the man more sure of his position. He could, after all, simply detain the pilgrims and their merchant hangers-on, and let English traders in his domain receive the same rough justice they have before. Even the apparent generosity of Charlemagne's gift giving is pointed. His mention of gifts to the bishoprics of 'Æthelred' is a reminder to

Offa that he is not the only power in the land. Æthelred, Offa's son-in-law, was also king of Northumbria, albeit he was murdered in a palace coup before he could appreciate Charlemagne's generosity. Likewise, the no doubt splendid 'Hunnish sword' Charlemagne gives to Offa is presumably one captured as spoils during Charlemagne's spectacular victory over the Hunnish Avars in 795, when he acquired massive amounts of treasure as booty. The Hunnish sword, therefore, stands as a reminder of Charlemagne's impressive fighting credentials and of his 'winning ways'. We only need to hink of the importance of other swords, such as 'Mimming' in *Waldere*, to northern Europeans in their heroic poems (see p. 117).

Even Charlemagne's apparently innocent reference to 'the priest Odberht' has an edge, if he is the same person as Eadberht Praen, a priest of royal Kentish blood who was exiled on the continent and returned in the last year of Offa's life to revolt and snatch back briefly the Kentish crown from the Mercian interlopers. If such is the case, then Charlemagne is gently reminding Offa that he happily harbours Offa's enemies, including those who fled England from Offa in fear of their lives and that he will not simply surrender them. The whole letter is a masterful example of high international politics. If it often cited as an example of Offa's reputation, it is also a salutary reminder that Charlemagne remained top dog.

Whether or not Charlemagne seems to have had his doubts about the iron man beyond his borders, both his contemporaries and later commentators in Anglo-Saxon England seems to have been suitably awed by Offa. Indeed, it is tempting to return to two passages in Old English poetry that speak approvingly of Offa's fifth-century ancestor and namesake, Offa of Angeln. As we have seen (pp. 104–5), the implication is that these passages were intended to flatter King Offa of Mercia. In the Old English poem *Widsith*, supposedly the eyewitness account of a poet who travelled between the courts of many kings, an extended passage brings together praise for the land-grabbing zeal of Offa of Angeln, a more telescoped account of the feud between the ancient pagan King Ingeld of the Heathobards and his father-in-law, King Hrothgar of the Danes, as well as the relations between Hrothgar and his nephew, Hrothulf, who eventually snatched his crown. The passage concludes with the author's own version of his life as a wandering poet, dependent on the generosity of noble patrons. I offer my own translation in prose:

> Offa ruled the Angles, Alewih the Danes: he was the bravest of all of those men, and yet he could not perform greater deeds than Offa, since Offa first of men carved out when still a boy the greatest of kingdoms. No one at that age did greater deeds in battle: with his one sword he marked out the border against the

Myrgings at the Eider-mouth; the Angles and the Swabians maintained it
afterwards just as Offa carved it out. [. . .]

  Hrothulf and Hrothgar maintained their truce together for a very long
time, nephew and uncle, after they had driven off the race of Vikings, and
forced back the cream of Ingeld's men, cut down at Heorot the might of the
Heathobards. [. . .]

  So I travelled through many foreign lands throughout the broad world.
I experienced both good and bad there, separated from my family, far from my
beloved kinsmen: I gave my service widely, so I can sing, and give an account,
utter before the multitude in the mead-hall how the well-born ones showed
their nobility.

The precise background to this passage is murky, but the compressed
form of the narrative of itself invites interpretation. Certainly, the fact that
Offa of Angeln is here celebrated as a king who carved out his own borders in his youth would have resonated with eighth-century and later
Anglo-Saxons familiar with the similarly ruthless achievements of Offa of
Mercia. It has been pointed out that this passage and Alcuin's letter of condemnation are the only places where an Offa and an Ingeld are held up as
examples, albeit that here the earlier Offa is held up for praise, whereas
Alcuin clearly condemns both Ingeld and the eighth-century king. Note how
the poet here tells us how Offa is an Angle, Alewih a Dane and Ingeld (if only
by implication) a Heathobard, but doesn't tell us what nationality Hrothgar
and Hrothulf are. Perhaps he expected his audience simply to know or to
infer it from the nationality of Alewih. In fact, we know from *Beowulf* and
other sources that (like Alewih) they are Danes; and that Heorot (the word
means 'hart' in Old English) is Hrothgar's mighty Danish hall, with sweep-
ing gables in the shape of a hart. It is also important, however, to note that
Widsith is precisely the kind of poet spouting tales of ancient pagan kings
that is condemned both at the Council of *Clofesho* and by Alcuin.

It is worth pointing out that *Beowulf* also contains an extended and
rather abruptly introduced passage in praise of Offa of the Angles, since
here to an oblique compliment to his namesake may be intended. The
Beowulf poet contrasts Hygd, the 'very young, wise, accomplished' queen of
Beowulf's uncle, King Hygelac of the Geats, with a dangerous queen, whom
I interpret as Queen 'Fremu'. The poet says that Fremu's wild and murderous ways in her youth were ended when she was married to Offa of the
Angles. The whole sequence (*Beowulf*, lines 1925–62) is worth translating,
beginning as it does with a description of King Hygelac's hall:

  The building was magnificent, the king a famous lord in the high hall, Hygd,
  the daughter of Hareth, very young, wise, accomplished, even though she spent

few years within the walled enclosure: nonetheless she was not mean, nor too stingy with gifts, costly treasures, for the people of the Geats.

Fremu, a nation's queen, acted with arrogance, grim wickedness; there was no one so bold among her own dear companions, except as her continual lord, who dared risk that he laid eyes on her in the daytime: he reckoned that bonds of slaughter, twisted by hand, would be laid on him: soon after that, once he was taken captive, he was doomed to the sword, that a twisted blade should settle it, proclaim a horrid death. That is not queenly behaviour for a woman to show, however matchless she may be, that a woman set to bring peace between peoples should deprive any dear man of his life for an imagined insult. Men at ale said more: that it was the kinsman of Hemming [Offa] who cut her off, so that she caused fewer mighty afflictions, cruel attacks, once she had been given, gold-adorned, to the young hero, the mighty noble, and came travelling to Offa's hall on her father's advice.

After that, good and famous as long as she lived, she enjoyed her allotted life on the throne, had deep love for that prince of men, the best of all men, as I have heard tell, of mankind between the seas. Because Offa was in both gifts and battles a spear-bold man, widely famed: he held his land with wisdom. From them was Eomer born, as an aid to warriors, a kinsman of Hemming, grandson of Garmund, and powerful in battles.

There are a number of things that are interesting about this extended passage, not least of which is the way in which it jumps so suddenly from Hygd to Fremu to praise of Offa of Angeln. We notice also the extent to which the implied genealogy given here differs significantly from what appears in the passage from *The Anglo-Saxon Chronicle* quoted earlier. There, Eomer is not Offa's son, but his grandson and Offa's father is not Garmund but Wermund. Despite these differences, it has been suggested that such elaborate focus on his ancestor and namesake is again intended to reflect on Offa of Mercia, Alcuin's contemporary: at the very least, his name appears alongside mighty pagan heroes celebrated in ancient poetry and apparently condemned by the church.

Of further interest in this context is the fact that, according to one of his biographers at least, Charlemagne himself caused to be written down and memorised what are described as 'barbarian and most ancient songs, in which the deeds and battles of bygone kings were sung' (see earlier p. 233). This is so even if his passion for such material was not universally shared: Charlemagne's son, the aptly named Louis the Pious, evidently rebelled against his father's un-Christian interests and, according to his own biographer, 'rejected the pagan songs he had learnt in his youth, and did not want them to be read or learnt or taught'. We might assume that similarly ambivalent attitudes towards the heroic pagan past may have existed at various times in Anglo-Saxon England and such ambivalence is surely reflected in the kinds of poetry that have so haphazardly survived.

By now, you will have read enough in this book to know that Anglo-Saxon poetry is justly celebrated for its range and variety. It includes examples of many different genres, such as riddles, saints' lives, elegies, biblical and historical narratives, prayers, meditations, descriptions of sea voyages, places, persons and battles and poems of advice and wisdom and learning, including both original compositions and works versified from Latin prose or adapted from existing Latin verse sources. It is perhaps curious, for this reason, that Alcuin is rarely discussed as a poet and still more rarely as a poet of any merit or interest at all. Alcuin is the only Anglo-Saxon we know to have composed poems in all of the aforementioned styles and genres and indeed the Anglo-Saxon to whom we can attribute the largest body of extant verse. And yet alongside all Alcuin's other letters, treatises, scholarly and educational texts, it is important to stress the fact that he has left us around 7000 lines of verse. This quantity is equivalent in terms of words (since in general Latin verse lines are longer than Old English ones) to two-and-a-half *Beowulf*s or a quarter of surviving Old English verse. Whatever his views on the celebration of pagan kings, Alcuin is one of a number of Anglo-Saxon authors composing in Latin whose works bear closer comparison with Old English texts than they sometimes receive.

Goodbye to all that? The poetry of exiles

One such area is in the way in which Alcuin responds as an exile (albeit a voluntary one) to the places he still calls home. A sense of Alcuin's nostalgia can be gleaned from one of his most celebrated poems, in which he bids farewell to the cell that has been his home. It has been argued that it is his cell at the imperial court at Aachen that is lamented here, but other factors of geography and phrasing would also fit York, his original home. The poem is notable for the way in which it fits an elegiac mood of yearning and regret that is also found in a number of the finest Old English poems that have survived. A key section of the poem reads as follows:

> Nothing remains for ever, nothing is truly unchanging;
>   dark night covers the sacred day.
> Cold winter suddenly shakes the beautiful flowers
>   and a harsher breeze disturbs the peaceful sea.
> In the fields where the holy youths used to chase stags,
>   now a tired old man leans on his staff.

> We wretches, why do we love you, fugitive world?
>> You always fly from us, failing ever.

Such laments for a lost age are widespread in Old English. For example, a typical passage from the poem *The Wanderer* ultimately derives from Latin models for its structure, but to the native tradition for its phrasing:

> What has become of the stallion? What has become of the youth? What has become of the treasure-giver? What has become of the feasting-place? Where are the joys of the hall? Ah, for the bright cup! Ah, for the mail-coated warrior! Ah, for the prince's power! How that time has passed, grown dark under the shadow of night, as though it had never been.

The speaker in *The Wanderer* portrays himself as a lordless man wandering through the land, a man whose very rootlessness renders him suspicious. Another Old English poem, *The Fortunes of Men*, has a sad section on the fate of exiles:

> One man has to travel on foot in ways remote and carry his provisions with him and tread the spray-flung track and the dangerous territory of alien peoples. He has few surviving providers; everywhere the friendless man is disliked because of his misfortunes.

Against this widespread literary sympathy for outsiders we should balance the fact that throughout the period many Anglo-Saxons found themselves exiles, whether voluntary (like Boniface or Alcuin) or involuntary (like the speaker in *The Wanderer* and like Æthelbald of Mercia and Alfred of Wessex, who had to win back their crowns). All these disoriented and disaffected folk would have felt a similar sense of longing, whether they expressed it in Old English or in Latin, in prose or in verse, at the beginning of the period or at the end. The beginning of *The Wanderer* expresses this longing in words which subvert the sense of our earliest 'Saxon proverb', while retaining much of its form. To take us out of this chapter, here is the classic Old English reflection on solitude, exile and fate:

> Oft him anhaga   are gebideð,
> metudes miltse,   þeah þe he modcearig
> geond lagulade   longe sceolde
> hreran mid hondum   hrimcealde sæ,
> wadan wræclastas.   Wyrd bið ful aræd! (*The Wanderer*, lines 1–5)

> Often a lonely person feels grace,
> the favour of the creator, even though, troubled in mind,
> he has had to stir with his hands the ice-cold sea,
> travel the paths of exile: fate is fully settled.

Translations and texts

Allott, Stephen, *Alcuin of York* (New York, 1974). A useful collection of selected translations of letters written by Alcuin to various correspondents.

Bullough, Donald, 'What Has Ingeld to do with Lindisfarne?', *Anglo-Saxon England* 22 (1993), pp. 93–125.

Orchard, Andy, 'Wish You Were Here: Alcuin's Courtly Verse and the Boys Back Home', in *Courts and Regions in Medieval Europe*, Jones, Sarah Rees, Richard Marks and A.J. Minnis, eds (Woodbridge, 2000), pp. 21–43.

Further reading

Fox, Michael, 'Alcuin as Exile and Educator: "uir undecunque doctissimus"', in *Latin Learning and English Lore*, O'Keeffe, Katherine O'Brien, and Andy Orchard, eds, 2 vols (Toronto, 2005) I, pp. 215–36.

Fulk, Robert D., 'The Name of Offa's Queen: *Beowulf* 1931–2', *Anglia* (2004), pp. 614–39.

Garrison, Mary, '"*Quid Hinieldus cum Christo?*"', in *Latin Learning and English Lore*, O'Keeffe, Katherine O'Brien, and Andy Orchard, eds, 2 vols (Toronto, 2005) I, pp. 237–59.

Gwara, Scott and David W. Porter, eds, *Anglo-Saxon Conversations: The Colloquies of Aelfric Bata* (Woodbridge, 1997).

Keynes, Simon, 'England, 700–900', in *The New Cambridge Medieval History*, II, *c. 700–c. 900*, McKitterick, Rosamund, ed. (Cambridge, 1995), pp. 18–42.

Keynes, Simon, 'Offa, King of the Mercians', in *Blackwell's Encyclopedia of Anglo-Saxon England*, Lapidge, Michael, John Blair, Simon Keynes and Don Scragg, eds (Oxford, 1998), pp. 340–1.

Kirby, D.P., *The Earliest English Kings* (London, 1991).

Lapidge, Michael, *Anglo-Latin Literature, 600–899* (London, 1996).

Lapidge, Michael, *Anglo-Latin Literature, 900–1066* (London, 1993).

Lapidge, Michael, *The Anglo-Saxon Library* (Oxford, 2006).

Orchard, Andy, 'Enigma Variations: the Anglo-Saxon Riddle-Tradition', in *Latin Learning and English Lore: Studies in Anglo-Saxon Literature for Michael Lapidge*, O'Keeffe, Katherine O'Brien, and Andy Orchard, eds, 2 vols (Toronto: University of Toronto Press, 2005) I, pp. 284–304.

Whitelock, Dorothy, *The Audience of 'Beowulf'* (Oxford, 1950).

Wormald, Patrick, 'The Age of Offa and Alcuin', in *The Anglo-Saxons*, Campbell, James, ed. (London, 1982), pp. 101–28.

Wormald, Patrick, 'Bede, *Beowulf*, and the Conversion of the Anglo-Saxon Aristocracy', in *Bede and Anglo-Saxon England*, Farrell, Robert T., ed., British Archaeological Reports 46 (Oxford, 1978), pp. 32–95.

CHAPTER 9

Old English prose: King Alfred and his books

Susan Irvine

Poetry isn't the whole story in Old English literature. In this chapter we shall look at the first Old English prose. Although it is not 'fiction' by any stretch of the word, the prose that the Anglo-Saxons, in particular the Mercians and West Saxons, began to write in the ninth century marked a key stage in their intellectual development. Ideas that had resided in Hebrew and Greek, then Latin, prose writings were now to be made available to Anglo-Saxons through the first form of an English prose. The daring of this enterprise is breathtaking. Given that the poetry of a traditional warlike idiom could not be expected to express all the thoughts of advanced theological, philosophical or historical discourse, so for nearly three centuries there had been a need for ubiquitous monastic Latin. And when the knowledge of this faded, due to economic decline and Viking invasions in the mid-ninth century, it was one royal figure, King Alfred of Wessex (849–99), who came to the rescue. How do you write prose in your own language if no one has really done this before?

For what the Old English language was, see Chapter 10. To be sure, there were Old English law codes and the like. By the 820s even some charters were written in Old English. But a lot more was needed for Anglo-Saxons to make their form of prose English match the power of Latin. King Alfred supplied the drive. In the process of creating the conditions for his and other writers' construction of Old English prose, Alfred laid the foundations for a level of rhetorical skill that reached its height in the later tenth century and was quite unparalleled at that time in western Europe (see Map 6).

Back in the 880s, the story of King Alfred and his books stands out as extraordinary, even in a period where so many interesting stories cry out to be told. How and why did an Anglo-Saxon king become one of the most

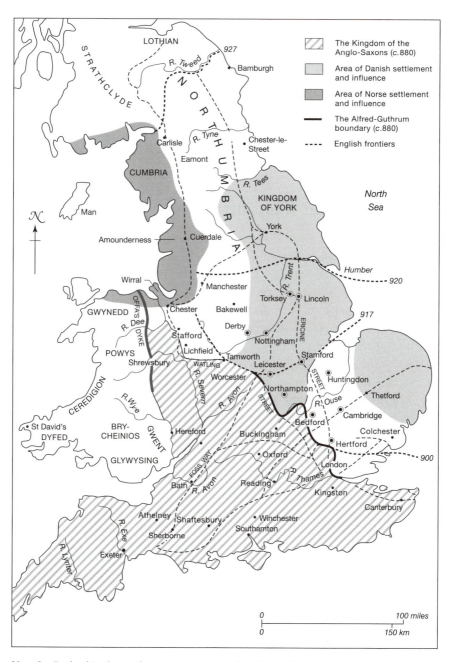

Map 6   England in the tenth century (courtesy of Professor Simon Keynes)

important literary figures of all time? How could one man engage so effectively not only with the ferocious Viking raiders who besieged his kingdom but also with the most profound philosophical issues of his day? The 'Alfredian Renaissance', the revival of intellectual culture that characterised the last part of the ninth century in England, is every bit as significant for the development of English literary tradition as its more famous sixteenth-century counterpart. This chapter will consider the motivations and achievements of this exceptionally gifted scholar–king, the only English king to be known as 'the Great'.

Stories about King Alfred

Not surprisingly, given his significance, a variety of stories have grown up around King Alfred, some told by those close to him, some by those rather further away. We probably have to accept that at least some of these need to be taken with a pinch of salt. But, however much one may want to dispute the details, the tales associated with Alfred tend to reflect the wisdom and intellectual disposition that must have underpinned his every activity. I want to look at just two of them as a way of introducing a man whose passion for knowledge changed the course of English literary history.

My first story is from Alfred's youth. It is told by Asser, the monk from Wales who became the king's advisor and biographer. Bishop Asser, as he became, explains in his biography how Alfred loved hearing English poems recited by others and how he easily learned them off by heart. His *Life of King Alfred* then continues:

> One day, therefore, when his mother was showing him and his brothers a book of English poetry which she held in her hand, she said: 'I shall give this book to whichever one of you can learn it the fastest.' Spurred on by these words, or rather by divine inspiration, and attracted by the beauty of the initial letter in the book, Alfred spoke as follows in reply to his mother, forestalling his brothers (ahead in years, though not in ability): 'Will you really give this book to the one of us who can understand it the soonest and recite it to you?' Whereupon, smiling with pleasure she reassured him, saying: 'Yes, I will.' He immediately took the book from her hand, went to his teacher and learnt it. When it was learnt, he took it back to his mother and recited it.

This story from over 1100 years ago of a child drawn to learning still speaks to us as twenty-first-century readers. Its ingredients – the bond between mother and child, the competition, the naive eagerness and precocity of the child, the delight in the physical beauty of the object, the satisfactory narrative closure – all contribute to its timeless appeal. In its particular context the story points to Alfred's love of words and wisdom from a very early age. He is shown to have God on his side ('divine inspiration'), and to have an instinctive appreciation for the way in which the beautifully decorated initial letter in the book might reflect the worthiness of its contents.

My second story, the best known of all stories associated with King Alfred, is the story of Alfred and the cakes. Even those who know very little else about Alfred have probably heard of how he, while sitting brooding over his troubles with the Vikings in a peasant's cottage, failed to notice some loaves of bread burning in the oven, for which he was roundly told off by the peasant's wife. This account was probably invented a century or so after Alfred's death in 899 by the anonymous author of the *Life of Saint Neot*, a saint's life composed in Latin around the end of the tenth century. The *Life of Saint Neot* includes the following passage (slightly abbreviated here):

> There is a place called Athelney which is surrounded on all sides by vast salt marshes and sustained by some level ground in the middle. King Alfred happened unexpectedly to come there as a lone traveller. Noticing the cottage of a certain unknown swineherd, he directed his path towards it and sought there a peaceful retreat; he was given refuge, and he stayed there for a number of days, impoverished, subdued and content with the bare necessities. Reflecting patiently that these things had befallen him through God's just judgement, he remained there awaiting God's mercy. Alfred patiently kept the picture of Job's astonishing constancy before his eyes every day. Now it happened by chance one day that the king remained alone at home with the swineherd's wife. The wife, concerned for her husband's return, had entrusted some kneaded flour to the oven. As is the custom among countrywomen, she was intent on other domestic occupations, until she saw the bread burning from the other side of the room. She immediately grew angry and said to the king (unknown to her as such): 'Look here, man, you hesitate to turn the loaves which you see to be burning, yet you're quite happy to eat them when they come warm from the oven!' But the king, reproached by these disparaging insults, ascribed them to his divine lot; somewhat shaken, and submitting to the woman's scolding, he not only turned the bread but even attended to it as she brought out the loaves when they were ready.

Alfred may be a king but it is his relationship with common humanity that is the focus of this story. He happily spends time in the swineherd's cottage. He is so bound up with his own thoughts that he takes his eye off the ball (or the bread). He accepts and learns from criticism. Here again his guide is a woman, but now it is the swineherd's wife rather than his mother. Most of all, Alfred's humble behaviour is implicitly linked to his love of learning and especially his awareness of the scriptures. His reflective and philosophical leanings are an essential part of the way he is characterised.

Filling in the facts

These two stories reflect facets of Alfred's character which the Anglo-Saxons felt to be distinctive and admirable. Yet we cannot fully understand Alfred's literary achievements without a sense of his wider historical and political cultural context. This section will provide a brief sketch of the background behind the Alfredian writing bonanza.

First, how did Alfred himself end up as king? When Alfred was born in 849 to Æthelwulf, king of Wessex since 839, and his wife Osburh, he was the youngest of six children, five of whom were male, and any prospect of his becoming ruler must have seemed very remote indeed. But circumstances were to intervene. His oldest brother Æthelstan died in the early 850s. His father Æthelwulf then arranged that in the event of his own death, the kingdom should be divided between the next two brothers, Æthelbald and Æthelberht. Æthelwulf died in 858, but Æthelbald had little time to enjoy his share of the inheritance, himself dying in 860. Æthelberht no sooner succeeded to the whole kingdom than he also died (in 865). The next brother down, Æthelred, became the next king of Wessex. But his reign too was cut short at his death in 871.

Even given the lower life expectancy of the Anglo-Saxon period, Wessex's poor record with three kings in the previous 12 years did not augur well for Alfred's own survival as king. The most evident source of danger for kings and their subjects in this period was the Vikings, whose ferocious and destructive tendencies should not be underestimated, even if they never actually wore the horned helmets so beloved of Hollywood. The Vikings had engaged periodically in assaults on parts of southern England from the 830s onwards (for more on this, see p. 303). From the 850s the raids seem to have been more sustained, involving larger armies and longer campaigns. The Vikings took control of East Anglia in 869–70 and continued their move westwards into Wessex. Alfred and his brother mounted fierce resistance against the Viking armies and even succeeded in putting them to flight in a battle at Ashdown early in 871. But by the time Alfred succeeded to the throne later in 871, the situation had worsened again. The first part of Alfred's reign, up to about 878, was largely dominated by his attempts to repel the Viking invaders. Bouts of conflict were interspersed with various peace treaties which entailed paying off the Vikings with substantial amounts of money. The Vikings imposed their presence on other areas of England as well, conquering Northumbria and parts of Mercia. In 877 the Vikings once again attacked Wessex, forcing Alfred into hiding. It is in this period that Alfred is supposed to have spent some time taking refuge in the swineherd's cottage and absent-mindedly neglected the burning loaves of bread. Alfred must have been more active, however, in organising resistance to the Vikings than this story would suggest. Around the middle of 878 Alfred and his army fought against the Vikings at Edington (in Wiltshire) and forced them to flee. They were pursued to their stronghold in Chippenham, where they were besieged by Alfred's army and eventually, two weeks later, surrendered. A peace treaty with terms extremely favourable to Alfred, including the baptism of the Viking King Guthrum, was agreed. By the end of the 870s the creation of the so-called Danelaw had been completed, which gave the Danes control of Northumbria, the eastern parts of Mercia and East Anglia.

Fortunately for Alfred, and for English literary history, this intensive period of conflict and negotiation with the Vikings was followed by a good dozen years of relative calm. Obviously Alfred had to get his country back into shape again and it is therefore not surprising to find that considerable time and effort was spent on rebuilding and reinforcing his kingdom. He exploited his hands-on military knowledge to reorganise the army and to establish a series of *burhs* or fortified sites. The foresight represented by these activities would reveal itself in the later years of his reign. Meantime Alfred also turned his attention to learning and education. It is fair to say that for Alfred this was all part of getting his country back into shape; not only had the depradations of the Vikings led to significant losses of the tools of learning such as books, but also people themselves were putting less priority on learning than they had done in the past. In order to counter this sorry state, Alfred brought in a number of scholars to Wessex from both Mercia and the continent and instituted an educational programme to disseminate learning more widely through his kingdom. The nature of this educational programme and its implications will be the subject of much of the rest of this chapter.

In 892 a new wave of Viking invasions assailed England. The Vikings marshalled their troops effectively, but were in the end unable to make significant headway in the face of the defensive strategies that Alfred had established. Alfred was clearly occupied with confronting the Viking threat up to about 896, after which the main danger seems to have subsided. It is possible that in the last three years of his reign Alfred was at last able to devote himself single-mindedly to the intellectual pursuits that he valued so highly.

Alfred's multicultural context

Alfred's books reflect a keen awareness of other cultures and their skills and traditions. When he set out to promote learning in his own kingdom, Alfred began by gathering some foreign scholars. As we saw in the last chapter (p. 231), he collected scholars from the neighbouring kingdom of Mercia, such as Bishop Wærferth of Worcester, Plegmund (who was appointed Archbishop of Canterbury in 890), and the priests Æthelstan and Werwulf. Alfred turned to Wales for another of his advisors, securing (after some delicate negotiation) the services of Asser, a monk at St David's. Some scholars came from even further afield. From the continent were brought over the colourfully named John the Old Saxon and Grimbald, a monk from St Bertin's in Flanders. This diverse group from England and abroad would have supplied Alfred with a wealth of intellectual traditions divergent from his own and Alfred clearly revelled in the opportunity to engage with their explanations and interpretations of literary works and other topics such as the nature of kingship. Alfred was interested in the ways in which continental kings exercised their authority. In many respects he modelled his kingship on their example.

Alfred's court then must have been a vibrant multicultural environment, buzzing with the interaction of scholars from the various English kingdoms and from the continent. Multicultural also implies multilingual and multilingualism was another important aspect of Alfred's cultural context. In Alfred's day, no less than in the centuries before him, Latin was considered the proper language for scholarly endeavour. The works which Alfred and his late ninth-century reading group met to read and discuss were Latin works. Latin manuscripts were copied and recopied; substantial libraries of these are known to have existed in England and on the continent. Alfred's advisors from the continent presumably brought over manuscripts of Latin writings with them. But the spoken language of England was English; the majority of Alfred's subjects would have understood only English and by the end of the ninth century knowledge of Latin was declining even among the clergy. Alfred, who wrote in English but drew on Latin sources, provided an insight into Latin intellectual culture for a much wider audience whose first (and often only) language was English.

In so many ways Alfred's horizons extended beyond the boundaries of his native Wessex. It is with Alfred that the idea of an English nation first seems to have become part of the Anglo-Saxon cultural perspective. The English nation as we now understand it was not a concept that would have meant anything to the inhabitants of England, at least at the beginning of Alfred's reign. England was a series of separate kingdoms when Alfred succeeded to the throne of Wessex and all three – Northumbria, Mercia, and Wessex – had their own rulers and ruling systems. An alliance between Mercia and Wessex had existed since the mid-ninth century, probably because these two kingdoms needed to stand together to fend off the Vikings. What seems to emerge during Alfred's reign, however, is more than an alliance, but rather a recognition of Alfred as the leader of all Englishmen, wherever they came from. Alfred, for example, is referred to as 'king of the Angles and of the Saxons' or 'king of the Anglo-Saxons' in various documents of the late 880s and 890s. Of course this might just reflect what the writers of these documents wanted people to think. On balance, however, the evidence suggests that the origins of English nationhood is something to be laid at Alfred's door.

There is another way in which we might view Alfred's books as emanating from a multicultural environment. As a king, Alfred's activities were inevitably bound up with the life of the court. We tend to think of the court as being rather remote and self-sufficient. But in Alfred's day the court's activities were very closely bound up with those of the church, that other ever important player in Anglo-Saxon England. Alfred wanted his bishops and clergy to be better educated, because he knew that it was through them that learning would filter through to other parts of society. As they had done before, religious culture and court culture interacted very closely with each other during Alfred's period. We will see this when we turn to the books themselves.

An Anglo-Saxon 'mission statement'

What occasionally frustrates the study of Old English literature is that Anglo-Saxon authors were not much given to explaining how and why they went about their literary activities. One important exception to this, however, is a letter that Alfred wrote early in his literary career to accompany one of his works. It is usually known as 'Alfred's Preface to his Translation of Gregory's *Pastoral Care*' or 'Alfred's Preface on the State of Learning in England' and I will refer to it as the Preface, but it is actually more like a circular letter or a covering letter – the sort of thing that one might send out with, say, a job application. In it Alfred gives a remarkable insight into his literary aims and ambitions.

Central to the Preface is Alfred's scheme for making learning available to a much wider audience than before. His aim, he explains, is to set up a programme of translation by which 'certain books which are the most necessary for all men to know' (*sumæ bec, ða ðe niedbeðearfosta sien eallum monnum to wiotonne*) will become available in 'the language that we can all understand' (*ðæt geðiode . . . ðe we ealle gecnawan mægen*), that is, English. These translations will enable the 'free-born young men now of England' (*sio gioguð ðe nu is on Angelcynne friora monna*) to become better educated; those who are persuaded to take their education further can do so by taking lessons in Latin. Alfred also explains why he feels the need for such a programme. Recalling the happy times of the past, when the Anglo-Saxon kings commanded power and respect and when religious life, learning and scholarship flourished in England, he draws a contrast with the grim situation at the time when he succeeded to the throne. He explains how a general air of prosperity in the churches of his own youth actually masked a fundamental breakdown in their tradition. Although they could boast an abundance of 'treasures and books' (*maðma ond boca*), the books were little more than museum pieces because their owners were unable to understand the Latin in which they were written. In the face of such a collapse of the tradition of Latin learning, Alfred argues, the best response must be a translation programme which would offer people the opportunity to become educated. Alfred ends his Preface by explaining how he translated Gregory's *Pastoral Care* into English with the help of his advisors and that he plans to despatch a copy of it to every monastery, where it can then be consulted and copied.

Innovation is at the heart of this translation programme. Never before in England had its native language been viewed as an appropriate medium for articulating the complex ideas found in Latin literature. The idea of translating Latin works into English as a way of informing and educating wide swathes of the population offered exciting educational opportunities. Books in English could open up avenues of communication that had not been available before.

In setting up this scheme, Alfred was doing something very new in England, but he did have in mind a continental precedent. A literary renaissance patronised by Charlemagne, who was crowned Emperor in 800, and his successors in the Carolingian Empire had heaped credit on these rulers and their kingdoms. Alfred sought for his kingdom too the cultural prestige which came from intellectual prowess. The scheme to make available a collection of works written in English must have seemed an ideal way to foster such prestige.

Ensuring that the books reached the audience for whom they were intended was not straightforward in the late ninth century. After all, there were no large publishing companies such as we take for granted as the means of producing and advertising books. Book production and circulation in Anglo-Saxon England, as we have seen, were in the hands of scribes and monasteries. Books were copied and stored in monasteries and indeed no manuscripts at all would have survived from the Anglo-Saxon period had it not been for the secure environment which the monastic libraries offered. It is no surprise to find then that the priority destinations for Alfred's books are the monasteries. The opening of Alfred's Preface consists of a greeting to the person for whom it was intended. Each copy would have been addressed to a particular individual; the manuscript copy of the Preface now in the Bodleian Library in Oxford, for example, is the one which Wærferth, Bishop of Worcester, was to receive: 'King Alfred sends words of greeting lovingly and amicably to Bishop Wærferth' (*Ælfred kyning hateð gretan Wærferð biscep his wordum luflice ond freondlice*). Just to avoid any confusion, the manuscript also contains in block capitals the note: 'This book must go to Worcester' (*Ðeos boc sceal to Wiogora Ceastre*) (see plate 12). The manuscript actually has some annotations, or glosses, written by a later Bishop of Worcester, which indicates that the manuscript did reach its target.

The Preface is important for the information it gives us about Alfred's programme of learning and its implementation. But in its content and style it points to wider issues and techniques that recur in Alfred's writing. In the rest of this chapter, I would like to consider some of these issues and techniques, in relation to both the Preface and Alfred's other books. Before doing that, however, we need to identify these 'other books'.

What are Alfred's books?

Tantalisingly, although Alfred refers to 'certain books which are the most necessary for all men to know', he never explicitly tells us what these books are. We can tell what Alfred probably had in mind, however, from the Old English translations of Latin works which were written in this period. It is important to note that the word 'translation' is a misnomer here. These works are not what we would call translations. They are rather Old English *adaptations* which show constant rewriting and interpretation of their sources (some more so than others). In his Preface to Gregory's *Pastoral Care*, Alfred explains that he translates 'sometimes word for word, sometimes sense for sense' (*hwilum word be worde, hwilum andgit of andgite*), where 'sense for sense' covers a multitude of expansions and reinterpretations of the original.

Alfred tells us in this Preface that he himself is responsible for the translation of Gregory's *Pastoral Care* into Old English:

Ða ongan ic ongemang oðrum mislicum ond manigfealdum bisgum ðisses kynerices ða boc wendan on Englisc ðe is genemned on Læden Pastoralis, ond on Englisc Hierdeboc.

Then I began, among the various and manifold afflictions of this kingdom, to translate into English the book which in Latin is called *Pastoralis*, and in English 'Shepherd-book'.

Alfred tells us that he went through the Latin with his advisers, Plegmund, Asser, Grimbald and John, and then 'translated it into English as I understood it and as I could most meaningfully render it' (*swæ swæ ic hie forstod, ond swæ ic hie andgitfullicost areccean meahte, ic hie on Englisc awende*). We can imagine a series of small group seminars in which each passage of the source was translated and analysed, with particular attention paid to how it might best be understood by a contemporary Alfredian audience. The process of 'translation' itself was presumably the distillation of such discussions into a written form, although the translator did not necessarily himself write down his work but perhaps dictated it to a scribe. It is clear that to call Alfred the 'author' of his works means something rather different from what 'author' implies to us today.

Gregory's *Pastoral Care* is the only work which Alfred himself explicitly claims to have translated. Although Gregory's work is essentially a manual for the clergy, it contained all kinds of general information about the qualities needed in anyone in a position of responsibility and it is easy to see the attraction of the work for Alfred as ruler of a kingdom. Of course, we cannot *prove* that Alfred was the translator. Indeed, some scholars doubt that Alfred actually did translate anything, arguing that his name was used because of the authority it conveyed. Neither, however, can we *disprove* his claim to have done so. The evidence of vocabulary and style suggests that three other translations were also the work of the translator of Gregory's *Pastoral Care* (assumed here to be Alfred). One of these is the translation of Boethius's *On the Consolation of Philosophy*. Boethius wrote this work in prison awaiting execution; he describes an imaginary dialogue between himself and a figure called Lady Philosophy through which he is gradually brought from despondency and despair to a recognition of the ultimate wisdom of God's providence. A prose Preface to the Old English translation attributes the work to Alfred: 'King Alfred was the translator of this book' (*Ælfred Kuning wæs wealhstod ðisse bec*). This Preface tells us, just as the Preface to Gregory's *Pastoral Care* did, that the translation was 'sometimes word for word, sometimes sense for sense' (*hwilum . . . word be worde, hwilum andgit of andgite*). It also alerts us to the fact that there are two different versions of the Old English Boethius, one of which is all in prose, the other in alternating prose and poetry (as in the Latin original). The Preface claims that Alfred first turned the *Consolation of Philosophy* into prose and then 'rendered it subsequently into verse' (*geworhte hi eft to leoðe*). The production of two different Old English versions of the same work would suggest that the structure and style, and not just the contents, of these Latin master-pieces attracted the attention of Alfred and his advisors.

The two other works for which Alfred himself may have been responsible are the prose translations of Augustine's *Soliloquies* and the first 50 psalms of the Psalter. Augustine's *Soliloquies* is an odd choice in some ways since it doesn't seem at any stage to have been one of Augustine's best sellers. It may have been its similarities to Boethius's *Consolation of Philosophy* that attracted Alfred's attention: it too offers a dialogue between two figures (here Augustine's mind and his reason) and treats complex philosophical issues (here the immortality of the soul). Alfred departs even further from his source in composing this work: the last part of his Book II and the whole of his Book III move away from the *Soliloquies* altogether and draw on a range of other sources instead. To find Alfred translating psalms is less sur-prising; given that the Latin Psalter was recognised as an ideal teaching text in Latin, it must have seemed appropriate to have an English version of the psalms available for a programme of teaching in English.

Among 'Alfred's books' should be included a number of other works which were not composed by Alfred himself, but which were almost cer-tainly produced as part of his scheme to make important books available in English. One of these is the translation of Gregory's *Dialogues*, which was probably done by Bishop Wærferth of Worcester (Asser tells us this in his biography of Alfred). It is another work which uses dialogue for its structure – here between the Pope and a deacon named Peter. The work tells the lives of various saints with lots of colourful details along the way. The translation of Gregory's *Dialogues* can be compared to another work with a focus on saints, the Old English *Martyrology*, which may also have been translated from a Latin original in Alfred's reign. Saints were the Anglo-Saxon equival-ent to modern celebrities: audiences revelled in the details of their lives (and deaths) just as many people today take an interest in the more lurid elements of celebrities' lives. We shouldn't take this comparison too far, however. Let's face it, it is not exemplary virtue which underpins the accounts of modern celebrities.

Two of the translations probably to be assigned to Alfred's programme were historical in their focus: Orosius's *Seven Books of History against the Pagans* (which offered a history of the world from the Creation to 417 AD) and Bede's *Ecclesiastical History of the English People* (whose focus was on England and the gradual establishment of Christianity there after the arrival of the monk Augustine in 597 AD). The interest in history implied by the selection of these works for translation is also reflected in another work which is thought to have been conceived and compiled in Alfred's reign, the *Anglo-Saxon Chronicle*. This offers a series of annals recounting the history of the Anglo-Saxons, with a particular emphasis (which the context of Alfred's court makes unsurprising) on the fortunes of the West Saxon kingdom. Although individual annals offer translations of passages from, for example, Bede's *Ecclesiastical History*, the idea of a chronicle of English history written in English was strikingly new in Alfred's day. The *Anglo-Saxon Chronicle* continued to circulate and to be updated well after Alfred's reign; at one centre, Peterborough, new entries were still being added right up to the middle of the twelfth century.

There were other works in English that were probably produced in the period: Alfred's law code, for one, and the wonderfully entitled Bald's *Leechbook*, with its copious collection of medical recipes. The suggestion there of eating a radish at night to prevent harm from a woman's chatter the next day is one of the many remedies that have not withstood the test of time. These works, like the *Anglo-Saxon Chronicle*, are important spin-offs from a programme that prioritised English as the language of communication. But, in literary terms at least, the pinnacle of Alfred's achievement is the provision of English versions of what were in his opinion the most important books for all men to know, inspirational Latin works by authors such as Gregory, Boethius, Augustine, Orosius and Bede. Some of the literary interests and techniques of the writings attributed to Alfred himself, his prefaces and his own translations, will be explored in the following sections.

A king's voice

Alfred's dual roles as king and author interact to interesting effect in his works. The voice of royal authority is combined with one of intense introspection. Not only does Alfred speak as a king, but he also explores the nature of kingship and the different types of responsibilities that it entails.

In his Preface to Gregory's *Pastoral Care* Alfred presents his royal credentials at the outset, with a brief formal address in the third person: 'King Alfred sends words of greeting lovingly and amicably to Bishop Wærferth' (*Ælfred kyning hateð gretan Wærferð biscep his wordum luflice ond freondlice*). Having imposed the stamp of regal authority, Alfred turns quickly to a more introspective approach. Moving into the first person ('I'), he recreates his own thinking process in order to explain his decision to set up a learning programme: 'And I would have it known that it has very often come to my mind . . .' (*ond ðe cyðan hate ðæt me com swiðe oft on gemynd . . .*). The word 'mind' here is the first of a pattern of words reverberating throughout the Preface which relate to thought and memory: 'suppose' (*wene* and *wendon*), 'think' (*geðencean* and *geðenc*), 'thinks' (*ðyncð*, twice), 'remembered' (*gemunde*, five times) and 'wondered' (*wundrade*). Alfred draws in his audience to understand and sympathise with his predicament. Despite its personal tone, however, it is clear that Alfred's role as king informs the Preface as a whole.

Near the beginning of the Preface, Alfred presents his view of ideal kingship among other recollections of England's glorious past:

> me com swiðe oft on gemynd . . . hu ða kyningas ðe ðone onwald hæfdon ðæs folces Gode ond his ærendwrecum hersumedon; ond hie ægðer ge hiora sibbe ge hiora siodu ge hiora onweald innanbordes gehioldon, ond eac ut hiora eðel gerymdon; ond hu him ða speow ægðer ge mid wige ge mid wisdome.

> It has very often come to my mind . . . how the kings who had authority over the people obeyed God and his messengers; and they maintained their peace, morality and authority at home and also extended their territory abroad; and how they succeeded both in war and in wisdom.

Alfred's learning programme is inspired by his desire to recreate ideal kingship in his own kingdom, by combining military and intellectual pre-eminence.

The same thoughtful engagement with the nature of kingship can be seen in another preface written from Alfred's first-person perspective. This is the Preface to Wærferth's translation of Gregory's *Dialogues*. The whole Preface is only two (admittedly quite lengthy) sentences in total:

> Ic Ælfred geofendum Criste mid cynehades mærnysse geweorðod, habbe gearolice ongyten and þurh haligra boca gesægene oft gehyred, þætte us, þam þe God swa micle heanesse worldgeþingða forgifen hafað, is seo mæste ðearf, þæt we hwilon ure mod betwix þas eorþlican ymbhigdo geleoðigen and gebigen to ðam godcundan and þam gastlican rihte. And forþan ic sohte and wilnade to minum getreowum freondum, þæt hi me of Godes bocum be haligra manna þeawum and wundrum awriten þas æfterfylgendan lare, þæt ic þurh þa mynegunge and lufe gescyrped on minum mode betwih þas eorðlican gedrefednese hwilum gehicge þa heofonlican.

> I, Alfred, honoured with the glory of kingship by Christ's gift, have clearly perceived and frequently heard from statements in holy books that for us, to whom God has granted such high platform of worldly office, there is the greatest need occasionally to calm our minds amid these earthly anxieties and

turn them to divine and spiritual law. And therefore I sought and asked of my true friends that they should write down for me from God's books the following teaching concerning the virtues and miracles of holy men, so that, strengthened through those exhortations and love, I might occasionally reflect in my mind on heavenly things amid these earthly tribulations.

In this preface, as in the Preface to Gregory's *Pastoral Care*, Alfred alludes explicitly at the very beginning to his own royal authority. He then moves to consider more generally the need for those in positions of power to calm their minds by devoting them to spiritual enlightenment. By commissioning the translation of Gregory's *Dialogues*, he too can fulfil in this respect the role of the ideal ruler. Alfred emphasises the link between serious thought and kingship: he 'clearly perceived' the need for rulers as a group to 'calm their minds' and he himself desires to reflect on heavenly things 'in his mind'.

Elsewhere too, Alfred addresses the nature of kingship. The Old English version of Boethius' *Consolation* offers a particularly striking example in a passage which is independent of the source. Here 'Mind' (*Mod*), which is the name Alfred gives to the character of Boethius within the work, expresses views to Wisdom (here called *Gesceadwisnes*) on kingship which apparently reflect Alfred's own:

> And þa andswarode þæt Mod and þus cwæð: Eala, Gesceadwisnes, hwæt, þu wast þæt me næfre seo gitsung and seo gemægð þisses eorðlican anwealdes forwel ne licode, ne ic ealles forswiðe ne girnde þisses eorðlican rices, buton tola ic wilnode þeah and andweorces to þam weorce þe me beboden was to wyrcanne; þæt was þæt ic unfracodlice and gerisenlice mihte steoran and reccan þone anwald þe me befæst wæs. . . . Þæt bið þonne cyninges andweorc and his tol mid to ricsianne, þæt he hæbbe his lond fullmonnad; he sceal habban gebedmen and fyrdmen and weorcmen. Hwæt þu wast þætte butan þissan tolan nan cyning his cræft ne mæg cyðan. . . . Forþy ic wilnode andweorces þone anwald mid to reccenne, þæt mine cræftas and anweald ne wurden forgitene and forholene. Forþam ælc cræft and ælc anweald bið sona forealdod and forsugod, gif he bið buton wisdome; forðæm ne mæg non mon nænne cræft bringan buton wisdome.

And then Mind answered and said thus: 'Look, Wisdom, you know that desire for and possession of earthly power never pleased me very much, and nor did I unduly desire this earthly rule, but that nevertheless I wished for tools and resources for the task that I was commanded to accomplish, which was that I should virtuously and worthily guide and direct the authority which was entrusted to me. . . . In the case of the king, the resources and tools with which to rule are that he have his land fully manned: he must have men who pray, men who fight, and men who work. Indeed you know that without these tools no king may make his ability known. . . . Therefore I sought the resources with which to exercise authority, so that my skills and authority would not be forgotten and concealed. For every skill and every authority is soon obsolete and passed over, if it is without wisdom; because no man may bring to bear any skill without wisdom.'

Alfred, through 'Mind', explains that a king must muster the resources he needs and put them to proper use. His most important resource is his subjects, divided here into three classes: the religious, the military and the labourers. The last part of the passage quoted focuses on the interaction of *cræft* (skill), *anweald* (authority) and *wisdom* (wisdom). It is these three qualities that together enable a king to rule effectively. This passage moves a long way from the practical account of the resources required by a king with which it begins. Alfred takes the opportunity here to offer a wider exploration of ideal kingship – a concept which for him combines not only authority and skill but also, above all, wisdom.

The pursuit of wisdom

For Alfred wisdom and learning from books go hand in hand. In the Preface to Gregory's *Pastoral Care*, Alfred describes as 'good wise men' (*godena wiotona*) those who in former times in England 'had thoroughly studied all the books' (*ða bec eallæ befullan geliornod hæfdon*). In another preface, that to the Old English *Soliloquies*, Alfred explains his own method of learning from books. He uses the metaphor of gathering wood as a way of describing his gathering of ideas from a range of literary sources:

Gaderode me þonne kigclas and stuþansceaftas, and lohsceaftas and hylfa to ælcum þara tola þe ic mid wircan cuðe, and bohtimbru and bolttimbru, and, to ælcum þara weorca þe ic wyrcan cuðe, þa wlitegostan treowo be þam dele ðe ic aberan meihte. Ne com ic naþer mid anre byrðene ham þe me ne lyste ealne þane wude ham brengan, gif ic hyne ealne aberan meihte; on ælcum treowo ic geseah hwæthwugu þæs þe ic æt ham beþorfte.

I then gathered for myself staves and props, and tie-shafts and handles for each of the tools which I knew how to work with, and cross-bars and beams, and, for each of the structures which I knew how to build, the finest pieces of wood I could carry. I never came home with a single load without wishing to bring home the whole forest, if I could have carried it all – in every tree I saw something which I needed at home.

The image used here is a wonderfully down-to-earth way of describing intellectual endeavours. Alfred goes on to advise everybody who can do so to take the opportunity to collect timbers in the same way that he has done – in other words, to apply themselves to book learning. Through reading authors such as Gregory and Augustine, Alfred explains, he hopes to acquire the understanding that will enable him to live more calmly in this world and also be more prepared for heaven.

It is not enough for Alfred in his pursuit of wisdom just to read; he is also determined to remember what he has read. It is worth bearing in mind that in the Anglo-Saxon period, people were much more used to having to learn things off by heart. We know that Alfred had a particularly good memory (at least according to his biographer Asser). But even Alfred is aware that the memory is fallible. In his translation of Augustine's *Soliloquies*, he offers independently of his source a picture of the kind of scholarly environment which he had probably found productive for his own learning:

> Ða cwæd ic: hwam wille ic ælles befæstan þæt ic elles gestryne butan minum geminde?
> Þa cwæd heo: is þin gemind swa mihtig þæt hit mage eall gehealden þæt þu geðengst and hym bebeotst to healdenne?
> Ða cwæð ic: nese, la nese, ne min ne nanes mannes nis to þam creftig þæt hit mage eall gehæaldan þæt him me on befæst.
> Þa cwæð heo: befæste hit þonne bocstafum and awrit hit. ac me þincð þath þeah, þæt þu si to unhal þæt ðu ne mage hit æall awritan; and þeah þu æall hal were, þu beþorftest þæt ðu hæfdest digele stoge and æmanne ælces oðres þinges, and fæawa cuðe men and creftige mid þe, ðe nan wiht ne amyrdan, ac fultmoden to þinum crefte.

> Then I [St Augustine] said: To what shall I entrust everything that I acquire, if not to my memory?
> Then it [Reason] said: Is your memory so powerful that it can contain everything that you reflect on and that you command it to retain?
> Then I said: No, not at all; neither my nor any man's memory is so powerful that it can retain everything entrusted to it.
> Then it said: Then commit it to letters and write it down. But it seems to me, however, that you are not well enough to write it all down; and even if you were completely well, you would need to have a private place, free from every other distraction, and a few learned and skilful men with you who would not disturb you at all, but would assist you in your work.

Ideally, Alfred implies, everything one learns would be written down. Ill health may make that impossible. Even without ill health, this activity requires such dedication that it is only possible if a quiet place and some learned advisors are available. The allusion to ill health here is interesting since we know that Alfred suffered ill health throughout his life. According to Asser, Alfred had contracted piles as a young man, apparently as the result of his praying to God for an illness that would make it easier for him to restrain his sexual desires. Alfred was later cured, when he prayed to God for a less severe illness, but was then struck down on his wedding night by a new illness that lasted from the age of 20 to 45. There has been much speculation about what this second illness might have been. It is not identified in the source, but Crohn's disease is one plausible theory. With the combined references here to ill health and to a few learned men as advisors, both of which apply to Alfred's own situation, Alfred is perhaps implying that his own learning environment is one through which the virtue of reason might be attained. This puts Alfred in a position which contrasts with the figure of Augustine who, according to the Old English *Soliloquies*, has neither solitude nor the help of other men.

For Alfred, the wisdom which can be attained through book learning is also a way of reaching towards an understanding of God's wisdom. In the Old English *Consolation*, Alfred identifies wisdom as the highest virtue, one that embodies within it other virtues:

> Swa swa wisdom is se hehsta cræft, and se hæfð on him feower oðre cræftas: ðara is an wærscipe, oðer gemetgung, ðridde is ellen, feorðe rihtwisnes. Se Wisdom gedeð his lufiendas wise and wære and gemetfæste and geþyldige and rihtwise, and ælces godes þeawes he gefyllð þone þe hine lufað. Þæt ne magon don þa ðe þone anweald habbað þisse worulde; ne magon hi nanne cræft forgifan þam ðe hi lufiað of hiora welan, gif hi hine on heora gecynde nabbað.

> Thus wisdom is the highest virtue, and it contains within it four other virtues: one of those is caution, the second moderation, the third courage, and the fourth justice. Wisdom makes its devotees wise and cautious and moderate and patient and just, and it fills him who loves it with every good quality. Those who have authority in this world cannot do that; they cannot give from their wealth any virtue to those who love them, if they do not have it in their nature.

Wisdom, the supreme virtue, incorporates a number of other virtues that it passes on to those who love it. Kings or other earthly rulers cannot emulate wisdom itself: they may be wise but, unlike wisdom, they cannot impart their virtues to people who do not already have them. Wisdom for Alfred encompasses different meanings. Not only is it the intellectual knowledge that can be achieved through book learning, but also a more spiritual quality associated with God's divine wisdom. The two of course are far from distinct: only through the wisdom achieved by book learning can someone move towards apprehending the ultimate wisdom of God.

Wealth

Just as the word 'wisdom' reverberates through Alfred's writings, so too does the word 'wealth' (*welan*). 'Wealth' can entail either material prosperity or a more spiritual enrichment. Alfred plays on the two meanings, sometimes allowing for both interpretations at the same time. Wisdom is often connected with wealth in Alfred's mind. In the passage cited earlier from the Old English *Consolation*, Alfred includes both 'wisdom' and 'wealth'. Earthly rulers, unlike wisdom itself, cannot grant virtue 'from their wealth' (*of hiora welan*) to those who love them. Here 'wealth' refers explicitly to the physical treasure rulers have at their disposal. The word also points implicitly in this context to a contrast between this worldly wealth, which cannot grant virtue, and spiritual wealth, which wisdom represents.

Elsewhere Alfred plays much more extensively on the notion that 'wisdom' is itself 'wealth'. In the Preface to Gregory's *Pastoral Care*, Alfred develops a multilayered word play on these two concepts. The idea that monetary wealth and the wisdom derived from books are inextricably tied up with one another reverberates through the Preface as a whole. Alfred connects treasure and books as he recalls how in the recent past, before the Viking raids, 'the churches throughout all England were filled with treasure and books' (*ða ciricean giond eall Angelcynn stodon maðma ond boca gefyldæ*). Alfred then goes on to imagine the guilt his ancestors must have felt at being unable to read these books owing to their ignorance of Latin:

> Swelce hie cwæden: Ure ieldran, ða ðe ðas stowa ær hioldon, hie lufodon wisdom, ond ðurh ðone hie begeaton welan ond us læfdon. Her mon mæg giet gesion hiora swæð, ac we him ne cunnon æfter spyrigean, ond forðæm we habbað nu ægðer forlæten ge ðone welan ge ðone wisdom, forðæmðe we noldon to ðæm spore mid ure mode onlutan.

> It is as if they had said: Our ancestors, who formerly occupied these places, loved wisdom, and through it they obtained wealth and left it to us. In this we can still see their tracks, but we cannot follow them. And therefore we have now lost both the wealth and the wisdom, because we would not bend down to their tracks with our minds.

Twice in this passage Alfred links 'wealth' (*welan*) and 'wisdom' (*wisdom*). Through wisdom wealth was gained; now both wealth and wisdom have been lost. Alfred intends to reverse this process: he will make it possible for wisdom to be recovered and through wisdom wealth, too, will be recovered. This wealth is both metaphorical (spiritual riches accumulated through wisdom) and literal (financial prosperity). The latter comes through success in war, too, and, earlier in the Preface, Alfred links wisdom with war, commenting on how kings in times past succeeded 'both in wisdome and in war' (*ge mid wige ge mid wisdome*). As Tom Shippey remarks, 'Wisdom, in Alfred's speech and mind, is linked with war and with wealth (*wig, wela*), and not just because they alliterate' (1979: 353).

The association between wealth and wisdom is also evident in Alfred's intention, stated in this Preface, to send to each bishop an *æstel* as an accompaniment to the book. It seems therefore that Alfred was not averse to offering the Anglo-Saxon equivalent of the goody bags handed out at Oscars ceremonies as a sweetener to his bishops. An *æstel* is probably a book marker, perhaps a rod-like pointer for following the line while reading or for inserting in book at a particular place. Alfred explicitly comments on the cost of the *æstel*: it is worth 50 mancuses (a *mancus* being a gold coin). This means that each one was expensive to make and presumably had gold or jewels worked into its construction. One particular object, now known as the 'Alfred Jewel', has been linked with this *æstel* (see plate 13). The Alfred Jewel is a beautiful and intricate piece of work. It consists of a pear-shaped frame enclosing a piece of rock crystal superimposed on a design made out of cloisonné enamel. The enamel design, which presents a figure wearing a tunic and holding the stems of objects that appear to be flowers, has been interpreted in different ways: as Christ, a particular saint, the Pope, Alexander the Great, a personification of Sight or, simply, Alfred himself. A gold extension in the form of an animal head comes out of the narrower end of the frame and a tube or socket comes out of the animal's mouth. This suggests that the jewel was originally attached to something else, something perishable such as wood, ivory or leather. The jewel is particularly associated with Alfred because of an inscription around the edge of the frame which reads 'ÆLFRED MEC HEHT GEWYRCAN' ('Alfred had me made'). Whether or not this particular jewel represents the *æstel* of the Preface, it is clear that Alfred wished to emphasise to his bishops the significance of his enterprise by associating with it objects of great value. The valuable *æstel* is an important pointer for us as modern readers towards understanding Alfred's perspective on learning: wealth and wisdom are inseparable.

Alfred's story telling

This chapter has been largely devoted to telling the story of Alfred and his books. In this section I want to turn to Alfred as a teller of stories. Clearly, Alfred didn't select books for translation on the basis of their having a strong narrative line. The ones chosen tend to be more discursive and philo-sophical in their approach. Often, however, they include mini-narratives to illustrate or develop their themes. The Old English version of Bede's *History* retells from its source some well-known stories. One of these is of Gregory, before he became Pope Gregory the Great, standing before a group of slave boys in Rome. On being informed that they are English, Gregory responds that they seem to him not 'Angles' but 'angels' (*non Angli sed angeli*). An-other story is of Cædmon, the cowherd who is divinely inspired to compose Old English poetry (see pp. 191–2). Similarly, Bishop Wærferth's translation of Gregory's *Dialogues* recounts stories of the virtues and miracles of vari-ous holy men and women. One of these is the extraordinary account of a woman who, against advice, refused to remarry and whose unsatisfied sexual desires then led her to grow a beard. In the Old English *Consolation*, Alfred exploits his own talents as a story teller. In this adaptation of a Latin version of Boethius' work, Alfred transforms the source's often brief allusions to classical stories, both historical and mythological, into compelling narra-tives. Presumably aware of the appeal of these stories to his audience, Alfred is quick to fill in their details. At one point, where Boethius refers in passing to the heads of the Hydra, Alfred offers a succinct version of the story of Hercules and this particular monster:

> Swa swa mon on ealdspellum sægð þæt an nædre wære þe hæfde nigon heafdu, and symle gif mon anra hwelc of aslog, þonne weoxon þær siofon on ðæm anum heafde. Þa geberede hit þæt þær com se foremæra Erculus to, se wæs Iobes sunu; þa ne meahte he geþencan hu he hi mid ænige cræfte ofercuman sceolde, ær he hi bewæg mid wuda utan and forbærnde þa mid fyre.

> So it is told in old stories that there was a serpent with nine heads, and whenever one was struck off, seven more grew on that head. It happened that the famous Hercules, son of Jove, came to that place. He could not think how he could overcome it with any skill, until he surrounded it with wood and burnt it up with fire.

No one is absolutely sure where all the details came from for this account. Alfred or his advisors may have read the classical stories elsewhere or they may have relied on commentaries which accompanied the *On the Consolation of Philosophy* (although no commentary survives that includes all the relevant details). In any case, it is clear that Hercules is the object of some admiration in this Old English retelling of his exploit.

In some cases, Alfred's desire to tell the stories from classical mythology puts him in a very awkward position indeed. Any involvement of pagan gods or pagan magic made the stories quite out of keeping with religious tradition and required an explicit reminder that they were a pack of lies. We can see this concern being addressed in the retelling of the story of Ulysses and Circe. The Old English version of the story has a back-to-front version of events and is curiously idiosyncratic. Whereas in the classical accounts (and in the Boethian source), Circe changes Ulysses's men to animals when she first encounters them, in the Old English version Ulysses and Circe initially have a love affair, as a result of which his men threaten to leave:

> Sona swa hio geseah þone fordrifenan cyning ðe we ær spræcon, þæs nama wæs Aulixes, þa ongan hio hine lufian, and hiora ægþer oðerne swiðe ungemetlice, swa þætte he for hire lufan forlet his rice eall and his cynren, and wunode mid hire oð ðone first þæt his ðegnas him ne mihton leng mid gewunian, ac for hiora eardes lufan and for þære wræce tihodon hine forlætenne.

> As soon as she saw the shipwrecked king, about whom we spoke before, whose name was Ulysses, she began to love him, and each of them loved the other very immoderately, so that he entirely abandoned his kingdom and his family out of love for her, and stayed with her until the time came when his thanes could no longer stay with him, but intended to abandon him out of love for their homeland and out of vengeance.

It is at this point in Alfred's version that Circe transforms Ulysses' men and her action is preceded by a warning that this story is purely fiction, made up by liars:

> Ða ongunnon lease men wyrcan spell, and sædon þæt hio sceolde mid hire drycræft þa men forbredan, and weorpan hi an wildedeora lic.

> Then false men made up the story, and said that she supposedly transformed the men with her sorcery, and changed them into the form of wild animals.

Alfred clearly enjoyed the classical myths and assumed his audience would too. Nonetheless, he is careful to draw the line, here and elsewhere, between true and false stories. He also knows that the inclusion of such material can only be justified by the moral lessons that it conveys. The story of Ulysses and Circe has been adapted by Alfred in such a way as to present a rather different moral from its source. Ulysses for Alfred is no hero, as Boethius would have it, but rather a lecherous philanderer, whose immoderate desires cause him to neglect his kingdom and family. Ulysses represents weakness of mind, just as much as his men represent weakness of body. However much Alfred revelled in the narrative details of these classical stories, their wider meanings were never far from his mind. And, like many later leaders, Alfred was not averse to manipulating a text to enforce a propaganda point.

Rhetorical strategies

For Alfred, not just what was said mattered, but also how it was said. He uses a variety of rhetorical devices and other literary strategies to convey his ideas as imaginatively and effectively as possible.

The majority of Alfred's books are in prose, both those attributed to him personally and those he commissioned. Alfred may also have composed poetry; certainly the prose preface to the Old English *Consolation* claims that he versified the prose version, and the verse preface to the same work proclaims his skill as a poet:

> Ðus Ælfred us   ealdspell reahte,
> cyning Westsexna,   cræft meldode,
> leoðwyrhta list.

> Thus Alfred, King of the West-Saxons,
> told us ancient stories, made known his ability,
> the skill of poets.

Whether or not Alfred composed poetry, it is clear that he was familiar with poetic techniques and exploited them in his work. He often uses, for example, the alliteration that is so characteristic of Old English poetry. His Preface to Gregory's *Pastoral Care* provides plenty of evidence. We looked earlier at the ways in which he connects *welan* ('wealth') and *wisdom* ('wisdom'), and *wige* ('war') and *wisdome*. Elsewhere he plays on the link through alliteration of *lufodon* and *lefdon*:

> Geðenc hwelc witu us ða becomon for ðisse worulde, ða ða we hit nohwæðer ne selfe ne **lufodon** ne eac oðrum monnum ne **lefdon**: ðone naman anne we **lufodon** ðætte we Cristne wæren, ond swiðe feawe ða ðeawas. [my bold]

> Think what punishments came upon us in this world when we neither loved learning ourselves, nor bequeathed it to other men; we loved only the name of being Christians and very few loved the virtues.

The similarity in sound of *lufodon* ('loved'), used twice in this short passage, and *lefdon* ('bequeathed', literally 'left') imposes, along with the accumulation of negatives, a suitably disparaging tone. Later in the Preface the same pairing of *lufodon* and *læfdon* is found again, this time in the context of praise for those who did pass on wealth and wisdom. Another good example of Alfred's use of alliteration for rhetorical purposes is his address to wise men in the Old English *Consolation*:

> Wella, wisan men, wel; gað ealle on þone weg ðe eow lærað þa foremæran bisna þara godena gumena and þara weorðgeornena wera þe ær eow wæron.

> Oh wise men, go, all of you, on the path which the famous examples of the
> good men and of those eager for honour who preceded you teach you.

In this short passage, Alfred uses three alliterative groupings: *Wella, wisan
men, wel, godena gumena* and *weorðgeornena wera*. This technique produces an
appropriately elevated tone for spurring on the wise to even greater heights.

Alfred also uses concrete and down-to-earth images and metaphors to
help make complex subject matter as accessible as possible. The metaphor
of gathering wood for house building in the Preface to the Old English
Soliloquies (see p. 261) to represent intellectual activity is one such example.
In the Old English *Consolation*, Alfred introduces an intricate image of the
axle of a wagon in relation to its wheel to explain the notion of God's
providence; God is the unmoving axle, while the wheel, the people, are
constantly in motion: 'the axle stands still and yet bears all the wagon and
controls all the movement' (*sio eax stint stille and byrð þeah ealne þone wæn,
and welt ealles þæs færeltes*). In the Old English *Soliloquies*, Alfred develops
the metaphor of a ship (a person) and its anchor (God) to describe how God
offers stability in the face of earthly turmoil:

> Gefastna þa eagan þines modes on gode swa se ancer byd gefastnoð on ðære
> eorðan. þeah þæt scyp si ute on ðære sæ on þam ydum, hyt byð gesund and
> untoslegen, gyf se streng aþolað; forðam hys byd se oðer ende fast on þære
> eorðan and se oðer on ðam scype.

> Fix your mind's eyes on God just as the anchor is fixed in the ground. Even
> though the ship is on the waves out at sea, it is safe and sound if the cable holds,
> because one of its ends is fixed in the ground and the other is fixed to the ship.

Alfred also exploits in his work the motif of the ideal past. The pictures
of the past that Alfred creates may never have existed exactly as he imagines
them. Through contrasting these pasts with the present, however, Alfred is
able to point to the values that underlie his vision for the future. In the
Old English *Consolation*, the Golden Age of the past is represented, as in its
source, as an unattainable time of innocence when people were satisfied
with the most simple existence and did not yearn for material wealth: 'oh
that our times could now be like that' (*eala þæt ure tida nu ne mihtan weorþan
swilce*), laments Alfred. In the Preface to Gregory's *Pastoral Care*, Alfred presents a more practical picture of the ideal past as those happy times in England when kings obeyed God and were successful in what they set out to do
and when learning flourished in England ('how people from abroad sought
wisdom and instruction in this county', *hu man utanbordes wisdom ond lare
hieder on lond sohte*). Here Alfred seems to have in mind the intellectual pre-
eminence of Northumbria a century or so before. Through allusions to the

glorious past, Alfred gives us an insight into the hopes and ideals which he aims to pass on to his people.

The end of the story?

Keenly aware as he was of the transience of earthly things, including literature and learning, Alfred could hardly have envisaged how his programme and the books that were produced as a result of it would play such a crucial role in the development of English literary tradition. Ironically, just as the Latin books so cherished by Alfred and his group of advisors in his day were on the verge of becoming cobwebbed antiquities, so now Old English literature is in danger of disappearing from the consciousness of the nation that created it. Rarely compulsory for English students at universities and by no means even an option in many, the oldest books in our language are in danger of death by neglect. The challenge for today's scholars and students is to take a leaf out of one of Alfred's many books and re-energise the study of Old English literature.

Translations and texts

Carnicelli, Thomas A., ed., *King Alfred's Old English Version of St Augustine's Soliloquies* (Cambridge, MA, 1969). This the standard edition of the work.

Hecht, H., ed., *Bischofs Wærferth von Worcester Übersetzung der Dialoge Gregors des Grossen*, Bibliothek der angelsächsischen Prosa 5 (Leipzig, 1900). The standard edition of Wærferth's translation of Gregory's *Dialogues*.

Keynes, Simon and Lapidge, Michael, trans., *Alfred the Great* (Harmondsworth, 1983). A valuable and accessible collection of translated excerpts from Alfred's works. This is a good starting point for further study of Alfred.

Krapp, G.P., ed., *The Paris Psalter and the Meters of Boethius*, Anglo-Saxon Poetic Records 5 (New York and London, 1932). The standard edition of the verse passages of the Old English *Consolation*.

Sedgefield, Walter J., ed., *King Alfred's Old English Version of Boethius De Consolatione Philosophiae* (Oxford, 1899). The standard edition of this work.

Sweet, Henry, ed., *King Alfred's West-Saxon Version of Gregory's Pastoral Care*, 2 vols., Early English Text Society, Original Series 45 and 50 (London, 1871–2). The standard edition of this work.

Further reading

Abels, Richard, *Alfred the Great: War, Kingship and Culture in Anglo-Saxon England* (Harlow, 1998). A useful general account of Alfred's achievements.

Bately, Janet, 'The Literary Prose of King Alfred's Reign: Translation or Transformation?', *Old English Prose: Basic Readings*, Szarmach, Paul E., ed. (New York and London, 2000), pp. 3–27. An accessible and learned discussion of Alfred's methods.

Discenza, Nicole Guenther, *The King's English: Strategies of Translation in the Old English Boethius* (Albany, NY, 2005). A recent book-length analysis of the Old English *Boethius* in relation to its source.

Godden, Malcolm, 'Wærferth and King Alfred: The Fate of the Old English *Dialogues*', *Alfred the Wise: Studies in Honour of Janet Bately on the Occasion of her Sixty-fifth Birthday*, Roberts, Jane, Janet L. Nelson and Malcolm Godden, eds (Cambridge, 1997), pp. 35–51. A useful study of this neglected work.

Irvine, Susan, 'Ulysses and Circe in King Alfred's *Boethius*: A Classical Myth Transformed', *Studies in English Language and Literature: 'Doubt Wisely': Papers in Honour of E.G. Stanley*, Toswell, M.J. and E.M. Tyler, eds (London, 1996), pp. 387–401. A detailed consideration of this story in the Old English *Consolation*.

Shippey, T.A., 'Wealth and Wisdom in King Alfred's *Preface* to the Old English *Pastoral Care*', *English Historical Review* 94 (1979), pp. 346–55. A refreshingly literary account of Alfred's Preface.

Sisam, Kenneth, *Studies in the History of Old English Literature* (Oxford, 1953). Contains an informative section on the circulation of the *Pastoral Care* Preface.

Whitelock, Dorothy, 'The Prose of Alfred's Reign', *Continuations and Beginnings: Studies in Old English Literature*, Stanley, E.G. ed. (London, 1966), pp. 67–103. A valuable overview.

Wittig, Joseph S., 'King Alfred's *Boethius* and its Latin Sources: A Reconsideration', *Anglo-Saxon England* 11 (1983), pp. 157–98. A seminal article on the various literary sources which might have been available in Alfred's reign.

CHAPTER 10

The Old English language

Peter S. Baker

How hard is Old English? The short answer is 'not very'. Of course, the English of the *The Dream of the Rood*, *The Wanderer* or Alfred's Preface to *The Pastoral Care* will inevitably present more barriers to comprehension than the fourteenth-century English of Chaucer, just as Chaucer's English is more difficult than Shakespeare's, Shakespeare's more difficult than the Brontës'. For one thing Old English has more than one dialect. Namely, you will have noticed that *The Dream* has an older version in Northumbrian, just like Bede's *Death Song* and two versions of Cædmon's *Hymn*, whereas the other literature you have seen is written in West Saxon. But don't worry. West Saxon *is* Old English for the purpose of learning this language, which, indeed, is far easier to learn than any other ancient language, easier, even, than French and Spanish – languages that are thought easy for English speakers to learn. While most people take years to learn Latin or Greek and a year or more to acquire even a reading knowledge of a modern language, most students of Old English are ready to read *Beowulf* after just one term of study.

The reason Old English can be learned so quickly is that, despite its 'foreign' look, it is recognisably English. The following sections will describe Old English mainly in terms of its resemblance to modern English. Naturally, I am going to take the position that Old English is not only easy but also worth learning. But along the way I shall try to give you enough information about the language to allow you to come to your own conclusion.

Old English is a language like other languages

OK, so Old English is a language. Why am I pointing out something as obvious as that? Old English used to be universally taught as a linguistics course, in which students learned not only the language, but also learned in great detail how each of its features had descended from Germanic and Indo-European originals. People who were forced to take such courses often moan (sometimes in the *Guardian* or *Times Literary Supplement*) about the pain and boredom of the experience.

Historical linguistics – the study of how languages change over time – is a lively field that a great many students find fascinating. Many find it worthwhile to know the place of English in the Germanic sub-family of languages and the place of Germanic in the enormous and ancient Indo-European language family (see Chapter 1, p. 8). Many also find it edifying to learn how and why English has changed over the centuries, if only because the language is still changing, more or less rapidly, everywhere it is spoken. But you don't need to become a historical linguist if your purpose is to read *Beowulf* or *The Anglo-Saxon Chronicle*, any more than you need to learn the history of French to read Flaubert or navigate the Champs Elysées. One would have thought it obvious to everyone that any language can be learned without resort to historical linguistics. But no, even today there are textbooks that insist, either explicitly or implicitly, that one must study certain 'sound changes' in order to learn Old English. Do they think Anglo-Saxon children had to learn consonant changes according to 'Grimm's Law' and 'Verner's Law' just to acquire their mother tongue? Pity the foreigners who immigrated to Anglo-Saxon England, such as Archbishop Theodore of Tarsus, the Frankish queens Bertha and Judith and countless other people who had to master all their vowel changes, details of 'breaking' and '*i*-mutation', before they could talk to people in their adopted country! How did they do it so long before linguistics were invented in the nineteenth century?

Fortunately, teachers and textbook writers increasingly recognise that the learning of Old English and the study of its history are quite separate projects. The best-selling textbook, *A Guide to Old English*, by Bruce Mitchell and Fred C. Robinson (2001), presents only as much historical material as is relevant to the grammar. My own more recent textbook, *Introduction to Old English* (2003), offers historical material only in asides for interested readers. Those who wish to go deeper into the history of the language are better off taking a course in the history of the English language or consulting a book such as Roger Lass's *Old English: A Historical Linguistic Companion* (1994) or the first volume, by Richard M. Hogg, of *The Cambridge History of the English Language* (2000).

Who knows, if you do decide to learn Old English, you may find yourself shanghaied into a course in Indo-European linguistics when your real aim was to learn to read *Beowulf*. Indeed if that were to happen, you might even like it. Otherwise, however, it is more likely you will find your course in Old English more or less resembling a course in any other language – with the important difference that you won't have to speak it.

The spelling of Old English disguises its familiarity

In the following, I am going to spell Old English words putting in various dots over consonants and length marks over vowels. Even though we don't speak it now, I have done this to help you understand how the language sounded. Outside the teaching of Old English language, you will find that no one bothers with dots or length marks. We don't go in for them in modern English either and the repertory of Old English sounds is more like that of modern English than any other language.

That said, Old English spelling is very different. One early enthusiast, the early American president Thomas Jefferson (1743–1826), complained that certain 'peculiarly Saxon' letters used by printers of Old English made the language look 'rugged, uncouth, and appalling to an eye accustomed to the roundness and symmetry of the Roman character'. 'This,' he continued, 'is a first discouragement to the English student'. Jefferson took the Anglo-Saxons seriously: looking at the British hold over America, he complained that: 'Our emigration to this country gave England no more rights over us than the emigration of the Danes and Saxons gave to the present authorities of their mother country over England.' Now there's a thought. Generally, Old English looked far more intimidating to students of the eighteenth century than it does to modern students, for early printers of the language used typefaces that imitated the look of Old English manuscripts. Modern printers use modern letter shapes where possible, but even so the student must cope with the oddball letters þ ('thorn') and ð ('eth') for the first sounds of modern *thin* and *then* and æ ('ash') for the vowel of modern *cat*. Textbook writers add length marks and other diacritics to help the modern student identify and pronounce words, making Old English texts for students look even more cluttered and foreign.

In the eighteenth century spelling reformers were lurking behind every tree, so it is only to be expected that Jefferson himself should have suggested reforming the spelling of Old English. His recommendations never got any traction among the learned, but his experiment in Old English spelling reform shows how accessible Old English can become when its spelling is altered to approximate that of modern English. The following box shows a passage from the Old English translation of Orosius' *History against the Pagans*, a sort of world history that King Alfred wanted his people to know (pp. 257–8). This passage is presented first as it might appear in a modern textbook, second in Jefferson's reformed Old English spelling and, finally, in modern English translation. To test yourself, see how often you need to look at the third column to understand what is in the second.

Hē wæs mid þǣm fyrstum mannum on þǣm lande. Næfde hē þēah mā þonne twentiġ hrȳðera and twentiġ scēapa and twentiġ swȳna, and þæt lȳtle þæt hē erede, hē erede mid horsan, ac hyra ār is mǣst on þǣm gafole þe þā Finnas him ġyldað.	He was mid them firstum mannum in them land. nhaved he tho ma then twenty hryther, & twenty sheep, & twenty swine, & that little that he eared, he eared mid horsen, ac hir ar is most in them gavel tha the Fins him yieldeth.	He was with the first men in the land. He did not then have more than twenty cattle, and twenty sheep, and twenty swine, and the little that he plowed, he plowed with horses, but their revenue is mostly in the tribute that the Finns give to them.

The unfamiliar nouns and verbs include *hryther* 'cattle', *eared* 'plowed', *ar* 'revenue' and *gavel* 'tribute'. Whether you had difficulty with 'grammar words' such as *mid* 'with', *them* 'the', *ma* 'more' and *ac* 'but' depends on whether you have some experience with Middle English or with such languages as Dutch and German. But if Jefferson's respelled Old English in the middle column is easier to read than the original on the left, then you have got the point of this exercise: you can make your life a good bit easier just by learning the Old English spelling system.

All right, so how does Old English spelling work? First, most vowels have their 'continental' or 'European' values. Note that the modern English examples in the following list are approximate: your pronunciation will be more or less like Old English depending on whether you're from London or Chicago, Canberra or Toronto:

a is like the a in *father*
æ is like the a in *cat*
e is like the a in *fate*
i is like the ee in *feet*
ie is like the i in *sit*
o is like the oa in *coat*
u is like the oo in *boot*
y is like the u in French *tu* or the *ü* in German *Tür*

In addition there are two diphthongs – two part vowels like the *i* of *fight* (which starts with the tongue low in the mouth and glides to a high position):

eo starts with a vowel like the a of *fate* and ends with a rounded sound, like o or u

ea starts with a vowel like the a of *cat* and ends with a lower sound, like a in *father*

All vowels come in long and short varieties, with 'length' understood as 'duration': long vowels are like their short equivalents except that they take about twice as long to pronounce.

Consonants are mostly like those of modern English, with these exceptions:

c is always pronounced like k, never like s

ċ (the dot is added by modern editors) is like the ch in *child*

cg is like the dg in *edge*

f is pronounced like v when it comes between vowels

g is pronounced like the g in *good*, never like the g in *gentle*

ġ is pronounced like the y in *yet*, but

nġ is pronounced like the ng in *angel*

g between 'back' vowels a, o or u is pronounced like Dutch g; if you don't know what that means, pronounce it like a w, for that is what becomes of the sound in later English

h when it comes at the end of a syllable is like German or Scottish ch

s is pronounced like z when it comes between vowels

sc is pronounced like sh in *should*

þ and **ð** are equivalent; they are like th in *thin* except between vowels, where they are like th in *then*

Sometimes ċ, ġ and sc are followed by an e or i which is not pronounced, but only indicates the quality of the preceding consonant. Otherwise, letters are never silent: you must do your best to pronounce everything you see, although it may take some effort to do so, as with *hlǣder* 'ladder', *hring* 'ring', *fnēsan* 'sneeze', and *gnæt* 'gnat'. Some letters that we use now, j, k, q, v and z, are almost never encountered in Old English.

This list of spelling rules may seem long. I confess that I have simplified them somewhat. But at least it can be learned quickly. One way is to practise using Old English spelling to write modern English. One nineteenth-century scholar, Thomas Oswald Cockayne, provided a precedent for the exercise by using þ in his own writing, but ġiu cæn tec þe præctiess furþer, ġiusing al the leters of þe Old Englisc ælfabet, or æt list þos þæt correspond approx-imætliġ tu modern Englisc saunds. Ġiu wil no daut ron intu æmbiguoss siċuescions (soċ æs hwat tu du abaut þe *u* of *but*, hwiċ is nat in Old Englisc – ai æm ġiusing *o* hir); bot part of þe fon is in pondering hau to adæpt the old spellings tu modern ġiuss. Wons ġiu hæf writen a fiu pecges ġiusing Cing Ælfred's spelling siestem, ai cæn gerantiġ þæt ġiu wil nefer forget it.

After you have had a bit of practice with this spelling system, you'll be ready to encounter simple sentences in Old English. It is easy to put together sentences that are good Old English and, at the same time, good modern English, albeit with some odd-looking endings which you may safely ignore (for the moment anyway). By now you can easily guess the meaning of the following made-up sentences:

> Sumor is lang and hāt.
> Ælfred hæfde fīf scēap.
> Þes man wile helpan his wīfe.
> Þæt scip sanc tō botme.
> Ġif mē his hors and his sweord.
> Wē ǣton buteran and ċēse and meolce and huniġ, and wē sāwon þā fiscas swimman on sǣ.

You can read more complicated sentences if you have read a bit of Chaucer or later authors. To read the following passage you only need to recognise the archaic pronouns *þū* 'thou' and *iċ* 'I':

> Ēadweard sæġde, 'hwȳ hæfst þū druncen eall mīn wīn?' Hē andswarode, 'iċ wæs þurstiġ, and iċ dranc þīn wīn'.

It must be admitted that an Old English sentence that uses only words that have survived to the present day is likely to be rather artificial, as these are. Anglo-Saxon writers did occasionally produce such sentences, as when a certain monster-fighting troubleshooter presents his credentials at the Danish royal court:

> Bēowulf is mīn nama.

But Old English writers are rarely so obliging.

If you have guessed from the samples presented so far that there are regular correspondences between Old and modern English vowels, you are right; and knowing these correspondences can ease the difficulty of learning vocabulary. Here are the most reliable ones:

a, *æ*, and *ea* correspond to modern *a* (*bacan* 'bake', *sæd* 'sad', *heard* 'hard')

ā corresponds to modern *o*, *oa* (*bāt* 'boat')

e and *eo* correspond to modern *e* or *ea* (*helpan* 'help', *heofon* 'heaven')

ē and *ēo* correspond to modern long *e* or *ee* (*hēr* 'here', *fēdan* 'feed', *dēop* 'deep')

i corresponds to modern *i* (*smið* 'smith')

ī corresponds to modern long *i* (*bītan* 'bite')

o corresponds to modern *o* (*rotian* 'rot')

ō corresponds to modern *oo* (*tōl* 'tool')

u corresponds to modern *u* (*þunor* 'thunder')

ū corresponds to modern *ou*, *ow* (*hūs* 'house', *hū* 'how')

y corresponds to modern *i* (*hype* 'hip')

Every now and then these correspondences will fail you. Some vowels have been shortened and others lengthened in the last 900 years. Some failures are because the dialect in which most Old English texts are written is not the one from which current 'standard English' is descended. And the modern English outcomes of *ēa*, *ǣ*, *īe* and *ȳ* are not easy to predict. But you will find the correspondences that are fairly reliable to be very helpful.

Old English and modern English share many words

Most Old English words are no longer in use. They have been replaced by upstarts from French, Latin, Old Norse and other languages. As the modern English lexicon is vastly greater than that of Old English, an even smaller proportion of the modern English lexicon comes from Old English. You can prove this to yourself simply by searching for 'OE' (a common abbreviation for Old English) in the 'Etymology' field of the online *Oxford English Dictionary*. The experiment has limitations, for some instances of 'OE' may be casual references rather than indicators of a word's actual origin. Nonetheless, you get an interesting result: 11,623 words. Since the *OED* contains well over a quarter of a million entries, you can see what a pitifully small proportion (well under 4%) of the English vocabulary is from Old English.

Don't stop reading. There is a fallacy in what I have just written and you must have spotted it. What the proportion of Old English words in the *OED* is means nothing. The *OED* includes a great deal of rare and specialised vocabulary, many thousands of words like *amphitype, amphivorous, amphodarch* and *amphodelite*. I found these at random just by opening Volume I. Of course, words like these are not from Old English, but since no one uses them, who cares? A better estimate was provided by a computerised survey of the 80,000 or so words in the *Shorter Oxford Dictionary*, which found that around 27% were certainly or probably from Old English (Finkenstaedt and Wolff). But the English vocabulary of daily life is much smaller than 80,000. How many everyday English words are derived from Old English? For an unscientific test, let's look at the opening of Charles Dickens's *Great Expectations*. In this passage all words and parts of words derived from Old English are in bold type:

> **My father's** family **name being** Pirrip, **and my** Christian **name** Philip, **my** infant **tongue could make of both names nothing longer or more** explicit **than** Pip. **So, I called myself Pip, and came to be called** Pip.
>
> **I give** Pirrip **as my father's** family **name, on the** authority **of his** tombstone **and my** sister, – Mrs. Joe Gargery, **who** married **the blacksmith. As I never saw my father or my mother, and never saw any likeness of either of them** (for their **days were long before the days of** photographs), **my first** fancies regarding **what they were like were** unreasonably derived **from** their tombstones. **The shape of the** letters **on my father's, gave me an** odd idea **that he was a** square, stout, **dark man, with** curly **black hair. From the** character **and** turn **of the** inscription, '**Also** Georgiana **Wife of the Above,' I drew a childish** conclusion **that my mother was** freckled **and sickly.**

Of the words in this passage, 117 are derived from Old English and 26 are later borrowings. I have excluded proper names from the count, and also the Old English–French hybrid *tombstone*. So 78% are from Old English and a mere 22% from elsewhere. The proportion of loanwords would be higher in a passage from the famously Latinate Samuel Johnson (1709–84) or in one from your maths textbook. But rare indeed is the English work in which the vocabulary is not predominantly Old English.

As you might guess from the Dickens passage, words likely to have survived from Old English include 'grammar words' such as pronouns ('I from *ic*, my from *mīn*, he from *hē*, his from *his*, what from *hwæt*), conjunctions (and from *and/ond*, as from *eall swā*, that from *þæt*) and prepositions (on from *on*, of from *of*, from from *fram/from*). There are also forms of 'to be' (*bēon*), auxiliary verbs (could from *can/cūðe*), and other common verbs (make from *macian*, call from *ċeallian*, give from *ġifan*, see from *sēon*, draw from *dragan*). There are nouns of relationship (father from *fæder*, mother from *mōdor*, sister from *sweostor*) and other people words (man from *mann*, child from *ċild*, wife from *wīf*). There are the names of body parts (tongue from *tunge*, hair from *hǣr*), other very common nouns (name from *nama*, day from *dæġ*, shape from *ġesceap*), adjectives (long from *lang*, first from *fyrst*, dark from *deorc*, black from *blæc*) and adverbs (never from *nǣfre*, also from *eall swā*). Other survivals include (to name just a few more):

- words for **domestic and other animals**: *cū* 'cow', *swīn* 'swine', *hors* 'horse', *hund* 'hound', *sċēap* 'sheep', *fisc* 'fish', *fugol* 'fowl', *wulf* 'wolf', *bera* 'bear', *hafoc* 'hawk'; **food and drink**: *mete* 'meat', *bēan* 'bean', *corn* 'corn, grain', *hwǣte* 'wheat', *meoluc* 'milk', *medu* 'mead', *wīn* 'wine', *bēor* 'beer'; **clothing**: *scyrte* 'shirt', *scōh* 'shoe', *cæppe* 'cap', *hōd* 'hood', *slīefe* 'sleeve'

- **weights and measures**: *pund* 'pound', *tunne* 'ton', *ynċe* 'inch', *fōt* 'foot', *ġierd* 'yard', *mīl* 'mile'

- **geographical features**: *woruld* 'world', *eorðe* 'earth', *hyll* 'hill', *clif* 'cliff', *īġland* 'island', *sǣ* 'sea'

- verbs of **counting and saying**: *tellan* 'tell, count', *spellian* 'spell, relate', *secgan* 'say', *sprecan* 'speak', *ċeallian* 'call', *nemnan* 'name', *grētan* 'greet', *ġiellan* 'yell'; verbs of **fighting**: *feohtan* 'fight', *hergian* 'harry', *winnan* 'win, struggle', *ofercuman* 'overcome'

- verbs of **perceiving, knowing and thinking**: *lōcian* 'look', *hȳran* 'hear', *fēlan* 'feel', *cnāwan* 'know', *understandan* 'understand', *þenċan* 'think', *hopian* 'hope'

- modern English **'irregular verbs'**, most of which are survivals from Old English: *brecan* 'break', *ċēosan* 'choose', *drincan* 'drink', *drīfan* 'drive', *etan* 'eat', *feallan* 'fall', *healdan* 'hold', *licgan* 'lie', *rīdan* 'ride', *rinnan* 'run', *singan* 'sing', *stelan* 'steal', *sittan* 'sit', *slēan* 'slay', *teran* 'tear', *werian* 'wear', *wrītan* 'write', and many more

- modern English **nouns with irregular plurals**: *oxa* 'ox', *gōs* 'goose', *tōð* 'tooth', *lūs* 'louse', *mūs* 'mouse' and others in addition to man, child and foot, just mentioned

- Old English **prefixes and suffixes** that are still productive (that is, they can still be used to make new words from old ones): *-isc* (-ish) to make adjectives from nouns, *-lēas* (-less) to express a lack, *-liċ* (-ly) to make adjectives, *-līċe* (-ly) to make adverbs, *-ness* (-ness) to form abstract nouns, *ofer-* (over-) to express excessiveness, *un-* (un-) to form negatives of adjectives or to reverse the action of a verb and *under-* (under-) to express insufficiency

It can be a pleasant challenge to recognise modern English words in their Old English disguises. See what you can make of these words (hint: the verbs end with *-an*):

āgan	efen	mūð	stedefæst
ǣfnung	faldian	nīwe	talu
ælf	fēond	nōn	tōmorgen
betst	frēond	offrian	þistel
brād	ġystrandæġ	ortġeard	þunor
cēpan	grund	peniġ	utera
cicen	hnappian	prēost	wascan
cyċene	hrēaw	rōwan	weddung
drǣdan	langian	Rūh	wiðūtan
dysiġ	līm	sceadu	wreċċa
earm	middel	Sōfte	yfel

Glancing at an Old English text or dictionary, you may grumble that there is still a lot of vocab. The base vocabulary of Old English is smaller than you might guess, however, from the thickness of a student-oriented dictionary such as Clark Hall and Meritt's *A Concise Anglo-Saxon Dictionary*. The reason is that the Old English lexicon is largely made up of families of words constructed around base elements or 'roots' by transforming the roots, adding prefixes and suffixes and making compounds. Once you grasp this principle, you can often make pretty accurate guesses at the meanings of words by recognising the family they belong to.

Here's an example. The Old English word *hāl* comes to us as 'whole' (the *w* is a fifteenth-century innovation); but in Old English, the base meaning is 'well' and 'entire' is a secondary meaning. From this adjective we can derive *hǣlð* 'health' by applying the same vowel-change-plus-suffix trans-formation that gives us *strength* from *strong* and *length* from *long*; with the same vowel change we get *hǣlu*, which also means 'health', and by adding verb endings we get *hǣlan* and *hāligan* 'heal'. With other suffixes we can derive more adjectives, such as *hālbǣre* 'wholesome', *hālwende* and *hālwendlic*, also 'wholesome', and nouns *hālness* 'wholeness', *hālwendness* 'healthful' and *hǣling* 'healing'. From a perfectly understandable association of physical with spiritual health we also derive words with religious meanings such as *hāliġ* 'holy', *hālga* 'saint' (the 'hallow' in 'All-Hallows' Eve' or 'Halloween'), *hāliġness* 'holiness', *hǣlness*, *hālor* and *hāls* 'salvation', *hǣlend* 'saviour' (i.e. healer = Christ), *hālgian* 'hallow, sanctify', *hālgung* 'sanctification', and *hǣlgere* 'sanctifier'. With an -*s* suffix added to the root we get words such as *hāls* 'salvation', *hālsian* 'adjure, swear, augur', *hālsung* 'exorcism, augury' and *hālsere* 'soothsayer'. This family of words yields a large number of compounds as well, such as *hāliġ-dæġ* 'holiday', *hāliġ-ern* 'holy place, sanctuary', *Hāliġ-mōnað* 'Holy Month, September', *hāliġ-wæter* 'holy water', *hǣl-wyrt* 'health plant, i.e. pennyroyal', *wan-hāl* 'unhealthy' and *efen-hāliġ* 'just as healthy'.

Among the many word families in Old English are these (the lists of family members are not exhaustive):

cynn 'kin, family', *cyning* 'king', *cennan* 'beget', *ġecynde* 'innate' (from which we get modern *kind*)

ġifan 'give', *ġifu* 'gift', *ġifeða* 'what is given, fate', *gafol* 'tribute'

gold 'gold', *gylden* 'golden', *gyldan* 'gild', *ġeolo* 'yellow'

þanc 'thanks, thought', *þenċan* 'think', *þynċan* 'seem', *þancol* 'thoughtful'

faran 'fare, go', *faru* 'journey', *ferian* 'ferry, convey', *ġefēra* 'fellow traveller, companion', *fyrd* 'army'

sittan 'sit', *settan* 'set', *ġeset* 'seat', *setl* 'seat, throne', *sadol* 'saddle'

beald, *bald* 'bold', *bealdian* 'be bold', *byldan* 'embolden, encourage', *bealdor* 'lord, leader'

From these are created many compounds, such as *wuldor-cyning* 'king of glory (God)', *gold-ġifa* 'gold giver' king', *mōd-ġeþanc* 'thought of the mind', *fyrd-scip* 'naval ship' and *medo-setl* 'mead seat (a seat in a hall, where mead is drunk)'. The meaning of most compounds is transparent once you have recognised the elements that comprise them. You can explore Old English word families further by browsing Stephen Barney's *Word Hoard*.

Old English grammar: a moderate number of inflections

Inflection is the marking of a word, usually by adding an ending or changing a vowel, to signal something about its grammar. The collection of all possible forms of a word is called a 'paradigm'. Here's a sample paradigm, for the masculine noun *stān* 'stone':

singular	nominative/accusative	stān
	genitive	stānes
	dative	stāne
plural	nominative/accusative	stānas
	genitive	stāna
	dative	stānum

Clearly more endings can be added to the Old English word than to *stone*, which like nearly all modern English nouns has only two forms: one with -*s* to make a possessive ('a stone's throw') or a plural ('a pile of stones'), and an unmarked form for all other purposes. This paradigm presents us with other puzzles as well: how can a word for 'stone' be masculine? and what do we mean by 'nominative', 'accusative', 'genitive' and 'dative'?

All nouns in Old English have gender: they are masculine, feminine or neuter. So, you may say, do nouns in modern English. But 'gender' for us is more an attribute of a thing than it is of the word that refers to the thing. Our nouns are not marked for gender like words in German or French. True, we use masculine or feminine pronouns (he, she) to refer to people or animals that are masculine or feminine and neuter pronouns (it) for things that we consider, accurately or not, to have no gender (stones, trees, sea anemones). But persons who care intensely about the sexuality of trees or sea anemones are free to refer to them using masculine or feminine pronouns. They may sound peculiar, but we would not say they are being ungrammatical. In Old English, by way of contrast, gender is a property of the word itself, is part of the package. This is much like saying it is a property of a modern English noun that it makes a plural by adding -*s* (stones) or -*en* (oxen) or by changing its vowel (teeth). The -*s* or -*en* or *oo*-to-*ee* is part of each package. In fact, Old English nouns often have different endings depending on their gender. For example, these three sentences illustrate the plurals of a masculine, a feminine and a neuter noun:

masculine	Þā **stānas** lǣgon on þǣre eorðan
	The **stones** lay on the earth
feminine	Þā **wyrta** sindon bitera
	The **herbs** are bitter
neuter	Þā **scipu** seġldon on þǣre sǣ
	The **ships** sailed on the sea

The plural of masculine *stān* is *stānas*, that of feminine *wyrt* is *wyrta* and that of neuter *scip* is *scipu*.

While I am delivering bad news, I may as well add here that noun endings vary by *declension* as well as by gender. A declension is a class of nouns whose endings are similar. In modern English there is only one declension (nouns that add -*s*, like *stone*). There are traces of a few more: nouns that change their vowels (like *man* and *tooth*), one noun that adds -*en* to make a plural (*ox*) and one that adds -*ren* (*child*). But in Old English, there are several declensions. Some of these look so alike that the differences are hardly interesting to any but historical linguists: we group these together as 'strong' nouns: for example, *stān*, *wyrt* and *scip*. Another major declension is called 'weak': the modern English noun *ox* is all that survives of this one, but the weak declension is quite large in Old English. Here is the paradigm for *stān* again, along with that of *nama* 'name', a weak masculine noun:

		strong	weak
singular	nominative	stān	nama
	accusative	stān	naman
	genitive	stānes	naman
	dative	stāne	naman
plural	nominative/accusative	stānas	naman
	genitive	stāna	namena
	dative	stānum	namum

Nouns that change their vowels make up another declension. In addition to those that survive in modern English, which have already been mentioned, several others have since moved into the dominant declension: for example, *bōc* 'book' (plural *bēċ*), *hnutu* 'nut' (*hnyte*) and *burg* 'fortress, town' (*byriġ*). In addition to these, there are several minor declensions: one for nouns of relationship ending in -*r* (*fæder* 'father', *mōdor* 'mother', *sweostor* 'sister', *brōðor* 'brother' and *dohter* 'daughter'), one for nouns that refer to young creatures (*ǣġ* 'egg', *lamb* 'lamb', *ċealf* 'calf' and in some dialects *ċild* 'child' – the *r* of our plural *children* is a remnant of this declension), one that inserts *þ* before the endings of most forms (*mōnað* 'month', *ealu* 'ale', *hæle* 'hero', *mæġð* 'maiden') and one called '*u*-stem nouns' for historical reasons, although the letter *u* is not prominent in its paradigm (*sunu* 'son', *hand* 'hand', *wudu* 'wood', *duru* 'door', *winter* 'winter' and a few more). As in modern English, these minor declensions are most likely to consist of very common nouns whose frequency keeps them from seeming strange. The result is that, although they make up a tiny proportion of the vocabulary, you meet them quite often. No question: it will take some work to learn the Old English nouns.

Now for the other bad news. *Case* is important in the Old English grammatical system: nouns, pronouns and adjectives are all marked for case as well as for gender and number. Case is the marking of nouns, pronouns and adjectives to indicate their function in the sentence. In modern English the case system is most fully preserved in certain pronouns. For example, the third-person pronoun *he* has three forms for three cases:

'subjective' for subjects	**He** gave Freddy his helmet
'objective' for direct and indirect objects	Freddy gave **him** his helmet
'possessive' to indicate possession	Freddy gave him **his** helmet

The modern English subjective corresponds to the Old English nominative and the possessive to the genitive; the modern English objective merges two Old English cases, the accusative for direct objects and the dative for indirect objects and several other functions:

nominative	**Hē** ġeaf Friðuwalde his helm
	He gave Freddy his helmet
accusative	Hē ġeaf **hine** Friðuwalde
	He gave **it** to Freddy
genitive	Friðuwald ġeaf him **his** helm
	Freddy gave him **his** helmet
dative	Friðuwald ġeaf **him** his helm
	Freddy gave **him** his helmet

Personal pronouns are not much more complicated in Old English than in modern English. Still, the case system takes some getting used to because of the case forms of other pronouns, nouns and adjectives. These short sentences illustrate the case forms of the pronoun usually translated 'the' and some common nouns:

masculine nominative	**Se cyning** ġeaf mē þis sweord
	The king gave me this sword
masculine accusative	Se eorl ofslōh **þone cyning**
	The earl slew **the king**
masculine genitive and dative	Iċ ġeaf **þæs cyninges** hēafod **þām munuce**
	I gave **the king's** head **to the monk**

Notice how the preposition 'to' becomes unnecessary when the case of 'the monk' is made explicit. Here are some more:

feminine nominative	**Sēo cwēn** hæfð ānne gyldenne hring
	The queen has a golden ring
feminine accusative	Godġifu forbærnde **þā healle**
	Godiva burned down **the hall**

feminine genitive	Se ende **þǣre worulde** is nēah
	The end **of the world** is near
feminine dative	Bēowulf truwode **þǣre strengðe** his handa
	Beowulf trusted **in the strength** of his hands

Where modern English uses a construction with *of* and a noun, Old English usually uses the genitive form of the noun. Here are some more:

neuter nominative	**Þæt wǣpen** forbærst
	The weapon broke
neuter accusative	Se þeġn ġēat **þæt bēor**
	The servant poured **the beer**
neuter genitive	**Þæs wīfes** gold is forloren
	The woman's gold is lost
neuter dative	Iċ sende þæt gold **þām mæġdene**
	I sent the gold **to the maiden**

The last two sentences illustrate one of the oddities of Old English gender: *wīf* 'woman' and *mæġden* 'maiden' are neuter rather than feminine. But that just goes to show that grammatical gender and biological sex are not the same thing.

The Old English verb system is structured like that of modern English; as to verb endings, if you have read any of Shakespeare or his contemporaries you will have no difficulty with the present singular endings and if you have read some Chaucer you will find very few surprises indeed. As in modern English, many verbs make the past tense by adding a -*d* or -*t* ending (these are called 'weak' verbs), while others make the past tense by changing the vowel of the root syllable (these are 'strong' verbs and they are both more regular and more numerous than in modern English). The irregular or anomalous verbs, which belong to neither group, include *bēon* 'to be', *willan* 'will', *dōn* 'to do', *gān* 'to go' and several auxiliary verbs, called 'preterite presents' in Old English grammar: these are pretty much the same verbs that are anomalous in modern English. The subjunctive is used more frequently than in modern English; the difference between singular and plural is always marked by inflectional endings; person is marked in the present singular indicative but not elsewhere. Some verbs are contracted in ways that make them look odd, and some feature odd consonant changes in the root syllable; but, all in all, the verbs won't cause much excitement in your life.

So how much memorising of paradigms do you need to do to learn Old English? The major paradigms fit on one side of a single sheet of paper (Baker, 'Magic Sheet'), which students often use as a reference while studying and reading. If you study this 'Magic Sheet' with an eye to minimising your labour you will notice that there are many fewer distinct grammatical forms than there are words on the sheet. For example, all strong nouns have the same dative ending; all masculine and neuter nouns are the same in the genitive and dative; all genitive plural nouns end in -*a* and all dative plural nouns and adjectives in -*um*; all feminine nouns are the same in the dative and genitive singular; all neuter nouns are the same in the nominative and accusative; adjective endings tend to look like either noun endings or pronouns; all strong and weak verbs look similar in the present tense. There are irregularities and annoying surprises here, as there are in any language; but the memorisation is fairly painless. Other languages, not only ancient ones but many in use today, have got far more inflexions to learn than Old English.

Old English word order is flexible, not chaotic

A commonplace is that Old English word order is 'free'. The reason given is that Old English inflections do much of the work that word order does in modern English. For example, in a simple statement we put the subject in front of the verb and the object (if any) behind:

Freddy slew Harry

There is no doubt that Freddy is the one doing the killing and that Harry is the unlucky object of his wrath. By contrast, Old English does the same work with case endings – right?

Friðuwald ofslōh Herebeald

Not *quite*. It looks the same but there is more to it. The Old English looks like the modern English case because each of the names *Friðuwald* and *Herebeald* is the same in nominative and accusative: neither has an ending for these cases. How, then, can you decide which of them is the subject of *ofslōh* 'slew' and which the object? If word order were actually 'free', so that speakers could put their words wherever they wanted, the many ambiguities of the Old English inflectional system would make communication difficult.

It turns out that, while word order in Old English clauses is more flexible than that of modern English, it is like modern English in being more fixed than the word order of some more heavily inflected languages, such as Latin, which is truly free. In other words, Old English is more modern than it looks, with a word order that takes on much of the burden of communicating information about the functions of words in clauses.

It is worth pausing to ask whether modern English word order is as inflexible as we often imply when we contrast it with that of Old English.

How far from the standard subject–verb–object order can we stray without putting at risk our ability to communicate? In my *Introduction to Old English*, I illustrate with the following lines from Thomas Gray's *Elegy Written in a Country Churchyard* (1750):

> The curfew tolls the knell of parting day,
>   The lowing herd winds slowly o'er the lea,
> The ploughman homeward plods his weary way,
>   And leaves the world to darkness and to me.
> Now fades the glimmering landscape on the sight,
>   And all the air a solemn stillness holds,
> Save where the beetle wheels his droning flight,
>   And drowsy tinklings lull the distant folds.

If we look at just the essential elements of the clause, the subject and verb, we can spot three different patterns in these lines. The most common pattern, as you might expect, is subject–verb, used in the first line and four others:

> S   V
> The <u>curfew</u> <u>tolls</u> the knell of parting day

But the first line of the second stanza has the reverse, verb–subject:

> V   S
> Now <u>fades</u> <u>the glimmering landscape</u> on the sight

And this pattern is common in early modern English clauses that begin with adverbs, as you can prove to yourself by flipping through any edition of Shakespeare's plays and poems. The next line has a third pattern, in which the subject comes early in the clause and the verb comes at the end:

> S   V
> And <u>all the air</u> a solemn stillness <u>holds</u>

This pattern, too, in which the matter that comes between the subject and the verb may be an object, an adverb or adverbial element, or both, is common in early modern English. For convenience, we will call these three patterns SV, VS and S . . . V. The last two of these look rather archaic now, but most readers find them perfectly intelligible.

It happens that the three patterns we have identified in Gray's *Elegy* are also the three basic patterns of Old English word order. Here are some brief examples, taken from *The Anglo-Saxon Chronicle*, along with literal translations:

> SV   And se here cōm þā tō Ðēodforda
>   And the army came then to Thetford

VS   Ðā cōm se here tō Hamtūne
          Then came the army to Northampton

S. . .V   And his hāliġe blōd on þā eorðan fēol
          And his holy blood on the earth fell

The placement of other elements in the clause (objects, indirect objects, adverbs, prepositional phrases) is 'free' compared to modern English, but you will find some patterns significantly more often than others. For example, in SV clauses the object usually follows the verb; in VS clauses it usually follows the subject; in S. . .V clauses it usually comes in the middle. Old English has a marked tendency to place 'light' elements near the beginning of a clause; so when the object or indirect object is a pronoun it will usually come early:

Ond hēo **hine** in þæt mynster onfēng
And she **him** into the monastery received

Him wæs ful boren
'(To) **him** was (a) cup borne'

The last of these examples shows a variation on the VS word order, in which an auxiliary verb comes early in the clause while the verbal (infinitive or past participle) that goes with it is deferred to the end. The reverse may also happen: the verbal may come early while the auxiliary comes at the end.

The rules of Old English word order can be learned as an elaboration of the familiar rules that govern the usage of such poets as Thomas Gray. The fiction that Old English word order is 'free', together with the failure of some older Old English textbooks to cover the subject adequately, no doubt has caused some students to despair in the presence of what may appear at first to be syntactial confusion. Fortunately, recent textbooks (Mitchell and Robinson and yours truly) devote considerable space to the demystification of word order.

The pleasures of Old English

It is easy to learn Old English. However, a skill's being easy of acquisition is not sufficient justification for actually acquiring it. We all of us pass up opportunities to learn skills (juggling, rock climbing, playing the nose harp) for which we might have no use. The corpus of Old English texts is relatively small and the texts that most people want to read have been translated; so what percentage is there in learning the language? It is a commonplace that something is always lost in translation. Seamus Heaney's translation of *Beowulf* is undeniably great, but the pleasures it affords the reader are distinctly different from those offered by the Old English text itself. The following sections outline several pleasures that can be experienced only by one who has learned to read Old English.

'O'er the lea': poetic vocabulary

The Old English lexicon includes a number of words that are found exclusively or mainly in poetry. That just shows how traditional Old English poetry was, even in its own time, as opposed to the new art of prose-writing pioneered and advanced by King Alfred and his successors (pp. 252–6). In Old English prose an 'old' man is merely *eald*, but in Old English poetry he is *gamol*. If you are *unrōt* 'unhappy' in prose you may *wēpan*, but in poetry if you are *ġeōmor* you will *grēotan*. In prose you must *fæstnian* your *scip* to keep it from floating away, but in poetry *sǽlan* your *nacan*; in a prose battle you can throw a *spere*, but in a poetic one you need a *gār* or a *daroð*; in prose you can swing a *sweord*, but in poetry you can also use a *mēċe* or a *bill*. In prose a woman will probably be a *wīf* or *wīfman*. In poetry she may be an *ides* or a *mæġð*, and perhaps she is *wunden-feax* or *wunden-locc* 'wavy haired'. If she is noble (and women in poetry usually are), she may also be *gold-hroden* 'gold adorned'. If she is married to a noble warrior, she may call him a *freca*, *hæleð*, *rinc* or *secg*. If he is young he may be a *byre* or *mago*. She may employ an enormous number of poetic terms for a royal husband, among them *bēag-ġifa* 'ring giver', *folc-āgend* 'possessor of the people', *hild-fruma* 'first in battle', *hlēo* 'shelter', *mon-dryhten* 'lord of men', *rǽswa* 'counsellor', *wil-ġeofa* 'giver of pleasure' or *wine* 'friend'.

Fans of Tolkien's fictions will notice how he drew on Old English poetic diction for names, among them *frōd* 'wise, mature' for Frodo, various king words, *þēoden*, *gold-wine*, *fengel*, *þengel*, for kings of Rohan, *mearh* 'horse' for the horses of Rohan and *medu-seld* 'mead hall' for their hall, and *hæleð* 'warrior' for Haleth son of Helm.

Some grammatical forms are reserved largely for poetry. Poetry has accusative *mec* for *mē* 'me' and *þec* for *þē* 'thee', and it sometimes uses a possessive adjective *sīn* for *his* 'his'. Certain verb forms are mostly poetic, for example *iċ hafo* for *iċ hæbbe* 'I have', *wē sēgon* for *wē sāwon* 'we saw' and *hē ġeong* for *hē ēode* 'he went'. Where West Saxon, the dialect that dominates Old English prose, usually makes a third-person singular with the ending -ð and a change of vowel in the root syllables of most strong verbs, poetry prefers a longer form -eð and forgoes the vowel change: prose has *hēo hilpð* 'she helps', but poetry would have *hēo helpeð*. This difference actually makes the verbs of poetry easier than those of prose for speakers of modern English.

Many poetic traditions employ a specialised diction; until recent times English poets enthusiastically employed archaic and dialect words such as the pronouns *thou, thee, thine* and *ye*; contractions and shortened forms like *e'er, mo, o'er* and *ope*; and replacements of common words like *bane, beauteous, darksome, ere, lea, plaint, tabor* and *welkin*. Such diction is sometimes dismissed as a crutch for the lexically disabled; but it was used by great poets as well as poetasters. We ought not to discount the pleasure of conventional elements in poetry, which served as stylistic markers and reminded poets and their audiences that they were sharers in a tradition which they experienced as ancient and powerful.

Swords and ice: the kenning

The Argentine writer and sage Jorge Luis Borges (1899–1986) once told an interviewer that he fell in love with the Old English language because of two words he encountered in books that he happened to have at home. 'Those two words, I can still recall them, those words were the name of London, *Lundenburh*; and then Rome, *Romeburh*.' These are ordinary enough place names, formed on a pattern familiar to anyone who has ever heard of, say, Edin-burgh or Canter-bury. Perhaps what drew Borges' notice was the way the addition of *-burh* 'stronghold, town' to otherwise familiar names (London, Rome) foregrounded a method of word formation that, as he said, was unavailable in his native Spanish. Old English commonly makes new words by compounding. Old English can combine two words into one. It is also possible to make compounds in modern English (as with such relatively modern formations as *highbrow* and *sidecar*), but we have a marked preference for other methods of making words, such as adding prefixes and suffixes (sometimes using Greek or Latin elements) and adapting words from other languages. Old English prefers to make compounds. Even when the origin of a word is Latin, Old English frequently 'borrows' it by translating its elements and making a compound out of them. So, for example, we have *leorning-cniht* 'young man who learns, disciple' from *discipulus*, itself formed from the roots that yield Latin *discere* 'learn' and *puer* 'boy'. Modern English prefers the direct loan *disciple* (also present in Old English as *discipul*).

Old English has great flexibility in the formation of compounds. These are most often made by either joining two nouns (*bere-ærn* 'barley house, barn'), an adjective and a noun (*gōd-dǣd* 'good deed'), a noun and an adjective (*wīf-fæst* 'wife-fast, married'), an adverb and a noun (*ofer-æt* 'over-eating'), an adverb and an adjective (*fela-sprecol* 'very talkative') and an adverb and a verb (*þurh-crēopan* 'creep through'). A compound can become an element of another compound. So, for example, *mān-āð* is 'false oath, perjury' and *mānāð-swaru* is 'the swearing of a false oath'. When the first element is an adjective or a noun it is generally not inflected, as it would be if the compound elements were separated to make the words of a phrase. So, for example, *mōd-glēaw* 'mind wise' is much the same as *mōdes glēaw* 'wise of mind'.

But note that the two constructions are not equivalent in every respect. The genitive ending of *mōdes* 'of mind' effectively makes the noun into an adverb modifying the adjective *glēaw* 'wise'. How is one wise? In mind, of course: mentally. By contrast, the compound construction *mōd-glēaw* merely juxtaposes a noun and an adjective while saying nothing about their relationship to each other; this information must be inferred, and it cannot be predicted from the elements' parts of speech. The compound *lim-wēriġ* 'limb weary, weary of limb' is rather like *mōd-glēaw* in that the second element describes a property of the first ('one's mind/limb is wise/weary'); but *mere-wēriġ* 'sea weary' is similarly constructed and we immediately suspect that it does not mean that the sea is weary, but rather that one is weary of the sea – the voyage has taken too long.

Such ambiguity is useful to poets. When a compound is metaphorical or metomymic we call it a *kenning*. Here's an example from *Beowulf*. It comes when the hero is fighting Grendel's mother:

> Ðā se ġist onfand
> þæt se beado-lēoma   bītan nolde. (*Beowulf*, lines 1522–3)
>   Then the stranger found out
> that the battle-light bite would not.

What is a *beado-lēoma* 'battle-light'? The context makes the first element *beado* 'battle' perfectly understandable, but *lēoma* is a riddle. The wider context clears everything up: Beowulf has just swung his mighty *hilde-bill* 'battle-sword', which has sung a 'greedy war-song' on his enemy's head. Now he finds that the 'battle-light' will not *bītan* 'bite'. So the *beado-lēoma* is his sword and it is so called because it reflects the light when he wields it in battle. It happens that we have already seen a use of this idea in a similar kenning, *hilde-lēoma*, in *Beowulf*, line 1143, at the moment Hengest accepts the Danish sword (p. 103).

Many kennings are conventional: you will encounter them repeatedly in *Beowulf* and other poems. Such are *bān-hūs* 'bone-house, the body', *hron-rād* 'whale-road, the sea', *niht-helm* 'helmet of night, nocturnal darkness' and many others. With such common kennings it can be difficult to tell whether an Anglo-Saxon audience would notice the figurative content. In the first lines of *Beowulf*, when we are told that various peoples *ofer hron-rāde* have to obey Scyld and pay him tribute, it is hard to see what the kenning contributes to the sense of the passage. But frequently a kenning brings us up short. A well-known example comes just after Beowulf has struck off Grendel's head and the sword he used for the purpose begins to melt:

> Þā þæt sweord ongan
> æfter heaþo-swāte   hilde-ġicelum
> wīġ-bil wanian. (*Beowulf*, lines 1605–607)

> Then the sword began
> on account of the battle-sweat in battle-icicles
> the war-sword, to wane.

There are some perfectly ordinary compounds here: the metaphor embedded in *heaþo-swāt* 'battle-sweat' is so common that it is hardly a metaphor at all and *wīġ-bil* 'war-sword' is quite literal. These belong to a type called 'poetic compounds': they contain conventional first elements (frequently one of the many poetic words for 'war, battle': *beado, gūð, heaðo, hild, wīġ*) which add little or nothing to the sense but supply a needed alliteration and (since they occur exclusively in poetry) a suitably ornate style. *Hilde-ġicel* is something else entirely: *ġicel* means 'icicle' (the modern word is derived from a compound of *īs* 'ice' and *ġicel*), an apt metaphor because it is shaped like a sword but is fragile and melts quickly in the sun. *Hilde* 'battle' looks like the first element of an ordinary poetic compound, but its very conventionality is now enlisted in the service of poetic effect, since the new construction is modeled on such poetic words for 'sword' as *hilde-bill* and *hilde-mēċe*. The comparison of the sword to an icicle is carried not only by the resemblances between swords and icicles, but also by the very shape of the word that expresses the metaphor. Even a Heaney cannot reproduce this effect precisely (he translates *hilde-ġicelum* as 'gory icicles'), because modern English is no longer capable of it.

The braided sentence: poetic variation

Variation is one of the most noticeable features of Old English poetry. It is, to put it simply, the repetition in others words of an element of a sentence or clause. Here's an example from *Beowulf*:

> þæt þām gōdan wæs
> hrēow on hreðre,   hyġe-sorga mæst. (*Beowulf*, lines 2327–8)

> That to the good (one) was
> distress in (his) breast, of mind-sorrows the greatest.

In this otherwise straightforward sentence, *hrēow* 'distress' is in variation with *hyǧe-sorga mǣst* 'greatest of mind-sorrows'. The characteristic that makes this pair of sentence elements a variation rather than a list is that they refer to the same thing, to Beowulf's sorrow. Similarly, two verbs in variation will name the same action and two adjectives in variation will name the same attribute of the same noun. These sentences exhibit variation:

> He slew the king, cut off his head.
> Today I telephoned customer service, the unhelpful clods!
> The room was green, a sort of chartreuse.

These sentences do not exhibit variation, even though they resemble the ones above:

> He slew the king and cut off his head. (The implication of 'and' is that he beheaded the king after killing him – the two verbs do not refer to the same action.)
> Today I telephoned customer service, Bobby and Grandmother. (I made three telephone calls or one conference call to three people: either way it is not variation.)
> The room was green, pink and purple. (All three colours were in the room.)

The modern (and classical) construction that most resembles variation is called 'apposition', that is, the placement of two grammatically parallel nouns, noun phrases or adjectives together in the same clause. Here is an example of apposition:

> John the carpenter had a bad day.

The elements in apposition are 'John' and 'the carpenter.' One of these explains or further identifies the other: 'the carpenter' tells us more about 'John'. In the classical definition of apposition the two elements occur side by side. In informal modern English the elements can be separated ('I telephoned customer service today, the unhelpful clods!'), but this is not the usual thing.

In Old English poetry, variation is a bit more complicated and much more interesting than apposition. First, verbs and other elements besides nouns and adjectives can be in variation. The following lines from *Beowulf* describe the young Danes riding back from the Mere, just before one of them composes a new poem about Beowulf (p. 99). In these lines, we have infinitives in variation and sharing an auxiliary verb:

Hwīlum heaþo-rōfe   hlēapan lēton
on ġeflit faran   fealwe mēaras. (*Beowulf*, lines 864–5)

At times the battle-famed (men) leap let (= made to leap)
in competition go the bay mares (= horses).

The infinitives *hlēapan* 'leap' and *faran* 'go' are in variation, sharing the auxiliary *lēton* 'allowed, made'. There is no rule that elements in variation must come together in a clause; in fact, they are often separated by other elements. In the first example above, *hrēow* and *hyġe-sorga mǣst* are separated by the prepositional phrase *on hreðre* 'in (his) breast', while in the second the two infinitives are separated by their shared auxiliary.

To understand more about how variation works, think back to what I said earlier about Old English word order. Another way of stating the relations among the basic clause patterns SV, VS and S. . .V is as a set of constraints, for example:

The subject may come before or after the verb.
The verb may come before or after the subject or at the end of the clause.

In prose, one makes a choice among the various positions in which it is legal to put a subject, verb, object or other element. The poet, by way of contrast, asks 'why not use more than one of the legal positions?' Look at this very simple instance of variation:

Wīġlāf maðelode,   Wīhstānes sunu
Wiglaf spoke, Wihstan's son

The subject is stated twice, as *Wīġlāf* and as *Wīhstānes sunu*. Each comes in a position where a subject is allowed – one in front of the verb (SV) and one behind (VS). Does the second subject create another position for a verb – can we have a pattern SVSV? Perhaps. Look at this:

Unferð maþelode,   Ecglāfes bearn,
þe æt fōtum sæt   frēan Scyldinga,
onband beadu-rūne. (*Beowulf*, lines 499–501)

Unferth spoke, Ecglaf's son,
who at the feet sat of the lord of the Scyldings,
unbound battle-runes.

Most readers take the long noun phrase *Ecglāfes bearn . . . Scyldinga* as a variation on *Unferð* and *onband beadu-rūne* as a clause with an unstated subject. Old English often carries over a subject from one clause to another, as we can still do when speaking informally ('Unferth spoke up, used fighting words'). But what's to prevent us from taking *Ecglāfes bearn . . . Scyldinga* as the subject of *onband*? In this case we might interpret our lines as two clauses as follows:

> Unferth spoke;
> The son of Ecglaf . . . unbound battle-runes.

But 'spoke' and 'unbound battle-runes' are clearly in variation, the second a restatement and elaboration of the first. What, then, is to stop us taking the whole passage as a pair of variations forming, as it were, a syntactical braid?

> Unferth . . .
>> spoke
> the son of Ecglaf . . .
>> unbound battle-runes

In modern apposition, one element always interrupts the normal flow of a sentence: it has a parenthetical quality (and indeed can be punctuated with parentheses). But elements in variation do not interrupt the flow of the sentence when they occur, as they almost always do, in grammatically appropriate positions: they often do not seem parenthetical at all. Often variations are placed together, like appositional elements in Beowulf's words to Wiglaf at the end of his life:

> 'Bēo nū on ofoste,   þæt iċ ǣr-welan,
> gold-ǣht onġite.' (*Beowulf*, lines 2747–8)

> 'Be now in haste, so that I the ancient wealth,
> the gold possessions may see.'

Looked at as a grammatical construction, *gold-ǣht* 'gold possessions' is parenthetical. Its sense seems less so, since it is no more specific than *ǣr-welan* 'ancient wealth'. Rather, the elements in variation foreground two different aspects of the dragon's treasure: its antiquity and its great value. The job that variation performs, especially in the better poetry, has less to do with clarification than with exploration: it leads an audience through an investigation of the boundaries of a concept.

The weirdness of *wyrd*, the moodiness of *mōd*

Perhaps the most famous word in the Old English lexicon is *wyrd*, which is generally translated as 'fate'. We have seen it as the theme of the opening of *The Wanderer* (p. 21). As a translation, 'fate' is probably the best we can do, but it is unfortunate choice in several ways, not least because in most readers' minds the word 'fate' is evocative of classical heroes who do not belong to the world of *Beowulf*. The concept of fate is a moving target even in classical literature, different for Homer, Sophocles and Virgil: we should not expect *wyrd* to be a good match for any of these. The reader who has encountered the implacability of fate in *Oedipus Rex* can only be confused by Beowulf's observation on his escape from the sea after his swimming match with Breca:

'Wyrd oft nereð
unfæġne eorl   þonne his ellen dēah' (*Beowulf*, lines 572–3)

'Fate often saves
the undoomed warrior when his valour is good'

As anyone who has read *Oedipus Rex* will know, Sophoclean fate does not save the valiant any more than it does the timorous. Old English *wyrd*, by allowing for individualism (p. 22), means something different.

Latin *fatum*, where we get 'fate' from, is literally 'what has been said'. Old English *wyrd*, contrariwise, belongs to the same root as *weorðan*, a word now unfortunately lost from our language, which means 'become, happen'. The base meaning of *wyrd* is 'what happens', and it is often used to mean 'event', as in *The Dream of the Rood* when the crosses are cut down:

Þæt wæs eġeslić wyrd! (*The Dream of the Rood*, line 74)
That was a terrible event!

Indeed we cannot always be sure of the proper translation of *wyrd*: 'fate' or merely 'event'. Yet it often appears as something that can have an effect in this world: it is *ārǣd* 'resolute' in *The Wanderer*, line 5, while in *Beowulf* it can *forniman* 'take away' warriors and others. In classical and also in Norse mythology the gods are subject to fate; but in Christian Anglo-Saxon England *wyrd* may appear as subordinate to or even identified with God. In *Beowulf*, lines 477–9, Hrothgar says that *wyrd* has swept away his warriors by means of Grendel's terror, but God can put a stop to his evil deeds. In lines 2526–7, before he goes into battle with the dragon, Beowulf uses *wyrd* in variation with *metod* 'God'.

The Old English noun *wyrd* has become an adjective, *weird*; if we want a noun we must add a noun ending to make *weirdness*. The result does not mean 'fate', even if, given the idea of coincidence, one of the meanings of 'That's really weird!', might have come from a feeling that the thing was predestined. For *wyrd*, however, the classical analogue 'fate' is a rather rough approximation of sense, 'weird' even more so. So *wyrd* is not only 'resolute' (*ārǣd*), but strictly untranslatable. Roy Liuzza, in his translation of *Beowulf*, leaves it alone: '*Wyrd* often spares an undoomed man, when his courage endures!' You, in yours, may of course respond to this challenge in your own way.

Wyrd is an extreme example of a phenomenon well known to translators: many of the key words in the original language have no exact counterparts in the language of the translation. This is true of Old and modern English, despite their kinship. Even such common words as *habban* 'have' and *healdan* 'hold', while their core meanings remain largely unaltered, have shed old meanings and taken on new ones, as you can prove to yourself by comparing the lists of definitions for these words in the scholarly Old English dictionary by Bosworth and Toller with those in the *Oxford English Dictionary*. The reader of Old English often experiences little jolts of surprise at the way words have changed their meanings: *drēam* means 'joy, music' and has little to do with dreaming; *scēawian* means 'look at', not 'show'; *līcian* means 'please', not 'like'; *mǣl* means 'occasion' as well as 'meal' (an occasion for eating); the *mete* you eat at a meal includes all kinds of food, not just 'meat'; *willa* means 'pleasure' as well as 'will'; *lust* stands for all kinds of desire, not only sexual.

The shifting definitions of words can sometimes give us a glimpse into the culture of Anglo-Saxon England. This is certainly the case with *mōd*, one of the most common Old English words for the mind. It comes to modern English as *mood*, but the meaning is very different. In prose *mōd* often is used of the conscious mind, which embraces emotion, will and reason. In poetry, it is especially associated with the emotional state and can be distinguished from understanding or reason. *Mōd* is also associated with courage and fighting spirit; but as such it is an unruly aspect of the mind, likely to drive one to violence if not restrained. In the 'Finnsburh Episode' of *Beowulf*, we are told that when Hengest, or the Danes (the subject is unclear), cannot restrain the *wǣfre mōd* 'restless mind', they avenge the death of their old lord Hnæf by slaying Finn (pp. 102–4). And *The Seafarer* admonishes:

> Stīeran mon sceal strongum mōde   ond þæt on staþelum healdan.
>
> (*The Seafarer*, line 109)
>
> [lit.] Steer one must the strong mind and it in steadiness hold.

The *mōd* requires steering, and one must hold it in a stable place; but God, we are told, rewards those who believe in his might by steadying the mind.

Those who wish to explore the subtleties of *mōd* and related words in more detail should consult Malcolm Godden's classic article 'Anglo-Saxons on the Mind'. There are lots of words for the mind in Old English: not only *mōd*, but also *hyge, sefa, ferhð, hreðer, myne, gehygd, mōdsefa, ferhðsefa, modgehygd, gemynd* . . . The list is not endless, but it's not short either, neither is it bad for a people who have been derided as muddled or thick. For our purposes it is enough to recognise that no modern English word can translate *mōd* precisely and no one who encounters Old English poetry only in translation can understand it fully.

Conclusion

Few students are now forced to study Old English. In the day when Old English was commonly required for undergraduate or graduate degrees, it was easy to imagine that the end of the requirement would mean the end of the discipline. And yet interest in Old English remains high in most major universities. This is not surprising, really. There are many reasons to learn Old English, among them the need to attain an accurate understanding of historical documents, the wish to understand one's own language better, and of course the pleasure of encountering some of the greatest English poetry in its original language. The effort required to learn the language is not negligible, but reasonable and, for many students, enjoyable. If you have read this chapter with attention, you have already made a good start.

(Answers to exercise on p. 281)			
own (v.)	even	mouth	steadfast
evening	fold	new	tale
elf	fiend	noon	tomorrow
best	friend	offer	thistle
broad	yesterday	orchard	thunder
keep	ground	penny	outer
chicken	nap	priest	wash
kitchen	raw	row	wedding
dread	long (v.)	rough	without
dizzy	lime	shadow	wretch
arm	middle	soft	evil

Further reading

Baker, Peter S., *Introduction to Old English* (Oxford, 2003). This is my textbook and I have aimed to make it accessible.

Baker, Peter S. 'Magic Sheet'. See http://www.engl.virginia.edu/OE/courses/handouts/magic.pdf. A one-page summary of Old English inflections.

Barney, Stephen A., *Word Hoard: An Introduction to Old English Vocabulary* (New Haven, CT, 1985). An entertaining book that shows how words are grouped into families.

Borges, Jorge Luis, 'A Conversation With Jorge Luis Borges', *Artful Dodge* online (http://www.wooster.edu/artfuldodge/interviews/borges.htm). Dated 1980; accessed 2 May 2006.

Bosworth, Joseph and T. Northcote Toller, *An Anglo-Saxon Dictionary* (Oxford, 1882–1921). The only complete scholarly dictionary of Old English. For a newer dictionary, not yet complete, see Cameron.

Cameron, Angus, comp. *Dictionary of Old English* (Toronto, 1986). A scholarly dictionary of Old English, originally published on microfiche but now being issued on CD-ROM. As of 2006 it is complete through F.

Clark Hall, J.R. and H.D. Meritt. *A Concise Anglo-Saxon Dictionary*, 4th edn (Cambridge, 1960). The best dictionary for students.

Finkenstaedt, Thomas and Dieter, Wolff, *Ordered Profusion: Studies in Dictionaries and the English Lexicon* (Heidelberg, 1973).

Godden, Malcolm, 'Anglo-Saxons on the Mind', *Old English Literature*, Liuzza, R.M., ed. (New Haven and London, 2002). Reprints an essay from 1985.

Heaney, Seamus, trans., *Beowulf: A New Verse Translation* (New York, 2000).

Hogg, Richard M., ed., *The Cambridge History of the English Language* (Cambridge, 2000), Vol. I: Beginnings to 1066.

Jefferson, Thomas, *An Essay Towards Facilitating Instruction in the Anglo-Saxon and Modern Dialects of the English Language for the Use of the University of Virginia.* (New York, 1851). Posthumously published musings on Old English by an early enthusiast.

Lass, Roger, *Old English: A Historical Linguistic Companion* (Cambridge, 1994). An excellent book for the linguistically inclined.

Liuzza, R.M., trans., *Beowulf: A New Verse Translation* (Peterborough, ON, 2000). An excellent piece of work.

Mitchell, Bruce and Fred C. Robinson, *A Guide to Old English*, 6th edn (Oxford, 2001). Probably the best-selling textbook on Old English.

Simpson, J.A. and E.S.C. Weiner, *Oxford English Dictionary*, 2nd edn (Oxford, 1989).

CHAPTER 11

Viking wars and *The Anglo-Saxon Chronicle*

Jayne Carroll

AN. .dcclxxxvii. Her nom Beorhtric cyning Offan dohtor Eadburge. 7 on his dagum cuomon ærest .iii. scipu, 7 þa se gerefa þærto rad 7 he wolde drifan to þæs cyninges tune þy he nyste hwæt hie wæron. 7 hiene mon ofslog. Þæt wæron þa ærestan scipu deniscra monna þe Angelcynnes lond gesohton.

(Manuscript A)

787 AD [actually it was 789]. In this year king Beorhtric married Eadburh, daughter of Offa. And in his days came for the first time three ships; and then the reeve rode there, and he wished to make them go to the king's manor, because he did not know what they were, and they killed him. Those were the first ships of the Danish men who sought the land of the English.

With these few words, the composer of this part of the *Anglo-Saxon Chronicle* ushered in a new age: the age of the Vikings. From the late eighth century to the end of the Anglo-Saxon period, England was a land dominated by Scandinavian activities, some murderous, as Beaduhard, the king's unfortunate reeve, discovered to his cost in 789, some friendly and fruitful, as the enduring Scandinavian contribution to our language illustrates.

For most people today, the word 'Viking' summons up a picture of a large and fearsome Scandinavian warrior, intent on pillage and murder, wielding a sword or perhaps an axe and most likely crowned with a horned helmet. While the chronicler who recorded the raid of 789 would, if we stripped our warrior of his Victorian horns, recognise this picture, it is nonetheless a decidedly partial representation of the activities of Scandinavians out and about during the Viking Age (*c*. 800–*c*. 1100). In England as elsewhere in Europe, they traded, settled, farmed, manufactured and became Christian, contributing to all levels of English society, from the very lowest to the very highest. Alfred the Great, ninth-century king of England and stalwart defender of the land against the Vikings, shares his epithet with Cnut the Great, the

Danish-born conqueror of eleventh-century England and commonly deemed more English than the English. The smash-and-grab raids for which the Vikings are famous are only one facet of a many-sided story.

The first Vikings in England

It was certainly violent pillage which concerned the 'first ships of the Danish men' and their immediate successors. The chronicler of the annal for 789 wrote with the benefit of hindsight. Unlike the poor reeve, he knew exactly 'what they were' (*hwæt hie wæron*). Writing in the late ninth century, he knew that these ships were the first of many to plague England's men and women – and, at this time, particularly England's holy men, for it was the wealthy monasteries which attracted the attention of the marauding Scandinavians. In 793, the monastery on the island of Lindisfarne, just off the coast of Northumbria and particularly vulnerable to ship-borne incursion, fell victim to raiders:

> AN.dccxciii. Her wæron reðe forebecna cumene ofer Norþanhymbra land 7
> þæt folc earmlice bregdon: þet wæron ormete ligræscas, 7 wæron geseowene
> fyrene dracan on þam lyfte fleogende. Þam tacnum sona fyligde mycel hunger,
> 7 litel æfter þam þæs ilcan geares on .vi. idus Ianuarii earmlice heðenra manna
> hergung adiligode Godes cyrican in Lindisfarenae þurh reaflac 7 mansleht.
>
> (Manuscript E)

> 793 AD. In this year terrible portents appeared over the land of the
> Northumbrians, and wretchedly frightened the people; there were excessive
> lightning flashes, and fiery dragons were seen flying in the air. A great famine
> soon followed these signs; and a little after that in that same year on 8 January
> the harrying of the heathen men wretchedly destroyed God's church in
> Lindisfarne through plunder and slaughter.

While the annal for 789 is a relatively straightforward narrative of what must have been the most significant event of the reign of Beorhtric, king of Wessex, the annal for 793 is more obviously interpretative. The comets that lit up the eighth-century sky are seen as dragons whose fiery breath heralds catastrophe and the disastrous famine is covertly presented as nature's corollary to the Viking scourge. In this annal, the raiders have lost their designation as Danes, and are called 'heathen men' (*heðenra manna*), a label used by the Christian Anglo-Saxons to refer to any non-Christians, but very often to the Vikings. The annal's subtext is easy to divine. The arrival of these warriors is punishment from God. It was not long before Christian writers made this point explicitly. Later that year, the English churchman Alcuin sent a letter from the court of Charlemagne (the Frankish emperor) to Æthelred, king of Northumbria, in response to the attack on Lindisfarne. While his account of the raid is hardly that of an eyewitness, it remains one of the most vivid contemporary responses to Viking violence, and is strikingly direct in its attribution of blame:

> Lo, it is nearly 350 years that we and our fathers have inhabited this most lovely land, and never before has such terror appeared in Britain as we have now suffered from a pagan race, nor was it thought that such an inroad from the sea could be possible. Behold, the church of St Cuthbert spattered with the blood of the priests of God, despoiled of all its ornaments; a place more venerable than all in Britain is given as a prey to pagan peoples. [. . .] Consider carefully, brothers, and examine diligently, lest perchance this unaccustomed and unheard-of evil was merited by some unheard-of evil practice. (translation by Whitelock)

These imagined evil practices do not remain 'unheard of' for long. In his highly rhetorical Latin, Alcuin proceeds to outline in some detail deeds which he believes merit God's wrath. Sexual crimes dominate, with fornication, adultery and incest listed first. Greed, robbery and 'violent judgments' are mentioned, too, and what we would think of as lesser crimes are dwelt on. Alcuin asks King Æthelred to consider the immoderate dress of his people and, in particular, their hairstyles, which are said to imitate those of the pagan Danes. His conclusion? That 'judgment has begun, with great terror, at the house of God, in which rest such lights of the whole of Britain. What should be expected for other places?' (translation by Whitelock). Alcuin clearly had his suspicions of what should be expected for other places. He wrote in warning to the monks of Wearmouth and Jarrow, also in Northumbria and similarly exposed to sea-borne raids, but to no avail. The *Chronicle* reports that a place at the mouth of the Don (*Donemuþe*), probably Jarrow, was sacked the following year by 'the heathens' (*þa hæðenan*).

The Vikings come back

For the next 30 years, the *Chronicle* does not report a single further attack. We know from other sources that the Vikings were busy ravaging the coasts of Ireland and the continent, and it may be that they were too busy elsewhere to trouble the Anglo-Saxons. Alternatively, it may be that the chronicler was not aware of raids in parts of the country unfamiliar to him or that the raids were not deemed significant enough to find their way into the written record – the *Chronicle* is by no means an exhaustive account of the events of the time. However, from the 830s on, the onslaught was relentless. The chronicler records Viking successes in Sheppey (835), in Portland (840), in Romney Marsh, Lindsey (part of Lincolnshire), East Anglia, and

Kent (841), in London and Rochester (842) and in Carhampton (843). The year 851 marked the arrival of 350 ships into the Thames. London and Canterbury were stormed and Beorhtwulf, the king of Mercia, was forced to flee before the Scandinavians turned southwards into Surrey. The chronicler's news is not entirely gloomy: there were successes on the English side, too. King Egbert of Wessex defeated a coalition of Danes and Cornishmen in 838; at Southampton (840), West Saxon ealdorman Wulfheard held off a force of either 33 or 25 ships (the figures vary according to which *Chronicle* manuscript is consulted). A united army of men from Somerset, led by ealdorman Eanwulf, and men from Dorset, led by ealdorman Osric and Ealhstan, bishop of Sherborne, overcame a Danish army at the mouth of the Parret (848). In Devon ealdorman Ceorl and his men 'made great slaughter' (*micel węl geslogon*), and at Sandwich King Æthelstan and ealdorman Ealhhere manage to capture nine Danish ships (850). It is clearly the aim of the chronicler to put as positive a gloss as possible on events. The victory, in 850, of West Saxon King Æthelwulf at an as-yet unidentified place named *Acleah* is described as 'the greatest slaughter made of a heathen army that we have heard tell of to this present day' (*þæt mæste węl geslogon on hępnum herige þe we secgan hierdon oþ þisne ondweardan dæg*). Even defeats are described in ways which emphasise the valiant performance of the Englishmen and the (reportedly) marginal nature of the Viking victories. Of the Dorset ealdorman Æthelhelm and his men it is said that, 'for a good while they drove back the army' (*7 gode hwile þone here gefliemde*; MS A, s.a. 837 [840]). The unsuccessful alliance of Ealhhere of Kent and Huda of Surrey in 853 is said to have 'at first taken the victory' (*7 ærest sige namon*) against 'the heathen army' and heavy losses on both sides are emphasised. Each English leader, whether victorious or not, is individually named and his status as king, ealdorman or churchman is carefully recorded. The *Chronicle*'s account of each is personalised and it sets these individuals against a massed and faceless enemy designated as 'heathens' (*hæðenan*), 'Danes' (*Dene*), 'shiploads' (*sciphlæstas*), and, increasingly, simply 'the army' (*se here*). The ubiquity of the raiding Scandinavians ensured that no further identification was needed. There was no danger that the readers of the annals would not know exactly to whom the chronicler was referring.

Vikings stay for longer: St Edmund and the Great Army

The second half of the ninth century saw significant changes in the pattern of Viking activity in England. The Scandinavian presence had hitherto been confined to seasonal raids, but in 850 'the heathen men for the first time remained over the winter' (*heðne men ærest ofer winter sæton*). It was only a matter of time before those winter-long stays turned into something more permanent. This change in Viking strategy was matched by a change in the English response. In 865, the English made the first of many ultimately unsuccessful attempts to buy off their enemies:

> AN. .dccclxi. Her sæt heþen here on Tenet 7 genamon friþ wiþ Cantwarum
> – 7 Cantware him feoh geheton wiþ þam friþe – 7 under þam feohgehate
> se here hiene on niht up bestel 7 oferhergeade alle Cent eastewearde.

> 865 AD. In this year the heathen army remained in Thanet, and made peace with the Kentish people; and the Kentish people promised them money in return for that peace; and during the period when that money-secured promise held, the army stole up in the night and harried all of eastern Kent.

This annal portrays the Vikings as deceitful and their actions as dishonourable, a characterisation that turns up repeatedly in later texts, as we shall see. Here, the chronicler's outrage that the army should harry despite having promised peace – and having accepted money as a guarantee – is almost tangible. Their actions are described with the verb *bestelan* 'to steal [up on], move stealthily', which in the *Chronicle* is used exclusively of the Vikings' actions, often referring to their movement during the night. In this context the word has clear overtones of devious wiliness.

The year 865 was a landmark in more ways than this. Most significantly, it marked the arrival of the Viking 'great army' (*micel here*), led by two brothers, Ivar 'the boneless' (Old Norse *Ívarr inn beinlauss*) and Halfdan, a third man, named Bacsecg, and various 'jarls' (Old English *eorl*, used as an equivalent to the Old Norse title *jarl* 'earl, nobleman'). While the previous attacks on England seem to have been the work of individual bands of Vikings working in an opportunistic way, this army seems to have been a larger, well-organised force with conquest on its mind. It arrived in East Anglia, where it over-wintered, and where its men were provided with horses in return for peace. In retrospect, this was rather a bad idea, as it was as a mounted force that the Vikings advanced through England in the following years. From East Anglia, the army proceeded to York, where it despatched the two contenders for Northumbria's throne. This was the first of the Anglo-Saxon kingdoms to fall to the Vikings and it remained under Scandinavian control – as the Viking kingdom of York – for most of the following 100 years. The next year (867) the great army moved from York to Nottingham, in the kingdom of Mercia, to spend a somewhat inconclusive winter in the town's fortified area, before returning north in 869. A further foray into East Anglia was decisive, however, resulting in the fall of that kingdom and a period of Danish rule. The circumstances of the kingdom's fall are variously documented. Under the year 870 (for 869), the *Chronicle* gives a customarily terse account of the events leading up to the death of Edmund, king of East Anglia:

> AN. .dccclxx. Her rad se here ofer Mierce innan Eastengle 7 wintersetl namon æt Þeodforda. 7 þy wintra Eadmund cyning him wiþ feaht, 7 þa Deniscan sige namon & þone cyning ofslogon 7 þæt lond all geeodon.

> 870 AD. In this year the army rode across Mercia into East Anglia and took winter-quarters at Thetford. And that winter, King Edmund fought with them, and the Danish had the victory and killed the king and overran all the land.

Shortly after his death, and certainly during the period of Danish rule, Edmund was venerated as a saint. It is quite possible that men who had had a hand in Edmund's killing later worshipped him as a martyr–saint! In the early tenth century his remains were translated to the monastery at Bury St Edmunds (then called *Bedricesworth*), which became the centre of his developing cult. This cult resulted in the production of two further accounts of Edmund's death, each in the form of a saint's life, one of the most popular genres of the medieval period. The first is in Latin and is generally known as the *Passio Sancti Eadmundi* ('Passion [suffering] of St Edmund'). It was written for the monks of Ramsey in 987/8 by Abbo of Fleury, who had spent time teaching there (985–87), and had heard Edmund's story from Dunstan, Archbishop of Canterbury, to whom he dedicated the account. The second account is based on Abbo's narrative and is in Old English. It was written in about 990 by Ælfric, who later became abbot of Eynsham (in 1005) and was the most prolific writer of the late tenth century (pp. 419–22). He included his translation in his *Lives of Saints*, a collection dedicated to a West Saxon nobleman, Æthelweard, who was at that time engaged in damage limitation during a later phase of Viking activity. Ælfric does not add anything substantial to Abbo's account of events, which is considerably richer in historical detail than the *Chronicle*'s short entry, giving names, places and a detailed sequence of events leading up to Edmund's death. Abbo was writing more than 100 years after Edmund's death, but nevertheless there are good reasons to place some faith in his account of the killing. His preface, addressed to Dunstan, shows him to be what we would think of as a 'responsible' historian – one who carefully cites his sources. Ælfric, in his own preface, follows Abbo's example and retraces the path that the account has taken to reach him:

> Sum swyðe gelæred munuc com suþan ofer sæ fram Sancte Benedictes stowe on Æþelredes cynincges dæge to Dunstane ærcebisceope þrim gearum ær he

forðferde, and se munuc hatte Abbo. Þa wurdon hi æt spræce oþ þæt Dunstan
rehte be Sancte Eadmunde, swa swa Eadmundes swurdbora hit rehte Æþelstane
cynincge, þa þa Dunstan geong man wæs and se swurdbora wæs forealdod man.
Þa gesette se munuc ealle þa gereccednysse on anre bec and eft, ða þa seo boc
com to us binnan feawum gearum, þa awende we hit on Englisc, swa swa hit
heræfter stent.

A certain very learned monk came from the south over the sea from
St Benedict's place [the monastery at Fleury], in King Æthelred's day, to
Archbishop Dunstan, three years before he died. And this monk was called Abbo.
They [Abbo and Dunstan] talked together until Dunstan talked of St Edmund,
just as Edmund's sword-bearer had talked of it to King Æthelstan when Dunstan
was a young man, and the sword-bearer was a very old man. Then the monk set
all of this down in a book, and afterwards when the book came to us within a
few years, we turned it into English, just as it hereafter stands.

Abbo and Ælfric retell Dunstan's own account and, as Dunstan himself
heard it from an eyewitness, there are only two links in the human chain
from Abbo to the eyewitness. We should therefore give the saint's life some
credence, despite the fact that its account is rather different from that in the
Chronicle. Where the *Chronicle* seems to suggest that Edmund was killed in
or after a battle, there is no such battle mentioned by Abbo and Ælfric. They
have the Vikings, led by Ivar the boneless (Old English *Hinguar*), indiscrim-
inately killing the men, women and children of East Anglia before sending
a messenger to Edmund, demanding that he submit to Ivar's overlordship
and reign under him as a puppet king. One of Edmund's bishops advises
him to comply, but he refuses to do so unless Ivar first converts to Christianity. Ivar's men seize the king, who has thrown away his weapons, then
bind and beat him. Edmund's constant calling on Christ is said to enrage
the pagan Vikings, who throw spears at him until, in Ælfric's translation,
'he was completely covered with their darts, like the bristles of a hedgehog'
(*oð þæt he eall wæs besæt mid heora scotungum swilce igles byrsta*; Lat. *uelut
asper hericius* 'like a prickly hedgehog'). When this fails to silence the
Christian king, Ivar commands his head to be chopped off, which – at least
at first – appears to do the job more satisfactorily. The Vikings leave the
body where it falls, but hide his head in nearby woodland in order to deny
Edmund a decent Christian burial. The rest of the Life is given over to the
miracles that follow Edmund's death. These begin almost immediately, with
the king's head crying out 'here, here, here' (*her, her, her*), guiding those who
search for it in the right direction, until they find it clasped safe in the paws
of a helpful guardian wolf. On the saint's translation, his body is found to
be uncorrupted, with head miraculously rejoined to body and in subsequent

years his hair and nails continue to grow. Edmund's sanctity is further proven when eight men who wish to rob his tomb are frozen to the spot for the duration of the night and, in the morning, are arrested and punished. Another unfortunate man called Leofstan, who insolently demands to see Edmund's uncorrupted body, is rewarded with instant insanity and he dies a horrible death, devoured by worms.

Much of Abbo's narrative is conditioned by the genre within which he was working and can be if not exactly discounted at least taken with a large pinch of salt. We need not take as historically accurate the extended portrait of Edmund as an ideal Christian king or the miracles that announce and prove his sanctity. Abbo is consciously enlisting Edmund in a rollcall of saints and these facets of the narrative are to show why he belongs there. This is often done through explicit comparison with other saints or biblical figures. The devil seeks to test Edmund's patience 'as in the case of St Job' (*sicut et sancti Iob*). After the Vikings have used Edmund for target practice he resembles not only a hedgehog, but also the Roman martyr St Sebastian (*in passione similis Sebastiano egregio martyri*; 'in suffering resembling Sebastian, the illustrious martyr'), who was shot with arrows and left for dead. The wolf's miraculous preservation of Edmund's head is compared to that of Daniel, who remained safe 'among the open jaws of hungry lions' (*esurientium rictus leonum*). All in all, Edmund is 'not inferior in merit to [St] Lawrence, blessed deacon and martyr' (*non . . . esse inferiorem meritis Laurentii beati leuitae et martyris*). The most frequent comparison, however, is with Christ. Abbo states three times that Edmund follows in the footsteps of Christ, and the account of the king's death is followed by an extended and highly rhetorical comparative passage:

> Ille quidem purus sceleris in columna ad quam uinctus fuit sanguinem non pro se sed pro nobis flagellorum suorum signa reliquit; iste pro adipiscenda gloria immarcescibili cruentato stipite similes poenas dedit. Ille integer uitae ob detergendam rubiginem nostrorum facinorum sustinuit benignissimus immanium clauorum acerbitatem in palmis et pedibus; iste propter amorem nominis Domini toto corpore grauibus sagittis horridus et medullitus asperitate tormentorum dilaniatus in confessione patienter perstitit, quam ad ultimum accepta capitali sententia finiuit.

> Indeed, the one [Christ], free from sin, left behind on the column to which he was bound blood, not for himself but for us, as a sign of his scourgings; the other [Edmund], for the attainment of unfading glory, paid a similar penalty on the blood-stained trunk. The one, perfect in life, endured, most benign, the affliction of the savage nails in his palms and feet in order to wipe away the blight of our sins; the other, for love of the name of the Lord, bristly with

painful arrows over his whole body, and pierced to the very core with the harshest of torments, steadfastly persisted in declaring his creed, which finally he ended when he had received the sentence of death.

Despite the formulaic elements of Abbo's *Passio*, it seems likely that the narrative outline of his account of Edmund's death has its roots in reality and that the Vikings, under Ivar, killed the king not in a battle but in the aftermath of the East Anglian campaign. The *Passio* offers us evidence for the kind of atrocity with which the Vikings are indelibly associated (see Map 7).

The differences between Abbo's and Ælfric's accounts may not be significant from a historical perspective, but the two works are stylistically distinct. Ælfric turns Abbo's complex and highly rhetorical Latin into relatively simple Old English. Four and half a thousand Latin words become two and a half thousand English ones, with the more florid passages, such as the comparative one just quoted, entirely omitted and the lengthy and ornate speeches greatly condensed – and, in the process, rendered much more believable. The pared-down remaining narrative is ordered into the distinctive 'rhythmical prose' that characterises many of Ælfric's later works, in which phrases containing two stresses are paired through alliteration. Ælfric's approach to his source is best illustrated by setting two passages side by side in the following box (see p. 311).

Abbo's vivid and detailed – and, of course, fictional – recreation of the slaughter is rejected in favour of a more measured, less descriptive statement. The horror of Abbo's account and the sense of outrage are nevertheless conveyed, but in few words: Ivar acts 'just like a wolf' (*swa swa wulf*) and 'shamefully tormented honest Christians' (*to bysmere tucode þa bilewitan cristenan*). To the modern reader Ælfric's account reads more like 'proper' history and it is easy to forget that Abbo's extravagant *Passio* was his sole source, to which no new historical information was added.

Mindful of his audience, Ælfric contextualises the East Anglian events of the narrative with reference to Alfred, king of Wessex (871–99) and great-great-grandfather of Æthelred, who was king of England at the time that the *Lives of Saints* were written (about 990). In doing so, he is reminding his readers and listeners of a leader who withstood the Viking threat when the kingdoms of Northumbria, East Anglia, and Mercia had fallen. Relating the overthrow of East Anglia, he alludes to the West Saxon king who, at the end of the ninth century, brought to an end the advance of the Scandinavian armies. As we shall see, in 990 Ælfric's king, Æthelred 'the unready' (Old English *unrǣd*, 'no counsel, ill counsel') was facing renewed and intensive Scandinavian assaults on England and Ælfric's brief reference to Alfred was undoubtedly a deliberate tactic to inspire hope and strength in his harassed

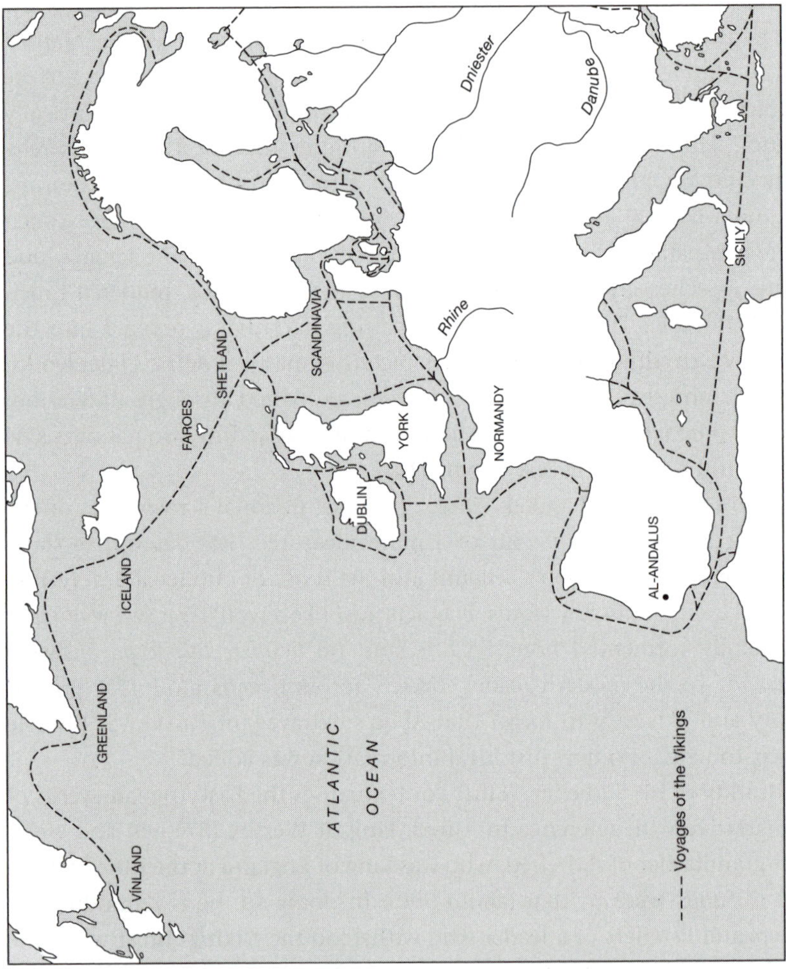

Map 7   Viking expansion

Hinguar reliquit ibi crudelitatis socium, et a boreali parte orientali subito astans cum magna classe ad eius quandam ciuitatem latenter appulit. Quam ignaris ciuibus introgressus ignibus cremandam dedit, pueros senes cum iunioribus in plateis ciuitatis obuiam factos iugulat, et matronalem seu uirginalem pudicitiam ludibrio tradendam mandat. Maritus cum coniuge aut mortuus aut moribundus iacebat in limine; infans raptus a matris uberibus ut maior esset heiulatus trucidabatur coram maternis obtutibus. Furebat impius miles lustrata urbe, ardendo ad flagitium quo posset placere tyranno, qui solo crudelitatis studio iusserat perire innoxios.

Þa gewende Hinguar east mid his scipum and Hubba belaf on Norðhymbra lande, gewunnenum sige mid wælhreownysse.

Hinguar þa becom to Eastenglum rowende, on þam geare þe ælfred æðelincg an and twentig geare wæs, se þe, Westsexena cynincg, siþþan wearð mære; and se foresæda Hinguar færlice swa swa wulf on lande bestalcode and þa leode sloh, weras and wif and þa ungewittigan cild, and to bysmore tucode þa bilewitan Cristenan.

Ivar left his partner in cruelty there [in Northumbria], and approaching from the north-east, all at once, standing by with a great fleet, he landed secretly at a certain city. When he had entered the city without the citizens' knowledge, he decreed that it should be consumed by flames. He slaughtered boys and old men along with the young whom he encountered in the streets of the city, and he ordered both matronly and virginal women to surrender their chastity. Husband and wife lay dead or dying on the street; an infant snatched from its mother's breasts was killed before the maternal eyes so as to make her lamentations greater. The wicked army raged through the wasted city, eager for that foulness with which it could please the tyrant, who from love of cruelty alone had ordered innocents to be killed.

Then Ivar turned east with his ships and Ubbi remained in Northumbria, having won victory with cruelty. Then Ivar came sailing to East Anglia, in the year in which Prince Alfred, who afterwards became the famous king of the West Saxons, was twenty-one years old. And the aforementioned Ivar suddenly, just like a wolf, stole up onto the land, and killed men and women, and innocent children, and shamefully tormented the honest Christians.

audience. Ælfric may have stated in the preface to his *Lives of Saints* that their purpose was 'to strengthen your faith', but 'to strengthen your resolve' in the face of heathen advance is the subtext of his life of Edmund. And there was no better way to do it than by evoking the age of Alfred the Great.

Alfred's first wars with the Danes

We know a good deal about Alfred's life not only from the relatively detailed account offered by the *Anglo-Saxon Chronicle*, but also from a contemporary Latin biography written by a Welsh monk called Asser. Asser had known Alfred for about eight years before he wrote the biography in 893 and he had supervised his learning of Latin and helped him with his programme of translation (p. 252). Asser relied in part on the relevant annals of the *Chronicle*, but much of his material must have come from direct observation, or from Alfred's own account of events past and present. His text offers valuable glimpses into Alfred's childhood and his religious and intellectual interests.

Alfred was not yet king when, at the beginning of 871 and having already conquered East Anglia, the Viking army turned its attention to Wessex, making Reading its base. The first battle was at Englefield and was fought and won by West Saxon ealdorman Æthelwulf. The remaining battles of the year were fought with mixed success by Alfred and, until he died after Easter, his brother, King Æthelred. Alfred inherited the kingdom at an extraordinarily difficult period of intense fighting. The *Chronicle* records a number of battles in some detail under the annal for 871, carefully listing the arrangements of the armies and the names of their leaders. Its conclusion, however, indicates that Wessex, like the other kingdoms before it, was unable to maintain this level of defence, particularly since an additional 'great summer army' (*micel sumorlida*) had arrived to join the Vikings in Reading. The West Saxons were forced to make the pragmatic decision to buy off the Vikings:

> 7 þæs geares wurdon .viiii. folgefeoht gefohton wiþ þone here on þy cynerice be suþan Temese, 7 butan þam þe him Ęlfred þæs cyninges broþur 7 anlipig aldormon 7 cyninges þegnas oft rades on ridon þe mon na ne rimde, 7 þæs geares wærun ofslægene .viiii. eorlas 7 an cyning; 7 þy geare namon Westseaxe friþ wiþ þone here.

> And during the year nine battles were fought against the army in the kingdom south of the Thames, besides those raids which Alfred, the king's brother, a single ealdorman, and the king's thanes rode out on, which are impossible to count. And during the year nine jarls were slain, and one king; and in this year the West Saxons made peace with the army.

This 'peace' resulted in the Viking army leaving Wessex and returning to Mercia, where it established a base at Repton and put to flight the Mercian king, thus dealing the ancient kingdom its deathblow (874). After the Vikings had 'conquered the entire kingdom' (*þæt lond eall geeodon*), they installed a puppet king, Ceolwulf. His willingness to cooperate with the occupying force inspired an unusually forthright response from the Chronicler:

> Hie sealdon anum unwisum cyninges þegne Miercna rice to haldanne, 7 he him aþas swor 7 gislas salde, þæt he him gearo wære swa hwelce dæge swa hie hit habban wolden 7 he gearo wære mid him selfum 7 on allum þam þe him læstan woldon to þæs heres þearfe.

> They gave the kingdom of Mercia to a foolish thane to control, and he swore them oaths and gave them hostages that Mercia might be ready for them any day that they wanted it, and he himself, and all those who would follow him, were ready to attend to the army's needs.

On the whole, this section of the *Chronicle* narrates the actions of the Vikings with relatively little in the way of condemnation, but the actions of the Anglo-Saxon Ceolwulf earn more explicit disapprobation – disloyalty is a crime indeed.

Following Mercia's fall, the great army split into two. One half, led by Halfdan, went back into Northumbria that same year (874). Halfdan raided and pillaged in the then-familiar way, but shortly afterwards, in 876, he 'shared out the land of the Northumbrians, and they [his men] proceeded to plough and support themselves' (*Norþanhymbra lond gedælde 7 ergende wæron 7 hiera tilgende*). The Vikings were here to stay, no longer just opportunistic pirate–raiders or well-organised conquering land forces, but settled individuals who worked the land, just as the native Northumbrians had done for some 400 years. The way was clear for the Vikings' lasting contribution to England's heritage. While Halfdan's men settled, however, the other half of the great army indulged in the more familiar Viking activities of raiding and terrorising further south.

In 874 these men, led by three leaders named in the *Chronicle* as Guthrum, Oscetel and Anwend went from Repton to Cambridge. In 875 they proceeded south into Wessex and broke the peace that had held there for the last four years. From 875 to 877 they were up to their old tricks, targeting Wareham and Exeter and breaking their promise to leave Wessex, a promise that they had made 'on the holy ring, which previously they would not do for any nation' (*on þam halgan beage, þe hie ær nanre þeode noldon*; MS A, 876). In 877 they made the same promise, but this time kept it, returning to Mercia, the eastern part of which they shared out (*gedældon*

– the same verb used of the sharing out of Northumbria) and settled. The western part they granted to Ceolwulf.

Despite the fact that members of the great army had settled in Northumbria and Mercia, there still remained a sufficient number to make a third invasion of Wessex possible. One of the leaders, Guthrum, returned with his men early in 878. Undoubtedly, his aim was to conquer Wessex as his comrades had conquered the kingdoms of Northumbria, East Anglia and Mercia. To begin with, it looked as though Guthrum's aims were well on the way to being fulfilled. The offensive forced King Alfred into hiding. The *Chronicle* tells us that 'he travelled in difficulties with a small troop through woods and moor-fastnesses' (*he lytle werede unieþelice æfter wudum for 7 on morfæstenum*; MS A, 878), and later legend tell us that he was so preoccupied with his troubles that he absent-mindedly allowed some loaves to burn while minding them for a swineherd's wife (p. 249). Although this well-known story is most likely entirely fictional, it is not hard to believe that at this time the king's mind was entirely taken over with Viking matters. At this point the future of Wessex – and England – looked bleak indeed. From this lowest point, however, Alfred managed not only to stay alive but to regroup sufficiently to trouble the Vikings. He did this from Athelney in the Somerset marshes, where he built a fortress, peopled with the fighting men of the Somerset shire. Shortly after this, Alfred and these men joined up with those from Wiltshire and Hampshire. As a combined force they met the Viking army at Edington in Wiltshire, fighting the most celebrated battle of Alfred's reign:

> [he] þær gefeaht wiþ alne þone here 7 hiene gefliemde, 7 him æfter rad oþ þæt geweorc 7 þær sæt .xiiii. niht; 7 þa salde se here him foregislas 7 micle aþas, þæt hie of his rice uuoldon 7 him eac geheton þæt hiera kyning fulwihte onfon wolde, 7 hie þæt gelæston swa, þæs ymb .iii. wiecon com se cyning to him Godrum þritiga sum þara monna þe in þam here weorþuste wæron æt Alre, 7 þæt is wiþ Eþelinggaeige, 7 his se cyning þær onfeng æt fulwihte, 7 his crismlising was æt Wedmor, 7 he was .xii. miht mid þam cyning, 7 he hine miclum 7 his geferan mid feo weorðude.

> [he] fought there with the entire army and put it to flight, and rode after them until they reached the fortification, and laid siege there for a fortnight; and then the army gave him preliminary hostages and great oaths that they would leave his kingdom and promised him also that their king would receive baptism, and they did so, so that after three weeks the king Guthrum – one of thirty of the most worthy men in the army – came to him at Aller which is is near Athelney, and the king stood sponsor to his baptism, and his confirmation was at Wedmore [in Somerset], and he was twelve nights with the king, and he [Alfred] honoured him and his companions with riches.

Guthrum and his men also kept their promise to leave Wessex, staying in Cirencester for a year and thence to East Anglia, where they 'settled and shared out the land' (*gesæt þæt lond 7 gedęlde*; MS A, 879). A further Viking army which had arrived in the Thames in 878 left for the continent. Alfred's victory at the battle of Edington appears to have discouraged them from trying their own hand at the conquest of Wessex.

Vikings defeated! Alfred builds up Wessex

The year 878 was without doubt a landmark for the West Saxons. Its events secured a period of relative peace and security for Wessex which lasted through the 880s. Alfred put this respite to good use, not only establishing an effective defensive system which would secure Wessex from future attack, but also setting up a programme to encourage religious and intellectual progress (p. 252). Alfred, like Alcuin and many other Christian authors of the time, interpreted the Viking raids as a form of divine punishment for the decline in learning and the irreligious behaviour of his people and he set about putting this to rights. In the preface to his translation of Pope Gregory's *Pastoral Care* (Latin *Cura Pastoralis*) he directs his readers to 'Remember what punishments befell us in this world when we ourselves did not cherish learning nor transmit it to other men' (*Geðenc hwelc witu us ða becomon for ðisse worulde, ða ða we hit nohwæðer ne selfe ne lufedon, ne eac oðrum monnum ne lefdon*).

While Alfred encouraged his priests to disseminate knowledge and did his best to provide them with Old English material fit for purpose, he knew that learning alone was not enough to keep Wessex out of the clutches of the Vikings. Military advances were vital as a safeguard for the future. The *Chronicle* retrospectively records Alfred's reorganisation of his army, which increased its efficiency and the length of time it was able to campaign continuously: 'the king had divided his army into two, so that always half the men were at home and half out [on active service], except for those who had to man the forts' (*hæfde se cyning his fierd on tu tonumen, swa þæt hie wæron simle healfe æt ham, healfe ute, butan þæm monnum þa burga healdan scolden*; MS A, 893).

The forts referred to in this annal were another aspect of Alfred's military reforms. The 880s saw the establishment of a system of fortified defensive sites (often called burhs – *burga* in the 893 annal). A document known as the *Burghal Hidage* records the maintenance and manning of 33 fortified places in the south of England as part of a coherent defence plan. These places were stategically positioned – they guarded the various routes through the kingdom, were largely situated on the coast or on inland waterways and their distribution ensured that the entire population of Wessex was within relatively easy reach of one or other of them. Some made use of existing forts (Roman sites, for example), others were new, designed as stoutly defended urban centres with a regular grid of streets, many of which eventually developed into our modern towns – yet another lasting testament to Alfred's greatness. Although the *Burghal Hidage* document dates to around 919, 20 years after Alfred's death, the arrangements that it describes relate to Alfred's reign. It lists for each fortified site the number of hides (a measure of land of about 120 acres) required for its maintenance:

> Þreo hund hida hyrð to Eorpeburnan. 7 xxiiii. hida To Hæstingaceastre hyrþ .v. hund hida 7 to Læwe hyrþ twelf hund hida. 7 to Burham hyrþ seofan hund hida [. . .]

> Three hundred hides belong to *Eorpeburnan* [unidentified site probably in Sussex], and 24 hides [And] to Hastings belong 5 hundred hides [And] to Lewes twelve hundred hides And to Burpham belong seven hundred hides [. . .]

What exactly is meant by these short statements is then clearly explained:

> To anes æceres bræde on wealstillinge 7 to þære wære gebirigeað .xvi. hida Gif ælc hid byþ be anum men gemannod þonne mæg man gesettan ælce gyrde mid feower mannum.

> For the establishment of a wall of one acre's breadth, and for its defence, 16 hides are required. If each hide is represented by one man, then each pole (of wall) can be furnished with four men.

In other words, for each 'pole' of wall (a defended length of about five metres), four men were required to defend it and one man was provided from every hide of land. So, 334 men manned the walls of the fortified site at *Eorpeburnan*, 500 at Hastings and 700 at Burpham. The *Burghal Hidage* is of immense interest to historians and archaeologists as it affords a valuable glimpse of the workings of the West Saxon government and gives the precise length of the defensive works at the various fortifications. However, as the short extracts demonstrate, its immediate appeal for students of Old English language and literature is rather limited! Nevertheless, the *Burghal Hidage* is important for us as a rare surviving example of the use of Old English for strictly administrative purposes – there must have been a good number of such documents floating around in the Anglo-Saxon period, each written in a similar workaday style. It is easy to forget, when immersed in the epic excitement of *Beowulf* and the gory and sometimes apocalyptic detail of saints' lives and homilies, that Old English's capacity for literary appeal was matched by its practical functionality.

Alfred's political and military achievements during this period were not confined to Wessex. In the early 880s, Ealdorman Æthelred of the (western) area of Mercia remaining in English hands acknowledged Alfred as overlord. This alliance was consolidated in 886, when Alfred captured London from the Vikings who had held the city and passed it into the care of Æthelred. This capture in itself was extremely important and can be seen as a preliminary step towards the tenth-century 'reconquest' of Scandinavian England (of which more later), but two further events of enormous significance followed. First, the *Chronicle* notes that 'all the English people – except those who were under subjection to the Danes – submitted to him' (*him all Angelcyn to cirde þæt buton deniscra monna hæftniede was*; MS A, 886). Second, Alfred negotiated a treaty with Guthrum, the Viking king of East Anglia who had accepted baptism in 878. The prologue of this treaty outlines the English in general and the Danish people in East Anglia as those to whom it applied. This treaty defines the boundary between that part of England under Scandinavian control (later known as the Danelaw), and that which remained in the hands of the English. It travels 'up the Thames, and then up the Lea, and along the Lea to its source, then in a straight line to Bedford, then up the Ouse to Watling Street'. The treaty establishes that English and Danish individuals in both parts of 'Anglo-Scandinavian' England have equal legal value, or *wergild* (literally 'man-payment', the amount payable in compensation if an individual were killed and a valuable disincentive to manslaughter). English and Danes were to cohabit their land on equal legal footing, regardless of the Danelaw boundary.

Both the statement in the 886 annal and the prologue of Alfred and Guthrum's treaty (concluded between 886 and 890) suggest that by this time Alfred's leadership was recognised beyond the borders of Wessex, well into English Mercia. The *Chronicle* uses *Angelcynn* 'the English people' to describe those who submitted to the West Saxon king. This term was rarely used before Alfred's reign, but the king and writers associated with him appear to have adopted it at about this time to refer to all those Christians in England who were united against Scandinavian advance. The vision of a united English people was not born as a result of the Viking threat – it was there in Bede's eighth-century notion of the *gens Anglorum* (Latin for 'English people', used in his *Ecclesiastical History*) – but it certainly flowered under the peculiar pressures of the late ninth century.

Vikings come back: Alfred's second wars with the Danes

The measures put in place by Alfred were put to the test in 892, when the Viking army returned from its extended continental campaign (879–91).

It was at about this time that the *Chronicle* itself was first circulated and it is perhaps likely that the two events were related. The *Chronicle* survives today in seven manuscripts, commonly referred to with the letters A to G (although most of G was destroyed in the Cotton Library fire of 1731). These manuscripts date from the late ninth century (the time at which the annals to about 890 were written into MS A) to the mid-twelfth century (MS E continues to 1154). Each of the seven manuscripts contains an 'original' compilation which was made during the very early 890s and then circulated for copying (the early medieval form of publication). This compilation is known as the 'Common Stock' or the 890 *Chronicle* and it was put together from a variety of sources, including Bede's *Ecclesiastical History*, various annals pertaining to local matters throughout the south of England and presumably to some extext the stock of oral narratives handed down from one generation to the next.

These sources were shaped into a text which attempted to give a coherent history of the various Germanic tribes who arrived in England from the mid-fifth century, set against the broader history of the island from its invasions by Julius Caesar in 55 and 54 BC. Although the Common Stock is indisputably a West Saxon product which is very obviously told from a West Saxon viewpoint, it tells the story – albeit rather patchily – of what we might aptly think of as Alfred's *Angelcynn* and not just the kingdom of Wessex. The timing of the compilation has been read as evidence that the Common Stock represents a piece of official West Saxon propaganda, developed in response to the impending threat of the Viking army which returned to England in 892 and designed to remind people that it was the West Saxons alone who resisted the invaders. However, it is not certain that the Common Stock was an 'official' product of Alfred's court (or even an unofficial product of one of his circle) and the text is rather more inclusive than the quotation suggests.

It is, of course, impossible for us to know whether the purpose of circulating the *Chronicle*'s Common Stock was to encourage the English people as a whole to come together under Alfred to resist the renewed Viking threat of 892. However, it is at least possible that it should be counted alongside the burghal organisation and the reform of the army as a factor contributing to the successful defence of southern England in the 890s, a defence recorded in the 'first continuation' of the *Chronicle* (in all manuscripts except E), which updates the Common Stock for the years 893–96, and gives a very detailed and lively account of Alfred's actions in these years. No longer do annals briefly record first an English victory then one or more 'Danish' victories. The simple paratactic style of the earlier entries ('and' . . .

'and' . . . 'and') has been replaced by a more syntactically complex and satisfy-ing narrative ('when' . . . 'then' . . . 'until' . . . 'because' . . . 'so that'). The annals are lengthy and gripping and depict in detail raids and sieges for which the mobile Viking army received support from Scandinavians already settled in the Danelaw. Each Viking offensive was quickly countered by stout and very well-organised responses on the part of the king and his army and the annals also provide evidence of a good deal of careful forward planning:

> Þa sume dæge rad se cyng up bi þære eæ 7 gehawade hwær mon mehte þa
> ea forwyrcan, þæt hie ne mehton þa scipu ut brengan; 7 hie ða swa dydon,
> worhton ða tu geweorc on twa healfe þære ea. (MS A, 895)

> Then one day the king rode up by the river and observed where it might
> be possible to block the river so that they [the Vikings] could not bring their
> ships out; and then they [the English] did so, building two forts on each side
> of the river.

To our picture of Alfred the military commander and Alfred the strategic thinker we can add a further dimension – Alfred the ship designer:

> Þa het Ælfred cyng timbran langscipu ongen ða æscas. Þa wæron fulneah tu
> swa lange swa þa oðru. Sume hæfdon .lx. ara, sume ma. Þa wæron ægðer ge
> swiftran ge unwealtran ge eac hieran þonne þa oðru; næron nawðer ne on
> fresisc gescæpene ne on denisc, bute swa him selfum ðuhte þæt hie
> nytwyrðoste beon meahten. (MS A, 896)

> Then King Alfred commanded longships to be built to combat the Viking ships
> [*æscas*]. They were almost twice as long as the others. Some had sixty oars, some
> more. They were both faster and more stable and also higher than the others;
> they were designed neither in Frisian nor Danish style, but as seemed to [Alfred]
> himself would be most useful.

Translator, civil reformer, military commander and now ship designer – it really was largely down to Alfred's extraordinary leadership that the chronicler was able to record that:

> Ða þæs on sumera on ðysum gere tofor se here, sum on Eastengle, sum on
> Norðhymbre, 7 þa þe feohlease wæron him þær scipu begeton 7 suð ofer sæ
> foron to Sigene. Næfde se here, Godes þonces, Angelcyn ealles forswiðe
> gebrocod. (MS A, 896)

> Then afterwards in the summer of this year the army dispersed, some to
> East Anglia, some to Northumbria, and those without property got ships for
> themselves and went south over the sea to the Seine. The army had not,
> through the mercy of God, very greatly afflicted the English people.

More Viking wars: Alfred's children carry on

Three years after the departure of the Viking army Alfred died, leaving a son, Edward, who became king of Wessex, and a daughter, Æthelflæd, who had married Æthelred, ealdorman of Mercia, shortly after the capture of London in 886 in an alliance which further cemented the links between Wessex and Mercia. These three individuals embarked on what is usually called the 'reconquest' of the Danish-ruled areas of England, a reconquest that had started with this capture. As with the word *reconquista* in Muslim Spain, the word 'reconquest' in Danish England is somewhat problematic, as in effect the campaigns of Edward and Æthelflæd represented a West Saxon takeover of areas that had never before been under West Saxon control. The first 20 years of the tenth century saw eastern Mercia and East Anglia come under the nominal control of Edward – after a highly successful and extended campaign the various Scandinavian leaders who had ruled, independently of each other, the various Danelaw land units submitted to his overlordship. Edward's campaigns are recorded in the *Chronicle*'s second and third continuations (897–914 MSS ABC and 915–920, MS A), but these are supplemented by a further – and discrete – set of annals for the years 902–24, preserved in MSS BCD. These annals are known as the *Mercian Register* and, as the name suggests, are mainly concerned with Mercian events, in particular the anti-Scandinavian measures taken by Æthelflæd 'lady of the Mercians' (*Myrcna hlæfdige*, MS B, Mercian Register 912). She was a fine military strategist, who ruled Mercia alone after the death of her husband in 911. Around this time she dealt also with new Vikings, Gaelicised Norwegians who were moving into Lancashire and Cheshire from their few generations' worth of settlement in eastern Ireland (see the *Gawain* poet in Chapter 15, p. 485). Together, Æthelred and Æthelflæd had fortified five towns, but between 912 and 915 Æthelflæd alone directed the building of nine Mercian fortresses – an extraordinary achievement narrated by the author of the Mercian Register in a matter-of-fact if rather breathless style:

> Her com Æthelflæd Myrcna hlæfdige on þone halgan æfen Iuentione Sancte Crucis to Scergeate 7 þær ða burh getimbrede, 7 þæs ilcan geares þa æt Bricge. Her Gode forgifendum for Æþelflæd Myrcna hlæfdige mid eallum Myrcum to Tamaweorðige 7 þa burh ðær getimbrede on foreweardne sumor, 7 þæs foran to Hlafmæssan þa æt Stafforda; ða þæs oþre geare þa æt Eadesbyrig on foreweardne sumor, 7 þæs ilcan geares eft on ufeweardne hærfest þa æt Wæringwicon; ða þæs oðre geare on ufan midne winter þa æt Cyricbyrig, 7 þa æt Weardbyrig, 7 þy ilcan geare foran to middan wintra þa æt Rumcofan.

In this year [912] on the eve of the Invention of the Holy Cross [2nd May] Æthelflæd, lady of the Mercians, went to *Scergeat* and built there a fortress, and the same year one at Bridgnorth. In this year God, by God's grace, Æthelflæd lady of the Mercians went to Tamworth and built a fortress there in the early summer, and afterwards before Lammas [1st August] one at Stafford; then in the following year one at Eddisbury in the early summer, and afterwards in the same year in late autumn one at Warwick; and the next year after midwinter one at Chirbury, and one at *Weardburh* [unidentified], and in the same year before midwinter one at Runcorn.

Æthelflæd's operations were coordinated with those of Edward, her brother, to whom she too vowed allegiance. When she died in 918 Edward succeeded her as direct ruler of Mercia. Its inhabitants, both Danish and English, submitted to him, but the 919 annal in the Mercian Register suggests that this submission was not of their choosing:

Her eac wearð Æþeredes dohtar Myrcna hlafordes ælces onwealdes on Myrcum benumen 7 on Westsexe alæded ðrim wucan ær middum wintra; seo wæs gehaten Ælfwyn. (MS B, 919)

In this year the daughter of Æthelred, lord of the Mercians, was deprived of all power over the Mercians and taken into Wessex three weeks before midwinter; she was called Ælfwynn.

A later historican, William of Malmesbury, recorded a Mercian revolt in Chester in the months before Edward died in 924. The *Mercian Register*'s discreet but tangible dissatisfaction with the events that followed Æthelflæd's death seems to have been shared by the men and women of the ancient midland kingdom. There is no mention of Ælfwyn and her claims in the Wessex-based A manuscript, which presents the conquest of eastern Mercia and East Anglia as entirely Edward's achievement, mentioning Æthelflæd only to record her death. Its annal for 920 expresses a triumphalist satisfaction in the expansionist achievements of the West Saxon king:

hine geces þa to fæder 7 to hlaforde Scotta cyning 7 eall Scotta þeod, 7 Rægnald 7 Eadulfes suna 7 ealle þa þe on Norþhymbran bugeaþ, ægðer ge Englisce ge Denisce ge Norþmen ge oþre, 7 eac Stræcledweala cyning 7 ealle Stræcledwealas. (MS A, 920)

the king of the Scots and all the Scottish nation accepted him as father and lord, and Ragnald and the son of Eadwulf, and all those who lived in Northumbria, both English and Danish and Norwegian, and also the king of Strathclyde and all the inhabitants of Strathclyde.

When Edward died in 924, he left to his son Æthelstan an ostensibly united England. Only the land north of the Humber – the Viking kingdom of York – remained independent and under Scandinavian control.

King Æthelstan and the Danelaw

Of course this newly 'united' kingdom by now comprised English and Scandinavian inhabitants. As we have seen, the *Chronicle* records, in 876, 877 and 879, Scandinavian settlement in Northumbria, eastern Mercia and East Anglia and also further settlement in the 890s, when some members of the Viking armies decided to settle rather than return to the continent and extend their life of raiding. In these areas English people and Scandinavian must have lived side by side, although the Scandinavians must have had the upper hand in the power stakes, at least initially, and their sons and grandsons must have manned the armies of the early tenth century to oppose Edward and Æthelflæd's incursions. The *Chronicle*, with its 'us and them' viewpoint and its focus on the military exploits of the age, does not cast light on how the ordinary folk of eastern and northern England, both English and Scandinavian, rubbed along beside each other. Neither does it tell us how many Scandinavians there actually were in Danelaw, although it provides evidence that some army members brought their families with them.

In 892 the English stormed the Viking fortress at Benfleet in Essex and seized 'both property, and women, and also children' (*ge feo, ge on wifum, ge eac on bearnum*; MS A, 893). A further annal, that for 895, notes that the Danes 'had placed their women in safety in East Anglia before they left the fort' (*hæfdon hira wif befæst innan Eastengle, ær hie ut of þæm geweorce foron*; MS A, 895). Some of these would have settled as family units in eastern and northern England, but there must also have been a great deal of intercourse – of all kinds! – between English and Scandinavian. While we have the official or semi-official accounts represented by the *Chronicle* in its various forms, we lack the voice of the ordinary settler; or at least we hear it only in the many Scandinavian place-names scattered unevenly through the Danelaw and the many different Scandinavian personal names recorded within place-names and historical documents, primarily the Domesday book. Place-name evidence is a complex linguistic matter, but the sheer number of parish names and more minor names (the names of streets and fields, for example) which are in some way indebted to the linguistic presence of the Scandinavians suggest a large-scale settlement. This was probably one that involved not only communities derived from the fighting men of the Viking armies, but also a secondary migration of those who came to settle in the wake of the Scandinavian conquest. Names ending in -*by* 'farmstead, village' and -*thorpe* 'secondary settlement' are easy to identify as Scandinavian in origin and there are plenty of them in today's East Midland counties of England (Bagsby, Grimsby, Ousby, Saxby etc.). Not every Scandinavian place name would have been coined by a man or woman of Scandinavian origin, speaking Old Norse, but there are so many of them that they indicate massive linguistic influence on the part of the settlers. These Old Norse speakers left their mark not only on present-day maps of England, but also on present-day English. So firmly are the Vikings linked with rape and pillage in the popular imagination, that it would come as a great surprise to many English speakers to learn that they use on a daily basis words imported by the Vikings 1000 years ago. The words include *take, get, anger, ill, egg, skirt, sister, law, leg, happy, husband, freckle, window, call* and *ransack*. All these words are loans into English from Old Norse. These borrowed words are of everyday character. They are not specialist technical terms that supplemented the Old English wordstock to describe new and foreign concepts. They replaced words that already existed in Old English and this indicates very extensive linguistic influence. Most strikingly, the Old English grammatical system was affected by the Vikings. The third-person plural pronouns *they*, *them* and *their* are not English in origin but Norse. There is no doubt about it, there were very many speakers of Danish and Norwegian in late Anglo-Saxon England. The following few pages will tell you more about what their 'Old Norse' language was. For those who want to skip this section, normal service will be resumed on p. 329.

Notes on the Old Norse language

Richard North

So far there have been many wild and whirling words in foreign languages in this book, chief of which is (now, we hope, the not-so-foreign) Old English. There will be more as well. But so far there has also been some quotation from Old Norse and this section is written to give you a sense of what that language was. For most of Anglo-Saxon history, Danish and Norwegian were roughly the same. There used to be a convention in English-speaking countries to call this language and its culture and derivative literature 'Old Norse', because it originated in Norway (Dutch for some reason, *noors*, 'Norwegian'). 'Old Icelandic', contrariwise, makes more sense, given that Iceland is where most of it was written down (see Chapters 12–13). Some people try to make up for the unfairness of this division of labour by saying 'Old Norse–Icelandic'. I am going to say 'Old Norse' for the name, and 'Old Icelandic' for the written form, of the language that was spoken by Scandinavians in England in the ninth to eleventh centuries.

Let's suppose Egill, an Icelander who has been staying in Norway, is now in Chester with the retinue of King Æthelstan of England. The big battle of Bromborough (*Brunanburh*) is over and Egill is waiting for a few days before taking ship for Norway. In comes the king's butler, a man named Edward:

Ēadweard sǣġde, 'hwȳ hæfst þū druncen eall mīn wīn?'

Egill is so surprised by this question that he answers politely:

Hē andswarode, 'iċ wæs þurstiġ, and iċ dranc þīn wīn'.

If you have read Chapter 10 (p. 272), you can make out the meaning of this exchange in modern English. Now, let's change it a little and dramatise it:

Edward: 'Hwȳ hæfst þū druncen eall mīn wīn?'
Egill: 'Ek var þyrstr, ok því drakk ek vín þitt.'
Edward: 'Eall mīn wīn?'
Egill: 'Já, allt þitt vín, þótt konungs vín er, en eigi þitt.'

Here Egill talks in his own language, knowing that the butler can understand him. Each in his own language is how Vikings and Anglo-Saxons communicated much of the time. Egill's word order is naturally Norse in style. In his first answer he puts the 'I'-pronoun *ek* after the verb *drakk* and the possessive adjective 'your' *þitt* (lit. 'thy') after *vín*, along with a new word *því* which means 'therefore' or 'for this reason'. But his meaning is the same as *iċ wæs þurstiġ, and iċ dranc þīn wīn*. Egill knows Edward can follow him and doesn't raise one of his eyebrows as he did with the king a few days ago. But when the butler says 'All my wine?', Egill has to make the position clear. His second answer means literally 'Yes, all your wine, though king's wine [it] is, and not yours'. *Eigi* is the only different-looking Norse word here, for Old English *nē* or *nāht* ('not'), but you can imagine that most Anglo-Saxons had had occasion to learn what this word means. By now the two speakers have gathered an audience. Edward appeals to them as follows:

'Hū mæġ þes blōdiġa wīċing eall þæs cyninges wīn up ādrincan? Iċ nē can hit understondan.'

Helpfully, one of the king's housecarls renders Edward's question into Egill's language, which we can set out in Old Icelandic:

'Hvé má inn blóðugi víkingr þessi drekka upp alla vínit konungsins?'

Unlike Old English *þes*, the Old Icelandic *þessi* ('this') usually goes after its noun, here *víkingr*. Also postponed is the Icelandic word for 'the', the definite article: literally *vín-it* means 'wine-the' and *konungs-ins* means 'king's-the' or 'of king-the'. Otherwise, it is a faithful translation. Egill gets the message. Years later, back in Iceland, one of his friends tells the story like this:

'Sumurin í Englandi váru þá lǫng ok heit [*the summers in England were then long and hot*]. Hafði Egill eigi drukkit of mikit enn þá [*Egill hadn't drunk too much by then*]. Mjúkr var hann ok ódrukkinn, ef sannliga er sagt [*Meek he was and sober (lit. "un-drunk"), if truly it is said*].'

At this point the sun sets behind the mountain and the narrator's audience shake their heads.

'Egill mælti, "Ek em engi víkingr, heldr em ek bónda sonr frá Íslandi [*Egill said, I'm no Viking, rather am I a farmer's son from Iceland*]. En eigi emk kallaðr ertinga maðr heldr [*But I'm not called a man who puts up with insults either*]".'

This looks more promising.

'Hǫfði vindr þá Egill [*his head Egill then turns (lit. "winds")*] ok segir þeim manni, er þá var konungs jarl inn mesti [*and says to that man who was then the greatest (lit. "most") earl of the king*], "Gef mér hross ok sverð hans ein" [*Just give me just his horse and sword*].'

In Old English, the king's earl turns nervously to his reeve and says *Ġif mē his hors and his sweord*. These sentences show some formal resemblances between Old Icelandic, on one hand, and Old and modern English, on the other. If you run over them for a couple of minutes, you will learn how to convert one into the other, *v-* for *w-*, *drakk* for *dranc*, *sverð* for *sweord*, *gef mér* for *ġif mē* and so on. As we have seen, the Icelandic 'the'-word is postponed (*vín-it*, 'wine-the') rather than placed in front as with us. Where an adjective is involved, however, the 'the' word does go in front. So you say *jarl-inn* for 'the earl' but *inn mesti jarl* for 'the greatest earl' or *inn blóðugasti jarl* for 'the bloodiest earl'. You will see variations in the word for 'the' as well: *inn* where it goes with a man, a masculine; *it*, with a neuter noun such as *vín*, 'wine'. There is a feminine gender as well, just as in Old English. The feminine definite article is *in* (with one *n*). Let's pick a feminine-gendered noun. For instance, where you say *sēo burh* in Old English for 'the borough' or 'the town' feminine, in Old (and modern) Icelandic you just say *borgin*. So *jarlinn, borgin ok vínit*, 'the earl, the town and the wine'. What a combination.

If you actually use these words, you have to go into cases, just like in Old English. Pretend we are in an eighteenth-century novel: 'The earl rode to York because he wanted to drink all the wine in the town.' In a tenth-century English novel that would have been:

se ealdorman rād tō Eoforwīċe, for þǣm þe hē wolde drincan eall þæt wīn on þǣre byriġ (*or* burġe).

Or in an Icelandic saga, one imagines:

Jarlinn reið til Jórvíkr, fyrir því at hann vildi drekka vín allt í borginni.

Fastened on to *borg* ('town'), a feminine noun, the feminine 'the' word that we just met has to go into a dative case after the preposition *í* ('in'). *Borg* doesn't change in the dative, although other nouns do. But if we say 'to the town', with *til* ('to'), as in 'the earl rode to the town', that would be *jarlinn reið til borgarinnar*. The preposition 'to', *til*, takes a genitive case (one of the few Old Icelandic prepositions that do). Genitive of *borg* is *borgar* ('town's', 'of a town'). Genitive of feminine *in* is *innar*. Stick them together: *til borgar-innar*. That's how the definite article in Old Icelandic works. If you go over these sentences again, you will learn many other things as well. To continue with the story:

'"Ek kalla á konung ok alla menn hans," segir Játvarðr [*I call on the king and all men his, says Edward*] "at eigi láti mik heyra slíkt illmæli útlends bóndasonar [*that they not make (lit. 'let') me hear such ill-talking of an outland farmer's son*]. Konungr gaf mér sverðit [*The king gave me the sword*] ok hross mitt fekk ek af dróttningunni [*and my mare I received from the queen*]. Bæði eru hlutir mínir [*Both are my things*] ok víst tekr hann þá aldri heðan á brott til Íslands [*and surely he is taking them never from here abroad to Iceland*]."

Egill kastar honum út ór hǫllunni í gegnum vindauga eitt [*Egill casts him out of the hall through a certain window*].'

At the time of the incident Edward speaks all his words in Old English. His last ones are:

'Hē ġewisslīċe nā ne ġenimeþ hīe heonon ūt on *Ultima Thule* nǣfre.'

Perhaps there has been a misunderstanding. We should note an ambiguity in what Edward says. The Old Norse is 'víst tekr hann þá aldri heðan á brott til Íslands' (*surely takes he them never from here abroad to Iceland*). The problem with the Old English version of this is not only Edward's pile-up of negatives such as *nā, ne, nǣfre* ('no time', 'not', 'never'). It is also the lack of difference between 'they', 'them' and 'her'. Edward's complaint also means 'he surely will never take (*ġenimeþ*) her (*hīe*) out of here to Iceland', referring to the queen. Give the queen to Egill?

For their part, the Anglo-Saxons were getting tired of confusing *hē, hēo, hīe* and similar words, especially when buying and selling was involved. That is why, by the end of the eleventh century, they had taken the pronoun *þeir* ('they') and its other forms genitive *þeirra* ('their') and dative *þeim* ('them') from the Danes. Of course, pronouns were not the only words which 'they took' (*þeir tóku*) from the Danes or which we 'get from them' (*getum af þeim*). There are lots of others, as we saw earlier in this chapter. 'An Englishman cannot **thrive** or be **ill** or **die** without Scandinavian words', wrote the Danish grammarian Otto Jespersen, '**they are** to the language what bread and **eggs** are to the daily **fare**'. The words *þrífa, illr, þeir, eru, deyja, egg* and *far* are indeed only some of these loans. What about *law* (*lǫg*)? In northern counties until the nineteenth century there was also 'wapentake' (*vápnatak*) for a 'hundred', a district where house-holders mustered for call-ups or committee meetings. Other terms, not so socially responsible, include 'to busk' (*búask*, 'to prepare oneself'), 'bag' (*baggi*), 'skill' (*skil*, 'discernment'), 'window' (*vindauga*, lit. 'wind-eye'), 'ransack' (*rannsaka*, lit. 'to house-hurt'), 'scrap' (*skrap*, 'bric-a-brac'), 'take' (*taka*), 'upstart' (*uppstertr*, lit. 'tail up') and 'gloat' (*glotta*, 'grin'). These words illuminate what was perceived to be going on in Yorkshire and the eastern Midlands in the tenth century. Next time you hear someone say English has no word for German *Schadenfreude* ('joy at (others') misfortunes'), think of *gloating* and how, perhaps, the Anglo-Saxons, by taking this word from their smiling Danish neighbours, believed that their language had no word for it either.

Let's look at some tables for Old Icelandic words we have just seen. Tables are used for the reflexes of these words to this day by people learning modern Icelandic. Like all Germanic languages, Icelandic puts the stress on the first syllable of the word: *bo:rgarinnar* and so on. Pronouns are much like ours, old and modern: *ek* ('I'), *þú* ('thou', 'you (singular)'), *hann, hon, þat* ('he, she, it'); *vér* ('we'), *þér* ('you (plural)'), *þeir, þær, þau* ('they (masculine, feminine, neuter)'). To take two verbs first, *kalla* ('to call') and *gefa* ('to give'). Note that whenever a stressed *a* is followed by *u*, it turns into *ǫ*:

pronoun	present	simple past		
ek	kalla	kallaða	*present participle* (-ing)	kallandi
þú	kallar	kallaðir	*past participle* (-ed)	kallaðr
hann	kallar	kallaði		
vér	kǫllum	kǫlluðum	*perfect*	ek hefi kallat etc.
þér	kallið	kǫlluðuð		
þeir	kalla	kǫlluðu		

The type of the verb *kalla* is called 'weak' because it is easier to master than the 'strong' type represented here by the verb *gefa*:

pronoun	present	simple past		
ek	gef	gaf	*present participle*	gefandi
þú	gefr	gaft	*past participle*	gefinn
hann	gefr	gaf		
vér	gefum	gáfum	*perfect*	ek hefi gefit etc.
þér	gefið	gáfuð		
þeir	gefa	gáfu		

The modern English past tenses analogy is -*ed* for 'weak' or regular verbs (*called*) and a change of vowel in the stem for the 'strong' or irregular verbs we still have (such as *give* – *gave* – *given*). In Old Icelandic just as in Old English, there are two or three 'weak' conjugations (i.e. classes) of verb (*kalla* is no. 2 weak) and seven 'strong' ones (*gefa* is no. 5 strong).

Old Icelandic nouns have three genders and four cases singular and plural like most Old English ones; and they also share with the latter a common system of endings. We can't go into this here, but I will give three examples, the counterparts of Old English *se stān* ('the stone', masculine), *sēo burh* ('the borough, town', feminine) and *þæt sumor* ('the summer', neuter).

To make life more interesting I shall tack on the definite article as well. Please remember that no hyphens are normally written between Old Icelandic nouns and enclitic definite articles; and that, for ease of snappy diction, the initial *i-* in the article is made to disappear if there are too many syllables:

singular	*nominative*	steinn-inn	borg-in	sumar-it
	accusative	stein-inn	borg-ina	sumar-it
	genitive	steins-ins	borgar-innar	sumars-ins
	dative	steini-num	borg-inni	sumri-nu
plural	*nominative*	steinar-nir	borgir-nar	sumur-in
	accusative	steina-na	borgir-nar	sumur-in
	genitive	steina-nna	borga-nna	sumra-nna
	dative	steinu-num	borgu-num	sumru-num

Once upon a time, the Vikings did say *steinar-inir* and *steina-inna*, even *steinum-inum*, *borgum-inum* and *sumurum-inum*. But it all took too long to say. The Vikings cut out the extra syllable clutter and shortened these words as in the table we have just seen.

We must shorten things now and go back to the chapter text. Before we do, however, let's read some Old Icelandic poetry. The following, from *The Lay of Atli* (*Atlakviða*), is probably of Norwegian origin from the later tenth century, composed when Egill Skalla-Grímsson was an old man. The following lines have been quoted already in Chapter 4 (on p. 122). Here I shall modernise their spelling, translate more literally and hyphenate to show the disposition of words in compounds:

Rín skal ráða   róg-málmi skatna,
á sú in ás-kunna,   arfi Niflunga.
Í veltanda vatni   lýsa-sk val-baugar
heldr en á hǫndum   gull skíni Húna bǫrnum. (stanza 27)

Rhine shall rule strife-metal of warriors,
that river the god-sprung, [shall rule] inheritance of Nibelungs.
In rolling water illuminate-themselves foreign-rings
rather than on hands of Huns' children the gold may shine.

But treasure *was* available in England. Land and treasure was, of course, why so many Scandinavians came here in the first place. Their language helped make ours. That is why the Vikings are part of our culture.

Further reading

Gordon, E.V., ed., rev. A.R. Taylor, *An Introduction to Old Norse*, 2nd edn (Oxford, 1956).

Townend, Matthew, *Language and History in Viking Age England: Linguistic Relations between Speakers of Old Norse and Old English*, Studies in the Early Middle Ages 6 (Turnhout, 2002). The definitive study of how Vikings and Anglo-Saxons communicated.

Egill is but one indication that Æthelstan succeeded to an Anglo-Scandinavian melting pot of a country. Æthelstan had been brought up with his aunt Æthelflæd and his uncle Æthelred, so he enjoyed a more secure position in Mercia. From there, he was able to extend his influence into Northumbria, which he did by forming an alliance with Sihtric (or Sigtryggr), the Viking king of York, shortly after becoming king himself.

Viking wars again: *The Battle of Brunanburh*

When king Sihtric died in 927, his young son Olaf succeeded to the kingdom. The arrival of Olaf's uncle Guthfrith from Viking Dublin, where he was king, prompted Æthelstan to invade Northumbria and drive both Olaf and Guthfrith out. Northumbria was, at least temporarily, under Æthelstan's control. This expulsion sowed the seeds for the most famous battle of the early tenth century: the Battle of Brunanburh. In 937, Guthfrith's son, Olaf, who had succeeded to the Viking kingdom of Dublin, allied himself with the kings of Strathclyde and Scotland and they invaded England. The *Anglo-Saxon Chronicle*'s record of Æthelstan's reign is otherwise meagre, but for 937 (MSS ABCD) it includes a 73-line poem now known as *The Battle of Brunanburh*, a verse celebration of the resounding victory of a united force of West Saxons and Mercians over Olaf (anglicised as *Anlaf* in the poem):

> Her Æþelstan cyning,   eorla dryhten,
> beorna beahgifa,   and his broþor eac,
> Eadmund æþeling,   ealdorlangne tir
> geslogon æt sæcce   sweorda ecgum
> ymbe Brunanburh. (*The Battle of Brunanburh*, lines 1–5)

> In this year Æthelstan, lord of men,
> ring-giver of warriors, and also his brother,
> Prince Edmund, struck long-lasting glory
> with swords' edges at the battle
> around *Brunanburh*.

Brunanburh's status as a *'Chronicle* poem' is fascinating. Scholars are divided on whether or not the poem was composed specifically for its place in the *Chronicle* but, regardless of this, its inclusion in what is otherwise a scanty and terse set of annals gives it the guise of factual representation. Its careful record of names and numbers just about fulfils its brief as informative reportage. However, it is very clearly and heavily indebted to traditional heroic poetry (see Chapter 4) in its alliterative style and its use of formulaic vocabulary. Æthelstan is immediately and conventionally styled as a 'lord of men' (*eorla dryten*, line 1) and a 'ring-giver of warriors' (*beorna beahgifa*, line 2), both of which phrases are used in *Beowulf* and elsewhere in the heroic corpus. The poem deliberately evokes the topos of the generous lord, surrounded by a loyal band of men (a 'comitatus'), to summon up a vision of heroic leadership. The traditional epithets are complemented by the poem's extended use of the beasts-of-battle topos. The West Saxons get most of the glory:

Leton him behindan   hræw bryttian
saluwigpadan,   þone sweartan hræfn,
hyrnednebban,   and þane hasewanpadan,
earn æftan hwit,   æses brucan,
grædigne guðhafoc   and þæt græge deor,
wulf on wealde. (lines 60–5)

They left behind them to enjoy the corpses
the dark-coated one, the black raven,
horny-beaked, and the dun-coated eagle,
white from behind, to enjoy the carrion,
greedy battle-hawk, and the grey beast,
the wolf in the forest.

Æthelstan and Edmund are thus enrolled in an ancient but continuing tradition of heroic warfare. The brothers are also referred to as 'sons of Edward' (*afaran Eadweardes*, line 7). This, too, is formulaic and traditional (think of the number of times that Beowulf is referred to as 'son of Ecgtheow'), but its significance is greater than this. When Edward is mentioned, we are being asked to recall and connect with Æthelstan and Edmund a king who also headed a united force of West Saxon and Mercians against Scandinavian enemies and who also had something approaching a legitimate claim on the title of king of a unified England. The formula implies continuity and the claims of birthright and, as such, is supported with further explicit references to family relationship. The fraternal bond between the poem's two heroes is emphasised. Edmund is named as Æthelstan's 'brother' at the onset of the poem (*broþor*, line 2), and they are 'brothers both together' (*gebroþer begen ætsamne*, line 57) towards its end. *Brunanburh* contains an explicit statement of the ideology of birthright. Æthelstan and Edmund defend their land 'as was befitting (or natural) to them from their ancestors' (*swa him geæþele wæs fram cneomagum*, lines 7–8). Their fitness to rule is in their blood. In fact, the poem's concluding passage links their victory at Brunanburh to the *adventus Saxonum* – the arrival of the first Germanic tribes to settle Britain in, tradition has it, 449, and appeals to the authority of written sources in a highly self-conscious manner:

> Ne wearð wæl mare
> on þis eiglande æfre gieta
> folces gefylled beforan þissum
> sweordes ecgum, þæs þe us secgað bec,
> ealde utwitan, siþþan eastan hider
> Engle and Seaxe up becoman,
> ofer brad brimu Brytene sohtan,
> wlance wigsmiþas, Wealas ofercoman,
> eorlas arhwate eard begeatan. (lines 65–73)

> Nor was there greater slaughter
> on this island ever yet
> of folk felled before this
> by the edges of swords, as books tell us,
> old sages, since hither from the east
> there came Angles and Saxons,
> over the broad ocean they sought Britain,
> proud battle-smiths, and overcame the Britons,
> glorious warriors and conquered the homeland.

Not only are Æthelstan and Edmund heirs to their father Edward, but also to those fifth-century warriors who made much of the island of Britain theirs through military conquest. The poet is clearly inviting us to draw parallels between the Germanic tribes and the West Saxon royals. Where the tribes 'sought Britain' (*Brytene sohton*, line 71), the brothers 'sought their homeland' (*cyþþe sohton*, line 58), which subtly suggests that their homeland is rather more than just Wessex. The suggestion, however, is not explicit: Æthelstan may head a united force, but the poem carefully distinguishes West Saxons (*Wesseaxe*, line 20) and Mercians (*Myrce*, line 24), and the home of Æthelstan and Edmund is explicitly detailed as 'the land of the West Saxons' (*Wesseaxena land*, line 59).

Also covert is the old opposition between Christian Englishman and heathen Scandinavian, craftily encoded in a reference to the sun, which follows the course of the fighting, as 'God's bright candle'. The blood flowed on the battlefield, we are told, 'from when the sun came up in the morning, glorious star, glided over the lands, bright candle of God, the eternal lord, until the noble creation sank to its resting place' (*siðþan sunne up on morgetid, mære tungol, glad ofer grundas, godes condel beorht, eces drihtnes, oð sio æpele gesceaft sah to setle*, lines 13–17). The implication is that the actions of the English are blessed by God.

Despite the fact that *Brunanburh* is a poem in praise of Æthelstan and Edmund, they feature rather less than we might imagine. A great deal of the poem is given over to lavish descriptions of flight and slaughter. The enemies are 'destroyed by spears' (*garum ageted*, line 18). Five young kings and seven earls lie dead on the battlefield, 'put to sleep with swords' (*sweordum aswefede*, line 30). Lest we are tempted to sympathise with the vanquished coalition, the poet effectively dehumanises them: the English 'hewed the fleeing soldiers' (*heawan herefleman*, line 23) just as they had hewn battle shields (*heawan heapolinde*, 6) – the verbal repetition achieves a striking objectification. The poet's delight in the coalition's trouncing is undisguised. His gaze lingers on the retreat of Olaf, 'driven by necessity' (*nede gebeded*, line 33), and that of Scottish king Constantine, who 'had no need to exult' (*hreman ne þorfte*, line 39), given that he had left behind a dead son on the battlefield, 'ground down by wounds, young at the battle' (*wundun forgrunden, giungne æt guðe*, lines 43–4).

This gloating may not be to the modern reader's taste. In this respect the poem is certainly distinct from other Old English poems, despite its conscious grounding in the Anglo-Saxon poetic tradition. The Old English heroic corpus is shot through with elegiac threads, but these are noticeably absent from *Brunanburh*. The poet's apparent enjoyment of descriptions of the dead and dying has prompted comparisons with Old Norse praise poetry (labelled 'skaldic', from ON *skáld* 'poet', on account of its non-anonymity; see Chapter 13, pp. 393–6), much of which is similarly preoccupied with celebrating victorious slaughter. It has been suggested that *Brunanburh* was the result of its poet's famility with the skaldic tradition. However, such praise poetry is common to many cultures and it may be that *Brunanburh* is a late surviving example of a native tradition. *Brunanburh*'s register is black and white, with no room for shades of grey. Æthelstan, Edmund, and their West Saxon and Mercian troops are rightly triumphant and their murderous victory is God given and justified by (written) history and their own innate nobility. Olaf Guthfrithson and Constantine are the 'wretched remnants of spears' (*dreorig daraða laf*, line 54; i.e. battle survivors) to whom no sympathy should be extended. On one side are the English and, on the other, is a motley crew of Scandinavians and Scots.

An alternative, more complex and altogether more interesting scenario is suggested by an episode in the thirteenth-century *Egils saga Skalla-Grímssonar*, one of the *Íslendinga sogu*, or Sagas of Icelanders (see Chapter 13). *Egils saga* tells the story of a tenth-century Norwegian family who settle in Iceland. Its hero, Egill Skalla-Grímsson, has already featured in 'Notes on the Old Norse Language'. Egill in this saga is a skilful poet and irrepressible Viking who offers both his poetic wares and his military strength to foreign leaders, including those in England. Chapter 54 of the saga tells of a great battle between Óláfr 'king of the Scots' and King Æthelstan, in which Egill and his brother Þórólfr fight for the English king, with Egill leading the bravest of the English troops and Þórólfr heading a division of Norwegians. Many scholars have associated this battle, which the saga places at an unidentified place called *Vínheiðr*, with that at Brunanburh (also unidentified, but probably Bromborough on the Wirral). The details of the saga are undoubtedly confused. Viking Óláfr and Scottish Constantine are conflated into a 'Scottish' king, Óláfr, and the saga's account of the prebattle negotiations between Óláfr and Aðalsteinn (i.e. Æthelstan) are totally incredible. However, the account does seem to be based on the Brunanburh tradition and it is not unthinkable that the English king should have employed Scandinavian mercenaries in his army. Æthelstan was renowned for the cosmopolitan character of his court, and Scandinavian tradition has it that Hákon Haraldsson, king of Norway (934–60), was the English king's foster son. He had the nickname *Aðalsteinsfóstri* ('Æthelstan's foster son'). A good number of scholars believe that Egill did indeed visit Æthelstan and he is said to have composed and performed a *drápa* – a long and elaborate poem with repeated refrain – in praise of the king. One verse and the refrain are preserved in Chapter 55 of the saga:

Nú hefr foldgnárr fellda,	Now has the land-dominating battle-increaser
fellr jǫrð und nið Ellu,	[warrior], chief-descendant of kings, felled three
hjaldsnerrandi, harra	princes; land falls under Ella's descendant.
hǫfuðbaðmr, þría jǫfra;	Æthelstan did more; everything is lower than
Aðalsteinn of vann annat,	the kin-famous king; this we swear, breaker of
allt's lægra kynfrægjum,	the fire of the wave [gold > generous ruler].[1]
hér sverjum þess, hyrjar	
hrannbrjótr, konungmanni.	[refrain:]
	Now the highest reindeer-road lies under
[stefit:]	valiant Æthelstan.
Nú liggr hæst und hraustum	
hreinbraut Aðalsteini.	

---

[1] *Hyrjar hrannbrjótr* 'breaker of the fire of the wave': 'fire of the sea' is a common kenning for 'gold' in Norse poetry and a breaker (distributor) of gold is a generous ruler.

The picture of Æthelstan presented to us here is not dissimilar to that in *Brunanburh*. *Brunanburh*'s 'ring-giver of men' (*beorna beahgifa*) is matched with Egill's 'gold-breaker' (couched in a complex kenning characteristic of the skaldic genre). Both present the king as a traditional, treasure-distributing heroic leader. We find the same emphasis on bloodlines, with Egill describing Æthelstan as 'kin-famous' (*kynfrægjum*) and a 'chief-descendant of kings' (*harra hǫfuðbaðmr*). Where *Brunanburh* looks back to the *adventus Saxonum* to place Æthelstan's victory within a broad historical context and to identify him as a worthy leader of a united England, Egill's reference to him as a 'descendant of Ælle' (*nið Ellu*) similarly refers back to an early phase of English history. The Ælle in question is probably the sixth-century king of the South Saxons, who Bede said was an overlord of all England south of the Humber – a position only slightly inferior to that which Æthelstan claimed for himself – and again we have the king cast as heir to a far-reaching kingdom. The king's martial prowess is brought to the fore too, although without *Brunanburh*'s detail. He is a 'battle-increaser' (*hjaldrsnerrandi*) who is able to fell princes. In fact, where *Brunanburh* is relatively restrained in its account of Æthelstan's conquest of land, sending its hero back to his ancestral homeland, Egill's poem is not. The matter of land is mentioned three times in this single stanza and refrain. The king is described as 'land-dominating' (*foldgnárr*); land falls (*fellr jǫrð*) under him; the highest reindeer road (Scotland?) lies under him (*liggr . . . und . . . hreinbraut Aðalsteini*). This offers a nice counterpoint to *Brunanburh*'s clear-cut depiction of Englishman versus Viking. Egill, an Icelandic Viking of Norwegian descent, celebrates the victory of an English king over Irish Vikings of Norwegian descent. This hints at an altogether more complex social (and political) situation and one that may be closer to the reality of tenth-century Anglo-Scandinavian England than Old English sources like the *Chronicle* would have their readers believe.

Back to the Danelaw: The Capture of the Five Boroughs

The complex reality of Anglo-Danish intermingling is hinted at in a second *Chronicle* poem, preserved as the annal for 942 in MSS ABCD, and generally known as *The Capture of the Five Boroughs*. Much had happened since Æthelstan's victory at Brunanburh in 937. When the king died in 939, his brother Edmund succeeded to a kingdom that included not only Wessex, but also East Anglia, Mercia and Northumbria. Edmund did not hang on to these last two for long. In 939, 'the Northumbrians were false to their pledges and chose Olaf of Ireland as their king' (*Norðhymbra alugon hira getreowaða 7 Anlaf of Yrlande him to cinge gecuron*; MS D, 941) – Olaf Guthfrithson was back and his shopping list included more than just Northumbria. From a base in York, he and his men proceeded into Mercia (940), where, following assaults and raiding, a treaty was drawn up between Olaf and Edmund. This gave Olaf power in Mercia north and east of Watling Street, including the East Midland shires: the 'Five Boroughs' of Leicester, Lincoln, Nottingham, Stamford and Derby. The mixed Anglo-Danish population of this area, which had been under English control since Edward the Elder's reign, now found itself in the hands of the 'Irish–Norwegian' Vikings. But not for long:

> Her Eadmund cyning,   Engla þeoden,
> mæcgea mundbora,   Myrce geeode,
> dyre dædfruma,   swa Dor scadeþ,
> Hwitanwyllesgeat   and Humbra ea,
> brada brimstream.   Burga fife,
> Ligoraceaster   and Lincylene
> and Snotingaham,   swylce Stanford eac
> and Deoraby.   Dæne wæran æror
> under Norðmannum   nyde gebegde
> on hæþenra   hæfteclommum
> lange þrage,   oþ hie alysde eft
> for his weorþscipe   wiggendra hleo,
> afera Eadweardes,   Eadmund cyning. (*The Capture of the Five Boroughs*,
> lines 1–13)

> In this year King Edmund, lord of the English,
> protector of men and beloved doer of deeds,
> conquered Mercia, as far as Dore borders it,
> the Whitwell Gap and the River Humber,
> broad rapid river; and the Five Boroughs,
> Leicester and Lincoln
> and Nottingham, also Stamford
> and Derby. The Danes were previously
> oppressed by force under the Norwegians,
> in the fetters of the heathens
> for a long time, until afterwards,
> because of his worthiness, King Edmund,
> protector of warriors and son of Edward, redeemed them.

This poem, which is quoted in full, packs a lot into a few short lines. It has a neat envelope construction, beginning and ending with three half-lines designating the king: *Eadmund cyning, Engla þeoden, mæcgea mundbora* (lines 1–2) . . . *wiggendra hleo, afera Eadweardes, Eadmund cyning* (lines 12–13). Like *Brunanburh*, it describes Edmund as *afera Eadweardes* 'son of Edward' and it makes full use of conventional heroic vocabulary – in fact three of the epithets used to describe Edmund are also found in *Beowulf* (*mundbora* 'protector', in *Beowulf*, lines 1480 and 2779; *dyre dædfruma* 'beloved doer of deeds', in *Beowulf*, line 2090; and *wiggendra hleo* 'protector of warriors', in *Beowulf*, lines 429, 899, 1972 and 2337). The poem's greatest interest, however, lies in a conception of a tenth-century 'English' population which is radically different from that imagined in *Brunanburh*, a record of events that took place only five years previously. As we have seen, the poem for 937 carefully differentiates West Saxons and Mercians and sends Æthelstan and Edmund back to Wessex at the poem's end.

The author of *Five Boroughs*, by way of contrast, labels his king *Engla þeoden* 'lord of the English, and replaces *Brunanburh*'s clear distinction between Mercians and West Saxons with a clear distinction between the Danes of the Danelaw and the newly arrived heathen Northmen. The Danelaw Danes are depicted as assimilated members of the Christian kingdom of England and, in fact, function metonymically for eastern Mercia's Anglo-Danish population as a whole. The age-old distinction between heathen Viking and Christian Englishman is reinvented – reinvigorated, in fact – in this new mixed-identity environment. Here, the emphasis on the oppressors' heathenness allows the poet to cast Edmund in the role of Christian redeemer. The verb used of the king's military conquest is *alysan* (past tense *alysde*, line 11). The primary sense given in the new *Dictionary of Old English* is 'to deliver, release, liberate, rescue, free' and these meanings are certainly present in *Five Boroughs'* use of the verb, particularly since the Danes are freed from 'fetters' (*hæfteclommum*). However, it is also the standard word used for spiritual redemption, often used with God or Christ in subject position ('Christ redeemed us'; sense '2(b)' in the *Dictionary of Old English*). Edmund's conquest is a spiritual victory, a redemption, and his subjects are united not by their racial origins but by their religious affiliation. The Common Stock's standard usage of 'heathen' as equivalent to 'Dane' was rendered obsolete in the new political reality of the mid-tenth century.

Blues of a frontier town: the Viking kingdom of York

England experienced a few more Viking hiccups in the mid-tenth century, the most significant involving Northumbria's independence under

Norwegian rulers from 949–954. For the last two years of this period Northumbria was ruled by King Eiríkr, associated in Scandinavian tradition and most modern scholarship with the fearsome Eiríkr 'Bloodaxe' (Old Norse *blóðøx*) of Norway. Eiríkr Bloodaxe was one of the sons of King Harald 'Finehair' (*hárfagri*) and he, too, had been Norwegian king during a short-lived and bloody reign that ended when he was driven out by his people. If we are to believe our Scandinavian sources, in 948 he made a first and failed attempt to make Northumbria his home. Four years later he was more successful and from 952 to 954 he ruled in York with Queen Gunnhildr and his Norwegian followers. The Viking poet Egill Skalla-Grímsson, whom we have already met in Æthelstan's court, was Eiríkr's sworn enemy. *Egils saga* relates a famous episode in which Egill appears before Eiríkr in York and recites a long praise poem, *Hǫfuðlausn* ('Head-Ransom'). The poem's title, which it shares with a number of other skaldic texts, derives from its function in the saga. Egill delivers the poem to Eiríkr in order to save his own head. Much of the poem is taken up with very general descriptions of battle in which Eiríkr is depicted as the prime mover: 'the king reddened the sword' (*rauð hilmir hjǫr*, stanza 10); 'arrows took life; bloody spears flew' (*fleinn hitti fjǫr, flugu dreyrug spjǫr*, stanza 10); 'the people's protector defied death' (*stózk folkhagi við fjǫrlagi*, stanza 14). The poem does not give us the who, the when and the where of these violent encounters, but it does succeed in evoking a clear picture of the poet standing before his patron. The opening stanzas, which take the form of a conventional 'bid for hearing', establish this performance context:

Vest fórk of ver,
en ek Viðris ber
munstrandar mar,
svá's mitt of far;
drók eik á flot
við ísa brot,
hlóðk mærðar hlut
míns kvarrar skut.

I travelled west over the sea, and I carry the sea of Óðinn's mind-shore [poetry]; thus was my journey; I launched a ship into the sea at ice-break [spring]; I loaded with a portion of praise the back-cabin of my ship.

Buðumk hilmr lǫð,
þar ák hróðrar kvǫð,
berk Óðins mjǫð
á Engla bjǫð;
lofat vísa vann,
víst mærik þann;
hljóðs biðjum hann,
því at hróðr of fann.

The king offered me hospitality; there I have a duty of praise; I carry Óðinn's mead [poetry] to England; praise for the prince is accomplished; assuredly I praise him; we ask him for a hearing because I have devised a praise-poem.

Here and in later stanzas, Egill focuses on his poetic role and his skill becomes evident not through novel and pertinent ways to describe martial exploits, but through his imagery-rich evocation of this role. This is apparent even in these first two verses, which introduce a string of liquid images running throughout the poem: Egill travels over the sea (*ver*) with his 'sea of Óðinn's mind-shore' (*Viðris munstrandar mar*), his 'Óðinn's mead' (*Óðins mjǫð*; two kennings for poetry that rely on myths narrated and explained by Snorri Sturluson in his *Edda*; see Chapter 12). Egill's poem fulfils its function and Eiríkr allows the poet to leave his court unscathed, provided that he never return.

Vikings come again: England's second Viking Age

When King Eiríkr was expelled from York in 954, Northumbria was absorbed once and for all into England and for 25 years England enjoyed peace and prosperity. That is, until the reign of Æthelred (978–1016). The C chronicler records, alongside his consecration in 979, the appearance of a 'bloody cloud in the likeness of fire' (*blodig wolcen . . . on fyres gelicnesse*; MS C, 979). Things did not look good for Æthelred's England. The bad press that bequeathed to Æthelred the nickname 'the Unready' had started. Æthelred's nickname dates from the twelfth century and derives from the Old English *unræd* 'no counsel, ill counsel'. It plays on the meaning of Æthelred, which means 'noble counsel': 'noble counsel' becomes 'no counsel' in the person of the English king. We can be certain that the author of the relevant section of the Chronicle (preserved in MSS CDE and sometimes called *The Chronicle of Æthelred and Cnut*) would have endorsed this harsh view of Æthelred's abilities. These annals were not contemporary but were written after the king's death, when the Danish king, Cnut, had taken the throne. This was the upshot of the Scandinavian raiding that had dominated Æthelred's reign for 30 years. The following annal (for 999) should give a good idea of the gloomy and frustrated tone of the chronicler's account:

> Her com se here eft abuton into Temese 7 wendon þa up andlang Medewægan
> 7 to Hrofeceastre, 7 com þa seo centisce fyrd þar ongean, 7 hi ða þær fæste
> togædere fengon, ac wala þæt hi to raðe bugon 7 flugon, 7 þa Deniscan ahton
> wælstowe geweald 7 namon þa hors 7 ridan swa hider swa hi sylf woldon &
> forneah ealle West Kentingas fordydon 7 forheregodon. Ða rædde se cyning
> wið his witan þæt man sceolde mid scypfyrde 7 eac mid landfyrde hym ongean
> faran, ac þa ða scipu gearwe wæron þa ylcodan þa deman fram dæge to dæge,
> 7 swencte þæt earmre folc þæt on ðam scipon læg, 7 a swa hit forðwerdre beon
> sceolde swa wæs hit lætre fram anre tid to oþre, 7 a hi leton heora feonda werod

wexan, 7 a man rymde fram þære sæ, 7 hi foron æfre forð æfter, 7 þonne æt
ðam ende ne beheold hit nan þing seo scypfyrding ne seo landfyrding buton
folces geswinc 7 feos spylling 7 heora feonda forðbylding. (MS C, 999)

In this year the Viking army came again into the Thames and then turned up
the Medway and to Rochester, and the Kentish division came against them
there and they vigorously engaged in battle together, but alas! too quickly they
turned and fled, and the Danes had possession of the battlefield and took the
horses and rode wheresoever they themselves wanted, and they destroyed and
harried almost all of West Kent. Then the king with his counsellors decided
that the ship- and land-armies should be sent against them, but when the
ships were ready then the officials delayed from day to day, and vexed the
poor people who remained in the ships, and always as things should have
been progressing they were slower from one hour to the next, and always they
allowed their enemies to grow stronger, and always they [the English] retreated
from the sea, and always they [the Danes] followed after, and then in the end
it effected nothing – neither the ship-army nor the land-army – except the
distress of the people and the wasting of money and the encouragement of
their enemies.

We are a long way here from the celebratory account of Alfred's final
wars against the Danes, although the army that plagued Æthelred in 999 is
in many ways similar to the Great Army that Alfred faced. It had been in
England for a number of years and represented a sustained, well-organised
threat to the country. It had arrived off the coast of Kent in 991 and was led
by Óláfr Tryggvason, who shortly afterwards became king of Norway, and
Sveinn (i.e. Sven) Forkbeard, king of Denmark.

Norwegians in 991: The Battle of Maldon

In 991, on 10 or 11 August, Óláfr Tryggvason's army fought the most
famous battle of Æthelred's reign, against Ealdorman Byrhtnoth at Maldon
in Essex. Byrhtnoth, ealdorman of Essex from 956, was one of the most
important men in England, possibly of royal descent, and his defeat at
Maldon was a severe and significant blow for England. All the surviving
Chronicle manuscripts record the event. MS A tells us (in an annal for 993)
that Óláfr arrived with a fleet of 93 ships and ravaged Sandwich and Ipswich
before proceeding to Maldon, where he fought and killed Ealdorman
Byrhtnoth and 'afterwards made peace' (*nam syððan frið*) with the English.
The account in MSS CDE (under the correct year, 991) records the event
rather more succinctly: 'Ealdorman Byrhtnoth was killed at Maldon' (*wæs
Brihtnoð ealdorman ofslegen at Mældune*).

This battle owes its fame not to the *Chronicle* accounts but to a poem known as *The Battle of Maldon*. The poem survives in fragmentary form in an eighteenth-century transcript. The medieval manuscript from which it was copied was destroyed in the Cotton Library fire of 1731, the same fire that left the edges of the *Beowulf* manuscript singed. Of the poem, 325 lines survive; neither the beginning nor the end is preserved. The verse is in standard Old English alliterative form and it tells the story of the battle in traditional poetic diction and style. Byrhtnoth is cast as the war-hardy and generous Germanic leader, a 'protector of warriors' (*hæleða hleo*, line 74) and a 'treasure-giver' (*sincgyfan*, line 278; *beahgifan*, line 290). His followers are a loyal 'comitatus' – a band of noble warriors who, in return for the wealth, protection and guidance offered by their leader, are prepared to fight to the death in defence of – or revenge for – their lord's life and who have committed themselves to him with public vows of loyalty. At the onset of battle, Byrhtnoth positions himself 'among those people where it most pleased him to be, where he knew his household companions to be most loyal' (*mid leodon þær him leofost wæs, þær he his heorðwerod holdost wiste*, lines 23–4). A number of these individuals are named in what survives of the poem. We are told of the vows that they have made to Byrhtnoth (lines 15, 213, 290); his past generosity to them and their less faithful companions (lines 188, 196–7); and of the to-the-death devotion that this inspires. After Byrhtnoth's death, 'they all intended then to do one of two things, / to lose their lives or to avenge their friend' (*hi woldon þa ealle oðer twega, lif forlætan oððe leofne gewrecan*, lines 207–8).

This kind of reciprocal relationship is described in some detail in Tacitus's *The Germany* (*Germania*), a Roman historian's account of the continental Germanic tribes from around 98 AD. Tacitus's description pertains to the warrior society of this early period up to Age of Migrations (roughly 400–600 AD). Its ethos of unswerving loyalty and commensurate reward – the 'heroic code' – underlies Old English poems such as *Beowulf*, *Widsith*, *Waldere* and *The Finnsburh Fragment* (see Chapter 4), all of which narrate events that are supposed to have taken place during this period, although they were written into their surviving manuscripts in the late tenth and early eleventh centuries. The events that *Maldon* describes, by way of contrast, occurred during the late tenth century, shortly before the poem was composed (which, at the very latest, was only a few decades after the battle, and most likely within a few years of it). The *Maldon* poet uses the lord-comitatus image not because it accurately represents the historical situation of Byrhtnoth and his men, but because it raises them to the level of the semi-mythological heroes that are celebrated in *Beowulf* and the other heroic

Plate 11 A symbol for the Gospel of St John in the Book of Durrow is emblematic of the cultural vision which took place in the British Isles: the form of the exotic lion is based upon that of the more familiar wild boar. Both animals were totemic of princely power (courtesy of Trinity College Library, Dublin)

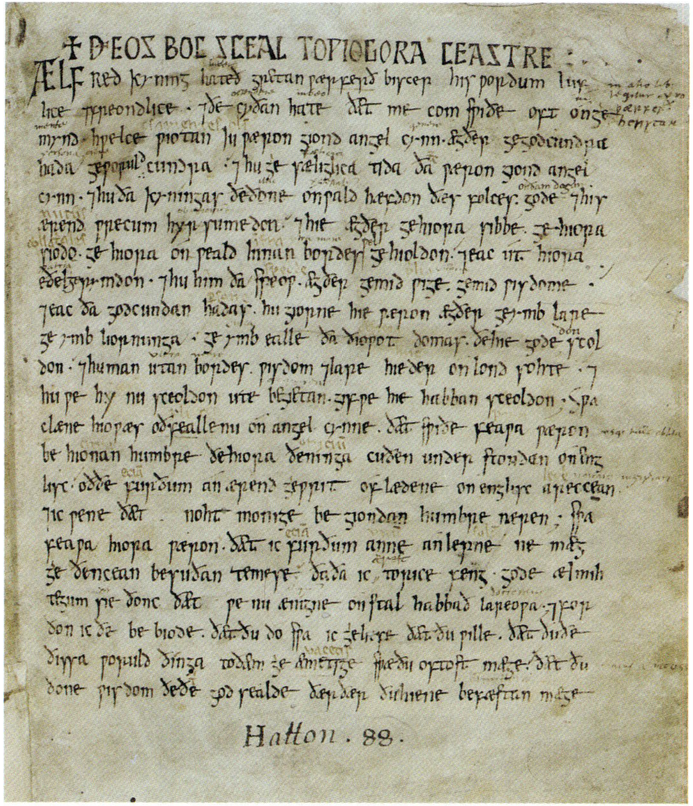

Plate 12 King Alfred's Preface to his translation of Gregory's *Pastoral Care* (courtesy of the Bodleian Library, University of Oxford, MS Hatton 20, fol. 1r)

Plate 13 King Alfred's Jewel (courtesy of the Ashmolean Museum, Oxford)

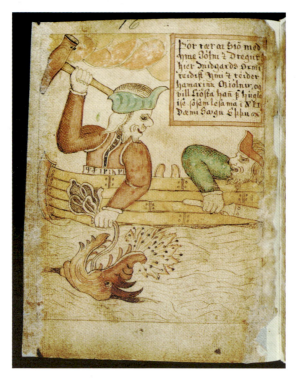

Plate 14 Þórr rising with the giant Hymir to catch the World Serpent. From Melsted's Edda (courtesy of Árni Magnússon Institute, Iceland)

Plate 15 Óðinn steals the mead of poetry in bird shape, from Melsted's Edda (courtesy of the Árni Magnússon Institute, Iceland)

Plate 16 Arthur Rackham's illustration of Freyja from 1911 to Wagner's *Das Rheingold* (courtesy of Mary Evans Picture Library)

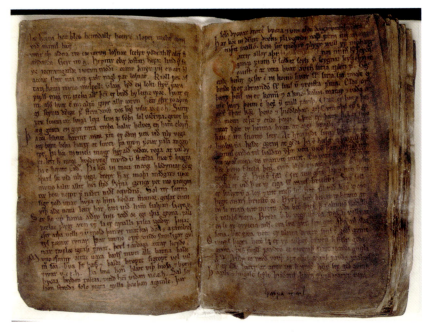

Plate 17 Codex Regius of the *Poetic Edda* (courtesy of the Árni Magnússon Institute, Iceland)

Plate 18 An Icelandic sitting-room at the beginning of the nineteenth century by Auguste Meyer (author's private collection)

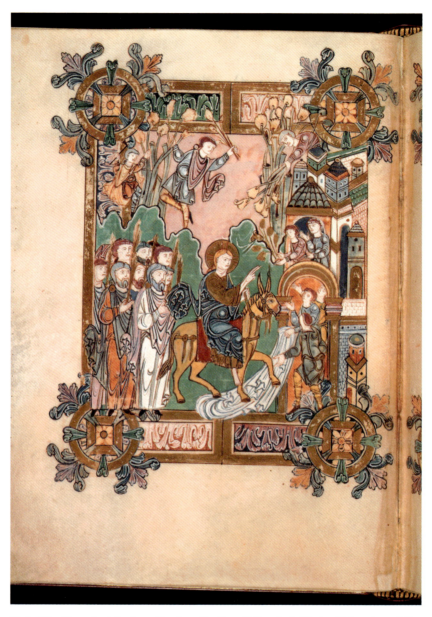

Plate 19 The entry into Jerusalem from the *Benedictional* of Æthelwold (courtesy of the British Library)

Plate 20 Elephant-like creatures from *The Return of the King* (dir. Peter Jackson 2002, courtesy of the British Film Institute)

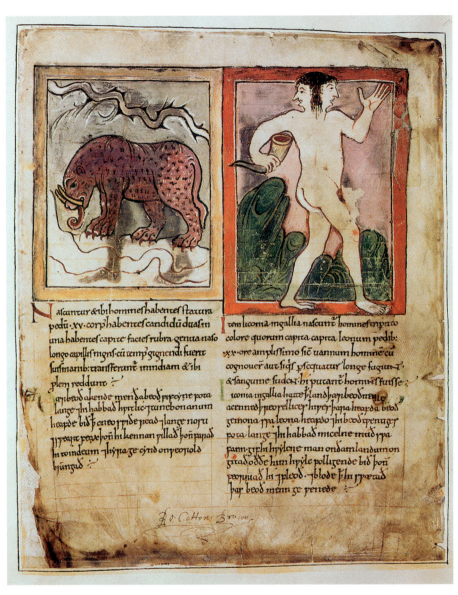

Plate 21 An elephant and a two-headed man in the *Marvels of the East* (courtesy of the British Library, Cotton Tiberius B. v; 11th century)

poems. The poet idealises his warriors, makes them larger than life. Some of the strengths that he bestows on them are more credible than others. We can believe in his portrait of Byrhtnoth as a responsible and charismatic leader, one who 'rode and instructed, told the soldiers how they should form up and hold the position and asked that they should hold their shields properly, firmly with their fists, and not be at all afraid' (*rad and rædde, rincum tæhte hu hi sceoldon standan and þone stede healdan, and bæd þæt hyra randan rihte heoldon, fæste mid folman, and ne forhtedon na*, lines 18–21), and who thanked, encouraged and urged on his men in the heat of battle (lines 127–8).

After all, the historical Byrhtnoth had assumed the position of ealdorman in 956 and so had enjoyed a position of great responsibility for the best part of 35 years before he met his death at Maldon. 'The military man was experienced' (*Frod was se fyrdrinc*, line 140), as the poet tells us. We may be less inclined to give credence to his eight-line 'death bed' speech, delivered after his arm is damaged and before he is cut down by 'heathen slaves' (*hæðene scealcas*, line 181), in which he thanks God for all the worldly joys he has experienced and asks for his soul's safe transport to heaven in words that echo the liturgical Latin of the Office for the Dead (lines 173–80). Having said that, however, there is good reason to believe that the individuals so carefully named did indeed fight loyally for their lord and for England. Some of the men bear Scandinavian names, others unusual names and, on more than one occasion, the poet distinguishes between two men of the same name – none of this is likely to have resulted from a list of invented heroes. The *Maldon* poet was celebrating and commemorating the bravery and loyalty of specific individuals, some of whom have been identified with reasonable confidence. By way of contrast, we may be less confident that Ælfwine, son of Ælfric, took some time out to proclaim his noble Mercian lineage and to declare that his fellow Mercians would not have reason to taunt him for cowardice, for leaving his lord dead behind him, when he got home; and less confident that Offa, Leofsunu, Dunnere and Byrhtwold in reality added their voices to his, each essentially repeating his commitment to die rather than to survive his dead lord. Two lines spoken by Byrhtwold, the final warrior to give voice to his noble sentiments, succinctly encapsulate the heroic ideal and are – with good reason – among the most famous in the Old English corpus:

'Hige sceal þe heardra,   heorte þe cenre,
mod sceal þe mare,   þe ure mægen lytlað.' (*The Battle of Maldon*, lines 312–13)

'The spirit must be the firmer, the heart the bolder,
courage must be the greater as our strength diminishes.'

The *Maldon* poet is not attempting to recreate the last hours of the men's lives, but to reinvent them so that his heroes of unquenchable courage meet fitting ends. We are not reading about the specifics of this particular battle, but about the timeless values of heroism as enshrined in the Old English literary tradition and in other heroic literatures. As Beowulf utters his boast ('When I was younger, I had great triumphs'; Heaney 1999: 15), so does Byrhtnoth ('here stands . . . an earl of unstained reputation'). As Beowulf demonstrates (at Unferth's expense) that his verbal skills match his ability to slay troublesome monsters, so Byrhtnoth wields his vaunting words wittily, declaring that the Vikings shall be paid not with the silver that they have requested, but 'with spears as tribute, deadly point and tried swords, payment in war-gear which will be of no benefit to you in battle' ('*to gafole garas . . . , ættynne ord and ealde swurd, þe heregeatu þe eow æt hilde ne deah'*, lines 46–8), playing on the double meaning of *heregeatu*, which denotes both war gear and tribute. The characteristics and behaviour of Byrhtnoth and his men can easily be compared to those of Beowulf and to a countless number of other heroes from different times, places and cultures.

For every hero, we have a villain and in the *Battle of Maldon* the villains come not only in the guise of the Viking 'wolves of slaughter' (*wælwulfas*, lines 96) but also in the guise of disloyal retainers who are not inclined to follow their lord's example and die on the battlefield. The bravery of Ælfwine, Offa, Leofsunu and the rest contrasts with the cowardly behaviour of Godric, Godwine and Godwig, the sons of Odda (lines 185–97). After Byrhtnoth's death, 'those who did not want to be there', the poet tells us, 'turned from the battle' (*bugon þa fram beadwe þe þær beon nolde*, line 185). Godric flees from the battlefield on Byrhtnoth's horse and 'too many men believed . . . that it was our lord' (*wende þæs formoni man . . . þæt wære hit ure hlaford*, lines 239–40). That we should read this as a shocking violation of the heroic code is underscored by the poet reminding us, at the moment of Godric's horseback flight, that Byrhtnoth 'had often made him a gift of many a horse' (*mænigne oft mear gesealde*, line 188). 'It was not right', the poet solemnly declares (*hit riht ne wæs*, line 190).

With Godric's behaviour we are offered one explanation of the battle's disastrous outcome – the actions of the many who believe he is Byrhtnoth results in a fragmented army (*folc totwæmed*, line 241) – but the poet gives us others, too. The all-round untrustworthiness of the Vikings is one, of course. At the outset of the battle, the 'heathens' (lines 55, 181) are situated on an island in the River Blackwater (then called the *Pante*, line 68), which was then and is now linked to the mainland by a narrow causeway (*bricge*, line 74). Following Byrhtnoth's cross-river – presumably shouted – promise of war trappings as 'tribute', the English and Viking armies face each other across the Blackwater, each prevented by the high tide from reaching the other (lines 64–5) but with the occasional well-aimed arrow fatally reaching its target (line 71). The poet has Byrhtnoth position Wulfstan, Ælfhere and Maccus on the causeway and these three men successfully prevent any Viking advance. When faced with such 'unrelenting guardians of the causeway' (*bricgweardas bitere*, line 85), the Vikings show their true colours. They reject straightforward 'honest' battle in favour of devious scheming: 'the hateful visitors began to use guile' (*ongunnon lytegian þa laðe gystas*, line 86).

Exactly what this 'guile' or deception might be is difficult to say, but it seems to refer to the Vikings asking for safe passage across the causeway. It may be that their gift of the gab is what is referred to here or perhaps their cunning lies in the fact that they are deviously appealing to Byrhtnoth's sense of fair play. The end result, however, is that Byrhtnoth allows them to cross the causeway and to gain 'too much land' (*landes to fela*, line 90). From a strategic point of view it is difficult to account for Byrhtnoth's decision. The poet tells us that he did it *for his ofermode* (line 89) and these three words have been the subject of much debate. *Ofermod* is used elsewhere in the Old English corpus and it usually means 'pride', one of the seven deadly sins. Given that the poet elsewhere presents Byrhtnoth in an encomiastic fashion as a good and wise leader and an exemplary Christian (of the militant variety), it is difficult to imagine that he dispatches his hero to eternal damnation. Where some scholars and translators stick to the orthodox translation (pride), others have suggested for *ofermod* a wider range of meanings based on context – excessive bravery and excessive belligerence being perhaps the most frequently suggested definitions. Byrhtnoth has, after all, declared himself ready and willing for a fight (lines 54–8). Whatever we think of the ealdorman's actions, the poet makes it clear that he understands the consequences of his actions:

'God ana wat
hwa þære wælstowe   wealdan mote.' (lines 94–5)

'God alone knows
who will control the battlefield'

The Vikings' control of the battlefield at Maldon in 991 not only deprived England of one of its most esteemed leaders, but also occasioned, at least in part, the first of Æthelred's many attempts to replace military encounters with the payment of 'Danegeld'. If the Vikings could not be defeated on the battlefield, they were to be bought off with English silver. It was at around this time that Ælfric wrote his *Life of St Edmund* and the account of a royal leader's decision to meet the early Viking challenge with a refusal to fight can profitably be read alongside the decision to meet this later challenge with money rather than battle. Ælfric offers his audience (and his high-standing patron, Ealdorman Æthelweard of Wessex) a saintly precedent for a more pacific means of dealing with the renewed Scandinavian threats than that espoused by Alfred and his children and grandchildren.

Danegeld: the English pay up

Between 991 and 1014 the English surrendered thousands of pounds of gold and silver to the Vikings. A 'pound' meant weight in old measure and from that came to mean a unit of currency: so here it means both. Æthelred's mints were busy churning out coins with which to pay them – the £10,000 payment which sufficed in 991 had increased to £48,000 in 1012 and it carried on rising. The Viking army that had enjoyed success at Maldon remained in England until 1005, although it was no longer led by Sveinn Forkbeard or Óláfr Tryggvason. At times it accepted payment in return for keeping other armies at bay, at other times it raided and ravaged the land. Two further forces arrived to be richly rewarded for plaguing England's inhabitants, but the stakes were certainly raised with the return of Sveinn Forkbeard in 1013. His activities forced Æthelred and his family to take refuge with his brother-in-law, the Duke of Normandy. Sveinn had achieved his conquest of England, but his hard-won status as ruler of England was short lived. He died early in 1014 and Æthelred returned to drive out Sveinn's son, Knútr. In Old English the son's name was 'Cnut' (i.e. Canute).

This was a desperate time for the English, portrayed in memorable fashion by Wulfstan, archbishop of York, in his *Sermon of the Wolf to the English* (*Sermo Lupi ad Anglos*; Latin *lupus* 'wolf' was Wulfstan's pen name):

> Ne dohte hit nu lange inne ne ute, ac wæs here and hete on gehwilcan ende oft and gelome, and Engle nu lange eal sigelease and to swyþe geyrigde þurh Godes yrre; and flotmen swa strange þurh Godes þafunge þæt oft on gefeohte an feseð tyne, and hwilum læs, hwilum ma, eal for urum synnum.

> For a long time now nothing has gone well either at home or abroad, but there has been devastation and persecution in every district time and again,
> and for a long time the English have been utterly defeated and too thoroughly disheartened through God's anger; and the pirates so strong with God's consent that often one puts ten to flight in battle, and sometimes less, sometimes more, all because of our sins.

Like Alcuin and Alfred before him, Wulfstan interprets the Viking incursions as God's punishing the English for their many sins. Many sins indeed – *The Sermon of the Wolf* reads like a catalogue of iniquities and their corresponding disasters and humiliations. Wulfstan presents them within an eschatological framework. The first sentence of his sermon informs us that 'the world is in haste and the end approaches' (*ðeos worold is on ofste, and hit nealæcð þam ende*). The deteriorating standards dwelt on by Wulfstan precede, prefigure and indeed will perhaps culminate in the reign of Antichrist, which the writer indirectly associates with Danish conquest. Wulfstan was preaching this to the English after Æthelred's return from Normandy in 1014, 'when the Danes persecuted them most', as the sermon's Latin rubric informs us. Wulfstan's impassioned call for repentance and increased worship of God was not new. He had been responsible for a number of Æthelred's law codes and these too had included pleas for the honouring of God's law as well those of the king in order to secure peace and security against the Vikings. None of these codes, however, has the sense of urgent desperation that is to be found in the extraordinary *Sermon of the Wolf* (see further Chapter 14).

Cnut returned in 1015 to campaign against first Æthelred and then, after Æthelred's death in April 1016, his son Edmund, 'called Ironside because of his bravery' (*Irensid . . . geclypod for his snellscipe*; MS D, 1057). A detailed account of his campaign is given in the *Chronicle* and in particular of the part played by the double-crossing ealdorman Eadric Streona, who vowed allegiance variously to Edmund and to Cnut and whose treacherous actions set the seal on Cnut's important victory at *Assandun* (18 October 1016). Following this battle, Edmund and Cnut came to terms, with Edmund's rule restricted to Wessex, and Cnut becoming king of 'Mercia' – all of England north of the Thames. When Edmund died just over a month later, Cnut assumed the throne of all England. Eadric Streona received his comeuppance in 1017, when Cnut had him executed in London.

The Danes rule England: King Cnut

Despite Wulfstan's dire predictions and his apocalyptic association of Danish rule with the reign of Antichrist, Cnut's reign (1016–35) is generally held to be one of the most successful of all pre-Conquest kings of England. The *Chronicle*'s annals for these years are scanty, and after the litany of the woes which made up its account of Æthelred's reign it is easy to understand how this can be taken to signify prosperous stability. Wulfstan himself was a key operator in Cnut's government, working towards a peace settlement between English and Danes and drafting Cnut's laws in the same way as he had drafted Æthelred's. Under Cnut, England's manuscript culture continued to thrive. The king and his new wife Emma, the politically astute second wife of the late King Æthelred, were generous patrons of religious institutions, but it was not only English and Latin literary culture that benefited from their munificence.

Cnut's court in Winchester became an important centre for the production of skaldic poetry. The king may have striven to present himself as an English monarch *par excellence*, but his northern roots were clearly of the utmost importance to him and it seems that Winchester was very much on the map for touring Icelandic skalds (Frank 1994; Townend 2002). There, the king of England's Danish heritage was celebrated – he was hailed as *Skjǫldungr*, i.e. 'Scylding' (as in the Scyldings of *Beowulf*) and his poets presented him not as protector of the English but protector of the Danes. His conquest of England was described in traditionally bloody skaldic terms as an occasion on which he 'gladdened the mew of the swordman [the raven, one of the beasts of battle]' (*mǫ reifðir sverðmans*; in Hallvarðr háreksblesi's poem *Knútsdrápa*). In other words, Cnut fed the raven with the corpses of English warriors. Perhaps the most explicit statement of conquest is to be found in a poem by Sighvatr Þórðarson, in which he records that: Cnut soon slew the sons of Æthelred, or else drove them out of the land' (*senn sonu sló, hvern ok þó, Aðalráðs, eða út flæmdi, Knútr*). As these poems were most likely recited at Winchester, the seat of the West Saxon royal line which had produced Æthelred and his exiled sons, it is safe to assume that tact was not a virtue prized in skalds. Skaldic poetry's arcane diction and tortuous syntax most likely rendered the verse on Cnut incomprehensible to an England audience and it was just as well – they are unlikely to have savoured the content if they had understood it. There is one aspect of the verse, however, which may well have met with English approval and that is its depiction of Cnut as a Christian king. (Cnut was not a convert but had been born into the Christian faith – kings of Denmark had been Christian since 965.) Skaldic poetry is inescapably indebted to rich pagan mythological traditions, but while references to the gods, giants and valkyries of Norse mythology pepper the verse on Cnut, his poets nevertheless emphasise his Christianity. He is 'under heaven the foremost prince' (*und himnum . . . hǫfuðfremstr jǫfurr*; Sighvatr's *Knútsdrápa*). He 'protects the land as does the Lord of all the splendid hall of the mountains [heaven]' (*verr jǫrð sem ítran alls dróttinn sal fjalla*; Hallvarðr's *Knútsdrápa*). The Viking who finally conquered England was not one of the chronicler's hated pagans but a Christian who went on pilgrimages to Rome and who was 'close to [St] Peter' (*klúss Pétrusi*; Sighvatr's *Knútsdrápa*). Even Alcuin would have approved.

With Cnut installed as king of England (and Denmark and indeed of Norway and parts of Sweden for a time), it is possible to draw to a close a narrative of the Vikings in England and there are merits in ending such a chapter with Cnut's accession and a discussion of skaldic verse. First, the Danish conquest is often overlooked in favour of the second, more revolutionary conquest of the eleventh century, that of the Normans. Second, the skaldic tradition is not usually considered as part of England's literary heritage (at least, not usually in textbooks), but the skaldic verse composed or recited in Anglo-Saxon England deserves its place alongside Old English and Latin texts. The stereotypical English or American person may be monoglot, but his or her literary heritage is most definitely not.

Translations and texts

The standard editions of the Chronicle manuscripts are:

MS A: Bately, Janet M., ed. (Cambridge, 1986) *The Anglo-Saxon Chronicle, A Collaborative Edition. Volume 3, MS A.*

MS B: Taylor, Simon, ed. (Cambridge, 1983) *The Anglo-Saxon Chronicle, A Collaborative Edition. Volume 4, MS B.*

MS D: Cubbin, G.P., ed. (Cambridge, 1996) *The Anglo-Saxon Chronicle, A Collaborative Edition. Volume 6, MS D.*

MS E: Irvine, Susan, ed. (Cambridge, 2004) *The Anglo-Saxon Chronicle, A Collaborative Edition. Volume 7, MS E.*

There is also:

Abbo of Fleury: *Passio Sancti Eadmundi Regis et Martyris*, in *Three Lives of Saints*, Winterbottom, Michael, ed. (Toronto, 1972) (reproduced in Szarmach 2003). This is the standard edition of Abbo's Latin *Life of St Edmund.*

Dobbie, E.V.K., *The Anglo-Saxon Minor Poems*, Anglo-Saxon Poetic Records 6 (New York, 1942). Contains standard editions of *Brunanburh, The Capture of the Five Boroughs* and *The Battle of Maldon.*

Fell, Christine, trans. and ed., revised edn (London, 1983) *Egils saga.*

Frank, Roberta, 'King Cnut in the Verse of his Skalds', in *The Reign of Cnut,* Rumble, Alexander R., ed. (Manchester, 1994), pp. 106–24. Very good on the politics of the eleventh century.

Guðnason, Bjarni, ed., *Danakonunga sögur* (Reykjavík, 1982). Includes the standard edition of *Knýtlinga saga*, which offers an account of Cnut's reign from the Scandinavian point of view. *But, it's in Icelandic!*

Hill, David and Alexander R. Rumble, eds, *The Defence of Wessex: The Burghal Hidage and Anglo-Saxon Fortifications* (Manchester, 1996). Text and translation of the *Burghal Hidage* and a related text, in a volume that explores all aspects of Wessex' fortified sites. This is an advanced and scholarly book – for enthusiasts only.

Keynes, Simon and Michael Lapidge, trans., *Alfred the Great: Asser's* Life of King Alfred *and Other Contemporary Sources* (Harmondsworth, 1983). An excellent collection of sources, in translation and with copious notes and introductory material, for the reign of King Alfred.

Mitchell, Bruce and Fred C. Robinson, *A Guide to Old English*, 6th edn (Oxford, 2001). A standard textbook with a selection of texts including Ælfric's *Life of St Edmund*.

Page, R.I., *Chronicles of the Vikings: Records, Memorials and Myths* (London, 1995). Many texts in translation from the period and later. Everything a Viking needs to know.

Scragg, D.G., ed., *The Battle of Maldon, AD 991* (Oxford, 1991). A collection of essays published on the 1000–year anniversary of the battle. The volume covers both literary and historical approaches and includes a text and translation of *The Battle of Maldon*.

Swanton, Michael J., *Anglo-Saxon Prose* (London, 1975). A useful collection of prose texts in modern English translation, including Ælfric's *Life of Edmund* (pp. 97–103) and his letter to brother Edward (p. 29), the treaty of Alfred and Guthrum (pp. 4–5) and Wulfstan's *Sermo Lupi* (pp. 116–22).

Swanton, Michael J., trans., *The Anglo-Saxon Chronicle* (London, 1996). This has got all the vernacular *Chronicles* in translation plus a huge amount of learning.

Szarmach, Paul, ed., *Edmund of East Anglia* (2003) (www.wmich.edu/medieval/research/rawl/edmund/index.html). This website gives texts and translations (of varying quality) of Ælfric's *Life of St Edmund* and Abbo of Fleury's *Passio Sancti Edmund* and reproduces Whitelock 1969 (see Further reading). The website is structured so that the different versions of the story can be viewed alongside each other and is therefore an excellent tool for comparative study.

Whitelock, Dorothy, *English Historical Documents, c. 500–1042* (London, 1955). A comprehensive collection of documents, in translation, pertaining to Anglo-Saxon England. Unfortunately, now out of print, but available in many libraries.

Whitelock, Dorothy, ed. and rev., *Sweet's Anglo-Saxon Reader in Prose and Verse*, 15th edn (Oxford, 1967). A collection of OE texts for beginning undergraduates, including Alfred's Preface to the Pastoral Care, Wulfstan's *Sermo Lupi* and *The Battle of Maldon*.

Further reading

Bately, Janet M., 'The Compilation of the Anglo-Saxon Chronicle Once Again', *Leeds Studies in English*, new series 16 (1985), pp. 7–26.

Bately, Janet M., *The Anglo-Saxon Chronicle: Texts and Textual Relationships* (Reading, 1991).

Cameron, Angus, comp. (Toronto, 2003) *Dictionary of Old English in Electronic Form A–F*. The first CD-ROM of this fantastic new research tool, the result of many years of lexicographical work.

Clark, Cecily, 'The Narrative Mode of *The Anglo-Saxon Chronicle* before the Conquest', in *England Before the Conquest: Studies in Primary Sources Presented to Dorothy Whitelock*, Clemoes, Peter and Kathleen Hughes, eds (Cambridge, 1971), pp. 215–35.

Cooper, Janet, ed., *The Battle of Maldon: Fiction and Fact* (London and Rio Grande, 1993). The second of two volumes of essays published in response to the 1000-year anniversary of the battle. The first is Scragg (1991).

Haywood, John, *The Penguin Historical Atlas of the Vikings* (Harmondsworth, 1995). A well-illustrated introduction to Viking activity in Scandinavia and elsewhere, notable for its excellent maps.

Keynes, Simon, 'The Vikings in England, *c.* 790–1016', in *The Oxford Illustrated History of the Vikings*, Sawyer, Peter, ed. (Oxford, 1997), pp. 48–82. This offers a good overview of the activities of the Vikings in England from the perspective of a distinguished historian.

Lapidge, Michael, John Blair, Simon Keynes and Donald Scragg, eds (Oxford, 1999). *The Blackwell Encyclopedia of Anglo-Saxon England*. This contains short articles on every imaginable aspect of Anglo-Saxon England – the entries yield a wealth of information presented concisely and with recommendations for further reading.

Richards, Julian D., *The Vikings: A Very Short Introduction* (Oxford, 2005). Does exactly what it says on the tin.

Sawyer, Peter, *The Age of the Vikings* (London, 1975). An influential publication which, famously, plays down the numbers of Danes involved.

Townend, Matthew, *Language and History in Viking Age England: Linguistic Relations between Speakers of Old Norse and Old English*, Studies in the Early Middle Ages 6 (Turnhout, 2002). The definitive study of how Vikings and Anglo-Saxons communicated.

Whitelock, Dorothy, 'Fact and Fiction in the Legend of Saint Edmund', *Proceedings of the Suffolk Institute of Archaeology* 31 (1969), pp. 217–33. This article assesses what historical truth we can glean from the various accounts of Edmund's martyrdom.

CHAPTER 12

Viking religion: Old Norse mythology

Terry Gunnell

When the first shocked accounts of the Viking raids on Anglo-Saxon England began to reverberate across Europe in the summer of 793 after a gang of violent Nordic youths equipped with axes and swords had appeared out of the sea to descend on the monastery of Lindisfarne, the horror was clearly not limited to the fact that the attackers were foreign, warlike and effectively sea borne. Writers regularly emphasised the fact that the new aggressors were 'pagans' (*pagani*) or 'heathens' (*hæðenan*), enemies of the Church.

But what was so horrific about their being heathen? Essentially, the writers were well aware that these newcomers did not believe in the same single God that was worshipped by the British, Irish and Frankish Christians and had little respect for the symbols that united these peoples and connected them to their rulers. On the contrary, it was clear that their view of the world harked back to various religious beliefs that the Church had been doing its level best to eradicate among the earlier Anglo-Saxon settlers of Britain: beliefs that were connected to the landscape of the 'barbarian' east rather than the classical south; beliefs that were closely tied up with natural forces and personal honour, which were shaped by the individual or his family rather than the centralised distant authorities. Even more problematic was the fact that, unlike the Christian religion, these beliefs were not codified in a single book; they lived and flourished in the oral tradition and as such were relatively fluid and changeable around a general (if variable) core of central names and ideas. The new organised Christian religion based on south-eastern philosophy was thus facing an apparently disorganised religious *system* that was closely tied up with the elements. Worst of all was the fact that the god that guided one shipload of Vikings might not be the same god that guided the next. For the Christians, everything about this new assault represented chaos. To some degree, it was like a Punk or Goth assault on a Moonie centre.

The religious beliefs of the new invaders were closely related to those once held by the various Anglo-Saxon peoples, many of whom had come from southern Scandinavia themselves. Many of the new Viking raiding parties (and later armies) originated from flat plains and islands of Denmark, like the earlier Angles and Jutes. Others had spiritual and family connections to the warrior societies of southern Sweden that had given birth to the character and culture of *Beowulf*.

Diversity of Germanic heathen beliefs

Most of the Vikings chasing monks up monastery paths in the ninth to eleventh centuries would have known the names of deities such as Óðinn (Old English Woden), Frigg, Þórr (Thor), Freyr and Freyja. By way of contrast, their understanding of what these figures were would have varied depending on their upbringing and home environment. Many of the Norse raiders, especially those that later took over the northern parts of England, Scotland and Ireland, came from the cramped and mountainous fjords of western Norway. This was an area the Anglo-Saxons later established close connections with, when they helped King Óláfr Tryggvason (ruled 995–1000) and later King Óláfr 'the Stout', later 'the Saint', Haraldsson (ruled 1015–30) to convert the local heathen communities. Initially, the beliefs of all these peoples, whether Danes, Anglo-Saxons and Norwegians, were bound up with the natural forces they faced in their day-to-day lives. If we bear this in mind, we understand the natural diversity of the religious worldviews of those living in Denmark, in the hills of southern Norway or Sweden or in the winter darkness and tundra of the far north, where people regularly encountered the shamanistic beliefs of 'Sami' or Lappish nomadic hunters.

Until quite recently, many scholars have suggested that the northern peoples had a largely systematised religion with an accepted hierarchy of gods (centring around the figure of Óðinn) and that they had a generally agreed body of mythology that was known throughout the Viking Age and probably for some time before that, all the way across the Nordic world. This approach was highly misleading. It has its roots in the work of the Brothers Grimm, grammarians and folktale gatherers who also, in the early nineteenth century, were determined to underline the earlier existence of a shared worldview that united not only the Germans themselves but also the Germanic peoples as a whole. The German states at the time of the Grimms was sandwiched between the French and Russian empires. Many Germans felt ideologically opposed to the Catholic church, the religion of Germany's main national rivals. The fact that similar myths, folktales and traditions seemed to be known in the other countries with Germanic languages, such as Scandinavia and the British Isles, was proof to the Grimms of some shared cultural features with very early roots. Furthermore, Óðinn, who was well known in German folklore and place names, was also called the 'All-father' (*Alfǫðr*), and a god of victory in Icelandic (and thus also Norwegian) mythology. This nomenclature appeared to confirm still further the existence of a common Germanic religion reaching far to the north. This simultaneously underlined the existence of a new, widespread, if locally based, mythology that was both colourful and influential.

The idea that this new Germanic mythology and worldview should be seen as a single, organised Germanic 'religion', was nonetheless more related to the overall political agenda and the model of the organised Christian church than it was to the disorganised folkloric world that the Grimms were discovering elsewhere in their studies. In folklore, 'local variation' was and has always been the keyword. Variation, however, was not a very useful means of unifying nations, even if it was clearly also the key word of the pre-Christian system of beliefs that was known across the enormous expanse of land that made up the Nordic countries.

Sources for Viking and Anglo-Saxon paganism

What, then, do we know about the religious beliefs of the Vikings and, thus, indirectly about the beliefs of the pre-Christian Anglo-Saxons that preceded them? In general it might be said that information has come down to us from both literary and archaeological sources. These data suggest an exciting amalgamation of three or more systems of belief. Central to the extant written accounts is the male-oriented 'religion' of the Norse sky gods, better known as Æsir. The cults of these deities had moved up Scandinavian coasts from southern Denmark, along with the mindset of the mobile, land-encroaching, hierarchical warrior band, each of which seems to have focused on a single semi-divine ruler. This type of warrior cult probably took root in the more northerly Scandinavian regions in around 500 AD. Another northern belief system looks far older. This is the apparently land and fertility-based 'religion' of the *Vanir* gods, which seems to have had its centre in the southeast of Sweden prior to the arrival of the Æsir. Tenth- to thirteenth-century sources imply that the Vanir centred around the figures of Njǫrðr, god of the sea, and his two children Freyr ('lord') and Freyja ('lady'), god and goddess of sex, fertility and procreation as well as success-ful harvests. Existing alongside both Vanir and Æsir throughout the Viking period was a third system, the shamanistic 'religion' of the Sami and other so-called 'Finno-Ugric' hunters of northern Norway and Sweden. As we saw in Chapter 4 (p. 109), Vǫlundr, the Norse Wayland the Smith, is defined as a kind of Sami craftsman in the Eddic poem *The Lay of Wayland*. The Sami people were in close contact with other Nordic peoples throughout the Viking Age. Behind all of these religious systems, however, are certain other earlier layers of belief like those reflected in the mystical Bronze Age rock carvings of gods and men found particularly in southwest Sweden (*c.* 1500–500 BC). Broadly speaking, we could call the Vanir system a relic of these old Bronze Age cults, the Æsir system a reflection of the early European Iron Age.

As noted already, the key sources of material about these beliefs are of two kinds. On one side there are archaeological finds which are still regularly coming to light, aided by modern building work like that at present happening around Stockholm and especially Gamla Uppsala in Sweden. According to *The History of the Church of the Bishops of Hamburg* (*Gesta Hammaburgensis ecclesiae pontificum*), by Adam of Bremen in the 1070s, huge outdoor festivals took place in Uppsala in pre-Christian times. To some extent the archaeology would confirm this, although the problem with such archaeological material is that it lacks labels: its meaning has to be recon-structed from its context. A bearded statuette with a hammer, like that found in Eyrarland, Iceland, does not have to be Þórr. It could just as well be a chess piece. While it may be dated as genuinely pre-Christian, it lacks any explanatory text.

The other type of source regarding Old Norse belief is literary. Here we are particularly fortunate because a number of early texts concerning Old Norse 'religion' were recorded in Iceland and Denmark in the twelfth, thirteenth and fourteenth centuries. Of central importance here is the Prose *Edda* of Snorri Sturluson (1179–1241), which includes two works concerning mythological matters, *The Beguiling of Gylfi* (*Gylfaginning*) and *The Language of Poetry* (*Skáldskaparmál*). These two works were written in stages in the 1220s and 1230s. They were written to provide budding poets in Iceland with the knowledge to compose mythological poems of their own. *The Beguiling of Gylfi* tells most of the Norse myths in prose form, set within a story framework telling how King Gylfi of Sweden set out to discover the magic of a mysterious race of beings called the Æsir who had once been wor-shipped as gods. A welcoming committee of three beings called High, Just as High, and Third tell Gylfi (and us) everything we need to know about

Norse cosmology from the creation of the Norse cosmos to its violent end, in the so-called Ragnarǫk. Of particular value is the fact that the Prose *Edda* contains numerous quotations from an older text, the Poetic *Edda*. Otherwise known as 'Eddic poems' or *Eddukvæði*, this is a collection of 31 anonymous poems about Old Norse gods and heroes which come in the form of monologues, dialogues and third-person accounts. More about this later.

Another feature of the Prose *Edda* is its preservation of skaldic poetry. In *The Language of Poetry*, probably written earlier than *The Beguiling of Gylfi*, Snorri sets out to explain the working of the skaldic kenning on which Old Norse–Icelandic court poetry was based. Skaldic poetry differs from 'Eddic' in that it commonly takes the shape of occasional verse produced in complex metres by poets whose names survive. These verses are otherwise largely preserved as the backbone of the Icelandic family sagas, or Sagas of Icelanders, which we will meet in the following chapter. Many of them are pre-Christian and have a great deal to tell us about the religion of Snorri's heathen ancestors in Iceland and Norway.

Unlike the extant Old English texts, many of the earlier noted Icelandic works in poetry and prose deal directly with heathen 'religion', in their case the Old Norse religion. These take the form both of religious mythology and descriptions of early religious practice. Some of the oldest poetic texts in the Poetic *Edda* and some skaldic poems even seem to have their roots in even earlier texts that may have been used in religious practice. The obvious problem with these texts, however, is that they were written down in Iceland at the earliest in the later eleventh century. In other words, their transcription took place in a largely Christian society around 300 years after 1000, when Christianity was accepted by the Icelanders as their religion. The Icelandic scribes and authors who did the writing were, for the main part, learned Christian writers who had their own agendas in keeping with the time. They were also living in a country which was some distance away from mainland Scandinavia where the old 'religion' had its roots. It is thus questionable whether similar texts to those found in Iceland would have been written in south-eastern Sweden, northern Norway or southern Denmark. Indeed, the one mythological work that comes from Denmark, Saxo Grammaticus' *History of the Danes* (*Gesta Danorum*), shows a number of key differences in emphasis.

Nonetheless, it seems likely that these texts (in both prose and poetry) must have either lived within – or had their roots in – an oral tradition that went back to the 'dark' pre-Christian times. This material was probably altered to some degree as it was passed from person to person in the oral tradition before it was first written down. It then went through some kind of editorial process before it appeared on the 'vellum' or calf-skin sheets in codices which preserved it for us today. It can nonetheless be effectively used alongside other more 'genuine' source materials such as archaeological artefacts, place names and, for example, earlier Latin or Anglo-Saxon texts dealing with the early Norse or Germanic religion. Particularly useful comparative material is found in earlier historical works, some of which are truly ancient. Top of the list here is *The Germany* (*Germania*), written in about 98 AD by the Roman patriot and moral historian Cornelius Tacitus, who also provides a few details about Germanic tribes in his contemporary *Annals of Rome* (*Annales*). Chapter 40 of *The Germany* is especially famous for giving the name 'Nerthus' for a deity said to be worshipped by seven north Germanic tribes including the *Anglii*, ancestors of the Angles who crossed to Britain. This divine name, though applied to a goddess (possibly in error), is the same name as Njǫrðr, father of Freyr and Freyja in the Old Norse Vanir. Tacitus, however, was not the only historian to write about Old Norse religious practice. There are other works by geographers, church fathers and historians, such as Strabo, Jordanes, Procopius, Bede, Alcuin and the earlier mentioned historian of the archbishops of Hamburg–Bremen, Adam of Bremen (writing around 1050–70). The advantage of the later Icelandic and Danish texts is that they provide a potential living voice to add to this earlier, relatively skeletal, historical and archaeological material. The Icelandic and Danish sources give us a chance to breathe the same air as the common Norse warrior or farmer.

To return to the primary texts. If we assess the importance of the later Icelandic and Danish mythological material, four texts are crucial. The most influential is Snorri Sturluson's *Edda*, a compilation which is often treated like a Bible of Old Norse mythology. The Poetic *Edda* is another important work, arguably even more precious than Snorri's Prose *Edda*. Alongside this come the skaldic poems, which were composed especially about kings and historical occurrences by named court poets from Viking times. It is likely that Snorri's writing of the Prose *Edda* saved the Eddic poetry for posterity by inspiring its original collection from the oral tradition. Even then, however, it is a miracle that anything survived, considering that the Poetic *Edda* reaches us mainly in the from of the 'Codex Regius', a phrase-book-sized manuscript which turned up in an Icelandic farmhouse in 1643. Without this manuscript and others like it, such as the four that preserve Snorri's Prose *Edda*, we would have hardly any knowledge of the beliefs of the early Norse peoples at all.

Many of the Old Norse–Icelandic poems were, of course, initially presented orally and seem to take us directly into the living rituals or initiation ceremonies that might have taken place within Viking halls. Particularly powerful in this sense is *The Words of Grimnir* (*Grímnismál*), a monologue in which the god Óðinn, here disguised as 'Grímnir' a travelling wizard, describes himself as being tortured between two fires for eight nights. As he undergoes his ordeal, Óðinn describes for his listeners the world of the gods that his spirit can see as it soars from his body. Many of our main ideas about Old Norse cosmology originate in this poem, which ends with Óðinn revealing his true identity and causing King Geirrøðr, his torturer, to fall on his own sword.

Alongside the Prose and the Poetic *Edda* (and the earlier mentioned skaldic poems) two other important early sources provide us with key material about the Old Norse gods. One is again by Snorri Sturluson, *The Saga of the Ynglings* (*Ynglinga saga*). This saga forms the opening section of a much larger book on the lives of the Norwegian kings, called *The Garland of the World* (*Heimskringla*). The fourth most informative source for Norse mythology is the earlier-mentioned *History of the Danes* (*Gesta Danorum*), which was written in Latin in the early thirteenth century, by the Danish chaplain Saxo Grammaticus. Both *The Saga of the Ynglings* and *The History of the Danes* begin with some account of the gods of earlier times, although their authors follow a medieval academic tradition known as 'euhemerism', whereby mythological accounts are described as history; the gods are said to have been people who were wrongly worshipped as divine. In *Ynglinga saga*, for example, we find Snorri describing Óðinn and the other gods as warrior kings with roots in Asia and thus reaching back to the Trojans.

Óðinn, Norse god of war and poetry

Both Saxo and Snorri imply that Óðinn was the accepted head of an accepted hierarchy of gods. Commonly depicted today as one eyed, with two ravens on his shoulders named Huginn ('endowed with thought') and Muninn ('endowed with memory'), wolves at his feet and a spear in his hand, Óðinn is said to be the father of Þórr ('Thor') and other gods as well. He is also one of the creators of the world, which was made, according to one account, from the body of a primeval giant called Ymir. Óðinn sits in a high seat, seeing over the world, constantly receiving new information about current events from his ravens. According to *The Seeress's Prophecy* (*Vǫluspá*), composed around the time Iceland was converted, Óðinn is also seen as being one of three gods who breathe life into the first human beings (called Askr and Embla), who are found on the borderline territory of the seashore in the form of two lumps of wood. It should be noted that this comparison between human beings and trees runs throughout extant Old Norse poetry. As the ruler of Ásgarðr, the home of the gods, Óðinn is more than a little untrustworthy. Accounts depict him as living on wine alone, being regularly on the move and constantly in touch with the ecstatic 'wild side', be it in the form of illicit sex with giants' daughters, through drink, battle, shape changing, contact with the dead, magic or poetic creation. Saxo, in *The History of the Danes*, depicts 'Othinus' (Óðinn) essentially as a dirty old man, a cheap magician whose only intention is to dupe innocent Danes and especially innocent women. Of particular interest is the fact that Saxo clearly knew other poems than those known by Snorri. It is also evident that he knew relatively little about the Vanir gods (Freyja is unmentioned). In short, Saxo's work effectively underlines what has been said earlier about different beliefs existing in different places. The main pity is that we lack the originals of the material that he translated or rewrote in Latin.

Óðinn was very popular with warriors, but it can never be certain from the extant literature whether he wants his followers carrying out his wishes alive or dead. Alive, they fight countless battles and offer him sacrifice by hanging and spearing the best warriors. Dead, they serve him as part of his regenerated armies in Ragnarǫk, the final battle at the end of the world. The place where these dead warriors eat, drink and sleep, before fighting, dying and being revived each following day, is known as 'Valhǫll' (often mistakenly written as Valhalla, the 'hall of the chosen'). Indeed, it is probably this intimate connection with two worlds, the living and the dead, that has resulted in Óðinn being depicted as having one living eye and one 'dead', even though one later account, in *The Seeress's Prophecy*, suggests that he gave away one eye as a personal sacrifice for greater knowledge.

Over and above Óðinn's central role as the crazed warrior leader of the living and dead, his main association is with poetic creation. Both Snorri, in *The Language of Poetry* (Chapter 6) and the Eddic poem *The Words of the High One* (*Hávamál*, stanzas 104–10) describe how, after a night of sex with Gunnlǫð, a giant's daughter, he steals the poetic mead (a mixture of spittle, blood and honey) from the giants and, in the form of an eagle, flies with it to the world of the gods. The girl's father, Suttungr, pursues him in the shape of an eagle. In his haste, Óðinn loses some of the mead 'backwards'. This accidental dollop of poetic mead, which lands in the world of men, is the source of inspiration for all inferior poets in Middle Earth. The end of this story describes Óðinn's safe arrival in the gods' citadel where he spews out the mead into vats that the Æsir have prepared. From then on the best poets, naturally Óðinn's worshippers, may expect to receive various draughts of 'Soul-Rouser' (Óðrørir) from the war god's mead vat whenever they need his divine guidance in composition. One example of this is Egill Skalla-Grímsson of Borg, in Iceland, is a historical person who refers to his relationship with Óðinn as the 'thief of the Mead of Poetry', in his *On the Loss of Sons* (*Sonatorrek*, c. 960), an elegy on the deaths of two of his sons which appears towards the end of *Egil's Saga* (*Egils saga Skalla-Grímssonar*, Chapter 78; see p. 396).

Elsewhere in *The Words of the High One*, Óðinn describes how he sacrificed himself (to himself) by hanging on a tree with a spear in his side, thereby gaining access to the knowledge of the magical runes, which could only be found within the realms of death. The relevant strophe is particularly powerful:

> Veit ek at ek hekk   vindga meiði á
> 　　　nætr allar níu,
> geiri undaðr   ok gefinn Óðni,
> 　　　sjálfr sjálfum mér,
> á þeim meiði   er manngi veit
> 　　　hvers hann af rótum renn. (*The Words of the High One*, stanza 138)

> I know that I hung on a windy tree
> 　　　nine long nights,
> wounded with a spear, dedicated to Óðinn,
> 　　　myself to myself
> on that tree of which no man knows
> from where its roots run. (Larrington 1996: 34)

Óðinn's connection with poetic creation explains in part why so much attention should have been placed on him by writers like Snorri Sturluson. Snorri was both a poet and a key member of a ruling family, the Sturlungs (*Sturlungar*) which had a mafia-like grip on Iceland until many of them died in battle in northern Iceland in 1238. It can surely come as little surprise either that Óðinn should have been taken as the favourite god of kings and other rulers or of those mercenary warriors who left their families to join the Viking bands or royal armies led by these figures.

Other Norse gods and goddesses

For other people living in the north, however, it seems clear that the Óðinn hegemony did not apply. Comparatively few place names in Norway and Sweden are dedicated to Óðinn (compared to those related to other gods like Freyr, Þórr, Njǫrðr or Freyja); and no mention is made of anyone worshipping him in the thirteenth-century foundation narrative, *The Book of*

Settlements (*Landnámabók*), which provides basic background information on settlers coming to Iceland from Norway and the northwest British Isles in *c.* 870 onwards. Here, as in several other historical accounts, the central figure is another Æsir god, Þórr, whose name is much more common in place names and personal names all over northern Europe (including, in England, place names like Thurstable and Thursoe). Unlike Óðinn, Þórr is never seen as a warrior *leader*, even if he might now be viewed as a good candidate for a course on anger management. Neither is Þórr associated with magic, words or death, apart from a sarcastic remark by Óðinn in a poem that Þórr receives dead slaves. His key role is in working mainly independently to keep natural forces in check, be they in the form of the sea (personified by the Middle Earth sea serpent) or the forces of mountain, ice and snow (personified by the giants). Þórr's name means 'thunder' and he fights giants with a hammer. He is seen as regularly traversing borderlines in a chariot drawn by a couple of bad-tempered goats that he nightly eats and then revives. Central here is the account in the Eddic poem *The Lay of Hymir* (*Hymiskviða*), which describes Þórr fishing for the Middle Earth sea serpent. In another ur-fairy tale account of a visit to another giant, Útgarða-Loki, he wrestles with old age in the form of an old woman, causes tides by drinking the sea (thinking he is drinking from a horn) and lifts the sea serpent (thinking it is a cat). In yet another Eddic poem, *The Lay of Thrymr* (*Þrymskviða*), he has to dress up as a bride (the love goddess Freyja) in order to get his hammer back from a giant. This last story underlines another threat posed by this religious system to Christianity: like the classical Greek religion, it had nothing against laughter serving as part of religious belief.

There is no doubt that for many farmers and sailors, particularly those living in western Norway, Þórr was seen as being the prime, if not the only, god. Apart from Loki, a kind of professional trickster, Þórr is rarely seen as interacting with other gods. For some, in his role as 'the good farmer' (as he is known in later Scandinavian folk belief), Þórr seems to have served as a fertility god, bringing thunder and rain. He is married to Sif ('kindred'), a goddess whose false golden wig replaces hair that was cut off by Loki. This myth has been compared to the cutting of harvest corn. Þórr's connection to weddings in *The Lay of Thrymr* and other later Norwegian ballads and folktales suggests that this role went even further. Some have even seen his hammer as serving a phallic role in ceremonies blessing the bride, as occurs in *The Lay of Thrymr*.

This theme brings us to Freyr, Freyja and Njǫrðr of the Vanir. These gods seem to have very old roots especially in Norway and Sweden. As noted earlier, accounts by Snorri Sturluson, Saxo Grammaticus and Adam of

Bremen, as well as place name evidence, point to some particularly close connections between these gods and the area around Uppsala in Sweden as well as other central kingdoms like the areas around Oslo and Trondheim in Norway. The Eddic poem *The Seeress's Prophecy*, Snorri's Prose *Edda* and *The Saga of the Ynglings* all talk of an ancient 'war' taking place between the Vanir and the Æsir gods which eventually led to a merger. Again, Óðinn and the Æsir seem to have come out best here, even though the Vanir were supposed to win the battle. This story probably reflects certain key changes that seem to have taken place in the practice of Old Norse 'religion' in around 500 AD as outdoor worship and sacrifice like that described by Tacitus (and echoed in the talk of figures like Grendel's mother, the Arthurian Lady of the Lake and Tolkien's Goldberry and Galadriel) came to a gradual end to be replaced by new indoor religious centres (the first move towards churches). It may also reflect earlier religious activity which was once dominated by females being gradually transferred into the hands of male rulers who over time came to control both the religious and the legal spheres. The latter idea might be broadly taken as synonymous with the shift from Bronze Age to Iron Age societies, with the latter more inclined to carry out warfare. But it is also seen, rather more clearly, in the use of the word *goði* ('god-spokesman') for a local magnate or powerbroker in Iceland, Sweden and Denmark. In its coinage and oldest uses, this word shows the chieftain blending his earthly role with that of the religious representative.

Nonetheless, it is evident that for some, Freyr, Freyja and possibly Njǫrðr as well (though his cult is much older) retained central power. Indeed, as we have seen, their names are really only descriptions meaning 'lord' and 'lady' (offering further parallels to Celeborn and Galadriel: indeed Tolkien makes several indirect connections between the Vanir and the elves, following up several hints given in the Old Norse texts). Their regal names underline the central roles that these gods had and also the fact that they were seen by many as being too important to mention by personal name (like the Christian God). Indeed, it is possible that an older Anglian counterpart of Freyr (under the personal name of Ingui or Ing) was the main god of the Germanic invaders in the north of England. 'Ingui' seems to have been the main threat as far as the Roman mission to Anglo-Saxon England was concerned. The arguments on which this idea depend are long and complicated (North 1997). However, they begin with evidence of an earlier tribal name (the *Ingvaeones*) which Tacitus, in *The Germany*, says was the name for peoples in the North Sea Germanic coastal area (approximating to modern Denmark). This is the region from which the Angles, whom Tacitus cites as Nerthus' worshippers in Chapter 40, migrated to Britain. Where Iceland is concerned, it is noteworthy that according to *The Book of Settlements*, Freyr is the only other god apart from Þórr who is said to have been worshipped by the original settlers.

It is noteworthy that Freyr seems to be included in a trio of Swedish gods at the religious centre of Gamla Uppsala, according to *The History of the Church of the Bishops of Hamburg*, by Adam of Bremen. While 'Thor' sits in the middle of their temple, with an armed 'Wodan, that is fury' (*id est furor*) standing to one side, on his other side there is a god named 'Fricco' who appears to be Freyr. Fricco's statue is described by Adam as being equipped 'with a huge phallus' (*cum ingenti priapo*). In general, it is clear that Freyr was viewed by many as having a wide range of functions ranging from connections with war (he is said to be an excellent rider), to the sea (he is supposed to own an wonderful ship that can be folded up) and connected to general human and agricultural fertility. Sometimes associated with the sun, he is also connected with earthly burial (unlike Óðinn who seems to prefer cremation) and 'good crop years and peace' (*ár ok friðr*), both of which were, and still are, the two main priorities for farmers.

A fourteenth-century prose account called *The Tale of Gunnarr Helmingr* (*Gunnars þáttr helmings*) describes how a talking statue of Freyr used to be annually taken around certain settlements in Sweden in a wagon in wintertime accompanied by Freyr's 'wife', a priestess who interpreted his words. Freyr's main purpose here was clearly to bring luck and fertility to the settlements. Support for similar events having actually been practised is found in the shape of certain rich 'ritual' wagons that have been found in archaeological digs at Oseberg in Norway and Dejbjerg in Denmark. Further support comes in Tacitus' much earlier account, which describes how certain tribes carried out similar ceremonies, involving processions that centred around the ritual wagon of the goddess Nerthus.

Understandably, since both Snorri and Saxo were writing some distance from Sweden, there are few recorded myths concerning Freyr. There is, however, a dramatic poem called *The Words of Skírnir* (*Skírnismál*) which is contained with the other Eddic poems and might have roots in living seasonal ritual. This work describes how Freyr, after having spied a beautiful giant girl called Gerðr ('fenced-off land') in the distance when sitting in his high seat, has lapsed into an unholy sulk because he feels that his parents will not approve of the potential relationship. This, of course, is something that is likely to have dire consequences for the world, since, as has been noted, Freyr rules general well-being and fertility. The only way to solve the problem is for Freyr's childhood friend Skírnir (lit. 'shining one') to take on the god's role, borrowing his horse, sword and riches and gallop off to

Jǫtunheimr (the land of the giants) to get Gerðr to agree to an assignation with the god in a grove. This takes time, threats of violence and several runic curses, but eventually succeeds. The world is brought back to rights and the rays of the sun return to the earth.

Quite naturally, the Christian male writers and collectors of the thirteenth century had less interest in, and probably less knowledge of, the goddesses. As a result, we have less information about Freyr's sister, Freyja, a figure that almost certainly lies to some extent behind Tolkien's image of the elven queen, Galadriel. In spite of the lack of information, it can be relatively confidently assumed that Freyja must have been a very powerful deity in mainland Scandinavia (especially Sweden and Norway, if not England and Iceland). As a model of womanhood, she is very different from Frigg, her counterpart among the Æsir. Despite, or because of, her name, Frigg is depicted as a matriarch relegated to staying at home where she serves her philandering warrior husband, Óðinn. Later she weeps for his death and that of her son, Baldr, whose death later represents the first stage towards the final downfall of the gods at Ragnarǫk (see later). Freyja, meanwhile, runs her own hall and chooses her own lovers. She is apparently not averse either to a spot of incest with her brother (another Vanir characteristic, reminiscent of the Egyptian pharaohs) or to sleeping with a trio of dwarfs if it is likely to end in her gaining a beautiful piece of jewellery. One of her identifying symbols is the necklace Brísingamen, of which we have seen an old English version in the *Brosinga mene* of Hama and Eormanric in *Beowulf*, lines 1198–1201 (Chapter 4, p. 111). Freyja was denounced by Christians and Æsir believers alike in the humorous poem *Loki's Flyting* (*Lokasenna*). Nonetheless, she had a large number of place names dedicated to her and is connected with the traditional female spheres of foresight, love, giving birth and death. Apparently, she also ran her own hall of the dead, where she received half of all those who died. Indeed, it may well be that she had close ties with the figure of Hel ('hell'), goddess of the underworld, and the figures of the valkyries (*valkyrjur*), as well as other types of female guardian spirit known in the Norse area in earlier times. Some archaeologists have even argued that the figure buried in the large Oseberg ship now kept in a museum in Oslo could have been both a priestess of Freyja and a ninth-century queen.

These, then, are the main gods and goddesses that the Vikings and their Anglo-Saxon predecessors seem to have actively worshipped when they were depositing bodies and weapons in Danish marshes and lakes in the early Iron Age and celebrating at the large-scale festivals of midwinter, midsummer and the start of winter and summer, which were later deftly transformed by the early spin doctors of the Christian Church into Christmas, St John's Eve, Hallowe'en and Easter.

There were, however, a number of other figures that mentioned several times in Old Norse mythology, figures that may have roots in other earlier or contemporaneous local gods that came to be adopted into the dominant Norse pantheon. We have previously encountered Njǫrðr, Freyr and Freyja, gods who supposedly joined the Æsir as hostages after the Æsir–Vanir cult war. Regarding Njǫrðr, one myth tells of how he found himself in a problem-ridden marriage with a giant's daughter after she was allowed to choose the god that had the most beautiful feet as a husband in recompense for the gods killing her father. The giantess, Skaði, had hoped to choose Baldr because he was allegedly the most beautiful of the gods. She forgot, however, that the god of the sea was bound to have the cleanest, most sparkling toes. The pair's ensuing problems were based on the fact that they could not decide where to set up a permanent abode, since neither could stand the dwelling place of the other. This appears to be yet another myth designed to explain natural phenomena: in this case the changing of the seasons.

Also central for the German tribes at some point in the past (even though little is said about him in later times in the works of either Snorri or Saxo) was the war god Týr (meaning simply 'god'), whose name was used as a translation for that of Mars when the Germanic speakers adopted the Roman system of seven days for the week. The other gods named here were Woden or Óðinn for Wednesday, Thunor or Þórr for Thursday and Frigg for Friday. Týr's name appears mainly in place names in Germany, Denmark and England. His only other extant claim to fame was that according to one myth he rather stupidly offered to put his hand in the mouth of the giant wolf, Fenrir, when the gods were trying to bind the beast that was destined to swallow Óðinn at the end of the world. This proved a bad move. When he realised he was trapped, Fenrir promptly bit off the hand.

Another two central male gods are Heimdallr and Loki. The former, with his horn and excellent hearing (he can hear the grass growing), has the role of the gatekeeper to Ásgarðr, waiting beside the rainbow which some accounts suggest served as a bridge between worlds. As numerous writers have shown, Heimdallr's later adversary, Loki, is one of the most attractive figures in the pantheon, especially for modern-day readers. Loki is the son of a giant named Fárbauti ('fear-beater') and a goddess named Laufey ('leaf-isle'). He is adopted as blood brother to Óðinn and becomes the occasional travelling companion of Þórr. Everything about Loki seems to defy simple classification. He does not just walk on the wild side like Óðinn, he *is* the wild side in all senses of the word: he regularly changes shape, becoming at different times a flea, a seal, a salmon and a female horse. In the last role, he/she gives birth to an Óðinn's eight-legged stallion, Sleipnir. On another occasion, he is said to have fathered the half-decayed figure of Hel, the Middle Earth sea serpent, and the giant wolf, Fenrir. If anything goes wrong in the world of the gods (from Þórr losing his hammer to Sif losing her hair), it is usually because Loki has caused it. Nonetheless, it is questionable whether Loki was initially seen as evil, rather than mischievous, and indeed whether the concept of moral 'evil' existed among the Norse nations in the way that the Christian Church viewed it. It was only in later years, as the Norse people came into ever increasing contact with the Church, that Loki gradually came to take on the attributes of Satan. Thus, Loki is said to cause the death of Baldr by directing Baldr's blind brother Hǫðr to throw a mistletoe spear at him. Baldr had previously secured an immunity from harm from all things living and lifeless – all things barring the mistletoe, however, which was left out of the general oath, as being too young to swear. Baldr now falls dead. For the Norse gods this is like the deaths of J.F. Kennedy, Martin Luther King and Princess Diana rolled into one. Loki is rounded up and punished by being chained below the earth beneath the dripping fangs of a poisonous serpent. His wife, Sigyn, catches the drips in a bowl, but each time she turns to empty it, a drop lands on Loki and he writhes in agony, causing earthquakes for the whole world. Loki, however, is destined to break free. When he does, he is different, more like the Christian idea of Antichrist, leading a horde of monsters to attack the gods at Ragnarǫk, thereby bringing about the end of the world.

As regards other goddesses, there is even less information. Most goddesses come in the form of wives owned by the gods (such as Frigg and Þórr's wife Sif) or desirable objects of kidnap for the giants, such as Freyja or Iðunn. The latter, whose name means 'the renewer', is the subject of another interesting seasonal myth described in the skaldic poem *Harvestlong* (*Haustlǫng*) and later in Snorri's Prose *Edda*. This story tells of how Iðunn is kidnapped by the giant Þjazi, along with her apples of youth which had previously been used by the gods to retain an appearance of youth. They now started aging rapidly and Loki (once again, the original initiator of the problem) is dispatched with Freyja's magical falcon cloak to bring her back in the form of an acorn.

Many of the myths like that just given underline the fact that behind the Old Norse cosmology was a worldview that, like many other religions, centred around the idea of 'us and them', and 'here and there'. The 'them' and the 'there' in this case are represented by the world of the so-called giants or *jǫtnar* (cf. *etins* in English). Some writers, once again following a Christian model, have tried to suggest that these beings were the evil, ugly antithesis of the gods and their main enemies at the final battle of Ragnarǫk. Others, considering the later folklore image of trolls into which the giants were changed over time, seek to suggest that they were stupid or bestial. While there are one or two images of the giants having three heads, for example, the approach just given ignores a number of key features in the Viking approach to the world. Among other things, this appears to have involved the idea that respect be accorded an enemy if he or she deserved it. The giants may thus live on the other side of a natural divide, like a mountain range, but they have very beautiful daughters and cultural objects worth stealing. Like women, they also have a much greater knowledge of the history of the world, past, present and future than their male partners in crime. Naturally, like any other Germanic tribe, they want to steal from their neighbours, but then so do the gods. Both races commonly resort to violence (perhaps the gods more than the giants). The 'jotuns', however, also represent the origin of both the world and the gods, since the world was originally formed from one of them (Ymir), and most of the Æsir gods either issue directly from their ranks (Óðinn) or from their daughters (Þórr). Indeed, it appears that the gods need the giants to survive since, for among other things, the gods must know that inbreeding is not a good idea. It is noteworthy that when they need sons to revenge their eventual deaths, both Óðinn and Þórr have to beget offspring with giantesses rather than their own wives. Óðinn also has to go to the giants to learn knowledge of the future (as in the Eddic poem, *The Words of Vafþrúðnir*, or *Vafþrúðnismál*) and in order to steal poetry. In short, the giants are simply adversaries rather than evil, but like any other adversaries, they need to be kept at bay (mainly by Þórr). If they have any symbolic meaning, they probably represent the untamed natural forces of rock, ice, snow and water that surrounded and threatened the local farm or the local valley represented by Ásgarðr and/or Middle Earth where humans were supposed to live.

As has been mentioned earlier, several myths are meant to explain natural phenomena and there seems to have been more than one Norse myth of how the world was created. One tells of how it was created from the body of the giant Ymir, another (in the poem *The Seeress's Prophecy*) how it rose from the sea. The variation in cosmological concept in different myths means that the mythographer Snorri Sturluson finds himself in great difficulties when trying to form a single image of the pagan Norse cosmology for his Prose *Edda*. The range in concept is nonetheless quite natural: as has previously been emphasised, the Norse area contained numerous peoples with different dialects who lived in very different habitats and within these peoples were, of course, numerous extended families. This explains both the number of gods and the variation in the form of the myths.

There are, nonetheless, a number of shared features and recurring mythological images over and above the central idea of the existence of two (or more) opposing forces. Essentially, the giants are not 'here'; they are either all around us (in 'the outer world' or 'Útgarðr'), in the east (the mountain ridge that lay at the end of the main populated Norwegian fjords) or, for the Icelanders, in the cold icy north (the Icelanders knowing that the 'east' was a pretty impractical term since they came from there initially). In the sea circling the world (if the Vikings ever really believed that the world was round) were various sea creatures and other spirits that needed warding off with the figureheads on their longships and somewhere among these was the Middle Earth sea serpent, Jǫrmungandr (lit. 'great monster'). This was why many Icelanders appear to have called on Þórr to help them survive the North Atlantic crossing to Iceland. Whether Ásgarðr, the home of the gods, was above Middle Earth or simply in a kind of parallel reality linked by the rainbow is also open to question (perhaps depending on whether you lived in mountains or on an island), but clearly the world of Ásgarðr itself was based on the image of the valleys or communities where the Norse people lived, which often centred around a central hall which might double as a temple on holy days. Central to all these worlds, however, was the image of the World Tree (paralleled by the main pillars in the chieftain's hall) which held up the sky (roof) and served to connect all the various worlds. Sometimes referred to as Yggdrasill (lit. 'the horse of Yggr' Óðinn, referring to the god's self-sacrifice hanging on the tree), the Norse world ash tree finds clear parallels in the Christian *rood* (the Tree of Knowledge that later becomes the cross; compare the Ruthwell Cross in Chapter 6, p. 178) and has direct connections to earlier descriptions by Tacitus and others of how worship in the early Iron Age often took place in holy groves. Further parallels can be seen in the close connections between human beings and trees in poetry and in the mention of the holy tree of the Saxons, Irminsul, which Charlemagne had cut down, and also in the sacrificial tree at Gamla Uppsala which stood near a pool and the statues of the gods according to Adam of Bremen. Recent archaeological finds in Sweden have supported such ideas. The remains of an ancient tree have been found beneath an early Christian church along with various bones, including those of a bear, scattered around it.

According to *The Seeress's Prophecy*, the tree began growing at the start of time and will collapse in fire at the time of Ragnarǫk. The poem suggests that until then it serves as the centre of the world and it is here that the so-called *Norns* of fate meet. Numerous accounts going back into Roman times testify to the belief and respect that Germanic peoples, no less than the Greeks, Romans or any others, had for ideas of fate. Tacitus, in *The Germany*, tells of Germanic tribes throwing pieces of wood marked with signs to find out about the future. The same idea is reiterated in a variety of sources up until the time between 1000, when Christianity was finally accepted in Iceland, and *c.* 1030, when it was properly consolidated in Norway. Apparently Norse people would not travel or go to war without checking up on the likely fate that might befall them and often they used female sooth-sayers, seeresses, for just this purpose. This was perhaps their weakest link, since, as certain Roman commanders and missionaries discovered, if you could control the interpretation of the prophecy, you could control the people. Indeed, this may well have been how the Icelanders were eventually won over to Christianity.

Fate, however, seems to have been personified in various ways by the Norse peoples. The image most commonly referred to (based again on *The Seeress's Prophecy*) is that of three 'Norns' or personified abstracts of time (the *nornir*), who are named Urðr, Verðandi and Skuld. As Past, Present and Future respectively, they come from 'outside' and sit by a well at the foot of the World Tree. The Norns are closely bound up with the idea of goddesses and seeresses being able to see into the future, also of other supernatural women such as the valkyries protecting warriors on the battlefield. The Norns are commonly seen as direct parallels to the Greek and Roman spinners of fate (the *Parcae* and *Moirai*). This misunderstanding has arisen partly because one poem talks of the Norns making threads when a person is born, while another account (in *Njal's Saga*) contains an image of supernatural women weaving with skulls and intestines before a battle takes place. However, it is worth noting that the Norns themselves are never shown as spinning or weaving. They simply sit by a well. Here the implication is that they alone deal out the water of fate from this well. This image may perhaps be represented in the numerous brooches and amulets that have been found, from Viking times, of women carrying horns.

Other central female figures in the lower levels of Old Norse 'religion' are the valkyries (*valkyrjur*), the fetches (*fylgjur*) and the so-called *dísir*. These beings seem to be different local manifestations of the same idea, since they are all forms of spirit that accompany human beings. While the fetches often appear in dreams in animal form, the valkyries and *dísir* are definitely female figures. The main difference is that the latter protect families or nations, while the valkyries appear alongside individual warrior heroes.

They are also mentioned in heroic romance and poetry rather than in the Sagas of Icelanders, which are drawn from daily life. This distribution suggests that they might be essentially a poetic image. The same does not apply to the unnamed *dísir*, which are said to have received sacrifices at the start and end of the winter and seem to be mainly connected to those areas where the powerful Yngling kings held sway in Scandinavia, around Uppsala and modern-day Oslo and Trondheim. While the *dísir* protected farms, the valkyries were directly associated with war and death, perhaps developing out of a blend of ravens and campaign followers. Over time, however, their role in poetry and warrior society changed and, by the end of the Viking period, their role has largely diminished to that of hostesses in Óðinn's hall of the dead. In earlier times, both of these groups of beings are described as taking on an independent male role, riding horses in chainmail and dealing out death to men whenever they feel so inclined.

This classical Wagnerian image of valkyries serving as buxom operatic barmaids threading the crowded benches of Valhǫll represents the final stage of the assimilation of at least two different concepts of death which seem to have existed in Old Norse mythology. The image of Óðinn's 'hall of the chosen' (*Valhǫll*), as we have seen, is that of a warrior heaven in the sky where dead heroes are greeted by maidens in armour who serve them endless horns of drink, all the food they could wish for, and sex, as they prepare themselves for the final battle at Ragnarǫk. This image is probably a relatively late development based on the image of the Germanic warrior elite living away from their families in their leader's hall or even a larger barracks (like that found at Trelleborg in Denmark). The other image of death as a cold, earthly realm called Hel possibly has closer connections to the Vanir cult. The journey to Hel is described twice in our extant sources: once when Óðinn goes there himself to find out from a dead seeress why his favourite son has been dreaming badly and then later when Baldr's brother, Hermóðr, goes there to try for Baldr's release. His mission fails because the price, that everything living and lifeless should weep for Baldr, is not fulfilled by Loki (here cast as a grumpy cave giantess). The essential feature about Hel, a gated and guarded place below the surface of our world, is that unlike Valhǫll, it is ruled by a *woman* called Hel. Depicted as having a face that is half black, she is said in one place to be one of the offspring of Loki, although it is natural to see her, Freyja and the valkyries as having a great deal in common. Certainly, as has been noted before, Freyja is said to receive half of the dead. Elsewhere, in *Egil's Saga*, a suggestion is made that all women go to Freyja, although no suggestion is ever made of an Amazon-like female parallel to the all-male world of Valhǫll ever having been conceived. Once again, though, these accounts make it clear that variation by time and place was a key feature of Old Norse mythology.

The valkyries and the *dísir* were not the only other types of being to exist in the 'lower levels' of Old Norse mythology. Other groups of beings were so deeply rooted in the cosmology of the local landscape that they were near impossible for the church to eradicate: namely the spirits of the local fore-fathers that lived in the farm grave mounds and then the local nature spirits that have lived on into our own times in the form of folk belief. Various legal and historical documents make it clear that most if not all of the Norse peoples believed that the landscape outside the farm was populated by a range of powerful nature spirits (originally called *landvættir*). In later times, these come to blend in concept with other slightly more powerful beings that appear here and there in Old Norse mythology, namely the dwarfs (*dvergar*) and the elves (*álfar*). There is nothing at all in the original sources to suggest that these dwarfs were small and bearded or that these elves had pointed ears and lived in forests. It is clear, however, that Tolkien followed the original Old Icelandic sources closely when creating both his dwarfs and his elves. He not only borrows the original names of the dwarfs from part of *The Seeress's Prophecy* (where we also find the name Gandálfr; see p. 53) but also follows the early suggestions of connections between the dwarfs and rock caverns and the fact that the original dwarfs were seen as being excel-lent creators of artefacts: among other things, they are said to have made Óðinn's spear, Þórr's hammer, Freyr's ship, Sif's hair, Freyr's gold boar, Óðinn's ring, Freyja's necklace and the fetter that kept the wolf Fenrir under control for a while.

Unlike the dwarfs, the so-called *álfar* (probably meaning 'bright ones') never appear directly in the Old Norse myths. However, it seems clear that they, like Tolkien's elves, were originally seen as being much closer to demi-gods than nature spirits, not least because they are regularly named alongside the giants and gods as one of the three key races in the poems: indeed, it may well even be that the word *álfar* was another word for Vanir gods in some circles. Certainly, as has been mentioned earlier, Freyr is said to be directly connected to the elves, since the Eddic poem *The Words of Grímnir* states that he is given the 'Elf-Home' (*Álfheim*) as a teething gift.

As noted earlier, the words 'elf', 'dwarf' and 'troll' have all lived on in the folklore of England, Scotland and various other countries in Germanic-speaking Europe, including Scandinavia, of course. This general survival testifies to the fact that the beliefs in natural spirits were more difficult to winkle out of rocks and trees than the beliefs in higher beings connected with ritual and royal ideology. Some of these deities could be relatively effectively transformed in accordance with Pope Gregory's earlier instruction, to the abbot Mellitus in 601 (preserved in Bede's *History of the English Church and People*, Book I, Chapter 30), that Christian missionaries should not burn the heathen temples, but instead find a way of transforming them and the activities that were carried out in them into features of the Christian cult. Thus, while Óðinn becomes a demon hunter, Þórr later finds himself transformed into St Óláfr, the patron saint of Norway; Óláfr, in turn, becomes a red-haired troll basher, his Christian axe conveniently replacing Þórr's hammer. Freyr, meanwhile seems to have been replaced by the Swedish St Staffan, and Freyja and Frigg amalgamate into the motherly, moral Marys. This process, however, was very gradual, since the official acceptance of Christianity in Denmark, Norway, Iceland and, eventually, Sweden only followed a long period of interaction between the two 'religions'. It should also be stressed that the contacts did not only take the form of raiding and war. At the same time, Norse merchants were engaged in selling wares to the English and Irish and in order to do this they often needed to take the first step of christening, known as 'first signing' (*prima signatio*). One archaeological artefact even points to both Þórr's hammer and crosses being made from the same mould. Elsewhere, as in Cumbria, we find images of Óðinn being swallowed by the wolf and Þórr fishing for the Middle Earth sea serpent appearing on Christian crosses. There can be little question that the two religions here have become intimately intertwined.

As has been noted before, ideas of fate and the acceptance of death were deeply rooted. However, the powerful idea that the world of the gods should come to an end at Ragnarǫk is almost certainly one that was strongly influenced by Christian thought and not least the popular Christian idea that the world was going to come to an end in around the year 1000. The Norse had always been travellers and were open to new ideas. Furthermore, as noted at the start, there was no one codified religion that their people had to follow. As the sagas show, people could effectively change their allegiance if their previous favourite god was not coming up with the goods. It is thus not surprising that we find motifs from Celtic and Christian mythology blending with those from Norse Britain and Scandinavia. Thus, for example, Heimdallr creates the Norse class system by sleeping with three different women, Great-Grandmother, Grandmother and Mother, begetting the races of thralls, churls and earls respectively. This is a story with Irish connections, preserved in *The Catalogue of Rígr* (*Rígsþula*), a poem which was probably composed in Norwegian Ireland or north-western England in the eleventh century. Elsewhere, as we have seen, Óðinn hangs from the World Tree with a spear in his side, rather like Jesus on the Cross. Similarly the main account of Ragnarǫk in the Eddic poem *The Seeress's Prophecy* seems to be strongly influenced by Christian teaching and symbolism, especially from the Book of Revelations. This likely combination only serves to strengthen the power of the some of the final images of this poem. Earlier in the chapter, a connection was noted between the Norse natural landscape and the stoic, heroic approach to life and death that is a characteristic of the mythology of the old north. Bearing all these points in mind, we can examine a selection of stanzas from the end of the world sequence in *The Seeress' Prophecy* (*Vǫluspá*; text and translation after Dronke 1997):

Geyr [nú] Garmr mjǫk   fyr Gnipahelli –
festr mun slitna,   en freki renna.
Fjǫlð veit hón frœða –   fram sé ek lengra,
um ragna rǫk   rǫmm, sigtíva. (stanza 43)

Brœðr munu beriaz   ok at bǫnom verða[z]
muno systrungar   sifiom spilla.
Hart er í heimi,   hórdómr mikill
– skeggǫld, skálmǫld –   skildir ro klofnir –
vindǫld, vargǫld –   áðr verǫld steypiz.
Mun engi maðr   ǫðrum þyrma. (stanza 44)

Leika Míms synir,   en miǫtuðr kyndiz
at en[o] galla   Giallarhorni.
Hátt blæss Heimdallr   – horn er á lopti –
mælir Óðinn   við Míms hǫfuð.
Skelfr Yggdrasils   askr standandi,
ymr it aldna tré   en iǫtunn losnar. (stanza 45)

Hrymr ekr austan,   hefiz lind fyrir.
snýz Iǫrmungandr   í iǫtunmóði.
Ormr knýr unnir,   en ari hlakkar –
slítr nái neffǫlr.   Naglfar losnar. (stanza 47)

Surtr fer sunnan   með sviga lævi:
skínn af sverði   sól valtíva.
Grjótbiǫrg gnata,   en gífr rata.
troða halir helveg,   en himinn klofnar. (stanza 50)

Þá kømr Hlínar   harmr annarr fram,
er Óðinn ferr   við úlf vega,
en bani Belia   biartr at Surti.
Þá mun Friggiar   falla angan. (stanza 51)

Þá kømr inn mæri   mǫgr Hlǫðyniar,
gengr Óðins sonr   við *orm* vega,

Drepr hann af móði   miðgarz véor[r]
– muno halir allir   heimstǫð ryðia –
gengr fet nío   Fiǫrgyniar burr
neppr frá naðri   níðs ókvíðnom. (stanza 53)

Sól tér sortna,   sígr fold í mar,
hverfa af himni   heiðar stiǫrnor.
Geisar eimi   við aldrnara,
leikr hár hiti   við himin siálfan. (stanza 54)

Now Garmr bays loud   before Looming Cave –
the fetter will break   and the ravener run free.
Much she knows of old knowledge, ahead I see further,
over the fate of the powers, virulent fate of victory's gods. (stanza 43)

Brothers will fight and kill each other,
sisters' children will defile kinship.
It is harsh in the world, whoredom rife
– an axe age, a sword age – shields are riven –
a wind age, a wolf age – before the world goes headlong.
No man will have mercy on another. (stanza 44)

Mímr's sons sport, but fate's measure is lit
at the sound of the clear Clarion Horn.
Loud blows Heimdallr – the horn points to the sky –
Óðinn talks with Mímr's head.
Yggdrasill shivers, the ash, as it stands.
The old tree groans, and the giant slips free. (stanza 45)

Hrymr drives from the east, hoists his shield before him.
Mighty Wraith [the world serpent] coils in giant wrath.
The snake flails the waves, and the eagle exults –
pale-beaked rips corpses. Nail Boat slips free. (stanza 47)

Surtr moves from the south with the scathe of branches:
there shines from his sword the sun of Gods of the Slain.
Stone peaks clash, and troll wives take to the road.
Warriors tread the path from Hel, and heaven breaks apart. (stanza 50)

Then is fulfilled Hlín's second sorrow,
when Óðinn goes to fight with the wolf,
and Beli's slayer, bright, against Surtr.
Then shall Frigg's sweet friend fall. (stanza 51)

Then comes the glorious child of Hlǫðyn,
Óðinn's son strides to fight the Serpent.
He smites in fury, shrine-guarder of Middle Earth
– all heroes will abandon the homestead of earth –

he steps nine paces, Fiǫrgyn's child,
failing – leaving slain the snake that had not feared its vile act. (stanza 53)

The sun starts to blacken, land sinks into sea,
the radiant stars recoil from the sky.
Fume rages against fire, fosterer of life,
the heat soars high against heaven itself. (stanza 54)

And so ends the present world. After this, however, *The Seeress's Prophecy* describes how a new world is born: the earth arises once again from the water and the second generation of gods return. Interestingly enough, nothing is said about a return of any goddesses. Even more interesting is an additional strophe that appears at the end of one later version of the poem, suggesting that a new greater god will now appear, greater than all those who have preceded him:

Þá kømr inn ríki   at regindómi
Ǫflugr ofan   sá er Ǫllo ræðr. (stanza 60.b)

Then the Powerful to the judgement place of gods,
The Mighty from above, He Who rules the universe.

And so, in the end, Christianity took over the world of the old Germanic gods in Iceland just as it did everywhere else. The warlike Vikings were now expected to love Jesus instead of Óðinn or Þórr. In a manner of speaking, you could say the monks of Lindisfarne had finally got their revenge.

Translations and texts

Dronke, Ursula, ed., comm. and trans., *The Poetic Edda II: Mythological Poems* (Oxford, 1997).

Evans, David A.H., ed., *Hávamál*, Viking Society for Northern Research, Text Series 7 (London, 1986).

Faulkes, Anthony, trans., *Snorri Sturluson: Edda*, Everyman Series (London, 1987).

Fisher, Peter, trans. and Hilda Ellis Davidson, ed., *Saxo Grammaticus: Gesta Danorum, Books I–IX* (Cambridge, 1979–80).

Larrington, Carolyne, trans., *The Poetic Edda*, Oxford World's Classics (Oxford, 1996). More accessible than Dronke, less accurate but more modern in style.

Mattingly, H., trans., *On Britain and Germany: Agricola and Germania* by Cornelius Tacitus, Penguin Classics (Harmondsworth, 1948).

Further reading

Aðalsteinsson, Jón Hnefill, *Under the Cloak* (Reykjavík, 1999).

DeBois, Thomas, *Nordic Religions in the Viking Age* (Philadelphia, PA, 1999).

Davidson, Hilda Ellis, *Gods and Myths of Northern Europe* (Harmondsworth, 1964).

Glob, P.V. *The Bog People*, Bruce-Mitford, Rupert, trans. (London, 1977).

Gunnell, Terry, *The Origins of Drama in Scandinavia* (Cambridge, 1995).

Lindow, John, *Handbook of Norse Mythology* (Santa Barbara, CA, 2001).

North, Richard, *Heathen Gods in Old English Literature*, Cambridge Studies in Anglo-Saxon England 22 (Cambridge, 1997).

Orchard, Andy, *Cassell's Dictionary of Norse Myth and Legend* (London, 1997).

Simek, Rudolf, *A Dictionary of Northern Mythology*, Hall, Angela, trans. (Cambridge, 1996).

Turville-Petre, Gabriel, *Myth and Religion of the North* (New York, 1964).

Wilson, David, *Anglo-Saxon Paganism* (London, 1992).

CHAPTER 13

Sagas of Icelanders

Joe Allard

Everyone has heard of the Vikings, most have heard of 'sagas' too, and some link one term with the other. If Vikings were the pirates among whom some early Icelanders, such as Egill Skalla-Grímsson, made their name, 'sagas' are the stories written about them and their descendants. These sagas were written in Old Icelandic prose and the best-known category of them is called 'Sagas of Icelanders' (modern Icelandic *Íslendinga Sögur*). These are better known than the 'sagas of ancient times' (*fornaldar sögur*), which consist of heroic stories in prose dealing with such Age of Migrations (400–600 AD) heroes as Sigmundr the Volsung and King Hrólfr of the Danes – heroes such as we have seen in the poetry described in Chapters 3 and 4. In their written form, the sagas are largely a product of the thirteenth and fourteenth centuries. It became a vogue during this period to record and elaborate on what had been a vigorous oral tradition of telling stories about the original settlers of Iceland, their ancestors and descendants. The years in question, broadly speaking, are from 850 to 1070. Forty of these sagas have survived, as well as over 50 short tales (*þættir*). Many others have been lost. The writers remain anonymous. In the following, I shall start with the English titles, then gradually introduce the titles in the original Icelandic so as to give you a better sense of what these sagas are.

Although the surviving sagas share a number of narrative and formal qualities there is otherwise a surprising variety of content and concern. Some deal with an extended family over many years like *Njal's Saga* ((*Brennu-*)*Njáls saga*), *Egil's Saga* (*Egils saga Skalla-Grímssonar*), and *The Saga of the People of Laxardal* (*Laxdæla saga*). These are several of the 'Family Sagas', a generic tag sometimes wrongly attached to the entire canon of Sagas of Icelanders. Some of these, like *The Saga of the People of Eyri* (*Eyrbyggja saga*), tell us about regional feuds that that might extend over decades. Others are biographies of individuals. Among the oldest are thought to be the 'Poet's Sagas' (*skáld-sögur*) of Hallfreðr the Troublesome Poet (*Hallfreðar saga Vandræðaskálds*), Gunnlaugr Serpent-Tongue (*Gunnlaugs saga Ormstungu*), Bjǫrn the Champion of the Hitardal People (*Bjarnar saga Hítdælakappa*) and Kormákr (*Kormáks saga*). Each is a story of crossed and doomed love, either through a quality of the poet's character, sorcery or both. And each saga is packed with poems. Other sagas and tales concern the fate of outlaws like Gísli Súrsson (*Gísla saga Súrssonar*) and Grettir the Strong (*Grettis saga Ásmundarsonar*) who are also masters of poetic form. There are several very effective comedies among the sagas, as well as stories and tales of the supernatural. Some are set mainly abroad in locations as varied as North America, Greenland, Scandinavia and the Mediterranean.

The sagas display a number of narrative and stylistic features that are unique in medieval European literature. They are largely realistic. The prose is laconic, terse and succinct. What is not stated directly is often as important as what is. The plot, the events of feud and conflict, of love and loss, dominates the stories. Once introduced, characters are shown in significant action. The larger sagas range over several generations and many years. *Njal's Saga* extends for over 70 years, *Egil's Saga* and *Laxardal* for 150. Years, sometimes decades, are telescoped into a paragraph, sometimes a sentence.

What we are told in the sagas resides in the communal memory ('it was said at the time', 'people thought that', 'some say . . . others say'). It would never occur to a saga teller to describe what a character might be thinking. This approach to character is perhaps the most profound literary difference with both other medieval and later European literatures. Without access to thought patterns the saga method suggests character in a manner just as fresh and exciting as other modes. Also notable in saga style is that characters seldom develop or change internally.

Europeans had been aware of the existence of Iceland since antiquity, but the island had never been inhabited on a permanent basis. It was too warm and isolated for the nomadic Inuit populations and too remote for anyone else. It was used as a summer base for some Irish hermit monks in the ninth century who are said to have left when the Norse heathens began to arrive to settle. Ingólfr Árnarson and Hallveig Fróðadóttir established the first permanent farmstead at Reykjavík (Smokey Bay) in the early 870s. Perhaps as many as 20,000 others arrived in the following decades. It was rumoured throughout the Viking world that in Iceland 'there was good land to be had at no cost, there were many stranded whales, an abundance of salmon and rich fishing grounds all year round' (*þar landskosti góða, ok þurfti*

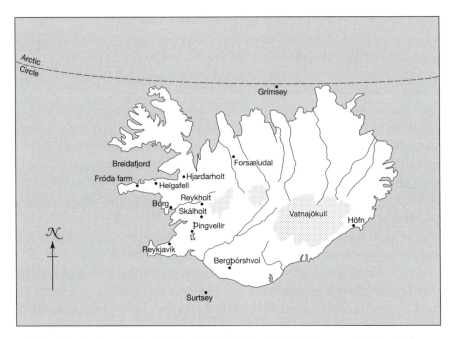

Iceland lies in the middle of the North Atlantic. The Arctic Circle crosses the island of Grímsey in the north. Its southern-most point is the island of Surtsey, at 63°23', which rose out of the sea in a series of dramatic volcanic eruptions in 1963. Iceland lies on the boundary of the North American and Eurasian tectonic plates and is the only bit of the Mid-Atlantic Ridge that rises about sea level. These features account for the high level of geothermal activity . . . eruptions, geysers and hot springs. Ten percent of the land mass is glaciated. The middle of the country is uninhabitable arctic desert, mountains and lava fields. It is prohibiting, inhospitable and, probably, haunted. Around the coast the land is arable, suitable for certain hardy crops and grazing for sheep, cows, horses and goats. The rivers run with salmon in season and the surrounding waters are rich with fish, seals and whales. The bird life is also remarkable. The Gulf Stream, that warm North Atlantic current that sweeps up from the Caribbean, moderates the climate so that is never as cold as one imagines it ought to be. The average winter temperature is higher than in New York City. It is said to be the windiest inhabited country on earth. The Gulf Stream is also an important source for driftage, an important resourece in a land that has become virtually treeless. Whatever woodland the early settlers found when they arrived was quickly used for building and fuel.

Map 8   Iceland in the settlement years

ekki fé at kaupa; kǫlluðu vera hvalrétt mikinn ok laxveiðar, en fiskastǫð Ǫllum misserum, in *Laxdœla saga*, Chapter 2).

According to saga accounts, the settlers were mainly landed Norwegians who felt under pressure and threat during the consolidation of power in Norway of King Haraldr Fine-Hair (ruled *c.* 885–930). A vivid account of this era forms the first part of *Egil's Saga*. The emigrants travelled to Iceland from Norway and the Norse Viking strongholds in Scotland and Ireland and the North Sea Islands of Orkney, Shetland, the Faroes and the Hebrides. They brought with them their Celtic women and slaves. The settlers were dominantly heathen, although there were Christians among them. Some of the settlers might have been literate in Latin, Gaelic or dialects of Old English, but their own language, which we call Old Icelandic or Old Norse, didn't develop a literary technology (i.e. an alphabet and grammar) until the eleventh century. That was because Christianity was not adopted as Iceland's religion until 1000. With the exception of runes for certain ceremonial, memorial and graffiti inscriptions, the early Icelanders were preliterate.

How do the sagas work?

By way of introduction, I want to run through the major events and techniques of the *Saga of the People of Laxardal* (*Laxdœla saga*). It is one of the great family sagas, covering eight generations and nearly 150 years. It was probably written down in the 1240s. Like many of the sagas it is a cracking good read. It gives us a vivid and compelling portrait of what life must have been like for the Norse and Celtic settlers of Iceland in the ninth, tenth and eleventh centuries but also, in some measure, for their Anglo-Saxon contemporaries. Many of the characters and locations in the following summary will appear in other sagas and other contexts, as we shall see.

One of the original settlers of Iceland is the imposing matriarch Unnr 'the Deep-Minded' (*in djúpúðga*). She leaves Norway (in around 890) with her father, the powerful and well-born lord Ketill 'Flat-Nose' (*flatnefr*), son of Bjǫrn Buna, and some of her siblings when Haraldr Fine-Hair is making life difficult for them in Norway. She settles first in Scotland with her father. Her son, Þórsteinn the Red, becomes ruler of half of the Scottish kingdom, but is then killed at Caithness. Ketill has died by now so Unnr has a cargo ship built secretly in the forest and sets off for Iceland taking with her many notable people of good family and a number of slaves. In a remarkable genealogy en route, it transpires that Unnr fixes marriages for her granddaughters that establish the ruling dynasties of the Orkney and the Faroe Islands. Having arrived in Iceland (in around 915), she lays claim to a large area of Breiðafjǫrðr, in the west, which becomes the setting for many later sagas. She gives the 'Salmon River Valley' (*Laxárdalr*) as a dowry to one of her distinguished followers, the chieftan Kollr, when he marries her grand-daughter Þorgerðr. Their son is Hǫskuldr, called Dala-Kolsson (son of Kollr of the Dales). Icelanders of the age of settlements used the patronymic naming system, that is, your given name and the name of your father. Hǫskuldr, therefore, is the son of Dala-Kollr. Hǫskuldr's son Þorleikr is Þorleikr Hǫskuldsson. His daughter Hallgerðr is Hallgerðr Hǫskuldsdóttir, that is, the daughter of Hǫskuldr. Today, 90% of Icelanders use the same system – which makes using the telephone book a bit of a nightmare!

Hǫskuldr marries the good-looking, imperious and exceptionally intel-ligent Jórunn Bjarnardóttir (i.e. Bjǫrn's daughter). Later Hǫskuldr travels to Norway to acquire timber to enlarge his estate. At a market in the Brenn Islands in Norway he decides to buy a slave girl from a rich Russian merchant named Gilli. In his tent Gilli shows him a row of a dozen young women. He takes a fancy to the one sitting at the end of the bench. She is beautiful but, according to Gilli, she has a major flaw: 'The woman is mute. I've tried every way of coaxing her into speech, but I've never got a word out of her. I'm quite convinced she cannot speak.' ('*Kona þessi er ómála; hefi ek marga vega leitat máls við hana, ok hefi ek aldri fengit orð af henni; er þat at vísu mín ætlan, at þessi kona kunni eigi at mæla*', Chapter 12).

Hǫskuldr pays three marks of silver, thrice the going rate for a slave girl. He sleeps with her the same night. On his return to Iceland, Jórunn is under-standably far from pleased with her husband's purchase. She stops his dalliance with the girl who, in due course, gives birth to the beautiful and promising Óláfr, nicknamed 'the Peacock' (*Pái*). The girl is still thought to be deaf and dumb. One morning, two years later, Hǫskuldr is out of doors seeing to the farm:

> Veðr var gott; skein sól ok var lítt á lopt komin; hann heyrði manna mál; hann gekk þangat til, sem lœkr fell fyrir túnbrekkunni; sá hann þar tvá menn ok kenndi; var þar Óláfr, sonr hans, ok móðir hanns; fær hann þá skilit, at hon var eigi mállaus, því at hon talaði þá mart við sveininn. (Chapter 13)

> It was a fine day, and the dawn sun was shining. He heard the sound of voices. He went over to the stream at the foot of the sloping homefield. There he saw two people he knew well: it was his son Óláfr, and the boy's mother. He realised then that she was not mute at all, for she was chatting busily to the child.

She admits that she is called Melkorka, daughter of the Irish King Mýrkjartan. She was taken captive in a Viking raid there when she was 15 and sold into slavery.

Sixteen years later Óláfr travels abroad. He goes first to Norway where his reception by Haraldr Grey-Cloak and his mother Gunnhildr is exemplary:

Gunnhildr lagði mikil mæti á Óláf, er hon vissi, at hann var bróðursonr Hrúts; en sumir menn kǫlluðu þat, at henni þœtti þó skemmtan at tala við Óláf, þótt hann nyti ekki annarra at. (Chapter 21)

Gunnhildr made much of Óláfr when she found out that Hrútr was his uncle, but there were some that said she enjoyed his conversation whether he had any family or not.

Óláfr then travels to Ireland to find his grandfather. His Irish is fluent. He shows the king the gold teething ring he had given his daughter years before. He is recognised by King Mýrkjartan as his grandson. He leaves Ireland having been accepted as a man of high birth, indeed with royal blood. He is, of course, still the bastard son of a slave woman.

Óláfr the Peacock returns from his travels with renown. At his father's urging he asks for the hand in marriage of Þorgerðr, the daughter of Egill Skalla-Grímsson. Yes, this is the same Egill whom you have met in *Egils saga* composing a praise poem in honour of King Æthelstan of England (see p. 333). Þorgerðr and Óláfr settle at Óláfr's new farm at Hjarðarholt ('herd wood'). In due course they have eight children. Later Óláfr returns from a trip abroad with the boisterous young Norwegian Geirmundr the Noisy whose prize possession is the sword 'Leg-Biter' (*Fótbít*). 'It was an impressive weapon: the pommel and guard were made of walrus ivory, without any silver, but the blade was very sharp and there was never any rust on it' (*Þat var mikit vápn ok gott, tannhjǫlt at; ekki var þar borið silfr á, en brandrinn var hvass, ok beið hvergi ryð á*). Geirmundr falls in love with Óláfr's daughter Þuríðr. Óláfr is opposed to the marriage but Geirmundr bribes Þorgerðr to gain approval and the wedding takes place in Óláfr's newly built, and lavishly decorated, hall at Hjarðarholt. A poet named Úlfr Uggason performs a famous poem on this occasion, called the 'House Lay' (*Húsdrápa*). But the marriage is a disaster and after the birth of their daughter, Gróa, Geimundr decides do a runner. Þuríðr hears that Geimundr has boarded a ship in Breiðafjǫrðr intending to sail off to Norway. She has herself rowed out in the middle of the night. She has holes drilled in the ship's towboat so she can't be chased. She then boards and finds Geimundr's hammock. She takes 'Leg-Biter' and replaces it with baby Gróa. She then gets back on her own boat. Geimundr wakes and realises what has happened. He begs Þuríðr to return the sword and take the baby but she refuses. He then utters the curse that 'Leg-Biter' will cause the death of someone the family would least like to lose. They then sail away. We are told that Geimundr and the rest of the crew (and the baby, presumably) shipwreck off Norway and are drowned.

Óláfr's eldest son is named Kjartan after his Irish great-grandfather. Kjartan grows up with his half-brother Bolli Þorleiksson whom Óláfr fosters. Kjartan is a real knockout:

> Hann var allra manna fríðastr, þeira er fœzk hafa á Íslandi; hann var mikilleitr ok vel farinn í andliti, manna bezt eygðr ok ljóslitaðr; mikit hár hafði hann ok fagrt sem silki, ok fell með lokkum, mikill maðr ok sterkr [. . .] betr var hann ok vígr en flestir menn aðrir; vel var hann hagr ok syndr manna bezt; allar íþróttir hafði hann mjǫk umfram aðra menn; hverjum manni var hann lítillátari ok vinsæll svá at hvert barn unni honum. (Chapter 28)

> He was the most handsome man ever been born in Iceland. He had a broad face and regular features, the most beautiful eyes and a fair complexion. His hair was thick and as shiny as silk [. . .] He was a big strong man, a better fighter than other men, skilled with his hands, and a top swimmer; he could perform all the sports far and away above other men; he was the humblest of men, and so popular that every child loved him.

Later Kjartan falls in love with Guðrún Ósvífrsdóttir. 'She was the most beautiful woman to have grown up in Iceland, both beautiful and intelligent [. . .] She was the shrewdest of women and highly articulate' (*Hon var kvenna vænst, er upp óxu á Íslandi, bæði at ásjánu ok vitsmunum* [. . .] *Allra kvenna var hon kœnst ok bezt orði farin*, Chapter 32). It seems to be a match made in heaven. Before becoming engaged to marry, however, Kjartan decides to go abroad for experience of travel and to win renown. Guðrún asks to come, but Kjartan rejects her company. He asks her to wait for three years, but she refuses. They part in disagreement.

The travellers, including Kjartan, Bolli and Hallfreðr the Troublesome Poet make landfall near modern-day Trondheim (in the year 998). Óláfr Tryggvason (reigned 995–1000) is king. He it is who has set his sights on converting Scandinavia and Iceland to Christianity. The king wants the visiting Icelanders to convert, but they hold back. During their stay Óláfr's missionary Þangbrandr returns from a mission to Iceland with the news that the islanders are proving diffcult. Some have converted but there is still a stubborn majority of heathens. He has killed two during his trip. We also learn that Hjalti Skeggjason has been outlawed at the Althing for blaspheming the heathen gods. Óláfr is furious and refuses to let any Icelanders leave Norway. The next summer he sends Hjalti and Gizurr the White (*hvíti*) to Iceland to preach the new faith. He allows others to leave but keeps Kjartan and three others as hostages.

On his return Bolli, who has always been in Kjartan's shadow, asks Guðrún to marry him. Kjartan, he tells her, is deeply involved with the King's sister, Ingibjǫrg (the most beautiful woman in Norway), and is unlikely to return. Her response is telling: 'I will never marry any other man as long as I know that Kjartan is alive' (*'Engum manni mun ek giptask, meðan ek spyr Kjartan á lífi'*). However, pressure is brought to bear by her father Ósvífr and her brothers. Grudgingly, almost against her will, Guðrún consents and marries Bolli. Kjartan returns soon after with a wedding gift from Ingibjǫrg for Guðrún. It is an elaborate headdress heavy with woven gold. Kjartan hears about Guðrún and Bolli's marriage, but says nothing. Soon after he marries a woman called Hrefna. They come to love each other, but it is not thought by everyone to be a suitable match.

Soon the temperature begins to rise. The headdress is stolen. One presumes by the people at Sælingsdale Tongue at Guðrún's urging. In retaliation Kjartan besieges the house there and denies everyone access to the privy for three days. Each escalation is fairly trivial, but the emotions are high. Finally, after Kjartan frustrates Bolli's and Guðrún's attempt to buy a property to enhance their prestige, she eggs Bolli on to ambush and deal with Kjartan. In the ambush Kjartan is set upon by the Ósvífssons. In the end it is Bolli who kills Kjartan with 'Leg-Biter'. He is immediately sorry as Kjartan dies in his arms. When he tells Guðrún her response is strangely enigmatic: 'Morning tasks are often mixed: I have spun yarn for twelve ells of cloth and you have killed Kjartan' (*'Misjǫfn verða morgunverkin; ek hefi spunnit tólf álna garn, en þú hefir vegit Kjartan'*). These words are the author's signal that he has got his story from Old Norse heroic poetry, from the tale of Brynhildr's jealous slaying of Sigurðr through her husband and his brothers (see Chapter 4, p. 121). Like Brynhildr, the heroine of this saga is still in love with the man she has had killed, as Bolli knows when he says he doubts this killing will make Hrefna, the widow, any paler than Guðrún, the instigator; or that his wife would have missed him more than she does Kjartan.

Once Kjartan has been killed the feud is set in full motion. It is only a matter of time before Bolli is killed in a shepherd's hut by a revenge party led by Helgi Harðbeinsson. They tell Guðrún, who is nearby, what they have done and Helgi callously wipes Bolli's blood off his sword onto the sash she is wearing around her waist. Helgi then suggests that under the sash is the one who will take his life in revenge. Guðrún is pregnant with Bolli Bollason. At this point she decides it would be politic to move from Sælingsdale. She arranges to exchange farms with an old friend and confidant named Snorri the Goði ('broker' or 'chieftain', *not* to be confused with his descendant Snorri Sturluson) from Helgafell in the west of Iceland. She enhances the estate there and brings up her sons Þorleikr and Bolli. In due course, with the advice of Snorri the Goði, young Bolli takes revenge and kills Helgi. The feud, now running for years, is finally settled. Guðrún marries her fourth husband, the distinguished and wealthy chieftain Þorkell Eyjólfsson. Gellir is their son. Tragically Þorkell drowns in a shipwreck in Breiðafjǫrðr.

Þorleikr and Bolli travel abroad to win fame and fortune. After a very honourable reception and treatment by King Óláfr later 'the Saint' Haraldsson (ruled *c.* 1015–30), Bolli travels on to Constantinople where he joins the Varangian Guard. In her later years Guðrún turns increasingly to the Christian faith. She becomes Iceland's first anchoress at Helgafell. Her son Bolli returns with great renown and in splendour. His nickname is Bolli 'the Courteous' (*inn prúði*). On a visit to his mother he asks a question the answer to which is wonderfully enigmatic and typical of the saga method at its best. 'Will you tell me something, mother, that I am very curious to know? Which man did you love the most?' ('*Muntu segja mér þat, móðir, at mér er forvitni á at vita? Hverjum hefir þú manni mest unnt?*'). Guðrún answers by outlining and comparing the qualities of her four husbands. But this, of course, is not Bolli's question. He presses her further. She weakens a little and Bolli begs her to tell. 'Guðrún answers, "I was worst to the one I loved the most." "I think", said Bolli, "that the truth has now been told" ' ('*Þá mælti Guðrún: "Þeim var ek verst, er ek unna mest." "Það hyggju vér", svarar Bolli, "at nú sé sagt alleinarðliga" '*). Once again, another interview with a man named Bolli. But in this case, we can see a later, flashier generation, looking back and marvelling at the passionate lives of their elders.

Old Icelandic law in the sagas

Concern with the law, its transmission, interpretation and enforcement plays a very large role in many of the sagas, most memorably in *Njal's Saga* where legal machinations, tricks and errors of interpretation are the narrative focus of many episodes, both at the Althing (the national assembly, *Alþingi*) and elsewhere. The final breakdown of legal procedure leads to the Battle of the Althing. After a series of exciting legal manoeuvres and challenges worthy of any finely honed courtroom drama of our era, the force of law loses its grip and the country is plunged into lawlessness.

By 930 all the land was claimed and the country fully settled. There were no villages or towns but, rather, farmsteads around the country. The rural community was roughly organised by *goðorð*, approximately 36 'chieftaincies' based, originally, on kinship alliances. The original *goði* [/goːaθi/] ('social broker' or 'chieftain', sometimes mistranslated as 'priest') seems to have combined secular and religious functions. The system was unique to Iceland. There was no king, no executive, no military or police. The only unifying force was the law. The earliest law code is said to have been brought to Iceland by a man named Úlfljótr from the Gula Assembly in Norway. During the early decades of the settlement there were a number of 'things' (*þingi*), local law assemblies held in the spring. Here the law was pronounced, cases were argued and decided by juries, settlements were reached and often, later, breached. In 930 the Althing was established as a national assembly, which met for two weeks in mid-summer at Thingvellir (*Þingvellir*), a plain of astonishing natural beauty, lava fields, lakes, cliffs, gorges and waterfalls, which straddles the meeting of the tectonic plates that divide North America and Europe. It is not far from the landtaker Ingólfr's farmstead at Reykjavík.

Here the lawspeaker, the only elected official in the land, would recite from memory one-third of the law each year of his three-year term. Here, too, old acquaintances were renewed, marriages were negotiated, trade was pursued and stories and poems were told and remembered. In the absence of any executive force it was up to the parties involved in disputes to enforce decisions of the court. Settlement might involve blood money (so many marks of silver for killing a slave; so many more for killing a free man). For more serious offences someone might be outlawed. Lesser outlawry was for a period of three years. The convicted lost all legal rights and protection for that period, his property was confiscated and he could be killed with impunity. To travel abroad was the best course. One viking, named Eiríkr the Red, is said to have been sentenced to this outlawry. It was his fame to settle the southwest tip of Greenland, from where North America was later discovered. The stories of these adventures, nearly half a millennium before Christopher Columbus sailed in 1492, are to be found in *Eirik the Red's Saga* (*Eiríks saga Rauða*) and *The Saga of the Greenlanders* (*Grænlendinga saga*), two works which are also called the *Vínland Sagas*. These tell of the voyages of discovery to North America led by Eiríkr's son Leifr 'the Lucky'. Full outlawry, by way of contrast, was a life sentence. As a narrative device, it gives the meat and muscle to several sagas, most vividly *Gísli Súrsson's Saga* (*Gísla saga Súrssonar*) and *The Saga of Grettir the Strong* (*Grettis saga*). The heroes of these sagas spend years surviving in the wilderness keeping alive by their wits, raiding farmers in an American Wild West fashion 1000 years before Hollywood. Grettir, who we shall meet later, spent nearly 20 years as an outlaw and was only finally defeated and killed with the help of witchcraft and sorcery.

Coming of Christianity to Iceland

As we have seen in *Laxdæla saga*, Iceland was converted by the Norwegian King Óláfr Tryggvason, a reformed Viking who was probably part of the 991 raid which is celebrated in *The Battle of Maldon* (see Chapter 11, p. 339). In 995, Óláfr set out to Christianise Scandinavia and the North Atlantic Viking settlements in Orkney, the Faroe Islands and Iceland. Chapters 100–105 of *Njáls saga* (*c.* 1280) relate the arrival of Óláfr's missionary priest Þangbrandr, son of Count Willibald of Saxony. The missionary lands with his Icelandic companions in the Eastfjords. There are Christians in Iceland already, but most people are heathen. Some are hostile to Þangbrandr's mission but others, like Hallr of Síða, give a cautious welcome. Hallr converts on the condition that Þangbrandr pledges his word that the Archangel Michael will become his own guardian angel.

Þangbrandr's evangelising isn't an especially smooth ride. Some of the heathens hire sorcerers and encourage berserks to thwart, and kill if possible, this man on a mission from God. They fail, of course, but several are speared or hacked to death by Þangbrandr and an Icelandic friend in the process. As they travel around the country, some households, like Njáll's at Bergþórshvol, willingly accept the new faith. Njáll has an Irish name, the same as *Níall* of the Uí Níaill (O'Neill) royal clan we have seen in seventh-century Northumbria (Chapter 6, p. 176), so perhaps he was partly Christian already. Other Icelanders resist strongly. In the summer before this one (i.e. 999), the atmosphere at the Althing was tense. Heathens and Christians were increasingly at odds and a young poet named Hjalti Skeggjason, before travelling abroad with a chieftain named Gizurr the White, made the memorable satiric verse about the old gods. In *Njáls Saga*, this is quoted as follows:

> Spari ek eigi goð geyja!
> Grey þykki mér Freyja;
> æ mun annat tveggja
> Óðinn grey eða Freyja. (*Njáls Saga*, Chapter 102)

> I don't mind mocking the gods,
> for I think that Freyja's a bitch;
> it must be one or the other –
> Óðinn's a dog or else Freyja. (after Magnus Magnusson and Hermann Pálsson)

On his return (in 1000), Hjalti has to deal with the fact that he has been sentenced to the lesser outlawry for blasphemy.

The final resolution is significant in the annals of both religion and politics. The situation looks ugly at the next Althing, in 1000. One day groups of Christians and heathens go to the Law Rock, name witnesses and renounce the community of laws. They want a law speaker of their own and name Hallr of Síða, but the latter approaches the existing law speaker, Þorgeirr, a heathen (he appears in six other sagas) and gives him three marks of silver to proclaim what their new common law shall be. This is a risk, for Þorgeirr is a heathen. He lies down all the next day with a cloak over his head, then addresses the gathering from the Law Rock, making everyone pledge to accept his judgement. They agree. His decision, a wonderful compromise, is that all people in the land should be Christian and renounce the worship of idols. They must not expose children at birth or eat horseflesh. The penalty for carrying out these practices openly will be outlawry, but they will not be punished if the business is done in private. In a land with no villages or towns perhaps most people lived in relative privacy most of the time! But in fact this, or an incident a bit like it, is how the Christians won.

Growth of literature in Iceland

With Christianity came literacy. In the next few decades of the eleventh century Iceland was visited by English and European priests and other learned men. Monasteries were soon founded on the island. An alphabet, based on Old English script, evolved along with some brilliant drafts of an Icelandic grammar. In 1056 a diocese, or episcopal see, was established at Skálholt, the family farm of Gizurr the White, whose son was consecrated in Bremen as Iceland's first native bishop. A second diocese was founded at Hólar in the north of Iceland in 1106. There were active centres of learning at important farms like Oddi and Haukadalr and at the cathedral schools of Skálholt and Hólar. That many early Icelanders became literate quickly is beyond question. Many modes of communication, however, like the laws, poetic and narrative entertainment, genealogy and kinds of history remained fixed firmly in the older oral tradition and would remain so for many years to come. The notion of literacy as an alternative technology was hardly alien.

Early vernacular literate work was essentially church related, but the early twelfth century witnessed the ripening of the secular fruit of writing. It was the new Icelandic script, of a usable and flexible vernacular, that made all this possible. The early Icelanders took to it with enthusiasm. In addition to the range of clerical concerns (homilies, saints' lives, stories of bishops and so on), they wrote down family trees or genealogies, Scandinavian royal history, law, grammar, recent Icelandic history, calendar reckoning and, later, the wonderful stories of the original settlers. Of course, during the later part of this century, they also began to write down Eddic and skaldic poems such as we have seen discussed and quoted in various chapters before this one: *The Lay of Wayland*, *The Lay of Atli*, *The Words of the High One*, *The Seeress' Prophecy* and many other great works of poetry.

Kvöldvaka and Ari the Learned

It is hard to imagine any secular literary development without a corresponding, and vigorous, oral tradition. Iceland has always been a nation of poets and storytellers and the telling of stories for entertainment (*sagnaskemmtun*) was a central element of most social occasions. *The Sagas of the Icelanders* have their genesis in shared communal entertainments, which were as much to do with performance as with writing and reading. For centuries poetic and narrative production was shared on the farms. There were no villages or towns in Iceland before the late nineteenth century. The evening entertainment on farms (*kvöldvaka*, literally 'evening wake') began in winter with the lighting of the oil lamp, usually an hour after sunset. As people attended to chores like knitting and the carding and spinning of wool, someone (the farmer, a boy, a guest) told, or read, sagas and recited or chanted poems. The Icelandic noun *saga* is from the verb *segja* 'to speak', 'to say', 'to tell'. What was 'said', then, about the settlers would have been an important feature of entertainments like these. Their literary inscription, however, in the thirteenth and fourteenth centuries, owes a huge debt to the pioneering historical work of a man named Ari the Learned.

Ari the Learned Þorgilsson (1068–1148), to give him his full name, was a scholar, priest and *goði* who compiled *The Book of Icelanders* (*Íslendingabók*) in the 1120s. This is a concentrated history of Iceland from the settlement to the early twelfth century. It includes a discussion of the settlement, the bringing of the laws from Norway, the establishment of the Althing, the settlement of Greenland by Eiríkr the Red and the journeys to Vínland (North America), the coming of Christianity (an account which formed the basis of the one in *Njáls Saga*) and brief lives of the first native-born bishops of Iceland, Ísleifr Gizurarson and his son, Gizurr Ísleifsson.

Ari's choice of the vernacular is significant for all later Icelandic literature. So, too, is his historiographical method. He used what he felt to be the most reliable informants and oral sources and always acknowledged them. His own circumspection leads him to say, in the preface to the second (and only surviving) draft of *Íslendingabók*, 'whatever is wrongly reported in this history, one is duty bound to accept what proves to be more true' (*En hvatki es missagt es í frœðum þessum, þá es skylt at hafa þat heldr, es sannara reynisk*). Finally, Ari wrote his history from a position of living memory. His sources were informants connecting him to the past in a living chain of memory. These included his paternal uncle Þorkell Gellison, the grandson of Guðrún, heroine of *Laxdœla saga*. In other words, Guðrún was his great-grandmother. The fact that the Icelandic for 'great-grandmother' is *edda* possibly explains why Snorri Sturluson, in the 1220s, chose this word for the name of his treatise on poetry and mythology: i.e. to illustrate the long transmission of poetry over many generations (see Chapter 12, p. 354).

Another important source for the sagas from the same period were the early written versions of *The Book of Settlements* (*Landnámabók*). This, as it survives in three redactions now, is a book of genealogy that, moving clockwise around the country, names some 3500 people, over 430 of whom were original settlers. It includes accounts of boundaries and homesteads and, sometimes, brief anecdotes about events and disputes some of which, later, became more fully fledged sagas. Genealogy is fundamental to Icelandic storytelling. For *The Sagas of the Icelanders* it is the genesis of a nation in all its variety and complexity. But the extended genealogies are a feature of the saga method that those encountering them for the first time often find curious or distracting. However, they serve a number of functions. They might establish an often exalted lineage in Norway in the past; they sometimes detail land claims and boundaries; they look forward sometimes as many as eight generations to the saga-writing age. And, of course, the complexities of kinship often lie at the root of disputes and feuds in the sagas themselves.

On first exposure such lists of names and relationships are baffling, but it becomes increasingly delightful to consider the significance of many of the players when other sagas are considered and such lists are compared. Over 700 people appear in more than one saga; some in many. Guðmundr Eyjólfsson the Powerful appears in 18 sagas, Snorri the Goði Þorgrímsson in 11, Óláfr the Peacock Hǫskuldsson in 8. The more sagas one reads, the more often will an already familiar character turn up in a new situation from a different angle.

Eight generations seems a long time to most of us, but is not so great in kin distance in a land whose language has a vocabulary for extended blood relations. For example, *fjórmenningar* means people who have the same great-grandmother; *fimmenningar*, who have the same great-great-grandmother, *sexmenningar*, who have the same great-great-great-grandmother . . . and so on. This can go back into the mists of the settlement years. In recent years a genealogical website has been developed for Icelanders, most of whom subscribe. It is modestly called the *Book of Icelanders* (*Íslendingabók*) and allows Icelanders instant access to genealogies some of which claim to lead back to the ninth and tenth centuries – 35 generations or more.

The genealogies and the stories they often contained were an important part of the oral social fabric in early Iceland and played a regular part in evening entertainments on most farms. We know from meteorological research that the climate was milder in the settlement years than in later centuries. The cooling of the climate during the fifteenth and sixteenth centuries (the so-called 'Mini-ice Age') spelt the end of the Greenland adventure. We shouldn't forget, however, that the latitude and extremes of light and dark haven't changed. Icelanders of all ages would have had very long winter nights to wile away. One of them was Snorri, the man who compiled the *Prose Edda, The Garland of the World* (*Heimskringla*) and possibly *Egils saga* as well.

Snorri Sturluson, writer and gentleman

The writers of the sagas are self-consciously in a literary tradition initiated by Ari the Learned. That saga writers remain anonymous suggests that the enterprise had a large element of the recording of stories that were already well known through an oral tradition. There are many today, however, who see *Egils saga* as the work of Snorri Sturluson (1179–1241), one of the most prolific and remarkable historians, critics and poets in thirteenth-century Europe. We know that he compiled *Heimskringla*, a comprehensive and meticulous series of biographies of the kings of Norway extending from the myths and mists of pre-history to the year 1177. As we saw in Chapter 12, Snorri also produced the *Prose Edda* or *Snorra Edda*, a three-section handbook for skaldic poets. Stories about the Norse gods form the core of *The Beguiling of Gylfi* (*Gylfaginning*). *The Language of Poetry* (*Skáldskaparmál*) is a brilliant and comprehensive discussion of kennings, the intricate metaphoric tropes often drawn from the old mythology, citing examples of poems by many named skalds. The final section is a long poem called the *List of Verse Forms* (*Háttatal*). This is a catalogue of 100 metrical verse forms composed by Snorri himself, in praise of King Hákon Hákonarson of Norway (ruled 1217–63) and the latter's enemy and father-in-law, Earl Skúli (died 1240).

In the biography of King Haraldr 'the Hard Ruler' (*Harðráði*) Sigurðsson in *Heimskringla* we find a number of answers to questions about the survival of stories and poems in an oral tradition and to the particular importance of skaldic poems to history. Taken with other sagas and tales from *The Sagas of the Icelanders* we have the most vivid and sometimes entertaining portrait of a period of critical historical importance for Norse and Anglo-Saxons alike. Leading a fleet of over 300 ships, Haraldr invaded England in September 1066. On Monday the 25th he met the army of King Harold Godwinsson at Stamford Bridge. This is where Haraldr was killed. Just 19 days later Harold of England fell at Hastings, his army defeated by the Norman invaders led by William the Bastard of Normandy. Between them, the battles of Stamford Bridge and Hastings mark the end of the Viking era in Britain, which began, according to *The Anglo-Saxon Chronicle*, with the raid on the monastery of Lindisfarne in 793 (p. 302).

As we have seen, Snorri was a member of the powerful Sturlung clan, which gives its name to the tumultuous age of Icelandic civil war in the middle of the thirteenth century. He was fostered at Oddi, in southern Iceland, whose owners had been drawn to the Norwegian royal family since marrying into them in the twelfth century. The men of Oddi wrote royal history, Icelandic history and poetry. As he grew up, Snorri became an active player in the politics of Iceland, and he remained so all his prolific literary life. The more equal power divisions between various *goðorð* in the earlier years of the Commonwealth, which are reported in the sagas, had become more narrowly and bitterly contested between several opposing families during the thirteenth century. Leaders like Snorri, himself lawspeaker from 1215–18 and again from 1222–31, courted Norwegian royalty. His own life is worthy of a saga. In 1241, at the age of 62, he was killed by his enemies in his cellar at Reykholt, just as he was about to take a bath (the geothermal bath, called *Snorralaug*, and parts of the cellar are still visible). The political turmoil spun further and further out of control until Iceland submitted to Norwegian rule in 1262–4 after nearly 400 years of self-governing commonwealth.

True and false and the writing of history

In the Prologue to *Heimskringla* Snorri acknowledges his debt to Ari the Learned:

> Því var eigi undarligt, at Ari væri sannfróðr at fornum tíðendum bæði hér ok útan lands, at hann hafði numit at gǫmlum mǫnnum ok vitrum, en var sjálfr námgjarn ok minnigr. (Prologue to *Heimskringla*)

> It is hardly surprising the Ari knew the truth about events of the past both here and in foreign lands, for he got his information from old and wise men and women, and he himself was keen to learn and had a long memory.

In his *King Harald's Saga*, Snorri echoes Ari's caution about his sources and methods. Many of Haraldr's accomplishments are not recorded here, he says.

> Kømr til þess ófrœði vár ok þat annat, at vér viljum eigi setja á bœkr vitnislausar sǫgur. Þott vér hafim heyrt rœður eða getit fleiri hluta, þá þykkir oss heðan í frá betra, at við sé aukit, en þetta sama þurfi ór at taka. (Chapter 36)

> This is because of our lack of knowledge, and partly because we are reluctant to record stories that are without witness. Although we have been told stories and

have heard about other deeds, it seems better that our account should later be expanded than it should have to be corrected.

These criteria of memory and writing take us to the heart of the saga enterprise. Early in his saga Haraldr travels to Constantinople where he becomes leader of the Varangian Guard, the Scandinavian mercenaries who served as bodyguards and warriors for the Byzantine Empire. After the Norman Conquest of England the Varangian Guard was almost entirely composed of Englishmen, no doubt Anglo-Saxon warriors defeated by the Normans at Hastings in 1066. Vividly described to us are a series of battles, sieges and manoeuvres in Asia Minor among the Saracens, in Sicily, then through Palestine to Jerusalem, where Haraldr bathes in the Jordan River, generously endows the shrine of Christ of the Holy Cross and clears the route to Jordan killing all robbers and troublemakers in the area.

How Snorri managed to give us such a compelling account of Byzantium and the Holy Land nearly 200 years before is flagged up in a passing reference to a couple of Icelanders who travelled with Haraldr. 'One was Halldórr Snorrason, the son of Snorri the Goði, who brought this story to Iceland, the other was Úlfr Óspaksson' (*Halldórr, sonr Snorra goða; hann hafði þessa frásǫgn hingat til lands; annarr var Úlfr, sonr Óspaks*, Chapter 9). Just how you 'bring' a story from Byzantium to Iceland is revealed to us the *Tale of Þorstein the Story-Wise* (*Þorsteins þáttr sǫgufróða*). Long after the events in Byzantium a bright young Icelander named Þorsteinn presents himself at Haraldr's court in Norway one summer. He is made welcome because he can tell good stories. He is given clothes and weapons but is obliged always to entertain anyone who asks him. As Yule approaches he grows melancholy. Always perceptive, Haraldr knows that the youth is running out of stories. The boy admits that he has only one story left and that is about Haraldr himself and his travels. The King proposes a ploy by which the young man can spin the story out to Twelfth Night. At the end of the festivities Haraldr asks where the youth learned the story. His answer is telling: 'It was my custom, Lord, to travel each summer to the Althing in my country, and I learned the story from Halldórr Snorrason' ('*Þat var vanði minn, herra, at ek hvert sumar til alþings á váru landi, ok nam ek svá sǫguna, er Halldórr Snorrason sagði*'). Here is almost a snapshot of an oral tradition in action. In addition to law disputes, marriage arrangements and drinking, the Althing was also the site of storytelling and poetry creation and recitation, stories and poems that people would commit to memory and retell later themselves.

Another important source for events in *Heimskringla* is skaldic poetry. The kings' histories and the Icelandic sagas are packed full of verses, which are often used to give authenticity to an event. This is what the poet said at the time. This is an eyewitness account, as it were. In the kings' histories of the preliterate Northern world the court poet was the equivalent of the media. What he said (and how he said it) during an important event, or reflected on it afterwards, was the only enduring record. It was said in such an intricate form to be memorable. There are over 90 poems in *King Harald's Saga*, some by Haraldr himself. Most of the others are attributed to Icelanders in his company. For centuries Icelanders were the court poets for Scandinavian royalty. The Icelandic word for these poets is *skáld*, probably because they were either 'scolded' by sarcastic listeners or themselves 'scolded' others.

Snorri, and other recorders of histories and sagas, placed great faith in the evidence of poems. A skald could offer lavish praise but he could not fabricate or lie. Nonsense or half-truths in verse would be an insult rather than praise if an audience, including the king, had been present at the event. Five poems in *King Harald's Saga* are attributed to Stúfr Þórðarson. A tale about Stúfr's first meeting with Haraldr survives in the vellum compilation *Morkinskinna* which contains a history of Haraldr that Snorri used as one of his sources. Stúfr the Blind is the son of Þórðr the Cat, who had been fostered by Snorri the Goði. It is Þórðr the Cat who helps exorcise the ghosts at Fróða farm, as we shall see. Stúfr's grandmother, like Ari's as it happens, was Guðrún Ósvífrsdóttir. Stúfr travels to Norway where he meets Haraldr at a prominent farm in Oppland. They hit it off and become drinking partners the first evening. Later the king asks Stúfr to entertain him with poems. After a long time he asks Stúfr how many *flokkar* (sequences of stanzas without refrains) he has recited. He has, it turns out, recited 30. The king asks if he knows any *drápur* (sequences of stanzas with one or more refrains at various intervals). 'I know no fewer *drápur* than *flokkar* and there are many of those that I haven't recited yet' ('*Eigi kann ek drápurnar færri en flokkana, ok eru þeir þó enn margir ókveðnir*'). This is both a prodigious feat of memory and evidence of the popularity of poetry both for recording events and for entertainment. At the end of the tale the king promises to let Stúfr compose a *drápa* in his honour. Sections of this, we presume, are found in the saga on King Haraldr Sigurðsson written by Snorri.

More on skaldic poetry

Over 5000 skaldic poems survive, most of them in the *dróttkvætt*, or court stanza form. Each stanza has eight lines (*vísuorð*) of six syllables each. End rhyme is seldom a feature of these verses, which are controlled by and heavy with alliteration (*stuðlun*) and internal full- (*aðalhending*) and half- (*skothending*) rhymes. Because the language is inflected, word order is far less important than in English. Unlike the prose, which is relatively straightforward and not unlike older forms of English, the poems can be monsters. The poets often use complex metaphor-like figures called kennings, which recall the heathen mythology. The following example is a stanza from Úlfr Uggason's 'House Lay' (*Húsdrápa*) which he performed at the wedding feast of Þuríðr and Geirmundr the Noisy at Óláfr the Peacock's new hall at Hjarðarholt as we have seen. The wainscoting and ceiling were decorated with fine carvings showing scenes from the old mythology. One represented the swimming contest between Heimdallr and Loki described in Snorri's *Edda* where this verse is preserved. They were fighting for the Brisings' necklace, stolen by Loki from Freyja. Loki, half-giant, is the trickster god, son of Fárbauti. Heimdallr is the watchman of the Æsir who guards the Bifrost Bridge. He is blind and has nine mothers. Note the density of the alliterative patterns. In bold letters is an alliteration pattern that is common to the form. There are two alliterating sounds in the odd line and one that comes at the start of the even line (*höfuðstafur*). I've also stressed with italics and underlining other rhyme and alliterative patterns here:

R**á**ð*ge*g*n*inn br**a**gð**r** r**a**g*n*a
r*ei*n – at Singast*ei*ni
fr*æ*gr við firna sl*æ*gjan
F**á**rbauta mǫg – v**á**ri.
M*ó*ðǫflugr ræð**r** **mœ**ðra
mǫgr hafnýra fǫgru
-ky*nn*ik- áð**r** ok *einn*ar
átta -mærðar þáttum.

A literal translation reveals the other complex and difficult problems that face any translator: 'Ready with a plan, the gods' land-warmer transforms for the blessing-jewel, renowned for facing the monstrously sly kinsman of Fárbauti. Mighty in spirit, the son of eight plus one mothers – I proclaim [Óláfr] in strands of renown – is the first to get control over the dazzling sea-kidney' (translation by Richard North).

The fiendish untranslatable complexity of the original poems has always been a challenge for translators. Although many of the translated poems in the sagas lie rather dead on the page (indeed, some of the originals are often rather dead themselves) there are a number of exceptional poems that more than merit efforts to come to terms with the form.

Take as a fairly gentle example the second poem in *Kormák's Saga*. Kormákr the skald has just caught a glimpse of the ankles, and then eyes, of

Steingerðr, with whom he falls in love. She is behind the door of a passage-way where wood is stored, standing at the threshold, only her feet and eyes visible in the hall. The following is Kormákr's response, which is the second of 85 of his poems in the saga. I've highlighted some of the sound patterns in the first two lines:

Brunnu beggja kinna
bjǫrt ljós á mik drósar,
oss hlœgir þat eigi,
eldhúss of við felldan
en til Ǫkkla svanna
ítrvaxins gatk líta,
þró muna oss of ævi
eldask, hjá þreskeldi.

The difficulty of the word order is clear in the following literal render-ing: 'Burned of both the cheeks the bright lights onto me of the girl, us makes laugh it not, from the fire-hall's wood felled but to the ankles of the girl wondrously grown could I look, yearning not us for life age, by the threshold.'

Any translator faces the task of writing a new poem in English that is, somehow, an equivalent or echo of the original. The syllable count and word order are virtually impossible to render into English, but a recent translation takes successful pains to give us quite a good impression of the alliterative density of the Icelandic and the spirit of the original:

The bright lights of both
her cheeks burned onto me
from the fire-hall's felled wood;
no cause of mirth for me in that.
By the threshold I gained a glance
at the ankles of this girl
of glorious shape; yet while I live
that longing will never leave me. (translation by Rory McTurk)

What results is a new poem in English equivalent in many important respects to the original.

Two memorable poems are by Egill Skalla-Grímsson, one for anecdotal reasons, the other as one of the greatest laments of the tenth century. In the first Egill's ship has run aground during a storm at the mouth of the Humber in England. This is when King Eiríkr Bloodaxe and his wife Gunnhildr rule Northumbria from York. Egill and Eiríkr are old enemies. His friend Arinbjǫrn advises him to submit himself to them as he has no obvious means of escape. Gunnhildr is keen to kill him on the spot, but because night has fallen they decide to execute him in the morning (killing at night was considered murder). Arinbjǫrn suggests that Egill compose a celebratory poem, a *drápa*, in Eiríkr's honour. He performs the poem next morning and Eiríkr gives him his head as a reward. It's the so-called 'Head Ransom' (*Hǫfuðlausn*) poem.

Later in his life and back in Iceland, there is a family tragedy. Egill's promising young son Bǫðvarr goes to fetch wood from the Hvítá river with five farmhands. On their return a wild south-westerly gale swamps their boat and they all drown. Egill recovers the body, places it in Skalla-Grímr's burial mound, then, such is his grief, he locks himself in his bed closet intending to starve himself to death. Egill's wife Ásgerðr sends a messenger to their daughter Þorgerðr at Hjarðarholt. She rides to Borg and begs Egill to let her into the bed closet so she can join him in death. Once in she tricks him to eating a bit of seaweed. 'Is it bad for you?' he asks. 'Terrible', she replies (*'Er það illt manni?' segir Egill. 'Allillt' segir hon*). Then he drinks some milk, thinking it would be water. His suicide has been frustrated. She then suggests that he compose a poem in the honour of Bǫðvarr and Gunnarr, another son who had died of a fever shortly before. In the morning he performs 'The Hard Loss of Sons' (*Sonatorrek*) which Þorgerðr promises to carve onto a rune stick. The poem, in 25 stanzas, relies completely on the old mythology. In it Egill expresses his frustration at being unable to take revenge on Óðinn, ultimately responsible for Bǫðvarr's death in the storm. But, finally, he takes comfort in one of Óðinn's gifts . . . the word mead, the god's prize: that is, poetry itself.

Character and action

In most sagas we are told what characters look like but it always their behaviour that is of most importance. We first meet Egill when he is three:

> En er hann óx upp, þá mátti brátt sjá á honum, at hann myndi verða mjǫk ljótr ok líkr feðr sínum, svartr á hár. En þá er hann var þrévetr, þá var hann mikill ok sterkr, svá sem þeir sveinar aðrir, er váru sex vetra eða sjau; hann var brátt málugr ok orðvíss; heldr var hann illr viðreignar, er hann var í leikum með ǫðrum ungmennum. (*Egil's Saga*, Chapter 31)

> As he grew up it soon became clear that he would turn out very ugly and resemble his father, with black hair. When he was three he was as big and strong as a boy of six or seven. He became very talkative at an early age and had a gift for words, but tended to be difficult to deal with in his games with other children.

When the family is invited to a feast that year Skalla-Grímr forbids Egill to join them:

> 'Ekki skaltu fara,' segir Skalla-Grímr, 'því at þú kannt ekki fyrir þér at vera í
> fjǫlmenni, þar er drykkjur eru miklar, er þú þykkir ekki góðr viðskiptis, at þú
> sér ódrukkinn.' (Chapter 31)

> 'You're not coming,' said Skalla-Grímr, 'because you don't know how to behave
> where adults are drinking heavily. You're bad enough when you're sober.'

Egill grows up, ages, loses his hair and, finally, his sight, but as a character he is much the same at 80 as he was at 3.

Manly accomplishments, skill at arms, physical prowess and swimming ability are often registered as heroic traits. Sometimes these are accompanied by Hollywood good looks like Gunnarr Hámundarson in *Njál's Saga* or Kjartan Ólafsson in *Laxárdal*. But physical beauty means little in the sagas. Consider the introduction of Njáll's eldest son Skarpheðinn. We are informed that he is skilled with arms and a good swimmer and runner. He is quick to speak and often scathing in his words. His physical description sounds honest and neutral but gives us an insight into the saga teller's more long-term intentions.

> Hann var jarpr á hár ok sveipr í hárinu, eygðr vel, fǫlleitr ok skarpleitr, liðr á
> nefi ok lá hátt tanngarðrinn, munnljótr nǫkkut ok þó manna hermannlegastr.
> (*Njáls Saga*, Chapter 25)

> He had curly auburn hair and handsome eyes. He was pale and sharp-featured
> with a crooked nose and protruding teeth, which made him ugly around the
> mouth. He looked a real warrior.

We'll return to Skarpheðinn and the subject of teeth in due course.

The descriptions of women follow the same direct, succinct pattern. The variety of powerful women in the sagas is impressive. Beauty is often a bonus, but qualities of intelligence and temperament carry more weight in the long run. Hallgerðr Hǫskuldr's daughter is:

> kvenna fríðust sýnum ok mikil vexti, ok því var hon langbrók kǫlluð. Hon
> var fagrhár ok svá mikit hárit, at hon mátti hylja sig með. Hon var ǫrlynd
> ok skaphǫrð. (*Njáls Saga*, Chapter 9)

> a woman of great beauty. She was very tall, which earned her the name Long-
> Legs, and her lovely hair was now so long that it could veil her whole body. She
> was extravagant and quick-tempered.

She is later responsible for the deaths of her three husbands, most notably the heroic Gunnarr Hámundarson. He has been sentenced to lesser outlawry at the Althing for some killings. On his way to the ship and three years' exile his horse stumbles and he looks back to the sloping fields of his farm at Hlíðarendi. His response has an understandably iconic status in the Icelandic imagination:

'Fǫgr er hlíðin, svá at mér hefir hon aldri jafnfǫgr sýnzk, bleikir akrar ok slegin tún, ok mun ek ríða heim aptr ok fara hvergi.' (*Njáls Saga*, Chapter 75)

'How lovely the slopes are: more lovely than they have ever seemed to me before, pale cornfields and new-mown hay. I am going back home, and I will not go away.'

Soon after this Gunnarr is besieged by his enemies at his house but can keep the attackers at bay with his bow and arrows. One of his enemies manages to slash his bowstring. He asks Hallgerðr for locks of her famously long hair to make repairs. She refuses. He had slapped her once, she reminds him. He is overcome and killed. That she is 'extravagant and quick-tempered' comes to count for much more in the saga than her long legs and beauty. Other, less significant, characters will often get a vivid (and loaded) sentence. Stýrr's daughter, Ásdís, in *Eyrbyggja saga*, is 'vigorous, very proud and rather temperamental' (*skǫrulig, ofláti mikill ok heldr skapstór*, Chapter 28).

Throughout the sagas we are given the impression of meeting real people from whose actions we can intuit qualities of their characters. Physical peculiarities or shortcomings are a normal part of the initial portrait as well as clues to future behaviour and event. Njáll Þorgeirsson of Bergþórshvol is 'wealthy and handsome, but he had one peculiarity: he could not grow a beard' (*vel auðigr at fé ok vænn at áliti, en sá hlutr var á ráði hans, at honum óx eigi skegg*, *Njáls Saga*, Chapter 20). In the build-up to the feud that reaches its climax with Gunnarr's death, Hallgerðr and her unsavoury cronies decide to call Njáll 'Old Beardless' (*karl inn skegglausi*) and his sons 'Little Dung-beards' (*taðskegglingar*), insults that Gunnarr finds intolerable.

Another memorable, and not very flattering, introduction to a character is Þórhallr'. His short saga, called Ale-hood's Story (*Ǫlkofra þáttr*), is one of several very fine comedies in the canon. He brews ale to sell at the Althing and always wears a hood. The way that he is described and dealt with is telling:

Lítill var hann ok ljótr. Engi var hann íþróttamaður [. . .] Engi var Þórhallr veifiskati kallaðr ok heldr sínkr. Honum váru augu þung.

He was small and ugly. He was a man of no great physical prowess [. . .] No one called Þórhallr a generous man. He was, in fact, rather stingy. His eyesight was poor.

In an unfortunate accident when making charcoal, Ale-hood burns up a wood belonging jointly to six powerful *goðar* ('chieftains'), all of whom appear as major characters in other sagas. They conspire, rather maliciously, to have Ale-hood outlawed so they can share out his wealth. Ale-hood appears so pitiful that his case is taken up by Broddi Bjarnason, brother-in-law of the powerful *goði* Þórsteinn Síðu-Hallsson. Broddi proceeds to humiliate the *goðar* one by one and save Ale-hood's miserable skin. He accuses them in court of greed, cowardice and sexual perversion. Þorkell Scarf, for example, blundered en route to last year's Spring Assembly, not on the lookout for Steingrímr's

> 'stóðhest selfeitan, ok lagðist hann upp at baki þér, en merrin sú, er þú reitt, var mǫgr, ok fell hon under þér, ok hefi ek eigi spurt til sans, hverjum þá slauðraði, en hitt sá menn, at þú vart lengi fastr, því at hestrinn lagði fœtrna fram yfir kápuna.' (Chapter 3)

> 'seal-fat stallion which mounted you from behind, while the bony mare you were riding collapsed under you, and I have not heard for a fact which of you got nailed. Everyone could see how long you were stuck there, the stallion's legs had got such a grip on your cloak.'

Or Eyjólfr Þórðarson, who, being pursued by his enemies, became 'so afraid that you turned yourself into the likeness of a mare, which was a great abomination' (*svá hræddr, at þú brátt þér í merar líki, ok váru slíkt firn mikil*).

It is the action, the give and take, the insults that inform the saga. Character, Ale-hood's especially, adds to the fun but is so clearly secondary that at the end of the third chapter the saga man informs us quite bluntly that 'Ale-hood is now out of the saga' (*Er nú Ǫlkofri ór sǫgunni*).

One of the *goði* dealt with so peremptorily by Broddi is Snorri the *goði* Þorgrímsson, the friend and confidante of Guðrún Ósvífr's daughter, as we've seen. He appears in 11 sagas but features most prominently in *The Saga of the People of Eyri (Eyrbyggja saga)*, which is a wonderful weaving together of many episodic strands, and contains some of the best ghost stories in the literature. The subtleties of saga characterisation and the invitation to the listener to construct motive and second guess are given brilliant exposition here:

> Snorri var meðalmaðr á hæð ok heldr grannligr, fríðr sýnum, réttleitr ok ljóslitaðr, bleikhárr ok rauðskeggjaðr; hann var hógværr hversdagliga; fann lítt á honum, hvárt honum þótti vel eða illa; hann var vitr maðr ok forspár um marga hluti, langrækr ok heiptúðigr, heilráðr vinum sínum, en óvinir hans þóttusk heldr kulða af kenna ráðum hans. (*Eyrbyggja saga*, Chapter 15)

> Snorri was a man of medium height but rather thin, and he was handsome, with regular features and fair skin. He had fair hair and a red beard. He was usually an even-tempered man, and did not readily show his likes and dislikes. Snorri was a wise man and had foresight about many things, a long memory

and a disposition to vengeance. He gave good counsel but his enemies felt the chill of his strategies.

After this we see him in action, listen to the words he speaks, or hear reports about him. It would never occur to the saga writer to presume to guess what Snorri might be thinking. That, of course, is left to us, and is one source of real delight in the saga style.

An episode later in the saga demonstrates the effect of the technique at its best. Stýrr Þorgrímsson from Hraun, one of Snorri's rather stormy neighbours, finds himself lumbered with two Swedish berserks, the brothers Halli and Leiknir. They had been the gift to Stýrr's brother Vermundr from Earl Hákon Sigurðarson of Lade in Norway. 'They both went into berserk fits and once they had worked themselves up into a frenzy they were not like human beings. They went mad like dogs and had no fear of either fire or iron' (*Þeir gengu berserksgang ok váru þá eigi í mannligu eðli, er þeir váru reiðir, ok fóru galnir sem hundar ok óttuðusk hvárki eld né járn*, Chapter 25).

Soon after moving in with Stýrr, Halli takes a fancy to Stýrr's daughter Ásdís who, as we know, 'is vigorous, very proud and rather temperamental'. She doesn't seem to resist the Swedish he-man's charm and chat. Much to the father's alarm Halli tells Stýrr that he want to marry Ásdís. Menacingly, Halli gives him three days to consult with his friends and bring him a positive answer. Stýrr rides over to Snorri's farm at Helgafell to seek advice. Snorri takes him up onto Helgafell to talk because plans made there have a better chance of bearing fruit. 'They walked up onto the mountain and sat there talking right up until evening. No one knew what they were talking about. Then Stýrr rode home' (*Síðan gengu þeir á fjallit upp ok sátu þar á tali allt til kvelds; vissi það engi maðr, hvat þeir tǫluðu. Síðan reið Stýrr heim*, Chapter 28).

Stýrr's offer to the brothers is that, as Halli has no money, Stýrr will set certain difficult tasks for them to perform. Once completed Halli may have Ásdís in marriage. The berserks are to clear a road through the lava field out to Bjarnarhǫfn, build a field wall over the lava between pastures and make an enclosure on Stýrr's side of the wall. These are prodigious tasks, indeed, and require all the additional power of berserk frenzy to accomplish. While the work is in progress Stýrr builds a new bathhouse at Hraun. It is deep in the ground and incredibly hot. When the berserks return they are exhausted by the work and the berserk frenzy they have been in. Stýrr suggests a rest and a warm soak in the new bathhouse. Once they're in, he blocks off the entrance and piles rocks on top. He then cranks up the heat and spreads a wet ox hide in front of the door. Halli finally manages to smash through the door, but slips on the hide and is killed by Stýrr. Leiknir has a spear thrust through him as he charges out and falls dead back through the door. They are dumped in a pit in the lava field so deep that nothing could be seen from the bottom but the sky:

> En er Snorri goði spyrr þetta, reið hann út undir Hraun, ok sátu þeir Snorri ok Stýrr enn allan dag. En af tali þeirra kom þat upp, at Stýrr fastnaði Snorra goða Ásdísi dóttur sína, ok tókust þessi ráð um haustið eptir. (Chapter 28)

> When Snorri the Goði heard about this he rode over to Hraun where he and Stýrr spent the whole day talking together. The outcome of their discussion was that Stýrr betrothed his daughter, Ásdís, to Snorri the Goði, and the wedding took place the next autumn.

We are left to reconstruct the conversation on Helgafell and to imagine the intrigues and thoughts of Snorri and Stýrr. The berserks are now safely out of the way, there is a useful road through the lava field (still called the *berserkjahraun*), Stýrr is freed from further threat and Snorri establishes an important kin relationship in the area and, of course, he gets the girl. We learn from another genealogical source that Snorri and Ásdís have four children: Þórðr, Þóroddr, Þorsteinn, and especially Guðlaugr, who became a monk at Lincoln in England.

Tenth-century jet set: Vikings see the world

Viking raids and battles loom large in the sagas. Many of the original settlers have Viking pasts and many young Icelanders, who travel abroad as a part of their coming of age, become involved in Viking expeditions of one kind or another. The most full blown and vivid of them all is our old favourite, Egill Skalla-Grímsson of Borg. In his career abroad he manifests all the qualities that the Anglo-Saxons feared about their northern neighbours and which the Victorians blew into the large-scale caricatures of these bearded bullies.

Egill is a ruthless warrior, a rune master, a bit of a berserk, a prodigious drinker, a sailor and a first rate skaldic poet. In his seventh year, at the autumnal ball games on the plains by the Hvítá river, he is roughed up by Grímr Heggsson, a 10- or 11-year-old who is strong for his age. Egill's response is to borrow a hand axe and drive it into Grímr's head, right through to the brain. Skalla-Grímr seems indifferent to the event, but Egill's mother Bera says he has 'the makings of a true Viking and would clearly be put in command of warships when he was old enough' (*Bera kvað Egil vera víkingsefni ok kvað þat mundu fyrir liggja, þegar hann hefði aldr til, at honum væri fengin herskip*). Egill answers with a skaldic verse:

Þat mælti mín móðir,
at mér skyldi kaupa
fley ok fagrar árar,
fara á brott með víkingum,
standa upp í stafni,
stýra dýrum knerri,
halda svá til hafnar,
hǫggva mann og annan. (*Egils saga Skalla-Grímssonar*, Chapter 40)

My mother said
I would be bought
a boat with fine oars
set off with Vikings
stand upon the prow
command the precious craft,
then enter port
kill a man and another. (translation by Bernard Scudder)

When he is 13, after another killing or two, he travels abroad with his elder brother Þórólfr, and the Viking episodes really come to life.

In Norway Egill journeys with a bailiff named Ǫlvir and his men to collect rents. After a rough passage they reach Atley Island, near an estate of King Eiríkr Bloodaxe and Queen Gunnhildr. It is run by Bárðr, who puts them up in an outbuilding and, protesting that he has no ale, gives them bread and butter and bowls of curds and whey. He twice states that he'd give them better if he had it. King Eiríkr and Queen Gunnhildr turn up shortly later and are given a feast with plenty of strong ale. Egill and his men then join in the drinking, which is a sort of competition in which men sit in pairs and must finish off each horn of ale in one. You can't put a horn down to rest on the table in any case. Bárðr's initial deception about the drink is clearly an unforgivable breach of Viking hospitality. After many a horn of ale, Bárðr and Gunnhildr put poison in Egill's drinking horn. Egill carves a few runes on the horn and splashes them with his own blood. The drinking horn shatters, spilling the poisoned ale onto the straw. Egill and Ǫlvir head for the door, pursued by Bárðr who insists that they drink more:

Myrkt var í forstofunni; hann lagði sverðinu á Bárði miðjum, svá at blóðrefillinn hljóp út um bakit; féll hann dauðr niðr, en blóð hljóp úr undinni. Þá fell Ǫlvir, ok gaus spýja ór honum. Egill hljóp út ór stofunni. (Chapter 44)

It was dark in the doorway. Egill thrust the sword so deep into Bárðr's stomach that the point came out through his back. Bárðr fell down dead, blood pouring from the wound. Then Ǫlvir dropped to the floor, spewing vomit. Egill ran out of the room.

The next spring Þórólfr and Egill equip a big longship and go raiding in the Baltic. The Viking's dealings in Courland (*Kúrland*) suggest, perhaps, the reality of international relations at that time. Sometimes they raid, kill and plunder, fight battles and win booty. On another occasion: 'They offered the people a fortnight's truce and traded with them. But when the truce was over they began plundering again' (*lǫgðu þar við land með hálfs mánaðar friði ok kaupstefnu; en er því var lokit, þá tóku þeir at herja*, Chapter 46).

On this expedition the Vikings split up into parties of a dozen each to find their own booty. Egill's group discover a large farm in the forest and, looking for loot, are captured by a band of Courlanders, who decide to torture and kill them the next morning, since night is falling and it will be more fun in daylight. They are tightly bound and locked in an outbuilding. Of course, Egill manages to free himself and his men. They discover a store-room which is full of valuable treasure and weapons. They arm themselves, take the treasure, and runs towards the ships. In the woods, however, the Viking Egill stops in his tracks:

> 'Þessi ferð er allill ok eigi hermannlig; vér hǫfum stolit fé bónda, svá at hann veit eigi til; skal oss aldregi þá skǫmm henda; fǫrum nú aptr til bœjarins ok látum þá vita, hvat títt er.' (Chapter 46)

> 'This is a poor and cowardly raid. We have stolen all the farmer's wealth without him knowing. We shall never suffer such shame. Let us go back to the farm and let people know what has happened.'

Very much against the wishes of his comrades, who simply want to clear off back to the ship, Egill rushes back by himself, takes burning logs from the fire room and sets the farmhouse alight. Moments later the main room flames up, the roof collapses and everyone inside perishes. Egill claims a chest of silver as his private booty.

There is an exceptionally vivid portrait of Egill in his mature years. This is after his taking part in a battle which has since been identified with the battle of *Brunanburh* (probably Bromborough on the Wirral), which, as we have seen in Chapter 11 (p. 323), is celebrated in a poem in the *Chronicle* entry for year 937. In *Egil's Saga* the battle is called Vinheiðr and is fought by King 'Aðalsteinn' of England (i.e. Æthelstan, ruled 927–39) against the Scots and Vikings from Ireland. In this battle Egill's brother, Þórólfr, has just been killed. After the battle is over, Egill sits in the high seat across from the king, menacing Aðalsteinn with his looks until he gets an appropriate financial recompense:

> Hann hafði hjálm á hǫfði ok lagði sverðit um kné sér ok dró annat skeið til hálfs, en þá skelldi hann aptr í slíðrin; hann sat uppréttr ok var gneypr mjǫk.

Egill var mikilleitr, ennibreiðr, brúnamikill, nefit ekki langt, en ákafliga digrt, granstœðit vítt ok langt, hakan breið furðuliga, ok svá allt um kjálkana, hálsdigr ok herðimikill, svá at þat bar frá því, sem aðrir menn váru, harðleitr ok grimmligr, þá er hann var reiðr; hann var vel í vexti ok hverjum manni hærri, úlfgrátt harit ok þykkt ok varð snimma skǫllóttr; nn er hann sat, sem fyrr var ritat, þá hleypði hann annarri brúninni ofan á kinnina, en annarri upp í hárrœtr; Egill var svarteygr ok skolbrúnn. (Chapter 55)

He was wearing a helmet and laid his sword across his knees, and now and again he would draw it half-way out of the scabbard, then thrust it back in again. He sat upright, but with his head bowed low. Egill had very distinctive features, with a wide forehead, bushy brows and a nose that was not long but extremely broad. His beard grew over a long, wide part of his face, and his chin and entire jaw were exceptionally broad. With his thick neck and broad shoulders, he stood out from other men. When he was angry, his face grew harsh and fierce. He was well built and taller than other men, with thick wolf-grey hair, although he had gone bald at an early age. When he was sitting in this particular scene, he wrinkled one eyebrow right down onto his cheek and raised the other up to the roots of his hair. Egill had dark eyes and his brows joined in the middle.

Later in the saga Egill is back in Norway. He is sent on a mission by the king to collect tribute in Vermaland. Travelling through a treacherous winter landscape, they arrive at a farm run by a man named Ármóðr. Like Bárðr in Atley earlier, Ármóðr gives them bowls of curds and a room for the night, protesting that he has nothing better. At her mother's suggestion Ármóðr's 10- or 11-year-old daughter speaks a verse and spills the beans. He slaps her but then brings in an exceptionally strong brew of ale. The drinking, rule governed and formulaic (and reminiscent of many a rough public bar in England today), commences. Egill's companions become incapacitated through drink one by one. As a matter of honour Egill finishes what they are incapable of drinking. When he feels he can go on no longer:

Stóð hann þá upp ok gekk um gólf þvert, þangat er Ármóðr sat; hann tók hǫndum í axlir honum ok kneikði hann upp at stǫfum. Síðan þeysti Egill upp ór sér spýju mikla, ok gaus í andlit Ármóði, í augun ok nasarnar ok í munninn; rann svá ofan um bringuna; en Ármóði varð við andhlaup, ok er hann fekk Ǫndinni frá sér hrundit, þá gaus upp spýja. (Chapter 71)

He stood up and walked across the floor to where Ármóðr was sitting, seized him by the shoulders and thrust him up against a wall-post. Then Egill spewed a torrent of vomit that gushed all over Ármóðr's face, filling his eyes and nostrils and mouth and pouring down his chest. Ármóðr was close to choking, and when he managed to let out his breath, a jet of vomit gushed out with it.

Next morning Egill goes to Ármóðr's bed closet intending to kill him. Wife and daughter plead for mercy. Obligingly, Egill cuts off the man's beard close to the chin and gouges out one of his eyes with his finger, leaving it hanging on his cheek. These are only a few examples of the rollicking, almost comic, good stuff of Viking Egill at his best.

The following day they arrive at Þorfinnr's farm in Eiðaskógr. The farmer's daughter, Helga, is lying on the cross-bench clearly very ill. Egill asks if anything has been done about her illness. 'We have had some runes carved. The son of a farmer who lives nearby did it and since then she's been much worse' (*'Ristnar hafa verit rúnar, ok er sá einn bóndason heðan skammt í brott. Er þat gerði, ok er síðan miklu verr en áðr'*). Egill examines the bed and finds a whalebone with runes carved on it. He reads the runes, then shaves them off into the fire. He burns the whalebone and speaks a verse:

> Skalat maðr rúnar rísta,
> nema ráða vel kunni,
> Þat verðr mǫrgum manni,
> es of myrkvan staf villisk;
> sák á telgðu talkni
> tíu launstafi ristna,
> Þat hefr lauka lindi
> langs oftrega fengit. (Chapter 72)

> No man should carve runes
> unless he can read them well;
> many a man goes astray
> around these dark letters.
> On the whalebone I saw
> ten secret letters carved
> from them the linden tree
> took her long harm. (translation by Bernard Scudder)

Egill then carves some new runes and places them under the pillow. Helga feels as if she were waking from a deep sleep. She is well again, but still very weak.

Foreign travel is a common currency in many of the sagas. Norwegian kings, queens and earls are often shown as anxious to meet, entertain and reward Icelandic visitors. One such is Queen Gunnhildr, Egill's nemesis. Gunnhildr is a bit of a sexy witch, a woman the Icelanders loved to hate. Early in *Njáls Saga* Hrútr ('ram') Herjólfsson, Hǫskuldr's half-brother, must journey to Norway to claim an inheritance left him by his mother. He leaves behind his fiancée Unnr Mǫrðr's daughter, promising to return within three years for the wedding. At the time Eirikr Bloodaxe has been killed and his son Haraldr Grey-Cloak rules with his mother Gunnhildr. She hears that a ship has arrived and is anxious to know what Icelanders are aboard. She arranges that Hrútr is well received by Haraldr and the terms of his inheritance are secured. She then places Hrútr on her throne, treats him to a feast, sits up drinking with him and takes him to bed every night for a fortnight. Before he leaves she asks him if he has a woman out in Iceland. He denies that he has, but Gunnhildr senses the truth. Because he hasn't been honest with her she casts a spell: he will be unable to consummate his marriage, but will be able to have normal sex with any other woman.

After a miserable two years back home his marriage to Unnr ends in divorce. Unnr confesses to her father that the marriage has not been consummated. We imagine impotence at first but, no, quite the contrary:

'Þegar hann kemr við mik, þá er hǫrund hans svá mikit, at hann má ekki eptirlæti hafa við mik, en þó hǫfum vit bæði breytni til þess á alla vega, at vit mættim njótask, en þat verðr ekki. En þó áðr vit skilim, sýnir hann þat af sér, at hann er í œði sínu rétt sem aðrir menn.' (*Njáls Saga*, Chapter 7)

'Whenever he touches me, his member is so engorged that he cannot have enjoyment of me, although we both passionately desire to reach consummation. But we have never succeeded. And yet, before we draw apart, he proves that he is by nature as normal as other men.'

These are the ironically determined grounds for divorce that leads to the first set of feuds that lead to Gunnarr's death and finally reach climax with the conflagration at Bergþórshvol many years later. We learn in *Laxdœla saga* that with his later two wives Hrútr has 16 sons and 10 daughters.

These wonderfully suggestive pieces of violence and erotica are in no way unique in the saga canon, but one wonders if the very distance from Iceland, and the passport to the imagination such distance allows, doesn't give the saga teller more rein to elaborate and embellish his story for the delight of his farm-bound audience. It is often the case that exploits and episodes abroad are much more colourful and vivid, more charged with sex and violence, than events in Iceland, on the farm, when the hero returns. The Egill that we see back home is rather different from the violent and vomiting berserk Viking we see in Norway, England, and the Baltic. He is still large, strong willed and difficult to deal with, but the liberty of distance and exciting fantasy is further removed. Young men regularly earn their reputation by seeing the world, by being received at the courts of Norway, Denmark, England, Orkney and Ireland. They are often rewarded for poems in praise of a king or earl and join their retainers for military or Viking adventures. There isn't a regular pattern to such narratives, however, and the variety is part of the spice of such stories.

Hauntings in the sagas

Although much of the saga literature is realistic, workaday and domestic, there is no shortage of the supernatural, eerie and thrilling. Trolls and giant-esses appear from time to time, but aren't usually a significant feature in most stories. We've met already a number of shape changers and berserks, but these are normally psychotic humans with little of the spirit world about them. It's the revenants, the living dead, that linger in the memory. The George A. Romero element in some Icelandic stories must have given many an Icelandic youngster uneasy moments after dark on long winter nights.

Ghosts in the sagas are corporeal, violent and malevolent. In *Eyrbyggja saga* Þórólfr Lame-Foot (*bægifótr*), father of Arnkell and neighbour of Snorri the Goði, dies an ugly death in a fit of rage. He's buried in a strongly built cairn. Soon after people realise that he's not resting in peace. Animals near the cairn run wild and bellow themselves to death. The shepherd is regularly chased home by Þórólfr. Later he is found dead near the cairn: his body is coal black and every bone in his body is broken. Later he is seen in Þórólfr's company. As winter advances, and darkness falls further and further, people hear someone riding the roof. No one dares graze animals in the valley. The farms are devastated, then deserted. Þórólfr kills some men, who are later seen in his company. In the spring Arnkell Þórólfsson decides to move the corpse. It is undecayed but hideous to look at. On the way to the new burial site on a headland, the oxen pulling the sledge go mad, break loose and run themselves to death. Þórólfr is buried in a new cairn and rests quietly for some time. This sort of malevolent creature, wreaking death, destruction and madness after its own death, is truly disturbing, and appears with some frequency.

In *Grettis saga*, it is a Swedish shepherd, named Glámr, who dies but then returns to haunt Forsœludal ('the valley of shadows') in Skagafjǫrðr in the north. Such valleys, with beautiful mountains to the south, enjoy 24 hours of daylight during the summer months. That's when you should go to Iceland. But then, aha, the sun sets in early December not to rise again until early February: the perfect setting for ghosts and hauntings. Glámr is easily as malevolent and destructive as Þórólfr Lame-Foot. He rides the roof at night, kills men and animals, drives some people out of their wits and to death. He clears the valley. Grettir the Strong is just the hero to deal with this. In another show of his strength and derring-do Grettir takes on Glámr. After an epic struggle in the farmhouse, during which they crash through the doorframe and out into the night, Grettir manages to pin Glámr to the ground. Before he can behead him (to settle a revenant you must chop off its head and place it by the buttocks) the moon appears from behind the swiftly flying clouds. Suddenly Grettir's strength deserts him, from exhaustion but also because of the fierce way Glámr is rolling his eyes. In this eerie moment Glámr pronounces his curse:

> 'Þú munt verða útlægr gọrr ok hljóta jafnan úti at búa einn samt. Þá legg ek þat á við þik, at þessi augu sé þér jafnan fyrir sjónum, sem ek ber eptir, ok mun þér þá erfitt þykkja einum at vera, ok þat mun þér til dauða draga.' (*Grettis saga*, Chapter 35)

> 'You will be made an outlaw and be forced to live alone and outdoors. And this curse I lay on you: my eyes will always be before your sight and this will make you find it difficult to be alone. And this will lead to your death.'

For the rest of his life Grettir will be afraid of the dark, a wonderfully sinister and effective curse on an outlaw, forced to live outside in a land with particularly dark winters!

Another set of memorable hauntings occur in *Eyrbyggja saga* centred on Fróða farm, to the west of Helgafell. Around the year 1000 a ship arrives from Dublin. One passenger is the Hebridean woman Þórgunna, who was once a lover of Leifr 'the Lucky' Eiríksson and bore his child. We know this from a story in *Eiríkr the Red's Saga*. She lodges at with Þuríðr, who is envious of her fine English linen and silk quilt. Her bed canopy is stunning, the like not seen before the Iceland. Þórgunna is in her 50s. She is blunt spoken, tall and stout, with dark eyelashes, narrow eyes and a full head of chestnut hair. She is well mannered and a churchgoer, but not very talkative. She takes a fancy to Þuríðr's 14-year-old son Kjartan, but he is reserved in her company (probably horrified), which irritates her.

One day during haymaking there is a sudden downpour from a mysterious black cloud that sweeps across the clear sky. It is a rain of blood. All the hay dries except for Þórgunna's. She thinks that the marvel forbodes the death of someone. She falls ill soon after. On her deathbed asks to be taken to Skálholt for burial because she senses that it will one day be a holy centre. She then divides her possessions. She gives Þuríðr a number of articles, but firmly stipulates that they must burn her bed and bedclothes. After her death Þuríðr pleads with her husband Þóroddr not to burn anything so fine as the English linen. He finally relents. On the way to Skálholt with the corpse the party is refused hospitality on a farm near the Hvítá river. They go to bed without food. In the middle of the night the farm is disturbed by a rustle in the pantry. It is Þórgunna, stark naked, baking bread for her pall bearers. The farmer then offers them whatever they want. Þórgunna leaves the room and isn't seen after that.

Soon at Fróða the hauntings begin. One evening a half-moon appears on the wainscoting and circles the room. Þórir Wood-Leg (*tréfótr*) explains that it is a 'fatal moon' (*urðarmána*) and will be followed by someone's death. The deaths begin. First a shepherd falls ill. A few days later he is found dead. Þórir Wood-Leg is then accosted by the dead shepherd on his way to the privy one evening. He is badly thrown around, becomes ill and dies. Þórir and the shepherd are seen in each other's company after that. One after another the farmhands die until there are six dead in all. While this is going on, something begins to eat the dried fish in the storeroom. One day Þóroddr sets off with five companions in a ten-oared boat to fetch more dried fish. During their absence a seal's head comes up out of the floor in the fireplace. A servant tries to beat it back down into the floor with a club, but it rises further and further, staring at Þórgunna's bed curtain. Young Kjartan attacks it with an iron sledge hammer and, finally, blow after blow, drives it back down through the floor. The next morning Þóroddr and his companions are reported to have drowned.

Kjartan and Þuríðr prepare a funeral feast using the Yule ale for the occasion. On the first night Þórodd and his companions come in, totally drenched. This is considered a good omen. There is still a vestige of the heathen belief that if the drowned attend their own funeral feast they've been well received by the sea goddess Rán. The drowned go though the sleeping hall and settle in the fire room. When the fire burns down they leave. This continues through the week. After all the guests have left the fire is lit as usual. Þóroddr and his companions return and begin to wring out their clothes. Then Þórir Wood-Leg and his five companions enter. They are covered with earth (as you would expect of the buried) and begin splattering mud on the drowned sailors. This goes on throughout Yule (and you thought *your* Christmas was awful!). While all this is going on a tail appears among the dried fish. The stockfish is being mysteriously consumed. Þorgríma Witch-Cheek (*galdrakinn*), Þórir Wood-Leg's widow, then falls ill and, shortly, she and five others die. By the end of the winter, 18 people have died and five servants have run away. From a farm community of 30 only seven remain.

Finally young Kjartan rides over the Helgafell to seek the advice of his uncle Snorri the Goði. Snorri sends a priest to Fróða. Snorri advises them to burn Þórgunna's bed canopy and prosecute all the revenants at a special court. The priest should then sing mass, consecrate water and hear confession. As usual, his advice is sound. Kjartan burns the bedclothes and Þórðr the Cat, Snorri's foster son and father of Stúfr the Blind, begins to summons the revenants for trespass and depriving people of life and health. The procedure follows that of an action at an assembly, decisions are heard and cases are summed up and judged. As each is sentenced he or she stands up and leaves, some with a comment like 'I sat here as long as I could' or 'I think there's little peace to be had here, so we will all get going.' They all seem reluctant to leave. So end the hauntings.

We must now return to Þórólfr Lame-Foot. He has been reburied on the headland in Chapter 34. Nearly 30 chapters later, Þórólfr returns, more malevolent and destructive than ever. He is killing both people and livestock and clearing the valley. Arnkell, his son, has by now been killed by Snorri the Goði, so it falls to Þóroddr Þorbrandsson (Snorri's blood brother) to take action. They break into the cairn. The corpse is black as hell, large as an ox, and still unrotted. It is monstrous to look at. This time they roll the body to the seashore and burn it. The strong wind blows the ashes far and wide. They collect what they can and throw it into the sea.

Such treatment should be enough to lay any ghost (it would work for me), but Þórólfr is more stubborn than most. One of Þóroddr's cows takes to wandering down to the foreshore and licking the stones where the funeral fire had been. Yes. Of course. The cow is later found to be with calf and gives birth to a heifer and then a bull. The bull prospers. When it bellows, Þóroddr's old foster mother, once thought to have foresight, but now blind and a bit batty, warns everyone, Cassandra-like, 'that's the sound of a troll, not the sound of a natural beast, and you'd do well to kill that illboding creature' ('Þetta eru trolls læti, en eigi annars kvikendis, ok gerið svá vel, skerið vábeiðu þessa.') It's Þórólfr again! Suddenly, after four years, through which Glæsir the bull has behaved like a pussy cat, with the foster mother tiring everyone with her warnings, the bull turns beastly. In a vivid final struggle, the Glæsir–Þórólfr creature tosses Þóroddr's torso into the air, twists him round and gores him deep in the stomach. The bull charges off with a terrible roar, pursued by the servants. He charges out into a bog, sinks down and never comes up again. Þóroddr, of course, is dead.

Episodes in the sagas

Sagas of Icelanders are, generally speaking, episodic. We are normally taken from one largely self-contained series of events to another. The 159 chapters of *Njáls Saga*, for example, break down into narrative units of around ten chapters, sometimes more in the case of a major confrontation like the Battle of the Althing, sometimes fewer, like the five chapters about the coming of Christianity (which was taken from another source in any case). Older scholarly opinion held that the episodes reflect the oral creation and performance of the stories. An evening's entertainment could comfortably accommodate two or three exciting episodes. The early decades of the twentieth century saw the rise of theories, called 'book prose', which maintained that sagas were authored works. Yes, there was an oral tradition that fed into the enterprise, but the saga men were literate authors creating long and structured works that could not have been retained in any individual performance memory. How much of the surviving saga corpus is editorial (transcribing older oral memories) and how much is authorial remains a vexed question in saga studies. But there is no question that sagas like *Njáls Saga* are highly coherent.

On this issue I'd like to return to Skarpheðinn Njálsson, with his 'crooked nose and protruding teeth'. In a series of increasingly serious misunderstandings after the killing of Gunnarr, the Njálssons become hostile to Þráinn Sigfússon, his brother Lambi and his sons. One winter's day Njáll's wife Bergþóra gets a report from some beggar women that Þráinn and his party have helped them across the frozen Markar River. The men had said unpleasant things about Njáll, calling him 'Old Beardless' his sons 'Little Dung-beards'. The women report that Þráinn with his seven companions will return to the district in four or five days.

On their return the Njálssons and their new brother-in-law, one Kári Sǫlmundarson, set an ambush. They are five against eight. Þráinn takes up position on the ice sheet opposite a floe that spans the channel of the river. Skarpheðinn's shoe thong breaks as they begin their attack (broken shoe laces in the sagas signal that something significant and exciting is about to happen). He reties it, then rushes down the hill towards the river:

> Skarpheðinn hefr sik á lopt ok hleypr yfir fljótit meðal hǫfuðísa ok stǫðvar sik ekki ok rennir þegar af fram fótskriðu. Svellit var hált mjǫk, ok fór hann svá hart sem fogl flygi. (Chapter 92)

> Skarpheðinn made a leap and cleared the channel between the ice banks, steadied himself, and at once went into a slide; the ice was glassy-smooth, and he skimmed along as fast as a bird.

What follows is justly famous:

> Þráinn ætlaði þá at setja á sik hjálminn. Skarpheðin berr nú at fyrri, ok hǫggr til Þráins með Ǫxinni, ok kom í hǫfuðit ok klauf ofan í jaxlana, svá at þeir fellu niðr á ísinn. Þessi atburðr varð með svá skjótrisvipan, at engi fekk hǫggvi á hann komit [. . .]
> 'Karlmannliga er at farit', segir Kári.

> Þráinn was about to put on his helmet. Skarpheðinn came swooping down on him and swung at him with his axe. The axe crashed down on his head and split it down to the jaw-bone, spilling the back teeth onto the ice. It all

happened so quickly that no one had time to land a blow on Skarpheðinn as he skimmed past at great speed [. . .]

'That was man's work', said Kári.'

The Njálssons and Kári kill Hrappr and Tjǫrvi in the ensuing battle, but spare the lives of the 'young puppies' including Gunnarr Lambason.

'Koma mun þar einu hverju sinni', segir Helgi, 'at þú mundir vilja hafa drepit hann, því at hann mun aldri trúr verða ok engi þeirra, er hér eru nú.'

Skarpheðinn mælti: 'Ekki mun ek hræðask þá.' (Chapter 92)

'Some day it will come about', said Helgi, 'that you will wish you had killed him, for he will never keep faith with you, nor will any of these who are here now.'

'I will not fear them', said Skarpheðinn.

And so it turns out. Sixteen years (and 37 chapters) later, the events on the frozen river might seem long past and forgotten, but actually the feuds and killings have raised the tension and temperature remorselessly. The Althing and the law have been unable to calm the various factions in the disputes. Finally a band of 100 enemies, led by Flosi Þórðarson of Svínafell, attack Njáll and his family at Bergþórshvol where they set the house alight and burn to death those inside. Eleven people die in the blaze including Njáll and Bergþóra, their sons Helgi, Grímr, and Skarpheðinn, Kári's 5-year-old boy Þórðr, who refuses to leave his grandmother, old Sæunn, Þórd Freedman (*leysingja*) and three others. Only Kári manages to escape the conflagration, later to wreak terrible revenge on the Burners.

As the flames rage, Gunnarr Lambason jumps up on the wall and taunts Skarpheðinn:

'Hvárt grætr þú nú Skarpheðinn?'

'Eigi er þat', segir hann, 'en hitt er satt, at súrnar í augunum. En svá sýnisk mér sem þú hlæir, eða hvárt er svá?'

'Svá er víst', segir Gunnarr, 'ok hefi ek aldri fyrr hlegit síðan þú vátt Þráin.'

Skarpheðinn mælti: 'Þá er þér hér minjagriprinn.' Tók hann þá jaxl ór pungi sínum, er hann hafði hǫggvit ór Þráni, ok kastaði í auga Gunnari, svá at þegar lá úti á kinninni; fell Gunnarr þá ofan af þekjunni. (Chapter 130)

'Are you crying now Skarpheðinn?' he asked.

'No', said Skarpheðinn 'but it is true that my eyes are smarting. Am I right that you are laughing?'

'I certainly am', said Gunnarr, 'and for the first time since you killed Þráinn.'

'Then here is something to remind you of it', said Skarpheðinn.

He took from his purse a molar he had cut out of Þráinn, and threw it straight at Gunnarr's eye; the eye was gouged out of the socket onto the cheek, and Gunnarr toppled off the wall.

Skarpheðinn burns to death soon after.

We meet the now one-eyed Gunnarr Lambason for the last time in a telling episode toward the end of all the hurly-burly. It is in Chapters 155–6. Kári has been taking his revenge on the Burners in Iceland, sometimes with the help of Bjǫrn of Mǫrk, a wonderfully drawn comic character. Flosi and others of the surviving Burners leave Iceland from Hornafjǫrðr in the east. After a rough passage, with huge waves, thick fog and gales, they are ship-wrecked on mainland Orkney. After fraught negotiations with Earl Sigurðr Hlǫðvisson (fraught because Flosi has killed Helgi Njálsson, once one of the earl's retainers) they are taken in. At Christmas they find themselves in the company of an Irish–Norse king, named Sigtryggr, who has come to seek support for a battle against King Brjánn (Brian) in Ireland. This is the great battle of Clontarf which is celebrated towards the end of *Njáls Saga*. While they wait for an answer, King Sigtryggr and Earl Gilli ask to hear about the burning of Njáll and his family and all the events since. Gunnarr is chosen 'to tell the story and a chair is placed for him to sit on' (*at segja sǫguna, ok var settr undir hann stóll*). The company is unaware that Kári and some of his supporters have landed secretly on mainland and that Kári is listening just outside the hall.

> Sigtryggr konungr spurði: 'Hversu þolði Skarpheðinn í brennunni?'
> 'Vel fyrst', segir Gunnarr, 'en þó lauk svá, at hann grét.'
> Um allar sagnir hallaði hann mjǫk til ok ló frá víða. (Chapter 155)

> King Sigtryggr asked 'How did Skarpheðinn bear the burning?'
> 'Well enough to start with', replied Gunnarr, 'but in the end he wept.'
> His whole account had been extremely biased and riddled with lies.

This is too much for Kári, who bursts into the hall and utters a skaldic verse affirming that he has indeed been avenging Njáll and the others.

> Hrósa hildar fúsir, –
> hvat hafa til fregit skarnar,
> hve ráfáka, rákum
> rennendr? – Níals brennu;
> Varðat veiti-Njǫrðum
> víðeims at þat síðan,
> hrátt gat hrafn at slíta
> hold, slæliga goldit. (Chapter 155)

> Men bold of battle
> boast the burning of Njáll,
> but have you heard
> how we harried them?
> Those givers of gold

had a good return:
ravens feasted
on their raw flesh. (translation after Robert Cook)

Then, to emphasise the point, he runs the length of the hall with his sword drawn and strikes Gunnarr on the neck with such force that the head flies off onto the table in front of the king and the earl. Kári makes good his escape and when the hubbub has subsided, the head and body removed and the tables scrubbed, Flosi 'took it upon himself to tell the story of the Burning. He gave every man his proper due and this account of it was trusted' (*tók til ok sagði søguna frá brennunni ok bar ǫllum mǫnnum vel, ok var því trúat*). What we can see in this episode, in a nutshell, is the saga in the making, one of its points of genesis. Within a few short paragraphs we have three versions of the Burning of Njáll: Gunnarr Lambason's, 'full of lies'; Flosi's, which is believed; and, of course, Kári's skaldic verse about his vengeance and, more dramatically, the Icelandic style of his literary critique.

The 'original' written version of *Njáls Saga* probably dates from around 1280, but we don't know who wrote it or where it was composed. It clearly reflects a range of earlier sources. These were genealogies like *The Book of Settlements*, which has material on Mǫrðr, Unnr, Gunnarr, Hǫskuldr and Hallgerðr and others. In addition, Hǫskuldr, Snorri the Goði and Óláfr the Peacock are central characters in *Laxdæla saga*, another important source, which is usually dated to the late 1240s. Behind the many scenes of legal give and take at the Althing, there are also sources like the *Grágás* ('Grey Goose'), an early record of Icelandic law from 1117. The chapters on the Icelanders' conversion to Christianity are from another saga; as, it seems, are the chapters at the end about the Battle of Clontarf.

What the Vikings have done for us

The Sagas of the Icelanders are a treasure trove of exciting stories that give us a unique insight into the ways of life of Europeans in the ninth, tenth and eleventh centuries. A common reflex in universities today is to treat them (if they are treated at all) as something alien to developments in Anglo-Saxon England, but we have seen by now that this is anything but the case. The Norwegian Vikings who settled in Iceland after 870 had regular dealings with the Irish and the Anglo-Saxons. And as we've seen, again and again, the Vikings and their skaldic poets were in regular residence (or raids) in what we now call England, Scotland, Wales and Ireland.

So, for example, Unnr the Deep-Minded Ketilsdóttir's son, Þorsteinn the Red, is said to be king of half of Scotland in the ninth century. Egill composed poems for Eiríkr and Gunnhildr in York, then served as a successful mercenary soldier for Æthelstan at Vinheiðr or *Brunanburh*. King Óláfr Tryggvason spent significant time in East Anglia in the 990s. The Hebridean Þórgunna brought some snazzy English linen with her to Iceland. Snorri Goði sent his son Guðlaugr to be a monk in England. King Cnut's court at Winchester was regularly entertained by Icelandic skalds (see p. 345), whether the Anglo-Saxon part of the audience understood them or not (probably not). Finally, as we have seen, Haraldr Harðráði Sigurdsson was a great friend of the Icelanders and brought some skalds with him in his ill-fated adventure to conquer England at Stamford Bridge in 1066. Had he prevailed against Harold Godwinson, then trumped William the Bastard at Hastings, history would read from a much more northerly direction.

It's now been made clear in our book how intrinsic Old Icelandic literature is to a full understanding of the development of the Anglo-Saxon world and its ideals of heroism, fate, battle and entertainment. To treat the Anglo-Saxon language and history in isolation is to miss the important fact that the northern European world in our long and complex period was always changing, that boundaries were fluid, that languages interacted and were sometimes mutually comprehensible, that stories of epic heroism, like *Beowulf*, were common property to England and a large swath of the continent. What we see, if we choose to look, is a true *Garland of the World*, a *Heimskringla* which shows all the world in its diversity, complexity, artistic achievement and thereby its legacy to us in the twenty-first century. We need only take the time to read it and we'll become more heroic and compassionate than we are now.

Translations and texts

All saga quotations are from *Íslenzk Fornrit*, Hið Íslenzka Fornritfélag, Reykjavík, ongoing since 1935. Quotations from Snorri Sturluson's *Edda* are from Anthony Faulkes' editions, London: The Viking Society for Northern Research, 1988 (*Gylfaginning*) and 1998 (*Skálskaparmál*). The most easily available English translations of the sagas are in Penguin Classics editions. Virtually all available translations (including G.W. Dasent and William Morris/Eiríkr Magnússon) have their own strengths and points of interest. See also *The Complete Sagas of Icelanders, Including 49 Tales*, editied by Viðar Hreinsson, Reykjavík: Leifur Eiríksson Publishing, 1997 (these have been acquired by Penguin and now form the core of Penguin Classics editions).

There are also a number of translations of the Eddic poetry, both Snorri Sturluson's Prose *Edda*, and the so-called *Elder* or Poetic *Edda*. These are important as the sources of Northern pagan mythologies. See also the Further reading for Chapter 12.

Further reading

Auden, W.H. and Louis MacNiece, *Letters from Iceland* (London, 1937).

Byock, Jesse L., *Feud in the Icelandic Saga* (Berkeley, CA, 1982).

Byock, Jesse L., *Viking Age Iceland* (Harmondsworth, 2001).

Clunies Ross, Margaret, ed., *Old Icelandic Literature and Society* (Cambridge, 2000).

Helgason, Jón Karl, *The Rewriting of Njál's Saga* (Clevedon, 1999).

Jones, Gwyn, *A History of the Vikings* (Oxford, 1984).

Kristjánsson, Jónas, *Eddas and Sagas*, 1988, Foote, Peter, trans. (Reykjavík, 1992).

Magnusson, Magnus, *Iceland Saga* (London, 1987).

McTurk, Rory, ed., *A Companion to Old Norse-Icelandic Literature* (Malden, MA, 2005).

Miller, William Ian, *Bloodtaking and Peacemaking: Feud, Law, and Society in Saga Iceland* (Chicago, 1990).

Morris, William, *Iceland Journals* (London, 1996).

Morris, William and Eiríkur Magnússon, *Saga Library* (London, 1901–1905).

O'Donoghue, Heather, *Old Norse–Icelandic Literature: A Short Introduction* (Malden, MA, 2004).

Poole, Russell, ed., *Skaldsagas: Text, Vocation and Desire in the Icelandic Sagas of Poets* (Berlin, 2001).

Sigurðsson, Gisli, *The Medieval Icelandic Saga and Oral Tradition: A Discourse on Method*, Jones, Nicholas, trans. (Cambridge, MA, 2004).

Wawn, Andrew, *The Vikings and the Victorians* (Cambridge, 2000).

CHAPTER 14

Prose writers of the English Benedictine Reform

Stewart Brookes

The Anglo-Saxons didn't write sagas, but they were great story-tellers. In the late Old English period, many of the stories they wrote were in prose. This was an age of outstanding cultural growth and artistic achievement and the later Old English prose is both stylish and sophisticated. At the heart of the renewed creative impulse was the Benedictine Reform movement of the tenth century, with its determination to restore learning and morality to the monasteries and abbeys. Given this degree of monastic influence, it is unsurprising that much of the writing of the period has a religious focus. Consequently, we will encounter stories that concern the miraculous doings of saints and adaptations of the Bible. Not everything produced has a religious theme, however. We will also examine travel journals, accounts of mythological creatures and even a romance (the fantastic rollercoaster ride of shipwrecks, love, and unlikely coincidences which is *Apollonius of Tyre*). There is drama, science, history, politics. Even the law gets a look in. And sermons, *lots* of them. Admittedly, these stories are often very different from those we tell, or appreciate, today. But with a little explanation, they not only become accessible, but turn out to be engaging.

The Benedictine Reform

Troubled by a widespread decline in learning, King Alfred had attempted to turn the tide with his policy decisions of the 880s–90s (see p. 252). The problem of low standards of learning persisted, however, and this was the impetus for the Benedictine Reform movement of the mid-tenth and eleventh centuries. The movement brought with it a spirit of religious and intellectual revival. The driving force was a formidable trio of bishops. These were Æthelwold, bishop of Winchester (c. 905–84), Dunstan, bishop of Worcester, then of London and then Archbishop of Canterbury (died 988) and Oswald, bishop of Worcester and then Archbishop of Canterbury (died 992). Inspired by the Benedictine revival on the continent, these men determined to reform the English monasteries according to the strict principles of the *Rule of St Benedict*, an originally sixth-century guide to monastic life. There seems to have been a genuine need for such reform. According to Æthelwold's bio-graphers, the monastery at Winchester was populated by drunken and gluttonous clerics. Not only had these clerics got married, which was contrary to Church law, but they had cast aside their wives for other women. If that wasn't enough, the Winchester clerics refused to celebrate Mass and so were not even fulfilling their basic duties.

The key moment for the Benedictine Reform movement was the accession of the boy king Edgar to the English throne (959–76). Edgar was King Alfred's great-grandson and in due course he became known as 'the Peacemaker' (*Pacifus*). As a former pupil of Æthelwold, bishop of Winchester (963–84), Edgar was sympathetic to the reform movement, and so Dunstan, Oswald, and Æthelwold found themselves in a position to influence royal policy and bring about change. With Edgar's backing, Æthelwold drove out the layabout clerics from Winchester and brought in his own people. The clerics slipped poison in Æthelwold's glass in revenge, but miraculously he survived. Expelling the clerics was only a first step, however. The reformers' ideal was to establish Benedictine principles as the standard for religious practice. In order to achieve this, they revitalised learning in the existing church institutions and founded new monasteries in the Benedictine image.

The Reform movement's focus on learning triggered a cultural renaissance. The reformers' personal interests encouraged the visual arts and crafts: Dunstan, bishop of Worcester and London (958) and then Archbishop of Canterbury (959–88), was a skilled metalworker and artist (a self-portrait survives). Æthelwold was a noted craftsman in gold. The Benedictional of Æthelwold (a benedictional is a book of a bishop's blessings) is a highly prized manuscript of Æthelwold's episcopacy. With its gold lettering, beautiful script, and lavish illuminations, it stands as tribute to the skill of the artists of Winchester (see plate 19). Service books were produced, music and chant were studied and architecture flourished. A noteworthy feat of engineering was the Winchester organ: the largest in northern Europe, it had 400 bronze pipes and was operated by a team of sweat-drenched men on the bellows. Most significantly, the monasteries developed into major centres of manuscript collection and production, fostering scholarship and writing.

It is in this period that the great collections of Old English poetry were written down (including the Exeter Book, the Vercelli Book and, most likely, the *Beowulf* manuscript). So, we owe the existence of most surviving Old English poetry to the best age of Old English prose.

Of course, Latin remained extremely important in this period. Latin was the language of the Church and essential to the daily routine of the monasteries: the Bible was in Latin, as were the commentaries on the Bible and also the psalms and prayers which the monks had to learn by heart. Latin was inescapable: Anglo-Saxon monks were even supposed to converse in it. And yet, despite that importance, another inescapable truth was that knowledge of Latin was poor, even among the monks. With immense practicality, Æthelwold tackled the problem head on, translating the key text of the Reform movement, *The Rule of St Benedict* (*Regula sancti Benedicti*) into Old English in the 940s or 950s. He set out his rationale for the translation in a highly significant sentence: 'It certainly cannot matter by what language a man is acquired and drawn to the true faith, as long only as he comes to God' (*Wel mæg dugan hit naht mid hwylcan gereorde mon sy gestryned and to þan soþan geleafan gewæmed, butan þæt an sy þæt he Gode gegange*). With the *Rule* in their own language, Æthelwold continues, the 'unlearned' (*ungelæreden*) won't be led to sin through ignorance. There was nothing on the continent to match this approach and it heralded a new wave of rhetorically poised and powerful Old English prose.

The initial drive to write in Old English, then, was a wish to educate those who had only limited Latin; just as it had been with Alfred several generations before. In one sense, everything that was written can be seen as a response to the decline in learning. There would have been no need for Old English prose if the population had been fluent in Latin. Although that may have been the starting point, those writers of Old English who responded to the educational challenge did so in an inventive and remarkable way. The Benedictine Reform produced a series of outstanding scholars and the needs of the populace meant that their best work was often in the vernacular, their own language. Even when following Latin texts, these writers did much more than just translate: they reshaped the texts to fit the needs of their audience, writing with a self-confidence which has its origins in Æthelwold's mission statement in his preface to the translation of *The Rule of St Benedict*.

Ælfric and his works: the *Colloquy*

When studying the prose literature of late Anglo-Saxon England, there's really only one place to begin; that is, with the writings of the Benedictine monk, Ælfric (*c.* 950–1010). Educated at Winchester, and a student of Bishop Æthelwold in the 960s and 970s, Ælfric [/ae:lfrich/] was the most prolific and versatile author of the period. His surviving works include translations of the Bible, stories about the lives of saints, a treatise on astronomy, a guide to Latin grammar, texts about the duties of monks and priests, an assortment of letters and about 130 sermons. The last are the two series of 40 homilies apiece named *Catholic Homilies* (*Sermones Catholici*) I and II, completed in 995; and *The Lives of Saints*, which followed. There are also many *Supplementary Homilies*. Fortunately, Ælfric didn't just write copiously, he also wrote well. His prose is attractive and lively, expressing even complex concepts with remarkable clarity. A conscious stylist, Ælfric borrowed the techniques of medieval rhetoric (such as repetition and parallelism) from Latin literature in order to make his sermons persuasive. In his later work, he employed alliterative rhythms which were broadly similar to those used in Old English poetry. Although he wrote prose, tending not to use the distinct vocabulary that is associated with Old English verse (for this see pp. 290–3), Ælfric's sentences can be, and sometimes are, set out as lines of poetry. A classic example is a sentence from the beginning of his *Life of St Edmund*:

> Eadmund se eadiga,   Eastengla cynincg,
> wæs snotor and wurðfull   and wurðode symble
> mid æþelum þeawum   þone ælmihtigan God.

> Edmund the blessed, king of East Angles,
> was wise and worshipful and worshipped ever
> with noble virtues the Almighty God.

Modern editors often set this out as prose, but as you can see from the underlines, it follows the alliterative rules, with four words stressed on a line, the third of which must alliterate with either or both of the two before (on Old English metrical rules, see Chapter 1, p. 23). Another example, from one of his sermons, demonstrates this effectiveness in a more expansive way:

> Swa swa se lichoma leofað be hlafe and drence, swa sceal seo sawl libban be lare and gebedum.

> Just as the body lives by food and drink, so shall the soul live by study and prayers.

Here, the use of paired phrases ('food and drink', 'study and prayers') gives the sentence a balanced structure and sets up a memorable contrast between *drence* ('drink'), on the one hand, and *gebedum* ('prayers'), on the other: almost as if the first should be traded in for the second. The effectiveness of that balance and contrast is enhanced by the repetition of forms of the verb *libban*, 'to live', while the alliteration makes the sentence easy on the ear. Combined, these features create a line which sticks in the mind. We would call this a 'sound bite' in our day and age. Memorability was an important quality given that this is a sermon and Ælfric wants the message to stay with those who hear it.

Ælfric's prose was designed to be listened to, either when performed by a preacher or read privately (in the medieval period, reading was always out loud, even to oneself). Writing for oral delivery, Ælfric often builds his sentences from short clauses, using alliteration to link the phrases. He aims for lucidity of style and utter clarity of meaning. The following extract is taken from a piece in which he rails against superstition, witchcraft and idolatry. Evidently, such practices were a problem that needed to be addressed, with many 'heathen' customs and beliefs filtering into Anglo-Saxon England via the Danish settlements in the north of England:

> Sume men synd swa ablende, þæt hi bringað heora lác
> to eorðfæstum stane, and eac to treowum,
> and to wylspringum, swa swa wiccan tæcað,
> and nellað understandan, hu stuntlice hi doð,
> oððe hu se deada stán, oððe þæt dumbe treow
> him mæge gehelpan, oððe hæle forgifan,
> þonne hi sylfe ne astyriað, of ðære stowe næfre.
> Se Cristene man sceall clypian to his drihtne
> mid mode, and mid muðe, and his munda abiddan. (lines 129–37)

> Some men are so misguided ('blinded') that they bring their offerings to a stone fixed in the ground, and also to trees, and to well-springs, just as witches teach. And they do not understand how foolishly they act, or how the dead stone or the dumb tree can help them, or give them healing when they don't ever move from the place. The Christian man must cry to his Lord with mind, and with mouth, and beseech his protection.

Ælfric's sarcasm is in full force when he describes the 'dead' stone and 'dumb' tree and he uses the alliterative potential to reinforce the point. The contrast between the stone, which is 'earthfast', and the men who can move, but are transfixed in their folly, builds on on this. The excerpt reaches its climax with the thumping alliteration of *mode, muðe, munda* ('mind, mouth, protection') in the final line, offering a powerfully constructed contrast to the imagery of the 'blinded minds', the 'dumb' and the absence of protection associated with the idolaters and their shrines.

Although the rhetorical power of Ælfric's prose is admirable, and his alliterative style aesthetically pleasing, his overriding concern was to produce clear and unpretentious writing. In this, he went directly against the predominant stylistic fashion of the time, which favoured flamboyant metaphors, obscure vocabulary, convoluted syntax and flowery language. The Benedictine reformers had championed this ornate and showy style, especially in their compositions in Anglo-Latin, and Ælfric would have known it well from his schooldays at Winchester. And yet Ælfric wasn't writing for the cliquey intellectual elite who valued such linguistic word games. He was writing for the 'unlearned' whom Æthelwold had identified as being in need of translations. In the Latin preface to his first series of Old English sermons, *Catholic Homilies* (*Sermones Catholici*), Ælfric makes this aim explicit, explaining that his project is:

> ob edificationem simplicium, qui hanc norunt tantummodo locutionem, sive legendo sive audiendo; ideoque nec obscura posuimus verba, sed simplicem Anglicam, quo facilius possit ad coe pervenire legentium vel audientium ad utilitatem animarum suarum, quia alia lingua nesciunt erudiri quam in qua nati sunt.

> for the edification of the simple who know only this language, either through reading or hearing it read; and for that reason we could not use obscure words, just plain English, by which it may more easily reach to the heart of the readers or listeners to the benefit of their souls, because they are unable to be instructed in a language other than the one to which they were born.

Ælfric's sermons can be quite complicated, so it is not necessarily the case that the audience he has in mind are intellectually challenged. Neither were they great scholars of Latin. There's a temptation to see this as an early reference to the stereotype of the English being 'unable' to learn foreign languages.

Ælfric's decision to adopt a straightforward prose style was hugely influential. As a consequence, he took centre stage in the development of literary prose. As part of his educational programme, Ælfric produced a set of resources to teach Latin to young monks. These resources included an Old English guide to Latin grammar and a Latin–Old English glossary so that the monks could learn the vocabulary of day-to-day life in the monastery. Ælfric's *Colloquy*, the third component in this set, is the most interesting from the 'stories' point of view. Written as prose, the *Colloquy* is an imaginary question and answer dialogue between a schoolmaster and his pupils. Instead of the format familiar from modern language classes ('What is your name?' My name is . . .'; 'What is the time?' The time is . . .'; 'How many siblings and pets do you have?' 'I have three sisters, one brother, and a Peruvian killer hamster'), each of the monastics takes the part of a character drawn from Anglo-Saxon village life and is then interrogated by the teacher on the nature of his work. The result is probably the closest thing we have to a play from this period and has a great deal of interest and appeal.

Although Ælfric wrote the *Colloquy* in Latin, an Old English translation was added between the lines of one of the manuscripts and it is that translation which will be our focus.

Pupils We cildra biddaþ þe, eala lareow, þæt þu tæce us sprecan forþam ungelærede we syndon and gewæmmodlice we sprecaþ.	*Pupils* Oh master, we children beg that you will teach us to speak correctly, because we are unlearned and speak badly.
Master Hwæt wille ge sprecan?	*Master* What do you want to talk about?
Pupils Hwæt rece we hwæt we sprecan, buton hit riht spræc sy and behefe, næs idel oþþe fracod.	*Pupils* We don't care what we talk about, as long as it is accurate and useful conversation, and not frivolous or filthy.
Master Wille beswungen on leornunge?	*Master* Are you prepared to be beaten while learning?
Pupils Leofre ys us beon beswungen for lare þænne hit ne cunnan. Ac we witun þe bilewitne wesan and ellan onbelæden swincgla us, buton þu bi togenydd fram us.	*Pupils* We would rather be beaten for the sake of learning than be ignorant. But we know that you are kind and unwilling to inflict blows on us unless we compel you to.

The opening line, articulated by the 'pupils', is Ælfric speaking from the heart. Much of what he wrote throughout his career was designed to cater for the needs of those that he felt were 'unlearned'. Whether his educational efforts were well received or not is another matter. He often notes that his role as teacher is a thankless task, and that he only continues because it is his duty. To have pupils eager for knowledge – and Latin at that! – is a wish-fulfilment fantasy. It is also part of the propaganda that can be detected throughout the *Colloquy*, with the real-life Anglo-Saxon pupils being conditioned into a certain way of thinking. Here, they are told to be hungry for knowledge and grateful for it, to strive for accurate and useful conversation, to avoid the frivolous and the filthy. They are also told that they should expect a beating, but in such a way that they welcome it and that the schoolteacher only does it for their own good. Evidently, beatings were a standard feature of Anglo-Saxon schooling: according to *The Rule of St Benedict*, children were to be whipped if they made mistakes when reading aloud in the refectory or during liturgical chants, which explains why the *Colloquy* students are eager to learn accurate pronunciation. And yet, for all that, I imagine that Ælfric himself was not quick to inflict blows, may have been kindly even, and perhaps reminds his fellow teachers that they should be slow to anger.

Moving beyond the classroom, the *Colloquy* introduces the male characters from village life. We can drop in on this now with the ploughman interview:

Master Hwæt sægest þu, yrþlingc? Hu begæst þu weorc þin?

Master What do you say ploughman? How do you carry out your work?

Ploughman Eala, leof hlaford, þearle ic deorfe. Ic ga ut on dægræd þywende oxon to felda, and iugie hig to syl. Nys hit swa stearc winter þæt ic durre lutian æt ham for ege hlafordes mines, ac geiukodan oxan, and gefæstnodon sceare and cultre mit þære syl, ælce dæg ic sceal erian fulne æcer oþþe mare.

Ploughman Oh, I work very hard, dear lord. I go out at daybreak driving the oxen to the field, and yoke them with the plough; for fear of my lord, there is not winter so severe that I dare hide at home; but the oxen, having been yoked and the share and coulter fastened to the plough, I must plough a full acre or more every day.

Master Hæfst þu ænigne geferan?

Master Have you any companion?

Ploughman Ic hæbbe sumne cnapan þywende oxan mid gadisene, þe eac swilce nu has ys for cylde and hreame.

Ploughman I have a lad driving the oxen with a goad, who is now also hoarse because of the cold and shouting.

Master Hwæt mare dest þu on dæg?

Master What else do you do in the day?

Ploughman Gewyslice þænne mare ic do. Ic sceal fyllan binnan oxan mid hig, and wæterian hig, and scearn heora beran ut.

Ploughman I do more than that, certainly. I have to fill the oxen's bins with hay, and water them, and carry their muck outside.

Master Hig; Hig; Micel gedeorf ys hyt.

Master Hee hee! It's hard work.

Ploughman Geleof, micel gedeorf hit ys, forþam ic neom freoh.

Ploughman It's hard work, sir, because I am not free.

This cameo supplies what appears to be a relatively realistic glimpse of daily life, showing a homely, low-status character of the kind that you would never see, for instance, in *Beowulf*. The emphasis on hard work and the young assistant, hoarse from cold and shouting, may well be a deliberate

Master Hu begæst þu cræft þinne?

Master How do you carry out your trade?

Huntsman Ic brede me max and sette hig on stowe gehæppre, and getihte hundas mine þæt wildeor hig ehton, oþþæt hig becuman to þam nettan unforsceawodlice and þæt hig swa beon begrynodo, and ic ofslea hig on þam maxum.

Huntsman I weave myself nets and set them in a suitable place, and urge on my dogs so that they chase the wild animals until they come into the nets unawares and are thus ensnared; and I kill them in the nets.

Master Ne canst þu huntian buton mid nettum?

Master Don't you know how to hunt without nets?

Huntsman Gea, butan nettum huntian ic mæg.

Huntsman I can hunt without nets certainly.

Master Hu?

Master How?

Huntsman Mid swiftum hundum ic betæce wildeor.

Huntsman I hunt for wild animals with fast dogs.

Master Hwilce wildeor swyþost gefehst þu?

Master Which animals do you mostly catch?

Huntsman Ic gefeo heortas and baras and rann and rægan and hwilon haran.

Huntsman I catch stags and wild boars and roe-buck and does, and sometimes hares.

Master Wære þu todæg on huntnoþe?

Master Were you out hunting today?

Huntsman Ic næs, forþam sunnandæg ys, ac gyrstandæg ic wæs on huntunge.

Huntsman I wasn't, because it's Sunday; but I was out hunting yesterday.

Master Hwæt gelæhtest þu?

Master What did you catch?

Huntsman Twegen heortas and ænne bar.

Huntsman Two stags and a boar.

Master Hu gefencge þu hig?

Master How did you take them?

Huntsman Heortas ic gefengc on nettum and bar ic ofsloh.

Huntsman I took the stags in nets, and the boar I killed.

Master Hu wære þu dyrstig ofstikian bar?

Master How did you dare stick a boar?

Huntsman Hundas bedrifon hyne to me, and ic þær togeanes standende færlice ofstikode hyne.

Huntsman The dogs drove it towards me, and I stuck it quickly, standing there in its path.

Master Swyþe þryste þu wære þa.

Master You were very brave then.

Huntsman Ne sceal hunta forhtfull wesan, forþam mislice wildeor wuniað on wudum.

Huntsman A huntsman mustn't be afraid, because all sorts of wild animals live in the woods.

hint from Ælfric to the young monks that they could be a lot worse off if they weren't in the monastery (beatings aside). One clever touch is the word play in the master's response to the ploughman: the master picks up on the close proximity of *hig* ('hay') to the pronoun *hig* ('them'), exclaiming *Hig; Hig* [/hee hee/]. The master's use of a word with a similar sound draws attention to the punning and adds a fun twist. The ploughman is a relatively servile character in comparison with the huntsman, our next interviewee (see p. 425).

This dialogue is interesting from a modern point of view because it offers an insight into Anglo-Saxon hunting practices (or, at least, Ælfric's understanding of them). All the same, it has to be admitted that the Master's style of questioning is somewhat naive and repetitive (how? which? what?). While such repetition may seem a literary weakness, it is central to the design of the *Colloquy* which is to reinforce vocabulary. In order to teach Latin most effectively, the *Colloquy* in its original Latin form opts for consistency over elegant variation and so it repeats the verb *capere* ('to capture') in a variety of forms (e.g. *capis, capio, cepesti, cepi*). The purpose of the Old English translation is rather different, however, and it uses a range of synonyms.

Once he has finished quizzing the huntsman, the master turns his attentions to a fisherman:

Master Hwilce fixas gefehst þu?

Fisherman Ælas and hacodas, mynas and æleputan, sceotan and lampredan, and swa wylce swa on wætere swymmaþ, sprote.

Master Which fish do you catch?

Fisherman Eels and pike, minnows and burbot, trout and lampreys and whatever swims in the water. Small fish.

The master's question provides an opportunity for the fisherman to reel off a catalogue of fish. Such lists were another function of the *Colloquy*, and were used to widen the vocabulary of the students. If some of the fish in the list seem unfamiliar, it is because they are decidedly eel-like in quality. Outside the East End or the Fens this may not be to modern taste. The lamprey is a case in point: with its toothed, funnel-like mouth it bores into the flesh of other fish and then sucks their blood. That might seem unattractive, but it was once a delicacy. Henry I of England (ruled 1100–35) is said to have died from a surfeit of lampreys. Perhaps the master isn't too keen on eels either, for he asks:

Master Forhwi ne fixast þu on sæ?

Fisherman Hwilon ic do, ac seldon, forþam micel rewyt me ys to sæ.

Master Hwæt fehst þu on sæ?

Fisherman Hærincgas and leaxas, mereswyn and stirian, ostran and crabban, muslan, winewinclan, sæcoccas, fagc and floc and lopystran and fela swylces.

Master Wylt þu fon sumne hwæl?

Fisherman Nic!

Master Forhwi?

Fisherman Forþam plyhtlic þingc hit ys gefon hwæl. Gebeorhlicre ys me faran to ea mid scype mynan, þænne faran mid manegum scypum on huntunge hranes.

Master Forhwi swa?

Fisherman Forþam leofre ys me gefon fisc þæne ic mæg ofslean, þonne fisc, þe na þæt an me ac eac swylce mine geferan mid anum slege he mæg besencean oþþe gecwylman.

Master And þeah mænige gefoþ hwælas, and ætberstaþ frecnysse, and micelne sceat þanon begytaþ.

Fisherman Soþ þu segst, ac ic ne geþristge for modes mines nytenyssæ.

Master Why don't you fish in the sea?

Fisherman Sometimes I do, but rarely, because it is a lot of rowing for me to the sea.

Master What do you catch in the sea?

Fisherman Herrings and salmon, porpoises and sturgeon, oysters and crabs, mussels, winkles, cockles, plaice and flounders and lobsters, and many similar things.

Master Would you like to catch a whale?

Fisherman Not me!

Master Why?

Fisherman Because it is a risky business catching a whale. It's safer for me to go on the river with my boat, than to go hunting whales with many boats.

Master Why so?

Fisherman Because I prefer to catch a fish that I can kill, rather than a fish that can sink or kill not only me but also my companions with a single blow.

Master Nevertheless, many catch whales and escape danger, and make a great profit by it.

Fisherman You are right, but I dare not because of my timid spirit!

The cowardly response of the fisherman (*ne geþristge*) is a nice touch of humour and is particularly effective because of the contrast with the bold huntsman (*þryste*). There's an engaging honesty in the characterisation, and the episode takes the imaginations of the young monks far outside the claustrophobic confines of the cloister.

Although the format works well, there are limits to how much of the master's questioning can be tolerated; at times he is reminiscent of a child with an insatiable appetite for 'why?'. This is a potential pitfall and Ælfric seems to be aware of it, to judge by an inventive change of direction that occurs when the fowler enters the picture:

Master Hæfst þu hafoc?	*Master* Have you got a hawk?
Fowler Ic hæbbe.	*Fowler* I have.
Master Canst þu temian hig?	*Master* Do you know how to tame them?
Fowler Gea, ic cann; hwæt sceoldon hig me buton ic cuþe temian hig?	*Fowler* Yes, I know how. What good would they be to me unless I knew how to tame them?
Huntsman Syle me ænne hafoc.	*Huntsman* Give me a hawk.
Fowler Ic sylle lustlice, gyf þu sylst me ænne swiftne hund. Hwilcne hafoc wilt þu habban, þone maran hwæþer þe þæne læss?	*Fowler* I will give you one willingly if you will give me a fast dog. Which hawk will you have, the bigger one or the smaller?
Huntsman Syle me þæne maran.	*Huntsman* Give me the bigger one.

So far the conversations have mostly been led by the master in a question-and-answer interview routine. What we have learnt has been in response to his prompting, just as you would expect within the conventions of a school-room dynamic. Although the replies have been engaging, some of the master's questions have been a bit predictable, unashamedly designed to allow for the recitation of lists of duties and chores. Even within this context, his question to the fowler seems particularly tame: outside the classroom scenario imagined, such a question would be patronising and so the fowler's snappy, sarcastic response is written with a degree of realism. Breaking the limitations of the question and answer format, Ælfric has the huntsman (the most likely candidate, although the speaker isn't named here) wade in, excited by the mention of the hawks. This introduces a refreshing spontaneity, with the characters addressing each other directly. The master soon regains control, asking 'How do you feed your hawks?' (*'Hu afest þu hafocas þine?'*), but the huntsman's intrusion has done the trick, renewing interest in the dialogue.

From this point on, the replies become rather lippier. The master is no longer dealing with the likes of the downtrodden ploughman who answers with servility and conforms to an English stereotype by complaining about the weather. The remaining characters are a much sharper bunch and they respond with frustration to the master's imperious tone. One imagines the students would have enjoyed playing these parts:

Master Wilt þu syllan þingc þine her eal swa þu hi gebohtest þær?	*Master* Do you want to sell your goods here for just what you paid for them there?
Merchant Ic nelle; hwæt þænne me fremode gedeorf min? Ac ic wille heora cypen her luflicor þonne gebicge þær, þæt sum gestreon me ic begyte, þanon ic me afede and min wif and minne sunu.	*Merchant* I don't want to. What would my labour benefit me then? I want to sell dearer here than I buy there so that I gain some profit, with which I may feed myself and my wife and my sons.

After this lesson in basic economics (perhaps for the benefit of those monks who may have to deal with canny door-to-door salesmen at some point) an array of tradesmen defend their professions with pride. The shoe-maker steps forward to explain that if it wasn't for the shoes and slippers he makes, not to mention leggings, leather flasks, bags and purses (actually, he *does* mention them), no one would survive the winter. Next is the turn of the salter, who insists that food would have no flavour were it not for his efforts. And were it not for the salt that he provides, then there would be no way to preserve butter and cheeses. One of my favourite responses is that of the cook:

The cook says Gif ge me ut adrifaþ fram eowrum geferscype, ge etaþ wyrta eowre grene, and flæscmettas eowre hreawe, and furþon fætt broþ ge magon [. . .]	*The cook says* If you expel me from your society, you'll eat your vegetables raw and your meat uncooked; and you can't even have a good broth without my art.
Master We ne reccaþ ne he us neodþearf ys, forþam we sylfe magon seoþan þa þingc þe to seoþenne synd, and brædan þa þingc þe to brædene synd.	*Master* We don't care about your art; it isn't necessary to us, because we can boil things that need boiling, and roast things that need roasting, for ourselves.
The cook says Gif ge forþy me fram adryfaþ, þæt ge þus don, þonne beo ge ealle þrælas, and nan eower ne biþ hlaford. And þeahhwæþere buton ge ne etaþ.	*The cook says* However, if you drive me out so as to do that, then you'll all be servants, and none of you will be lord. And without my craft you still won't be able to eat.

It is clear that the master has little respect for the cook's efforts. So disrespectful is the master's attitude that it leads me to suspect that Ælfric is echoing a real conversation that took place. Cooks, after all, are often undervalued (in *The Canterbury Tales* with good reason). If that is so, Ælfric may be using the opportunity to give the monks a few home truths about food preparation. The cook certainly argues with tenacity, even if there is no evidence to support the final assertion that they'll not be able to feed themselves, however much they slave over a hot stove.

Eventually, after having trodden on more than a few toes, the master enlists the aid of a wise counsellor:

Master Wisa, hwilc cræft þe geþuht betwux þas furþra wesan?	*Master* What do you say, wise man? Which trade among these seems to you to be superior?
Counsellor Me ys geþuht Godes þeowdom betweoh þas cræftas ealdorscype healdan, swa swa hit geræd on godspelle. Fyrmest seceað rice Godes and rihtwisnesse hys and þas þingc ealle beoþ togehyhte eow.	*Counsellor* I tell you, to me the service of God seems to hold the first place among these crafts, just as it reads in the gospel: 'Seek first the kingdom of God and his righteousness, and all these things shall be added unto you.' (Matthew 6: 33)

It is perhaps inevitable that the counsellor, as mouthpiece for the Benedictine monk Ælfric, would decide matters in that way. If the *Colloquy* had been written by the shoemakers' guild, for example, the counsellor would have given a different answer. Accepting the counsellor's judgement in this matter, the master then asks which of the secular trades is the most important. The counsellor decides that it is agriculture, because the ploughman feeds everyone and this provokes outraged protest from the other professions:

Se smiþ secgð Hwanon sylan scear oþþe culter, þe na gade hæfþ buton of cræfte minon? Hwanon fiscere ancgel, oþþe sceowyrhton æl, oþþe seamere nædl, nis hit of minon geweorce?	*The smith says* Where does the ploughman get his plough-share or coulter or goad, except by my craft? Where the fisherman his hook, or the shoemaker his awl, or the tailor his needle? Isn't it from my work?

Se geþeahtend andsweraþ Soþ witodlice sægst, ac eallum us leofre ys wikian mid þe, yrþlincge, þonne mid þe, forþam se yrþling sylð us hlaf and drenc; þu, hwæt sylst us on smiþþan þinre buton isenne fyrspearcan and swegincga beatendra slecgea and blawendra byliga?

The counsellor answers What you say is in fact true. But we would all prefer to live with you, ploughman, than with you, because the ploughman gives us bread and drink. You, what do you give us in your smithy but iron sparks, and the noise of hammers beating and bellows blowing?

Se treowwyrhta segð Hwilc eower ne notaþ cræfte minon, þonne hus and mistlice fata and scypa eow eallum ic wyrce?

The carpenter says Which of you doesn't make use of my craft, when I make houses and various vessels and boats for you all?

Se golsmiþ andwyrt Eala, trywwyrhta, forhwi swa sprycst þu þonne ne furþon an þyrl þu ne miht don?

The goldsmith answers Oh carpenter, why do you talk like that when you couldn't pierce even one hole without my craft?

Before things turn nasty, the counsellor steps in with words designed to placate:

Se geþeahtend sægþ Eala, geferan and gode wyrhtan, uton towurpon hwætlicor þas geflitu, and sy sibb and geþwærnyss betweoh us and framige anra gehwylc oþron on cræfte hys, and gedwærian symble mid þam yrþlinge þær we bigleofan us and foddor horsum urum habbaþ. And þis geþeaht ic sylle eallum wyrhtum, þæt anra gehwylc cræft his geornlice begange, forþam se þe cræft his forlæt, he byþ forlæten fram þam cræfte. Swa hwæðer þu sy, swa mæsseprest, swa munuc, swa ceorl, swa kempa, bega oþþe behwyrf þe sylfne on þisum, and beo þæt þu eart, forþam micel hynð and sceamu hyt is menn nellan wesan þæt þæt he ys and þæt þe he wesan sceal.

The counsellor says Oh, friends and good workmen, let us bring these arguments to an end quickly, and let there be peace and concord between us, and let each one of us help the other by his craft. And let us always agree with the ploughman, where we find food for ourselves and fodder for our horses. And I give this advice to all workmen, that each one pursue his trade diligently: for he who abandons his craft will be abandoned by his craft. Whoever you are, whether priest or monk or peasant or soldier, exercise yourself in this, and be what you are; because it is a great disgrace and shame for a man not to want to be what he is, and what he has to be.

The counsellor resolves the quarrel by saying that they should help each other, although it is noticeable that like the cook, he stands his ground and stubbornly insists on backing the ploughman. His insistence on unity is, in effect, an expression of the monastic ideal of a community working for the common good. The counsellor goes on to make plain a theme that was implict from the beginning: that each should be content with his or her lot. At the heart of this is the dismay that Ælfric expresses elsewhere about monks who have abandoned their vows to take up arms against the Viking invaders. The categories that the counsellor cites (priest, monk, peasant, soldier) make it clear that this is his concern. In effect, the *Colloquy* is more than an exercise in correct Latin; it is also a guide to correct living. This brings us neatly to the next topic: sermons.

Repent! It's Archbishop Wulfstan

Secretly, most Anglo-Saxons believed that the world was going to end in the year 1000. Literally. Obviously, this was rather depressing news for people in Europe in the last years of the tenth century. Over in Iceland (compare p. 37), the fear of End Time may have been the driving force behind the composition of the extraordinary poem *The Seeress's Prophecy* (*Vǫluspá*). And yet anywhere in western Europe, England, Iceland or Germany, if you were a fire-and-brimstone preacher, ready for a stint of doomsaying, the time was simply ideal. The best sermon writers of the age rose to the challenge. Ælfric warned of signs, and strange natural phenomena and men withering away from fear. For him, it was an opportunity to achieve redemption through repentance and he tended to avoid speculating about the precise date of the end. This wasn't really Ælfric's thing. For Byrhtferth, a monk of Ramsey in Huntingdonshire (*c*. 960–*c*. 1020), it was a mathematical conundrum: John's gospel had said that the devil would be unbound after 1000 years, and so it was just a case of waiting, and in the meanwhile investigating the symbolic possibilities of the number 1000.

The homilist Wulfstan, however, was significantly more animated. Wulfstan became bishop of London in 996 and then of Worcester in 1002. The Worcester job also included the archdiocese of York, because the Danes had caused so much damage to the diocesan infrastructure in the former Danelaw and in Yorkshire. In 1016 Wulfstan handed over Worcester to a suffragan bishop and concentrated on York. He died in 1023, an old man, although how old is unknown. Twenty-six sermons are attributed to him, of which 22 are in English and four in Latin. Probably he wrote more.

Wulfstan used the fears about the end of the world as a way of injecting urgency into his audience, trying to persuade them to change their ways and fix society's ills. One sermon, of which he had written three versions before 1016, is known as *The Sermon of the Wolf to the English when the Danes were most greatly persecuting them* (*Sermo Lupi ad Anglos quando Dani maxime persecuti sunt eos*), or *Sermo Lupi* for short:

> Leofan men, gecnawað þæt soð is: ðeos worold is on ofste, and hit nealæcð þam ende, and þy hit is on worolde aa swa leng swa wyrse; and swa hit sceal nyde for folces synnan ær Antecristes tocyme yfelian swyþe, and huru hit wyrð þænne egeslic and grimlic wide on worolde.

> Beloved men, recognise what the truth is: this world is in haste and nearing the end, and therefore the longer it is, the worse it will get in the world. And it needs must thus become very much worse as a result of the people's sins prior to the advent of Antichrist; and then, indeed, it will be terrible and cruel throughout the world.

Another homilist, the anonymous author of a sermon in the late tenth-century Blickling Homily collection (now kept in Princeton, New Jersey), took on the same issue. He attacked it head on, pulling no punches:

> Uton we forþon geþencean hwylc handlean we him forþ to berenne habban, þonne he eal þis recþ ond sægþ æt þisse ilcan tide þonne he gesiteþ on his dom setle; þonne sceolan we mid ure anre saule forgyldan ond gebétan ealle þa þing þe we ær ofor his bebod gedydon, oþþe þæs awægdon þe we dón sceoldan. Uton nu geþencean hu mycel egsa gelimpeþ eallum gesceaftum on þás ondweardan tíd þonne se dom nealæceþ. Ond seo openung þæs dæges is swiþe egesfull eallum gesceaftum. On þæm dæge gewiteþ heofon, ond eorþe, ond sæ, ond ealle þa þing þe on þæm syndon. Swa eac for þære ilcan wyrde gewíteþ sunne ond mona, ond eal tungla leoht aspringeþ. Ond seo rod ures Drihtnes bið aræred on þæt gewrixle þara tungla, seo nu on middangearde awergde gastas flemeþ. Ond on þæm dæge heofon biþ befealden swa swa bóc. Ond on þæm dæge eorþe biþ forbærned to axan. Ond on þæm dæge sæ adrugaþ. Ond on þæm dæge eall heofona mægen biþ onwended ond onhrered. Ond syx dagum ær þissum dæge gelimpeþ syllice tacn æghwylce ane dæge. Þa ærestan dæge on midne dæg gelimpeþ mycel gnornung ealra gesceafta, ond men gehyraþ myccle stefne on heofenum swylce þær man fýrde trymme and samnige. Þonne astigeþ blodig wolcen mycel from norþdæle ond oforþecþ ealne þysne heofon, ond æfter þæm wolcne cymeþ legetu and þunor ealne þone dæg. Ond rineþ blodig regn æt æfen.

> Therefore, we ought now to consider how much awe will come upon all created beings in this present time when the Judgement draws near. The manifestation of that Doomsday will be very terrible to all creation. On that day, heaven,

earth and the sea, together with all the life forms that are therein will be no more. So also on account of the same happening the sun and moon will pass away, as will all the light of the stars. Our Lord's Rood, which now puts wicked people to flight upon the earth, will be raised up into the concourse of the stars. On that day, heaven will be folded up like a book. On that day, the earth will be burned to ashes. On that day, the sea will dry up. And on that day, all the power of the skies will be turned and stirred. Six days before the day of reckoning extraordinary signs will occur each day. At noon on the first day there will occur a great lamentation of all living things, and humankind will hear a great noise in the skies as if an army is being assembled and set in order there. A great bloody cloud will then arise out of the North and cover all this heaven, and after this cloud will come lightning and thunder all day. In the evening, bloody rain will pour down.

The imagery here is vivid and quite startling. The Blickling sermon continues with the advice that everyone should repent, give charity and mend their wicked ways. One can indeed see an audience sitting up and paying attention after that particular description of Doomsday. It's hard to be sure what happened on 1 January 1000, but modern historians tell us the world didn't end after all. That could have come as an embarrassment for those preachers who had predicted the end, but luckily for them, there was an uncertainty about whether the 1000 years was counted from Christ's birth or from his death. That meant they had until at least 1033 before they had to rewrite their sermons.

So, the millennium turned out not to be the end of the world. This was scant consolation, however, for the many caught up in the misery and chaos of the following years. Viking attacks grew in frequency and ferocity and they met little resistance due to the cowardice of the leaders of the English forces who often fled before battle commenced. One of the worst offenders was Ealdorman Ælfric of Hampshire (another Ælfric) who would feign illness before running away and was even prepared to warn the enemy in order to avoid a fight. The *Chronicle* entry for 1003 is typical of his antics:

Þa gegaderede man swiðe micle fyrde of Wiltunscire and of Hamtunscire, and swiðe anrædlice wið þæs heres werd wæran. Þa sceolde se ealdorman ælfric lædan þa fyrde, ac he teah ða forð his ealdan wrencas. Sona swa hi wæron swa gehende þæt ægðer here on operne hawede, þa gebræd he hine seocne and ongan hine brecan to spiwenne and cwæð þæt he gesicled wære, and swa þæt folc becyrde þæt he lædan sceolde, swa hit gecweden ys, þonne se heretoga wacað, þonne bið eall se here swiðe gehindrad. Þa Swegen geseah þæt hi anræde næron and þæt hi ealle toforan, þa lædde he his here into Wiltune, and hi þa buruh geheregodon and forbærndon, and eode him þa to Searbyrig and þanone eft to sæ ferde.

> Then a very great army was gathered from Wiltshire and from Hampshire, and were very resolutely going towards the raiding-army; then Ealdorman Ælfric should have led the army, but he took to his old tricks: as soon as they were close enough for each force to see the other, then he pretended to be ill, and made violent efforts to vomit, saying he was taken ill, and thus deceived the people he should have led. As the saying goes: 'When the commander grows faint-hearted, then the whole army is greatly hindered.' Then when Sveinn saw that they were not resolute, and all dispersed, he led his raiding-army into Wilton and raided and burnt down the town, and then went to Salisbury and from there back to sea.

Understandably, there is a strong note of censure in the *Chronicle*'s account. Although the consequences of his cowardice are tragic, there is something comic (to me, at least) in the chronicler's description of the weak-kneed Ælfric desperately trying to vomit. It is impossible to know whether this was funny to an Anglo-Saxon reader as well, but I suspect that it may have been. Another unknown is how Ælfric of Hampshire, despite his 'tricks', remained one of the king's most trusted leaders. Like many a modern failed politician, Ælfric stayed on. He was still there in 1016 when his luck finally ran out quicker than he could. Clearly, King Æthelred was a poor judge of character, for the *Chronicle* for 1015 records that another of his chosen leaders, Ealdorman (i.e. earl) Eadric Streona of Mercia, enticed 40 ships away from the English fleet and then joined the Danes who were led by Cnut. Later, the *Chronicle* shows Eadric in Cnut's forces, plundering, burning and killing the English. No wonder that when Eadric is finally killed, one version of the *Chronicle* adds the comment 'very justly'.

Aside from *The Anglo-Saxon Chronicle*, the best known account of the Anglo-Saxon struggle against the Viking attack is that contained within the poem *The Battle of Maldon* (see Chapter 11, pp. 339–44). The *Maldon* poem can be seen as an attempt to rally a fighting spirit among the English, celebrating the bravery of the heroic Ealdorman Byrhtnoth of Essex while criticising the cowardly sons of Odda and the others who flee from the battlefield. Certainly, that is the approach taken by the homilist Ælfric, who responds to the contemporary situation – and particularly the issue of cowardice – in a number of his writings. For instance, when summarising the contents of the Bible in a letter written to a landowner by the name of Sigeweard, Ælfric explains that he has translated the story of the victory of Judith over the Assyrian general Holofernes 'as an example for you, so that also will defend your country against the attack of the enemy army with weapons' (*eow mannum to bysne, þæt ge eowerne eard mid wæpnum bewerian wið onwinnedne here*). He then goes on to note that in the Book of Maccabees (which he has also translated as a worthy example), the valiant Maccabees 'fought against the enemy army much more frequently than you will believe' (*feaht wið þone here miccle gelomlicor ðonne þu gelyan wylle*). The sarcasm in Ælfric's tone is undisguised when he says that his audience (he intends more than just Sigeweard to read the letter) will find it difficult to believe how often the Maccabees fought back: in the light of the cowardice outlined in the *Chronicle*, that might well be so.

The main issue seems to have been that many spoke courageously but failed to deliver what they had promised. Ælfric, still in sarcastic mode, notes that the Maccabees 'did not fight with brave words alone' (*hig noldon na feohtan mid fægerum wordum anum*), but kept their vows and were valiant on the battlefield. Significantly, the same theme surfaces in *The Battle of Maldon* when Ælfwine, son of Ælfric (not our Ælfric, not vomiting Ælfric – but yet another Ælfric), encourages his companions to make good on the courageous boasts that they raised up in the mead hall (*Maldon*, lines 212–15) and also in *Beowulf* when Wiglaf berates the cowardly warriors who hide in the woods instead of assisting Beowulf in his struggle against the fire-spewing dragon (*Beowulf*, lines 2633–40). Oath breaking and cowardice were clearly an ongoing problem, and the literature (both poetry and prose) responds to that with examples of heroic valour.

With the efforts to resist the Vikings ending in humiliation and defeat, Æthelred's counsellors advised a policy of buying off the invaders, but this, too, was little short of disastrous. Although the raiding parties were prepared to accept the money, they demanded ever larger sums in exchange for peace: first £10,000 in 991 (year of the defeat of Byrhtnoth at Maldon), then £16,000 in 994, £24,000 in 1002, £36,000 in 1007 and by 1012, a staggering £48,000. In addition to the suffering caused by the raiding parties, the population had to contend with the heavy taxation that was required to raise the funds to buy off the aggressors. Rubbing salt in the wounds, the Vikings often took the money and went ahead with their worst anyway. The English must have seemed a soft touch.

Meeting little effective opposition, the raiders got bolder. In 1011 Canterbury was captured (due to the treacherous acts of one Ælfmær) and Ælfheah, Archbishop of Canterbury, was taken prisoner. When he refused to allow a ransom to be paid to release him, the Vikings, in a drunken spree, murdered Ælfheah by pelting him with bones and bottles. This was a sign of what was to come. In due course the opportunistic attacks turned into a full-scale invasion. In 1013 Swein (Sveinn) Forkbeard Haraldsson, King of Denmark, came with a sufficiently large force to drive Æthelred into exile in Normandy and took the English throne. England was under Danish rule and many of those who should have fought back were complicit. But at least there was some peace. When Cnut took the throne, his giant kingdom of England, Denmark, Norway and parts of Sweden (1016–35) was in some ways a northern precursor to the Normans and their Plantagenet successors, Henry II and his sons, who, in 1152–1202, ruled an Angevin empire that stretched from the Scottish borders down to Catalonia in Spain.

Looking back on all the mayhem before Cnut took power, one has to marvel at the national political role of Archbishop Wulfstan of York. Besides sermons, he wrote law codes for both kings Æthelred and Cnut, canons (ecclesiastical laws) for the clergy, a couple of *Chronicle* entries for the tenth century and *The Institutes of Polity*, a thorough analysis of the roles of church and state. Wulfstan had seen it all. One of the most startling, and disturbing, accounts of this troubled period is the one he offers in his *Sermon of the Wolf* (*Sermo Lupi*). The year was 1014, Æthelred had been deposed and Wulfstan aims to capture the chaos of his time. First, he lists some of the wrongdoing around him. Then Wulfstan presents a litany of disasters afflicting the English while leaving it to them, life's walking wounded, to make the connection between their suffering and their sins. The disasters sound palpable to the ear. Try speaking some of this for yourself, if you doubt its power:

> Ne dohte hit nu lange inne ne ute, ac wæs here and hunger, bryne and blodgyte on gewelhwylcan ende oft and gelome; and us stalu and cwalu, stric and steorfa, orfcwealm and uncoðu, hol and hete and rypera reaflac derede swiðe þearle, and us ungylda swyðe gedrehtan, and us unwedera foroft weoldan unwæstma.

> For long now nothing has prospered here or abroad, but in every region there has been devastation and famine, burning and bloodshed over and again. And stealing and slaughter, plague and pestilence, cattle fever and disease, slander and hatred and the plundering of robbers have damaged us very severely; and excessive taxes have greatly oppressed us, and bad weather has very often caused us crop-failures.

There is a thundering emphatic technique. Unlike Ælfric, who likes long alliteratively regular lines, Wulfstan goes for alliterative word pairs, *inne ne ute*, *here and hunger*, *stric ond steorfa* with a more primitive, less academic, style. His writing is often called 'rhythmical prose'. Words such as *stric* and *hol*, not being found in any other writer, also seem to suggest that Wulfstan's English was of the racy, streetwise kind. He was all for making an impression on a huddled suffering mass. It was their sins, he makes clear, that brought the Vikings in the first place, while only their turning back to God can bring relief. In the meantime, disasters bring out the worst in people:

> Forðam on þysan earde wæs, swa hit þyncan mæg, nu fela geara unrihta fela and tealte getreowða æghwær mid mannum. Ne bearh nu foroft gesib gesibban

þe ma þe fremdan, ne fæder his suna, ne hwilum bearn his agenum fæder, ne
broðer oðrum; ne ure ænig his lif ne fadode swa swa he sceolde, ne gehadode
regollice, ne læwede lahlice; ne ænig wið oðerne getreowlice ne þohte swa rihte
swa he sceolde.

Because of this, it seems that for many years now there have been in this
country many injustices and unsteady loyalties among men everywhere. Neither
did one family member very often protect another any more than he would a
stranger, not a father his son, nor sometimes a child his own father, nor a man
his brother; nor did any of us order his life as he should have done, neither
clergy by the rule, nor laity by the law; nor did anyone intend to act loyally
towards another as justly as he should have done.

These phrases had been used by Wulfstan before, in other sermons, with the
difference that this time he reports family breakdowns as having happened,
rather than being in risk of happening. Having pummelled his audience
with the 'one-two, one-two' of alliterative word pairs, he engenders in them
a sense of temporary despair. To be sure, he gathers them up to him at the
end of the sermon, but not before shaming them first with an image of the
trafficking of women into slavery and prostitution:

And eal þæt is Gode lað, gelyfe se ðe wille. And scandlic is to specenne þæt
geworden is to wide and egeslic is to witanne þæt oft doð to manege þe dreogað
þa yrmþe, þæt sceotað togædere and ane cwenan gemænum ceape bicgað
gemæne, and wið þa ane fylþe adreogað, an æfter anum and ælc æfter oðrum,
hundum gelicost þe for fylþe ne scrifað, and syððan wið weorðe syllað of lande
feondum to gewealde Godes gesceafte and his agenne ceap þe he deore gebohte.

And all this is hateful to God, believe it who will. And it is shameful to speak
of something that has happened all too widely and it is frightful to know of
something that is often done by too many, by men who carry out the depravity
of pooling their money and buying a woman together in a joint purchase, then
carrying out a filthy act against her, one after the other and each man after the
other in turn, most like dogs that have no care for filth, and then selling, for a
price, out of the country into the power of enemies God's creature and His own
purchase dearly paid for by Him.

These are the most wretched crimes, and, sadly, there are parts of the world
where they still continue. The difference is that England was then the war
zone, and women were being trafficked into Europe. Wulfstan's sentences
are structured so as to emphasise an idea by repeating it in a variant form
and the idea here is not only frightful but also frightening. By focusing on
the female consigned to an earthly hell of men's making, Wulfstan succeeds
in persuading his audience, maybe women as well, that society has already

condemned itself to a living hell through its habitual neglect of the individual's human rights. In all this Archbishop Wulfstan comes across as a powerful orator. One can imagine him thundering out his message, fist banging on the lectern to emphasise his rhythmic prose pairings, the congregation quaking at the momentum of all his fire-and-brimstone words.

Old English maths and science: Byrhtferth of Ramsey

In a chapter about Anglo-Saxon literature, you probably weren't counting on science. And yet, counting is precisely what we're about to do. One of the key sciences was computus, the science of ecclesiastical arithmetic. As one of their duties, Anglo-Saxon priests had to calculate the date of Easter and there was a whole science dedicated to working out that date. Unlike most Christian festivals, which are tied to a fixed date in the solar calendar (for example, 25 December), the timing of Easter relies on both the lunar and solar calendars and so it moves about from year to year. The calculation of Easter's date is quite complex, requiring an understanding of astronomy and an ability to predict the phases of the moon accurately. To help with this, guides to computus were produced, which explained the principles involved. The most comprehensive and impressive of these explanatory manuals was the *Enchiridion*, produced by Byrhtferth of Ramsey (*c*. 960–*c*. 1020).

Byrthferth was a monk and schoolmaster at Ramsey Abbey, one of the main Benedictine abbeys in the later Anglo-Saxon period. As he admits in his writings, his obsession with computus and arithmology may be traced to Abbo of Fleury's two-year visit to Ramsey (985–7). One of the greatest scholars of his day, Abbo was expert in the disciplines of geometry, astronomy, arithmetic and music, as well as the arts of grammar, rhetoric and dialectic. Abbo hated the cold, damp of the marshy fenlands of Ramsey, despised English beer and had little that was good to say about his stay in Angleterre. Still, Byrhtferth couldn't have had a more learned teacher when it came to computus and the *Enchiridion* is one of the most comprehensive scientific works from the Anglo-Saxon period. The main aim of the *Enchiridion* was to make the complexities of computistical theory comprehensible even to those ill-educated students that Byrhtferth imagines will be struggling with the subject. Byrhtferth tried to teach them kindly: 'Often the brooding hen,' he says, 'though she clucks sorrowfully, spreads her wings and warms her chicks. So we intend to comfort young ones with this teaching' (*Oft seo brodige henn, þeah heo sarlice cloccige, heo tospræt hyre fyðera and þa briddas gewyrmð. Swa we þenceað iunglingas to frefrianne mid þissere lare*). Another extract gives an idea of the detail his students had to contend with:

> Þas twelf monðas þe we habbað ymbe gereht, hig habbað ealra daga þreohund daga and fif and syxtig daga and syx tida, þæt ys twa and fiftig wucan. Ealle þas monðas habbað ætgædere eahta þusend tida and seofonhund tida and syx and syxtig tida. Se monð þe hæfð þrittig daga and anne dæg, he hæfð seofonhund tida and feower and feowertig. Swa Ianuarius and Martius and Maius and Iulius, Augustus, October and December þas habbað swa fela tida swa we nu cwædon. Aprelis, Iunius, September and Nouember habbað feower and twentig læs: and Februarius, forðon he ys se læsta and he hæfð twegra daga læs þonne þa oðre, forþon he forlæt eahta and feowertig tida.

> The twelve months that we have spoken of have in all 365 days and six hours, that is fifty-two weeks. All those months have 8,766 hours. The month that has thirty-one days has 744 hours. So January, March, May, July, August, October and December have as many hours as we have just said. April, June, September and November have twenty-four fewer, and February, since it is the shortest and has two fewer days than the others, loses forty-eight hours.

The *Enchiridion* is written in both Latin and Old English and the Latin passages are often more detailed than the Old English which follows them. Byrthferth explains that this is because he has to bear in mind the ignorant, lazy, slacker (*sleacan*) students and priests who may be unable to fathom the intricacies of the subject:

> Vs þingð to langsum þæt we ealne þisne cwide on Englisc clericum geswutelion, ac we heom secgað soð to soðe þæt syx cynna ger synt on gerime. Þæt forme ys solaris geciged and þæt oðer þæs monan and þæt þridde communis, þæt ys gemæne ger. Þonne beouð þi geare þreo hund daga and feower and fiftig daga fram Eastertide þæt he eft cume. And þonne hyt byð embolismus oðð embolismaris (þæt ys eal an), þonne beoð þi geare þreo hund daga and feower and hundeahtatig daga. Gif hyt beo bissextus do þærto anne dæg. Ic þe secge, la cleric, on þin eare þæt ælce geare hyt byð solaris annus and lunaris and decennouenalis; forðon ælce geare þu scealt habban sum uers of þam circule þe ys nonas Aprelis, se hatte decennouenalis, and se de hatte nulle, se ys lunaris and he yrnð nigotyne gear all swa se oðer. Romanisce men habbað heora circul, and se fehð on Ianuario and þær wft geendað. Se circul ongynð on þam feorðan geare decennouenali and geendað on þam þriddan.

> It seems too tedious to explain this whole passage to clerks in English, but we tell then truly a truth, that there are six kinds of year in the computus. The first is called solar, the second lunar and the third *communis* – the common year. In the common year there are 354 days from one Easter festival to the next. And when the year is *embolismus* or *embolismaris* (it is all the same) there are 384 days in the year. If it is leap year add one day. O clerk I tell you in your ear that

every year is solar, lunar, and decennovenal, and so each year you must have a verse from the cycle *Nonae Aprelis*, called decennovenal; and the cycle called *nulle* is lunar and runs for nineteen years just like the decennovenal cycle. The Romans have their cycle, and it begins in January and ends there again. That cycle begins in the fourth year of the decennovenal cycle and ends in the third.

That's the simple version. Those decennovenals are enough to *cause* an embolism. Luckily, you won't be tested on this afterwards, whereas the monks who couldn't remember it, as you will have guessed, were liable to a beating.

Despite Byrhtferth's continual references to the ignorant in his audience, his writing is often ostentatious and obscure, utilising rare vocabulary and borrowings from Greek. He can also be remarkably wordy, using high-flown language and flowery expressions. It's not difficult to find examples of this in the *Enchiridion*. Here is Byrhtferth explaining his aims:

We æthrynon mid urum arun þa yðan þæs deopan wælis; we gesawon eac þa muntas ymbe þære sealtan sæ strand, and we mid æðenedum hrægle and gesundfullum windum þær gewicedon on þam gemærum þære fægerestan þeode. Þa yðan getacniað þisne deopan cræft, and þa muntas getacniað eac þa mycelnyssa þises cræftes. Hyt cwyð forðon, 'þær we gesawon þære lilian blosman' (þæt ys þæs gerimes fægernyssa), 'þær we onfengon þære rosena swæc' (þæt ys, þæt we ongeton þæs gerimes deopnyssa). On þære stowe se æðela feld us gearcode swete hunig and wynsumes swæcces. On þære ylcan stowe we onfengon myrran (þæt is wyrtgemang mid þam smyraðricra manna lic þæt hig rotian ne magon) and gutta (þætis hunigswete dropa – gif se adliga hyre geþigð he sona arist) and thus (þæt ys stor). Þas þing we gemetton on Ramegsige þurh Godes miltisigendan gife. Forþan ic ne swigie for ðæra bocra getingnyssum ne for þæra gelæredra manna þingum þe þas þing ne behofiað betweox heom to wealkynne. Ac we æthrynon þa deopan sæ and þa muntas þisses weorces. Nu wylle we þurh Godes willan þis agunnene weorc mid rumlicum wæstme began.

We have touched with our oars the waves of the deep water; we have seen as well the mountains by the shore of the salty sea, and with billowing sails and prosperous winds we have harboured on the coast of the fairest nation. The waves stand for this profound science, and the mountains stand for the magnitude of this science. Therefore it says 'where we saw the lily's blossoms' (the beauty of the computus) 'there we sensed the roses' fragrance' (we perceived the profundity of the computus). In that place the noble field provided us with honey, sweet and delightful to taste. In the same place we gathered myrrh, an excellent spice, with which one anoints the corpses of rich men so they will not decay, and *gutta* (honey-sweet drops – if a sick man takes them he will immediately arise) and *tus* (frankincense). We found these things in Ramsey through God's merciful grace. Therefore I shall not be silent either on account of the eloquence of the literate or for the sake of those learned men who have no need to discuss these things among themselves. But we have touched the deep sea and the mountains of this work. Now by the will of God we shall carry on this work with abundant fruit.

The gist seems to be: 'Computus is well complicated, but I'm a teacher and I totally know my stuff. I won't be initimidated by any bright so-and-sos who may think that they know it all already.' The prolixity is typical of Byrhtferth. At times, he seems utterly incapable of saying anything either simply or directly. Given the choice of one word or three, he opts for 12. As we saw earlier, this is precisely the style that Ælfric rejected. Still, for all its wordiness, Byrhtferth's imagery is carefully crafted and he plays the literary game of his time with great skill.

Of course, the primary purpose of the *Enchiridion* is to teach computus and not to showcase Byrhtferth's literary prowess. In this next passage Byrhtferth has more to say (always!) on the subject of the solar year:

> Þære sunnan geares dagas æfter þære sunnan ryne synt to asmeagenne, and synt eac to asmuganne mid scrutniendre scrutnunge, forðon naþætan þæt man sceal findan þa concurrentes, ac to eacan man sceal gemetan þa rihtinga þæra daga, and eac þæs monan. We todælað þa dagas þæs geares þurh seofon, and swa glædlice we becumað to þam andgite swa myceles gerenes. We wilniað þæt ne beo behydd þæs cynlica weg heononforð fram þæra eagum þe þis sceawiað.

> The days of the solar year, according to the sun's course, must be examined, and must also be studied with scrutinising scrutiny, for one must determine not only the concurrents, but also the ferial and lunar regulars. We divide the days of the year by seven, and so we arrive joyfully at an understanding of a very great mystery. We desire henceforth that this royal road not be hidden from the eyes of those who look at this.

So what is the 'royal road' that must be studied 'with scrutinising scrutiny' (*scrutniendre scrutnunge*)? The talk of concurrents and ferials is a-little worrying. Another decennovenal? It turns out to be something rather more mundane and infinitely more manageable. The seven times table!

The *Enchiridion* is a 'handbook'. As well as being a science book, it gives a strong sense of Byrhtferth's presence as he narrates, journal-like, his experience of writing it. We learn that he has been ill and unable to work; that he's finding the task laborious; and that he likes living in Ramsey. The following, from one of the Latin sections, offers an interesting insight into the pastimes of the clerics for whom he writes:

> Cum quodam tempore silens residerem in loco oportuno et perscrutatus essem multiplicem computandi prudentiam, cepi cordetenus ruminare pauca ex

plurimis, quali medicamine possem clericis proficere ut alee ludos relaxerent et huius artis notitiam haberent. Superius eis pulmentarium aduexi non modicum; nunc libet eis et poculum propinare.

When once I was sitting quietly in an appropriate place and was contemplating the manifold wisdom of the computus, I began inwardly to ruminate on a few things among many, concerning what medicine I might apply to the clerics so they would ease up on the dice and acquire some knowledge of this science. Previously I supplied a sizable repast; now is the time to administer a drink.

That's nice. Byrhtferth is offering to buy his students a drink. We've got a good idea of what the monks drank from the *Old English Colloquy*:

Master And hwæt drincst þu?

Pupil Ealu, gif ic hæbbe, oþþe wæter gif ic næbbe ealu.

Master Ne drincst þu win?

Pupil Ic ne eom swa spedig þæt ic mæge bicgean me win. And win nys drenc cilda ne dysgra, ac ealdra and wisra.

Master What do you drink?

Pupil Ale if I have it, or water if I have no ale.

Master Don't you drink wine?

Pupil I'm not rich enough to buy myself wine; and wine isn't a drink for children or the foolish, but for the old and wise.

Byrthferth's 'drink', however, is more of his arithmology. If you are thirsty, then you can look for yourself.

Old English fantasy literature

Biblical texts and the stories of saints often contain details that would have seemed alien, or just plain confusing, to an Anglo-Saxon audience. Ælfric is very aware of these cultural differences and so, whenever possible, he leaves out information that would require explanation. A delightful exception to this rule comes when Ælfric describes one of the big set-piece battles from the biblical Book of Maccabees (the scene which will be familiar to those who have seen Peter Jackson's *The Return of the King* (see plate 20). As so often in the Book of Maccabees, Judah and his Israelite army find themselves wildly outnumbered by the enemy forces of the Assyrians. As a template for Theoden in *The Lord of the Rings*, Judah and Co stand their ground, preparing to confront a new terror, war elephants:

Fif hund gehorsedra manna ferdon mid ælcum ylpe, and on ælcum ylpe wæs an wighus getimbrod, and on ælcum wighuse wæron þrittig manna feohtende mid cræfte, and mid gecneordnysse farende. Sumum menn wile þincan syllic þis to gehyrenne, forþan þe ylpas ne comon næfre on Engla lande. Ylp is ormæte nyten mare þonne sum hus, eall mid banum befangen binnan þam felle butan æt ðam nauelan, and he næfre ne lið. Feower and twentig monða gæð seo modor mid folan, and þreo hund geara hi libbað gif hi alefede ne beoð, and hi man mæg wenian wundorlice to gefeohte. Hwæl is ealra fixa mæst, and ylp is eallra nytena mæst, ac swaþeah mannes gescead hi mæg gewyldan.

Five hundred mounted men went with every elephant, and a war-house was built on each of the elephants, and in each war-house were thirty men, fighting with courage and advancing with eagerness. Some people will think it wondrous to hear this, because elephants have never come to England. An elephant is an immense animal, larger than a house, completely surrounded with bones within its hide, except at the navel, and it never lies down. The mother carries the foal for twenty-four months; and they live for three hundred years, if they are not injured, and man can tame them wonderfully for battle. The whale is the largest of all fishes, and the elephant is the largest of all beasts, but nevertheless man's skill may tame them.

The explanatory detail isn't part of the biblical account and Ælfric has taken it from descriptions of elephants in the 'natural history' writings of the classical world. For instance, when Ælfric states that elephants never lie down, he is relying on a long-held view that elephants couldn't bend their knees and so had to sleep standing up (or leaning against trees). That belief wasn't universal and so it is interesting to find it repeated in later medieval English writers and even by Shakespeare (*Troilus and Cressida* II, iii, 113), placing the Elizabethans in the same line of intellectual descent as the Anglo-Saxons. Tolkien has a place in that literary continuum too, noting that Oliphaunts never lie on the ground in Sam's poem in *The Two Towers*. Indeed, Tolkien's Oliphaunts are an affectionate nod to Ælfric: 'To his astonishment and terror, and lasting delight, Sam saw a vast shape crash out of the trees and come careering down the slope. Big as a house, much bigger than a house it looked to him, a grey-clad moving hill.' To an Anglo-Saxon, as to Samwise Gamgee, an elephant *might* have seemed larger than a house.

It is easy for a modern reader to smile at the information that Ælfric provides. But how long *do* elephants live? And what *is* their gestation period? Living in the Age of Google, it is easy to check: about 80 years and the gestation is 22 months (Ælfric's sources were fairly accurate on that one). Ælfric returns to elephants in another of his writings, explaining that 'the mighty elephant, which completely batters to death fierce bulls with its terrible trunk, is greatly afraid if it sees a mouse, even though the mouse cannot injure its greatness' (*se micela ylp, þe ða modigan fearras mid ealle ofbeat mid his egeslican nypele, ondræt him forþearle, gif he gesihð ane mus, ðeah ðe seo mus ne mage his micelnysse derian*). So Ælfric seems to have a personal fascination for these extraordinary creatures. The idea of an elephant's mouse terror is a universal, I suspect. In case you are wondering, modern psychologists have proved that elephants are not in fact, scared of rodents.

It was not only Ælfric who was fascinated by elephants. In the Nowell Codex, which also contains the poem *Beowulf*, there is a prose composition called *The Marvels of the East*, in which we find an artist's impression of an elephant (see plate 21). This image proves Ælfric's point: judging by the picture, it is clear that elephants hadn't come to England. Is that a tongue or a trunk? Claws on an elephant? And where are its ears? It is significant that the *The Marvels of the East* places the elephant in the same category as a range of mythological creatures, such as dragons, the phoenix and headless men with eyes and mouths in their breasts. Indeed, the picture we see here of such a creature is a literal giant of a man, 15 feet high, with two faces and a remarkably large 'erasure' by a later censor who wished to protect the public morals. We don't know whether Ælfric had seen such images, but his enthusiasm for elephants is clear. And Ælfric, as a gifted storyteller, understands his audience and their interests. He gives them wonders and miracles in his stories of saints. And in his adaptation of Maccabees, which is very long, he recaptures the audience's attention by offering a brief journey into the fantastic.

Another text that deals with journeys into the fantastic (and elephants) is *The Letter of Alexander to Aristotle*, a (probably) tenth-century Old English adaptation of a Latin composition, the *Epistola Alexandri ad Aristotelem*, that was popular in the Europe in the early Middle Ages. In this letter, which is also preserved in the *Beowulf* manuscript, Alexander the Great tells his former teacher, Aristotle, of all the wondrous things he and his army have encountered while campaigning in India. This was the Far East as far as the Anglo-Saxons were concerned. The letter tells of flying mice, men called the 'fish-eaters', two-headed snakes, not to mention crocodiles and hippopotami. Using a text of *Beowulf* to help him, the adapter focused more on Alexander than did the authors of his Latin source, presenting this king as rather proud:

> Ond eall min weorod wæs on þa gelicnesse tungles oððe ligite for þære micelnisse þæs goldes. [. . .] Ða sceawede ic seolfa and geseah mine gesælinesse and min wuldor and þa fromnisse minre iuguðe and gesælignisse mines lifes, þa wæs ic hwæthwugo in gefean in minum mode ahafen.

> And all my troop looked liked stars or lighting because of the amount of the gold. [. . .] When I myself gazed and saw my prosperity and my glory and the success of my youth and the prosperity of my life, I was somewhat uplifted with joy in my heart.

The Old English points up Alexander's relationship with his men, particularly the thrill which the conqueror obtains from the idea that his men love him more than themselves. This occurs on the march to Persepolis back west through southern Iran, when most of Alexander's army died of thirst:

> Ac swa hit oft gesæleð on þæm selran þingum and on þæm gesundrum, þæt seo wyrd and sio hiow hie oft oncyrreð and on oþer hworfeð, þa gelomp us þæt we wurdon earfoðlice mid þurste geswencte and gewæcte. Ðone þurst we þonne earfoðlice abæron and aræfndon, þa wæs haten Seferus min þegn funde þa wæter in anum holan stane and þa mid ane helme hlod hit and me to brohte. And he sylfa þursti wæs se min þegn, and hwæþre he swiðor mines feores and gesynto wilnade þonne his selfes. Þa he þa þæt wæter me to brohte swa ic ær sægde þa het ic min weorod and ealle mine duguþe tosomne, and hit þa beforan heora ealra onsyne niðer ageat, þy læs ic drunce and þone minne þegn þyrste and minne here and ealne þe mid me wæs. Ond ic þa beforan him eallum herede Seferes dæde þæs mines þegnes, and hine beforan hiora ealra onsione mid deorweorðum gyfum gegeafede for ðære dæde.

But as turns out so often in better and sounder things, fate and appearance often change them, and turn them into something else, and at that time it happened to us that we were sorely vexed and afflicted with thirst. We bore and suffered that thirst sorely, when one of my thanes who was called Seferus found water in a hollow stone and poured it into a helmet and brought it to me. And that thane of mine was himself thirsty, and yet he cared more for my life and health than for his own. And when, as I have said, he brought that water to me, I ordered together all my troop and all my trusted band and poured it away in the sight of them all, so that I should not drink and leave thirsty my thane and my army and all who were with me. And then before them all I praised the deed of Seferus my thane, and gave him precious gifts for that deed in the sight of them all.

An early prose romance: *Apollonius of Tyre*

While the Anglo-Saxons didn't have sages, they did have a taste for the fantastic, as we have just seen, and this was also expressed in the writing of prose romances. Only one survives, unfortunately, and this is incomplete. This is the *Apollonius of Tyre*, from the early eleventh century, which re-counts the adventures and misadventures of Apollonius, a young nobleman of a kingdom in the eastern Mediterranean. This tale is set in the ideal play-ground for shipwrecked sailors, a world of Greek gods and goddesses. No longer does an author, like Alfred in the 890s, feel obliged to explain these pagan creatures away as a pack of lies, or euhemeristically, as men wrongly worshipped as gods (compare p. 357). In the later period these gods take their place in a tale of love and adventure, shipwreck and betrayal, separation and reunion, brothels and pirates. Even from that brief summary, it will be clear that *Apollonius* is very different from anything that we've looked at so far, even if it is preserved in a manuscript which also contains Archbishop Wulfstan's *Institutes of Polity* together with a large collection of his sermons. The Old English *Apollonius* is a translation from a Latin original (*Historia Apollonii Regis Tyri*), itself based on a Greek romance, and was the first translation of the story into a vernacular language anywhere in western Europe. John Gower used the story in his *Confessio Amantis* (1360s) and Shakespeare in his romance play *Pericles, Prince of Tyre* (1608). The Old English *Apollonius* is also the earliest surviving example of the romance genre that was to flourish in the Middle English period.

The story opens with a shocking scenario, that of a king lusting after his daughter. In a terrible sequence of events, the king overpowers and rapes his daughter and she, on the verge of suicide, is then counselled by her nurse to submit to her father's will rather than take her own life. In order to conceal his crime from his people, the king sets a riddle for potential suitors, of which the solution points to his crime. He says that whoever solves the conundrum may marry his daughter, but whoever gets the answer wrong will be beheaded. Many try, spurred on by the princess's amazing beauty, but even those who get the right answer find themselves beheaded by the king, whose name is Antiochus. In due course the city gates are lined with severed heads. All the while, Antiochus continues to force himself on his daughter, but parades himself as a caring father; as Chaucer's Man of Law puts it, the opening of *Apollonius* is a 'cursed' story, 'so horrible a tale for to rede' (*The Man of Law's Tale*, lines 80–84).

Of course, every romance requires a dashing hero. So it is that we are introduced to the noble Apollonius, another suitor for the princess. When Apollonius solves the riddle, the king pretends that he has got it wrong, but (curiously) allows him 30 days to discover the correct solution. Apollonius leaves with an assassin of the king in pursuit. Afraid for his life (perhaps he is not so dashing after all), Apollonius sets sail and journeys into exile. Disturbingly, we never hear any more about the cruelly abused princess. After other adventures, Apollonius's ship is destroyed in a great storm and he is left as sole survivor, completely destitute. However, Apollonius's fortunes soon begin to recover. First he meets an old fisherman who offers him a share of his meagre food, even tearing his cloak in half so that Apollonius can enter the city clothed. Next, he impresses Archestrates, the local king, with his skill at a ball game and wins himself an invitation to the palace. Despite the delights of the banquet that he is served, Apollonius remains sad, reminded by the splendour of all that he has lost.

The story then brightens with the appearance of the king's daughter, named as Archestrate after her father. In an attempt to cheer Apollonius, Archestrate plays and sings at the harp, but while all others praise the princess, Apollonius remains silent. When the king asks him why, Apollonius replies, in a somewhat schoolmasterly tone, that Archestrate *could do better*. To make his point, Apollonius takes up the harp for himself (the very opposite of Bede's Cædmon at the 'beer party', *beorscipe* (p. 206)). This part we could compare with the Danish bard in *Beowulf*, lines 867–74 (pp. 96–9), with the difference that here we get some audience response:

> Ða wearð stilnes and swige geworden innon ðare healle. And Apollonius his hearpenægl genam and he þa hearpestrengas mid cræfte astirian ongan and þare hearpan sweg mid winsumum sange gemægnde. And se cyngc silf and ealle þe þar andwearde wæron micelre stæfne cliopodon and hine heredon.

> Then there was stillness and silence within the hall. And Apollonius took the plectrum and began to strike the harp-strings with skill, and accompanied the sound of the harp with beautiful song. And the king himself, and all who were present there, cried out with a loud voice and praised him.

Apollonius goes in for audience requests. What a talent he is, thinks the lonely princess, who begs her father for the right to reward him. This is in every way the vision of a good family relationship such as we saw violated in the anti-family with which the story began:

> Æfter þisum forlet Apollonius þa hearpan and plegode and fela fægera þinga þar forð teah, þe þam folce ungecnawen wæs and ungewunelic, and heom eallum þearle licode ælc þara þinga ðe he forð teah. Soðlice mid þy þe þæs cynges dohtor geseah þæt Apollonius on eallum godum cræftum swa wel wæs getogen, þa gefeol hyre mod on his lufe. Ða æfter þæs beorscipes geendunge cwæð þæt mæden to ðam cynge: 'Leofa fæder, þu lyfdest me litle ær þæt ic moste gifan Apollonio swa hwæt swa ic wolde of þinum goldhorde.'
>
> Archestrates se cyng cwæð to hyre: 'Gif him swa hwæt swa ðu wille.' Heo ða swiðe bliðe ut eode and cwæð: 'Lareow Apolloni, ic gife þe be mines fæder leafe twa hund punda goldes and feower hund punda gewihte seolfres and þone mæstan dæl deorwurðan reafes and twentig ðeowa manna.'

> After this Apollonius left the harp and played and performed there many pleasing things, which were unknown and unfamiliar in that country; and each of the things he performed pleased them greatly. Truly, when the king's daughter saw that Apollonius was so well educated in all accomplishments, then her heart fell in love with him. At the end of the entertainment, the girl then said to the king: 'Dear father, a little earlier you gave me permission to give

Apollonius whatever I wanted from your treasure.' Archestrates the king said to her: 'Give him whatever you want.' She then went out very happy and said: 'Master Apollonius, with my father's permission, I give you two hundred pounds in gold and four hundred pounds weight of silver, and a great quantity of costly clothing, and twenty serving men.'

Although she has managed to improve Apollonius's fortunes as she wished, the lovestruck Archestrate is now afraid that she will not see him again. In order to keep him near, she employs a clever stratagem, telling her father that she fears that Apollonius will be robbed if he leaves. And so, at the king's command, Apollonius is given a room at the palace. The princess Archestrate, however, cannot get him out of her mind:

> Ac þæt mæden hæfde unstille niht, mid þare lufe onæled þara worda and sanga þe heo gehyrde æt Apollonige, and na leng heo ne gebad ðonne hit dæg wæs, ac eode sona swa hit leoht wæs and gesæt beforan hire fæder bedde.

> But the girl had a restless night, inflamed with love of the works and songs that she had heard from Apollonius. And when it was day she could wait no longer but as soon as it was light went and stood beside her father's bed.

This king has his daughter's best interests at heart. He gladly acquiesces to her request that Apollonius become her teacher. This method of bringing lovers together was beloved both of medieval romance and the Shakespearean plays that were based on it.

Shortly afterwards, however, three eligible suitors approach the king asking for his daughter's hand. The king says that they have chosen a bad time to ask because his daughter is busy with her studies. But he promises that if they write down their names and their marriage gift, then he will get Apollonius to take their letters to his daughter and she will choose. On receipt of the missives, Archestrate replies in a letter of her own:

> 'Þu goda cyngc and min se leofesta fæder, nu þin mildheortnesse me leafe sealde þæt ic silf moste ceosan hwilcne wer ic wolde, ic secge ðe to soðan þone forlidenan man ic wille. And gif ðu wundrige þæt swa scamfæst fæmne swa unforwandigendlice ðas word awrat, þonne wite þu þæt ic hæbbe þurh weax aboden, ðe nane scame ne can, þæt ic silf ðe for scame secgan ne mihte.'

> 'Good king, and my dearest father, now that your kindness has given me permission to choose for myself what husband I wanted, I say to you truly, I want the shipwrecked man; and if you should wonder that so modest a woman wrote those words so shamelessly, then know that I have declared by means of wax, which knows no shame, what I could not for shame say to you myself.'

The story then takes a comic turn. The king assumes that his daughter is referring to one of the three young men standing before him, but doesn't know which of them is the 'shipwrecked man'. 'Which of you has been ship-wrecked?', he asks (*Hwilc eower is forliden?*'). Like an ugly sister in Cinderella, one crams his foot into this story's equivalent of the glass slipper, exclaiming:

> 'Ic eom forliden.'
> Se oðer him andwirde and cwæð:
> 'Swiga ðu; adl þe fornime þæt ðu ne beo hal ne gesund. Mid me þu boccræft leornodest and ðu næfre buton þare ceastre geate fram me ne come. Hwar gefore ðu forlidennesse?'

> 'I have been shipwrecked.'
> Another answered him and said:
> 'You keep quiet! Plague take you and make you neither whole nor sound! You studied book-learning with me and you have never been outside the city gates without me. Where was it you suffered shipwreck?'

Perplexed with the suitors, the king asks Apollonius to read the letter. The penny drops and Apollonius understands for the first time that Archestrate loves him. 'His face completely reddened' (*his andwlita eal gereodode*) and 'was all suffused with blushes' (*mid rosan rude wæs eal oferbræded*). The king is delighted by this turn of events and, in another wonderfully comic moment, promises to send word to the young men as soon as Archestrate is free from her studies. Of course, her learning is now synonymous with marriage to Apollonius, her teacher.

Having rid himself of the trio of suitors, the king confirms matters with his daughter. She, however, is unaware that her father is amenable to the idea and falls at his feet:

> 'Ðu arfæsta fæder, gehyr þinre dohtor willan. Ic lufige þone forlidenan man ðe wæs þurh ungelymp beswicen, ac þi læs þe þe tweonige þare spræce,
> Apollonium ic wille, minne lareow, and gif þu me him ne silst, þu forlætst ðine dohtor.'
>
>   Se cyng ða soðlice ne mihte aræfnian his dohtor tearas, ac arærde hi up and hire to cwæð:
> 'Leofe dohtor, ne ondræt þu ðe æniges þinges. Þu hafast gecoren þone wer þe me wel licað.'

> 'Kind father, listen to your daughter's desire. I love the shipwrecked man who was betrayed by misfortune. But lest you are unclear as to those words, I want Apollonius, my teacher, and if you will not give him to me you forsake your daughter.'
>
>   Truly the king could not bear his daughter's tears then, but raised her up and said to her,
> 'Dear daughter, do not be afraid for anything. You have chosen the man that pleases me well.'

There is another touch of the comic in her 'in case you are unclear'; as we saw the king, *had* been confused by her reference, although it is clear enough to an audience. Archestrate's behaviour is of particular interest because it is so different from the Germanic warrior–woman mould of Old English poetry: this is the first time that tears and emotional blackmail appear in English literature.

So, everyone is happy and, in true fairytale tradition, we might expect that the couple would go on to live happily ever afterwards. There are several mishaps that prevent this. The most immediate of these is that there are several pages missing from the manuscript at this point and so a good chunk of the story is lost (anticipating the tale of loss which is to follow). Fortunately, we can fill in the missing portion of the story from the Latin versions: Apollonius marries Archestrate and, after some time, learns that the evil king is dead and so decides to journey back to his own kingdom, Tyre. During the journey, the heavily pregnant Archestrate gives birth and appears to die and Apollonius seals her body in a chest and throws it overboard. The chest washes up at Ephesus and Archestrate, alive after all, ends up as high priestess at the temple of the goddess Diana. In the meanwhile, Apollonius gives his daughter Thasia into the keeping of Dionysia and Stranguillo. Thasia grows into a beautiful young woman and, in a fit of jealousy, Dionysia orders Thasia killed. Before this can happen, however, Thasia is abducted by pirates and then sold to a brothel keeper; although things look bad for her, Thasia manages to remain a virgin by telling her sad story. Apollonius then thinks that his daughter is dead too, but following a series of improbable events, he rediscovers her and then they are both reunited with Archestrate in the Temple of Diana. And then, finally, he can have his happily ever after: 'he lived in peace and happiness all the days of his life after his hardship' (*he leofode on stilnesse and on blisse ealle þa tid his lifes æfter his earfoðnesse*).

Apollonius of Tyre has a story which is certainly entertaining. And yet it is so different from most other Old English texts that its existence raises all sorts of interesting questions. Why was it translated? Who read it? How come it was copied into a manuscript containing Wulfstan's laws, *Institutes of Polity*, sermons and pieces of a religious nature? One way of explaining its inclusion is to try and interpret it as an extended moral lesson, perhaps as a warning about an over-reliance on worldly goods or as a model for princely behaviour. Certainly, there are aspects of the story which support that. Contrariwise, there are better choices than *Apollonius* to demonstrate such ideals. An Anglo-Saxon reader is likely to have noticed links between certain episodes in the story and those found in the lives of saints. For instance, the brothel scene (lost from the Old English manuscript) is a mainstay of virgin saints' lives and equivalent scenes are found in Ælfric's lives of Saint Agatha and Saint Lucy. Another parallel is the episode in which the fisherman cuts his cloak in half to clothe Apollonius: famously, St Martin does the same thing for a naked beggar and the episode is found in two versions of the life of Martin by Ælfric and also in the version of Martin in the *Blickling Homilies*.

In the end, the very existence of *Apollonius* suggests that the Anglo-Saxons had a taste for tales of excitement, adventure and even love: escapist entertainment, in other words. The translator of *Apollonius* is a skilled prose stylist, capably expressing the emotions, thoughts and subtleties of the original story and adding deft touches unique to this version. His work demonstrates above all how flexible and adaptable the Old English prose language had become. It is no wonder that *Apollonius* has been called the first English novel. Even before the Conquest, and certainly before the influence of the French romance genre, there was a taste for such stories and love tales. This taste was satisfied, as we shall see in the following chapter, throughout the Anglo-Norman period in the late eleventh century and early twelfth and especially when Queen Eleanor of Aquitaine arrived in England from Provence and Paris just after the mid-twelfth century. We lack most of the evidence, but that evidence, such as it is, shows that the later Old English literature was leading towards the poetic and prose romances of the French-dominated twelfth and thirteenth centuries. The achievement of the Benedictine Reform movement, puritanical as it was when it started, was to make Old English prose into an instrument of the highest calibre, whether this was for saints' lives, sermons, legal treatises and *Chronicle* entries, fantasy books, travel journals or eastern prose romances. In the earlier centuries, from the seventh to the tenth, the Anglo-Saxons had a great poetic tradition, as we have seen. But with the diversity of their prose writing, particularly in the tenth and eleventh centuries, we can say Old English literature came of age.

Translations and texts

Assmann, Bruno, ed., *Angelsächsische Homilien und Heiligenleben* (Kassel, 1889).

Baker, Peter S., and Michael Lapidge, eds, *Byrhtferth's Enchiridion* (London, 1995).

Bethurum, Dorothy, ed., *The Homilies of Wulfstan* (Oxford, 1957).

Crawford, Samuel J., ed., *The Old English Version of the Heptateuch, Ælfric's Treatise on the Old and New Testament and his Preface to Genesis* (London, 1922, revised 1969).

Garmonsway, G.N., rev. edn, *Ælfric's Colloquy* (Exeter, 1991).

Goolden, Peter, *The Old English Apollonius of Tyre* (London, 1958).

Kelly, Richard J., ed. and trans., *The Blickling Homilies (with General Introduction, Textual Notes, Tables and Appendices, and Select Bibliography)* (London and New York, 2003).

Lee, Stuart D., *Ælfric's Homilies on Judith, Esther and The Maccabees* (1999), http://users.ox.ac.uk/~stuart/kings/.

Orchard, Andy, *Pride and Prodigies: Studies in the Monsters of the Beowulf-Manuscript* (Cambridge, 1995).

Skeat, Walter W., ed. and trans., *Ælfric's Lives of Saints: Being a Set of Sermons on Saints' Days Formerly observed by the English Church*, Early English Texts, Original Series 94 and 114 (London, 1881–1900, repr. as one vol., 1966).

Swanton, Michael J., trans., *The Anglo-Saxon Chronicle* (London, 1996).

Swanton, Michael J., trans., *Anglo-Saxon Prose* (London, 1993).

Thorpe, Benjamin, *The Anglo-Saxon Version of the Story of Apollonius of Tyre* (London, 1834), http://www.georgetown.edu/faculty/ballc/apt/apt.html.

Whitelock, Dorothy, ed., and Martin Brett and Christopher N.L. Brooke, rev. edn, *Councils and Synods with Other Documents Relating to the English Church, Volume I: 871–1066* (Oxford, 1981).

Wilcox, Jonathan, ed., *Ælfric's Prefaces* (Durham, 1994).

Wright, C.E., *The Cultivation of Saga in Anglo-Saxon England* (Edinburgh, 1939).

CHAPTER 15

Anglo-Norman literature: the road to Middle English

Patricia Gillies

Most people have heard of William the Conqueror and the Battle of Hastings in 1066. That is when the Normans arrived, when they took England from the English and when everything changed. Anglo-Saxon earls became churls, so the story goes. While French became the ruling language, Old English went under and was hardly written again until well into the thirteenth century, some 200 years later. There is some truth in this story. And yet the Anglo-Saxons didn't sink into the ground and neither did their language. We don't speak French, as you must have observed. By now indeed this book will have shown you that our language has Anglo-Saxon roots, a Danish stiffening and some additional French, Latin, Greek and other linguistic flowering. The time when all this fusion began to happen was the first century after the Norman Conquest, an event which is better regarded as the prelude to a period of linguistic and literary diversity, innovation and expansion. This chapter will show how.

How the Conquest happened

Already in the tenth century, the shields and swords of Anglo-Saxon and Viking warfare were forging a cosmopolitan culture of rulership, where Vikings and Saxons negotiated and their peoples learned to exploit international connections even if amid high-priced exactions and painful anxieties. The Normans were part of the same deal. As the name says, they were descended from Norwegian Vikings who took land in the north French peninsular, *Normandia* ('zone of the Northmen'), in the tenth century. Later, the court of King Cnut brought Norse, Norman and Anglo-Saxon leaders together in a culture that celebrated Viking power in the artful blood, sweat and sharp edges of skaldic verse. This spiky foreign culture was menacing no doubt, but not entirely alien to the Anglo-Saxon world of *Beowulf* and *The Battle of Maldon*, where loss, lamentation and mutilated corpses express the dark side of a warrior's battle price. Somehow, however, the rhythm of attack and compensation faltered when Anglo-Saxons, Scandinavians and Normans started making deals about who would inherit what. The proximity and a shared Scandinavian heritage meant that contacts and relationships with Normans across the channel were common. The crowning example is King Edward the Confessor (ruled 1042–66), half-brother of the unpopular Harthacnut Cnutson (ruled 1035–42). Their mother Emma lived a long time (*c*. 980–1052). First she had married King Æthelred the Unready (ruled 978–1016), then his supplanter Cnut (ruled 1016–35). Emma was daughter of Richard I, Count of Rouen, so her son Edward was cousin to the dukes of Normandy whose men were coming and going at Anglo-Saxon courts for most of his reign. In a move typical of the racy times, Edward named his own Norman cousin William heir to the throne. To do this he had to exile the power behind his throne, the Anglo-Saxon magnate Earl Godwine, who was his father-in-law but had actually killed Edward's older brother Alfred in the determination over who would be king after Harthacnut. Godwine's incompetent henchmen had beheaded Alfred when all that was needed was a good job of blinding to get Edward's rival out of the way. This story is told after a fashion in *The Praise of Queen Emma* (*Encomium Emmae Reginae*), a poem commissioned by the mother of this lunatic family and written in Latin in 1041 by a monk in Flanders just over the Channel.

You can't keep a man like Earl Godwine down or out of a kingdom once he has fastened on. Godwine was soon back to discourage the swarm of Norman courtiers and he set up his two sons, Tostig and Harold, with their own earldoms in line for the throne. These boys had been named with English forms of *Þorsteinn* and *Haraldr*, so as to reflect the heritage of Gytha, their Danish mother. If you are getting the idea that who had what right to the English throne was a rather murky business, you are well on the way to seeing through the myth of the Norman Conquest. Eventually Tostig was exiled from his earldom of Northumbria. For his part, Harold was shipwrecked on the Normandy coast, so falling into the clutches of Duke William. For the Norman this was a heaven-sent opportunity, and he made Harold swear an oath promising to help him follow up King Edward's earlier dangle of the throne.

Harold's other ideas became clear when he renounced this oath and accepted the kingship on the death of Edward the Confessor in winter 1066. As the spring and summer war season approached, William defied all reasonable advice and began preparations for the immense enterprise of a cross-Channel invasion. It is unclear why he should want so badly a kingdom that carried such risk, but it does seem part of a vision of empire shared by other powerful men at that time and indeed in the future. In fact King Haraldr the 'Harsh-ruler' (*Harðráði*) of Norway (hard-ruled 1046–66) was thinking much the same thing. Feeling that he had rights to the throne of England via Cnut and various Norse royal relatives, 'Harald' (we will call him) prepared an expedition as well. There was nothing very new in his plans but the scale of them, given the Viking taste for raiding parties, invasion and overseas rulership. There was perhaps also a sense of the epic moment when heroism and its reward of kingship were to be achieved. But 1066 was a very bad year for kings named Harold, and a very bad year for rivers and bridges in Yorkshire. King Harald took advice from Tostig Godwinson and invaded Yorkshire. He seemed on his way to winning when he defeated the Saxon Earls Edwin and Morcar at Fulford Bridge near York. Quick to meet this disaster in the north, King Harold marched his troops up to what would eventually be called Stamford Bridge. He won a great victory with immense slaughter and King Harald died, together with Harold's treacherous brother Tostig, on 25 September. From the river Derwent choked with hacked and dying Vikings, the English Harold then led his tired troops on a lightning march from Yorkshire down to the East Sussex coast. Duke William had truly arrived.

Harold met William's army at Hastings barely three weeks later, on 14 October. After stoutly holding their line the English troops were repeatedly lured into pursuit of Norman troops in flight. King Harold and his brothers Gyrth and Leofwine were killed in the chaos, but even with the day lost, the Saxons made a last attack. The Norman cavalry, however, wheeled round and swept back, finishing most of them off. Now the kingship was William's. Real power had won, real death and agony endured, but in the scrimmage of axes, swords and shields of Hastings in 1066 we can see how a culture of 'epic deeds' (*chanson de geste*) was actually common to Anglo-Saxons, Scandinavians and Normans.

Anglo-Norman poetry and *The Song of Roland*

You will have a good idea of Anglo-Scandinavian warrior culture and poetry from Chapters 11–13. Now it is time to take a look at how this culture was re-interpreted following the Conquest, in what is called Anglo-Norman England. First of all, Anglo-Norman is both a culture and a language. As a language it is a dialect of French as it was written or copied in the British Isles. 'Anglo-Norman' means that a story may be constructed from tales from Brittany and written in continental French by an author, such as Marie de France, living in England yet insistent on French identity. That Marie was writing in England and acknowledged 20 years' residence there argues that her ideas and language were shaped by the Anglo-Norman context. In language use, French speakers were interacting with English speakers and culture, so naturally tastes changed in the very sound and feel of words. From the differences in the spelling of French texts copied in manuscripts, we can see that the Anglo-Norman dialect prefers the more Germanic 'w' and 'ch' sounds to regular French 'v' and 'c'. 'Ou' has more speakers than 'u', but 'u' is preferred to 'ui'. Nasal sounds are not much in favour. These are some of many examples. What is at work here is speakers' preference in a world separated, but not isolated, from continental tastes. Such features are found in French dialects, but the rich production of texts in what became known as *Insular culture* asserted a strong and vibrant Anglo-Norman cultural identity.

One of the landmark texts of Anglo-Norman England is a martial epic, a *chanson de geste*, known as *The Song of Roland* (*La Chanson de Roland*). This poem was probably first written down in continental French in the early twelfth century, but the best version (the so-called 'Oxford *Roland*') was copied by an Anglo-Norman scribe in late twelfth century England (*c.* 1170), during the reign of King Henry II and Eleanor of Aquitaine (1154–89). At the end of some 4002 lines appears the name 'Turold', which could indicate a scribe or author or a reference to another text. The plot of treachery, massacre of great knights and victory in this poem has all the ingredients of 1066, including Danes, Saxons and Normans as well as many other peoples. In this poem the knight Roland dies nobly in a rearguard action to cover the escape of Charlemagne's forces over the Pyrenees. As he dies he blows his great horn to summon help which will not come (almost like Boromir, one might suppose, in the battle with the orcs in *The Fellowship of the Ring*). The enemy in this poem is not the bandits who historically killed Roland in the mountain pass, but the grand Muslim rulers of Spain. *The Song of Roland* fits type scenes of extraordinary courage and strength to many fictitious battles between Christian and Muslim forces. In short, it reflects the imperial vision of William the Conqueror now revised by King Henry as the new Alexander the Great. Being set in Spain, the battles are a comfortable distance away and perhaps a nice place to think about during after-dinner entertainments in the cold English weather. England and the Saxons are listed among Roland's conquests for Charlemagne (as in lines 372 and 2330–32). And heroic identity is figured out in the timing of Roland's decision to blow his horn. The poet's theme of Christian–Muslim confrontation reflects the upper-class crusading mentality of the twelfth century. This theme leads scholars to place the written version of the poem in the aftermath of the First Crusade which took place in 1096–9 (and perhaps of the Second, in 1147–9). That was also the time when secular culture and literature got clear of religion, as did the crusading impulse itself. Going on crusade offered riches and adventures, a career option that flourished for the next 100 years and became a default activity for the next few centuries.

If the Conquest matches the scale and flow of the poem, the actual historic events at its origin are murky. No doubt it is rooted in an oral tradition about the massacre of the some of Emperor Charlemagne's best warriors in 778 in his army's rearguard at Rencesvals, now known as 'Roncesvalles' in Spanish and 'Roncevaux' in French. Apparently the emperor's men were protecting his baggage train when they were wiped out by Basques or Gascons (*Wascones*) bent on capturing Charlemagne's loot from his campaign against the rich Christian and Muslim cities of Spain. The poem makes the disaster more like a medieval cavalry battle with heavily armed knights foundering under a swift moving attack by lightly armed men. To this day Rencesvals is celebrated as a great victory among Basques who are worried, perhaps, lest the credit go to the Gascons. You would think that the French, however, would have little reason to hail this as a triumph. And yet if their conscription of a massive Carolingian foul-up into epic seems odd, the scale and aim of the event does match many stories of opportunistic warfare and spontaneous bravery in the Icelandic sagas. Indeed there are numerous other parallels, with the focus on internal conflict and treachery leading to the destruction of heroes found in Arthurian poetry in Welsh, Anglo-Norman and early medieval English. In all but name this is the great culture of *chanson de geste*.

As a poem of great deeds, *The Song of Roland* is the prime example of *geste* ('deeds' but also 'lineage') in the French tradition. As we have seen, it is called the 'Oxford *Roland*' and this is because the manuscript is kept in the Bodleian Library at Oxford University where it was discovered and published by a young French scholar Francisque Michel in 1837. The 'Oxford *Roland*' name declares the particular identity and importance of this poem in British culture. There are many other versions of the *Song of Roland* in widely varying lengths, episodes and languages. The Oxford text is one of the shorter versions with 4002 ten-syllable lines, generally with a pause, called a caesura, or pause for breath, always after the fourth syllable. Each half of the single line thus divided is called a 'hemistich'. In fact, it all looks rather like Old English verse, but without the alliteration and kennings. The verses are arranged in strophes of a number and lengths that vary according to the eye of the scholarly editor. In Old French studies a strophe is known

as a *laisse*. There is a taste for repeated sound patterns in the use of asso-
nance where all the lines in a *laisse* end in words that have the same final
accented vowel. Frequent use of formulaic expressions, in the exchange of
speeches, description of war equipment and in battle scenes, recalls Germanic
epic technique and points towards a layer of oral composition in the mists
of time surrounding the development of the narrative. Oral performance is
suggested by the letters 'AOI' that are written to mark the start and often the
end of many a good *laisse*. AOI may be a musical cue, a melodic pattern or
a cry of some type perhaps a more insistent version of *Hwæt!* at the beginning of *Beowulf* and other Old English poems.

Taste for repetition also emerges in the use of the *laisses similaires* where
the same event is repeated from differing points of view in a cluster of
laisses. It lends a filmic quality to the narration, as though a camera were
tracking round the action, but also allows for the richer development of
emotion or symbolic meaning depending how you like to read it. One of
the most resonant and fateful formulaic statements is used repeatedly to
invoke the perilous pass of Rencesvals. 'High are the mountains, dark and
great' (*Halt sunt li pui e tenebrus e grant*, AOI, line 1830). So here is a Valley
of Death that would not seem out of place in the neighbourhood of the
Grendel family Mere in *Beowulf*. The actual scene of battle, however, if
it really is the present-day Roncevaux, shows the great hillsides of the
Pyrenees sloping down into a wide valley with a few dark rocks but otherwise with lots of room to maneouvre. Oddly enough, the ugly things that
happen to the Grendel monsters in *Beowulf*, fingers and sinews bursting,
happen to Roland the hero. Once it's too late not to die gloriously in battle,
Roland bursts his brains by blowing his hunting horn (his *olifant*) to summon Charlemagne:

> Rollant ad mis l'olifan a sa buche,
> Empreint le ben, par grant vertut le sunet.
> Halt sunt li pui e la voiz est mult lunge,
> Granz .xxx. liwes l'oïrent il respundre.
> Karles l'oït e ses cumpaignes tutes.
> Co dit li reis: Bataille funt nostre hume.'
> E Guenelon li respundit encuntre:
> 'S'altre le desist, ja semblast grant mençunge.' (*laisse* 133, lines 1753–60)

> Roland put the olifant to his mouth, placed it firmly, using his heroic strength
> he blew the horn. High are the mountains and the voice of the horn sounds in
> the far distance. A full thirty leagues on people hear it resound. Charlemagne
> hears it and all his troops. The king says, 'Our men are in battle.' But Ganelon
> says, 'If anyone else said that, it would be a terrible lie.'

Ganelon is the traitor who makes sure Roland gets his comeuppance. Later he is drawn apart by wild horses. To go on with the story:

> Li quens Rollant par peine e par ahans,
> Par grant dulor sunet sun olifan.
> Parmi la buche en salt ford li cler sancs,
> De sun cervel le temple en est rumpant.
> Del corn qu'il tient l'oïe en est mult grant:
> Karles l'entent ki est as porz passant. (*laisse* 134, lines 1761–5)

> Count Roland in struggle and pain, in great agony blows his olifant. Bright blood spouts from his mouth. The veins of his temples are bursting out from his skull. Out from the horn the sound carries to ears far away. Charlemagne hears it as he goes through the narrow pass.

> Li quens Rollant ad la buche sanglente,
> De sun cervel rumput en est li temples,
> L'olifant sunet a dulor e a peine.
> Karles l'oït e ses franceis l'entendent;
> Ço dist li reis: 'Cel corn ad lunge aleine.' (*laisse* 135, lines 1785–9)

> Count Roland's mouth is bloody. His temples burst out from his skull. He blows the olifant in agony and pain. Charlemagne and the French hear it. The king says, 'That horn is blown with a long breath.'

The great debate in *Roland* studies is whether he deserves to start dying that way – there's quite a bit of fight in him even after his temples burst. Roland can be called 'a monster of pride'. Or he is fulfilling his feudal obligation to fight to the death and making sure that everyone else does too. Perhaps his *desmesure* ('pride') is like the *ofermod* of Ealdorman Byrhtnoth in *The Battle of Maldon* (p. 339). Is he acting, Christ like, god like, according to some secret knowledge that places his actions beyond the logical little world of human motivations? Folly, sin, martyrdom, sacrifice, warrior code or bloody-mindedness are all options here. You can join this debate as well.

The Oxford version opens with a council at the court of the Muslim King Marsile at the mountain-top city of Saragossa, the only holdout in Charlemagne's victorious sweep through Spain. Treachery is in the air, as Marsile's scheming counsellor Blancandrin suggests they promise to follow Charlemagne home to Aix in what is now Belgium and convert to Christianity. All Charlemagne has to do is leave Spain. When the Saragossans fail to show up as promised at Christmas, their hostages in Aix will lose their heads. That's a price Marsile and company are ready to pay. Looking for some peace and quiet after seven years of war, the Moors think this is a good plan, so messengers are sent to Charlemagne. Much as in *Beowulf*, messengers, deliberations and speeches are important in demonstrating the values and natures of the rival courts and characters. The grand old Charlemagne, at some 200 years old, is celebrating the fall of Cordoba and the massacre of all its Moorish citizens who failed to convert on the spot. The scene of his rejoicing is an open-air version of a hall where his knights are playing games and engaging in military sports. Into this idyll come Blancandrin and his party with their proposal. A council is called and a debate erupts among the knights that pits one of them, Ganelon, against the 'fool' he calls his stepson Roland. It is a kind of 'Peace in our Time' situation with Roland taking the Churchill role to insist that the enemy understands only war. As in September 1938, Ganelon's Chamberlain option proves more attractive and so it is decided to send a messenger to Marsile. No one is under any illusions about the danger of the mission, since other messengers have been beheaded, but after more logical debate and submerged motives, Roland names himself. He is opposed in this, however, by his best friend Oliver. Other knights then name themselves until Roland names Ganelon whom Charlemagne accepts. Ganelon is furious, but why? He has argued for trusting Marsile and has won out. In this epic the monster is both within and without. Jealousy and unseen compulsions are at work. The Oxford *Roland* is an elusive poem. To read it is to debate it.

Ganelon goes on the mission, but in order to save himself, strikes a bargain with the Moors to put an end to the warfare by betraying Roland into their hands. He returns to Charlemagne in triumph with the keys to Saragossa. Although plagued by nightmares, Charlemagne agrees to go home and Ganelon cunningly names Roland to the rearguard. Roland and his friend Oliver and other great warriors fall into line there. From on high in the Pyrenees, Oliver spots the immense army assembled in ambush. He tells Roland to blow his horn to call for help and Roland refuses, either once or three times depending on how you read the poem. Once again the spotlight is on a round of negotiation with obscure motives: 'Roland is honourable and Oliver is wise' (*Rollant est proz e Oliver est sage*, line 1093) The words 'honourable' and 'wise' appear to place the warriors in different categories, but each word can mean 'skilful' and each can mean 'wise' or 'prudent'. But is it one conversation or three? Once they are attacked and the fight becomes desperate, Roland does quite literally blow his brains out in summoning Charlemagne to honour the corpses. He places the bodies of Oliver and his principal warriors together so that the dying Archbishop Turpin, lying in his own entrails, can give them all a final blessing. It seems that the poem is really about a noble death. And yet a Christian death seems to be only part of what is going on. Roland's own death scene – where he offers his glove to God and tries to break his sacred sword Durendal on the rocks – takes place across three *laisses* (known as *laisses similaires*) that may be separate scenes or different aspects of one. Appropriately enough for the soul of a Christian martyr, angels carry his soul to heaven. Yet even at this holy moment, much is made of courage and cowardice is scorned. A counterpart in modern mythology would be Churchill's stated resolve to fight Nazi Germany until he and his War Cabinet lie on the floor choking on their own blood. Charlemagne discovers the scene and laments his great loss.

Charlemagne has more dark and terrifying dreams as Marsile now plots with Baligant, emir of Babylon who has finally arrived with an even vaster army to destroy Charlemagne. This is another debatable area in the *Roland*, because this episode can seem tacked on to an already powerful and complete poem, rather like the place of the Dragon episode has been questioned in *Beowulf*. Like Beowulf with the dragon, the emperor wins his apocalyptic battle with Baligant's great force from the east and destroys the kingdom of Marsile in the process. But ethical and motivational ambiguities remain. Perhaps that was part of the entertainment value of performances of this epic.

Ganelon's treachery is now revealed and his fate decided in council. His family pledges 30 hostages and defends his honour in the person of the noble Pinabel, who fights Charlemagne's champion Thierry in a trial by combat. Like Roland, Pinabel ends up with his brains on the ground. The family hostages are hanged, but as suits a traitor, Ganelon is stretched between four horses and torn to pieces. Marsile's queen, Bramimonde, turns into the Christian convert Juliana, baptized at Aix after all. Oliver's sister and Roland's betrothed, the very Christian Aude, falls dead at the news of his death. Nuns take her body to a convent and receive a gift of land for their trouble. Everyone is being paid off in some way, but there is much room to discuss the logic of the rewards. At the very end of the epic, the Archangel Gabriel calls on white-haired Charlemagne to go on a new crusade. The Emperor, now a kind of Christian Baligant, weeps at the prospect of endless war that opens before him. Or is he weeping about something else?

Eleanor of Aquitaine and Marie de France

In due course, when Henry II married Eleanor of Aquitaine in 1154, Anglo-Norman England became the heart of the Angevin Plantagenet empire. Henry was an Angevin because he was from the family of Anjou, in France, on both sides, being the son of Count Geoffrey of Anjou and Matilda, daughter of Fulk of Anjou. With Eleanor came a perhaps welcome addition to the literature of burst brains and spilled guts. Love and magic also flourished as themes in a secular culture influenced by her presence. Eleanor, who lived from 1122 to 1204, was a queen from the south of France, land of the itinerant minstrels known as 'troubadours'. When she met young Henry of Anjou at the French court in Paris in 1151, she was 29 years old and already married to King Louis VII of France. In three years' time, however, her loveless marriage would be annulled, she would be married to Henry, nine years her junior, and both would cross the Channel to become the crowned rulers of England.

Eleanor was rich in lands, well educated and scandalous in reputation. Having had an affair with her uncle in Antioch, she had already led a life that could furnish the text for many romances. In the mid-twelfth century, romances are the narratives adapted into a medieval French (*roman*) literature that was fast becoming the alternative to Latin literature. Eleanor's life with Henry produced some nine children who peopled the thrones of England and Europe. But Henry suspected her of involvement in the early 1170s' rebellion of her sons Henry the Young King (crowned in his father's lifetime), Richard (later the Lionheart) and Geoffrey. That meant that from 1174 onwards she would spend most of her life under guard, imprisoned in relative luxury, mainly at Winchester and Sarum (near Salisbury), until her son Richard became king on Henry's death in 1189. Eleanor's literary influence was probably more circumstantial than direct. She was a figure to inspire singers and writers looking to understand how this new era and culture connected with the past. Eleanor was familiar with several languages including her native 'Occitan' or Provençal from the south of France. Occitan is so called because people used the way they said 'yes' to identify the language spoken in the south, where *oc* means 'yes', as Occitan or the *langue d'Oc*. Today this language is still spoken and written in Languedoc and Provence. The language spoken in the north, where *oui* still means 'yes', was called the *langue d'Uil*. Eleanor's grandfather, Duke William IX of Aquitaine, brought in some culture from even further south. When he fought the Moors around Cordoba in the early 1120s, he acquainted himself there with Castillian versions of Arabic love poetry such as *The Dove's Neck-Ring*, which was written by the Maghrebi poet Ibn Hazm in the 1030s under the partial influence of Ovid. From Duke William and others like him in southern Europe, through Queen Eleanor, it could be said that the northern European culture of England was becoming more sophisticated.

This period of twelfth-century Angevin rule is a key one for the literature of epic (*geste*) and romance (*roman*). The twelfth century, in its own time or much later, is about kings and queens and medieval texts and images that function as icons or models – for good or ill. It is a watershed period when a secular culture, one that has much in common with our own, began to gain power in society and expression by questioning and sidelining religious concepts and values. When Marie de France was writing her *Lays* or 12 short stories translated from Breton sources in verse (more or less 500 lines each), somewhere in England around the 1160s, Queen Eleanor was still active in court life. It is thought that Eleanor's interests inspired Marie. The 'noble king' (*nobles reis*), who is addressed in the prologue to Marie's story *Guigemar*, is probably Eleanor's second husband, Henry II. Marie tells us that 'all good things take root in his heart' (*E en ki quoer tuz biens racine*, line 46). The compliment is perhaps double-edged, in view of the recentness with which the Angevin stock, calling itself *Planta-genet* ('taken root'), had done so in England. In *Guigemar*, a tale addressed to lords but not to ladies, the eponymous insensitive, hunt-loving protagonist is doomed by a magical animal to learn about love. In doing so he might reflect in some way on the contrast between the often brutal Henry and the cultivated Eleanor. If Marie is thinking about Eleanor, her reputation and a taste for the artistically and psychologically complex songs of the troubadours, she is careful to distance it by insisting that she translates old Breton lays to keep the memory of the past alive. Yet a response to the tales about Eleanor's unconventional behaviour may also be found not only in *Guigemar* but also in *Eliduc*. In both these poems, Marie highlights the evils caused by slanderers and their terrible fates once their lies have been discovered. Similarly Marie's introductions and conclusions to her stories on the joining of Breton and Anglo-Norman and English languages and culture may have show sensitivity to Eleanor's position as a foreign queen. Not only foreign languages and cultures are grafted, but Marie also tells stories about problems resulting from the interaction of beings from different worlds, animals and humans, fairy and human. In *Eliduc*, the devoted behaviour of weasels provides a lesson to brutal and confused humans. By observing and exploiting the behaviour of the weasels, two lovers manage to resolve the life and death issues that falling in love abroad poses to both men and women when a man has a wife at home. Marie's sensitive and nuanced portrayal of a werewolf in *Bisclavret* has made it a model text for understanding how close the link is between ruling power and the excluded and how that power can act to integrate the excluded for the good of all. Although the starring roles in this story go to king and wolf-man, the facial disfigurement of the adulterous wife and her lineage may be Marie's way of arguing for the essential goodness of the glamorous yet seductive Eleanor.

Whereas much is known about the charismatic Eleanor of Aquitaine, little survives concerning the Marie who wrote her *Lays* in Anglo-Norman. Even the choice of title (*Lays*, suggesting music and song) is elusive because Marie uses verbs of speaking and writing to express the making of her stories in verses. There are references to harps at the end of *Guigemar* that allow us to imagine that it can be made into a song:

De cest cunte ke oï avez
Fu *Guigemar* le lai trovez,
Que hum fait en harpe e en rote;
Bone en est a oïr la note. (*Guigemar*, lines 883–8)

From this story that I have heard, *Guigemar* was made into a lay that people play on harp and string; it is a good song to hear.

Yet we can only hear Marie's voice echo somehow through the writing of the tale that begins: 'Hear, gentlemen, what Marie says, she who does not want to be forgotten in her own time' (*Oëz, seignurs, ke dit Marie/Ki en sun tens pas ne s'oblie*, lines 3–4). Like Marie herself and the sound of her voice, the music remains beyond our grasp. What we have is narrative verse composed in octosyllabic (eight-syllabled) couplets. Whether the author was a man or a woman is subject to debate if not outright myth making. Scholars generally agree that the stories were written in England between the 1150s and 1160s based on influences from other types of medieval romances. The earliest and most reliable manuscript dates from the thirteenth century (Harley 978 in the British Library). In a coincidence that may show a Regency interest in these times, the *Lays* of Marie de France were first published in 1819, the same year Sir Walter Scott published *Ivanhoe*, a novel which foregrounds the Anglo-Norman period in England.

Marie refers frequently to lays as ways to remember or record the past, but the past that they relate cannot be fully heard. Only Marie has full access to the sounds. She leaves her readers feeling that they are on the edge of something when they thought they were in the middle. That's a trick that a twenty-first century popular writer would never try. Marie is playing a delightful game with us where we may learn something valuable but we must keep trying to find the past that she holds out. She doesn't give us all the answers, any more than the Oxford *Roland* does. The debate and questions that the texts provoke suggest the way that they made the past live in their own time. They provide a living entry to the past for us now. Marie's verse is charged with some kind of secret knowledge or charm. Other references to birds and bird song are linked to the general themes of love, nature and memory but add another dimension to the secret musicality of

Marie's expression. In *The Nightingale* (*Le Rossignol*, also called *Laüstic*) the link between the lovers and languages is in the song of a nightingale:

> Une aventure vus dirai
> Dunt li bretun firent un lai.
> *Laüstic* ad nun, ceo m'est vis,
> Si l'apelent en lur pais:
> Ceo est 'rossignol' en franceis
> E 'nihtegale' en dreit engleis. (*The Nightingale*, lines 1–6)

> I'll tell you an adventure that the Bretons made into a lay. *Laüstic* is the title, that's what I think, that's how they call it in their land; that is *rossignol* in French and *nihtegale* in proper English.

The woman stands by the window each night waiting to exchange words with her lover. She tells her husband that it is to listen to a songbird. When the woman's jealous husband brutally kills the nightingale, the bird's death marks the end of the lovers' contact. To commemorate their loss, the wife wraps the body of the bird in fine brocade where she has embroidered the story of their love in gold letters. When her servant tells the lover the story and gives him the little corpse, wrapped in another version of the story, he has a little coffer made of pure gold, adorned with jewels. Therein he places the dead nightingale, seals him within it. The box remains with him always. What at first seems an amusing story of a sudden taste for birdsong used to fool a gullible husband becomes a story where the nightingale is both contained in the love story and embodies it at the same time. So the forbidden yet conventional love of two human beings becomes a secret mating with another kind of being. The creation of this hybrid union perhaps marks the release of some magical harmony in the universe. The story does not stay sealed in the end but circulates in a Breton lay, unheard by us until released by Marie. From her, in turn, it was passed down into *The Owl and the Nightingale*, a poem from southern England in the early thirteenth century.

Marie's *Honeysuckle* (*Chevrefoil*) also pulls together different languages. It is particularly interesting because it is a brief (118 lines) yet powerful episode in the famously doomed love of Trist(r)an and Iseut. To sketch out the plot, Tristan escorts Princess Iseut from Ireland to marry his uncle King Mark of Cornwall, but a potion makes the two youngsters fall in love and their affair continues until rumbled by King Mark. They live in exile in the Wild Wood for a while, but when the potion's effect rubs off the lovers split, Tristan for Wales and then Brittany and Iseut back to her husband. Then the real love takes over. Although Tristan marries, but does not husband, another Iseut (of the Fair Hands), he cannot forget the first Iseut and manages to get her to his side after being mortally wounded in a local scrape. She arrives too late. Marie touched on an episode from this tale in her *Honeysuckle*. While most of her stories stem from sources we can only speculate about, they retain their individuality in that they do not link up with other well-known story networks. Even though there are many versions of the story of Tristan and Iseut or Isolde, including a saga version from 1260s' Norway, Marie's episode is of special value because she wrote *Honeysuckle* (*Chevrefoil*) close to the 1160s, which is when the earliest *roman* on Tristan in verse by Beroul appeared in Old French. There is also a more elaborate Anglo-Norman *Tristan* by Thomas, a *roman* which dates from the 1170s; and a work on King Mark and Iseut, now lost, composed by the northern French poet Chrétien de Troyes in 1150s or 1160s.

In *Chevrefoil*, Tristan, trickster and doomed lover writes his name on a hazel stick in a code language that he and his beloved Iseut share. Returning from Wales for a few days, Tristan hides in the Cornish forest (like the were-wolf hides in *Bisclavret*, exiled to the forest by his wife's treacherous theft of his human clothing). But this time Marie's sympathy is on the side of the lovers who betray king and country to live their passion. From trusty peasants who show him hospitality, Tristan discovers that he will have a chance to use the stick code to communicate with Queen Iseut as she passes through the forest. Just as there is a narrative about the bond between animal and human, king and exile, husband and wife, society and those who are different in *Bisclavret*, *Chevrefoil* is also about the vital link between different kinds: between the hazel tree and the honeysuckle vine that twines around it but also between the French and English languages and between Cornwall where Mark and Iseut live and Wales where Tristan was born. Tristan carves his name on a hazel stick because he and Iseut must be together or die just as the hazel and honeysuckle. As in *The Nightingale* (*Rossignol* or *Laüstic*), there seems to be some secret link between the natural world and the union of the lovers. The code works: Tristan and Iseut spend some quality time together in the forest and then he returns to Wales. Tristan then uses his skill as a harpist to make a lay as a way of keeping alive the memory of how he worded his love for Iseut:

Pur la joie qu'il ot eüe
De s'amie qu'il ot veüe
E pur ceo k'il aveit escrit
Si cum la reine l'ot dit,
Pur les paroles remembrer,
Tristram, ki bien saveit harper
En aveit fet un nuvel lai;

> Asez brefment le numerai:
> *Gotelef* l'apelent Engleis,
> *Chievrefoil* le nument Franceis.
> Dit vus en ai la verité
> Del lai que j'ai ici cunté. (*Chevrefoil*, lines 107–117)
>
> Because of the joy that he had from seeing his lover, and because of what he
> wrote and because the queen told him that he could do it, to keep the memory
> of their conversation, Tristan, who knew how to play the harp well, made a
> new lay out of it all. I'll name it briefly: the English call it Goatleaf, *Gotelef*,
> the French call it Goatleaf, *Chevrefeuille*. I have told you the truth about it from
> the lay that I have told here.

Conserving moments of love and love words, holding episodes of a love
story, is linked to keeping Anglo-Norman and Anglo-Saxon words together:
As she closes her lay, Marie laces her audience together in their languages like
hazel and goatleaf, which we call, in more mellifluous terms, honeysuckle.
But the suggestions of animal appetite that 'goatleaf' mingles with the mystery
of desire brings the reader to recognise the ancient urges that bind both
English and French speakers.

Eleanor's daughter Marie

The erotic joy of the *roman courtois* was really unstoppable. In around 1174,
Countess Marie de Champagne, daughter of Eleanor by her first marriage to
Louis VII, encouraged her chaplain, named Andrew (Andreas Capellanus),
to write an Ovidian treatise *On the Art of Fine Loving* (*De arte honeste amandi*).
This work attempts (and succeeds) to codify the rules of loving according
to whichever station the man or woman variously belongs to. Generally
the man talks less the lower in rank is the object of his passion. By placing
ladies in all powerful positions, however, this kind of literature inverted
baronial social norms. This treatise and the lyrics around it were driven by
highborn women. The language of feudalism was purloined to represent
them as *dangerous* or frightening lords of love. The influence of Marie de
Champagne in establishing this literature cannot be underestimated. From
1159 onwards she was the patron of Chrétien de Troyes, from whom no
fewer than five Arthurian romances survive. This poet, perhaps the most
famous from France in the medieval period, is sometimes known as the
'father' of Arthurian romance. The influence of Countess Marie's court
culture is still with us today, not only in Mills and Boon but also in the conventions of so-called 'romantic' love. These are the rules to which also Marie
de France subscribed.

Eleanor's daughter Matilda

The Plantagenet royals came from Anjou, on the upper border of the Occitan-speaking region of southern France. Nonetheless, they were happy to emphasise their descent from the Anglo-Saxon King Alfred and the Norman King William the Conqueror. The lineage of King Henry II (1154–89) in this way was already positioned at a cultural crossroads. Henry styled himself as a new Alexander and had a taste for *romans* based on the matter of Troy and Rome. Although this taste was shared by many medieval monarchs and their peoples across Europe, the British Isles was an especially suitable place for such an interest in the international and multicultural. Around 1160–70, the French poet Benoît de Sainte-Maure dedicated *The Story of Troy* (*Le Roman de Troie*), all 30,000 French lines of it, to Henry's Queen Eleanor. Anglo-Norman interest in the conqueror Alexander and his importance as a model for ambitious courtiers is reflected in the over 8000 Anglo-Norman lines of Englishman Thomas of Kent's *The Story of Alexander or How to be a Highly Effective Knight* (*Le Roman d'Alexandre Ou Le Roman de Toute Chevalerie*, 1175–1185).

We can see how popular the matter of Troy and Rome was with the Angevin royals when in 1182, the troubadour Bertran de Born complimented Princess Matilda, the daughter of Henry and Eleanor, in his native Occitan, as a new model Helen of Troy. Bertran calls Matilda 'a frisky, gay Elena' (*una gaia fresc'Elena*). Matilda's name echoes the imperial role of her father Henry's mother, Empress Matilda, who married Geoffrey of Anjou. This Matilda was the grand-daughter of William the Conqueror. All the more reason, then, for the lovelorn Bertran to tremble with fear when he beholds the princess:

Casutz sui de mal en pena
e vau lai o.l cors mi mena,
   don ja mais
no.m descargarai del fais;
car mes m'a en tal cadena
don mailla no.is descontena
   Car m'atrais
ab un esgart en biais
una gaia fresc'Elena.
Faich ai longa carantena,
   mas oimais
sui al digous de la Cena. (I, lines 1–12)

I have fallen from evil into pain, and I go where my body leads me, unable to unload its weight, one link in a chain never broken. A frisky, gay Elena attracted me with a sidelong look. I went through a long Lent, but from now on I am at the Thursday of the Last Supper.

Yet these lines are also cheeky as well as profound. Bertran was no wimp. He joined a revolt against Henry II in 1183. In this poem he might surprise us by taking on the burden of Matilda's dynastic body. At the time of composition the princess was heavily pregnant with her fourth child. He hails her as the newly proclaimed Trojan matriarch of the British. Yet Bertran is also both literally and metaphorically in drag, for his gambit presents Matilda as no dignified wife and mother but rather a young and sexy version of a royal woman at court. And that's just the first stanza. By the fourth, he or she is stripping the royal daughter to reveal the full sexual power of her dynasty-producing body. Such a tone reflects the charge of Henry's famously erotic and powerful courts (this one was at Argentan, in Normandy, late in 1182).

Another poem of Bertran's, produced for Matilda on the same occasion, is called *You shouldn't spend a whole morning just eating* (*Ges de disnar non for'oimais maitis*). This one trades the power of the flesh for the Roman imperial role coveted by the Angevins. With reference to Khorassan, a Persian city, the poet makes an intriguing reference to Oriental dominion:

> E car etz tant sobr'autras sobeirana,
>   vostra valors n'es plus au.
> Q'onrada n'er la corona romana
>   si.l vostre caps s'i enclau. (III, lines 21–4)

> Mais aic de joi que qi.m des Corrozana
>   car a son grat m'en esgau. (V, lines 39–40)

> Because you are so superior to the others, your worth appears even higher. The Roman crown will be honored if it encircles your head.

> I have more joy than if someone had given me Khorassan because, at her pleasure, I rejoice in her.

Eventually, one of Matilda's sons was crowned Holy Roman Emperor in 1209 (not holy, Roman or an empire, but covering the German-speaking area north of the Alps). This was a dynastic triumph that neither Matilda nor her father Henry II lived to see, for both died in 1189. Eleanor had died in 1204. Truly an old era was passing. In a later poem, *To all I say I don't want to live any longer* (*A totz dic qe ja mais non voil viure*), Bertran laments the even earlier death, in 1186, of Prince Geoffrey of Britany, son of Henry and Eleanor. Geoffrey was a church robber and reluctant rebel, but still Bertran, in his poem, hoped he would be received into the celestial company of Alexander, Roland and Oliver, even the church-robbing and mother-burning Raoul de Cambrai and a legendary Viking known as Ogier the Dane ('Holger

Dansker'). Bertran's 'code name' (*senhal*) for Geoffrey was 'Rassa', while he called Geoffrey's brother, the future King Richard the Lionheart, 'Oc e No' ('Yes and No'):

> Verais coms, Alixandres voil
> qe.us fassa compagnia lai;
> Ogiers e Raols de Canbrai,
> Rolantz ab tota sa vertut
> et Oliviers son aizinat (III, lines 17–21)

> De Lerida jusq'a Vernoil
> ni dal Far tro qu'a Roncisvai
> ni d'outra la mar ni de zai
> non portava princeps escut
> tan s'agues de bon pretz levat (IV, lines 25–9)
> lo segner

> S'Artus, losegner de Carduoil
> cui Breton atendon e mai,
> agues poder qe tornes sai,
> Breton i aurian perdut
> E nostre Segner gazagnat.
> Si lor i tornava Galvain
> non lur auria esmendat
> qe mais non lor agues tolut. (V, lines 33–40)

True Count, Alexander wants to keep you company there; Ogier and Raoul de Cambrai, Roland with all his strength and Oliver are your close friends.

From Llerida [in Catalonia] to Verneuil, from the straits of Messina to Roncesvaux, beyond the sea or here, no prince has borne a shield who has raised himself so high in good esteem.

If Arthur, lord of Carlisle, whom the Bretons await and always will, had the power to return here, the Bretons would lose in the exchange and God would win. If He returned Gawain to them in place of Rassa, He would not have given as much as he took.

For Bertran the treacherous Geoffrey was worth more alive than any prophetic return of King Arthur and Gawain, an idea with which the Welsh had tormented themselves while the Anglo-Saxons ruled England. Bertran was actually a rebel lord himself, as well as a poet. He was no believer in legends, for all the use he made of them in his often ironic verse. To show the Celtic connection, Prince Geoffrey did leave a son named 'Arthur' to his Breton subjects, although the poor boy was disappeared by his uncle, Prince John (in a way that anticipates the legend of the princes in the tower and their bad uncle King Richard III). Geoffrey named his son 'Arthur' because he was following a twelfth-century trend. However much people have doubted the Arthurian tales, from the Middle Ages to the present, King Arthur represents an enduring and sometimes disturbing vision of Britain's engagement with the rest of the world and particularly the east.

King Arthur of the Britons

In the twelfth century the Anglo-Normans could not get enough of the Celtic origins of Britain and King Arthur's brave fight against the vile Saxons. This period of Angevin rule is a key one for the literature of epic (*geste*) and romance (*roman*). The twelfth century was a watershed period when a secular culture, one that has much in common with our own, began to gain power in society and expression by questioning and sidelining religious concepts and values. The Arthurian history of Britain was very much a creation of this era. In its usually secular way, it purports to mix the most ancient Celtic, Trojan and Roman levels of multicultural tale telling. Arthur stands for a quasi-mythical Roman of British origins who is supposed to have held off the Saxon invasions in the mid sixth century. A Romano-British leader 'Ambrosius Aurelianus' is mentioned in writers such as Gildas (*c.* 550) and the Venerable Bede (*c.* 731), but it is *The History of the Britons* (*Historia Brittonum*, of the 820s, attributed to a fictitious 'Nennius') which adds 'Artorius' to the mix, by telling the story of how Britains fought and then succumbed to the Saxons. The earliest known vernacular reference to this figure shows just how slippery the truth about Arthur is. A manuscript from the late thirteenth century contains a copy of what appears to be a sixth-century Welsh poem, *Gododdin* [/godo:thin/] by a poet named Aneurin, who laments the loss of fighting men from the Gododdin tribe (near the borders of Scotland) in a battle with the Saxons near Catterick. Straightforward enough. This would be reminiscent of the poems on the death of Charlemagne's hero Roland, except that it mourns a warrior, who is now fodder for ravens, as 'no Arthur', simply because he lost. In the 1130s, Welsh clerics such as Geoffrey of Monmouth, in his *History of the Kings of Britain* (*Historia regum Brittanniae*, 1138–47) marketed this material to an Anglo-Norman audience by highlighting the Celtic king's vain fight against the vile Saxons. Then, as now, Anglo-Saxons were *personae non gratae*.

Arthur's story is part-history, part-Celtic mythology and part an infusion of the most diverse European and Middle Eastern influences you could imagine. There is an interesting argument that the Arthurian stories have been grafted to tales originating in north-eastern Persia brought to Britain by Sarmatian cavalry from Pannonia, present-day Hungary. At this time, however, the twelfth century, the emergence of tales of King Arthur reflected a new freedom to tell Celtic tales at the expense of the now less fashionable or politic Saxon stories. Perhaps the sense of rupture dating from the Conquest fuelled enthusiasm for stories that put peoples and languages together into a purposeful community.

Some sense of the multicultural origins of Arthur's legend may be reflected in the references to the east, the ability to unite different peoples for a common goal and an interest in languages. All this is featured in *The Story of Youth*, otherwise known as the *Mabinogion* (now in fourteenth-century manuscripts). One of the 11 tales in this collection, *Culhwch and Olwen*, was written in *c.* 1100 but probably pre-dates the Norman Conquest. In this tale Culhwch is made to accomplish a set of feats in King Arthur's court in order to win the hand of Olwen, daughter of the giant Ysbaddaden [/isbathah:den/]. Culhwch's name means 'pig run', so named because his mother cures her madness at a pig run but loses her young baby to the swineherd when frightened by his pigs. Growing up among pigs, Culhwch is nonetheless a king's son and first cousin to Arthur. They meet when Culhwch needs his help to get Olwen for a wife. It's her or no woman at all, thanks to Culhwch's wicked stepmother, who curses him thus for his lack of interest in her daughter. Through Arthur's leadership, the series of magical challenges are met. When the king himself finally gets the blood of this woman, the Black Witch, by slicing her into what looks like two convenient tubs, Culhwch gets his bride. There are traces of Alexander in this and the other tales, in the emphasis on marvels and in references to India and Africa. Like Alexander, King Arthur is a fierce warrior, but he has ability to unite peoples under his rulership. The international focus features in the other ten tales of *The Mabinogion* along with magic, beasts, games, prophecies, tale telling, shape shifting, rebirth and intimate treachery. But it is the multicultural yet mysterious aspect of Arthur linked to the theme of rebirth that is picked up in the twelfth-century versions of the 'matter of Britain'.

King Arthur took a star turn with the half-Welsh half-Breton cleric Geoffrey of Monmouth, whose *History of the Kings of Britain* joined an account of the settlement of Britain by 'Brutus', Roman grandson of Aeneas, to his clear exposition of what had been a murky Celtic Britain. Apparently, digesting traditional materials from oral and written sources, thanks to his native knowledge of Brythonic Celtic languages, Geoffrey completed his *History of the Kings of Britain* (*Historia regum Britanniae*) in 1138–1147. He was well placed in Monmouth on the Welsh border to draw on local resources for a Celtic chronicle. In doing so here, Geoffrey incorporated his earlier

Prophecies of Merlin (*Prophetiae Merlini*, in 1130). And in 1150 Geoffrey completed his *Life of Merlin* (*Vita Merlini*), a biography which claims Merlin as an important figure for the history of British kingship. In the later *Black Book of Camarthen* (*c.* 1250) there are poems on 'Myrddin' [/me:rthin/] or Merlin that may be much earlier than Geoffrey and which may shed some light on why he thought of Merlin so highly.

The association of Merlin with the magical kingship of Arthur echoes a story of Alexander the Great, which held that he was born from the adultery of his mother Olimpias with a shape-shifting Egyptian magician named Nectanebus. Perhaps with this influence, Geoffrey tells us that Merlin helped the warlord Uther pen Dragon, scourge of the Saxon invaders, to realise his adulterous desire for the faithful Ygerne by giving him the shape of her husband Gorlois. The real Gorlois dies in battle and later Arthur is born. Arthur goes on to unite the British Isles and then to rampage across France and Italy, defeating the Roman emperor Lucius and his eastern allies at the Battle of Saussy. But while abroad Arthur is betrayed by Mordred, his sister's (and his own!) son, along with his wife Queen Guinevere. At this setback Arthur does not wander off like Apollonius of Tyre, but goes back to Britain and besieges Mordred's force of Saxons, Irish, Scots and Picts at Winchester. All the then peoples of Britain are involved. Britons and Scandinavians fall on Arthur's side as the fight continues after Mordred's death until Arthur is badly wounded. He retires to the healing graces of the Isle of Avalon, where legend had it he was buried. In fact the local rulers claimed to have discovered Arthur's grave at Glastonbury in around 1190. They knew the unifying value of this legend and Arthur is most certainly the dead king who keeps on living.

He lives on, for example, in an Anglo-Norman adaptation of Geoffrey's tale. The poet Wace, from the Channel Islands, composed *The Story of Brut* (*Roman de Brut*) in *c.* 1155. Writing less than 12 years after Geoffrey, he could already draw on other historical narratives that referred briefly to Arthur's struggle against the Saxons. Wace famously summed up his common sense view of the magical kingship of Arthur as 'not all lies, not all truth, neither total folly nor total wisdom' (*Ne tut mençunge, ne tut veir,/Ne tut folie ne tut saveir*, lines 9793–4). Then Wace goes all out to convince his reader that it all rings true anyway. He humanises the enigmatic events of Arthur's story together with their shadowy actors. In developing the emotional reactions of the characters to meet all the treacheries and tragedies that engulf them, Wace also socialises their interactions by showing the courtly scenes and manners of Arthur's world. Other comments of Wace indicate his desire to impress on the audience that the fiction is real: 'The raconteurs', he says, 'have told so many yarns, the story-tellers so many stories, to embellish their tales that they have made it all appear fiction' (*Tant unt li cunteür cunté/ E li fableür tant flablé/Pur lur cuntes enbeleter,/Que tut unt fait fable sembler*, lines 9795–8). If Arthur's marriage is ill fated, it is because he and Guinevere have no children (lines 9657–8). To portray the preparations for Arthur's coronation, Wace uses a series of verbs to convey all the different activities and movements to show that what could be a formal and distant setting actually lies within the reader's own experience of a fair (lines 10337–60):

> Quant la curt le rei fu justee,
> Mult veïssez bele assemblee,
> Mult veïssez cité fremir,
> Servanz aler, servanz venir,
> Ostels saisir, ostels purprendre,
> Maisuns vuider, curtines tendre,
> Les mareschals ostels livrer,
> Soliers e chambres delivrer,
> A cels ki n'aveient ostels
> Faire loges e tendre trés.
> Mult veïssez as esquiers
> Palefreiz mener e destriers,
> Faire estables, paissuns fichier,
> Chevals mener, chevals lier,
> Chevals furbir e abevrer,
> Aveine, foerre, herbe porter.
> Mult veïssez en plusurs sens
> Errer vaslez e chamberlens,
> Mantels pendre, mantels plaier,
> Mantels escurre e atachier,
> Peliçuns porter vairs e gris,
> Feire semblast, ço vus fust vis. (*The Story of Brut*, lines 10337–58)

When the king's court was assembled, a fine gathering could be seen, and the city was in tumult, with servants coming and going, seizing and occupying lodgings, emptying houses, hanging tapestries, giving marshalls apartments, clearing upper and lower rooms, and erecting lodges and tents for those who had nowhere to stay. The squires could be seen busy leading palfreys and war-horses, arranging, stabling, sinking tethering-posts, bringing and tethering horses, rubbing them down and watering them, and carrying oats, straw and grass. You could see servants and chamberlains moving in several directions, hanging up and folding away mantles, shaking their dust off and fastening them, carrying grey and white furs: you would have thought it just like a fair.

In the *Mabinogion*, the descriptions of extraordinary fabrics, objects and beings allow the audience to visualise a strange and fascinating world from the outside in. Wace, by way of contrast, tells a tale that goes beyond the flatness of a list. In his poetry we inhabit the scene, which becomes increasingly more chaotic and vividly present as the energy of all the activities seems to build. The above passage provides a feeling for the real competition and pressures running beneath the surface of court life. The reader is offered the backstage view that is the focus of movie realism or of a reality television show. It is all in the 'fine gathering' (*bele assemblee*), 'fine equipment' (*de beles armes*) and 'fine clothing' (*de bels dras*, lines 10338, 10325). The courtiers themselves act much like fairgoers in their gaming, quarrelling, cheating and shouting, even betting all until they are stark naked (lines 10553–88). In the midst of this 'Carry on Courtier' the matchless king Arthur ends up looking pretty solitary. Once again there is a sense of isolation and desperation that underlies all the activity and stiff formality that plays into Arthur's great confrontation with Lucius and the Roman Empire that follows. Once in Europe, things do not end according to plan. Not long after the slaughter that accompanies Arthur's imperial conquest of Rome, Mordred betrays him and the brilliant court disintegrates into a violent civil war that is only redeemed by Arthur's mysterious withdrawal to Avalon. Wace has a talent for developing scenes and comedy, one which also conveys the real undercurrent of challenge and destruction in court life. We can see this if we look again at the songs of Bertran de Born, who was discussed earlier. This castle-holding troubadour addresses compliments to Henry II's daughter just before he urges Henry's sons into rebellion against their father in the great Revolt of 1183. For Arthur, read Henry II. If Wace's Arthur has prophetic dreams and masters a far-flung empire, he and his court are nonetheless intimate to the humanity of his readers. That, too, is the power of the story of Arthur.

In France the image of King Arthur underwent further humiliations until he became Guinevere's *mari complaisant*, the husband who winks at another man's love of his wife. This other man was Lancelot, a knight whom the French poets refined on the model of the randy Tristan of Cornwall and Wales. In due course a 'Continental' tradition of Lancelot's adulterous role developed away from the 'Insular' tradition (whereby it is Mordred who brings down King Arthur by an act of treachery while the king is abroad). Lancelot's affair with Guinevere becomes the love of their lives, the sole impediment to his perfection, the great flaw in his loyalty to Arthur and the court of Camelot. In due course it prevents him from beholding the Grail, a perfection which is granted to Galahad, a son of Lancelot especially created for the occasion as Jesus' hypostasis on earth. The Continental tradition, in which these tales developed, really starts with Chrétien de Troyes. As we have seen, Chrétien composed long poems on Arthur's knights for Countess Marie de Champagne, Eleanor's daughter, in her court in the 1170s; also for Count Philip of Alsace a bit further south. Perhaps Chrétien's most famous romances are *Lancelot or the Knight of the Cart* (*Lancelot, ou Le Chevalier de la charette*, in 1177–81) and his unfinished *Percival, or the Story of the Grail* (*Perceval, ou Le Conte du Graal, c.* 1182). In the one, he reluctantly tells the story everyone wanted to hear, how Lancelot made love to Guinevere while maintaining his friendship with Arthur, the *mari complaisant*. Chrétien was too reluctant to finish the other. He took a story which ultimately may have derived from ancient Celtic mythology involving a horn of plenty and some human sacrifice. You can catch up with this in 'The Waste Land' (1922), which reinvents the mythology with the aid of Jessie L. Weston's *From Ritual to Romance* (1920). In his time, Chrétien turned all his probably Breton source material into a Christian religious allegory involving Camelot's quest for the Holy Grail, the eucharistic cup of the Last Supper, together with an appearance of the very lance which stabbed Jesus as he hung on the cross. These were very powerful symbols for the time. Long before, in 1098, during the First Crusade (1096–9), when the *faransis* ('crusaders') broke into Antioch, they were pleased to liberate the same lance from the Seljuq Turks who then held the city. Chrétien's *Percival*, in particular, reintroduced some hard Christianity into Arthurian legend, of the kind which would later produce many creative conflicts in the behaviour of Lancelot and other adulterers in the French prose romances of the thirteenth century (the Vulgate Cycle), in the *Stanzaic Morte Arthur* of the fourteenth century, and in Sir Thomas Malory's English adaptations of both in his *Le Morte D'Arthur* (1467–70). In these works it is the love of Lancelot for Guinevere which provokes the civil war which gives the ever-faithless Mordred his chance for the throne. With the *Stanzaic Morte* and with Malory, at last, we can say that the sexy Continental Lancelot tradition arrived in England – a bit late, but better late than never.

Where the historicising 'Insular' tradition is concerned, Lancelot isn't in there. Arthur is the real Norman dark lord, all blood and guts just like his sister's son Gawain. Arthur got his first surviving English portrayal of this kind in the early thirteenth century. In the Severn Valley in England at this time lived a priest by the name of 'Layamon' or 'Laghamon' (normally it is written La3amon, with a *yogh* (3) pronounced like 'gh'). That is all we know of Layamon, although, as the name comes from Old Norse *lǫgmaðr* ('lawman'), it is possible this poet was descended from the Danish captains to whom King Cnut granted estates in the southwest Midlands in the 1020s (see p. 345). Probably about 200 years after this time, Layamon composed a massive poem adapting Wace, which is now known simply as *Brut* (*The Britain*). The *Brut* blends Old English and French verse forms in a new and independent manner in a hybrid alliterating and rhyming verse. Layamon doesn't just translate Wace but seems to be using other and particularly Celtic sources. Proceeding from the same creative intent, this represents a return to the multicultural emphasis of the *Mabinogion*. The hero Gawain is Arthur's sister's son, his right-hand man (Gwalchmai in *The Mabinogion*). Gawain is often sent to speak with different peoples in their own languages. Whatever the project at hand, Arthur's special power resides in his ability to lead and inspire 'many kinds of people' (*monni ennes cunnes men*, line 10005), but many kinds of people are also out to defeat him. Used in this double-edged sense, 'All' is the word that grows in power through the thousands of lines of Layamon's Arthurian verse until it echoes through Arthur's conquest of Rome, the imperial gathering of 'all'.

> Þa yet dude Arður mære,   aðelest alre Brutte:
> Arður asechen lette   alle þa riche
> kinges and eorles   and þa riccheste beornes
> þa i þan fehte weoren islayen   and idon of lif-dæyen;
> he lette heom burien   mid baldere pruten.
> Buten þreo kinges he beren lette   Luces þan kaisere,
> and lette makien beren   riche and swiðe maren,
> and lette heom sone   senden to Rome.
> And grette Rom-weren alle   mid græten ane huxe,
> And seide þat he heom sende   þat gauel of his londe,
> and efte wold heom alswa   senden heom gretinge ma
> yif heo irnen wolden   of Arðures golden;
> And þerafter wulle sone   riden into Rome
> And tellen heom tiðinge   of Brutlondes kinge,
> And Rome walles rihten   þe yare weoren tofallen –
> 'and swa ich wulle awelden   þe wode Rom-leoden!'
> Al þis yelp wes idel ido,   for eoðer weis hit eode,
> al oðer hit itidde   – þe leoden he bilæfen,
> al þurh Modred is mæien   forcuðest alle monnen!
> A þan muchele fihte   Arður of his cnihtes losede
> fif and twenti þusend   a uolden tohawen
> of Brutten swiðe balde,   biræued at liue. (*Brut*, lines 13908–928)

Then Arthur, the noblest of all Britons, does still more: Arthur caused all the mighty kings and earls and the greatest warriors who had been cut down and deprived of life in battle to be sought out; he had them buried with great splendour. But he ordered three kings to take the emperor Lucius and, having had a costly and magnificent bier made, dispatched them at once to Rome. And he greeted all the citizens of Rome with a gross insult, saying that he was sending them that tribute from his land, and, moreover, would send them more such greetings thereafter if they should still yearn for Arthur's treasure; and shortly thereafter he would ride into Rome and bring them tidings of the king of Britain, and secure the walls of Rome which once upon a time were overthrown – 'and so I will rule the unruly Romans!' All this vaunting was quite futile, for it turned out otherwise, turned out quite differently – he departed from his people, all through the might of Modred, the basest of all men!

In the great battle Arthur lost five and twenty thousand of his warriors, the bravest of Britons cut down and deprived of life.

Perhaps Danish in character, Layamon shows Arthur to have something of a Viking's sense of humour in the way he makes his point as the new world leader. Underlying his point to the Romans, with the bodies of their slain leaders, is the presence of the slain bodies of his own greatest warriors and the even more all-encompassing treachery of Modred which will engulf him and his empire (lines 13907–926). For Layamon the basic message of the Arthurian legend is a response to the famous problem of the one and the many and it is the many who win out. Arthur goes down like he should. But Wace seems to have had that idea too.

The Insular Arthurian tradition went on in England into the fourteenth century. In the *Alliterative Morte Arthure*, a poem perhaps from Leicestershire in the middle of that century, Arthur has the brute generalship of King Edward I, who had campaigned in Scotland and Wales. When a haughty senator of Emperor Lucius demands that Arthur give an account of himself and the Round Table in Rome, having not paid tribute in a while, Arthur reacts as everything his weakened Continental version could not be:

The king blushed [looked] on the berne   with his brode eyen,
That full bremly [fiercely] for brethe   brent [burned] as the gledes [coals],
Cast colours as the king   with cruel lates [expression]
Looked as a lion   and on his lip bites.
The Romanes for radness [fear]   rusht to the erthe,
For ferdness of his face   as they fey were;
Couched as kennetes [dogs]   before the king selven;
Because of his countenance   confused them seemed! (*Alliterative Morte Arthure*,
                                                                                                      lines 116–23)

In this poem, Gawain, too, is not the chivalrous type that we see in Malory's *Le Morte D'Arthur* or earlier, French, works. Rather this version of Arthur's sister's son is as Beowulf to Uncle Hygelac in *Beowulf*, or the hot-blooded

Anglo-Scandinavian warrior in a new guise. Take his last fight, for example, in the battle with his cousin Mordred:

> Then he moves to Sir Mordred   among all his knightes,
> And met him in the mid-sheld   and malles [hammers] him through,
> But the shalk [man] for the sharp [blade   he shuntes a little;
> He share [cut] him on the short ribbes   a shaftmond [six-inch] large.
> The shaft shuddered and shot   in the shire berne [shining man]
> That the sheddand blood   over his shank runnes
> And shewed on his shinbawde [shin-plate]   that was shire [brightly] burnisht!
> And so [as] they shift and shove   he shot to the erthe
> With the lush [blow] of the launce   he light on his shoulders
> An acre-lenghe [full-length] on a laund [hillock]   full lothly wounded.
> Then Gawan gird to the gome [man]   and on the grouf [his face] falles;
> All his gref was graithed;   his grace [luck] was no better!
> He shockes out a short knife   shethed with silver
> And sholde have slotted him in   but no slit happened;
> His hand slipped and slode [slid]   oslant on the mailes
> And the tother slely [slyly]   slines him under;
> With a trenchand knife   the traitour him hittes
> Through the helm and the hed   on high on the brain;
> And thus Sir Gawain is gone,   the good man of armes
> Withouten rescue of renk [man]   and rewe is the more! (lines 3840–59)

Uncle Arthur's grief is unimaginable, while he thinks little of Guinevere, here a momentary distraction. Now and again, from the East Midland area which Danes settled in the ninth and tenth centuries, the Insular tradition delivers pure saga style. The spirit of the hero lives on.

English in Anglo-Norman England

An idea of the Norman period as the new Dark Ages is still current in the study of early medieval language and literature. This is a myth founded on the fact of Norman oppression. According to this myth, an Anglo-Saxon vocabulary barely clings on in the place names and farmyard usage of the underclass. *Cow* and *calf* in the field, *beef* and *veal* on the table and so on. There's truth in every myth, but let us examine this one. It says that aristocrats, clerics and administrators share a sophisticated but provincial insular culture that breeds the hybrid languages of Anglo-Norman and Anglo-Latin. To be sure, there is great and unique literary expression in Anglo-Norman epics like the *Song of Roland*, in the historicising accounts of Arthur, the Celtic king whose prophetic return echoes down the ages, as well as in the

Breton love stories translated into the Anglo-Norman *Lays of Marie de France*. But the texts themselves? Of these, the myth says they are localised copies surviving in the backwaters of the innovative fast moving continental culture which produced the originals and then read the manuscripts to pieces or tossed them away as a new fashion took hold. Years later, hard on the dusty blood-stained heels of the Peasant Rebellion plotted and led by unruly Essex men in 1381, a new English literary culture boils up from a rising mercantile and artisan class. It is they who make use of an English where the cases are largely stripped out to serve the expressive needs of people concerned with trade, craft, barnyard and law. It's only a coincidence that Anglo-Norman shows the similar simplification of case structures and genres in Old French. Percolating through the dominant Anglo-Norman and Latin cultures, Middle English springs out like Athene, fully formed, ready to serve all societal functions. It is a tool fit for literary use thanks to a strongly French and Latinate vocabulary and the 'Alliterative Revival', a resurgence of poetry with the thumping consonant rhyme of the old Anglo-Saxon verse style. Thus the beginning of 'English literature'. Now there is only a flicker of those dusty old thanes and scops and the Anglo-Saxon world is so foreign that you have to study Old English as a language that has cases like Classical Latin or Modern German.

You can see that this myth shouldn't be trusted too far. In some ways it reflects the actual disinheritance of Anglo-Saxon noble families, for William the Conqueror, like King Cnut 40 years before him, shared out great parcels of Anglo-Saxon land. In his case the landholdings went to supporters from northern France, Brittany, and Flanders. King William spread his largesse further (and so further added to the mix of languages and cultures) by rewarding companions from the Angevin and the neighbouring Occitan-speaking areas of what would much later become central and southern France. The convergence of languages and cultures here likely worked to the advantage of England's majority Anglo-Saxon culture. Both the Old English and Old French languages were simplified in the same ways. This argues that there was a good deal of interchange on both sides by practical-minded people.

If the Norman yoke bore so heavily, why are there no writings addressed to the task of teaching French to English speakers for over 200 years after the Conquest? Shaped by its multicultural context into Anglo-Norman, French ran along side Anglo-Latin and Anglo-Saxon and other languages that suited the changing circumstances and needs of their users. In the mid-thirteenth century French seems to become a language to be taught because it is of literary interest rather than in general use. This sense of language streams and convergences is suggested in the use of Norman names often as additions to place names such as 'Swaffham Bulbeck'. Research shows that this place name comes from Old English *Swæfa hām* ('homestead of the Swabians') and *de Bolebech* for the Norman lord of the manor. Norse place names tend to pool in the Danelaw of north Essex, Norfolk and Suffolk, in the East Midlands, Yorkshire, Lancashire and Cumbria, Scotland and often feature in coastal areas further out as well. The local continuity of Anglo-Saxon structures is shown in so many place names derived from Anglo-Saxon kin or chieftain groups. Just think of all the village names that end with the suffix *-ing*. This is fixed to the name of a leader to show membership among his family or followers. Thus 'Brightling', from *Beorhtlingas*, means 'family or followers of Beorhtel'. Not to mention *-ton* (OE *tūn* 'farmstead, estate'), *-ham* (OE *hām* 'homestead' or *hamm* 'spit of land') and *-burgh* or *-bury* (OE *burh*, 'fort'). English survived to become the default language of fourteenth-century Britain.

Contrast this with Celtic languages, which left relatively few traces, often in names of the waters they held sacred, as the Anglo-Saxons moved into Romano-Britain. Still, there must have been language interchange between Celts and Saxons for those Celtic elements to remain. Don't these cultures really graft with each other, instead of the earlier being erased by the later? The remarkable literary texts of the Anglo-Norman period show much inter-action with the values and taste in stories of the Old English, Celtic and Old Norse cultures in their own environments. How different ethnicities and cultures interact is a theme that is often found in the literature of our period as well, although most moderns would claim that ours is the first time in which any mixture like this can be found. That is the real myth we live with now.

Finding the Anglo-Saxon past

The hybrid style of Romanesque architecture in late eleventh century is one reflection of the general cultural mix that took place. It also provides a clue to an otherwise mysterious element in the fourteenth-century *Life of St Erkenwald*, the patron saint of London. Here there is a concern with keeping the past alive in verse, one to match that of the twelfth-century Anglo-Norman *Lays* of Marie de France. This concern had become a real source of anxiety by Chaucer's lifetime, the fourteenth century. The poem tells us how an old tomb is discovered and opened at St Paul's Church in London, the elaborate shape and ornament of the lid shows both the age and worthiness of its yet fresh pagan corpse:

And as þai makkyd and mynyd a mervayle þai founden
As yet in crafty cronecles is kydde þe memorie,
For as þai dyght and dalfe so depe into þe erthe
Wai founden fourmyt on a flore a ferly faire toumbe;
Hit was a throgh of thykke ston thryvandly hewen,
With gargeles garnysht about alle of gray marbre.
The sperl of þe spelunke þat spradde hit olofte
was metely made of þe marbre and menskefully planed
And þe bordure enbelicit with bryght golde lettres;
Bot roynyshe were þe resones þat þer on row stoden.
Full verray were þe vigures, þer avisyd hom mony,
Bot all muset hit to mouth and quat hit mene shuld;
[. . .]
And als freshe hym þe face and the flesh nakyd
Bi his eres and bi his hondes þat openly shewid
with ronke rode as þe rose and two rede lippes.
[. . .]
And we have oure librarie laitid þes long seven dayes
Bot one cronicle of þis kyng con we never fynde. (*St Erkenwald*, lines 43–54,
                                                          89–92, 155–6)

As they built and dug they found a marvel the memory of which is still
recorded in learned chronicles, for as they worked and dug deep into the
earth they found an extremely fine tomb constructed on a floor; it was a
sarcophagus of thick stone, excellently cut, with gargoyles decorated around
it of grey marble. The lid of the tomb that enclosed it on the top was made
fittingly of marble and elegantly smoothed, and the border embellished with
letters of bright gold, but the letters that stood in a row there were mysterious.
The outlines were quite clear, as many saw, but everyone was at a loss to
pronounce the text or understand what it meant [lines 43–54]. As fresh was his
face and his bare skin by his ears and hands that were openly displayed, with
complexion as ruddy as the rose, and with two red lips [lines 89–92]. And we
have searched our library these seven long days, but we couldn't find a single
account of this king [lines 155–6].

A marvel indeed. In this saint's life the pagan has been granted the privilege
to stay untouched by Death's corruption until a Christian cleric, St Erkenwald,
can sanctify his just deeds with baptism and give him a place in heaven.
But when he gets what he has been waiting for all this time – to be duly
baptised by a Christian cleric – the pagan corpse falls to dust as his 'marble'
monument remains.

    This scene from *The Life of St Erkenwald* is proof of how much enthusiasm
there was in the fourteenth century for the Anglo-Saxon past and how

important it was for Chaucer's contemporaries to seek out its meaning and record it as their own. The discoverers of the tomb find themselves before a language still living in its bright runes, but they cannot voice or decipher either. Neither can they find any chronicles that match this figure. In this way we know that the poem's audience thought that carefully preserved chronicles were the true source for stories about past kings. We can also see their fear that already much of this information had been lost.

It matters to people to be able not only to decipher the past, but to interact with it as well. Just as the pagan in *The Life of St Erkenwald* needs the Christian present to complete his story, so his Christian finders need him to work out their own religious historical identity. The search for the past and its link to the forces of life itself that we see in the *Life of St Erkenwald* echo in the opening lines of the *Prologue* to *The Canterbury Tales*, composed later in the fourteenth century:

> Whan that Aprill with his shoures soote
> The droghte of March hath perced to the roote,
> And bathed every veyne in swich licour
> Of which vertu engendred is the flour;
> Whan Zephirus eek with his sweete breeth
> Inspired hath in every holt and heeth
> The tendre croppes, and the yonge sonne
> Hath in the Ram his halve cours yronne,
> And smale foweles maken melodye,
> That slepen al the nyght with open ye
> (So priketh hem nature in hir corages);
> Thanne longen folk to goon on pilgrimages,
> And palmeres for to seken straunge strondes,
> To ferne halwes, kowthe in sondry londes;
> And specially from every shires ende
> Of Engelond to Caunterbury they wende,
> The hooly blisful martir for to seke,
> That hem had holpen whan that they were seeke. (*General Prologue*, lines 1–18)

The past from which these people draw renewed life is rooted in the cult of the late twelfth-century archbishop of Canterbury and martyr Thomas à Becket, his brains dashed out *Roland* style on 29 December 1170, by rogue knights of the complicit King Henry II. Through this saint's body and through other relics, artefacts, books and poems, the world of Chaucer felt a deep connection with the past. Much as in the *Lays* of Marie de France, we see the force of spring compelling Chaucer's contemporaries to join together in some greater and more harmonious union. As nature unleashes its vitally connective power throughout the universe, English people desire to get in touch with the potent sites and figures of their past.

Losing the Anglo-Saxon past?

The wish to get back is no less true of people today than it was for those of Chaucer's time. Neither is the risk of losing the Anglo-Saxon past less potent for us than it was for them. In fact, it has increased quite naturally the further removed we are from 1066 and the six centuries of Anglo-Saxon history before it. Let's finish with some more words from the fourteenth century. These are about about losing the unlosable:

> Perle plesaunte, to prynces paye
> To clanly clos in golde so clere:
> Oute of oryent, I hardyly saye,
> Ne proved I never her precios pere.
> So round, so reken in uche araye,
> So smal, so smoþe her sydez were;
> Queresoever I jugged gemmez gaye
> I sette hyr sengeley in synglure.
> Allas! I leste hyr in on erbere;
> þurgh gresse to grounde hit fro me yot.
> I dewine, fordolked of lufdaungere
> Of þat pryvy perle withouten spot. (*Pearl*, I, lines 1–12)

This is the work of the '*Gawain* poet', an anonymous author living in London but probably from somewhere south of Manchester, whose four surviving poems (*Pearl, Cleanness, Patience* and *Sir Gawain and the Green Knight*) stand comparison with the best works of Geoffrey Chaucer. Like the younger Chaucer, this poet follows the French tradition with rhyming, mostly octosyllabic, lines. But in his case the rhyme scheme (A-B-A-B-A-B-A-B-A-B-C-B-C-B) is even more demanding than the stanzas of Chaucer's mature work, *Troilus and Criseyde* (c. 1385). Note also how this poet follows a Germanic style of verse craft. As well as intensifying the French rhyme scheme of the day, he writes each line with two, three or sometimes four alliterating words. In many cases, he makes the alliteration harder for himself by choosing initial clusters of consonants. This is expected in Old English or Old Icelandic poetry. In his opening sentence, however, he makes the *p(r)* alliteration of the fourth line rejoin that of the first. This is a highly literate device, contrived to match the circularity of the pearl, the very structure of his poem. By the same token, this poet from Cheshire, where the Irish Norwegians settled in the tenth century, has one line ('I sette hyr sengeley in synglure', line 8) with imperfect internal rhyme. This device was also known to the illiterate Norse skalds, who regarded it as essential and called it *skothending* (p. 393). And yet the poet also speaks to us in the idiom of the lyrical *roman courtois*, a form whose origins lay in Occitan France. So, borrowing doubtless from the thirteenth-century *Romance of the Rose*, he describes himself as 'stabbed through by the distance of the beloved' (*fordolked of lufdaungere*, line 11). In other words, he admits that losing the un-losable, his daughter, has brought him as much anguish as a dream brings the lover who finds himself unable to return.

Old English literature might be looked on as just such a pearl, as Clive Tolley has said. However, this is not a pearl that has to be lost. We are keeping it for you in this book. You may return, if you like, to Chapter 2 (on p. 38), where you will find the *Pearl* stanza translated by J.R.R. Tolkien, author of *The Lord of the Rings*. So we go full circle. In any case you may find yourself revisiting the beginning of this book of your own accord, for the sake of *Beowulf* and the other stories inside it. Then, who knows, you may wish to go outside this book to find more of the Old English, Old Icelandic, Old French literature which the contributors have discussed. After getting this far, it should come as no surprise to you to find the *Gawain* poet, any English poet, drawing on a hybrid culture that can be called Anglo-Scandinavian-Norman-French. You are doing this yourself whenever you read 'English literature'. In the end it will be up to you, one of a new generation of readers and thinkers, to save the cosmopolitan reality of medieval texts and the entertainment and wisdom that they offer.

Translations and texts

Andrew, Malcolm and Ronald Waldron, eds, *The Poems of the Pearl Manuscript: Pearl, Cleanness, Patience, Sir Gawain and the Green Knight* (Exeter, rev. 1987).

Barron, W.R.J. and S.C. Weinberg, ed. and trans., *La3amon's Arthur: The Arthurian Section of La3amon's Brut (9229–14297)* (London, 1989).

Baumgartner, Emmanèle and Françoise Vieilliard, ed. and trans. (abridged), *Benoît de Sainte-Maure. Le Roman de Troie* (Paris, 1998).

Benson, Larry D., ed., *King Arthur's Death: The Middle English 'Stanzaic Morte Arthur' and 'Alliterative Morte Arthure'* (Exeter, 1986).

Benson, Larry D., ed., *The Riverside Chaucer* (Boston, MA, 1987).

Burgess, Glyn S., trans., *The History of the Norman People: Wace's Roman de Rou* (Woodbridge, 2004).

Burgess, Glyn S., trans., *The Song of Roland* (Harmondsworth, 1990).

Burgess, Glyn S. and Keith Busby, trans., *The Lais of Marie de France* (Harmondsworth, 2003).

Davis, Norman, *et al.*, *A Chaucer Glossary* (Oxford, 1979).

Duggan, Hoyt N. and Thorlac Turville-Petre, eds, *The Wars of Alexander*, Early English Texts Society, Second Series 10 (Oxford, 1989).

Elwin, Malcolm, ed. and preface, *Ivanhoe* by Sir Walter Scott (London, 1968).

Emden, Wolfgang van, ed., *La Chanson de Roland*, Critical Guides to French Texts (London, 1995).

Fedrick, Alan S., trans., *The Romance of Tristan by Beroul and The Tale of Tristan's Madness* (Harmondsworth, 1970).

Foster, Brian and Ian Short, eds, trans., intro. and Catherine Gaullier-Bougassas and Laurence Harf-Lancner, notes, *Thomas de Kent. Le Roman d'Alexandre ou Le Roman de Toute Chevalerie* (Paris, 2003).

Jones, Gwyn and Thomas Jones, trans. and intro., *The Mabinogion* (London 1949, rev. 1970).

Kibler, William W., trans. and intro. with Carleton W. Carroll, *Chrétien de Troyes: Arthurian Romances* (Harmondsworth, 1991).

Micha, Alexander, ed. and trans., *Lais de Marie de France* (Paris, 1994).

Mills, Maldwyn, trans., *Six Middle English Romances* (London, 1992).

Paden, William D. and Tilde A. Sankovitch and Patricia H. Stablein [now Gillies], ed. and trans., *The Poems of the Troubadour Bertran de Born* (Berkeley, CA, and London, 1986).

Short, Ian, trans. and intro., *La Chanson de Roland* (Paris, 1997).

Thorpe, Lewis, trans., *Geoffrey of Monmouth. The History of the Kings of Britain* (Harmondsworth, 1966, rev. 1979).

Treharne, Elaine, ed. and trans., *Old and Middle English* (Oxford, 2000), includes Anglo-Saxon *Apollonius of Tyre*, Middle English *King Alisaunder* and *The Owl and the Nightingale*.

Turville-Petre, Thorlac and J.A. Burrow, eds, *A Book of Middle English*, 3rd edn (Oxford, 2005).

Weiss, Judith, trans., *The Birth of Romance; An Anthology, Four Twelfth-Century Anglo-Norman Romances* (London, 1992).

Weiss, Judith, ed. and trans., Wace's *Roman de Brut: A History of the British* (Exeter, 1999, rev. 2002).

Further reading

Barron, W.R.J., *English Medieval Romance*, Longman Literature in English Series (London and New York, 1987).

Brooke, Christopher, *The Saxon and Norman Kings*, 3rd edn (Oxford, 2001).

Campbell, Emma and Robert Mills, eds, *Troubled Vision: Gender, Sexuality and Sight in Medieval Text and Image* (New York, 2004).

Gaunt, Simon, *Retelling the Tale: An Introduction to Medieval French Literature* (London, 2001).

Golding, Brian, *Conquest and Colonization: The Normans in Britain, 1066–1100*, British History in Perspective (London, 1994).

Kibbee, Douglas A., *For to Speke Frenche Trewely*, Studies in the History of the Language Sciences 60 (Amsterdam, 1991).

Krueger, Roberta L., ed., *The Cambridge Companion to Medieval Romance* (Cambridge, 2000).

Lupack, Alan, *The Oxford Guide to Arthurian Literature and Legend* (Oxford, 2005).

Meale, Carol M., ed., *Women and Literature in Britain 1150–1500*, 2nd edn (Cambridge, 1996).

Menocal, María Rosa, *The Arabic Role in Medieval Literary History*: *A Forgotten Heritage* (Philadelphia, PA, 1987).

Mills, A.D., *Oxford Dictionary of British Place Names* (Oxford, 2000).

Mitchell, Jerome, *Scott, Chaucer and Medieval Romance: A Study in Sir Walter Scott's Indebtedness to the Literature of the Middle Ages* (Lexington, KY, 1987).

Pearsall, Derek, *Arthurian Romance: A Short Introduction* (Oxford, 2003).

Swanton, Michael J., trans., *The Anglo-Saxon Chronicle* (London, 1996).

Weir, Alison, *Eleanor of Aquitaine: By the Wrath of God, Queen of England* (London, 2000).

The end of Old English?

David Crystal

A ccording to Toronto University's *Dictionary of Old English Corpus* the entire body of Old English material from 600 to 1150 consists of only 3037 texts (excluding manuscripts with minor variants), amounting to a mere three million words. A single prolific modern author easily exceeds this total: Charles Dickens' fiction, for example, amounts to over four million. Three million words is not a great deal of data for a period in linguistic history extending over five centuries. But we should be grateful for small mercies. Given that the Vikings destroyed so many monasteries and the libraries they contained, we are lucky to have even three million words to explore. And it is enough to illustrate a literature which, as we have seen, is vivid, vibrant, and varied.

Old English dialects

Most of the texts illustrated in this book were written in the dialect of a single part of the country – Wessex. The prestige of a dialect always reflects the power of its speakers; and in Anglo-Saxon times the emergence of Wessex as the dominant and eventually unifying force in English politics inevitably resulted in an increase in the status of its dialect. But standards do not develop overnight; and in the case of Old English, the process took over a century.

Early West Saxon is the name given to the dialect that characterises the literature of the first part of the period. It is a literature almost entirely due to the motivation and influence of King Alfred, who introduced a revival of religion and learning – a programme designed to win God's support for victory over the pagan Danes and to consolidate loyalty to himself as a Christian king. The results of Alfred's assiduous language planning were remarkable. Almost all prose texts during the late ninth century and throughout the tenth display a dialect that is very largely West Saxon and it is this which has been used as the primary input for introductory grammars and manuals of Old English today.

Late West Saxon is the name given to the development of this dialect towards the end of the tenth century, when we find the writings of Ælfric, Wulfstan, Athelwold, Byrhtferth and others, as well as the continuation of the *Chronicle*, all of which were widely and officially distributed through the political and church networks. But there is an important difference between the Early and Late periods. In the Early period, the texts contain a great deal of variation, displaying dialect mixture, personal variation and scribal inconsistency. There is no sign of any real attempt to produce a consistent, universally standardised form of expression.

During the second half of the tenth century, just such an effort began to be made. A noticeable consistency appears in the work of scribes from monasteries all over the country. Writers as far apart as modern Wiltshire (Æthelwold), Dorset and Oxfordshire (Ælfric) and Worcestershire (Wulfstan) show remarkable similarity in spellings, words and constructions. Many scholars think that the influence of the Winchester school was especially strong. We can even see signs of revision taking place, with authorial corrections suggesting a concern to use 'correct' language.

Alongside West Saxon, three other dialects are known from the Old English period, deriving from the names of the Anglo-Saxon kingdoms: Kentish, Mercian and Northumbrian, with the last two sometimes grouped together as a northern variety, Anglian. In reality, there must have been many more. East Anglia is an example of a major gap. There would have been many dialects in this area, from what we know of early patterns of settlement, but there are no Old English texts to represent them. Thousands of dialect manuscripts must have been destroyed in the Viking invasions.

The evidence for a Kentish dialect is thin, with just a few documents, glosses and poetic texts, chiefly ninth/tenth century, displaying features that seem to be south-eastern in character. Although not numerous, these features are nonetheless among the most interesting in the early history of English. Several, indeed, exercise a permanent influence on the language, being taken up by some Middle English writers (notably, Chaucer) and eventually entering standard English.

The early appearance of Northumbrian texts is not surprising when we recall that by 700 several major centres of learning had emerged in the north, notably at Jarrow, Durham and Lindisfarne, with Bede and later Alcuin producing influential works. The amount of language in these texts is not large, but there are enough variant forms used in a consistent way to indicate that a distinctive Northumbrian dialect existed by the beginning of the eighth century. Interlinear glosses from the late tenth century confirm the character of this dialect, notably those added to the Lindisfarne and Rushworth Gospels. The absence of Northumbrian texts between the eighth and tenth centuries is a further result of the Viking burnings.

The growth of Mercia as a political power and a centre of culture and learning, during the eighth century, is reflected in the survival of several texts from that period. The most important are glossaries in which many of the forms display a distinctive West Midlands character, notably the Corpus and Vespasian Psalter texts. A surprising number of charters, land records and other official documents have also survived, reflecting the growth of political and legal frameworks during the period, especially under Offa, and they show many Mercian features.

Many texts display a mixture of dialect features. Mixing takes place when people from different dialect backgrounds come into contact and let themselves be influenced by each other. We have only hints about the social background of individual Anglo-Saxon scribes, but we do know there was considerable mobility. Travel records of the time suggest that the monks moved around the country a great deal, often bringing copies of books with them and staying for long periods in their host monasteries. There they would continue their scribal activities, working in association with others who might display different dialect backgrounds, and influencing – and being influenced by – different scribal practices and conventions.

Because the entire corpus is the product of a scribal elite, it gives no information about the dialect variations that ordinary people would have used. Most of the material belongs to specialised stylistic varieties, such as religious and legal language, or is consciously innovative and poetic. A record of everyday conversational speech is hardly ever found. There is one recorded example of a fairly extensive Old English conversation – the pupil/teacher dialogue forming the *Colloquy* of Ælfric. But we can hardly take this as representative, for the Old English text is actually made up of lines glossing a Latin original designed to teach Latin to boys in monastic schools. However, it is probably the closest we will ever get to Old English conversational style.

The four major dialect areas are the ones which have received all the attention; but undoubtedly there were further divisions within them. Over and above the question of their social diversity, three of the areas they covered were huge. Mercian and Northumbrian, in particular, covered a territory which in later centuries would each be home to several distinct dialects. These later dialects did not suddenly appear. They slowly evolved; and it is likely that some of their linguistic features were present in Anglo-Saxon times. Certainly there are enough variations within both Mercian and

Northumbrian for scholars to postulate northern forms of the former and southern forms of the latter. There is also evidence in Mercian of a division between the West and East Midlands.

What is particularly unclear – but highly intriguing – is whether we should be thinking exclusively in geographical terms in attempting to explain these variations. Some scholars think that, in the final analysis, what we have is a dialect picture not of regions of the country but of diocesan preferences, given that most scribes came from just a few monasteries, such as Jarrow, Winchester, Lichfield and Canterbury. The study of different handwriting preferences, illustration styles and page layout conventions – part of the subject of palaeography – is especially important in this connection.

Vocabulary change

No language has ever been found that displays lexical purity: there is always a mixture, arising from the contact of its speakers with other communities at different periods in its history. In the case of English there is a special irony, for its vocabulary has never been purely Anglo-Saxon – not even in the Anglo-Saxon period. By the time the Anglo-Saxons arrived in Britain, there had already been four centuries of linguistic interchange between Germanic and Roman people on the European mainland. The Roman soldiers and traders borrowed Germanic words and the Germanic people borrowed Latin ones. The integration was at times quite marked: many Roman cohorts consisted of men from Germanic tribes. Language mixing was there from the very beginning.

Latin

A Latin word might have arrived in English through any of several possible routes. To begin with, Latin words must have entered the Celtic speech of the Britons during the Roman occupation and some might have remained in daily use after the Romans finally left in the early fifth century, so that they were picked up by the Anglo-Saxons in due course. Or perhaps Latin continued to exercise its influence following the Roman departure: it is possible that aristocratic Britons would have continued to use the language as a medium of upper-class communication. If so, then we might expect a significant number of Latin words to be in daily use, some of which would eventually be assimilated by the Anglo-Saxons. Some Latin words would also have been brought in by the Anglo-Saxons invaders. And, following the arrival of St Augustine in 597, the influence of the monks must have grown, with Latinisms being dropped into speech much as they still are today.

The Latin words express a considerable semantic range. They include words for plants and animals, food and drink, household objects, coins, metals, items of clothing, settlements, houses and building materials, as well as several notions to do with military, legal, medical and commercial matters. Most are nouns, such as *camp*, *street* and *monk*, with a sprinkling of verbs and adjectives. As we move into the period of early Anglo-Saxon settlement in England, we find these semantic areas continuing to expand, with the growing influence of missionary activity reflected in an increase in words to do with religion and learning.

Nearly half of all Latin borrowings during this early period died out. In some cases, they were replaced during the Old English period: *fossere*, for example, was in early competition with *spade* and *spade* won. More often, the word that formed the replacement arrived in medieval times, as with *pocket*, which entered English from Norman French in the thirteenth century, taking over the function earlier performed by Old English *bisæcc* 'pocket' (from *bisaccium*).

Borrowing from Latin continued throughout the Old English period, but it changed its character as church influence grew. Whereas most of the earlier words entered the language through the medium of speech, later words came in through the medium of writing and were more learned and religious in character, such as *deacon* and *grammar*. This trend is not surprising: the teaching of the church had to be communicated to the Anglo-Saxon people and new vocabulary was needed to express the new concepts, personnel and organisational procedures.

Borrowing Latin words was not the only way in which the missionaries engaged with this task. Rather more important, in fact, were other linguistic techniques. One method was to take a Germanic word and adapt its meaning so that it expressed the sense of a Latin word: examples include *rod*, originally meaning 'rod, pole', which came to mean 'cross'; and *gast*, originally 'demon, evil spirit', which came to mean 'soul' or 'Holy Ghost'. Another technique, relying on a type of word creation that permeates Old English poetry, was to create new compound words – in this case, by translating the elements of a Latin word into Germanic equivalents: so, *liber evangelii* became *godspellboc* 'gospel book' and *trinitas* became *priness* 'threeness' = 'trinity'.

Scandinavian

The Vikings made their presence felt in Britain in the 780s, but it was a further century before Old Norse words began to arrive in Old English. In *c.* 880 Alfred made a treaty with Guthrum which left Alfred in control of London and Guthrum in control over an area of eastern England which, because it was subject to Danish laws, came to be known as the Danelaw. This area ran from the northern shore of the Thames as far west as the River Lea (the boundary of Essex), then north along the Lea into Bedfordshire and from there along the Ouse to the line of Watling Street. The boundaries further north are unclear, but it is evident from the place names that eventually appeared that Danes were present in the whole of the northern and north-eastern third of the country, roughly between Cheshire and Essex.

Over 2000 Scandinavian place names are found throughout the Danelaw, chiefly in Yorkshire, Lincolnshire and the East Midlands. The distribution of Scandinavian family names – such as those that end in -son (*Johnson, Henderson, Jackson* and so on) – also shows a concentration throughout the area. In Yorkshire and north Lincolnshire, 60% of the names recorded in early Middle English sources are of Scandinavian origins.

The Scandinavian place names are one of the most important linguistic developments of the period. Many are easily recognised. Over 600 end in -*by*, the Old Norse word for 'farmstead' or 'town', as in *Rugby* and *Grimsby*, the other element often referring to a person's name (Hroca's and Grim's farm, in these two cases), but sometimes to general features, as in *Burnby* ('farm by a stream') and *Westerby* ('western farm'). Many end in -*thorpe* ('village, outlying farm'), -*thwaite* ('clearing') or -*toft* ('homestead'), such as *Althorp, Millthorpe, Braithwaite, Applethwaite, Lowestoft* and *Sandtoft*.

We might expect Scandinavian place names to be recorded relatively quickly after the period of Norse settlement began; but what about general words in speech and writing? The treaty between Alfred and Guthrum con-tains the first Scandinavian loans known in Old English texts: *healfmarc* 'half a mark' and *liesengum*, a variant of *liesing* 'freedmen'. But only about 30 Norse words came into Old English during this period. Most are terms reflecting the imposition of Danish law and administration throughout the region, social structure, or cultural objects or practices, such as seafaring and fighting. Very few had enough broad applicability to survive into later periods of English, once Scandinavian culture and power declined.

Despite the extensive period of settlement and Danish becoming the language of power for a generation, the overall impact of Scandinavian words on Old English vocabulary continued to be slight during the eleventh century – just a few dozen more items being identifiable in English texts. Indeed, when we count up all the Scandinavian words that entered Old English between the ninth and the twelfth centuries, we arrive at a surpris-ingly small total – about 150. Why?

One important factor would have been the rise of the West Saxon dialect as the literary language following King Alfred's extensive use of it. By the year 1000 it had achieved the status of a scribal standard, used throughout the country as a result. It would have been difficult for regionally restricted Danish forms to achieve public prominence. The political centres were in the south, at Winchester and later London, outside the Danelaw. Then, in the later period, the rise of Norman influence made Danish words less prestigious. But perhaps most important is the very short period of time overall that received Danish rule – little more than 50 years in the age of the Danelaw and only 26 years in the age of Cnut. No creative literature with a Danish theme, which might have shown a typical Scandinavian vocabulary, has survived from this period.

If that was the end of the linguistic dimension to the Scandinavian story, it would be no more than a ripple in English linguistic history. But something remarkable was taking place in the period between Old and Middle English. Although there are no written records to show it, a considerable Scandinavian vocabulary was gradually being established in the language. We know that this must have been so, because the earliest Middle English literature, from around 1200, shows thousands of Old Norse words being used, especially in texts coming from the northern and eastern parts of the country, such as the *Orrmulum* and *Havelok the Dane*. They could not suddenly have arrived in the twelfth century, for historically there was no significant connection with Scandinavia at that time; England was under Norman French rule. And as it takes time for loanwords to become established, what we must be seeing is a written manifestation of an underlying current of Old Norse words that had been developing a widespread vernacular use over the course of two centuries or more.

There is no doubt that many of these words *were* well established, because they began to replace some common Anglo-Saxon words. The word for 'take', for example, was *niman* in Old English; Old Norse *taka* is first recorded in an English form, *toc* (= *took*) during the late eleventh century, but by the end of the Middle English period *take* had completely taken over the function of *niman* in general English. The everyday flavour of the Scandinavian loans can be seen, for example, in these two dozen words, all of which survived into modern Standard English:

> anger, awkward, bond, cake, crooked, dirt, dregs, egg, fog, freckle, get, kid, leg, lurk, meek, muggy, neck, seem, sister, skill, skirt, smile, Thursday, window

We mustn't overrate the impact Scandinavian words on English: they are only a fraction of the thousands of French words that entered the language during the Middle Ages. Moreover, the majority fell out of use. Yet some of the ones that did survive exercised a disproportionate influence, because (like *take* and *get*) they were very frequently used. And they were supplemented by another set of changes that were even more influential, because they made a permanent impact on the grammar of the language.

Grammatical change

The most important of these changes was the introduction of a new set of third-person plural pronouns, *they*, *them* and *their*. These replaced the earlier Old English inflected forms: *hi* or *hie* (in the nominative and accusative cases, 'they/them'), *hira* or *heora* (in the genitive case, 'their, of them') and *him* or *heom* (in the dative case, 'to them, for them'). Pronouns do not change very often, in the history of a language and to see one set of forms replaced by another is truly noteworthy.

Another grammatical influence was the use of *are* as the third-person plural of the verb *to be*. This form had already been used sporadically in northern texts during the late Old English period – for example, in the Lindisfarne Gospels – but in Middle English it steadily moves south, eventually replacing the competing plural forms *sindon* and *be*. *Sindon* disappeared completely by the mid-1200s, but *be* remained in use for several centuries, entering generations of intuitions through the style of the Book of Common Prayer and the King James' Bible (e.g. *They be blind leaders of the blind*, Matthew 15: 14). It continues to be a major feature of the language in regional dialects, both in Britain and abroad.

Among other Scandinavian grammatical features that survived are the pronouns *both* and *same* and the prepositions *til* 'till, to' and *fro* 'from'. The negative response word, *nay*, is also Norse in origin (*nei*). And the *-s* ending for the third-person singular present tense form of the verb (as in *she runs*) was almost certainly a Scandinavian feature. In Old English, this ending was usually *-ð*, as in *hebbað* 'raises' and *gæð* 'goes'; but in late Northumbrian texts we find an *-s* ending and this too spread south to become the standard form.

The transition from Old English to Middle English is primarily defined by the linguistic changes that were taking place in grammar. Old English, as we have seen (Chapter 10), was a language that contained a great deal of inflectional variation; modern English has hardly any. And it is during Middle English that we see the eventual disappearance of most of the earlier inflections and the increasing reliance on alternative means of expression, using word order and prepositional constructions rather than word endings to express meaning relationships.

We must be careful not to overstate the nature of the change. The phrase 'increasing reliance' is meant to suggest that there is a great deal of continuity between the grammatical systems of Old and Middle English. Word order was by no means random in Old English, neither was it totally fixed in Middle English. We can hear echoes of Old English word order even today. When we meet Yoda, in the *Star Wars* films, we find him regularly inverting his word order, placing the object initially: *If a Jedi knight you will become* . . . This was a common Old English pattern – and we have no difficulty understanding it 1000 years later.

However, a major grammatical change of this kind – from inflection to word order – is of real significance in the history of a language. Grammar is, after all, the basis of the way in which we organise our utterances so that they make sense, through the processes of sentence construction, and it is not an aspect of language that changes very easily – unlike vocabulary and pronunciation. New words come into English on a daily basis, but new habits of grammatical construction do not. Indeed, only a handful of minor grammatical changes have taken place during the past four centuries, although that period saw huge numbers of new words and many changes in accent. So when we see English altering its balance of grammatical con-structions so radically, as happened chiefly during the eleventh and twelfth centuries, the kind of language which emerges as a consequence, Middle English, is rightly dignified by a different name. At that stage, from a stand-point of linguistic structure, the Old English language was history.

End of an era

And from the standpoint of language use? Here we see a more gentle pro-cess operating. People often talk about a 'break' between Old and Middle English, but there was never any break. From a linguistic point of view, there could not have been. A spoken language does not evolve in sudden jumps: it consists of many thousands of working parts – in the case of English, over three dozen vowels and consonants, some three or four thousand features of sentence structure and tens of thousands of domestic words – and they do not all shift at once. If they did, different generations would not be able to understand each other. So, although the pace of linguistic change between Anglo-Saxon and early medieval times does seem to have been quite rapid, it was still gradual, and we encounter texts that are amalgams of Old and Middle English and texts that fall 'midway' between Old and Middle English.

The continuity is mainly to be seen in texts of a religious, political or administrative character, thousands of which have survived. Most of the surviving material in English is religious in character – about one-third are collections of homilies, especially by Ælfric and Wulfstan. The writings of

Ælfric, in particular, continued to be copied throughout the eleventh and twelfth centuries and these overlap with sermons from the twelfth century that are very clearly in an early form of Middle English.

The overlap is not difficult to identify. A copy of the Old English Gospels (Bodleian MS Hatton 38), made in Christ Church, Canterbury, probably in the 1190s, has been called 'the last Old English text'. That is very much later than a manuscript which has been called 'the earliest Middle English text': the *Sermo in festis Sancti Marie uirginis* ('Homily for Feasts of the Blessed Virgin Mary'), a translation of a Latin sermon by Ralph d'Escures, who was Archbishop of Canterbury between 1114 and 1122. It forms one of the *Kentish Homilies*, compiled *c.* 1150 or somewhat earlier, most of which are copied straight from Ælfric's *Catholic Homilies*.

The copying practices of twelfth-century scribes are especially important, because they provide evidence of an ongoing oral tradition between Old and Middle English. In several texts it is possible to identify examples of formulaic phrases, aphoristic expressions and other rhetorical features, dealing with a particular theme, which cannot be related to any known written source. When such locutions are found in several texts of different times and places, the conclusion is unavoidable: we are seeing here examples of oral transmission. The only way such material could have been incorporated into a piece of 'copying' is for the scribe to have been remembering such expressions and judging them to be appropriate for the text he was working on.

The religious material is of great sociolinguistic significance. If Ælfric's work was still being copied or quoted as late as around the year 1200, this gives us the strongest of hints that the language had not moved so far from Old English as to be totally unintelligible. It is inconceivable that the huge labour involved in copying would have been undertaken if nobody had been able to understand them. Contrariwise, we can sometimes sense a growing linguistic difficulty from some of the contemporary decision making, as when the monks of Worcester requested William of Malmesbury to have the Old English life of Wulfstan translated into Latin – presumably because they found it easier.

Eventually, there is a frank admission of failure. Around 1300, we find someone adding the following note in the margin of an Old English text: *non apreciatum propter ydioma incognita* ('not appreciated because an unknown language'). At that point, the Old English period was very definitely over. But its influence lives on, as this book has shown you.

The editors and the contributors

The editors

Joe Allard discovered Iceland almost by chance in the mid-1980s and has never looked back. He teaches at the University of Essex. He writes about, translates, and publishes (Mare's Nest Publishers, Festival Books) contemporary Icelandic poetry and fiction. He also writes about and teaches medieval Icelandic prose and poetry. He eats shark, puffin and whale and enjoys 57% Icelandic spirits. Hobbies include piano and watching volcanos.

Richard North was made to read Old English at Oxford and now teaches it for a living at UCL. He would like to be known for writing fiction, but is instead known – if that's the right word – for publications including *Heathen Gods in Old English Literature* (1997), *The Origins of 'Beowulf'* (2006), as well as some poems and short stories in the UCL English students' literary magazine. Hobbies include piano, reading the sagas and collecting students.

The contributors

Peter S. Baker is Professor of Medieval Literature at the University of Virginia. He has edited a number of Old English and eighteenth-century texts, and is the author of a textbook, *An Introduction to Old English*.

Stewart Brookes has a PhD in Old English Language and Literature from King's College London. His doctorate presents a new edition of Ælfric's adaptation of the biblical Book of Kings, addressing questions of Latin sources, textual transmission, and the significance of the Latin liturgical cycle. His publications include an essay on Ælfric's adaptation of the Book of Esther (2000) and entries on Byrhtferth of Ramsey, Dunstan, and the Old English poem *Daniel* in *The Literary Encyclopedia* (www.LitEncyc.com). His research interests are Old English literature, biblical textualities in the medieval period, and the interface between Hebrew manuscript painting and midrash.

Jayne Carroll was made to read Old English by Richard North at UCL, and much to her – and possibly his – surprise, she developed a taste for it. Further studies at King's College London and Nottingham introduced her to Old Norse and to English place names, and a year in Iceland sealed her fate and damaged her liver. She now lectures at the University of Leicester. Her first book, on place names, comes out in 2007.

David Crystal is honorary professor of linguistics at the University of Wales, Bangor. He learned his Old English in the English Department at University College London in the late 1950s, then went on to hold academic posts at London, Bangor and Reading. Although his field is general linguistics, he has always specialised in English language studies, where his best-known books include *The Cambridge Encyclopedia of the English Language* (2nd edn 2003), *English as a Global Language* (2nd edn 2003), *The Stories of English* (2004), and *The Fight for English* (2006). He received an OBE for services to the English language in 1995.

Patricia Harris Gillies graduated with honours in history (Phi Beta Kappa) and a doctorate in French Language and Literature at Northwestern University. Her thesis ('War and the Hero: Imagery in the *Aeneid, Beowulf, Chanson de Roland* and the Lyrics of Bertran de Born') was directed by William Paden. Together with William Paden and Tilde Sankovitch she is the co-editor of *The Poetry of Bertran de Born* (University of California Press, 1986). She is the co-editor of the *Song of Ganelon's Betrayal* (*Carmen de Prodicione Guenonis*) from the only known manuscript held in the British Library (*Traditio*, 1988). She has held an NDEA doctoral Fellowship, NEH Summer Fellowships at Princeton and Harvard and a Folger Shakespeare Library Summer Fellowship. She has been Scholar-in-Residence for twelve years at the Folger Shakespeare Library. Author of numerous articles on medieval French and comparative literature published in France and the USA, she has taught languages and literature everywhere from middle schools and high schools to the University of Maryland-College Park and American University, Washington, DC. She currently teaches in the Department of Literature, Film and Theatre Studies at the University of Essex where she is Associate Fellow. She is a regular member of the University of London Old Icelandic Reading Group, the Royal Holloway Old English Reading Group and the Cambridge Medieval French Research Seminar.

Terry Gunnell is a Senior Lecturer in Folkloristics at the University of Iceland, where he has worked full time since 1998. He is the author of *The Origins of Drama in Scandinavia* (1995), which deals in part with the possible dramatic presentation of the Old Icelandic Eddic poems, and is based largely on a thesis defended at the University of Leeds in 1991. In addition to this, he has published a number of articles on Old Norse religion and mythology, performance, drama, folk legends and belief, and folk customs past and present (particularly folk drama). He is at present engaged in editing a book on Nordic Masks and Mumming, and preparing a large database of Icelandic legends.

Susan Irvine is Professor of English at University College London. She has published widely on Old English literature and language, including *Old English Homilies from MS Bodley 343* (Oxford University Press 1993), *The Anglo-Saxon Chronicle MS E* (in *The Anglo-Saxon Chronicle: a Collaborative Series*, D.S. Brewer 2004), and articles on the writings of King Alfred. She is currently working on the *Old English Boethius*.

Jennifer Neville is originally from Canada and studied at the Universities of Alberta and Toronto before undertaking her PhD at Cambridge on representations of the natural world in Old English poetry. She is currently a Senior Lecturer in the Department of English at Royal Holloway, University of London, where she teaches Old and Middle English literature to a more or less captive audience of students. They are, of course, ultimately grateful to have had it forced on them, once they know better, and some actually go on to study it further, of their own free will. She also occasionally teaches Tolkien to a rather more willing crowd, but only if they agree to translate Old English literature as well. She maintains a fervent belief that no one can possibly function well in modern society without learning Old English.

Éamonn Ó Carragáin is Professor of Old and Middle English at University College Cork. He has varied research interests, including: the Vercelli Book; the *Beowulf* Manuscript; Liturgy and Culture; *The Dream of the Rood* and its contexts; the City of Rome; and the relationships between word and image. He has taught and lectured on Old English around the world.

Andy Orchard is Professor of English and Medieval Studies at the University of Toronto, and is Director of the Centre for Medieval Studies. He spent nine happy summers as a mountain guide in Iceland, before settling down to teach Anglo-Saxon, Norse, Celtic and Medieval Latin. He has written books on Aldhelm, *Beowulf*, and Norse myth and legend, and is currently writing others on Cynewulf, Wulfstan, and the Poetic Edda. He generally hangs out in 'Andy's Orchard' in Mullin's Irish pub in Toronto, where he can frequently be found muttering 'Hello darkness, my old friend' to serial pints of Guinness.

Clive Tolley studied at New College, Oxford, beginning with Classics before moving on to Old English and Old Norse. After two years in Finland he continued with his doctorate at New College on comparative Norse and Finnish mythology. He has long been interested in Tolkien and his fellow writers, and has acted as warden of The Kilns, C.S. Lewis's former home in Oxford. He now runs his own business in Chester, editing and typesetting academic books, as well as translating from Finnish and pursuing research in Norse and Finnish mythology and pre-Christian religion. Apart from an obsessive interest in obscure languages, he also enjoys renaissance and baroque music, which he sings and plays on the viola da gamba.

Bryan Weston Wyly is a researcher in English language and translation at the Unversité de la Vallée d'Aoste. His main focus is on language as instrument for thought, particularly in applications involving metaphor and metonymy, and in contrasts between linguistic systems operating primarily through auditory and visual channels. He is especially interested in contextualising this work in the historical transitions which took place among the Anglo-Saxon, Nordic and Celtic peoples in the Early Middle Ages.

Index

'Æ' follows on from 'Ad' and comes before 'Ae'. The letter 'ð' (lower case for 'Ð') comes after 'd'. 'Þ' follows 'T' as a new letter. 'Q' always goes near the end.

Brontës, The, 272
Brussels Cross, 185–7
Brynhildr, wife of Gunnarr and admirer
    of Sigurðr, 27, 34, 383
Burghal Hidage, The, West Saxon defence
    document (880s), 315–16
Burgundians, 8, 30
Burns, Robert (Robbie), 196
Byrhtferth (*c*. 960–*c*. 1020), monk of
    Ramsey and mathematician, 432
    Enchiridion (*Handbook*) of, 439–43
    prolixity of, 442
Byrhtnoth, ealdorman of Essex
    (governed 956–91), 5, 89–90
    ofermod ('pride') of, 468 (as compared
        with the *desmesure* of Roland in
        La Chanson de Roland)
    killed in the Battle of Maldon, 339
    celebrated in *The Battle of Maldon*,
        340–3, 435–6
Byrhtwold (d. 991), rallier at Maldon,
    341–2
Bǫðvarr bjarki, 27, 31, 108, 127
    see also Beowulf
Bǫðvarr Egilsson, 27, 36, 396
Bǫðvildr, raped by Vǫlundr, 27, 110
    see also Beadohild

Cædmon, 4, 176, 184, 266
    life sketch of, 189–209
    afraid of the lyre, 191
    unlike the hero of *Apollonius of Tyre*,
        448
    sings in a midnight vision, 191–2
    Hymn of, 189–91, 181–2, 197–9,
        272
    said to put most of the Bible into
        verse, 192, 211
    poetic legacy of, 208–16
    and praise poetry, 195
    dwelling of, 201
    name of as Welsh, 205
Caesar, Julius (d. 44 BC), 318
Cain, 6, 67, 72
Caistor-by-Norwich deer ankle-bone
    runic inscription, 12
Canterbury Tales, The, *see* Chaucer,
    Geoffrey
Canute, *see* Cnut

Capture of the Five Boroughs, The, OE
    Chronicle poem, 334–6
    see also Anglo-Saxon Chronicle, Old
        English literature
Carroll, Lewis, 49–52
    Wonderland of, 51
    'Jabberwocky' of, 48–50
    Through the Looking Glass of, 49, 51
    The Hunting of the Snark of, 51
Carthage, 6
Catalogue of Dwarfs, The, *see Dvergatal*
Catalogue of Rígr, The, *see Rígsþula*
Catholic Homilies (I and II series), *see
    Sermones Catholici*
Cattle Raid of Cooley, The, *see Táin Bó
    Cuailnge*
Celts, 2, 13–16 (Romano-British), 202,
    371
Ceolfrith, abbot of Monkwearmouth-
    Jarrow (ruled 688–716), 176,
    177
Ceolwulf, puppet king in Mercia (874),
    313
Ceorl, ealdorman of Devon, 304
Chamberlain, Neville, 461
Chanson de Roland, La, *see* Anglo-
    Norman literature
Chansons de geste, *see* Old French
    literature
Charlemagne, emperor of western
    Europe (ruled 771–814), 4, 33,
    107, 112, 226, 229, 230, 231, 234,
    237, 254, 303
    letter of to Offa, 238
    celebrated in *La Chanson de Roland*,
        457–62
Charles the Bald, king of Western
    Francia (ruled 840–75) and
    Emperor of Francia (875–7), 116
Charles the Younger (d. 811), son of
    Charlemagne, 237
Chaucer, Geoffrey (*c*. 1340–*c*. 1399), 2,
    272, 277, 286, 482
    Troilus and Criseyde of, 115–16
    The Canterbury Tales of, 1, 430 (cooks,
        undervaluing of)
    edition of by Thomas Speght, 59
    The Merchant's Tale, 115–16, 145
    The Man of Law's Tale, 447